Using

OLE 2.x in Application Development

John Toohey

QUE

Using OLE 2.x in Application Development

Library of Congress Catalog Number: 94-68558

ISBN: 1-56529-991-4

97 96 95 94 5 4 3 2 1

Interpretation of the printing code: The rightmost double-digit number is the year of the book's printing; the rightmost single-digit number, the number of the book's printing. For example, a printing code of 94-1 shows that the first printing of the book occurred in 1994.

Publisher: David P. Ewing

Associate Publisher: Joseph B. Wikert

Managing Editors: Michael Cunningham and Kelli Widdifield

Product Marketing Manager: Greg Wiegand

Dedication

This book is dedicated to my wife Hafdís for everything and then some.

Credits

Publishing Manager
Steven M. Schafer

Acquisitions Editor
Fred Slone

Acquisitions Coordinator
Patricia J. Brooks

Product Development Specialists
Robin Drake
Bryan Gambrel

Production Editor
Mike LaBonne

Copy Editor
Andy Saff

Technical Editor
Charlie Kindel

Cover Designer
Dan Armstrong

Book Designer
Amy Peppler-Adams

Production Team
Stephen Adams
Cameron Booker
Stephen Carlin
Kim Cofer
Amy Cornwell
Chad Dressler
Joelynn Gifford
Bob LaRoche
Elizabeth Lewis
Erika Millen
Angel Perez
Vic Peterson
Beth Rago
Kaylene Riemen
Clair Schweinler
Dennis Sheehan
Michael Thomas
Mary Beth Wakefield

Editorial Assistant
Michelle Williams

Indexer
Chris Cleveland

Composed in *Stone Serif* and *MCPdigital* by Macmillan Computer Publishing

About the Author

John Toohey is the development manager at Traffic Software, a leading developer of network fax products for Windows. He is the chief architect of Object-Fax, one of the first commercially available OLE 2.0 products. He has worked with Windows since release 1.0 and with OLE since the beta program for the first release. Though originally from Ireland, he lives and works in Reykjavík, Iceland with his wife and two children.

Acknowledgments

John Toohey would like to acknowledge the following persons:

First, I would like to thank Joe Wikert of Que Corporation for getting me involved in this project.

To Fred Slone, my acquisitions editor, for all his help.

To Bryan Gambrel and Andy Saff for editing the manuscript.

To all the other people at Que, including Robin Drake, Patty Brooks, Angie Lee, and those whose names I do not know.

I especially thank Charlie Kindel of Microsoft Corporation for all his help. Charlie read each chapter of the book and made sure that I stayed on track and that the information that I used was always up to date. I am extremely grateful to Charlie for all his help and advice.

To Kraig Brockschmidt. After six months of ploughing through the early alpha documentation for OLE, it was the early drafts of his book that finally brought everything together for me and lifted the clouds.

To Srini Koppolu of Microsoft Corporation, for teaching me the mechanism of in-place activation.

To Vim at Microsoft Europe, for first getting me involved in the OLE 2.0 program.

To Bill and Steve for starting it all (lest we forget).

And finally to my son Alexander James and daughter Selma Dröfn, for their patience and sometimes (thankfully) total lack of understanding during the past months when all my time was devoted to writing this book.

Trademarks

All terms mentioned in this book that are known to be trademarks or service marks have been appropriately capitalized. Que cannot attest to the accuracy of this information. Use of a term in this book should not be regarded as affecting the validity of any trademark or service mark.

Screen Reproductions in this book were created using Collage Plus from Inner Media, Inc., Hollis, New Hampshire.

Contents at a Glance

Foreword 1

Introduction 3

Introduction to OLE 7

1 General Concepts 9

2 The Component Object Model 33

3 A Sample C++ Application 53

4 The OLE SDK 91

Introduction to OLE

Using MFC To Implement OLE 115

5 Introduction to the MFC Document View Model 117

6 A Simple Container 167

7 An MDI Linking Container 201

8 OLE Compound Files 225

9 A Simple MFC OLE Server 263

10 A Full OLE Server 305

Using MFC

OLE Automation 343

11 General Concepts of OLE Automation 345

12 Creating a Simple Automation Controller 371

13 Creating a Simple Automation Server 397

14 MFC and Automation 425

15 An MFC Automation Client 447

16 An MFC Automation Server 479

OLE Automation

Beyond OLE 2.0 513

17 OLE Custom Interfaces 515

18 Thirty-two-bit OLE 549

19 Distributed Objects 591

20 The Future of OLE 601

Index 613

Beyond OLE 2.0

Contents

Foreword 1

Introduction 3

Source Code Issues ... 4

I Introduction to OLE 7

1 General Concepts 9

The History of OLE ... 10
Lightweight Remote Procedure Call (LRPC) ... 12
The Structured Storage System ... 13
Monikers ... 14
The Document-oriented Paradigm ... 14
Component Software ... 15
The Principal Technologies ... 16
Visual Editing ... 17
Link Tracking and Management ... 19
Compound Files and Structured Storage ... 24
Access Modes ... 25
Sharing Storage Objects ... 26
The *LockBytes* Object ... 26
Special Streams ... 27
The Future of Structured Storage ... 27
Uniform Data Transfer ... 27
OLE Automation ... 30
From Here... ... 31

2 The Component Object Model 33

Object Interfaces ... 33
The Interface *IUnknown* ... 34
Reference Counting ... 36
How the System Finds Objects ... 37
The *VersionIndependentProgID* Field ... 39
The *Conversion* Field ... 40
The *ProgID* Field ... 40
The *InprocHandler* Field ... 40
The *LocalServer* Field ... 40
The *InProcServer* Field ... 40
The *Verb* Field ... 40

The *AuxUserType* Field 41
The *DefaultIcon* Field 41
The *DataFormats* Field 41
The *MiscStatus* Field 41
The *Insertable* Key 42
The *Control* Key 42
Object Return Codes 42
The COM Memory Allocator 44
Enumerators 45
Object Inheritance, Aggregation, and Delegation 46
Aggregation 47
Delegation 49
Marshaling 50
From Here... 51

3 A Sample C++ Application 53

The Initialization Code 53
The Shutdown Code 54
The Sample Application 54
The *CDropTarget* Class 58
The Macros Used in OLE Headers 59
The Code for the *CDropTarget* Class 60
External Locks 67
Strong Locks 67
Weak Locks 68
The *IUnknown* Implementation 68
The *CDropTarget* Implementation 69
The Constructor 69
The Destructor 70
The *Create* Method 70
The *GetDragRect* Method 71
The *DragEnter* Method 72
The *DragOver* Method 74
The *DragLeave* Method 75
The Drop Operation 75
Storing the Dropped Object 76
Displaying the Stored Object 82
The *OnCreate* Method 83
The *OnDestroy* Method 83
The *DrawGhostRect* Method 84
The *OnDraw* Method 84
From Here... 89

4 The OLE SDK 91

The DocFile Viewer 92
The DISPTEST Automation Test 93
The *IDataObject* Viewer 95
The Class ID Generator 96

The Running Object Table Viewer 97
The LRPC Message Monitor 98
The OLE 2.0 Free Module Utility 99
The Ole2View Utility 100
The Windows Process Status Utility 110
The Type Library Generator 111
The Type Library Browser 112
The WXSRVR Program 112
The Debugging Handler 113
From Here... 114

II Using MFC To Implement OLE 115

5 Introduction to the MFC Document View Model 117

Application Frameworks 117
The MFC Document View Architecture 118
The Document Class 119
The View Class 120
The Document Template Class 121
The MFC OLE Classes 121
The Base Classes 122
The *COleDialog* Class 122
The *CDocItem* Class 123
The *COleDispatchDriver* Class 124
The *COleDocument* Class 124
The Container Classes 127
The *COleLinkingDoc* Class 127
The *COleClientItem* Class 129
The Server Classes 136
The *COleObjectFactory* Class 136
The *COleTemplateServer* Class 137
The *COleServerDoc* Class 137
The *COleServerItem* Class 142
The *OleIPFrame* Class 146
The *COleResizeBar* Class 148
Uniform Data Transfer Classes 148
The *COleDropSource* Class 149
The *COleDropTarget* Class 149
The *COleDataSource* Class 151
The *COleDataObject* Class 153
The OLE Dialog Classes 154
The *COleInsertDialog* Class 154
The *COleConvertDialog* Class 155
The *COleChangeIconDialog* Class 156
The *COlePasteSpecialDialog* Class 157
The *COleLinksDialog* Class 157
The *COleUpdateDialog* Class 158

The *COleBusyDialog* Class 159
Miscellaneous Classes 159
The *COleException* Class 160
The *CRectTracker* Class 160
The *COleStreamFile* Class 161
The *COleDispatchException* Class 162
The *COleMessageFilter* Class 163
AppWizard Support for OLE 164
From Here... 165

6 A Simple Container 167

Creating the Skeleton with the AppWizard 167
The Application Module 168
The *AfxOleInit* Function 168
The *SetContainerInfo* Method 168
The View Module 172
Inserting an Object 172
Drawing the Object 173
Activating the Object 174
Deactivating the Object 177
Sizing the Object 177
Assigning the Context Menu 179
The Document Module 190
The Object Interface Module 193
The *OnChange* Method 194
The *OnChangeItemPosition* Method 194
The *OnGetItemPosition* Method 194
The *OnDeactivateUI* Method 194
The *Move* Method 195
The *Serialize* Method 195
The Completed Container Skeleton 200
From Here... 200

7 An MDI Linking Container 201

COM Data Objects 201
The FORMATETC Structure 202
The *cfFormat* Field 202
The *ptd* Field 203
The *dwAspect* Field 203
The *lindex* Field 204
The *tymed* Field 204
The STGMEDIUM Structure 205
The *IDataObject* Interface 206
MFC's *IDataObject* Support 207
The Clipboard and OLE 208
The *OnEditPaste* Method 209
The *OnEditPasteLink* Method 212
The *OnEditPasteSpecial* Method 212

The *OnUpdatePaste* Method 213
The *OnEditCopy*, *OnEditCut*, and *OnEditClear* Methods 214
MFC Drag-drop Support 215
Registering the Application 215
The *OnDragEnter* Method 216
The *OnDragOver* Method 218
The *OnDrop* Method 219
The *OnDragLeave* Method 220
The *OnScrollBy* Method 220
Linking Support 221
From Here... 224

8 OLE Compound Files 225

The Structured Storage Model 225
The *LockBytes* Object 226
Storages 227
Enumerating Storages 230
Streams 230
Compound Files 233
Creating a Compound File 233
Access Modes 235
The Transaction Model 236
Lazy Reading of Streams 237
Special OLE Streams 238
The *CompObj* Stream 238
The OLE Stream 239
The Presentation Stream 240
The Downside of Compound Files 241
OLE's Use of Compound Files 241
The *IPersist* Interface 241
The *IPersistStorage* Interface 242
The *IPersistStream* Interface 243
The *IPersistFile* Interface 244
Property Sets 244
MFC's Implementation of Compound Files 256
From Here... 262

9 A Simple MFC OLE Server 263

The Server Architecture 263
GDI Mapping Modes 265
Metafiles 266
Examining the Code 267
The Window Application Class 267
The In-place Frame Class 272
The Document Class 275
The Document Constructor 280
The *OnSetItemRects* Method 280

The *OnOpenDocument* Method ... 281
The *OnGetEmbeddedItem* Method ... 281
The *OnSetExtent* Method ... 282
The *OnGetExtent* Method ... 282
The *Serialize* Method ... 282
The View Class ... 283
The *OnDraw* Method ... 287
The *OnEditBitmaps* Method ... 287
The Object Interface Class ... 287
The *Serialize* Method ... 291
The *OnSetExtent* Method ... 291
The *OnGetExtent* Method ... 291
The *OnDraw* Method ... 291
The Bitmap Class ... 292
Understanding What Happened ... 301
Testing the Server ... 302
From Here... ... 303

10 A Full OLE Server 305

Examining the Code ... 306
The Window Application Class ... 306
The In-place Frame Class ... 312
The Document Class ... 316
The Document Constructor ... 323
The *OnSaveDocument* Method ... 323
The *OnNewDocument* Method ... 323
The *OnOpenDocument* Method ... 323
The *OnGetEmbeddedItem* Method ... 323
The *OnSetItemRects* Method ... 324
The *OnSetExtents* Method ... 324
The *OnGetExtents* Method ... 324
The *Serialize* Method ... 324
The *OnSetTitle* Method ... 325
The Title Class ... 325
The View Class ... 327
The *OnDraw* Method ... 331
The *OnEditCopy* Method ... 331
The *OnEditChangeTitle* Method ... 332
The Object Interface Class ... 332
The Object Interface Constructor ... 336
The *Serialize* Method ... 336
The *OnSetExtent* Method ... 336
The *OnGetExtent* Method ... 337
The *OnDraw* Method ... 337
The *OnRenderGlobalData* Method ... 337
Testing the Server ... 338
A Closer Look at Linking ... 340
From Here... ... 341

III OLE Automation 343

11 General Concepts of OLE Automation 345

Background 345
Automation Objects 347
The *IDispatch* Interface 348
Using *CreateStdDispatch* To Implement *IDispatch* 352
Delegating the *IDispatch* Calls 354
Implementing the Dispatch Methods Directly 355
Automation Controllers 356
Script Languages 356
C++ Controllers 357
Object Browsers 357
Ole2View 358
The Excel 5.0 Object Browser 359
Exposing Objects in Your Application 360
The *Application* Object 361
The *Document* Object 362
The *Documents* Collection 364
The *Font* Object 365
A Real-World Example 366
Restricting Access to Objects 368
National Language Support 368
Using Type Libraries 369
From Here... 370

12 Creating a Simple Automation Controller 371

A Simple Automation Controller 371
Initializing the OLE Libraries 372
Creating an Instance of a Word Object 376
Error Reporting 378
Accessing the Automation Methods 382
From Here... 395

13 Creating a Simple Automation Server 397

A Simple Automation Server 397
The Initialization Code 398
Shutting Down 400
Creating Objects 404
IUnknown Implementation 405
IClassFactory Implementation 406
The *CObject* Implementation 412
The Type Library 414
Registering the Object and the Type Information 419
Generating the CLSIDs 420
Testing the Object 421
From Here... 423

14 MFC and Automation 425

Creating an Application with the AppWizard 425
Supporting Automation with the ClassWizard 427
Creating the Class 427
Adding a Method 428
Supporting Automation Clients 430
Examining the Code 430
The OLECREATE Macro 431
The DECLARE_DISPATCH_MAP Macro 432
The IMPLEMENT_OLECREATE Macro 436
Moving on to the Next Steps 436
Automation Client Support Revisited 436
Reading the Type Library 437
Creating the Dispatch Pointer 439
Invoking the Exposed Methods 439
Getting and Setting Property Values 444
From Here... 445

15 An MFC Automation Client 447

The Excel Object Model 447
The Test Application 448
Reading the Type Library 453
Changing the Generated Code 454
Accessing Excel 458
Running the Application 477
From Here... 477

16 An MFC Automation Server 479

The Test Application 479
The Initialization Code 480
The View Class 483
The Document Class 488
Initializing the Document Class 488
Adding Methods with the ClassWizard 489
Implementing the *CShape* Object 490
Implementing the Collection Object 495
The *IEnumVARIANT* Implementation 502
The *IUnknown* and *IEnumVARIANT* Methods 505
The *CVarEnum* Methods 505
The Test Script 510
From Here... 512

IV Beyond OLE 2.0 513

17 OLE Custom Interfaces 515

Custom Interface Architecture 516
Standard Interfaces 516
Marshaling 518
Custom Interfaces 518
The Service Control Manager 519
The Proxy 520
The Stub 521
A Sample Custom Interface Implementation 521
Creating the Proxy and Stub 522
Designing the Interface 522
The IDL File 523
Building the DLL 526
The Server Code 535
The MAIN.CPP File 535
The AUTOSRV.CPP Module 540
The Client Code 544
Registering the Server, Proxy, and Stub 547
Testing the Application 547
From Here... 548

18 Thirty-two-bit OLE 549

Background to Win32 550
The Flat Memory Model 550
The Asynchronous Input Model 551
Threads 552
Thread Synchronization 553
Critical Sections 553
Synchronization Objects 554
Memory Mapped Files 555
Issues in 32-bit Programming 556
Message Parameters 557
The Graphic Device Interface 559
Structure Alignments 560
The Application's Command Line 560
Checking for Multiple Instances of an Application 561
Unicode 561
Background 561
Using Unicode in Your Application 562
Changing Your Code 562
Unicode Font Support 572
Structured Exception Handling 572
OLE in a 32-bit Environment 574
Interoperability 575
Long File Names 575

Compound Files ... 576
Security Issues ... 576
Shared Memory ... 576
Enhanced Metafiles ... 576
OLE and Unicode ... 577
The Registry ... 578
Examining the Code ... 579
The OLE1.CPP File ... 579
The OLEDOC.CPP ... 582
Linking the Application ... 587
From Here... ... 589

19 Distributed Objects 591

The Promise of Distributed Objects ... 591
The Distributed Computing Environment ... 592
Threads ... 593
Remote Procedure Call (RPC) ... 593
Directory Services ... 594
Security Services ... 595
The Distributed File System ... 595
Time Services ... 596
Diskless Support Services ... 596
OMG CORBA ... 596
The Common Object Model ... 597
Distributed OLE ... 598
From Here... ... 600

20 The Future of OLE 601

Property Inheritance ... 602
Extended Object Layout ... 602
Object Tunneling ... 603
Support for Irregularly Shaped Objects ... 604
In-place Editing of Linked Objects ... 605
Shared Toolbars ... 605
Cross-platform Interoperability ... 606
Interoperability and the Macintosh ... 606
Interoperability and Windows NT ... 606
OLE Controls ... 607
Distributed Objects ... 608
True Link Tracking ... 609
Document Objects ... 609
The Windows Open Services Architecture Extensions for Real-time Market Data ... 610
Windows 95 File Viewers ... 611
The Windows 95 Shell ... 612

Index 613

Foreword

It never ceases to amaze me how rapidly computing technology is advancing. I remember not that long ago upgrading my TRS-80 Model III to 64K RAM and thinking "this is one hot machine." But looking back on the history of application development, it occurs to me that there are relatively few events which marked major turning points for the software industry during its rapid evolution. One of these, of course, was the introduction of the personal computer. With the introduction of the personal computer, application development entered a new phase—a phase that can be called a renaissance.

Starting in the late 1970s, a new generation of brash and creative developers began to take advantage of the accessibility of the personal computer. They began to build incredibly imaginative applications that opened our minds to the true potential of software to positively impact almost every aspect of our society. Not much later, we witnessed another major turning point with the introduction of the graphical user interface (GUI). While developing GUI-based applications required a significant learning investment on the part of developers, the value to users clearly justified this investment. Today, the Microsoft Windows graphical application environment has become a critical part of everyday computing, and is a major boon to the widespread deployment of computers into businesses and homes.

Looking back from the perspective we have today, it is easy to see that the introduction of PCs, and later the introduction of the GUI, were major turning points for the entire computing industry—not only for developers but for users as well. Today, I am equally convinced that the introduction of OLE 2 represents the next major turning point in the history of application development. With the introduction of OLE 2, we sit on the edge of a new era of computing—the component software era.

OLE 2 allows developers to design and build unique, value-added applications, yet be assured that these applications will dynamically interoperate with other OLE-enabled applications. The implications of the component software standard that OLE represents are staggering. Software developers can focus on using their core competencies to build software components that can be combined by users and software integrators with other components built by other developers. Components developed in different programming languages, coded by developers in different parts of the world, can be so seamlessly combined via OLE that they appear to be a single, integrated application. Corporations can, in turn, use prefabricated OLE components to quickly develop custom business applications, by purchasing and plugging together specialized components built by experts. Finally, users can use the rich document facilities OLE provides to seamlessly work with multiple applications, accomplishing tasks more quickly and efficiently.

In writing *Using OLE 2.x in Application Development*, John Toohey has provided an excellent resource for those developers who want to leverage the OLE 2 technology and become immediate players in the growing component software market. With clear explanations and insights into the OLE technology, John concentrates on providing real code examples that truly make learning OLE 2 straightforward and fun. He starts with an introduction to the Component Object Model, the foundation for all OLE 2 features, and covers OLE 2 all the way through to the future distributed capabilities Microsoft is currently building into the OLE architecture. John covers not only the compound document capabilities of OLE, but also provides in-depth coverage of OLE Automation, developing custom OLE interfaces, and developing 32-bit OLE applications for Windows NT and Windows 95. *Using OLE 2.x in Application Development* is an invaluable resource tailored for you, the imaginative application developer who will apply OLE 2 and help usher in the era of component software.

L. Gregory Leake
OLE Product Manager, Microsoft
Redmond, Washington
September, 1994

Introduction

OLE is without a doubt one of the most important technologies ever released by Microsoft. Like Win32, OLE will have an effect on every Windows developer in the coming years.

OLE is Microsoft's object system and the foundation for future releases of Windows and Windows NT. The promise of OLE is a world of component software that will bring true integration to the desktop. With a forthcoming release of OLE, users will be able to access distributed objects across the enterprise. The current level of integration that is available in Microsoft Office is but a hint of things to come.

To take part in this brave new world, developers must begin now to learn the fundamentals of OLE, its architecture, and its application.

My goal in writing this book is to provide you with the necessary background and code samples to get you up and running using OLE in your own applications.

Unfortunately, implementing OLE has received a reputation for being extremely difficult and time-consuming. The only thing that is difficult about OLE is the fact that it is new and that people are not yet used to it. With the release of the next generation of Windows (Windows 95) and new releases of Windows NT, programming with the OLE Component Object Model will become as familiar and easy as working with the Windows API.

This book is divided into four parts:

- Part I deals with OLE's architecture and background. Chapter 1 provides an introduction to OLE, including its history and an overview of the principal technologies. Chapter 2 covers OLE's object model, the Component Object Model (COM). In Chapter 3, you develop a sample C++

application that demonstrates how to write a simple OLE application. Chapter 4 covers the Software Development Kit (SDK) that is supplied with OLE.

- In Part II, you learn how to use the Microsoft Foundation Classes (MFC) libraries to implement OLE, and explore in depth OLE compound documents and files. Chapter 5 is an introduction to using MFC to create OLE applications. Chapter 6 describes how to develop a simple OLE container application using MFC. In Chapter 7, you continue developing the container by adding more advanced features. Chapter 8 examines in detail the OLE structured storage model. In Chapter 9, you develop an OLE object server using MFC. You continue developing the object server in Chapter 10, where you convert the server from a simple server to a full server.
- Part III examines OLE Automation with both standard C++ and MFC. Chapter 11 covers the general concepts of OLE Automation. In Chapters 12 and 13, you develop a simple OLE Automation client and server with C++. Chapter 14 introduces the OLE Automation support supplied with MFC. In Chapters 15 and 16, you develop an OLE Automation client and server using MFC.
- Finally, Part IV examines the future of OLE. Chapter 17 describes OLE custom interfaces and shows you how to build your own COM interface using the Interface Description Language (IDL) and the MIDL compiler. In Chapter 18, you learn about 32-bit OLE and develop a sample 32-bit NT application. Chapter 19 covers distributed objects, and Chapter 20 explores future OLE developments.

Source Code Issues

On the disk that accompanies this book, you can find the source code for each of the chapters' programs. The code demonstrates various OLE programming techniques and concepts. Although this code is not primarily intended to be used in real-world applications, you could use it for that purpose with the addition of better error checking.

Source code is the best source of information about new systems. When the documentation is unclear about something, sample code usually explains it best. I encourage you to read the sample code that accompanies the book, the sample code supplied with the OLE SDK, and finally the MFC sample code.

No code is ever 100-percent bug free, and I know that my code is no exception. If you find any bugs, please report them to me on CompuServe (72251,2140).

Code lines that are too long to fit within the margins of this book are joined by the following special line-wrap icon:

➥

In your programs, you should type the two lines as one.

All the 16-bit sample code was compiled with Visual C++ 1.5. The 32-bit code was built with Visual C++ 2.0. When working with the custom interfaces, I also used the Win32 SDK.

As always, the best way to learn is to try these techniques in your own applications. As the Chinese proverb says:

> I hear and I forget
>
> I see and I remember
>
> I do and I understand

Part I

Introduction to OLE

1 General Concepts

2 The Component Object Model

3 A Sample C++ Application

4 The OLE SDK

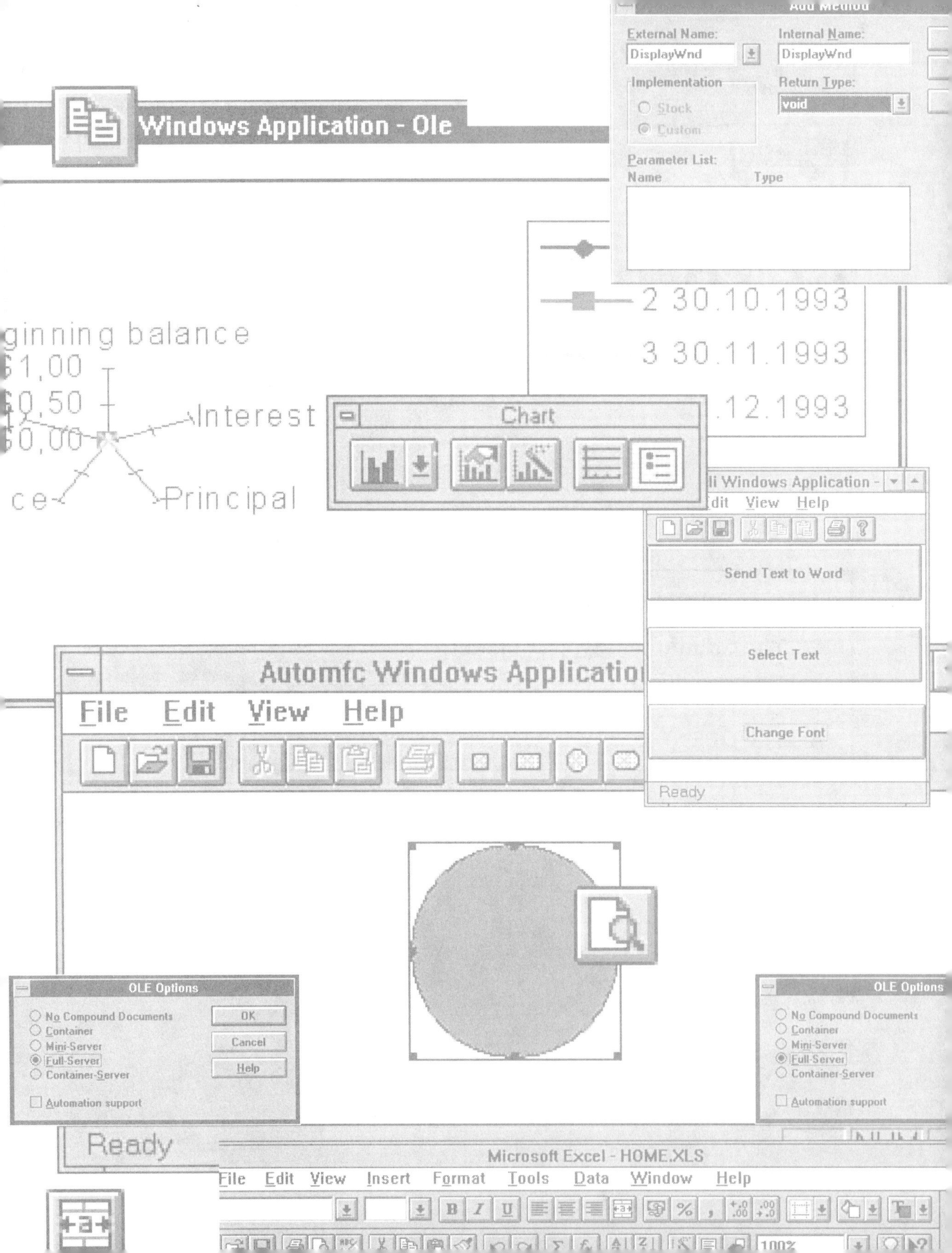
Windows Application - Ole
Add Method
External Name:
DisplayWnd
Internal Name:
DisplayWnd
Implementation
Stock
Custom
Return Type:
void
Parameter List:
Name
Type
2 30.10.1993
3 30.11.1993
.12.1993
ginning balance
Interest
Principal
Chart
li Windows Application -
dit View Help
Send Text to Word
Select Text
Change Font
Ready
Automfc Windows Applicatio
File Edit View Help
OLE Options
No Compound Documents
Container
Mini-Server
Full-Server
Container-Server
Automation support
OK
Cancel
Help
Ready
Microsoft Excel - HOME.XLS
File Edit View Insert Format Tools Data Window Help
100%

Chapter 1

General Concepts

This chapter introduces some of the background of Microsoft's OLE 2.0 technology. You also take a look at the Document-Oriented Interface (DOI) and see how it is changing the way that computers are used today. The DOI is an important part of OLE 2.0 that is probably, from a user's perspective, the most visible part of OLE 2.0.

Finally, you examine each of the major technologies that OLE 2.0 offers. These technologies form the core of Microsoft's system strategies for the next generation of operating systems. Future releases of both Windows 95 and Windows NT will use OLE 2.0 extensively. A sound understanding of the concepts and principles of OLE is a prerequisite for developing real-world OLE applications. Although you can go some of the distance using such tools as the Microsoft Foundation Classes (MFC) and Visual C++, knowing how all the parts fit together will help you move beyond the support provided by these tools.

In this chapter, you learn about the following:

- The history of OLE
- Two of OLE 2.0's underlying concepts: the document-oriented paradigm and component software
- The principal technologies behind OLE 2.0, including visual editing, linking tracking and management, compound files and structured storage, Uniform Data Transfer (UDT), and Automation

The History of OLE

An important feature of OLE is application integration. This idea is not new. It was first introduced in Microsoft Windows through dynamic data exchange (DDE). DDE was not actually a feature of Windows; rather, it was a protocol that defined how two applications could communicate and exchange data with each other. DDE was originally developed for Microsoft Excel, the application that developers always used to test against their own DDE applications. It was always a case of doing what Excel did and not what the protocol said. DDE was built around a client-server model and was difficult and idiosyncratic for both users and developers.

OLE 1.0, which Microsoft introduced in June 1991, was Microsoft's first attempt to deliver an object-oriented model for Windows (see fig. 1.1). OLE 1.0 was built on top of DDE and introduced the concept of compound documents. Like DDE, OLE was originally developed to solve a problem for a Microsoft application. The developers of Microsoft PowerPoint wanted a way to use Microsoft Graph as a presentation element in their application, so they developed a protocol called the Microsoft PowerPoint Graph. In Microsoft PowerPoint, a graph is embedded in a presentation as an object. The protocols used to develop the original specification for Microsoft PowerPoint formed the basis for OLE 1.0, and the concept of an application being used as a container for an object forms the core concepts for OLE 2.0.

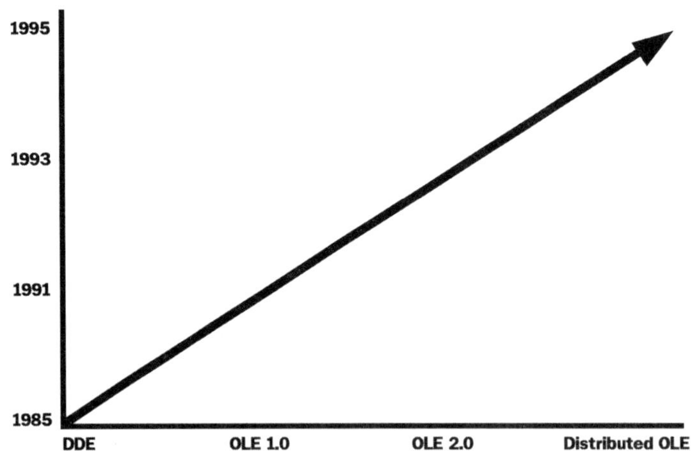

Fig. 1.1
The origins of OLE 2.0.

The concepts of *linked* and *embedded* objects were first introduced through compound documents. A *compound document* is a document that consists of data objects from various applications. You can either embed or link these objects. An embedded object is fully contained within the document. A linked object contains the path to a data source that contains the original data. To edit an embedded or linked object, you simply double-click on the object. The OLE libraries then execute the OLE server associated with that object. When you are finished editing the data, you quit the server application and the OLE libraries update the presentation data. The container does not have to display or print the object, because the OLE libraries take care of rendering the object to the printer or display.

The OLE 1.0 libraries, which shipped with Windows 3.1, were intended as a means of integrating applications. However, programming for OLE 1.0 proved difficult for developers outside Microsoft Corporation. Although this difficulty was partially due to the lack of documentation and example code from Microsoft, a major part of the problem was due to the underlying DDE protocols. DDE is an asynchronous protocol, which means that when you call a function, the function call returns immediately even though the OLE libraries have not completed the requested task. You then have to wait in a message loop, constantly polling a status function. Because you are passing data between the object and the container, you have to make copies of the data in memory and pass pointers to the data. This works fine for small amount of data, but if you embed a sound clip or a large graph in a container such as Write, you can bring the entire system to its knees. Linked objects caused major problems when the user moved the data source. The user would receive an unfriendly `broken links` error message and had to attempt to restore the link manually.

In May 1993, Microsoft formally released OLE 2.0, after undergoing a series of design previews and extensive beta testing by many independent software vendors (ISVs). The OLE 2.0 architects addressed all the shortcomings of OLE 1.0 and delivered a robust, scaleable object system for Windows. OLE 2.0 goes far beyond the capabilities of OLE 1.0 and beyond being a mechanism for creating compound files.

The features of OLE 2.0 are powerful and compelling. OLE 2.0 introduces a powerful interapplication drag-drop protocol, in-place editing of embedded objects, object programmability, Uniform Data Transfer (UDT), and structured storage for objects. The object model used in OLE 2.0, the Component

Object Model (COM), defines a binary object standard. Because COM defines a binary model, OLE 2.0 is independent of the applications and programming languages that you use to create your applications. This independence ensures interoperability between objects created by different vendors. If you write an object in C++, a Visual Basic programmer can use your object in his application because the methods of connecting to objects and exchanging data are provided through a common interface.

OLE 2.0 provides the foundation for future object systems from Microsoft. You can see how the system is designed from the ground up to be extensible and scaleable by examining three major parts of the current release:

- Lightweight remote procedure call (LRPC)
- The structured storage system
- Monikers

The following sections discuss each of these three new features. These features were key elements to the OLE architects. Although they knew that some of these features would not be available in the initial release of OLE 2.0, by designing the architecture as they did, the architects have assured a long future for OLE.

Lightweight Remote Procedure Call (LRPC)

The mechanism by which objects communicate with each other in OLE 2.0 is called lightweight remote procedure call (LRPC). LRPC takes care of marshaling parameters and interface calls from one process to another. This mechanism even handles the translation of calls and parameters from a 16-bit environment to a 32-bit one, and vice versa.

At any time, you can change the subsystem for true remote procedure call (RPC) to make OLE 2.0 a distributed object system (see fig. 1.2). In fact, this is what Microsoft has done with Distributed OLE, in which the LRPC system is replaced with an RPC compatible with the standard defined by the Open Software Foundation (OSF) in its Distributed Computing Environment (DCE) model. Microsoft and Digital have demonstrated just such a system. In the demonstration, an OSF/1 server ran a stock quote object that updated an Excel spreadsheet running on a Windows NT machine. Excel was not aware that the data was being sent to it from a remote machine or that the originating object was running on a UNIX machine. The entire process was transparent to both the user and the application. Every OLE 2.0 compliant application can connect remotely to other objects without requiring any changes to the application's code; in fact, you don't even have to recompile such applications. Chapter 19, "Distributed Objects," discusses Distributed OLE in more detail.

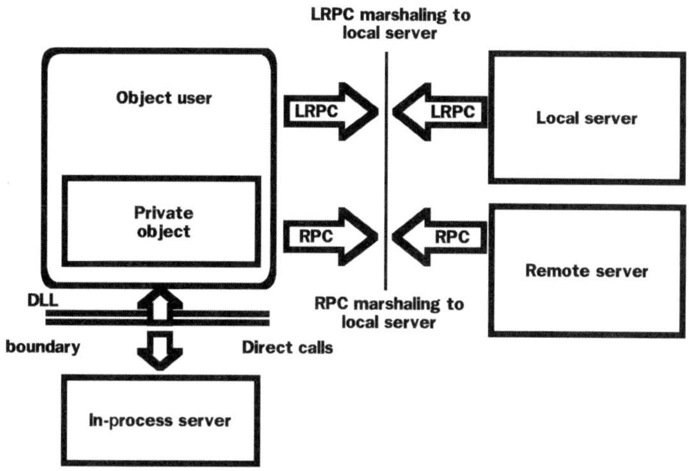

Fig. 1.2
Scaleable components.

The Structured Storage System

OLE 2.0 incorporates a structured storage system that provides persistent storage for objects. Compound files (OLE's implementation of structured storage) provide a file system within a file system. Compound files are structured similar to the DOS file system with *streams* (files) and *storages* (directories). Stream names can be as long as 32 characters.

Compound files provide *transacted storages*, in which changes are not written until you actually commit them. The specification also defines special streams called *property sets* that conform to a standard layout. Any application that can read property sets can extract information from your files. This feature is particularly powerful if the system shell can also read property sets.

In fact, this is the case in Windows 95. One special property set is the Summary Information stream, which can include such information about the document as the author's name, the last time the document was saved, the full name of the documents, thumbnails, and keywords. The Windows 95 shell can search through compound files for Summary Information fields.

Chapter 8, "OLE Compound Files," examines property sets in greater detail.

The current implementation of compound files runs under Windows 3.1, but a future version of Windows NT provides a native object file system (OFS). This new file system provides full searching of the contents of streams and property sets. However, the system is fully compatible with the current implementation of compound files and, like Distributed OLE, is completely transparent to the application.

Monikers

A new type of object, called a *moniker*, addresses link tracking. In OLE 1.0, a major annoyance was the broken links created by moving files. Links were so easily broken because they were stored as absolute path names. OLE 2.0 partially solves this problem by providing object monikers, which enable you to store relative path names with the absolute path names. The operating system (OS) actually moves the files, so the problem of broken links will be completely solved only when support from the OS is implemented. Microsoft promises this support in the OFS of a future release of Windows NT. Current OLE applications, when running on this release of Windows NT, will automatically receive this support through the system's implementation of object monikers. Again, no changes to the application's code will be required.

The Document-oriented Paradigm

Before delving further into the OLE technologies, you take a small detour in this section to examine the concept of compound documents and the document-oriented paradigm.

For some time now, programmers have bought into the promise of object-oriented programming (OOP), making a sometimes painful transition from traditional procedural languages like C and Pascal to modern object-oriented languages like C++. Along the way, programmers have also discovered the benefits of code reuse, class libraries, and frameworks. By delegating the "grunt work" to a particular class library or framework, you can focus your programming efforts on the application or problem at hand and thus shorten the development cycle. By inheriting a particular object's methods and data, you can extend the object's functionality to suit a particular task. Through the Microsoft Foundation Classes (MFC) and ObjectWindows Library (OWL) frameworks, Microsoft and Borland have demonstrated how object-oriented frameworks can both simplify and enhance the Microsoft Windows APIs. OOP techniques have unquestionably delivered on their promise.

Although programmers have enjoyed the benefits of object-oriented development techniques in their work, little of this object technology has been passed along to the user. Instead, programmers continue to deliver to the customer traditional monolithic applications. Fortunately, this is slowly starting to change, as the industry begins to move toward a more document-centered model of software development.

In the Document-Oriented Interface (DOI) model, the document itself is the focus of all the user's work. To begin working with a document, the user does not start an application and then choose Open from the File menu; instead, the document is simply opened. The underlying OS or system shell understands how to open a generic container to display the document for viewing or editing. This container is simply a storage place for various types of objects. These objects can be formatted text, graphics, numbers, video clips, or even embedded sound clips.

Objects can be moved around the containers or dragged and dropped to another container. To manipulate these objects, users invoke the object servers that support the objects. In the DOI paradigm, each object contains both the data and the code that can edit or view the data. Clicking on any object with a right mouse button usually brings up a popup menu that displays the various verbs that the user can invoke on that object.

In fact, the DOI paradigm fundamentally changes the definition of the word *document*. You normally associate the term *document* with a specific type; for example, you might associate a word-processing document with Microsoft Word or a spreadsheet document with Microsoft Excel. A compound document, on the other hand, is a collection of parts or objects; the document itself simply keeps all these objects in one place.

Component Software

The DOI introduces the notion of *component software*. Applications as you currently recognize them will disappear. The functionality of these applications will be broken into components or tools. If you want to write a letter, you will create an empty text object that provides basic text formatting facilities but not a spell checker. To spell-check the document, you invoke a separate spell-checking object.

Because the tools are separate objects, they will not necessarily come from the same software vendor. This will give users the choice of using the tools that best suit the particular task at hand. It also gives tool vendors the opportunity to concentrate all their resources on a particular tool.

The operating system also helps by providing standard viewers for various types of objects. Objects will let other tools open and edit them. If you receive a document that contains figures created with Excel, but you have only Lotus 1-2-3 available, you simply tell the object to convert itself to a 1-2-3 object.

As software developers start to develop components, the cost and time of the development cycle will decrease. Developers can leverage each other's objects in their own work. This availability of third-party objects will enable developers to concentrate on specific features of their product while delivering to their customers products that include the standard features—like spell checkers and graphing tools—that users have come to expect from modern software.

Note

Although this book is about OLE 2.0, Microsoft did not invent the DOI paradigm, nor is OLE 2.0 the only technology that supports this paradigm. OpenDoc from Apple, IBM, Novell, and WordPerfect is an architecture designed to create compound documents and component software. This architecture provides scripting technology based on Apple's AppleScript and Apple Events, object storage based on Apple's Bento technology, and a distributed object model based on IBM's Distributed System Object Model (DSOM). OpenDoc promises cross-platform interoperability and is an open standard. (OpenDoc will be licensed by CILabs [Component Integration Laboratories].) However, OLE 2.0 is already available, with hundreds of shipping applications already supporting it. Development tools such as MFC provide developers with the support necessary for developing OLE-compliant applications. Currently, OpenDoc is still only a specification. In fact, OpenDoc's survival in the marketplace will depend largely on its capability to interoperate with OLE.

The Principal Technologies

This section examines the principal technologies behind OLE 2.0. Although all the mechanisms to create compound documents are available in OLE 2.0, much more is provided. OLE 2.0 provides a set of layered technologies (see fig. 1.3) that you can implement independently of each other. You delve more deeply into all these technologies when you begin to develop code in later chapters.

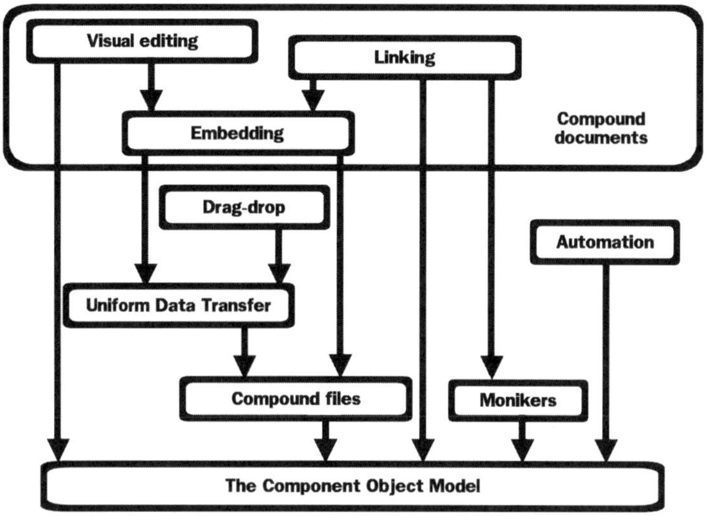

Fig. 1.3
OLE 2.0 technologies.

Visual Editing

Visual editing, or the in-place editing of embedded objects, is probably the most discussed aspect of OLE 2.0. From a user's perspective, one of the most difficult aspects of OLE 1.0's user interface (UI) is the context switch that occurs when the user double-clicks an object. The object's server is invoked and executed in a separate window. Instead, visual editing does what most users would naturally expect: the data is edited within the container. Visual editing is the first step toward achieving a true document-oriented interface. In visual editing, the application comes to the user, instead of forcing the user to come to the application.

So what actually happens during visual editing? The user first selects the object and double-clicks it. At this stage, the data that the user is viewing is simply a presentation metafile, that, with the help of the OLE libraries, the container draws in its client area. By double-clicking the object, the user invokes the object server. The object server then attempts to negotiate with the container for space for its toolbars and other adornments. If this negotiation succeeds, the server creates an editing window and awaits user input.

A major part of this complex series of negotiations involves menus. While the object is in-place active, its menu merges with the container's menu. Each object contains a special set of menus that are used for in-place activation.

The rules are simple. The container supplies three submenu groups: the File group, the Container group, and the Window group. The object supplies the Edit group, the Object group, and the Help group. These submenu groups are combined to form the menu for the activated object (see fig. 1.4). The implementation of merged menus is made more complex by having to deal with context-sensitive help and keyboard accelerators. Help or error messages that are normally displayed on the object server's status bar are routed to that container's status bar.

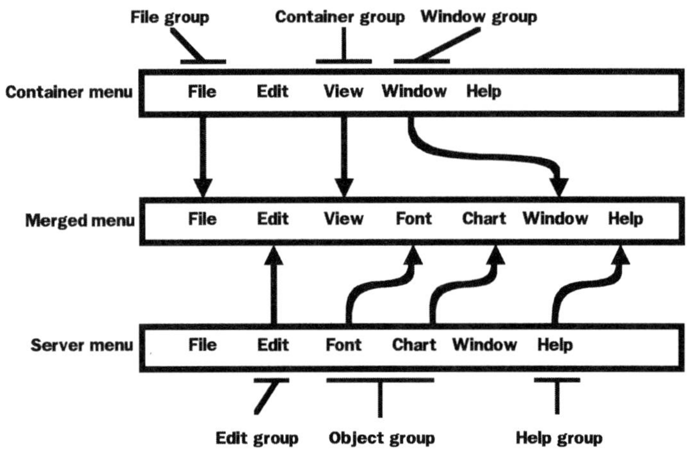

Fig. 1.4 Visual editing and menu merging.

This seamless integration with the container makes the object appear to be part of the container. When finished with the object, the user simply clicks on the client area to deactivate the object. The object removes its frame adornments and floating windows, and removes the merged menu. The server shuts down and the updated data returns to the container for storage.

Like so many software features, visual editing, while making it easy for the user to edit embedded objects, is extremely difficult for the developer to implement. You return to the details of implementing visual editing in Chapter 9, "A Simple MFC OLE Server," when you develop an OLE in-place server.

Visual editing applies only to embedded objects. Because the container stores an embedded object's data, you can edit it. A linked object's data, on the other hand, is stored elsewhere, so you must edit it within the object server.

Visual editing as provided in the initial release of OLE 2.0 is not perfect. Currently, OLE provides no support for irregularly shaped objects (those that are not rectangular). Likewise, large objects that straddle page boundaries in the container are not supported. For example, when a large spreadsheet object is embedded in a container, the user may want to activate a part of the object that lies on a particular page. This process, known as extended layout negotiation, is mentioned in the OLE 2.0 design specification but did not make it into the current release.

Another area of importance for visual editing is toolbar negotiation. Unfortunately, vendors have a long way to go before agreeing on a standard appearance for toolbars. The merging of menus during visual editing is possible only because Microsoft has laid down all standards and guidelines for an application's menus since the first release of Windows. All applications that adhere to the Windows interface guidelines include File, Edit, and, in the case of Multiple Document Interface (MDI) applications, Window menus. This standardization greatly simplifies the process of merging menus. The same standardization has not yet been done for toolbars.

Link Tracking and Management

Before you can understand link tracking and management technology, you need to be familiar with the following terms:

- A *link* or *linked object* is an OLE object that contains a reference to a link source.
- A *link source* is an object that provides the source data for the linked object.
- A *moniker* is a handle to a link source that is persistently stored with the linked object.
- *Moniker binding* is the process of getting from the linked object's moniker a pointer to a running instance of the link source.

These terms often are a source of confusion for developers when they begin to work with OLE.

Object linking (the *L* in OLE) has existed since the inception of DDE. OLE 1.0 introduced two distinct types of compound document objects:

- *Embedded* objects, the data of which is completely contained by the document
- *Linked* objects, the source data of which is stored apart from the document

OLE 1.0 also had four major restrictions that frustrated both users and developers:

- The definition of the link source was an object with two parts: the document name and the item name. Therefore, you could not link to embedded objects in the document or use nested links.
- The document name was stored as an absolute path. This was the source of the `broken links` error messages that users often encountered. If you moved the source document from its original location, you broke the link.
- Automatic links were a problem. If you linked a chart to your document and opened the chart is a separate application, no automatic updating of the linked chart would take place. To effect automatic linking in OLE 1.0, you had to open the linked chart from within the document.
- If you opened an OLE 1.0 compound document that contained linked objects, you had no way to determine whether the presentation data was up to date.

OLE 2.0 addresses each of these problems. The release supports linking to embedded objects, arbitrary deep nested linking, linking to files with absolute and relative path names, and linking to ranges (such as bookmarks or spreadsheet cells).

So, from a container's point of view, what is the difference between a linked and an embedded object? A linked object in a container is actually an embedded object. The major difference (apart from the COM interfaces supported) is that the native data for a linked object is a special OLE object called a *moniker*. (Chapter 2, "The Component Object Model," covers COM interfaces in detail.) The moniker object contains a reference to the actual source object.

A moniker is an object that contains a reference to a link source. The most basic operation that you perform on a moniker is that of binding it to the object that it references. In binding, the linked object is connected to the link source and an interface pointer is returned. You can then use this pointer to retrieve the updated presentation data for an object or to activate the object for editing.

Monikers come in different types, some defined by the user and some predefined by OLE. There are five predefined monikers:

- A *composite moniker*, as its name suggests, is composed of other monikers. Each of these simple monikers contains information that enables the containers to access the link source. For example, if your Microsoft Excel spreadsheet contains a quarterly report, the current sales figures are actually an embedded database object. Furthermore, the pie chart on the sheet is actually linked to the figures in the database object (see fig. 1.5). The composite moniker that references the figures would be composed of three monikers (see fig. 1.6). Each moniker within the composite moniker has information that leads to the actual link source.

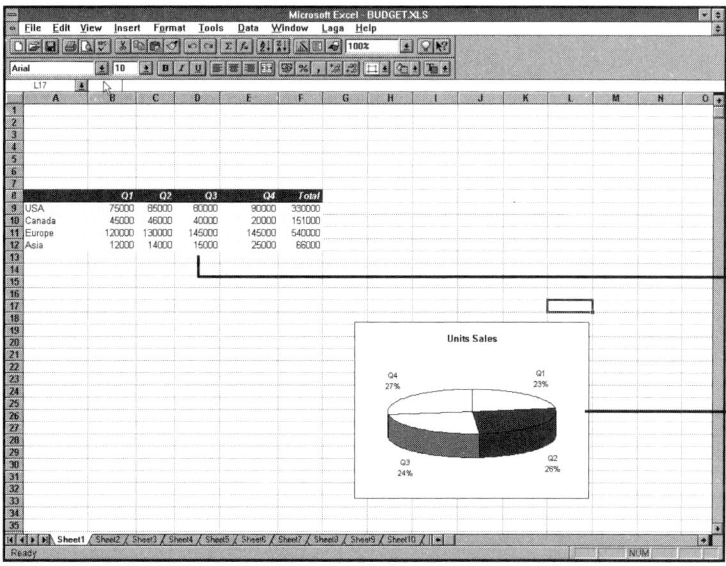

Fig. 1.5
A spreadsheet with an embedded database object.

Fig. 1.6
A composite moniker.

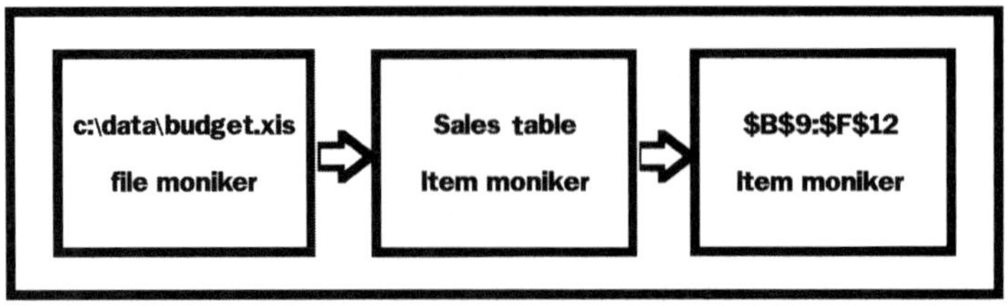

Although you create monikers from left to right, they are bound from *right to left*. The reason for this right-to-left direction is that binding is a potentially expensive process, and if you are already positioned somewhere on the moniker, the process is much quicker if you begin at the right. You'll see an example of this in Chapter 10, "A Full OLE Server."

- A *file moniker* is a simple moniker that contains a path name to a link source. The path name can be absolute or relative. When you bind to a file moniker, the creating application is determined (with `GetClassFile`), executed, and asked to open the file described in the moniker. Opening files can be an expensive process, particularly on busy networks, which is one of the reasons that the composite monikers bind from right to left. If the file is already opened, you do not want to reopen it. Even if you create an absolute file moniker for a particular object, OLE will also create a relative moniker from the absolute one. This relative moniker always takes precedence over the absolute one when binding. The absolute moniker is used only if the relative moniker fails to bind.

- An *item moniker* is actually a generalization of the OLE 1.0 *document, item* referencing system. Item monikers are application-defined references to items of data within a particular document. Examples include cell ranges in a spreadsheet and bookmarks in a word-processing program. You can nest item monikers arbitrarily deep, as in the following example:

  ```
  document[,item[,item[,item]]]
  ```

  In this case, the rightmost moniker binds to the moniker on the left, and so on, until the reference is resolved.

- An *antimoniker* removes the moniker that precedes it in a composite moniker. When you create a composite moniker, you constantly append new monikers to it, which are added from left to right. However, no mechanism exists for removing or deleting one of these simple monikers. Instead, you use an antimoniker. These monikers cannot be bound to and perform no other useful function.

- *Pointer monikers,* instead of referencing objects in passive space (on disk), reference objects only in active space (process memory). You cannot serialize pointer monikers, but you can marshal them to a different process.

OLE 2.0 provides relative path link tracking. Therefore, if you have a link to a file that resides in C:\DATA\EXCEL and move the entire tree structure to D:, the relative moniker \EXCEL\BUDGET.XLS may be enough to locate the file. However, if you move the file to D:\REPORTS\BUDGET.XLS, the moniker binding fails.

The current implementation method works in two cases:

- When the link source and the container are moved or copied but retain the same relative directory structure. This happens especially if both documents are in the same directory. In this case, the relative moniker binding always works.
- When the link source remains constant and the document is moved elsewhere. In this case, although the relative moniker fails to bind, the absolute moniker succeeds.

For general link tracking to work, support from the underlying OS is required. This support will probably come with a new type of moniker called a *tracking moniker*. This moniker will be responsible for recording the tracking information for a particular object. Although the new moniker will require changes to the OLE libraries, these changes will not result in the breaking of existing applications.

One problem with OLE 1.0 involves automatic links. If you open a linked source separately from the container that contains the linked object, the presentation data for the link is not updated. The OLE 2.0 architects decided to solve this problem with the alert object table (AOT). This table is basically a list of objects and monikers that must be updated. Unfortunately, the OLE 2.0 architects omitted the alert object table from OLE 2.0, so automatic links remain a problem. If you are curious about the proposed implementation of the alert object table, the OLE 2.0 design specification includes its documentation.

Compound Files and Structured Storage

The OLE 2.0 design specification describes a means of providing persistent storage for objects. Compound files are the implementation of the structured storage concept. Structured storage involves two types of objects: storage and stream. These object types are analogous to the directories and files in a file system.

In structured storage, each object can have its own stream. During the lifetime of the object, it can read and write to this stream. The object has full control over the amount of data that is read or written. This solves a major problem of OLE 1.0, in which an object had to read its entire data into memory to access the data. Although each object has its own stream, a compound document, such as a word-processing document, that contains many types of objects is physically stored as a single disk file. Thus Microsoft uses the phrase "a file system within a file" when referring to structured storage. The internal structure of a compound file is similar to the structure of your hard disk.

Within any compound file, several storage and stream objects exist (see fig. 1.7). The first storage object, the *root storage*, is the parent of all other storages and streams. You create storages and streams much as you create files and directories. The current implementation of compound files is implemented on top of the file allocation table (FAT) file system of Windows 3.1 and NTFS (NT File System) under Windows NT. A future version of Windows NT will implement a native OFS that will directly support storage and stream objects. Compound files provide binary compatibility across all platforms on which OLE is implemented.

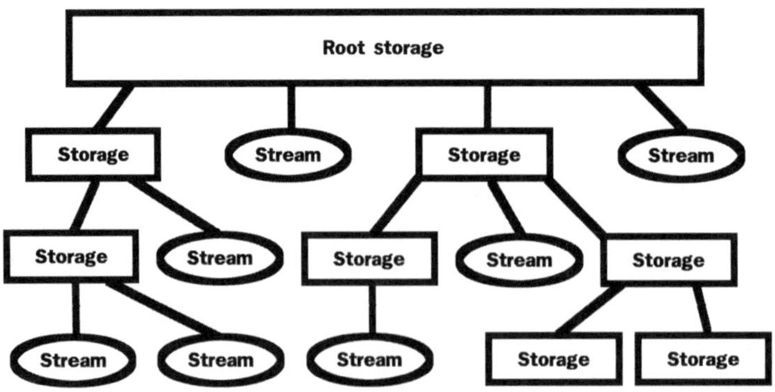

Fig. 1.7
OLE compound files.

Note

Compound files were originally known as *docfiles*, but have since been renamed *compound files* by Microsoft's marketing experts.

Access Modes

Structured storage supports two modes of access:

- In *direct* mode, any changes made to the object's data are immediately written to the file.
- In *transacted* mode, the changes are buffered until either a commit or rollback operation is performed.

One of the reasons that transacted mode is so important involves the use of compound documents. For example, suppose that you have a Word 6.0 document that contains an embedded spreadsheet object from Excel. You decide to change some of the figures in the spreadsheet and activate the object. When you finish, you save the changes and deactivate the object to return to Word. You then decide to exit Word *without* saving the changes that you made to the text. You now have a problem: what should be done to the changes that you made to the spreadsheet object? This is precisely the problem that transacted storage tries to solve. If you open the spreadsheet object in transacted mode, the container (Word in this case) can simply close the storage without committing the changes. When you reopen the document, the changes that you made to the text and to the spreadsheet figures have been discarded.

Transacted mode has its price. Performance suffers because the mode takes a "snapshot" of the original data and stores it in an unused portion of the file. For large objects, this process can take time. Normally, this performance hit would not be a problem: if you want to take advantage of rollback and commit in your application, you use transacted mode access and accept the performance hit; if speed is more important, you open the storage in direct mode.

However, with structured storage, the choice is not that simple. Unfortunately, in the current implementation of compound files, any storage that you open in direct access mode must also be opened exclusively. In other words, no other process can open that storage, not even in read-only mode.

While not a problem in a single-user environment, this constraint is a major headache in a network environment. Perhaps future releases of compound files will solve these problems.

Transacted access applies only to storage objects, not to stream objects. All stream objects are opened in direct and therefore exclusive mode.

Sharing Storage Objects

One important feature of structured storage is that you can marshal storage objects between processes. In the compound document scenario, the container creates the actual storage object and receives a pointer to the storage object. This pointer enables the container to retain control over when the storage is committed. Instead of transferring data through global memory, you can transfer a pointer to a storage object.

The *LockBytes* Object

In addition to the stream and storage object types, structured storage includes a third type of object: `LockBytes`. This object sits between the root storage object and the actual file system. The root storage object should not have to concern itself with the details of the storage device. For example, the storage medium may be global memory rather than a disk device. The root storage object need not be concerned about any difference between these mediums; instead, the `LockBytes` object takes care of the details (see fig. 1.8).

Fig. 1.8
The *LockBytes* object.

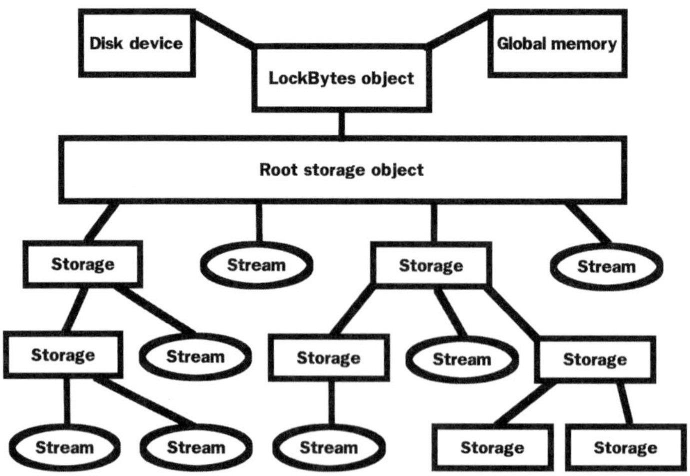

Special Streams

When an embedded object from a compound document is stored, the OLE libraries create a storage object for that object. The object's native data is stored in a stream under that storage object. OLE also creates several other streams. According to the OLE specification, any streams whose names begin with 0x01 to 0x1F (hexadecimal) are reserved. Currently, four such streams are in use:

0x01...	Control streams
0x02...	At least one and perhaps more presentation data streams
0x03...	Streams used by the container
0x04...	Property sets

In Chapter 4, "The OLE SDK," you examine the contents of each of these streams in detail as you use the compound file viewer provided with the OLE 2.0 SDK.

The Future of Structured Storage

How far can Microsoft go with structured storage? One direction in which Microsoft is heading is toward a unified namespace represented by a root storage. Network nodes would be substorages, and the volumes on these nodes would also be substorage objects. In fact, remote and local volumes and their directories and files would be storage and stream objects. If Microsoft accomplishes this goal, you will be able to place the system shell on top of root storage, and then browse or search the entire namespace—truly information at your fingertips.

Uniform Data Transfer

In the current release of Windows, you transfer data from one application to another in one of two ways. The most common method is clipboard transfer. Users select the data they want to transfer and copy it to the clipboard. The contents of the clipboard are then pasted into the receiving application. The second method is to establish a DDE link between the applications and then *poke* the data into the receiving application. Both of these methods use global memory to transfer the data. For large objects such a color bitmaps, the latter method of storing data in global memory can be prohibitive because of the amount of data involved.

After the clipboard receives data or the receiving application accepts the data through a DDE transfer, the receiving application's only information about the data itself is described by a clipboard data type. This data type is represented by a 16-bit integer and usually refers to a standard type such as CF_TEXT or CF_BITMAP. To add to the confusion, you have to use different protocols to effect each type of transfer. Obviously the OLE 2.0 architects had to address this problem, and their solution is Uniform Data Transfer (UDT) through OLE data objects.

Uniform Data Transfer provides a single protocol for data transfer, whether it is through the clipboard, drag-drop operations, or any other method. This single protocol is possible because of the separation of the actual transfer protocol from the exchange of data. Most important, the protocol transfers the *description* of the data, not the actual data itself. The data remains in storage until the receiver agrees to accept the data. After you develop the code to exchange data through the clipboard with OLE data objects, you can use the same code for drag-drop operations. The receiving container isn't concerned about how you actually transferred the data to it. Data transfer is provided through a special type of OLE object called a *data object.*

An important feature of Uniform Data Transfer is the addition of two new data structures. One structure provides a way to describe the data's storage medium, and the other contains a full description of the data.

The first of these structures, STGMEDIUM, describes the data's location. The data can exist in a global memory buffer, a disk file, a compound file stream, or a compound file storage object (see fig. 1.9).

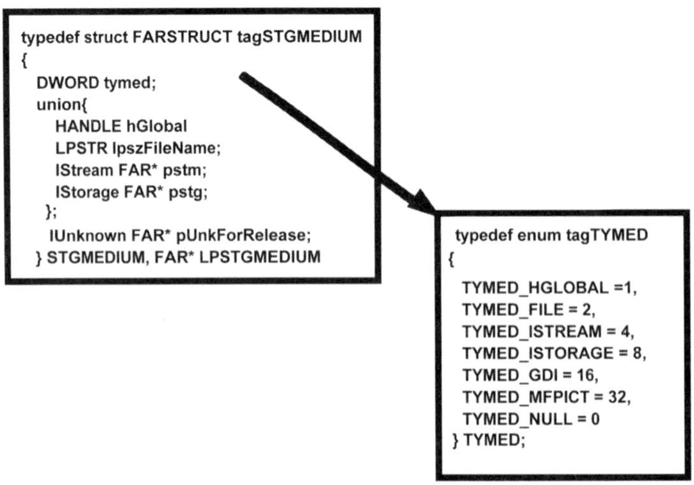

Fig. 1.9
The STGMEDIUM data structure.

The other data structure, FORMATETC, provides a rich description of the data, including information about the device to which the data was rendered (see fig. 1.10).

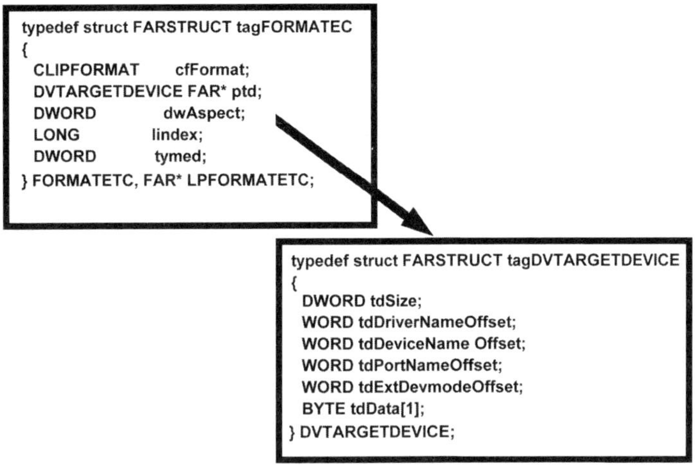

Fig. 1.10
The FORMATETC data structure.

One result of these two new data structures is that you can use the most convenient data medium with the most descriptive data description for each transfer.

DDE introduced the concept of warm and hot data links. In a *warm* link, the source of the data sends a notification of changes in the data to the data's consumer. The consumer can then request the new data. In a *hot* link, data is automatically sent each time that it changes. Notification is very important, especially in applications that constantly update data. To establish a notification link, an application creates an special object called an *advise sink*. This object is then connected to the data object and receives notification whenever the data changes. A series of flags that you set when creating the object determines how often and when the notifications are sent. As with DDE, warm or hot links can be used.

The drag-drop protocol of OLE is one of its most visible features. Drag-drop support is a major UI feature that provides the user with instant visual feedback of a data transfer operation. You simply select the object that you want to copy or move with the mouse and drag it to its destination.

The operation actually is just an extension of the clipboard I/O without the clipboard. Using the same code as you develop for clipboard I/O, you can drag and drop data within your application and also between applications.

OLE 2.0 drag-drop support provides instant and dynamic feedback to the user. For example, if a container refuses to accept the offered data, the mouse cursor changes into the international symbol for "no" (a circle with a line drawn diagonally through it); if, on the other hand, the container agrees to accept the data, the data's outline appears, showing the user immediately the data's size and where the data will be placed. By holding down the Ctrl key, you can control whether the data is moved or copied. The mouse cursor changes to reflect this choice by providing visual feedback to the user.

Implementing OLE's drag-drop support in your application is not difficult, as you will see when you develop your first sample application in Chapter 3, "A Sample C++ Application." Closely related to the transfer of data between or within applications is the process of displaying the presentation data of the object. Chapter 3 also demonstrates how you do this and describes the support provided by OLE.

OLE Automation

OLE Automation, or programmable objects, is the mechanism by which an object can expose its methods and properties to another application. Microsoft originally conceived OLE Automation as a means of providing a global macro language for Windows. Ultimately Microsoft decided against this, however, opting instead to let ISVs develop their own macros languages and tools and thus give the user a greater choice. Microsoft did, however, develop a version of Visual Basic, called Visual Basic for Applications (VBA), which provides this global macro language to Microsoft Office products such as Excel 5.0.

With an OLE Automation tool such as Visual Basic 3.0, a user can get a list of all Automation servers in the system and the available methods and properties for each. Visual Basic 3.0 then provides the user with the means to access these methods. Microsoft Word 6.0, for example, exposes its entire macro language (WordBasic) through one Automation object. This one object enables the user of a Visual Basic 3.0 program to control Microsoft Word completely from within the Visual Basic application.

This mechanism opens up enormous possibilities for writing custom applications, especially for corporate developers. Excel 5.0 supports over 128 programmable objects. As more developers add OLE Automation support to their applications, the boundaries between applications will begin to blur and you will see tighter application integration on the desktop.

Why would you want to expose your application's functionality? Every software developer knows what it is like to deliver a product to a customer only to be asked why certain features and functions were not included in the application. By exposing your application's methods through OLE Automation, you enable the user to decide how best to use this functionality. Using an OLE Automation tool such as Visual Basic 3.0, your customer can completely customize your application. You no longer have to read your customer's mind, anticipating all his favorite features, and can instead concentrate on delivering a tool set that the customer can use in many ways. In fact, the programming tool that the user uses to drive your application can be any application that supports OLE Automation.

One useful feature of OLE Automation is National Language Support (NLS). This feature enables you to translate exposed object and property names into the user's native language. In the past, a problem with macros was that they were often dependent on English names in menus and dialog boxes. For example, if you ran the macro on a machine running the German version of Windows, the macro would break. NLS also extends to support such things as data formats and decimal points. Therefore, a spreadsheet object, for example, can interpret a number differently depending the location information given to the object. This interpretation can be critical. For example, the number 500.00 is interpreted as 500 in the United States but 50,000 in Scandinavia.

From Here...

OLE Automation is a broad subject that is examined in much greater detail in Part III of this book. Interestingly, OLE Automation was developed at Microsoft separately from the rest of OLE. A separate group handled everything from the design and development to the documentation of OLE Automation. Even though OLE Automation uses the Component Object Model, you can implement OLE Automation apart from OLE 2.0. This is also the case for Extended MAPI (Microsoft's messaging APIs for e-mail), which uses the COM model but has nothing to do with OLE.

In the next chapter, you examine the Component Object Model in greater detail.

Chapter 2

The Component Object Model

The object model on which OLE is built is the Component Object Model (COM). This model describes a binary standard for creating component software. If you understand the concepts and architecture of the Component Object Model, you will understand OLE. However, if you don't grasp these principles, OLE will always be a confusing and frustrating system with which you will never be truly comfortable.

This chapter looks closely at the implementation details of COM, including the following:

- Object interfaces, and how they work.
- Sharing objects between multiple clients through reference counting.
- Locating and loading objects. You will also examine the structure of the registration database and see how to use it in OLE.
- Reusing objects with OLE. Object reuse is a major feature of all object systems, and OLE is no exception. The OLE method, aggregation and delegation, defines a mechanism for binary object reuse.
- Some miscellaneous features of the COM, including memory management, enumerators, and marshaling.

Object Interfaces

In the Component Object Model, objects communicate with each other through *interfaces*. The OLE design specification defines an interface as "a grouping of a set of semantically related functions into a named unit." In other words, an interface is an atomic unit in the COM. The model guarantees that if you receive a pointer to an interface, the object supports all the methods defined for that interface. An interface defines a contract between the object and the object user.

Interfaces are a core concept in the COM. When you work with OLE, you constantly work with interfaces. Component objects are similar to C++ objects, with some important differences:

- All methods defined by an interface are public. No private or protected methods are defined.
- OLE objects do not allow any access to their data. The interface mechanism exposes only the methods of an object. However, the COM does define special data objects that are used to transfer data between processes.
- Component objects do not support traditional inheritance. You reuse objects in OLE by using either aggregation or delegation. You will look closely at both of these methods at the end of this chapter, in the section "Object Inheritance, Aggregation, and Delegation."

The compiler implements interfaces as pointers to virtual function tables, or *vtables*. This implementation is useful, because C++ compilers use the same method to dispatch functions. You don't have to use C++ to implement COM interfaces (remember, such interfaces are binary), but the language does make implementation much easier.

> **Note**
>
> To see just how much easier implementing interfaces is with C++, take a look at code in the C samples supplied with the OLE SDK.

By convention, all interfaces are named so that the first letter of their name is *I*.

The Interface *IUnknown*

To qualify as a COM object, an object must support at least one special interface: `IUnknown`. The OLE headers define this interface as follows:

```
interface IUnknown
{
      virtual HRESULT      QueryInterface(IID& iid, void **ppvObj) = 0;
      virtual ULONG     AddRef() = 0;
      virtual ULONG     Release() = 0;
}
```

Note that the interface is defined as `struct`.

As you can see, this code defines all the functions as virtual. The code defines an interface, but does not implement it. Only the order of a set of function signatures is defined. Any object that supports the `IUnknown` interface also implements the interface.

Figure 2.1 shows an object that implements `IUnknown`. Notice the double-indirection that is used to access the member functions, and the fact that data can never be accessed through a COM interface.

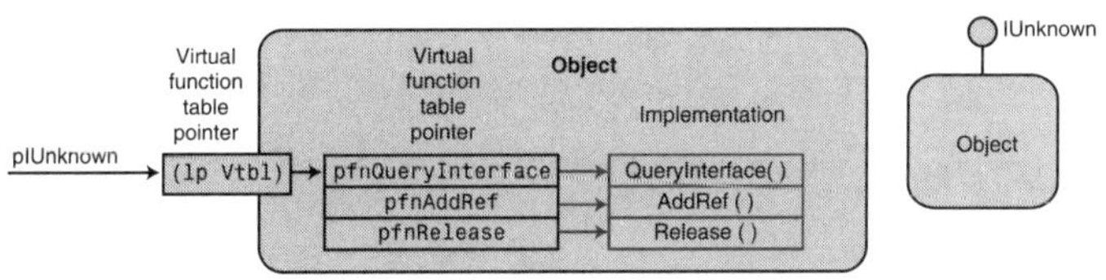

Fig. 2.1
An object that implements *IUnknown*.

COM provides the method `QueryInterface`, which enables objects to support multiple interfaces. This method enables the user to ask the object whether it supports a particular interface.

For example, suppose that you have a pointer to an OLE object defined as `pUnk`, and you want to see whether this particular object supports the interface `IOleObject`. The following code segment demonstrates how you can find out:

```
{
      LPOLEOBJECT pOle;
      HRESULT hr;
      .
      .
      .
      // Ask the object, through the pointer that you already have,
      // whether it supports the interface IOleObject.
      hr = pUnk->QueryInterface(IID_OleObject,(void **)&pOle);
      if(SUCCEEDED(hr))
      {
            // The object supports the IOleObject interface.
            // pOle now is the pointer to the object's implementation
            // of IOleObject
      }
}
```

If the `QueryInterface` method succeeds, you are returned to a pointer to the interface. The interfaces supported by an object are static; if your `QueryInterface` method succeeds for a particular interface of an object once, the method will also succeed if you query again. The object may not decide to implement the interface, and then later decline a request for the interface. Object interfaces are static, primarily to allow remote access to the object.

The `QueryInterface` method also enables you to update an object so that it can support additional interfaces without causing problems for the object's users. The object's user can support new features and still work with older objects. If an object does not support a new interface, the object simply returns E_NOINTERFACE to indicate to the caller that the interface is not supported.

The `IUnknown` interface supports two functions that are used in reference counting: `AddRef` increases a object's reference count, and `Release` decreases the reference count.

Reference Counting

After they are loaded into memory, objects can support multiple clients. Then, when all the clients finish using an object, it is unloaded from memory. But how does the object know when it is no longer needed? How does the object know how many clients are currently using it?

The answer to these questions lies in the COM *reference counting mechanism.* This mechanism ensures that the object is active and available as long as clients are using it. The object itself is responsible for managing the reference count.

However, the object's users must adhere to the reference-counting rules. When you receive a pointer to an interface through `QueryInterface`, the object calls `AddRef` for itself. However, if you copy that pointer, you are responsible for calling `AddRef` on the new pointer. When you finish using the object, you call `Release`, which decreases the object's reference count. When the reference count reaches zero, the object is free to destroy itself.

These rules sound simple, and they are. However, forgetting to call `AddRef` for an interface pointer can result in the object destroying itself while you are using it. Also, forgetting to call `Release` for an interface pointer condemns the object to remain forever in memory. Remember, you must call `AddRef` for each *new* copy of an interface pointer, and call `Released` to destroy each pointer.

These rules have some exceptions. If you have special knowledge about the lifetime of an interface pointer, you can skip the reference counting. In the following example, you can see how special knowledge of the nested lifetime of `pOle2` enables you to skip calling `AddRef` for this pointer:

```
{
    LPOLEOBJECT pOle1 = NULL, pOle2 = NULL;
    HRESULT hr;

    hr = pUnk->QueryInterface(IID_IOleObject,(void **)&pOle1);
    if(SUCCEEDED(hr))
    {
        // You now make a copy of this pointer:
        pOle2 = pOle1;
        // You have already locked the object in memory, so you
        // don't have to call AddRef() for the copied pointer.

        // Use the interfaces
        pOle1->CallSomeMethod();
        pOle2->CallSomeMethod();

        // You are finished with the object, so you release
        // the reference count.
        pOle1->Release();
        // If the reference count reaches zero, the object
        // destroys itself.
        pOle1 = NULL ;    // pointer no longer valid
        pOle2 = NULL ;    // pointer no longer valid
    }
}
```

As long as you do not release the object's reference count, you can copy the pointer and use it without calling `AddRef`.

How the System Finds Objects

Objects are dynamically loaded into the system whenever a user demands the object's services. The objects themselves may already be in memory, on the user's hard disk, or perhaps running remotely on another workstation. How do the OLE libraries know which objects to load and where they are located?

To support systems that can potentially have millions of independent objects running simultaneously, the COM architects at Microsoft needed a way to identify objects uniquely. The architects borrowed the concept of a globally unique identifier (GUID) from Apollo Computer, Inc. (The Open Software Foundation [OSF], in its Distributed Computing Environment [DCE] specification, also adopted GUIDs.) GUIDs are 128-bit (16-byte) numbers that are statistically guaranteed to be unique. The OLE API function `CoCreateGUID` can be used to generate GUIDs on the fly (the function makes the GUIDs unique by using the network adapter ID if present, the current date and time, and other information found on the machine).

Each object is identified by a special ID, *CLSID* (class ID). A CLSID is a GUID. OLE uses this and several other similar IDs extensively. Besides using a CLSID, OLE uses an *IID* (interface ID) and a *UUID* (universally unique ID), which is sometimes called a *GUID* (globally unique ID). A special program that comes with the OLE 2.0 SDK, UUIDGEN.EXE, generates these numbers. This utility uses the OLE API function `CoCreateGUID` to generate the GUIDs. These GUIDs are guaranteed to be statistically unique. This method for naming objects is essential in a distributed environment, which might include millions of objects.

After obtaining the CLSID for an object, the client calls the OLE API function `CoGetClassObject`. The following is the function's prototype:

```
HRESULT CoGetClassObject(clsid,grfContext,pReserved,iid,ppv);
```

This function locates the object identified by the CLSID in the first parameter, searching the system registration database (see fig 2.2) for the name of the OLE server associated with that CLSID.

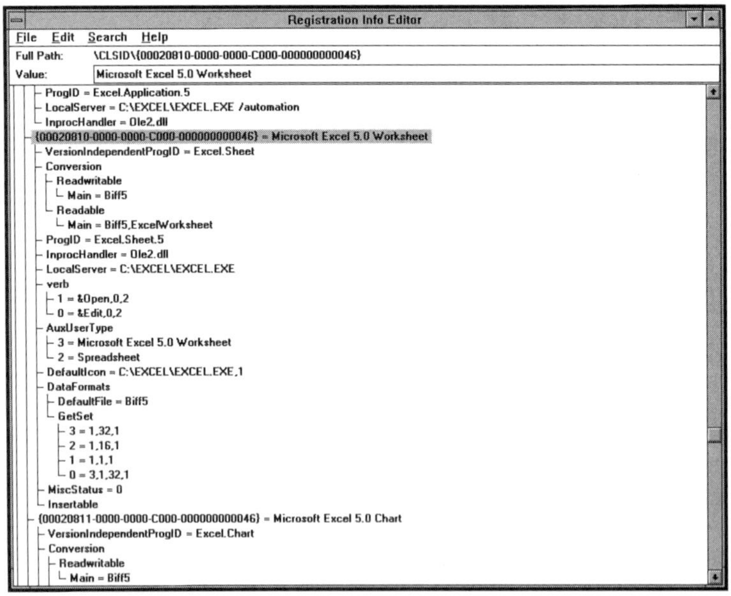

Fig. 2.2
The system registration database.

The pointer returned by this function points to the class object for the COM object. If you want to create a COM object in this way, the COM object must implement two objects: a class object and the object that actually implements the functionality of the COM object.

Note

After an object is loaded and the client creates an instance of the object, the container cannot determine whether the object was remote or local. The location of the object is completely transparent to the client code.

When the server is located, it is activated and `QueryInterfaced` for the interface defined in the fourth parameter, `iid`. As you can see in figure 2.1, the registration database stores much information about the object. In fact, the database is a central repository for all information regarding OLE objects and libraries. The following sections examine each of the database's fields.

The first line is as follows:

```
{00020810-0000-0000-C000-000000000046} = Microsoft Excel 5.0 Worksheet
```

This line describes the CLSID of Microsoft Excel 5.0. The CLSID is the key that the OLE libraries use to locate information about a particular object. The text to the right of the CLSID is the *main user type*. This text usually is presented when users choose the Paste Special option in an application.

Note

Most of the keys described in the following sections are not required. In fact, only the `LocalServer` and `InProcServer` keys are actually required. Otherwise, the object's purpose determines which keys are necessary. For example, a simple COM object that provides services to a client through a custom interface needs only `InProcServer` or `LocalServer`. However, an OLE compound document that supports conversion and more requires other keys.

The *VersionIndependentProgID* Field

The `ProgID` field that is used in OLE Automation usually contains version information. In figure 2.1, the `ProgID` is `Excel.Sheet.5`. The number 5 indicates version 5.0 of Excel. OLE Automation is discussed in detail starting in Chapter 11, "General Concepts of OLE Automation."

However, an object that supports Automation should have a `ProgID` that is independent of the product's version, so that users do not have to change their code when a new version of the product is released. In figure 2.1, the `VersionIndependentProgID` is simply `Excel.Sheet`.

The *Conversion* Field

The `Conversion` field lists the conversion types displayed in the Change Type dialog box. The `Readwritable` key shows types of objects that the object can emulate, and the `Readable` key shows the object types that the application can read and convert.

As Chapter 1 mentioned, the document-centered model of computing enables you to create a compound document with objects of type A and then e-mail the document to another user; that user may not possess server A, but can convert the A object to B-type objects.

The *ProgID* Field

The `ProgID` field is the programmatic identifier for the object. This field is used in Automation, and thus is discussed in more detail in Part III, "OLE Automation."

The *InprocHandler* Field

The `InprocHandler` field identifies the search path to the in-process handler for this type of object. This handler is usually the default implemented in OLE2.DLL.

The *LocalServer* Field

The `LocalServer` field identifies the name of the object's local server.

The *InProcServer* Field

The `InProcServer` field holds the name of the object's in-process (in-proc) server. Local servers typically are implemented in DLLs, and are loaded into the process space of the client. Win32 platforms also have `InProcServer32`, which points to the 32-bit implementation of the local server.

The *Verb* Field

The `Verb` field presents the verbs that the object supports. These verbs are usually displayed on the object's context menu. The field's format is as follows:

verb number = name,menu flags,verb flags

Verb 0 is always the object's default verb.

The *AuxUserType* Field

The AuxUserType field contains the auxiliary user types. Type 2 is the application's short name and type 3 is the application's full name. This contrasts to the Main user type, which is used in the Paste Special dialog box.

The *DefaultIcon* Field

The DefaultIcon field specifies the default icon that the API call ExtractIcon returns for this object.

The *DataFormats* Field

The DefaultFile key shows the default type of objects of this class. The GetSet key lists the default data types returned by the default handler during an EnumFormatEtc method call. Because these data types are stored in the DataFormats field, when a container queries an object, the default handler doesn't have to start the object to retrieve the data formats that the object supports.

The *MiscStatus* Field

The MiscStatus field contains varied status information about the object. The default handler returns this value during an IOleObject::GetMiscStatus call. If the object is running, it gets the status from the running object. In short, these bits are "hints" to containers on how to treat the object (the containers may ignore these hints). Table 2.1 lists all the possible values.

Table 2.1 Miscellaneous Status Information about an Object

Status Bits	Description
OLEMISC_RECOMPOSEONRESIZE	If the object's container resizes the space allocated to the object, the object will resize itself.
OLEMISC_ONLYICONIC	The object can be displayed only as an icon.
OLEMISC_INSERTNOTREPLACE	The object is not to replace the current selection during insertion, particularly if the object is being created as a link to the current selection.

(continues)

Table 2.1 Continued

Status Bits	Description
OLEMISC_STATIC	The object is static.
OLEMISC_CANTLINKINSIDE	The object cannot be a link source for a link. For example, a static object cannot be a link source.
OLEMISC_CANLINKBYOLE1	The object can be linked by an OLE 1.0 server.
OLEMISC_ISLINK	The object is linked, and is being used in OLE 1.0 compatibility code.
OLEMISC_INSIDEOUT	The object can be activated in place without being UI active (that is, without activating its menus, toolbars, and so on).
OLEMISC_ACTIVATEWHENVISIBLE	The object should be active whenever it is visible.

The *Insertable* Key

If the `Insertable` key is present, the object appears in all Insert Object dialog boxes.

The *Control* Key

If the `Control` key is present, the object is an OLE custom control and appears in Insert Control dialog boxes, as well as in the tool palettes of OLE Control Container applications.

This concludes your tour of the registration database. The database includes many other fields. Some concern OLE 1.0 servers and the shell commands for the Windows Program Manager. Others concern CLSID and server information for all the OLE 2.0 standard interfaces. However, this discussion covered the most useful and common fields.

Object Return Codes

As you read the OLE reference manual, you will notice that all interface methods return a new kind of error code called HRESULT (handle to a result code). HRESULT encapsulates both a SCODE (status code) and a handle to some extended error-handling information.

A SCODE type is 32 bits wide and consists of four fields (see fig 2.3). The topmost bit is the *severity* field. A value of 0 indicates that the function succeeded, and a value of 1 indicates an error. Next is the *context* field. OLE 2.0 does not implement this field. (In fact, the difference between a SCODE and an HRESULT is that in the HRESULT structure the context field is filled in.)

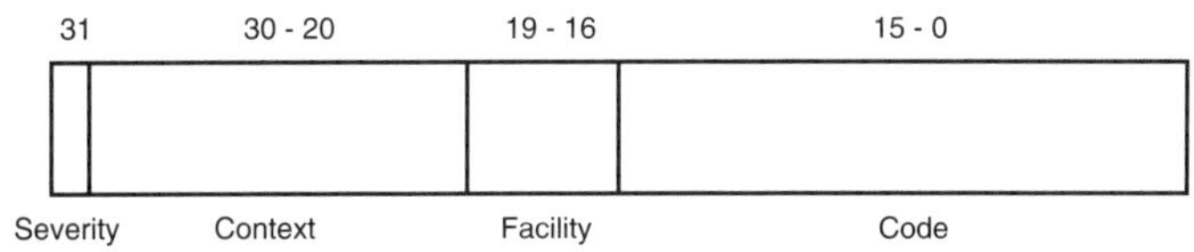

Fig. 2.3
The structure of a *SCODE.*

Next comes the *facility* field, which indicates the category of the error. Microsoft controls the allocation of facilities. Table 2.2 lists the currently defined facilities.

Table 2.2 Currently Defined Facilities

Facility	Description
FACILITY_NULL	Common status codes, such as S_OK
FACILITY_RPC	RPC (remote procedure call) error codes
FACILITY_STORAGE	Storage errors (if the lower 16 bits correspond to DOS error codes, the codes' meaning is the same as that of the DOS error codes)
FACILITY_DISPATCH	Automation errors
FACILITY_ITF	Interface-defined error codes

Last is the *code* field, which describes the actual error code.

If you examine the OLE header files, you will see that error codes have the following structure:

Facility_Severity_Reason

For example, the error code STG_E_MEDIUMFULL (which the `GetDataHere` method call returns from an `IDataObject` interface) tells you that the preferred storage medium is not large enough for the requested data. The OLE SDK provides several useful macros for dealing with SCODEs. Table 2.3 lists these macros.

Table 2.3 OLE 2.0 SDK Macros for Handling SCODEs

Macro	Definition	Description
SCODE_CODE	#define SCODE_CODE(sc)	Extracts the error code from a status code
SCODE_FACILITY	#define SCODE_FACILITY(sc)	Extracts the facility from the SCODE
SCODE_SEVERITY	#define SCODE_SEVERITY(sc)	Extracts the severity field from the SCODE
SUCCEEDED	#define SUCCEEDED(sc)	Returns true if the severity code indicates success
FAILED	#define FAILED(sc)	Returns true if the severity code indicates failure
MAKE_SCODE	#define MAKE_SCODE (sev,fac,code)	Makes a new SCODE

The API function

```
HRESULT GetScode(SCODE)
```

returns a SCODE extracted from an HRESULT. The companion to the function is

```
HRESULT ReturnFromScode(SCODE)
```

which generates an HRESULT from a SCODE.

The following function wraps a previously returned HRESULT with a SCODE, and returns the new HRESULT to the caller:

```
HRESULT PropagateResult(HRESULT,SCODE)
```

Although originally intending to use HRESULTs in a future release of OLE, Microsoft has now decided to use SCODEs exclusively. So, whenever you see a reference to HRESULT in the OLE documention, you can treat it as if it were a SCODE.

The COM Memory Allocator

A problem commonly arises when multiple processes use global memory to transfer data: who should allocate the initial memory block, and who should be responsible for freeing it? Although you can force applications to agree on a convention for managing memory, it is much simpler for the system to provide this memory management.

The OLE solution to this problem is an interface called `IMalloc`. The interface is defined as follows:

```
interface IMalloc : IUnknown
{
     virtual void * Alloc(cb) = 0;
     virtual void * ReAlloc(pv,cb) = 0;
     virtual void    Free(pv) = 0;
     virtual ULONG GetSize(pv) = 0;
     virtual int DidAlloc(pv) = 0;
     virtual void HeapMinimize() = 0;
}
```

OLE defines two types of memory: local and shared. The OLE libraries define and implement two allocator objects to manage memory. The user can define the *local allocator* by passing a pointer to an `IMalloc` object during a call to `CoInitialize` or `OleInitialize`. The OLE libraries maintain the *shared memory allocator*, which the user cannot modify.

The default implementation uses a subsegment-allocation scheme that is familiar to OS/2 programmers. This scheme, which is based on multiple local heaps, provides efficient access to memory but is constrained by a maximum block size of 64K. However, this constraint is completely lifted on Win32.

Note

For an excellent discussion and implementation of a subsegment-allocation scheme in Windows, see *Windows 3 Power Programming Techniques* by Paul Yao (Bantam Computer Books, 1990).

Whenever you need memory, you call the API function `CoGetMalloc`, specifying the type of memory you want and passing an `IMalloc` interface pointer. The returned pointer gives you access to the allocator object.

As the interface definition indicates, the methods supplied are similar to standard Windows memory-allocation functions.

Enumerators

You probably have already enumerated system objects in Windows. To do this, you call an enumerator function, such as `EnumFonts`, and pass a callback function. The enumerator then uses this callback to communicate with your application.

The COM simplifies this operation by eliminating the need for callbacks. Instead, the COM creates an *enumerator object* for each object that you want to enumerate. Each object that can be enumerated needs a special enumerator defined for it. So, COM defines the *concept* of an enumerator for each object, but not an actual enumerator interface.

Therefore, for each object to be enumerated, a special interface is created—`IEnumString` for strings, `IEnumUnknown` for `IUnknown` pointers, and so on. The interface for a string enumerator is defined as follows:

```
interface IEnumString : IUknown
{
      // Get the next string in the collection
      virtual HRESULT Next(ULONG, LPLPSTR,ULONG *) = 0;
      // Skip n elements
      virtual HRESULT Skip(ULONG) = 0;
      // Reset internal counter
      virtual HRESULT Reset() = 0;
      // Copy a string
      virtual HRESULT Clone(LPLPSTR) = 0;
}
```

A sample function to use this enumerator might look like the following:

```
{
      LPSTR lpStr;
      IEnumString *pEnum;

      pEnum = GetEnumSomeWhere();
      pEnum->AddRef();
      while(S_OK == pEnum->Next(1,&lpStr,NULL))
      {
           MessageBox(GetFocus(),lpStr,"String Enumerator",0);
      }
      pEnum->Release();
}
```

OLE uses enumerators extensively, so you will see more of them in upcoming chapters.

Object Inheritance, Aggregation, and Delegation

A familiar feature of object-oriented programming systems (OOPS) is class or object inheritance. The idea is simple: a class implements perhaps 75 percent of the functionality that you need to handle a particular problem; you then create a new object that inherits from the class and adds the missing 25 percent. Although this concept of code reuse works quite well, it has some problems.

The main problem is that you must know the details of the implementation of the base class. You need to know when you must override specific methods and when you can delegate them to the base class. You also must have the source code. (For this reason, all frameworks, including Microsoft Foundation Class and ObjectWindows Library, ship with complete source code.) If you override some of the methods of the base class and make an assumption about the state of the object when you call those methods, the code could break if the base class is revised later. This "fragile base class" problem is always possible when you redefine the base class.

However, a deeper issue is also involved: the basic difference between object-oriented programming (OOP) and object-oriented systems (OOS). Languages such as C++ and Objective C were designed to enable code reuse between developers and development groups. They were never intended to enable code reuse across multiple development groups or companies.

The Component Object Model helps solve this problem, by providing a binary standard that enables developers to use different languages to create component objects that anyone can reuse. These objects can even provide reuse across multiple platforms.

The OLE architects chose to use different methods, *aggregation* and *delegation*, for object reuse.

Aggregation

An *aggregate* is like any other object. It implements `IUnknown` and several other interfaces, and functions like any other Windows object. Internally, however, an aggregate is actually a composite object consisting of two or more objects. The object's user is unaware of how the object is implemented. Figure 2.4 shows how the aggregate looks conceptually.

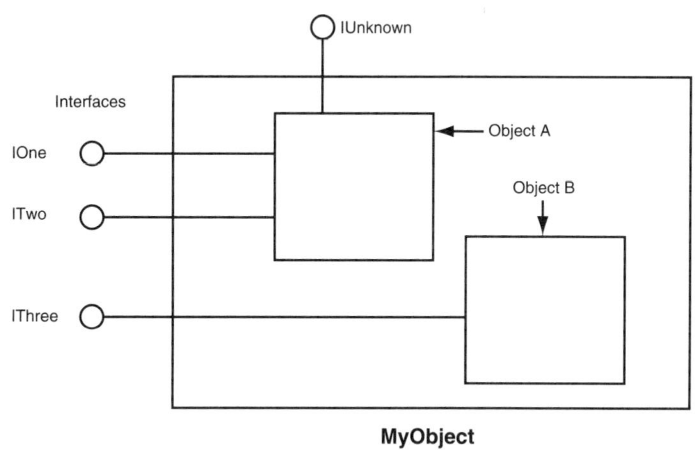

Fig. 2.4
An aggregate object.

For this model to work, the two objects must be capable of communicating. A `QueryInterface` call on interface `IThree` should be capable of returning an interface pointer to interface `IOne` or interface `ITwo`. A `Release` call on `IThree` should release the entire object if `IOne` or `ITwo` has no outstanding reference count.

The solution to this problem is a *controlling unknown*, which is a special instance of an `IUnknown` interface that is responsible for maintaining the reference count for the entire aggregate. The instance is also responsible for exposing the internal interfaces of the composite objects as its own.

To be part of an aggregate, an object must be prepared to forward to the controlling unknown all calls on its `IUnknown` interface. In other words, if you call the `QueryInterface` method for an object that is part of an aggregate, the method simply returns a call on the `QueryInterface` of the controlling unknown. This `QueryInterface` in turn either returns an interface pointer if it supports that interface or directly calls the `QueryInterface` of the aggregated object.

Figure 2.5 shows an object, `MyObject`, that supports four interfaces: `IOne`, `ITwo`, `IThree`, and `IUnknown`. The object is implemented with two internal objects: Object A and Object B. While creating Object B, Object A passed its `IUnknown` interface pointer to Object B. This interface pointer then became the controlling unknown for Object A. If a user has a pointer to interface `IThree`, a `QueryInterface` on that pointer for interface `IOne` would succeed, because the object would delegate the `QueryInterface` method call to the controlling unknown. The controlling unknown, which is the `IUnknown` interface for Object A, returns a pointer to interface `IOne`.

Fig. 2.5
An aggregate object with a controlling unknown.

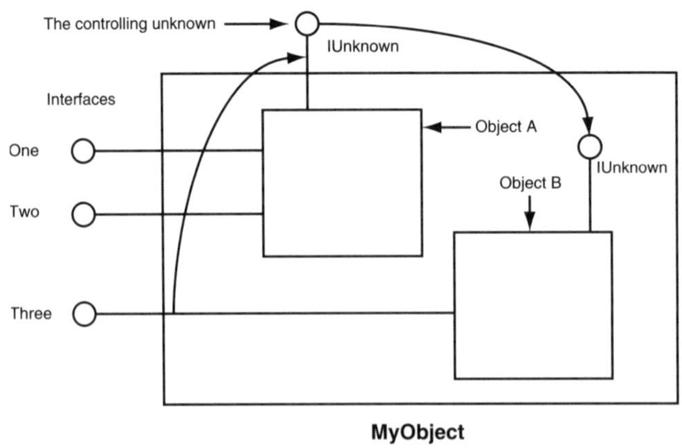

How does an object know that it is part of an aggregate, and where does the object get the pointer to the controlling unknown interface? An object knows that it is part of an aggregate only while an instance of the object is being created. The object that wants to create an aggregate passes its `IUnknown` interface pointer to `IClassFactory::CreateInstance` when creating a contained object. The object can refuse to become part of an aggregate by failing this call whenever the `punkOuter` parameter is not equal to NULL.

Several rules also govern reference counting for an aggregate. These rules are intended to prevent circular references. The OLE programmer's guide provides a full description of each of these rules.

Aggregation is not particularly difficult to implement and incurs little overhead. The main problem is conceptual. Although familiar with object reuse in a C++ world, most programmers have never before seen this type of object reuse. Like all new techniques, aggregation seems strange and difficult at first, but after you overcome your initial resistance, you will find that this method of object reuse is as good as any other.

Note

The aggregation method of object reuse has become quite controversial and the subject of much debate. The object model developed by IBM, SOM (System Object Model), uses traditional inheritance, as does Sun Microsystems DOE (Distributed Objects Everywhere). In fact, Microsoft is the only developer that does not support inheritance in its object model. Naturally, both camps believe that their method is the best. For developers, the arguments are mostly academic: if you choose to implement OLE in your application, you must use the COM method of object reuse; if you decide to implement SOM, you must then use SOM's inheritance.

Delegation

Reusing objects with the *delegation* method involves one object being completely contained by another. To reuse Object B, Object A creates an object of type B while being created. Object A then exposes all of B methods by overriding them. When the object user calls a method that is exposed by Object B, the overridden method is called and you can change the default implementation of that method. If you do not want to change the default implementation, you simply delegate to Object B's implementation.

Use the delegation method when you want to change some of the default implementation of a particular object. If you do not intend to change anything, however, you should use the aggregation method. Implementing stubs for all of an object's methods just to delegate to the object for their implementation can become tiresome.

Marshaling

The OLE design specification defines *marshaling* as "the packaging up of method arguments for transmission to a remote process." As you learned in Chapter 1, one of the design goals of OLE is to make objects accessible to remote processes while keeping the process transparent to both object servers and users. Marshaling is the key technique for achieving this goal.

The OLE design specification defines two kinds of marshaling: standard and custom. The OLE libraries provide standard marshaling, but you must provide custom marshaling when you develop custom interfaces. The OLE libraries know only about the standard interfaces and therefore cannot marshal custom interfaces.

Marshaling requires two objects: a proxy and a stub. Suppose that you have an OLE container that contains an embedded object. If you call an interface method for that object, the actual call is routed to a *proxy* object created by OLE. This proxy, which is located in COMPOBJ.DLL, validates the parameters, translates parameters from 32 bit to 16 bit (and vice versa) if necessary, and then calls the object using an LRPC (lightweight remote procedure call). The LRPC actually calls a *stub*, which "unmarshals" the parameters and then calls the object. This "unmarshaling" involves recreating the parameters that were marshaled originally. All this marshaling and unmarshaling is completely transparent to the object and container.

This design enables you to replace the LRPC mechanism with RPC (remote procedure call), which in turn enables the server object to exist on a remote workstation. Therefore, the design makes it possible to access all objects the same way.

OLE offers three kinds of servers: *remote*, *local*, and *in-process*. In-process servers, which are implemented as DLLs, do not require marshaling support. However, local and remote servers do require such support.

This look at marshaling has been brief and perhaps simplistic. As you can imagine, the implementation details of this technique can be quite complicated. Fortunately, standard marshaling, which you use whenever you use the standard COM interfaces, is completely implemented in the OLE libraries. You will return to marshaling in Chapter 17, "OLE Custom Interfaces."

From Here...

Now it is time to see how this technique works in practice. In the next chapter, you develop your first OLE application.

Chapter 3

A Sample C++ Application

It is now time to see how the Component Object Model works in practice. In this chapter, you develop an application that lets itself become a target for a drag-drop operation. The application accepts embedded objects from any application and stores the object in an OLE compound file. This application also displays the object in its client area.

You implement the COM interfaces for `IDropTarget` and `IUnknown`, and create a C++ class, `CDropTarget`, that provides the implementation. Although you will use the Microsoft Foundation Classes (MFC) library to create the application, you will not use any of MFC's OLE support.

So, let's take at look at what it takes to implement OLE support in your application.

The Initialization Code

You begin by enlarging the message queue to 96. You should enlarge the message queues for all of your applications that use OLE, to accommodate the amount of traffic generated by the OLE communication mechanism, LRPC. The MFC class libraries enlarge the queues for you automatically. If you use 32-bit OLE, this enlargement is not required.

Enlarging your message queue after your application begins to pump messages can lead to unpredictable results. You should always call the `SetMessageQueue` function before you enter your application's message pump.

In the `InitInstance` method, you check for the version number of the OLE libraries, comparing the build numbers to the build number that you used when you built the application. The OLE2VER.H header file defines the external variables `rmm` and `rup`. The `rmm` variable contains the major version number of the libraries, and `rup` contains the minor version number. If the major version of the libraries in memory differs from the libraries that you used, or if the minor number is less than what you used, you simply exit the application.

After you verify the libraries' build numbers, you call `OleInitialize` to initialize the libraries. The `OleInitialize` function takes a pointer to an `IMalloc` interface as a parameter. If you intend to use the default memory allocator, you should pass NULL for this parameter.

```
dwVersion  = OleBuildVersion();
if (HIWORD(dwVersion) != rmm || LOWORD(dwVersion) < rup)
{
     AfxMessageBox("Error: Incompatible OLE libraries");
     // Any error code will do
     hResult = ResultFromScode(E_FAIL);
     return FALSE;
}

// Initialize the OLE libraries
if((hResult = OleInitialize(NULL)) != NOERROR)
     return FALSE;
```

When you have successfully loaded the OLE libraries, you continue creating the application's main window.

The Shutdown Code

The shutdown code calls `OleUninitialize` to release the OLE libraries and then calls the base class' `ExitInstance` method. This method enables the framework to shut down the application.

The Sample Application

Listings 3.1 and 3.2 contain the complete source code for the sample application.

Listing 3.1 OLE1.H

```
#ifndef __AFXWIN_H__
     #error include 'stdafx.h' before including this file for PCH
#endif

#include "resource.h"       // main symbols
#include "iodnd.h"

//////////////////////////////////////////////////////////////////////
// COleApp:
// See ole1.cpp for the implementation of this class
//

class COleApp : public CWinApp
{
public:
     COleApp();

// Overrides
     virtual BOOL InitInstance();
     virtual int ExitInstance();


// Implementation

     //{{AFX_MSG(COleApp)
     afx_msg void OnAppAbout();
          // NOTE - the ClassWizard will add and remove member
          // functions here.
          // DO NOT EDIT what you see in these blocks of generated code!
     //}}AFX_MSG
     DECLARE_MESSAGE_MAP()
};
```

Listing 3.2 OLE1.CPP

```
#include "stdafx.h"
#include "ole1.h"

#include "mainfrm.h"
#include "oledoc.h"
#include "oleview.h"
#include "iodnd.h"

#ifdef _DEBUG
#undef THIS_FILE
static char BASED_CODE THIS_FILE[] = __FILE__;
#endif
```

(continues)

Listing 3.2 Continued

```
/////////////////////////////////////////////////////////////////////////////
// COleApp

BEGIN_MESSAGE_MAP(COleApp, CWinApp)
     //{{AFX_MSG_MAP(COleApp)
     ON_COMMAND(ID_APP_ABOUT, OnAppAbout)
          // NOTE - the ClassWizard will add and remove mapping
          // macros here.
          // DO NOT EDIT what you see in these blocks of generated code!
     //}}AFX_MSG_MAP
     // Standard file based document commands
     ON_COMMAND(ID_FILE_NEW, CWinApp::OnFileNew)
     ON_COMMAND(ID_FILE_OPEN, CWinApp::OnFileOpen)
END_MESSAGE_MAP()

/////////////////////////////////////////////////////////////////////////////
// COleApp construction

COleApp::COleApp()
{
     // This is a requirement of OLE, due to the amount
     // of traffic that the LRPC protocol can generate.
     SetMessageQueue(96);
}

/////////////////////////////////////////////////////////////////////////////
// The one and only COleApp object

COleApp NEAR theApp;

/////////////////////////////////////////////////////////////////////////////
// COleApp initialization
int COleApp::ExitInstance()
{

     // Shut down the OLE libraries
     OleUninitialize();

     return CWinApp::ExitInstance();
}
//---------------------------------------------------------------
BOOL COleApp::InitInstance()
{
     HRESULT hResult;
     DWORD dwVersion;

     //----------
     // Always check that the version of the OLE libraries
     // is compatible with the libraries you used to build
     // your application.
     dwVersion  = OleBuildVersion();
     if (HIWORD(dwVersion) != rmm ¦¦ LOWORD(dwVersion) < rup)
     {
          AfxMessageBox("Error: Incompatible OLE libraries");
          // Any error code will do
          hResult = ResultFromScode(E_FAIL);
```

```
            return FALSE;
        }

        // Initialize the OLE libraries
        if((hResult = OleInitialize(NULL)) != NOERROR)
            return FALSE;


        // Standard initialization
        // If you are not using these features and want to reduce the size
        // of your final executable, you should remove from the following
        // the specific initialization routines you do not need.

        SetDialogBkColor();        // Set dialog background color to gray
        LoadStdProfileSettings();  // Load standard INI file options
                                   // (including MRU)

        // Register the application's document templates.
        // Document templates serve as the connection between documents,
        // frame windows, and views.

        CSingleDocTemplate* pDocTemplate;
        pDocTemplate = new CSingleDocTemplate(
            IDR_MAINFRAME,
            RUNTIME_CLASS(COleDoc),
            RUNTIME_CLASS(CMainFrame),     // main SDI frame window
            RUNTIME_CLASS(COleView));

        AddDocTemplate(pDocTemplate);

        OnFileNew();

        return TRUE;
}

/////////////////////////////////////////////////////////////////////////////
// CAboutDlg dialog used for App About

class CAboutDlg : public CDialog
{
public:
        CAboutDlg();

// Dialog Data
        //{{AFX_DATA(CAboutDlg)
        enum { IDD = IDD_ABOUTBOX };
        //}}AFX_DATA

// Implementation
protected:
        virtual void DoDataExchange(CDataExchange* pDX);  // DDX/DDV support
        //{{AFX_MSG(CAboutDlg)
            // No message handlers
```

(continues)

Listing 3.2 Continued

```
    //}}AFX_MSG
    DECLARE_MESSAGE_MAP()
};

CAboutDlg::CAboutDlg() : CDialog(CAboutDlg::IDD)
{
    //{{AFX_DATA_INIT(CAboutDlg)
    //}}AFX_DATA_INIT
}

void CAboutDlg::DoDataExchange(CDataExchange* pDX)
{
    CDialog::DoDataExchange(pDX);
    //{{AFX_DATA_MAP(CAboutDlg)
    //}}AFX_DATA_MAP
}

BEGIN_MESSAGE_MAP(CAboutDlg, CDialog)
    //{{AFX_MSG_MAP(CAboutDlg)
        // No message handlers
    //}}AFX_MSG_MAP
END_MESSAGE_MAP()

// App command to run the dialog
void COleApp::OnAppAbout()
{
    CAboutDlg aboutDlg;
    aboutDlg.DoModal();
}
```

The *CDropTarget* Class

The `CDropTarget` class is an implementation of the COM interface, `IDropTarget`. OLE2.H defines the interface as follows:

```
DECLARE_INTERFACE_(IDropTarget, IUnknown)
{
    // *** IUnknown methods ***
    STDMETHOD(QueryInterface) (THIS REFIID riid, LPVOID FAR* ppvObj) PURE;
    STDMETHOD_(ULONG,AddRef) (THIS)  PURE;
    STDMETHOD_(ULONG,Release) (THIS) PURE;

    // *** IDropTarget methods ***
    STDMETHOD(DragEnter)
            (THIS_ LPDATAOBJECT pDataObj,
            DWORD grfKeyState, POINTL pt,
            LPDWORD pdwEffect) PURE;
    STDMETHOD(DragOver) (THIS_ DWORD grfKeyState, POINTL pt,
          LPDWORD pdwEffect) PURE;
    STDMETHOD(DragLeave) (THIS) PURE;
    STDMETHOD(Drop)
```

```
                (THIS_ LPDATAOBJECT pDataObj, DWORD grfKeyState, POINTL pt,
                 LPDWORD pdwEffect) PURE;
};
typedef         IDropTarget FAR* LPDROPTARGET;
```

Notice that OLE2.H declares the `IUnknown` interface methods. As Chapter 2 mentioned, all COM objects must implement this interface. However, although these methods are required, their implementation is trivial.

The Macros Used in OLE Headers

The OLE include file, COMPOBJ.H, declares many macros, some of which you will use in the sample code. The purpose of these macros is to provide a standard way of declaring classes and methods that is independent of the compiler that you are using, the platform you are targeting (Win16, Win32, or Mac), and the programming language that you are using (C or C++).

You use the DECLARE_INTERFACE_ macro to declare an interface that derives from another. The way that the interface expands depends on whether you are using C or C++. In the sample application, the `IDropTarget` declaration expands as follows in C:

```
typedef struct IDropTarget
{
    const struct IDropTargetVtbl FAR* lpVtbl;
} IDropTarget;

typedef struct IDropTargetVtbl IDropTargetVtbl;

struct IDropTargetVtbl
{
    HRESULT (STDMETHODCALLTYPE * QueryInterface) (
                                      IClassFactory FAR* This,
                                      IID FAR* riid,
                                      LPVOID FAR* ppvObj) ;
    HRESULT (STDMETHODCALLTYPE * AddRef) ;
    HRESULT (STDMETHODCALLTYPE * Release) ;
.
.
.
.
};
```

In C++, the same interface declaration expands as follows:

```
struct FAR IDropTarget : public IUnknown
 {
     virtual HRESULT STDMETHODCALLTYPE QueryInterface(
                                       IID FAR& riid,
                                       LPVOID FAR* ppvObj) = 0;
     virtual HRESULT STDMETHODCALLTYPE AddRef(void) = 0;
     virtual HRESULT STDMETHODCALLTYPE Release(void) = 0;
```

```
    .
    .
    .
    .
};
```

Notice that the C++ expansion is declared as a structure. This is because in C++, all structure members are public by default, and using the `struct` keyword rather than `class` eliminates unnecessary public declarations. Remember, these COM interface declarations are merely templates. All the methods in each interface are declared as pure virtual, so you must always provide the implementation of each method. (In other words, the interface declaration literally defines a structure containing function pointers—a virtual function pointer table.)

If you use the Borland compiler, the struct HUGE replaces the struct FAR.

The STDMETHOD macro expands to the virtual HRESULT STDMETHODCALLTYPE method. The way that STDMETHODCALLTYPE expands depends on the target platform. Under Win32, it expands as `__export __cdecl`, but under Win16 it expands as `__export FAR CDECL`.

These macros help tremendously to create portable code. In fact, the macros are excellent examples of how you can use the preprocessor to write portable code.

For a complete list of all the macros, read the OLE header files.

The Code for the *CDropTarget* Class

You implement all these methods in the `CDropTarget` class. Listing 3.3 declares the class.

Listing 3.3 IODND.H

```
#if !defined( _IODND_H_ )
#define _IODND_H_

#include "stdafx.h"
#include <assert.h>
#include <ole2.h>
#include <olestd.h>
#include <ole2ver.h>
#include "oledoc.h"
#include "oleview.h"

interface CDropTarget : public IDropTarget
{
```

```
public:

     CDropTarget();
     virtual ~CDropTarget();


     BOOL Create(HWND hTargetWnd,COleDoc *pDoc, COleView *pView);
     void GetDragRect(LPDATAOBJECT pDataObj, POINTL pointl);


     STDMETHODIMP QueryInterface(REFIID riid, LPVOID FAR* ppvObj);
     STDMETHODIMP_(ULONG) AddRef();
     STDMETHODIMP_(ULONG) Release();

     STDMETHODIMP DragEnter(LPDATAOBJECT pDataObj,
         DWORD grfKeyState,POINTL pt,LPDWORD pdwEffect);
     STDMETHODIMP DragOver(DWORD grfKeyState,POINTL pt,
         LPDWORD pdwEffect);
     STDMETHODIMP DragLeave();
     STDMETHODIMP Drop(LPDATAOBJECT pDataObj,DWORD grfKeyState,
         POINTL pt,LPDWORD pdwEffect);
private:
     int m_nCount;
     COleDoc *m_pDoc;
     COleView *m_pView;

     BOOL m_fCanAcceptData;
     CRect *m_DragRect;
     CLIPFORMAT m_cfObjectDescriptor;
     CLIPFORMAT m_cfEmbeddedObject;
     POINT m_ptOld;
     BOOL m_fGhost;
};

#endif
```

The module shown in listing 3.3 declares the `Create` method as well as the methods for `IUnknown` and `IDropTarget`, this time using the STDMETHODIMP definition instead of STDMETHOD. This macro is defined as follows:

```
#define STDMETHODIMP  HRESULT STDMETHODCALLTYPE
```

As you can see, STDMETHODIMP declares *nonvirtual* functions that have an implementation. The `CDropTarget` class inherits from the pure virtual class functions. The C++ compiler sets up things so that whenever a pointer to an instance of the `CDropTarget` class is used, it is actually a pointer to the vtable—and the first entry in that table is `QueryInterface()`.

You have also declared the `Create` method. The `m_nCount` variable keeps track of the object's reference counter, and the `m_hwnd` variable contains the handle to the drop target window. `ColeDoc` and `ColeView` are pointers to the MFC View and Document classes.

The m_fCanAcceptData variable is set to true if the application can accept the data that is being dropped on it. The m_DragRect variable contains the feedback rectangle that the application displays when the user draws an object in the client area. The feedback rectangle coordinates are in screen coordinates.

The module shown in listing 3.3 also declares the clipboard formats, because the application must register them itself. You will look at these formats shortly.

Finally, the POINT and BOOL parameters are used for housekeeping later in the code.

Listing 3.4 contains the source code for the implementation of the IDropTarget interface.

Listing 3.4 IODND.CPP

```
#include "stdafx.h"
#include "iodnd.h"

static char near  _szAssertFile[]= __FILE__;
extern char near g_szDbgPrefix[];
#if defined( __cplusplus )
extern "C" {
#endif
#if defined( __cplusplus )
}
#endif
//-----------------------------------------------------------------
CDropTarget::CDropTarget()
{
     m_DragRect = new CRect();
     m_DragRect->SetRectEmpty();
        m_nCount = 0;
        m_fCanAcceptData = FALSE;
        m_cfObjectDescriptor =
        ➥RegisterClipboardFormat(CF_OBJECTDESCRIPTOR);
        m_cfEmbeddedObject = RegisterClipboardFormat(CF_EMBEDDEDOBJECT);
        m_fGhost = FALSE;
}
//-----------------------------------------------------------------
CDropTarget::~CDropTarget()
{
     ASSERT(m_nCount == 0);
     CoLockObjectExternal(this,FALSE,TRUE);
}
//-----------------------------------------------------------------
BOOL CDropTarget::Create(HWND hTargetWnd,COleDoc *pDoc, COleView *pView)
{
```

```
    BOOL fRC = FALSE;

    ASSERT(IsWindow(hTargetWnd));

    m_hwnd = hTargetWnd;
    m_pDoc = pDoc;
    m_pView = pView;

    if(S_OK == CoLockObjectExternal(this,TRUE,TRUE))
    {
         AddRef();
         fRC = TRUE;
    }

    return fRC;
}
//--------------------------------------------------------------
STDMETHODIMP CDropTarget::QueryInterface(REFIID riid, LPVOID FAR* ppvObj)
{
    if (IsEqualIID(riid, IID_IUnknown))
     {
          *ppvObj=this;
          AddRef();
          return ResultFromScode(S_OK);
     }
    if (IsEqualIID(riid, IID_IDropTarget))
     {
          *ppvObj=this;
          AddRef();
          return ResultFromScode(S_OK);
     }
     return ResultFromScode(S_FALSE);
}
//--------------------------------------------------------------
STDMETHODIMP_(ULONG) CDropTarget::AddRef()
{
     m_nCount++;
     return(m_nCount);
}
//--------------------------------------------------------------
STDMETHODIMP_(ULONG) CDropTarget::Release()
{
     m_nCount—;
     if(0 == m_nCount)
          delete this;
     return(m_nCount);
}
//--------------------------------------------------------------
void CDropTarget::GetDragRect(LPDATAOBJECT pDataObj, POINTL pointl)
{
     FORMATETC fetc;
     STGMEDIUM stg;
```

(continues)

Listing 3.4 Continued

```
POINT pt;
LPOBJECTDESCRIPTOR pObjDesc;

m_DragRect->SetRectEmpty();
m_fGhost = FALSE;

pt.x = (int)pointl.x;
pt.y = (int)pointl.y;

fetc.cfFormat = m_cfObjectDescriptor;
fetc.ptd = NULL;
fetc.lindex = -1;
fetc.dwAspect = DVASPECT_CONTENT;
fetc.tymed = TYMED_HGLOBAL;

//------
// The main concern here is to retrieve the extent
// of the data object so that you can calculate a ghost
// rectangle to provide feedback to the user.
HRESULT hr = pDataObj->GetData(&fetc,&stg);
if (NOERROR == hr)
{
     pObjDesc =(LPOBJECTDESCRIPTOR)GlobalLock(stg.hGlobal);
     if (NULL != pObjDesc)
     {
          CDC *pDC;
          SIZE sz;

          sz.cx = (int)pObjDesc->sizel.cx;
          sz.cy = (int)pObjDesc->sizel.cy;

          //------
          // For apps that do not set the sizel field.
          if(0 == sz.cx)
          {
               sz.cx = 100;
               sz.cy = 100;
          }

          pDC = AfxGetApp()->m_pMainWnd->GetDC();
          pDC->HIMETRICtoDP(&sz);
          AfxGetApp()->m_pMainWnd->ReleaseDC(pDC);

          m_DragRect->OffsetRect(pt);
          m_DragRect->right += sz.cx;
          m_DragRect->bottom += sz.cy;
     }

     GlobalUnlock(stg.hGlobal);
     ReleaseStgMedium(&stg);
}

m_ptOld.x = (int)pointl.x;
```

```
    m_ptOld.y = (int)pointl.y;
}
//------------------------------------------------------------
STDMETHODIMP CDropTarget::DragEnter(LPDATAOBJECT pDataObj,
    DWORD grfKeyState,POINTL pt,LPDWORD pdwEffect)
{
    HRESULT hr;
    LPENUMFORMATETC ppEnumFormatEtc;
    ULONG pcelt;
    FORMATETC fetc;

    ASSERT(pDataObj != NULL);

    //------
    *pdwEffect = DROPEFFECT_MOVE;

    hr = pDataObj->EnumFormatEtc(DATADIR_GET,&ppEnumFormatEtc);
    if(S_OK == hr)
    {

        while(S_OK == ppEnumFormatEtc->Next(1,&fetc,
            (ULONG FAR *)&pcelt))
        {
            if(fetc.cfFormat == CF_TEXT ||
               fetc.cfFormat == m_cfEmbeddedObject)
            {
                m_fCanAcceptData = TRUE;
                break;
            }
        }
        ppEnumFormatEtc->Release();
    }

    //----
    // Check the state of the keyboard
    // modifier keys.
    // This sample app does not check for the mouse.
    if(MK_SHIFT == (grfKeyState & MK_SHIFT))
    {
        *pdwEffect = DROPEFFECT_MOVE;
    }
    else if (MK_CONTROL == (grfKeyState & MK_CONTROL))
    {
        *pdwEffect = DROPEFFECT_COPY;
    }

    //----
    // If the data is acceptable,
    // start the rubberband.
    if(m_fCanAcceptData)
    {
        GetDragRect(pDataObj,pt);
    }
    return ResultFromScode(S_OK);
}
```

(continues)

Listing 3.4 Continued

```
//------------------------------------------------------------------
STDMETHODIMP CDropTarget::DragOver(DWORD grfKeyState,
                                   POINTL pointl,LPDWORD pdwEffect)
{
     POINT pt;

     if(MK_SHIFT == (grfKeyState & MK_SHIFT))
     {
          *pdwEffect = DROPEFFECT_MOVE;
          m_fCanAcceptData = TRUE;
     }
     else if (MK_CONTROL == (grfKeyState & MK_CONTROL))
     {
          *pdwEffect = DROPEFFECT_COPY;
          m_fCanAcceptData = TRUE;
     }


     pt.x = (int)pointl.x;
     pt.y = (int)pointl.y;

     POINT ptDelta;

     ptDelta.x = (int)pointl.x - m_ptOld.x;
     ptDelta.y = (int)pointl.y - m_ptOld.y;

     if (ptDelta.x != 0 || ptDelta.y != 0)
     {
          // You have some movement.
          if(m_fGhost)
               m_pView->DrawGhostRect(m_DragRect);

          m_DragRect->OffsetRect(ptDelta);
          m_pView->DrawGhostRect(m_DragRect);
          m_fGhost = TRUE;
     }

     m_ptOld.x = (int)pointl.x;
     m_ptOld.y = (int)pointl.y;

     *pdwEffect = DROPEFFECT_COPY;
     return ResultFromScode(S_OK);
}
//------------------------------------------------------------------
STDMETHODIMP CDropTarget::DragLeave()
{
     m_fCanAcceptData = FALSE;

     if(m_fGhost)
          m_pView->DrawGhostRect(m_DragRect);

     return ResultFromScode(S_OK);
}
```

```
//------------------------------------------------------------
STDMETHODIMP CDropTarget::Drop(LPDATAOBJECT pDataObj,
            DWORD grfKeyState,POINTL pt,LPDWORD pdwEffect)
{
     if(m_fGhost)
          m_pView->DrawGhostRect(m_DragRect);

     m_pDoc->SaveObject(pDataObj);
     m_pDoc->UpdateAllViews(NULL);

     return ResultFromScode(S_OK);
}
//------------------------------------------------------------
//------------------------------------------------------------
```

External Locks

In listing 3.4, the object's `Create` method features a call to the OLE API function `CoLockObjectExternal`. This function call places a so-called "strong" lock on the object. Calling this function before calling `RegisterDragDrop` is absolutely required. If you fail to call `CoLockObjectExternal`, your application works the first time that an object is dragged over it, but then prematurely destroys itself when the object moves away. To understand why this happens, you must first understand the two types of locks used by the COM: strong and weak locks.

Strong Locks

Strong locks on an object are external locks. Such locks are often required when links to embedded objects must be updated. In this case, the container that contains the embedded object must remain in memory until all the links are updated. Objects that have strong locks placed on them always remain in memory.

During a drag-drop operation, for example, an object that does not have a strong lock placed on it is released by the remote connection when it finishes the operation. After the object is released, the application cannot accept any more drag-drop operations because the object that implements the `IDropTarget` interface is destroyed. You can demonstrate this for yourself by removing from the code the call to `CoLockObjectExternal` and then attempting to drop an object in the application's client area.

The function `CoLockObjectExternal` ensures that an object's reference count never reaches 0. Only the same process that creates the object (that is, the server itself) can call the function.

I have also used this function in IClassFactory::LockServer implementations. This method call locks an object in memory and is an excellent optimization method if you frequently create and destroy objects of the same type in your application. By using this method call, you can avoid having to load and unload the server application constantly.

Internally, OLE creates a stub manager to keep track of an object's external locks. As with all reference counts, each lock call must be paired with an unlock call. For the CoLockObjectExternal function, the second parameter determines whether a lock is placed or removed.

Weak Locks

You apply weak locks to an object when it registers itself in the running object table or, as in this sample application, when you register the object as a drag-drop target. For the sample application, the last user of the object releases it when it finishes.

The main difference between weak and strong locks is that weak locks give the object's user control of the object's lifetime. (The object's lifetime is the time from when it is created until it is destroyed.) In contrast, strong locks give the object itself control of its lifetime.

The *IUnknown* Implementation

As was mentioned earlier, the implementation of IUnknown is trivial. During the AddRef method call, you simply increase the internal reference counter. The application also returns the current reference count, as an aid for debugging. Forgetting to pair AddRef and Release calls is a common mistake, and not releasing objects can doom them to remain in memory forever. Checking the return values can help eliminate these potential bugs. If the reference count drops to 0 during a release, the object normally deletes itself. If no clients are using the object, it should remove itself from memory.

The QueryInterface method takes two parameters: the interface for which the object is being queried, and a placeholder for the returned interface pointer.

You first check whether the interface being queried for is IUnknown. All COM objects must support the IUnknown interface. You support this interface so that if the client queries you for it, you place the this pointer in the return pointer placeholder, increase the reference count, and return the S_OK code to the caller.

The other interface that you support is, of course, IDropTarget. You handle this interface the same way that you handle IUnknown.

Finally, if the application is queried for any other interface, the call simply fails. As Chapter 1, "General Concepts," explained, an interface is a contract between the object and the object user. COM contracts are very strict—if you support an interface, you must support it in its entirety. You cannot support some methods but not others.

The *CDropTarget* Implementation

Now let's examine each of the methods in the `CDropTarget` class.

The Constructor

You begin by initializing all the variables that the application uses during the object's lifetime. The only noteworthy aspect of this initialization is the clipboard formats that you register.

The CF_OBJECTDESCRIPTOR is made available whenever two OLE applications are transferring data. The structure contains information that describes the object. Table 3.1 describes each of this structure's fields. You use some of this information later.

Table 3.1 The CF_OBJECTDESCRIPTION Structure's Fields

Type	Field	Description
ULONG	cbSize	The size of the structure in bytes.
CLSID	clsid	The CLSID is used to find the application's icon. This is available only if the object is in an embedded source or embedded object format.
DWORD	dwDrawAspect	Usually DVASPECT_ICON or DVASPECT_CONTENT, but may also be 0. The aspect refers to whether the object will be drawn as an icon or whether the object's contents will be drawn.
SIZEL	sizel	The object's extents (the sizes of the object). This field is optional.
POINTL	pointl	The offset, in HIMETRIC units, from the upper-left corner of the area at which a drag operation was initiated within an object. This field is meaningful only for a drag-drop transfer operation. The value is (0,0) for other transfer situations, such as a clipboard copy and paste.

(continues)

Table 3.1 Continued

Type	Field	Description
DWORD	dwStatus	The same status bits returned by `IOleObject::GetMiscStatus`.
DWORD	dwFullUserTypeName	The offset from the beginning of the data structure to the null-terminated string that specifies the full user type name of the object. The value is 0 if the string is not present.
DWORD	dwSrcOfCopy	The offset from the beginning of the data structure to the null-terminated string that specifies the source of the transfer. The `dwSrcOfCopy` field is typically implemented as the display name of the temporary moniker that identifies the data source. The value for `dwSrcOfCopy` is displayed in the Source line of the Paste Special dialog box. A 0 value indicates that the string is not present. If `dwSrcOfCopy` is 0, the string `Unknown Source` is displayed in the Paste Special dialog box.

The other clipboard format that you register, CF_EMBEDDEDOBJECT, is offered when the data is either an embedded object or a linked object. In all OLE data transfers, this clipboard type is always the first offered. The sample application accepts only this type of data.

The Destructor

The destructor is fairly simple. The only requirement is to release the external lock that you initially placed on the object.

The *Create* Method

The `Create` method is the second half of the two-stage construction. This method accepts three parameters: the window handle for the frame windows, a pointer to the Document class, and a pointer to the View class.

The class stores these parameters for later use. You place an external lock on the object by calling `CoLockObjectExternal` to ensure that the object doesn't die prematurely.

Finally, you increase the reference counter and return to the caller.

The *GetDragRect* Method

The `GetDragRect` method calculates the size of the object that is being dragged. You use this calculated size to create a rubberband that is used to provide feedback to the user.

To extract the extents of the object, use the OBJECTDESCRIPTOR. Note that the extents field of the object is optional. Not all applications support such a field; in fact, neither Microsoft Word 6.0 nor Excel 5.0 support this field. I have tested the sample application with the `Cltest` test application supplied with the OLE SDK. If you drop any object into this application and then drag it to the sample application, the object extents field is filled in correctly.

To retrieve the object description, you must first fill out a FORMATETC structure and pass it to the object:

```
fetc.cfFormat = m_cfObjectDescriptor;
fetc.ptd = NULL;
fetc.lindex = -1;
fetc.dwAspect = DVASPECT_CONTENT;
fetc.tymed = TYMED_HGLOBAL;
```

The first field in the FORMATETC structure is the clipboard type. Use the return value from the previous `RegisterClipboardFormat` call. The `targetdevice` field and the `lindex` fields are not used. You want to extract the size of the object when it is represented by a DVASPECT_CONTENT metafile. Finally, the storage medium that you want is simply a global memory handle.

You now can call the `IDataObject::GetData` method to retrieve the information that you want. If the call succeeds, the `hGlobal` field of the STGMEDIUM structure should contain a valid memory handle. Locking the handle returns a pointer to a filled-in OBJECTDESCRIPTOR data structure:

```
HRESULT hr = pDataObj->GetData(&fetc,&stg);
if (NOERROR == hr)
{
     pObjDesc =(LPOBJECTDESCRIPTOR)GlobalLock(stg.hGlobal);
     if (NULL != pObjDesc)
     {
          CDC *pDC;
          SIZE sz;

          sz.cx = (int)pObjDesc->sizel.cx;
          sz.cy = (int)pObjDesc->sizel.cy;

          //—
          // For apps that do not set the sizel field.
          if(0 == sz.cx)
          {
               sz.cx = 100;
```

```
                sz.cy = 100;
            }

            pDC = AfxGetApp()->m_pMainWnd->GetDC();
            pDC->HIMETRICtoDP(&sz);
            AfxGetApp()->m_pMainWnd->ReleaseDC(pDC);

            m_DragRect->OffsetRect(pt);
            m_DragRect->right += sz.cx;
            m_DragRect->bottom += sz.cy;
        }

        GlobalUnlock(stg.hGlobal);
        ReleaseStgMedium(&stg);
```

The field in which you are interested is the SIZEL field. This field should contain the extents of the object. The extents, like all OLE object extents, are in HIMETRIC units. For the sample application, you must convert these units to device units. The application converts the units by using the `CDC` class' `HIMETRICtoDP` method. As was previously mentioned, not all applications support this field; if this is true for your application, set the size to a nonzero value.

The origin of the rectangle is set to the current mouse coordinates. The size of the rectangle is then set to the extents of the object.

Finally, you unlock the global memory handle and release the returned storage medium. The `ReleaseStgMedium` function uses the `tymed` member of the STGMEDIUM structure to determine the type of storage and perform the appropriate action. For the sample application, the function calls `GlobalFree` in the unlocked memory handle.

The *DragEnter* Method

The first time that the mouse enters the registered drag-drop window, the OLE libraries call the `IDropTarget::DragEnter` method. The primary function of this method is to determine whether the window can accept the type of data that is being offered.

The sample application accepts only embedded objects, so you can simply call the API function `OleQueryCreateFromData` to see whether you can create an embedded object from the data. You can also use an `OleQueryLinkFromData` function to check whether you can create a linked object.

For demonstration purposes, the sample application instead queries the object directly by creating an enumerator and iterating over the offered data formats until the application finds the data format that it wants.

The application uses a FORMATETC enumerator. The `IDataObject` interface has a method that returns such an enumerator. On receiving an enumerator, the application loops through the formats until it either encounters a CF_EMBEDDEDOBJECT format or the end of the offered formats. The application releases the enumerator when it is finished with it. (Remember the reference counting rules presented in Chapter 2.)

```
hr = pDataObj->EnumFormatEtc(DATADIR_GET,&ppEnumFormatEtc);
if(S_OK == hr)
{
     while(S_OK == ppEnumFormatEtc->Next(1,&fetc,(ULONG FAR *)&pcelt))
     {
          if(fetc.cfFormat == CF_TEXT
              || fetc.cfFormat == m_cfEmbeddedObject)
          {
               m_fCanAcceptData = TRUE;
               break;
          }
     }
     ppEnumFormatEtc->Release();
}
```

You must also provide feedback to the user. To do so, you change the mouse cursor to reflect the operation which is to be performed. (The OLE UI guidelines describe the various cursors that must be used.) Actually, the OLE libraries change the cursor; the application simply passes through the `pdwEffect` pointer the operation that it is going to perform.

Several factors affect the operation that the application is going to perform on the data. First, you must determine whether the application can accept the data. If not, you return DROPEFFECT_NONE to indicate that a drag-drop operation will not be performed. In this case, the cursor remains the standard Windows cursor.

If the data is acceptable, and the user has not pressed any modifier key, the operation will be a move. This is equivalent to a cut-and-paste operation. If the user is pressing the Shift key, the operation is also considered a move. You return DROPEFFECT_MOVE and the cursor changes to include a tiny rectangle at the base of the arrow.

If the user is pressing the Ctrl key, the operation will be a copy. Again, this is similar to a copy-and-paste clipboard operation. You return a DROPEFFECT_COPY and the cursor changes to include a small plus sign to indicate a copy operation.

The following code shows how you check for the keyboard during the drag-drop operation:

```
if(MK_SHIFT == (grfKeyState & MK_SHIFT))
{
     *pdwEffect = DROPEFFECT_MOVE;
}
else if (MK_CONTROL == (grfKeyState & MK_CONTROL))
{
     *pdwEffect = DROPEFFECT_COPY;
}
```

Finally, by pressing both the Shift and Ctrl keys, the user requests a drag-and-link operation. In this case, the cursor changes to include an equals sign. The sample application does not support this operation.

Before you return, you call `GetDragRect` to calculate the initial feedback rectangle.

The *DragOver* Method

Every time that you move the mouse over the target window, the `DragOver` method is called. The method's primary function is to continue to provide visual feedback to the user.

The application monitors the keyboard to see whether the user still wants to move or copy data to the application. One of the parameters passed is the current mouse coordinates. You use them to update the drag rectangle:

```
pt.x = (int)pointl.x;
pt.y = (int)pointl.y;

POINT ptDelta;

ptDelta.x = (int)pointl.x - m_ptOld.x;
ptDelta.y = (int)pointl.y - m_ptOld.y;

if (ptDelta.x != 0 || ptDelta.y != 0)
{
     // You have some movement.
     if(m_fGhost)
          m_pView->DrawGhostRect(m_DragRect);

     m_DragRect->OffsetRect(ptDelta);
     m_pView->DrawGhostRect(m_DragRect);
     m_fGhost = TRUE;
}

m_ptOld.x = (int)pointl.x;
m_ptOld.y = (int)pointl.y;
```

Because this method is called so often, the actual data object is not passed as a parameter. You should return from this function as quickly as possible, to ensure that the user continues to receive steady feedback from your application.

The sample application does not implement an important part of supporting a drag-drop operation: a scrolling feature that enables the user to select a part of your client area that is currently out of view.

To implement scrolling, you must create a hot zone, usually at the bottom of the target window. When the cursor passes into this area and remains for a certain time (determined by the `DragScrollDelay` parameters in the Windows section of WIN.INI), you should begin to scroll your client area. You also must pass DROPEFFECT_SCROLL to the drag source so the cursor can be changed. WIN.INI's `DragScrollInterval` parameters determine the speed of the scrolling.

The *DragLeave* Method

The `DragLeave` method is called if the mouse leaves the target window. In this case, you must assume that the user wants to abort the operation.

If the rubberband is visible, you remove it and set the data accept flag to false. If you were holding on to the data object pointer, you would also release it now.

The Drop Operation

When the user releases the mouse button over the target window, you first remove the rubberband, because it is no longer required. You then call the `SaveObject` method, passing it a pointer to the data object:

```
if(m_fGhost)
     m_pView->DrawGhostRect(m_DragRect);

m_pDoc->SaveObject(pDataObj);
m_pDoc->UpdateAllViews(NULL);
```

Finally, you call `UpdateAllViews` to update the application's client area so that the user can see the dropped object, as shown in figure 3.1.

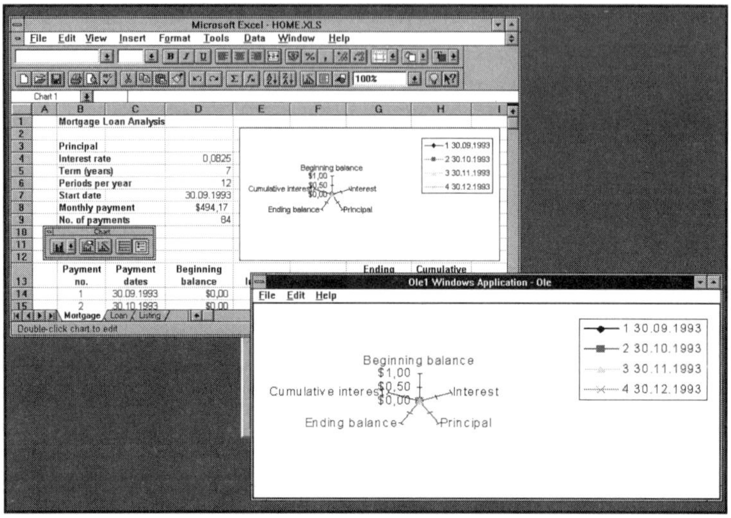

Fig. 3.1
A completed drag-drop operation.

Storing the Dropped Object

To store the dropped object, you first must find a place to store it. For the sample application, you create an OLE compound file to store the object.

You first check whether the compound file already exists. The API function `StgIsStorageDocFile` will fail if the passed-in file name is not a compound file. You then call either `StgCreatDocFile` or `StgOpenStorage`, depending on whether you created the file. In either case, the last parameter is a pointer to a pointer to an `IStorage` interface. If the API call succeeds, this variable returns a valid interface pointer.

After you have a compound file and a pointer to its root storage, you create substorage to hold the embedded object. To use the return root storage pointer, you call the `IStorage::CreateStorage` method, which creates the substorage. Again, the last parameter is a placeholder for a returned `IStorage` interface pointer.

```
HRESULT hr;
IStorage  *pStorage, *pSubStorage;

// Create or open the docfile.
if (FAILED(StgIsStorageFile(STORAGE)))
{
     hr = StgCreateDocfile(STORAGE,STGM_READWRITE
         |STGM_SHARE_EXCLUSIVE,0,&pStorage);
}
else
{
```

```
        hr = StgOpenStorage(STORAGE, NULL, STGM_READWRITE
             ¦STGM_SHARE_EXCLUSIVE,NULL,
             , &pStorage);
    }
    // Create the storage for this object.
    if (S_OK == hr)
    {
        hr = pStorage->CreateStorage(SUBSTORAGE,STGM_CREATE
        STGM_READWRITE¦STGM_SHARE_EXCLUSIVE, 0,0,&pSubStorage);
    }
    else
    {
        AfxMessageBox("Error: Failed to create docfile");
        return;
    }
```

The drag-drop operation passed a data transfer object to the application. Before you can store this object, you must first create an embedded object from it. To do so, you call the API function `OleCreateFromData`. This function should succeed, because you have already queried the object to see whether it could be an embedded object.

After you create the object, you communicate with it through the interface pointer that you passed in the seventh parameter. In this case, it is a pointer to an `IOleObject` interface.

```
IPersistStorage *pps;
// ------
// Here you create the embedded object from the data transfer object.
hr = OleCreateFromData(lpDataObj,IID_IOleObject,
    OLERENDER_DRAW,NULL,NULL,pSubStorage,
    (LPVOID FAR *)&m_lpOleObj);
if (S_OK == hr)
{
    hr = m_lpOleObj->QueryInterface(IID_IPersistStorage,
        (LPVOID FAR *)&pps);
    if (S_OK == hr)
    {
        // Save the object in the newly created stream
        hr = OleSave(pps,pSubStorage,TRUE);
        pps->SaveCompleted(NULL);
        pps->Release();
    }
}
m_lpOleObj->Release();
pSubStorage->Release();
```

You then ask the object, through `QueryInterface`, whether it supports the `IPersistObject` interface. This interface loads and saves objects in storages. To save the object, use the OLE helper function `OleSave`. This function performs four separate steps:

1. Calls the API function `WriteClassStg` to save the object's CLSID to a special stream
2. Saves the object's presentation data from the cache into the presentation stream
3. Saves the object's native data to a separate stream
4. Calls `IStorage::Commit` to commit the changes to the compound file's root storage

On returning from `OleSave`, you call the `IPersistStorage::SaveCompleted` method to change the object from the "no-scribble" state back to a normal storage state. You then release the interface pointer.

Now that you have safely stored the object, you can release the object interface pointers that you still have. Releasing the root storage pointer closes the file.

Listings 3.5 and 3.6 contain the code for the `CDocument` implementation.

Listing 3.5 OLEDOC.H

```
#if !defined( _OLEDOC_H_ )
#define _OLEDOC_H_


// oledoc.h : interface of the COleDoc class
/////////////////////////////////////////////////////////////////////////////
// Forward reference
interface CDropTarget;

class COleDoc : public CDocument
{
protected: // create from serialization only
     COleDoc();
     DECLARE_DYNCREATE(COleDoc)

// Attributes
public:
     CDropTarget FAR *m_pCDropTarget;
     HWND m_TargetWnd;
     LPOLEOBJECT m_lpOleObj;
// Operations
public:
     void SaveObject(LPDATAOBJECT lpDataObj);
     void DrawObject(CDC *pDC, LPRECT lprc);
// Implementation
```

```
public:
     virtual ~COleDoc();
     virtual void Serialize(CArchive& ar); // overridden for document I/O
#ifdef _DEBUG
     virtual void AssertValid() const;
     virtual void Dump(CDumpContext& dc) const;
#endif

protected:
     virtual BOOL OnNewDocument();

// Generated message map functions
protected:
     //{{AFX_MSG(COleDoc)
          // NOTE - the ClassWizard will add and remove
          // member functions here.
          // DO NOT EDIT what you see in these blocks of generated code!
     //}}AFX_MSG
     DECLARE_MESSAGE_MAP()
};

/////////////////////////////////////////////////////////////////////////////
#endif
```

Listing 3.6 OLEDOC.CPP

```
#include "stdafx.h"
#include "ole1.h"

#include "oledoc.h"

#ifdef _DEBUG
#undef THIS_FILE
static char BASED_CODE THIS_FILE[] = __FILE__;
#endif

#define STORAGE      "\\mydoc.dfl"
#define      SUBSTORAGE      "mystream"
/////////////////////////////////////////////////////////////////////////////
// COleDoc

IMPLEMENT_DYNCREATE(COleDoc, CDocument)

BEGIN_MESSAGE_MAP(COleDoc, CDocument)
     //{{AFX_MSG_MAP(COleDoc)
          // NOTE - the ClassWizard adds and removes mapping macros here.
          // DO NOT EDIT what you see in these blocks of generated code!
     //}}AFX_MSG_MAP
END_MESSAGE_MAP()
```

(continues)

Listing 3.6 Continued

```
//////////////////////////////////////////////////////////////////////
// COleDoc construction/destruction

COleDoc::COleDoc()
{
     m_lpOleObj = NULL;
}
//-------------------------------------------------------------------
COleDoc::~COleDoc()
{
}
//-------------------------------------------------------------------
BOOL COleDoc::OnNewDocument()
{
     if (!CDocument::OnNewDocument())
          return FALSE;

     return TRUE;
}

//////////////////////////////////////////////////////////////////////
// COleDoc serialization

void COleDoc::Serialize(CArchive& ar)
{
     if (ar.IsStoring())
     {
          // TODO: add storing code here
     }
     else
     {
          // TODO: add loading code here
     }
}

//////////////////////////////////////////////////////////////////////
// COleDoc diagnostics

#ifdef _DEBUG
void COleDoc::AssertValid() const
{
     CDocument::AssertValid();
}

void COleDoc::Dump(CDumpContext& dc) const
{
     CDocument::Dump(dc);
}
#endif //_DEBUG

//////////////////////////////////////////////////////////////////////
// COleDoc commands
void COleDoc::DrawObject(CDC *pDC, LPRECT lprc)
```

```
{
     HRESULT hr;
     IStorage  *pStorage, *pSubStorage;
     IUnknown *punk;

     // Open the compound file and the substorage
     // containing the embedded object.
     hr = StgOpenStorage(STORAGE,NULL,STGM_READWRITE¦
                        STGM_SHARE_EXCLUSIVE,NULL,0,&pStorage);
     hr = pStorage->OpenStorage(SUBSTORAGE,NULL,
                        STGM_READWRITE ¦ STGM_SHARE_EXCLUSIVE, 0,
                        0 , &pSubStorage);

     // Load the object into memory
     hr = OleLoad(pSubStorage,IID_IUnknown,NULL,(LPVOID FAR *) &punk);
     // Draw the presentation data
     hr = OleDraw(punk,DVASPECT_CONTENT,pDC->m_hDC,lprc);

     // Release the storage refs
     pSubStorage->Release();
     pStorage->Release();

     // Release the object
     punk->Release();

}
//-------------------------------------------------------------------
void COleDoc::SaveObject(LPDATAOBJECT lpDataObj)
{
     //----------
     // Create an OLE compound file and save the
     // data transfer object as an embedded object.
     //

     HRESULT hr;
     IStorage  *pStorage, *pSubStorage;


     // Create or open the docfile.
     if (FAILED(StgIsStorageFile(STORAGE)))
     {
          hr = StgCreateDocfile(STORAGE,STGM_READWRITE¦
                              STGM_SHARE_EXCLUSIVE,0,&pStorage);
     }
     else
     {
          hr = StgOpenStorage(STORAGE, NULL, STGM_READWRITE
               ¦STGM_SHARE_EXCLUSIVE,NULL,
               , &pStorage);
     }
```

(continues)

Listing 3.6 Continued

```
        // Create the storage for this object.
        if (S_OK == hr)
        {
             hr = pStorage->CreateStorage(SUBSTORAGE,STGM_CREATE
             STGM_READWRITE¦STGM_SHARE_EXCLUSIVE, 0,0,&pSubStorage);
        }
        else
        {
             AfxMessageBox("Error: Failed to create docfile");
             return;
        }

        if (S_OK == hr)
        {
             IPersistStorage *pps;
             // ------
             // Create the embedded object from the data transfer object.
             hr = OleCreateFromData(lpDataObj,
                     IID_IOleObject,OLERENDER_DRAW,NULL,NULL,
                    pSubStorage,(LPVOID FAR *)&m_lpOleObj);
             if (S_OK == hr)
             {
                    hr = m_lpOleObj->QueryInterface(IID_IPersistStorage,
                                                (LPVOID FAR *)&pps);
                    if (S_OK == hr)
                    {
                          // Save the object in the newly created stream
                          hr = OleSave(pps,pSubStorage,TRUE);
                          pps->SaveCompleted(NULL);
                          pps->Release();
                    }

             }
             m_lpOleObj->Release();
             pSubStorage->Release();
        }
        // Releasing the reference counter closes the file.
        pStorage->Release();


}
//--------------------------------------------------------------
//--------------------------------------------------------------
```

Displaying the Stored Object

The final step for the sample application is to display the dropped object in its client area. First, let's examine the `OnCreate` and `OnDestroy` methods of the View class.

The *OnCreate* Method

The drag-drop target is the frame window's client area, so the best place to create the drag-drop object is in the view creation method.

You start by calling the base class' `OnCreate` method to complete the actual creation of the frame window. You then create an instance of the `CDropTarget` class.

As you may be familiar with from MFC, I am using a two-stage object-construction method. This method enables the `Create` method to return an error code.

The two-stage construction process overcomes a major problem with C++ constructors: constructors cannot return error codes. But by creating a second stage to the construction process, namely a `Create` method, you can return the appropriate error codes.

After you successfully create the object, you call the OLE API function `RegisterDragDrop` to register the window that is to accept the dropped objects and the COM object that is to handle the data transfer.

The function takes two parameters:

```
pDoc->m_pCDropTarget = new CDropTarget();
pDoc->m_pCDropTarget->Create(m_hWnd,pDoc,this);
RegisterDragDrop(m_hWnd,pDoc->m_pCDropTarget);
```

The first parameter is the handle of the window that will accept the drop. You must explicitly register each window that you want to use as a drag-drop target. The second parameter is a pointer to a COM object that implements the `IDropTarget` interface. In this parameter, you pass in a pointer to the object, which is an instance of the class `CDropTarget`.

The *OnDestroy* Method

In the `OnDestroy` method, you need to reverse the process. You begin the shutdown process by calling the OLE API function `RevokeDrapDrop`. You pass in the handle of the window that was registered initially for the drag-drop target. This function enables OLE to remove the window handle from a table that OLE maintains internally.

You then release the reference count that you have on the object and delete the object:

```
RevokeDragDrop(m_hWnd);
// The object will destroy itself
// because the reference count will be zero.
pDoc->m_pCDropTarget->Release();
```

The *DrawGhostRect* Method

`DrawGhostRect` is a helper method that draws the feedback rubberband during the drag process. The code is simple. You set the ROP code in the device context to R2_NOT, which flips the pixels. In other words, drawing the same rectangle twice effectively erases the initial rectangle and restores the original background—a simple XOR operation.

```
CClientDC dc(this);
CPen pen(PS_SOLID,2,::GetSysColor(COLOR_ACTIVEBORDER));
CPen *oldPen;
CBrush brush;
CBrush *oldBrush;
CRect rcClient;
int oldROP;

oldROP = dc.SetROP2(R2_NOT);
brush.CreateStockObject(HOLLOW_BRUSH);

rcClient.CopyRect(rc);
ScreenToClient(&rcClient);

oldBrush = (CBrush*)dc.SelectObject((CBrush*)&brush);
oldPen = (CPen*)dc.SelectObject((CPen*)&pen);

dc.Rectangle(&rcClient);

dc.SetROP2(oldROP);

dc.SelectObject(oldPen);
dc.SelectObject(oldBrush);
```

The *OnDraw* Method

The `OnDraw` method is responsible for drawing the actual object. To achieve this, the method delegates to the `DrawObject` method from the Document class.

`DrawObject` begins by opening the compound file and opening the substorage that contains the object. You now have a pointer to the object storage; using that pointer, you call the API function `OleLoad` to load the object into memory.

Like all other OLE functions, this API call is simply a "wrapper" function for several OLE methods. The `OleLoad` function performs six steps:

1. Checks whether the object is marked for Automation object conversion. Some objects may be marked as such, for example, when a user installs a new version of an application. The installation program marks all the old CLSIDs to be automatically converted to the new format when they are loaded.

2. Retrieves the CLSID of the stored object.
3. Creates an instance of the object handler. If an object hander does not exist for this object (as is often the case), the default handler is used.
4. Passes the object an interface pointer to `IOleClientSite` if the object is being loaded into an OLE container.
5. Queries the object for `IPersistStorage` and calls `IPersistStorage::Load` to load the object.
6. Queries the object for the requested interface pointer passed in its fourth parameter.

As you can see, the `OleLoad` function packs quite a bit of functionality.

The following code shows the `OnDraw` method:

```
HRESULT hr;
IStorage  *pStorage, *pSubStorage;
IUnknown *punk;

// Open the compound file and the substorage
// containing the embedded object.
hr = StgOpenStorage(STORAGE,NULL,STGM_READWRITE¦
                    STGM_SHARE_EXCLUSIVE,NULL,0,&pStorage);
hr = pStorage->OpenStorage(SUBSTORAGE,NULL,
                           STGM_READWRITE ¦ STGM_SHARE_EXCLUSIVE, 0,
                           0 , &pSubStorage);

// Load the object into memory
hr = OleLoad(pSubStorage,IID_IUnknown,NULL,(LPVOID FAR *) &punk);
// Draw the presentation data
hr = OleDraw(punk,DVASPECT_CONTENT,pDC->m_hDC,lprc);

// Release the storage refs
pSubStorage->Release();
pStorage->Release();

// Release the object
punk->Release();
```

The object is now in the loaded state. Note that the object server has *not* been executed. The server itself is required only when you need to edit the native data. Because a metafile representing the object is stored separately and can be displayed by the default handle, this process is usually quite fast. With OLE 1.0, the object server would have been executed just to display the data. This speed is one of major improvements that OLE 2.0 introduces.

The API function `OleDraw` draws the object's presentation data. Again, this function call is a wrapper for some COM interface calls. In this case, the object is queried for `IViewObject`. The `IViewObject::Draw` method is then called to complete the drawing.

Listings 3.7 and 3.8 contain the code for the `CView` class.

Listing 3.7 OLEVIEW.H

```
#if !defined( _OLEVIEW_H_ )
#define _OLEVIEW_H_


// oleview.h : interface of the COleView class
//
/////////////////////////////////////////////////////////////////////////////

class COleView : public CView
{
protected: // create from serialization only
     COleView();
     DECLARE_DYNCREATE(COleView)

// Attributes
public:
     COleDoc* GetDocument();

// Operations
public:
     void DrawGhostRect(CRect *rc);
// Implementation
public:
     virtual ~COleView();
     virtual void OnDraw(CDC* pDC);  // overridden to draw this view
#ifdef _DEBUG
     virtual void AssertValid() const;
     virtual void Dump(CDumpContext& dc) const;
#endif

protected:

// Generated message map functions
protected:
     //{{AFX_MSG(COleView)
     afx_msg int OnCreate(LPCREATESTRUCT lpCreateStruct);
     afx_msg void OnDestroy();
     //}}AFX_MSG
     DECLARE_MESSAGE_MAP()
};

#ifndef _DEBUG  // debug version in oleview.cpp
inline COleDoc* COleView::GetDocument()
   { return (COleDoc*)m_pDocument; }
#endif
```

```
/////////////////////////////////////////////////////////////////////
//
#endif
```

Listing 3.8 OLEVIEW.CPP

```
#include "stdafx.h"
#include "ole1.h"

#include "oledoc.h"
#include "oleview.h"

#ifdef _DEBUG
#undef THIS_FILE
static char BASED_CODE THIS_FILE[] = __FILE__;
#endif

/////////////////////////////////////////////////////////////////////
// COleView

IMPLEMENT_DYNCREATE(COleView, CView)

BEGIN_MESSAGE_MAP(COleView, CView)
     //{{AFX_MSG_MAP(COleView)
     ON_WM_CREATE()
     ON_WM_DESTROY()
     //}}AFX_MSG_MAP
END_MESSAGE_MAP()

/////////////////////////////////////////////////////////////////////
// COleView construction/destruction

COleView::COleView()
{
     // TODO: add construction code here
}

COleView::~COleView()
{
}

/////////////////////////////////////////////////////////////////////
// COleView drawing

void COleView::OnDraw(CDC* pDC)
{
     RECT rc;
     COleDoc* pDoc = GetDocument();
     ASSERT_VALID(pDoc);
```

(continues)

Listing 3.8 Continued

```
     GetClientRect(&rc);
     pDoc->DrawObject(pDC,&rc);
}
//----------------------------------------------------------------
void COleView::DrawGhostRect(CRect *rc)
{
     CClientDC dc(this);
     CPen pen(PS_SOLID,2,::GetSysColor(COLOR_ACTIVEBORDER));
     CPen *oldPen;
     CBrush brush;
     CBrush *oldBrush;
     CRect rcClient;
     int oldROP;

     TRACE("DrawChostRect\n");

     oldROP = dc.SetROP2(R2_NOT);
     brush.CreateStockObject(HOLLOW_BRUSH);

     rcClient.CopyRect(rc);
     ScreenToClient(&rcClient);

     oldBrush = (CBrush*)dc.SelectObject((CBrush*)&brush);
     oldPen = (CPen*)dc.SelectObject((CPen*)&pen);

     dc.Rectangle(&rcClient);

     dc.SetROP2(oldROP);

     dc.SelectObject(oldPen);
     dc.SelectObject(oldBrush);
}
/////////////////////////////////////////////////////////////////////
// COleView diagnostics

#ifdef _DEBUG
void COleView::AssertValid() const
{
     CView::AssertValid();
}

void COleView::Dump(CDumpContext& dc) const
{
     CView::Dump(dc);
}

COleDoc* COleView::GetDocument() // nondebug version is inline
{
     ASSERT(m_pDocument->IsKindOf(RUNTIME_CLASS(COleDoc)));
     return (COleDoc*)m_pDocument;
}
#endif //_DEBUG
```

```
/////////////////////////////////////////////////////////////////////
// COleView message handlers

int COleView::OnCreate(LPCREATESTRUCT lpCreateStruct)
{
      if (CView::OnCreate(lpCreateStruct) == -1)
            return -1;

      COleDoc* pDoc = GetDocument();
      ASSERT_VALID(pDoc);

      //--------------
      // Create the object that supports
      // the IDropTarget interface and then
      // register the frame window as a
      // drop target.
      pDoc->m_pCDropTarget = new CDropTarget();
      pDoc->m_pCDropTarget->Create(m_hWnd,pDoc,this);
      RegisterDragDrop(m_hWnd,pDoc->m_pCDropTarget);

      return 0;
}
//-------------------------------------------------------------------
void COleView::OnDestroy()
{
      COleDoc* pDoc = GetDocument();
      ASSERT_VALID(pDoc);

      CView::OnDestroy();

      RevokeDragDrop(m_hWnd);

      // The object will destroy itself
      // because the reference count will be zero.
      pDoc->m_pCDropTarget->Release();


}
//------------------------------------------------------------------
//------------------------------------------------------------------
```

From Here...

This concludes your look at creating an OLE application with standard C++ and the OLE API. In the next chapter, you examine the OLE SDK and take a close look at some of the tools available for debugging OLE applications.

4

Chapter 4

The OLE SDK

Microsoft offers the OLE 2.01 Software Development Kit (SDK) for Win16 development on its own CD-ROM, and as part of the Microsoft Visual C++ product. For Win32 OLE development, the OLE SDK is available as part of the Win32 Software Development Kit for Windows NT 3.5 and will also be part of the Visual C++ 2.0 product. The kit consists of all the libraries, DLLs, and header files that you need to develop an OLE application.

The documentation for OLE is also shipped on the CD. The documentation includes the OLE design specification, the programmer's guide, and the Automation guide. The SDK also includes numerous tech-notes and Microsoft PowerPoint presentations. A Visual Basic application demonstrating various aspects of the OLE user interface (UI) guidelines can be found in the UIDEMO directory.

The CD includes sample code in C and C++ for 21 applications. This source code is an invaluable resource for every programmer, because it explores most aspects of OLE 2.0. You should examine this code and try using it in your own work.

The SDK also includes several useful tools, including utilities for browsing compound files and type libraries, and for writing scripts that test Automation servers. This chapter explores each of the following tools:

- The DocFile Viewer
- The DISPTEST Automation Test
- The `IDateObject` Viewer
- The Class ID Generator
- The Running Object Table Viewer

- The OLE 2.0 Free Module utility
- The Ole2View utility
- The Windows Process Status (WPS) utility
- The Type Library Browser
- The WXSRVR program
- The Debugging Handler

The DocFile Viewer

The DocFile Viewer (fig. 4.1) displays a hierarchical view of an OLE compound file's contents. The viewer initially displays the root storage for the file. By double-clicking the mouse, you display the child storages and streams. The contents of the actual streams are also displayed as a standard hexadecimal dump.

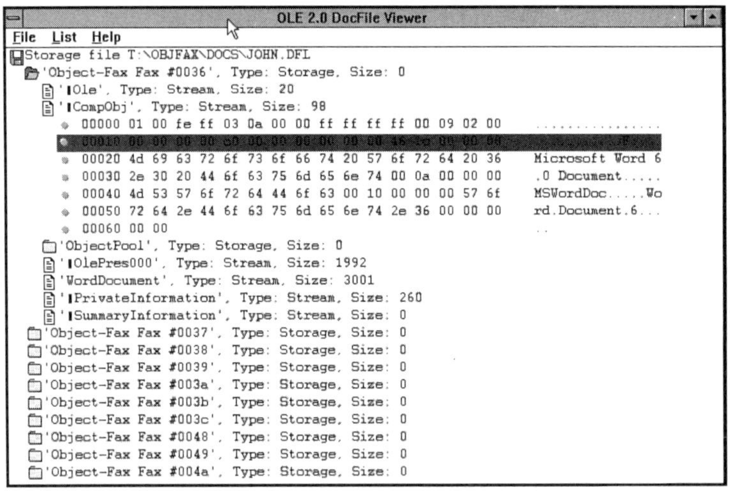

Fig. 4.1 The DocFile Viewer.

This utility is useful for debugging structured storage problems. The DocFile Viewer also enables you to dump the contents of the special OLE streams that are written out for stored compound document objects. Unfortunately, reading the contents of a large file can be quite slow, because the entire listing is read into memory.

The SDK's CD-ROM includes the viewer's full source code. This gives you an opportunity to develop the utility further and shows you how to write code that accesses compound files.

The DISPTEST Automation Test

The DISPTEST program provided with the OLE SDK is a scaled-down version of Visual Basic. The program provides a means for quickly testing your OLE Automation servers. In Chapter 13, "Creating a Simple Automation Server," you develop a DISPTEST script that tests your first Automation server. Figure 4.2 shows that DISPTEST program running under Windows NT.

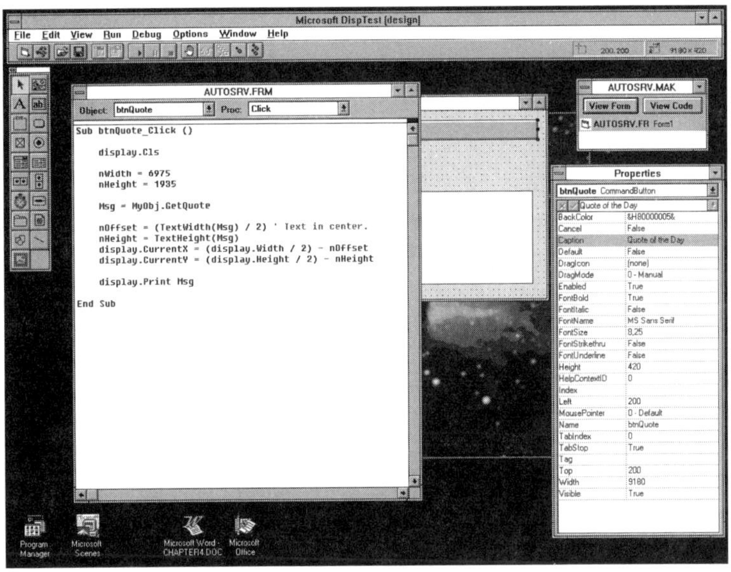

Fig. 4.2
The DISPTEST program.

DISPTEST implements the `IDispatch` interface to manipulate exposed methods and properties from Automation objects.

Using DISPTEST to load and initialize an object is simple: you declare a variable as a type `Object`, as in the following example:

```
Dim MyObj As Object
```

You have now created an empty object. To initialize this object to point to an Automation object, you use the following syntax:

```
Set MyObj = CreateObject("ProgID.ObjectName")
```

The variable `MyObj` now contains a fully initialized `IDispatch` interface pointer. Any methods exposed by this object can now be invoked through this variable.

To invoke a method on this object, you use the standard Visual Basic syntax. For example, to invoke the `GetQuote` method on the object that you develop in Chapter 13, you use the following code:

```
Msg = MyObj.GetQuote
```

To get or set an object's properties, you use the standard Visual Basic syntax:

```
object.property
```

A useful feature of the DISPTEST program is the OLE custom control call MSOLE2.VBX. You can use this control in a DISPTEST application to implement linking and embedding.

DISPTEST has some noteworthy limitations:

- *Little support for handing arrays.* You cannot pass an array as an argument to a method, nor can you set a property by using an array. If a method returns an array, you can access only individual members of the array; you cannot access the array as a whole.
- *No support for named arguments.* Such arguments are used extensively in WordBasic, for example. If you are using an object to access Microsoft Word 6.0, you cannot use named arguments. In WordBasic, you can issue the following call:

  ```
  EditFindFont .Point=12,.Font="Arial"
  ```

  This function call uses named parameters to the `EditFindFont` function, which actually takes 18 parameters. Therefore, if you use DISPTEST, you must make the following call:

  ```
  MyObj.EditFindFont 12,,,,,,,,,,,,,,,"Arial"
  ```

  Each parameter must be in its own position.

If you want to develop applications, you should purchase Visual Basic 3.0, which lacks these limitations. DISPTEST is best used strictly as a developer's tool for testing applications.

The *IDataObject* Viewer

The `IDataObject` Viewer is a tool that enables you to view the data formats of an `IDataObject` either on the clipboard or as used in a drag-drop operation.

To view a data object used during a drag-drop operation, choose GetDataObject from the **D**ataObject menu. Figure 4.3 shows the output generated when you drag this paragraph from a Microsoft Word 6.0 document to the `IDataObject` Viewer.

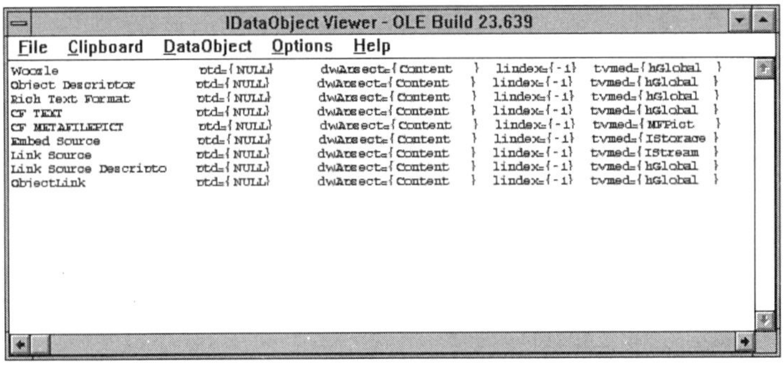

Fig. 4.3
The *IDataObject* Viewer.

The viewer shows the FORMATETC descriptors for the data formats that Word is offering. (See Chapter 1, "General Concepts," for a description of FORMATETC.) You can enumerate these formats by selecting the **E**numerate FormatEtc option from the **D**ataObject menu. This option enables you to move forward or backward through the next FORMATETC structure or to skip over elements. This enumerator feature functions exactly like all other enumerator objects. (See Chapter 1 for a more detailed explanation of COM enumerators.)

You can access the Object Descriptor information by choosing Show **O**bject Descriptor from the **D**ataObject menu. The data structure (OBJECTDESCRIPTOR) is made available during a data copy operation. Table 4.1 describes each of the fields.

Table 4.1 The Object Descriptor Fields

Field	Specifies
`cbSize`	The structure's size in bytes.
`clsid`	The icon for the data object, to be shown in a Paste Special dialog box.

(continues)

Table 4.1 Continued

Field	Specifies
dwDrawAspect	The aspect of the presentation metafile; usually DVASPECT_CONTENT or DVASPECT_ICON, but 0 if the data source did not originally draw the object.
sizel	The object's true extents. These extents are the same as those returned by IOleObject::GetExtent.
pointl	The offset, in HIMETRIC units, of the upper-left corner of the object in which the drag-drop operation began.
dwStatus	The MisStatus bits. See Chapter 2 for a more detailed explanation of these bits.
dwFullUserTypeName	The offset from the beginning of the data structure to the ASCIIZ string that specifies the full name of the object.
dwSrcOfCopy	The offset from the beginning of the data structure to the ASCIIZ string that specifies the source of the copy.

You access the Link Source Descriptor information by choosing Show **L**ink Source Descriptor from the **D**ataObject menu. The data structure is the same as that used in the Object Descriptor. Only the contents of the `dwSrcOfCopy` field differ. The source can represent either a pseudo object (an *outside link*) or a running embedded object (an *inside link*).

The `IDataObject` Viewer includes two menu options that call `OleQueryCreateFromData` and `OleQueryLinkFromData`. These functions are called with the `IDataObject` pointer, and the result of the function call is displayed.

The Class ID Generator

You have already seen how OLE identifies objects. The use of UUIDs (universally unique IDs) guarantees that object names are unique. This uniqueness is extremely important, particularly in a distributed environment in which millions of objects may exist.

To guarantee the uniqueness of these IDs, the OLE architects used a 128-bit ID. The ID is generated from a combination of the network card ID in your workstation, the current date and time, and a random-number generator.

The tool that generates these IDs is the Class ID Generator. When you execute this program, it places a new UUID on the clipboard. The program formats the number on the clipboard so that you can include the number directly in your application. The following GUID is pasted directly into this text from the clipboard:

```
6AA28941-5B17-101B-9948-7EF9E6AF2243
DEFINE_GUID(varNameHere, 0x6AA28941L,0x5B17, 0x101B, 0x99,
0x48, 0x7E, 0xF9, 0xE6, 0xAF, 0x22, 0x43);
```

The class ID generator formats the UUID in hexadecimal and also includes the DEFINE_GUID macro format.

The Class ID Generator tool, GUIDGEN, simply calls the OLE 2.0 API function `CoCreateGUID` to do its work.

The Running Object Table Viewer

The Running Object Table (ROT) Viewer (see fig. 4.4) helps you keep track of all objects currently open on a workstation. The ROT is used when a container must open a link to a linked object that is already running. It is preferable to connect to the running instance instead of starting a new instance.

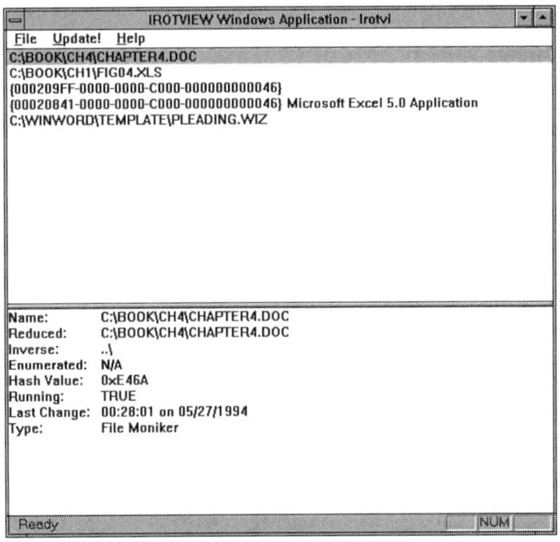

Fig. 4.4
The Running Object Table Viewer.

As objects are opened, they are registered in the ROT. When the alert object table (AOT) is finally implemented, each entry that is entered in the ROT is checked against entries in the AOT for automatic link updating.

The viewer utility displays the current contents of the ROT.

The LRPC Message Monitor

The LRPC Message Monitor, which is similar to the Spy utility included with the Windows SDK, provides insight into what happens when two processes use COM interfaces to communicate. For example, figure 4.5 shows the LRPC Message Monitor's output after you drag and drop an object from Microsoft Excel 5.0 to Microsoft Word 6.0.

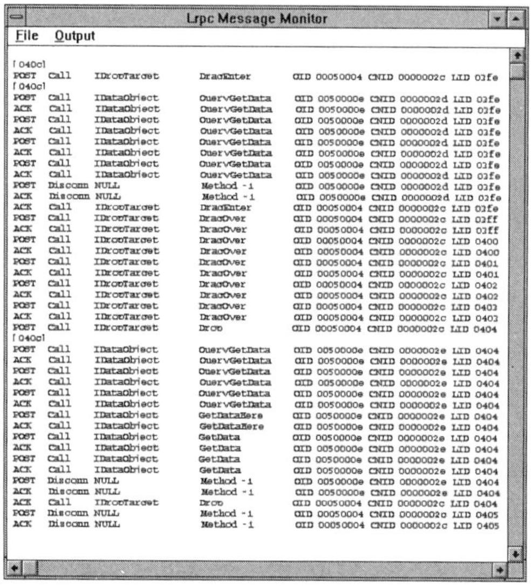

Fig. 4.5
The LRPC Message Monitor.

The first message posted is `DragEnter`. All applications that want to accept data in a drag-drop operation must implement the interface `IDropTarget`. One of the methods of this interface is `DragEnter`, which the OLE libraries call to inform the target application that a drag-drop operation is currently positioned within that application's registered drag-drop window. One of the parameters passed during this call is a pointer to an `IDataObject` interface.

The next message is a call to `IDataObject::QueryGetData`. Word is now trying to determine the type of data being offered and whether it can accept that type of data. As you can see, this method is called several times. Word also must determine whether a link or embedded data is being offered.

After Word receives an acknowledgment of the initial `DragEnter` message, the OLE libraries call the `DragOverv` method. This method generates visual feedback to the user by changing the mouse cursor's appearance.

A `Drop` message is then posted to signify that the user has released the mouse button. In the `Drop` method, Word receives an `IDataObject` pointer to the data. Word then calls `IDataObject::QueryGetData` again to determine the data type.

Finally, an `IDataObject::GetDataHere` is posted. Word provides a STGMEDIUM structure into which Excel can copy the data. This method is usually called for embedded objects. The OLE libraries in turn call `IDataObject::GetData` to retrieve the data. After an acknowledgment of the `Drop` message is posted, the transfer is complete.

The LRPC Message Monitor provides a fascinating glimpse into the inner workings of the LRPC (lightweight remote procedure call) protocol. Although you can easily get swamped by all the messages generated, the tool is still useful for debugging.

You can select where to send the debugging stream: to a file, terminal, or window. For closer inspection, you can save the message stream's entire contents to a file.

The OLE 2.0 Free Module Utility

Every programmer who has ever worked with DLLs has faced the problem of having DLLs locked in memory because the main application terminated abnormally. The simple Free Module (see fig. 4.6) utility excels at one task: unloading OLE DLLs from memory. The program is a baby brother to the more powerful Window Process Status (WPS) utility discussed later in this chapter.

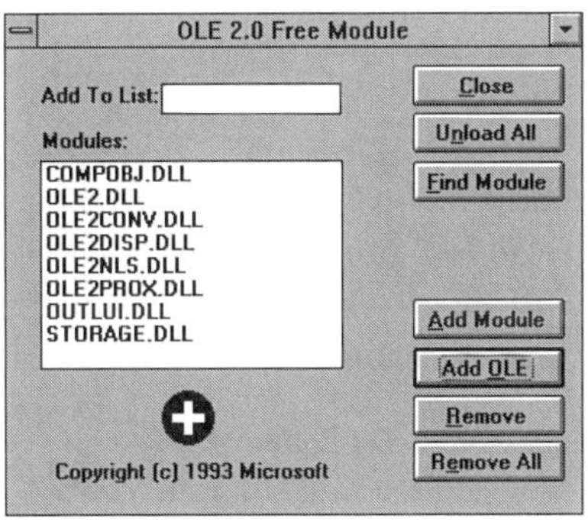

Fig. 4.6
The OLE 2.0 Free Module utility.

When you encounter a General Protection error in an OLE application, you can use this tool to unload the OLE libraries. After you run this utility, you see a list of all the OLE DLLs that are loaded in memory. You can then unload and free the DLLs individually or collectively.

The Ole2View Utility

Ole2View is the jewel among the SDK's collection of utilities. This utility provides the following features:

- A list of all the objects registered in the system
- A list of the interfaces that each object supports
- The full registration database information for each object
- A list of the data formats that each `IDataObject` interface supports
- A list of the methods and properties supported by `IDispatch` interfaces
- The current build numbers of all the OLE DLLs
- A full-featured type library viewer
- A means of extending itself to support interface viewers other than those supplied with the utility

Figure 4.7 shows Ole2View running with a sample application selected. The list box on the left shows all the objects registered in the system. Every container, object server, and type library is displayed. This list includes OLE 1.0 objects. The icons to the left of the objects indicate the various types. The **O**bjects menu includes a **S**how CLSIDs option that displays each object's CLSID in the list box.

The top-right window displays information about the selected object from the registration database. If you want to change some of this information, you can invoke REGEDIT (the system registry editor supplied with Windows) from the **F**ile menu by choosing **R**un the Registry Editor.

Double-clicking an object causes Ole2View to start the object and query it for its interfaces. The bottom-right list box then displays the interfaces.

If an interface viewer is available for a particular interface (Ole2View ships with interface viewers for `IDataObject`, `IDispatch`, `ITypeInfo`, and `ITypeLib`), that viewer displays information about the interface. The format of the display depends on the interface itself. The `IDataObject` viewer displays the results of `EnumFormatEtc`. To display this information, you select the interface and double-click it.

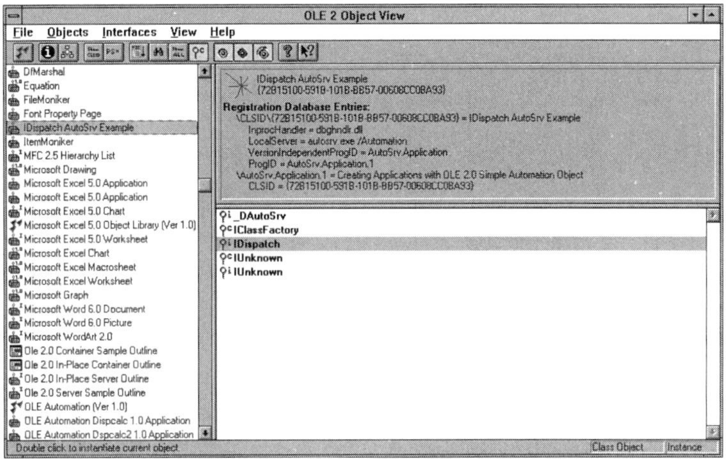

Fig. 4.7
Ole2View in action.

The `IDispatch` viewer displays the methods and properties that the object supports. One advantageous feature of this viewer is its capability to save the contents of a type library to a text file. The file is in Visual Basic format and is useful as a documentation aid.

Ole2View can display the current build numbers of all the OLE libraries, as well as the fully qualified path to those DLLs.

As was mentioned earlier, you can extend the functionality of Ole2View by writing a special interface viewer. To create an interface viewer, you must develop a DLL that exports the following function:

```
HRESULT WINAPI _export  DisplayInterface(
        HWND        hwndParent, // Ole2View's main frame wnd
        LPUNKNOWN   lpunk,      // Pointer to valid interface
        LPIID       lpiid,      // pointer to interface id
        LPSTR       lpszName    // Interface name
    } ;
```

This function is called with a valid pointer to the interface in question. You can then do anything you want with this interface pointer. The sample code that ships with the SDK shows an implementation for `IDataObject`, `IDispatch`, `ITypeLib`, and `ITypeInfo`.

As an example, you can add the following simple viewer for the `IRunnableObject` interface. You implement this interface with object handlers and DLL objects. Objects use this interface to determine when the objects should enter the running state and when to become a contained object.

Instead of writing a separate DLL, you can use the sample code provided with the SDK to compile and link your interface viewer. After you build the DLL, you must register it with the Ole2View program by adding the following entry to the OLE2VIEW.INI file:

```
[Interface Viewers]
{00000126-0000-0000-C000-000000000046}=defo2v.dll,DisplayIRunnableObject
```

You implement three methods in the interface viewer:

```
IRunnableObject::Run
IRunnableObject::IsRunning
IRunnableObject::GetRunningClass
```

Clicking the Run button sets the object in the running state (see fig. 4.8). You can verify this state by checking the results of the `IsRunning` call and by running the WPS utility, which is described in the next section.

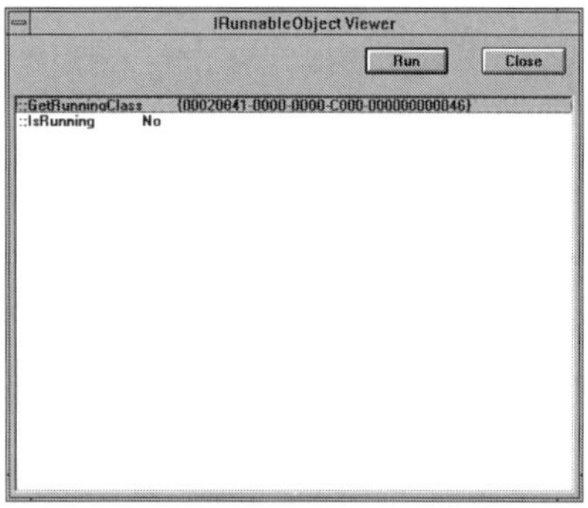

Fig. 4.8
The *IRunnableObject* Viewer.

The class ID of the object and its current running state are displayed in the viewer window.

Listings 4.1 and 4.2 are the implementation files for the interface viewer.

Listing 4.1 IRUNOBJ.H

```
#ifndef _IRUNOBJ_H_
#define _IRUNOBJ_H_

extern "C"
BOOL WINAPI __export fnIRunnableObjectDlg( HWND hDlg, UINT uiMsg,
    WPARAM wParam, LPARAM lParam ) ;

//-------------------------------------------------------------
class _far IRunnableObjectDlg
{
friend BOOL WINAPI __export fnIRunnableObjectDlg( HWND hDlg,
     UINT uiMsg, WPARAM wParam, LPARAM lParam ) ;
public:
     IRunnableObjectDlg( HWND hwnd, LPRUNNABLEOBJECT lpDO,
         LPIID lpiid, LPSTR lpszName ) ;
     ~IRunnableObjectDlg() ;
     int DoModal( void ) ;

     LPRUNNABLEOBJECT  m_lpRO ;
     LPIID           m_lpiid ;
     LPSTR           m_lpszName ;

     HWND        m_hWndParent ;
     HWND        m_hDlg ;

     HWND        m_lbGet ;

// Implementation
protected:
     BOOL DoIRunnableObject( UINT nLevel, LPRUNNABLEOBJECT pI) ;

     int AddItem( UINT nLevel, LPSTR sz, UINT uiType, int cColumns,
         LPCOLUMNSTRUCT  rgCol ) ;
     int AddItem( UINT nLevel, LPSTR sz, UINT uiType ) ;
     int AddItem( UINT nLevel, LPSTR sz ) ;

     BOOL OnInitDialog();
     void OnSize(UINT nType, int cx, int cy);
     void OnDrawItem(int nIDCtl, LPDRAWITEMSTRUCT lpDrawItemStruct);
     void OnMeasureItem(int nIDCtl,
          LPMEASUREITEMSTRUCT lpMeasureItemStruct);
     void OnDblclk();
     void OnSelchange();
     void OnDestroy();
     void OnRun();
};

typedef IRunnableObjectDlg FAR * LPIRUNNABLEOBJECTDLG ;

#endif
//-------------------------------------------------------------
//-------------------------------------------------------------
```

Listing 4.2 IRUNOBJ.CPP

```
#include "precomp.h"
#include "defo2v.h"
#include "irunobj.h"

static HFONT       g_hFont ;
static HFONT       g_hFontBold ;
static UINT        g_cyFont ;
//----------------------------------------------------------------
extern "C"
HRESULT WINAPI _export DisplayIRunnableObject( HWND hwndParent,
    LPRUNNABLEOBJECT lpRO, LPIID lpiid, LPSTR lpszName )
{
     HRESULT hr = NULL ;

     IRunnableObjectDlg dlg(hwndParent, lpRO, lpiid, lpszName ) ;
     dlg.DoModal() ;

     return hr ;
}
//----------------------------------------------------------------
IRunnableObjectDlg::IRunnableObjectDlg(HWND hwnd,
    LPRUNNABLEOBJECT lpRO, LPIID lpiid, LPSTR lpszName )
{
     m_lbGet = NULL ;
     m_hWndParent = hwnd ;
     m_lpRO = lpRO ;
     m_lpiid = lpiid ;
     m_lpszName = lpszName ;
}
//----------------------------------------------------------------
IRunnableObjectDlg::~IRunnableObjectDlg()
{
}
//----------------------------------------------------------------
int IRunnableObjectDlg::DoModal( void )
{
     return DialogBoxParam( g_hInst,
         MAKEINTRESOURCE( IDD_IRUNNABLEOBJDLG ), m_hWndParent,
         (DLGPROC)fnIRunnableObjectDlg, (LONG)this ) ;
}
//----------------------------------------------------------------
BOOL WINAPI __export fnIRunnableObjectDlg( HWND hDlg, UINT uiMsg,
    WPARAM wParam, LPARAM lParam )
{
     LPIRUNNABLEOBJECTDLG pIROD =
     ➥(LPIRUNNABLEOBJECTDLG)GetWindowLong( hDlg, DWL_USER ) ;
     switch (uiMsg)
     {
          case WM_INITDIALOG:
               pIROD=(LPIRUNNABLEOBJECTDLG)lParam ;
               if (pIROD==NULL)
               {
                    EndDialog( hDlg, 0 ) ;
```

```
                return TRUE ;
            }
            SetWindowLong( hDlg, DWL_USER, (LONG)pIROD ) ;
            pIROD->m_hDlg = hDlg ;
            return pIROD->OnInitDialog() ;
            break;
        case WM_DESTROY:
            if (pIROD)
                pIROD->OnDestroy() ;
            break;
        case WM_SIZE:
            if (pIROD)
                pIROD->OnSize( (UINT)wParam, LOWORD( lParam ),
                    HIWORD( lParam ) ) ;
            break;
        case WM_COMMAND:
        {
#ifdef WIN32
            WORD wNotifyCode = HIWORD(wParam);
            WORD wID = LOWORD(wParam);
            HWND hwndCtl = (HWND) lParam;
#else
            WORD wNotifyCode = HIWORD(lParam) ;
            WORD wID = wParam ;
            HWND hwndCtl = (HWND)LOWORD(lParam) ;
#endif

            switch (wID)
            {
                case IDCANCEL:
                    EndDialog( hDlg, IDCANCEL ) ;
                    break;
                case IDRUN:
                    if(pIROD)
                        pIROD->OnRun();
                    break;
            }
        }
        break;
        case WM_DRAWITEM:
            if (pIROD)
                pIROD->OnDrawItem( wParam,
                    (LPDRAWITEMSTRUCT)lParam ) ;
            break;

        case WM_MEASUREITEM:
            if (pIROD)
                pIROD->OnMeasureItem( wParam,
                    (LPMEASUREITEMSTRUCT)lParam ) ;
            break;
        default:
           return FALSE ;
    }
    return TRUE ;
```

(continues)

Listing 4.2 Continued

```
}
//----------------------------------------------------------------
BOOL IRunnableObjectDlg::OnInitDialog()
{
     m_lbGet = GetDlgItem( m_hDlg, IDC_IFACE_PROPS ) ;

     TEXTMETRIC  tm ;
     HDC hdc = GetDC(NULL);
     g_hFont = ReallyCreateFont( hdc, "MS Sans Serif", "Regular", 8, 0 ) ;
     g_hFontBold = ReallyCreateFont( hdc, "MS Sans Serif",
         "Bold", 8, 0 ) ;
     g_hFont = SelectObject( hdc, g_hFont ) ;
     GetTextMetrics( hdc, &tm ) ;
     g_hFont = SelectObject( hdc, g_hFont ) ;
     ReleaseDC( NULL, hdc ) ;
     g_cyFont = tm.tmHeight + tm.tmExternalLeading ;

     SetWindowFont( m_lbGet, g_hFont, TRUE ) ;

     if (IsEqualCLSID( IID_IRunnableObject, *m_lpiid ))
     {
          DoIRunnableObject( 0, (LPRUNNABLEOBJECT)m_lpRO ) ;
     }
     else
     {
          MessageBox( m_hDlg, "Wrong IID", "Error", MB_OK ) ;
     }

     DlgCenter( m_hDlg, m_hWndParent, FALSE ) ;
     RECT rc ;
     GetWindowRect( m_hDlg, &rc ) ;
     SetWindowPos( m_hDlg, NULL, rc.left, rc.top, rc.right - rc.left + 1,
                   rc.bottom - rc.top +1,
                   SWP_NOMOVE|SWP_NOZORDER | SWP_NOACTIVATE ) ;
     return TRUE;
}
//----------------------------------------------------------------
void IRunnableObjectDlg::OnRun()
{
     m_lpRO->Run(NULL);
     DoIRunnableObject( 0, (LPRUNNABLEOBJECT)m_lpRO ) ;
}
//----------------------------------------------------------------
void IRunnableObjectDlg::OnDestroy()
{
     int c = ListBox_GetCount( m_lbGet ) ;
     for (int i = 0 ; i < c ; i++)
     {
          LPITEMDATA lpID = (LPITEMDATA)ListBox_GetItemData( m_lbGet,
              i ) ;
          if (lpID)
          {
```

```
                if (lpID->uiType == I_COLUMNHEAD)
                    delete lpID->rgCol ;
                delete lpID ;
            }
        }

        if (g_hFont)
            DeleteObject( g_hFont );

        if (g_hFontBold)
            DeleteObject (g_hFontBold) ;
}
//-----------------------------------------------------------------
void IRunnableObjectDlg::OnSize(UINT nType, int cx, int cy)
{
    if (m_lbGet && !IsWindow( m_lbGet ) )
        return ;

    RECT    rc ;
    RECT    rcWnd ;
    GetClientRect( m_hDlg, &rcWnd ) ;
    GetWindowRect( m_lbGet, &rc ) ;
    MapWindowPoints( NULL, m_hDlg, (POINT FAR*)&rc, 2 ) ;
    rc.left = rcWnd.left + 5 ;
    SetWindowPos( m_lbGet, NULL, rcWnd.left + 5, rc.top, cx - 10,
                  cy - rc.top - 5, SWP_NOZORDER ¦ SWP_NOACTIVATE ) ;
}
//-----------------------------------------------------------------
void IRunnableObjectDlg::OnDrawItem(int nIDCtl, LPDRAWITEMSTRUCT lpDIS )
{
    if (lpDIS->itemID == LB_ERR)
        return ;

    LPITEMDATA      lpID ;
    COLORREF        rgbBack ;
    RECT            rcFocus ;
    BOOL            fSelected ;
    int             x, y, cy ;
    char            szItem[128] ;

    lpID = (LPITEMDATA)lpDIS->itemData ;
    rcFocus = lpDIS->rcItem ;
    ListBox_GetText( m_lbGet, lpDIS->itemID, szItem ) ;

    if (fSelected = (lpDIS->itemState & ODS_SELECTED) ? TRUE : FALSE)
    {
        SetTextColor( lpDIS->hDC, GetSysColor( COLOR_HIGHLIGHTTEXT ) ) ;
        SetBkColor( lpDIS->hDC,
            rgbBack = GetSysColor( COLOR_HIGHLIGHT ) ) ;
    }
    else
    {
        SetTextColor( lpDIS->hDC, GetSysColor( COLOR_WINDOWTEXT ) ) ;
```

(continues)

Listing 4.2 Continued

```
     SetBkColor( lpDIS->hDC,
         rgbBack = GetSysColor( COLOR_WINDOW ) ) ;
}

// if you are losing focus, remove the focus rect before
// drawing.
//
if ((lpDIS->itemAction) & (ODA_FOCUS))
     if (!((lpDIS->itemState) & (ODS_FOCUS)))
          DrawFocusRect( lpDIS->hDC, &rcFocus ) ;

y = lpDIS->rcItem.top ;
x = lpDIS->rcItem.left ;

int cxChar = GetTextMetricsCorrectly( lpDIS->hDC, NULL ) ;

if (lpID && (lpID->uiType == I_COLUMNHEAD ¦¦ lpID->uiType
➥== I_LABEL))
     g_hFontBold = SelectObject( lpDIS->hDC, g_hFontBold ) ;

cy = (rcFocus.bottom - rcFocus.top - g_cyFont) / 2 ;

ExtTextOut( lpDIS->hDC, x+2, y + cy, ETO_OPAQUE, &lpDIS->rcItem,
    NULL, 0, NULL ) ;
if (lpID)
     ColumnTextOut( lpDIS->hDC, x + 2 + ((cxChar*3) * lpID->nLevel),
     y + cy, szItem, lpID->cColumns, lpID->rgCol ) ;

if (lpID && lpID->uiType == I_COLUMNHEAD )
{
     COLORREF    rgb ;
     RECT        rc = rcFocus ;
     rgb = SetBkColor( lpDIS->hDC, GetTextColor( lpDIS->hDC ) ) ;
     rc.top = rc.bottom - 1 ;
     rc.left = x + 2 + ((cxChar*3) * lpID->nLevel) ;
     ExtTextOut( lpDIS->hDC, 0, 0, ETO_OPAQUE, &rc, NULL, 0, NULL ) ;
     SetBkColor( lpDIS->hDC, rgb ) ;
}

if (lpID && (lpID->uiType == I_COLUMNHEAD ¦¦ lpID->uiType
➥== I_LABEL))
     g_hFontBold = SelectObject( lpDIS->hDC, g_hFontBold ) ;

// if you are gaining focus, draw the focus rect after drawing
// the text.
if ((lpDIS->itemAction) & (ODA_FOCUS))
     if ((lpDIS->itemState) & (ODS_FOCUS))
          DrawFocusRect( lpDIS->hDC, &rcFocus ) ;

if (fSelected)
{
```

```
            SetTextColor( lpDIS->hDC, GetSysColor( COLOR_WINDOWTEXT ) ) ;
            SetBkColor( lpDIS->hDC, GetSysColor( COLOR_WINDOW ) ) ;
        }

}
//-----------------------------------------------------------------
void IRunnableObjectDlg::OnMeasureItem(int nIDCtl,
        LPMEASUREITEMSTRUCT lpMeasureItemStruct)
{
        lpMeasureItemStruct->itemHeight = g_cyFont ;
}
//-----------------------------------------------------------------
void IRunnableObjectDlg::OnDblclk()
{
}
//-----------------------------------------------------------------
void IRunnableObjectDlg::OnSelchange()
{
}
//-----------------------------------------------------------------
BOOL IRunnableObjectDlg::DoIRunnableObject( UINT nLevel,
    LPRUNNABLEOBJECT pIRunnableObject )
{

        HRESULT     hr ;
        CLSID clsid;
        static char szCLSID[144], szText[144];
        LPSTR lpStr = (LPSTR)&szCLSID;

        hr = pIRunnableObject->GetRunningClass(&clsid);
        if (SUCCEEDED( hr ))
        {
            StringFromCLSID(clsid,&lpStr);
            wsprintf(szText,"::GetRunningClass          %s",lpStr);
            AddItem( nLevel,szText, I_LABEL ) ;
        }

        BOOL fRunning = pIRunnableObject->IsRunning();
        if(fRunning)
            wsprintf(szText,"::IsRunning               Yes");
        else
            wsprintf(szText,"::IsRunning               No");
        AddItem( nLevel,szText, I_LABEL ) ;

        return TRUE ;
}
//-----------------------------------------------------------------
int IRunnableObjectDlg::AddItem( UINT nLevel, LPSTR sz, UINT uiType,
    int cColumns, LPCOLUMNSTRUCT  rgCol )
{
        int i ;
        LPITEMDATA      lpID ;
        i = ListBox_AddString( m_lbGet,  sz ) ;
```

(continues)

Listing 4.2 Continued

```
        lpID = new ITEMDATA ;
        lpID->uiType = uiType ;
        lpID->cColumns = cColumns ;
        lpID->rgCol = rgCol ;
        lpID->nLevel = nLevel ;
        ListBox_SetItemData( m_lbGet, i, (DWORD)lpID ) ;
        return i ;
}
//-------------------------------------------------------------
int IRunnableObjectDlg::AddItem( UINT nLevel, LPSTR sz, UINT uiType
)
{
        return AddItem( nLevel, sz, uiType, 0, NULL ) ;
}
//-------------------------------------------------------------
int IRunnableObjectDlg::AddItem( UINT nLevel, LPSTR sz )
{
        return AddItem( nLevel, sz, I_NORMAL, 0, NULL ) ;
}
//-------------------------------------------------------------
//-------------------------------------------------------------
```

The Windows Process Status Utility

The Windows Process Status (WPS) utility actually has little to do with OLE. Nevertheless, the tool is invaluable. WPS displays a list of all the tasks and modules in the system. The main window is split into two separate windows (see fig. 4.9).

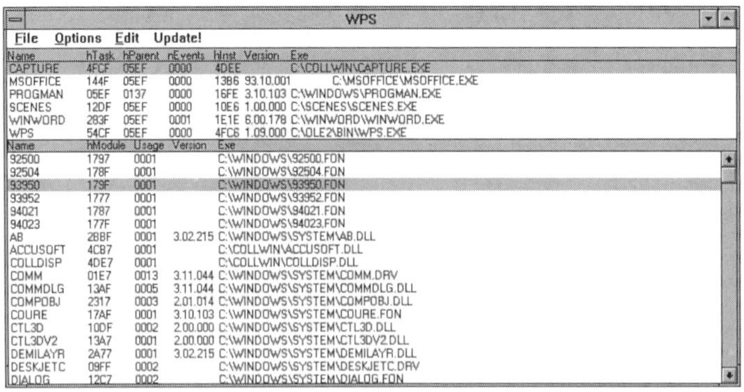

Fig. 4.9
The Windows Process Status utility.

The top window lists all the tasks in the system. For each task, this window displays the task name, task handle, parent handle, and instance handler. Two of the most useful fields are the version information field and the fully qualified path to the program. The version information is important especially for the OLE libraries. Most modern applications include a version resource in their executables, which certainly aids in debugging. The path name shows you exactly which executable is currently running. This name can be useful particularly if you keep many versions of the same program.

The module window at the bottom of the split screen displays information about each DLL and driver loaded in the system. This information includes the module name (as defined in the module's DEF file), the module handle, the current usage count, the version information, and the path to the disk file. The module usage count is useful if you are having problems loading or unloading DLLs. Like component objects, DLLs are locked in memory until their reference count reaches zero.

When you develop DLLs, one annoyance is that you have to remove them from memory if a crash occurs. If a DLL is locked in memory, you cannot load the new version that you have just compiled. However, the WPS utility enables you to select and remove modules from memory by double-clicking them. Be careful, though, not to remove a system module from memory inadvertently. WPS also enables you to reload a module from disk.

Caution

Removing modules with WPS is not bullet-proof, and can sometimes destabilize your system.

A useful aid in debugging is to save the state of the system before and after you load your application. WPS enables you to dump the system state to a disk file. You can then load the "before" and "after" files into an editor and compare them.

The Type Library Generator

MyTypLib is the compiler that Microsoft supplies to create type libraries. The compiler compiles scripts written in the Microsoft Object Description Language (MODL). You can supply the resulting type library to the user as a stand-alone library that you merge into a DLL as a resource or as a stream in a compound file. The name of the stream within the compound file must be `\006typelib`.

Type libraries expose an application's objects and describe each method and property. Chapter 11, "General Concepts of OLE Automation," examines type libraries in greater detail.

The Type Library Browser

You can find the Type Library Browser and its source code in the SAMPLES directory on the SDK's CD-ROM. You can open a type library and browse the type information available. Figure 4.10 shows the information available when you open the type library that you develop in Chapter 13, "Creating a Simple Automation Server."

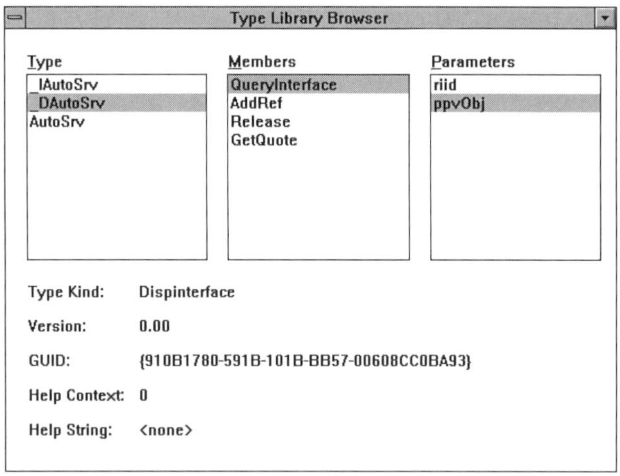

Fig. 4.10
The Type Library Browser.

The WXSRVR Program

One advantage of the Windows NT is the capability to execute a Windows application directly from a DOS box. This feature is especially useful when you want to execute a Windows development tool from a make file.

The WXSRVR program supplies this capability for Windows 3.X. To use this system, you must install VMB.386 in the 386enh section of your SYSTEM.INI file. Then, from the Program Manager, you must execute WXSRVR.EXE.

To start any Windows program from the DOS box, type **WX** *progname*. The Windows application is then executed.

For example, you can execute MyTypLib in this way. When you want to generate type libraries, you simply include the following line in your make files:

```
wx mktypelib...
```

The Debugging Handler

Included in the SAMP\HANDLER directory of the SDK's CD-ROM is an example of how you can create an in-process (in-proc) handler. This handler, which sits between the container and the default handler, logs all interface calls and their parameters to a window and a log file.

The code is a good example of how to write an inproc handler, and also is a useful debugging tool. Figure 4.11 shows the results of inserting an object whose in-proc handler has been replaced by the Debugging Handler.

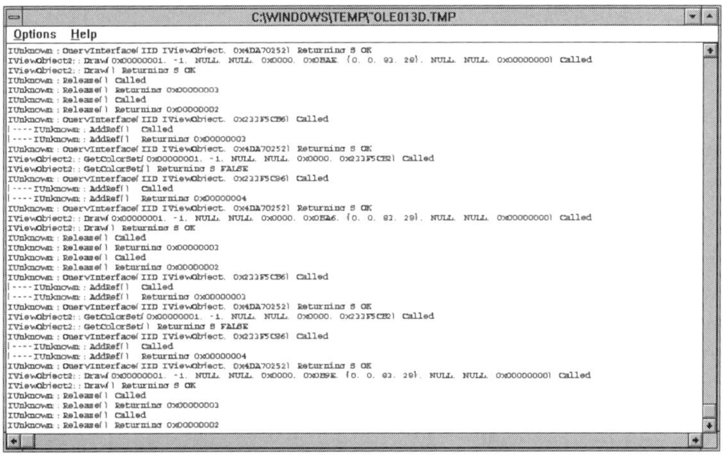

Fig. 4.11
The Debugging Handler in action.

The SDK also provides an installer tool that enables you to install the Debugging Handler for each object. When you examine the registration database of an object that you have selected for debugging, you will notice that the `InProcServer` key is updated to point to DBGHNDLR.DLL (the Debugging Handler).

After you finish debugging an object, you can remove the Debugging Handler and restore the default handler by using the installer program.

From Here...

In this chapter, you explored the OLE SDK. As you have seen, Microsoft provides several useful tools both for debugging OLE applications and also for increasing your understanding of how the pieces of such applications fit together.

The best tool that Microsoft provides, however, is the sample source code that demonstrates almost all areas of OLE development.

Part II

Using MFC To Implement OLE

5 Introduction to the MFC Document View Model

6 A Simple Container

7 An MDI Linking Container

8 OLE Compound Files

9 A Simple MFC OLE Server

10 A Full OLE Server

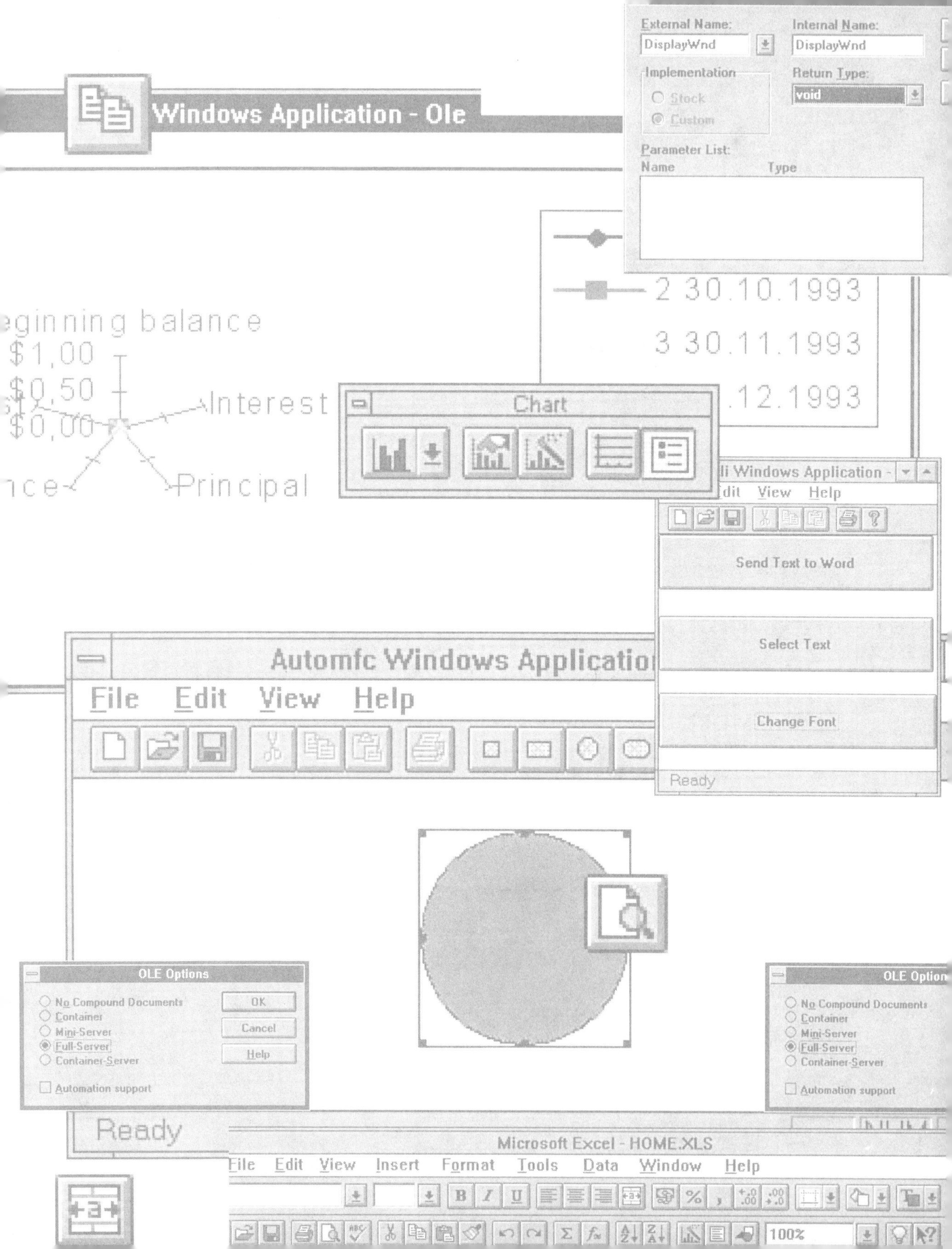

Windows Application - Ole
External Name:
DisplayWnd
Internal Name:
DisplayWnd
Implementation
Stock
Custom
Return Type:
void
Parameter List:
Name
Type
2 30.10.1993
3 30.11.1993
.12.1993
Interest
Principal
Chart
Windows Application -
View
Help
Send Text to Word
Select Text
Change Font
Ready
Automfc Windows Applicatio
File
Edit
View
Help
OLE Options
No Compound Documents
Container
Mini-Server
Full-Server
Container-Server
Automation support
OK
Cancel
Help
Ready
Microsoft Excel - HOME.XLS
File
Edit
View
Insert
Format
Tools
Data
Window
Help
100%

Chapter 5

Introduction to the MFC Document View Model

In this chapter, you examine the Microsoft Foundation Classes (MFC) framework and how you can use it to create OLE applications.

You learn about the following:

- The MFC Document View architecture, and how you can use it to create Windows applications
- The support for OLE that Microsoft added to the MFC framework
- The classes that wrap the functionality of the OLE interfaces
- The parts of OLE that MFC does not implement

Application Frameworks

Application frameworks have being making news for the past few years. In fact, their history goes back to Smalltalk-80. Smalltalk does not distinguish between its environment or framework and the application itself. In Smalltalk, you constantly reuse or subclass objects from the framework.

This concept of an application framework is much different from that of a class library. If you use a class library in your application, you are in effect adding value or functionality to your application with the aid of a third-party class library. When you use an application framework, on the other hand, you must accept the framework's architecture and design philosophy. In general, frameworks are not meant to be used on a piecemeal basis; instead, you use them in their entirety.

This is not as bad as it sounds. In return for structuring your application to fit the framework, you receive an enormous amount of "canned" functionality. The code within the framework usually is highly optimized and tuned. Also, you can extend frameworks like regular class libraries.

Frameworks provide you with the application-building blocks necessary in any commercial application, and free you to concentrate on the details of your particular application. MFC, for example, provides print preview functionality that is implemented in over 2,000 lines of code. One look at this code will more than convince you of the benefits of using a framework.

Another major benefit of using a framework is portability. Frameworks are very good at encapsulating and isolating platform-dependent code. MFC, for example, is available on both 16-bit and 32-bit Windows. A future release will also provide portability to the Macintosh.

Selecting a framework for your development work is not a decision to be taken lightly. Frameworks tend to be all-encompassing, so you cannot easily switch between them. Also, because modern frameworks are so large and complex, you have to spend significant time and resources to master them.

A full discussion of frameworks in general and MFC in particular is beyond the scope of this book. Instead, this chapter focuses on the part of the framework that affects OLE.

The MFC Document View Architecture

Before delving into the details of the MFC OLE implementation, you must first understand the Document View architecture of MFC. You must understand this important part of MFC before you can create OLE compound documents.

The MFC framework defines two types of classes for manipulating data: a Document class for saving and retrieving the disk-based data, and a View class for displaying and editing the data. In other words, this architecture attempts to separate the data, which may or may not be a disk file, from the user's view of the data.

An additional class is also used for the application's frame window. The class, `CMainFrame`, is responsible for creating the frame window and the application's toolbars and status bars.

The Document class is usually attached to a View class, but a particular Document object may have more than one view. For example, you can create an application that provides both a hexidecimal and an ASCII view of a text file. To do so, you would have one Document class, to manipulate the text file, and two View classes; one View class would provide the hexidecimal dump, and the other would provide the normal view of the data.

The diagram in figure 5.1 shows how the Document and View classes fit together.

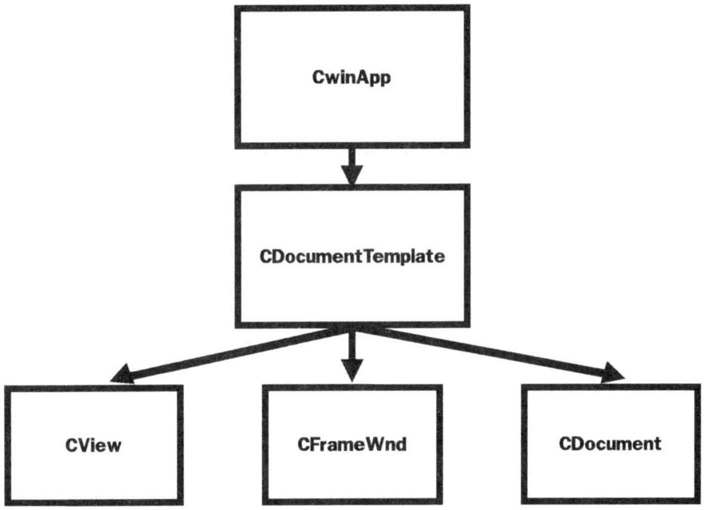

Fig. 5.1
The Document and View classes.

The Document Class

The `CDocument` class is responsible for all your application's file input and output (I/O). Usually you derive a class for the `CDocument` class to handle the specifics of your particular file or database format. MFC provides most of the functionality of this class for you.

The following are the principal steps that MFC goes through when you select File Open from your application:

1. The `CWinApp::FileOpen` method invokes Windows' common dialog box for opening files.

2. After you select a file, the `CWinApp::OpenDocumentFile` method is called. This method determines the document type and calls that document template object's `OpenDocumentFile` member.

3. The document template then dynamically creates an object of the type that you derived from `CDocument`. The framework's capability to create objects dynamically at run-time is one of MFC's advanced features. Any class can accomplish this feat by using the DECLARE_DYNAMIC and DECLARE_DYNCREATE macros and the `CRunTimeClass` structure. A View object is also created dynamically and associated with the Document object. The framework then calls the document's `OnOpenDocument` object.

4. The default implementation of the `CDocument::OnOpenDocument` method creates a `CFile` object and opens the actual disk file by using this object.

5. A `CArchive` object is created and attached to the `CFile` object. The `Serialize` method is then called. This is the only `CDocument` method that you must override. Your `Serialize` method reads the actual data into your object's member variables.

As you can see, the framework does most of the work for you. All that you have to do is interpret the data stream being read in from the `CArchive` object and store the data within your class.

The View Class

After your data is read in, you must provide a means by which the user can view the data. The `CView` class that you use to derive your class in turn derives from `CWnd`. This class provides everything that is required to display or print data.

To display or print your data, you override the `OnDraw` method. This method, which accepts a CDC device context as a parameter, is used for both displaying and printing. The framework prepares the necessary device context, depending on the output device. This device context can even be a Print Preview device context that implements Print Preview in your application.

The `OnDraw` method helps to isolate all your output in one place.

The `CView` class also supports several optimization methods that can dramatically increase performance. These methods include the use of "hints" that are passed to the drawing and device context methods. These hints can include pointers to invalid rectangles or to entire objects that need to be updated.

The Document Template Class

The `CDocTemplate` class is responsible for creating and linking together the View, Frame, and Document classes. Two framework classes derive from this class: `CSingleDocTemplate` creates Single Document Interface (SDI) applications, and `CMultiDocTemplate` creates Multiple Document Interface (MDI) applications.

You must create a separate `CDocTemplate` object for each type of document that your application supports. This class is responsible for implementing the dynamic object creation features.

The MFC OLE Classes

Now that you have briefly examined MFC's Document View architecture, it is now time to examine in detail the OLE support provided by MFC.

The OLE 2.0 specification defines over 96 interfaces. As OLE continues to evolve, Microsoft and others will continue to add more interfaces. One of the goals of Microsoft's AFX development team was to group together and encapsulate the most commonly used interfaces into fewer C++ classes.

As with COM interfaces, not all of these classes are required for each application that you develop, and most of the classes have a default implementation that is more than adequate for most implementations.

MFC 2.5 does not implement all the functionality of OLE. Later in this chapter, you examine some of the features and interfaces that MFC 2.5 omits. Figure 5.2 shows the classes added to MFC 2.5 to support OLE.

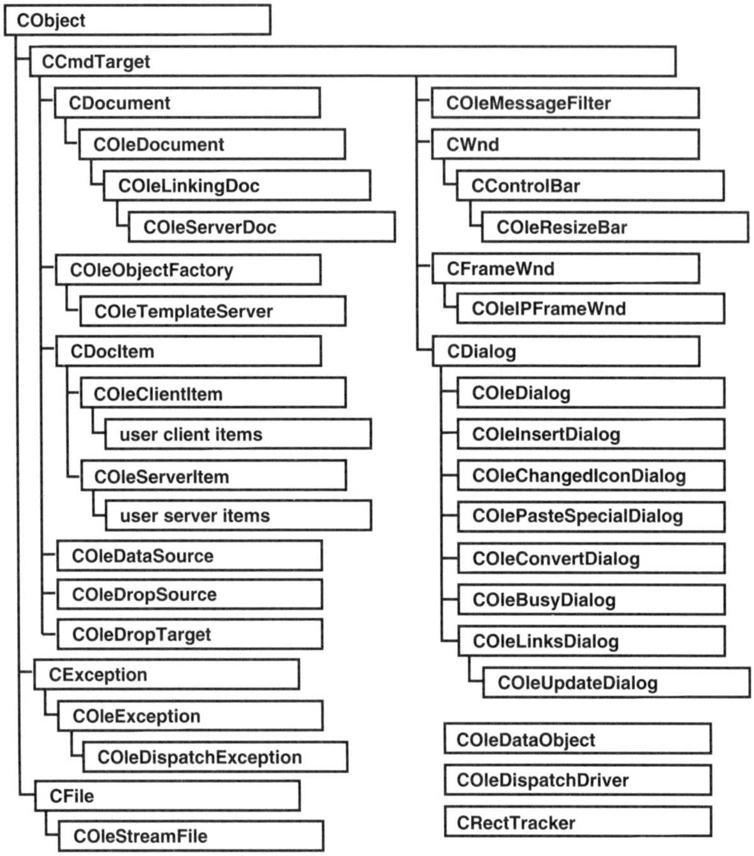

Fig. 5.2
The MFC OLE classes.

The Base Classes

MFC has four base classes: `COleDialog`, `CDocItem`, `COleDispatchDriver`, and `COleDocument`. The following sections describe these classes. You will not normally use any of these classes directly. These base classes contain most of the OLE functionality contained within MFC.

The *COleDialog* Class

This class, which derives from `CDialog`, provides the base class for the more specialized OLE dialog boxes:

```
class COleDialog : public CDialog
{
    DECLARE_DYNAMIC(COleDialog)

// Attributes
public:
    UINT GetLastError() const;
```

```
// Implementation
public:
     int MapResult(UINT nResult);
     COleDialog(CWnd* pParentWnd);
#ifdef _DEBUG
     virtual void Dump(CDumpContext& dc) const;
#endif

protected:
     virtual void OnOK();
     virtual void OnCancel();

     UINT  m_nLastError;

protected:
     friend UINT CALLBACK AFX_EXPORT
     ➥_AfxOleHookProc(HWND, UINT, WPARAM, LPARAM);

};
```

The *CDocItem* Class

The `CDocItem` is an abstract base class that is used to share common functionality between the `COleClientItem` and `COleServerItem` classes:

```
class CDocItem : public CCmdTarget
{
     DECLARE_SERIAL(CDocItem)

// Constructors
protected:      // abstract class
     CDocItem();

// Attributes
public:
     CDocument* GetDocument() const; // return container document

// Overridables
public:
     // Raw data access (native format)
     virtual BOOL IsBlank() const;

// Implementation
protected:
     COleDocument* m_pDocument;

public:
     virtual void Serialize(CArchive& ar);   // for native data
     virtual ~CDocItem();
#ifdef _DEBUG
     virtual void AssertValid() const;
     virtual void Dump(CDumpContext& dc) const;
#endif

     friend class COleDocument;          // for access to back pointer
};
```

The *COleDispatchDriver* Class

The `COleDispatchDriver` class implements Automation clients. It includes a method to create an `IDispatch` interface for an object and helper methods to access the exposed Automation methods and properties. You use this class later in this book when you begin to use OLE Automation.

```
class COleDispatchDriver
{
// Constructors
public:
     COleDispatchDriver();

// Operations
     BOOL CreateDispatch(REFCLSID clsid, COleException* pError = NULL);
     BOOL CreateDispatch(LPCSTR lpszProgID,
                         COleException* pError = NULL);

     void AttachDispatch(LPDISPATCH lpDispatch,
                         BOOL bAutoRelease = TRUE);
     LPDISPATCH DetachDispatch();
          // detach and get ownership of m_lpDispatch
     void ReleaseDispatch();

     // helpers for IDispatch::Invoke
     void InvokeHelper(DISPID dwDispID, WORD wFlags,
          VARTYPE vtRet, void* pvRet, const BYTE FAR* pbParamInfo, ...);
     void SetProperty(DISPID dwDispID, VARTYPE vtProp, ...);
     void GetProperty(DISPID dwDispID, VARTYPE vtProp, void* pvProp)
     ➥const;

// Implementation
public:
     LPDISPATCH m_lpDispatch;

     ~COleDispatchDriver();
     void InvokeHelperV(DISPID dwDispID, WORD wFlags, VARTYPE vtRet,
          void* pvRet, const BYTE FAR* pbParamInfo, va_list argList);

protected:
     BOOL m_bAutoRelease;    // TRUE if destructor should call Release

private:
     // Disable the copy constructor and assignment by default
     //   so you will get compiler errors rather than unexpected
     //   behavior if you pass objects by value or assign objects.
     COleDispatchDriver(const COleDispatchDriver&);
                                               // no implementation
     void operator=(const COleDispatchDriver&);  // no implementation
};
```

The *COleDocument* Class

`COleDocument`, which derives from `CDocument`, is the class that you use if your application is going to support visual editing. As you can see, this class is quite large:

```
class COleDocument : public CDocument
{
     DECLARE_DYNAMIC(COleDocument)

// Constructors
public:
     COleDocument();

// Attributes
     BOOL HasBlankItems() const; // check for BLANK items
     COleClientItem* GetInPlaceActiveItem(CWnd* pWnd);
          // return in-place active item for this view, or NULL if none

// Operations
     // iterating over existing items
     virtual POSITION GetStartPosition() const;
     virtual CDocItem* GetNextItem(POSITION& pos) const;

     // iterator helpers (helpers use virtual GetNextItem)
     COleClientItem* GetNextClientItem(POSITION& pos) const;
     COleServerItem* GetNextServerItem(POSITION& pos) const;

     // adding new items - called from item constructors
     virtual void AddItem(CDocItem* pItem);
     virtual void RemoveItem(CDocItem* pItem);

     void EnableCompoundFile(BOOL bEnable = TRUE);
          // enable compound file support (call only during constructor)
     void UpdateModifiedFlag();
          // scan for modified items -- mark document modified

     // printer-device caching/control
     BOOL ApplyPrintDevice(const DVTARGETDEVICE FAR* ptd);
     BOOL ApplyPrintDevice(const PRINTDLG* ppd);
          // these apply the target device to all COleClientItem objects

// Overridables
     virtual COleClientItem* GetPrimarySelectedItem(CView* pView);
          // return primary selected item, or NULL if none
     virtual void OnShowViews(BOOL bVisible);
          // called during app-idle if a document's visibility changed

// Implementation
public:
     CObList m_docItemList;  // not owned items

#ifdef _DEBUG
     virtual void AssertValid() const;
     virtual void Dump(CDumpContext& dc) const;
#endif
     CFrameWnd* GetFirstFrame();

     // document-handling overrides
     virtual void SetPathName(const char* pszPathName,
         BOOL bAddToMRU = TRUE);
     virtual ~COleDocument();
```

```
    virtual void DeleteContents(); // delete client items in list
    virtual void Serialize(CArchive& ar);   // serialize items to file
    virtual void PreCloseFrame(CFrameWnd* pFrame);
    virtual BOOL SaveModified();
    virtual void OnIdle();

    // compound file implementation
    virtual BOOL OnNewDocument();
    virtual BOOL OnOpenDocument(const char* pszPathName);
    virtual BOOL OnSaveDocument(const char* pszPathName);
    virtual void OnCloseDocument();
    void CommitItems(BOOL bSuccess);    // called during File.Save &
                                        // File.Save As

    // minimal linking protocol
    virtual LPMONIKER GetMoniker(OLEGETMONIKER nAssign);
    virtual LPOLEITEMCONTAINER GetContainer();

protected:
    DWORD m_dwNextItemNumber;
                        // serial number for next item in document
    BOOL m_bLastVisible;
                        // TRUE if one or more views were last visible

    // 'docfile' support
    BOOL m_bCompoundFile;   // TRUE if compound files are used
    LPSTORAGE m_lpRootStg;  // root storage for the document
    BOOL m_bSameAsLoad;     // TRUE = file-save, FALSE = Save [Copy] As
    BOOL m_bRemember;       // if FALSE, indicates Save Copy As

    DVTARGETDEVICE FAR* m_ptd;  // current document target device

    // implementation helpers
    virtual void LoadFromStorage();
    virtual void SaveToStorage(CObject* pObject = NULL);
    CDocItem* GetNextItemOfKind(POSITION& pos,
        CRuntimeClass* pClass) const;

    // command handling
    virtual BOOL OnCmdMsg(UINT nID, int nCode, void* pExtra,
        AFX_CMDHANDLERINFO* pHandlerInfo);

    afx_msg void OnUpdatePasteMenu(CCmdUI* pCmdUI);
    afx_msg void OnUpdatePasteLinkMenu(CCmdUI* pCmdUI);
    afx_msg void OnUpdateEditLinksMenu(CCmdUI* pCmdUI);
    afx_msg void OnEditLinks();
    afx_msg void OnEditConvert();
    afx_msg void OnUpdateEditChangeIcon(CCmdUI* pCmdUI);
    afx_msg void OnEditChangeIcon();
    afx_msg void OnUpdateObjectVerbMenu(CCmdUI* pCmdUI);

    friend class COleClientItem;
    friend class COleServerItem;
};
```

OLE documents are considered containers for OLE objects. Notice in the class declaration the methods to add and remove items from the document. There are also methods that enumerate the contained objects.

This class also contains the MFC support for OLE compound files. To use compound files in your application, you call the method `EnableCompoundFile` from your `COleDocument` constructor.

You see much more of this class and its methods in Chapter 6, "A Simple Container," when you begin to implement OLE containers.

The Container Classes

The `COleDocument` class provides most of the functionality for OLE containers, but two other classes are used by containers: `COleLinkingDoc` and `COleClientItem`. The following sections describe these classes in detail.

The *COleLinkingDoc* Class

The `COleLinkingDoc` class creates link containers. These containers support linking to embedded items within the container. Such linking is useful, for example, if you have an embedded spreadsheet in a container. If the user wants to create a chart from the embedded object's figures, he or she simply links to the embedded object. Subsequently, when the figures are updated in the embedded object, the chart that is linked to this object is also updated.

A more complicated scenario occurs when the chart is linked to an embedded object in another document. In this case, the linked object must be capable of launching the document that contains the link source.

To support this scenario, you must use the `COleLinkingDoc` and `COleTemplateServer` classes to enable your application object to be created programmatically. The `COleTemplateServer` class derives from `COleObjectFactory`, which in turn implements the COM interface `IClassFactory`.

The `COleLinkingDoc` class also directly implements the COM interfaces for `IPersistFile` and `IOleItemContainer`. (For a full discussion of how MFC implements COM interfaces and to see an example of how to implement an interface not supported by MFC, see Chapter 16, "An MFC Automation Server." In Chapter 7, "An MDI Linking Container," you implement a linking container.)

```
class COleLinkingDoc : public COleDocument
{
    DECLARE_DYNAMIC(COleLinkingDoc)
```

```
// Constructors
public:
     COleLinkingDoc();

// Operations
     BOOL Register(COleObjectFactory* pFactory,
                   const char* pszPathName);
          // notify the running object table and connect to pServer
     void Revoke();
          // revoke from running object table

// Overridables
protected:
     virtual COleServerItem* OnGetLinkedItem(LPCSTR lpszItemName);
          // return item for the named linked item (for supporting
links)
     virtual COleClientItem* OnFindEmbeddedItem(LPCSTR lpszItemName);
          // return item for the named embedded item
          // (for links to embeddings)

// Implementation
public:
     COleObjectFactory* m_pFactory;  // back-pointer to server

#ifdef _DEBUG
     virtual void AssertValid() const;
     virtual void Dump(CDumpContext& dc) const;
#endif
     virtual ~COleLinkingDoc();

     // overrides for updating monikers and
     // running object table registration
     virtual BOOL OnNewDocument();
     virtual BOOL OnOpenDocument(const char* pszPathName);
     virtual BOOL OnSaveDocument(const char* pszPathName);
     virtual void OnCloseDocument();
     virtual LPOLEITEMCONTAINER GetContainer();
     virtual void OnShowViews(BOOL bVisible);

protected:
     DWORD m_dwRegister;      // file moniker's registration in the ROT
     BOOL m_bVisibleLock;     // TRUE if user is holding lock on document

     // implementation helpers
     void RegisterIfServerAttached(const char* pszPathName);
     void LockExternal(BOOL bLock, BOOL bRemoveRefs);
     void UpdateVisibleLock(BOOL bVisible, BOOL bRemoveRefs);

     virtual void SaveToStorage(CObject* pObject = NULL);

// Interface Maps
protected:
     BEGIN_INTERFACE_PART(PersistFile, IPersistFile)
          STDMETHOD(GetClassID)(LPCLSID);
          STDMETHOD(IsDirty)();
          STDMETHOD(Load)(LPCSTR, DWORD);
```

```
        STDMETHOD(Save)(LPCSTR, BOOL);
        STDMETHOD(SaveCompleted)(LPCSTR);
        STDMETHOD(GetCurFile)(LPSTR FAR*);
    END_INTERFACE_PART(PersistFile)

    BEGIN_INTERFACE_PART(OleItemContainer, IOleItemContainer)
        STDMETHOD(ParseDisplayName)(LPBC, LPSTR, ULONG FAR*,
            LPMONIKER FAR*);
        STDMETHOD(EnumObjects)(DWORD, LPENUMUNKNOWN FAR*);
        STDMETHOD(LockContainer)(BOOL);
        STDMETHOD(GetObject)(LPSTR, DWORD, LPBINDCTX,
            REFIID, LPVOID FAR*);
        STDMETHOD(GetObjectStorage)(LPSTR, LPBINDCTX,
            REFIID, LPVOID FAR*);
        STDMETHOD(IsRunning)(LPSTR);
    END_INTERFACE_PART(OleItemContainer)

    DECLARE_INTERFACE_MAP()

    friend class COleClientItem;
    friend class COleClientItem::XOleClientSite;
    friend class COleServerItem::XOleObject;
};
```

The *COleClientItem* Class

The `COleClientItem` class defines the interface between the container (`COleDocument`) and the OLE object.

The class provides several methods to create objects. The objects created can be from files or the clipboard or be data transfer objects. The methods are wrappers for the `OleCreate` functions supplied by the OLE API. Several methods extract data from the embedded or linked objects and query them for the current status. Other methods activate and deactivate objects.

The class implements three COM interfaces: `IOleClientSite`, `IAdviseSink`, and `IOleInPlaceSite`.

As you can see, `COleClientItem` is huge class. However, you need to override only a few of its methods. The default implementation of the other methods usually suffices.

```
class COleClientItem : public CDocItem
{
    DECLARE_DYNAMIC(COleClientItem)

// Constructors
public:
    COleClientItem(COleDocument* pContainerDoc = NULL);

    // create from the clipboard
    BOOL CreateFromClipboard(OLERENDER render = OLERENDER_DRAW,
        CLIPFORMAT cfFormat = 0, LPFORMATETC lpFormatEtc = NULL);
```

II

Using MFC

```
	BOOL CreateLinkFromClipboard(OLERENDER render = OLERENDER_DRAW,
		CLIPFORMAT cfFormat = 0, LPFORMATETC lpFormatEtc = NULL);
	BOOL CreateStaticFromClipboard(OLERENDER render = OLERENDER_DRAW,
		CLIPFORMAT cfFormat = 0, LPFORMATETC lpFormatEtc = NULL);

	// create from a class ID (Insert New Object dialog)
	BOOL CreateNewItem(REFCLSID clsid,
		OLERENDER render = OLERENDER_DRAW,
		CLIPFORMAT cfFormat = 0, LPFORMATETC lpFormatEtc = NULL);

	// create from COleDataObject
	BOOL CreateFromData(COleDataObject* pDataObject,
		OLERENDER render = OLERENDER_DRAW,
		CLIPFORMAT cfFormat = 0, LPFORMATETC lpFormatEtc = NULL);
	BOOL CreateLinkFromData(COleDataObject* pDataObject,
		OLERENDER render = OLERENDER_DRAW,
		CLIPFORMAT cfFormat = 0, LPFORMATETC lpFormatEtc = NULL);
	BOOL CreateStaticFromData(COleDataObject* pDataObject,
		OLERENDER render = OLERENDER_DRAW,
		CLIPFORMAT cfFormat = 0, LPFORMATETC lpFormatEtc = NULL);

	// create from file (package support)
	BOOL CreateFromFile(LPCSTR lpszFileName,
		REFCLSID clsid = CLSID_NULL,
		OLERENDER render = OLERENDER_DRAW,
		CLIPFORMAT cfFormat = 0, LPFORMATETC lpFormatEtc = NULL);
	BOOL CreateLinkFromFile(LPCSTR lpszFileName,
		OLERENDER render = OLERENDER_DRAW,
		CLIPFORMAT cfFormat = 0, LPFORMATETC lpFormatEtc = NULL);

	// create a copy
	BOOL CreateCloneFrom(COleClientItem* pSrcItem);

// General Attributes
public:
	SCODE GetLastStatus() const;
	OLE_OBJTYPE GetType() const; // OT_LINK, OT_EMBEDDED, OT_STATIC
	void GetClassID(CLSID FAR* pClassID) const;
	void GetUserType(USERCLASSTYPE nUserClassType, CString& rString);
	BOOL GetExtent(LPSIZE lpSize, DVASPECT nDrawAspect = (DVASPECT)-1);
		// will return FALSE if item is BLANK

	HGLOBAL GetIconicMetafile();
	BOOL SetIconicMetafile(HGLOBAL hMetaPict);
		// getting/setting iconic cache

	DVASPECT GetDrawAspect() const;
	void SetDrawAspect(DVASPECT nDrawAspect);
		// setting/getting default display aspect

	// for printer presentation cache
	BOOL SetPrintDevice(const DVTARGETDEVICE FAR* ptd);
	BOOL SetPrintDevice(const PRINTDLG* ppd);

	// Item state
	enum ItemState
```

```
        { emptyState, loadedState, openState, activeState,
          activeUIState };
    UINT GetItemState() const;

    BOOL IsModified() const;
    BOOL IsRunning() const;
    BOOL IsInPlaceActive() const;
    BOOL IsOpen() const;
    CView* GetActiveView() const;

    // Data access
    void AttachDataObject(COleDataObject& rDataObject) const;

    // other rare access information
    COleDocument* GetDocument() const; // return container

    // helpers for checking clipboard data availability
    static BOOL PASCAL CanPaste();
    static BOOL PASCAL CanPasteLink();

    // helpers for checking COleDataObject, useful in drag-drop
    static BOOL PASCAL CanCreateFromData(const COleDataObject*
        pDataObject);
    static BOOL PASCAL CanCreateLinkFromData(const COleDataObject*
        pDataObject);

// General Operations
    virtual void Release(OLECLOSE dwCloseOption = OLECLOSE_NOSAVE);
        // clean up, detach (close if needed)
    void Close(OLECLOSE dwCloseOption = OLECLOSE_SAVEIFDIRTY);
        // close without releasing the item
    void Delete(BOOL bAutoDelete = TRUE);
        // logically delete from file -- no longer part of the document
    void Run(); // ensure item is in running state

    // Drawing
    BOOL Draw(CDC* pDC, LPCRECT lpBounds,
        DVASPECT nDrawAspect = (DVASPECT)-1);  // defaults to
                                               // m_nDrawAspect

    // Activation
    virtual BOOL DoVerb(LONG nVerb, CView* pView, LPMSG lpMsg = NULL);
    void Activate(LONG nVerb, CView* pView, LPMSG lpMsg = NULL);

    // In-place Activation
    void Deactivate();          // completely deactivate
    void DeactivateUI();        // deactivate the user interface
    BOOL ReactivateAndUndo();   // reactivate, then perform undo command
    BOOL SetItemRects(LPCRECT lpPosRect = NULL,
        LPCRECT lpClipRect = NULL);
    CWnd* GetInPlaceWindow();

    // Clipboard operations
    void CopyToClipboard(BOOL bIncludeLink = FALSE);
```

```
    DROPEFFECT DoDragDrop(LPCRECT lpItemRect, CPoint ptOffset,
         BOOL bIncludeLink = FALSE,
         DWORD dwEffects = DROPEFFECT_COPY¦DROPEFFECT_MOVE,
         LPCRECT lpRectStartDrag = NULL);
    void GetClipboardData(COleDataSource* pDataSource,
         BOOL bIncludeLink = FALSE, LPPOINT lpOffset = NULL,
         LPSIZE lpSize = NULL);

    // called for creating a COleDataSource by CopyToClipboard
    // and DoDragDrop
    virtual COleDataSource* OnGetClipboardData(BOOL bIncludeLink,
         LPPOINT lpOffset, LPSIZE lpSize);

    // Operations that apply to embedded items only
    void SetHostNames(LPCSTR lpszHost, LPCSTR lpszHostObj);
    void SetExtent(const CSize& size,
    DVASPECT nDrawAspect = DVASPECT_CONTENT);

    // Operations that apply to linked items only
    //  (link options are rarely changed, except through Links dialog)
    OLEUPDATE GetLinkUpdateOptions();
    void SetLinkUpdateOptions(OLEUPDATE dwUpdateOpt);

    // Link-source update status
    // (also useful for embeddings that contain links)
    BOOL UpdateLink();  // make up-to-date
    BOOL IsLinkUpToDate() const;    // is link up-to-date

    // object conversion
    BOOL ConvertTo(REFCLSID clsidNew);
    BOOL ActivateAs(LPCSTR lpszUserType, REFCLSID clsidOld,
        REFCLSID clsidNew);
    BOOL Reload();  // for lazy reload after ActivateAs

// Overridables (notifications of IAdviseSink, IOleClientSite,
//              and IOleInPlaceSite)
    // Callbacks/notifications from the server you must/should
    // implement
    virtual void OnChange(OLE_NOTIFICATION nCode, DWORD dwParam);
         // implement OnChange to invalidate when item changes

protected:
    virtual void OnGetItemPosition(CRect& rPosition);
        // implement OnGetItemPosition if you support in-place
        // activation

    // Common overrides for in-place activation
    virtual BOOL OnScrollBy(CSize sizeExtent);

protected:
    // Common overrides for applications supporting undo
    virtual void OnDeactivateUI(BOOL bUndoable);
    virtual void OnDiscardUndoState();
    virtual void OnDeactivateAndUndo();

    // Common overrides for applications supporting links to embeddings
    virtual void OnShowItem();
```

```
	// Advanced overrides for in-place activation
	virtual void OnGetClipRect(CRect& rClipRect);
	virtual BOOL CanActivate();
	virtual void OnActivate();
	virtual void OnActivateUI();
	virtual BOOL OnGetWindowContext(CFrameWnd** ppMainFrame,
		CFrameWnd** ppDocFrame, LPOLEINPLACEFRAMEINFO lpFrameInfo);
	virtual void OnDeactivate();
	virtual BOOL OnChangeItemPosition(const CRect& rectPos);
		// default calls SetItemRects and caches the pos rect

public:
	// Advanced overrides for menu/title handling (rarely overridden)
	virtual void OnInsertMenus(CMenu* pMenuShared,
		LPOLEMENUGROUPWIDTHS lpMenuWidths);
	virtual void OnSetMenu(CMenu* pMenuShared, HOLEMENU holemenu,
		HWND hwndActiveObject);
	virtual void OnRemoveMenus(CMenu* pMenuShared);
	virtual void OnUpdateFrameTitle();

	// Advanced override for control bar handling
	virtual BOOL OnShowControlBars(CFrameWnd* pFrameWnd, BOOL bShow);

// Implementation
public:
	// data to support non-in-place activated items
	LPOLEOBJECT m_lpObject; // in case you want direct access
	                        // to the OLE object
	DWORD m_dwItemNumber;   // serial number for this item
	                        // in this document
	DVASPECT m_nDrawAspect; // current default display aspect
	SCODE m_scLast;         // last error code encountered
	LPSTORAGE m_lpStorage;  // provides storage for m_lpObject
	LPLOCKBYTES m_lpLockBytes;
	                       // part of implementation of m_lpStorage
	DWORD m_dwConnection;   // advise connection to the m_lpObject
	BYTE m_bLinkUnavail;    // TRUE if link is currently unavailable
	BYTE m_bMoniker;        // TRUE if moniker is assigned
	BYTE m_bLocked;         // TRUE if object has external lock
	BYTE m_bNeedCommit;     // TRUE if need CommitItem
	BYTE m_bClosing;        // TRUE if currently
	                        // doing COleClientItem::Close
	BYTE m_bReserved;       // (reserved for future use)

	// for compound file support
	LPSTORAGE m_lpNewStorage;   // used during Save As situations

	// item state & item type
	ItemState m_nItemState; // item state (see ItemState enumeration)
	OLE_OBJTYPE m_nItemType;    // item type (depends on how created)

	// data valid when in-place activated
	CView* m_pView;            // view when object is in-place activated
	DWORD m_dwContainerStyle;       // style of the container wnd
	                                // before activation
	COleFrameHook* m_pInPlaceFrame;// frame window when in-place active
```

```
    COleFrameHook* m_pInPlaceDoc;   // doc window when in place
                                    // (may be NULL)
    HWND m_hWndServer;              // HWND of in-place server window

public:
    virtual ~COleClientItem();
    virtual void Serialize(CArchive& ar);
#ifdef _DEBUG
    virtual void AssertValid() const;
    virtual void Dump(CDumpContext& dc) const;
#endif

// Implementation
public:
    virtual BOOL ReportError(SCODE sc) const;
    virtual BOOL FreezeLink();  // converts to static:
                                // for edit links dialog

    DWORD GetNewItemNumber();   // generates new item number
    void GetItemName(char* pszItemName) const;
                                // gets readable item name

    void UpdateItemType();  // update m_nItemType

protected:
    // clipboard helpers
    void GetEmbeddedItemData(LPSTGMEDIUM lpStgMedium);
    void AddCachedData(COleDataSource* pDataSource);
    BOOL GetLinkSourceData(LPSTGMEDIUM lpStgMedium);
    void GetObjectDescriptorData(LPPOINT lpOffset, LPSIZE lpSize,
        LPSTGMEDIUM lpStgMedium);

    // interface helpers
    LPOLECLIENTSITE GetClientSite();

    // helpers for printer-cached representation
    BOOL GetPrintDeviceInfo(LPOLECACHE* plpOleCache,
        DVTARGETDEVICE FAR** pptd, DWORD* pdwConnection);

// Advanced Overridables for implementation
protected:
    virtual BOOL FinishCreate(HRESULT hr);
    virtual void CheckGeneral(HRESULT hr);

    virtual void OnDataChange(LPFORMATETC lpFormatEtc,
        LPSTGMEDIUM lpStgMedium);

public:
    // for storage hookability (override to use 'docfiles')
    virtual void GetItemStorage();  // allocate storage for new item
    virtual void ReadItem(CArchive& ar);    // read item from archive
    virtual void WriteItem(CArchive& ar);   // write item to archive
    virtual void CommitItem(BOOL bSuccess); // commit item's storage
```

```
    // compound & flat file implementations of the preceding
    void GetItemStorageFlat();
    void ReadItemFlat(CArchive& ar);
    void WriteItemFlat(CArchive& ar);
    void GetItemStorageCompound();
    void ReadItemCompound(CArchive& ar);
    void WriteItemCompound(CArchive& ar);

private:
    static CView* pActivateView;    // activation view

// Interface Maps
protected:
    BEGIN_INTERFACE_PART(OleClientSite, IOleClientSite)
        STDMETHOD(SaveObject)();
        STDMETHOD(GetMoniker)(DWORD, DWORD, LPMONIKER FAR*);
        STDMETHOD(GetContainer)(LPOLECONTAINER FAR*);
        STDMETHOD(ShowObject)();
        STDMETHOD(OnShowWindow)(BOOL);
        STDMETHOD(RequestNewObjectLayout)();
    END_INTERFACE_PART(OleClientSite)

    BEGIN_INTERFACE_PART(AdviseSink, IAdviseSink)
        STDMETHOD_(void,OnDataChange)(LPFORMATETC, LPSTGMEDIUM);
        STDMETHOD_(void,OnViewChange)(DWORD, LONG);
        STDMETHOD_(void,OnRename)(LPMONIKER);
        STDMETHOD_(void,OnSave)();
        STDMETHOD_(void,OnClose)();
    END_INTERFACE_PART(AdviseSink)

    BEGIN_INTERFACE_PART(OleIPSite, IOleInPlaceSite)
        STDMETHOD(GetWindow)(HWND FAR*);
        STDMETHOD(ContextSensitiveHelp)(BOOL);
        STDMETHOD(CanInPlaceActivate)();
        STDMETHOD(OnInPlaceActivate)();
        STDMETHOD(OnUIActivate)();
        STDMETHOD(GetWindowContext)(LPOLEINPLACEFRAME FAR*,
            LPOLEINPLACEUIWINDOW FAR*, LPRECT, LPRECT,
            LPOLEINPLACEFRAMEINFO);
        STDMETHOD(Scroll)(SIZE);
        STDMETHOD(OnUIDeactivate)(BOOL);
        STDMETHOD(OnInPlaceDeactivate)();
        STDMETHOD(DiscardUndoState)();
        STDMETHOD(DeactivateAndUndo)();
        STDMETHOD(OnPosRectChange)(LPCRECT);
    END_INTERFACE_PART(OleIPSite)

    DECLARE_INTERFACE_MAP()

// Friendship declarations (to avoid many public members)
    friend class COleUIWindow;
    friend class COleFrameWindow;
    friend class COleLinkingDoc;
};
```

The Server Classes

Six classes are categorized as server classes: `COleObjectFactory`, `COleTemplateServer`, `COleServerDoc`, `COleServerItem`, `COleIPFrame`, and `COleResizeBar`. The following sections describe these classes.

The *COleObjectFactory* Class

The `COleObjectFactory` class, which implements the `IClassFactory` COM interface, is used to create objects. The class also includes methods that update the application's registration database. `COleObjectFactory` is usually used as a base class; in fact, the `COleTemplateServer` class derives from it.

```
class COleObjectFactory : public CCmdTarget
{
     DECLARE_DYNAMIC(COleObjectFactory)

// Construction
public:
     COleObjectFactory(REFCLSID clsid,
          CRuntimeClass* pRuntimeClass,
          BOOL bMultiInstance, LPCSTR lpszProgID);

// Attributes
     BOOL IsRegistered() const;
     REFCLSID GetClassID() const;

// Operations
     BOOL Register();
     void Revoke();
     void UpdateRegistry(LPCSTR lpszProgID = NULL);
          // default uses m_lpszProgID if not NULL

     static BOOL PASCAL RegisterAll();
     static void PASCAL RevokeAll();
     static void PASCAL UpdateRegistryAll();

// Overridables
protected:
     virtual CCmdTarget* OnCreateObject();

// Implementation
public:
     virtual ~COleObjectFactory();
#ifdef _DEBUG
     void AssertValid() const;
     void Dump(CDumpContext& dc) const;
#endif

protected:
     COleObjectFactory* m_pNextFactory;
                                   // list of factories maintained
     DWORD m_dwRegister;           // registry identifier
     CLSID m_clsid;                // registered class ID
```

```
    CRuntimeClass* m_pRuntimeClass; // run-time class
                                    // of CCmdTarget derivative
    BOOL m_bMultiInstance;          // multiple instance?
    LPCSTR m_lpszProgID;            // human readable class ID

// Interface Maps
protected:
    BEGIN_INTERFACE_PART(ClassFactory, IClassFactory)
        STDMETHOD(CreateInstance)(LPUNKNOWN, REFIID, LPVOID FAR*);
        STDMETHOD(LockServer)(BOOL);
    END_INTERFACE_PART(ClassFactory)

    DECLARE_INTERFACE_MAP()

    friend HRESULT STDAPICALLTYPE
        DllGetClassObject(REFCLSID, REFIID, LPVOID FAR*);
};
```

The *COleTemplateServer* Class

When you are implementing a full server or a linking container, you use the `COleTemplateServer` class rather than `CDocTemplate`. As you can see, this class uses a `CDocTemplate` member to handle the Document and View interaction.

```
class COleTemplateServer : public COleObjectFactory
{
// Constructors
public:
    COleTemplateServer();

// Operations
    void ConnectTemplate(REFCLSID clsid, CDocTemplate* pDocTemplate,
        BOOL bMultiInstance);
        // set doc template after creating it in InitInstance
    void UpdateRegistry(OLE_APPTYPE nAppType = OAT_INPLACE_SERVER,
       LPCSTR FAR* rglpszRegister = NULL,
       LPCSTR FAR* rglpszOverwrite = NULL);
        // may want to UpdateRegistry if not run with /Embedded

// Implementation
protected:
    virtual CCmdTarget* OnCreateObject();
    CDocTemplate* m_pDocTemplate;

private:
    void UpdateRegistry(LPCSTR lpszProgID);
        // hide base class version of UpdateRegistry
};
```

The *COleServerDoc* Class

`COleServerDoc` is the base class for all OLE server documents. `COleServerDoc` is a collection class for `COleServerItem` objects. If the server supports only embedding, only one item is created per document and that item represents the

II

Using MFC

entire document. If the server also supports links, a `COleServerItem` object is created for each link. Server documents can also contain `COleClientItem` objects. Such is the case when you implement a full server that is also a container.

The main method that you must override in the `COleServerDoc` class is `OnGetEmbeddedItem`, which returns the embedded item object to the container.

The `COleServerDoc` class implements five COM interfaces: `IPersistStorage`, `IOleObject`, `IDataObject`, `IOleInPlaceObject`, and `IOleInPlaceActiveObject`.

```
class COleServerDoc : public COleLinkingDoc
{
     DECLARE_DYNAMIC(COleServerDoc)

// Constructors and Destructors
public:
     COleServerDoc();

// Attributes
     BOOL IsEmbedded() const;
     COleServerItem* GetEmbeddedItem();
         // return embedded item for document (will allocate if
         // necessary)

     // attributes specific to in-place activation
     BOOL IsInPlaceActive() const;
     void GetItemPosition(LPRECT lpPosRect) const;
          // get current position rectangle of in-place edit
     void GetItemClipRect(LPRECT lpClipRect) const;
          // get current clipping rectangle of in-place edit
     BOOL GetZoomFactor(LPSIZE lpSizeNum = NULL,
                        LPSIZE lpSizeDenom = NULL,
          LPCRECT lpPosRect = NULL) const;
          // returns the zoom factor in pixels

// Operations
     void NotifyChanged();
          // call this after you change some global attribute like
          //  document dimensions
     void UpdateAllItems(COleServerItem* pSender,
          LPARAM lHint = 0L, CObject* pHint = NULL,
          DVASPECT nDrawAspect = DVASPECT_CONTENT);

     // changes to the entire document (automatically notifies clients)
     void NotifyRename(LPCSTR lpszNewName);
     void NotifySaved();
     void NotifyClosed();        // call this after you close document

     // specific operations for embedded documents
     void SaveEmbedding();  // call this to save embedded objects
                            // (before closing)
```

```
    // specific to in-place activation
    BOOL ActivateInPlace();
    void RequestPositionChange(LPCRECT lpPosRect);
    BOOL ScrollContainerBy(CSize sizeScroll);
    BOOL DeactivateAndUndo();
    BOOL DiscardUndoState();

public:
// Overridables for standard user interface (full server)
    virtual BOOL OnUpdateDocument();
        // implementation of embedded update

protected:
// Overridables you must implement for yourself
    virtual COleServerItem* OnGetEmbeddedItem() = 0;
        // return item representing entire (embedded) document

// Overridables you do not have to implement
    virtual void OnClose(OLECLOSE dwCloseOption);
    virtual void OnSetHostNames(LPCSTR lpszHost, LPCSTR lpszHostObj);

// Advanced overridables
    virtual void OnShowDocument(BOOL bShow);
        // show first frame for document or hide all frames for
        // document

// Advanced overridables for in-place activation
    virtual void OnDeactivate();
    virtual void OnDeactivateUI(BOOL bUndoable);
    virtual void OnSetItemRects(LPCRECT lpPosRect,
        LPCRECT lpClipRect);
    virtual BOOL OnReactivateAndUndo();

    virtual void OnFrameWindowActivate(BOOL bActivate);
    virtual void OnDocWindowActivate(BOOL bActivate);
    virtual void OnShowControlBars(LPOLEINPLACEUIWINDOW lpUIWindow,
        BOOL bShow);
    virtual void OnResizeBorder(LPCRECT lpRectBorder,
        LPOLEINPLACEUIWINDOW lpUIWindow, BOOL bFrame);

    virtual COleIPFrameWnd* CreateInPlaceFrame(CWnd* pParentWnd);
    virtual void DestroyInPlaceFrame(COleIPFrameWnd* pFrameWnd);

// Implementation
protected:
    LPOLECLIENTSITE m_lpClientSite;  // for embedded item
    CString m_strHostObj;            // name of document in container
    BOOL m_bCntrVisible;             // TRUE if OnShowWindow(TRUE)
                                     // called
    BOOL m_bClosing;                 // TRUE if shutting down
    COleServerItem* m_pEmbeddedItem; // pointer to embedded item
                                     // for document

    COleIPFrameWnd* m_pInPlaceFrame; // not NULL if in-place activated
    CWnd* m_pOrigParent;             // not NULL if existing view used
```

II

Using MFC

```
    DWORD m_dwOrigStyle;            // original style of in-place view

public:
    virtual ~COleServerDoc();
#ifdef _DEBUG
    virtual void AssertValid() const;
    virtual void Dump(CDumpContext& dc) const;
#endif

    // overridables for implementation
    virtual BOOL OnSaveDocument(const char* pszPathName);
    virtual void OnCloseDocument();
    virtual void DeleteContents(); // delete auto-delete server items
    virtual LPMONIKER GetMoniker(OLEGETMONIKER nAssign);
    virtual COleServerItem* OnGetLinkedItem(LPCSTR lpszItemName);
      // return item for the named linked item (only if supporting
      // links)
    virtual BOOL CanCloseFrame(CFrameWnd* pFrame);

protected:
    // overrides to handle server user-interface
    virtual BOOL SaveModified();
                                // return TRUE if OK to continue
    virtual HMENU GetDefaultMenu();
                                // return menu based on doc type
    virtual HACCEL GetDefaultAccelerator(); // return accel table
                                            // based on doc type
    virtual BOOL GetFileTypeString(CString& rString);

    // IPersistStorage implementation
    virtual void OnNewEmbedding(LPSTORAGE lpStorage);
    virtual void OnOpenEmbedding(LPSTORAGE lpStorage);
    virtual void OnSaveEmbedding(LPSTORAGE lpStorage);

    // Implementation helpers
    void NotifyAllItems(OLE_NOTIFICATION wNotification, DWORD dwParam);
    BOOL SaveModifiedPrompt();
    void ConnectView(CWnd* pParentWnd, CView* pView);
    void UpdateUsingHostObj(UINT nIDS, CCmdUI* pCmdUI);

// Message Maps
    //{{AFX_MSG(COleServerDoc)
    afx_msg void OnFileUpdate();
    afx_msg void OnFileSaveCopyAs();
    afx_msg void OnUpdateFileUpdate(CCmdUI* pCmdUI);
    afx_msg void OnUpdateFileExit(CCmdUI* pCmdUI);
    //}}AFX_MSG
    DECLARE_MESSAGE_MAP()

// Interface Maps
protected:
    BEGIN_INTERFACE_PART(PersistStorage, IPersistStorage)
        STDMETHOD(GetClassID)(LPCLSID);
        STDMETHOD(IsDirty)();
        STDMETHOD(InitNew)(LPSTORAGE);
        STDMETHOD(Load)(LPSTORAGE);
```

```
        STDMETHOD(Save)(LPSTORAGE, BOOL);
        STDMETHOD(SaveCompleted)(LPSTORAGE);
        STDMETHOD(HandsOffStorage)();
    END_INTERFACE_PART(PersistStorage)

    BEGIN_INTERFACE_PART(OleObject, IOleObject)
        STDMETHOD(SetClientSite)(LPOLECLIENTSITE);
        STDMETHOD(GetClientSite)(LPOLECLIENTSITE FAR*);
        STDMETHOD(SetHostNames)(LPCSTR, LPCSTR);
        STDMETHOD(Close)(DWORD);
        STDMETHOD(SetMoniker)(DWORD, LPMONIKER);
        STDMETHOD(GetMoniker)(DWORD, DWORD, LPMONIKER FAR*);
        STDMETHOD(InitFromData)(LPDATAOBJECT, BOOL, DWORD);
        STDMETHOD(GetClipboardData)(DWORD, LPDATAOBJECT FAR*);
        STDMETHOD(DoVerb)(LONG, LPMSG, LPOLECLIENTSITE, LONG,
            HWND, LPCRECT);
        STDMETHOD(EnumVerbs)(IEnumOLEVERB FAR* FAR*);
        STDMETHOD(Update)();
        STDMETHOD(IsUpToDate)();
        STDMETHOD(GetUserClassID)(CLSID FAR*);
        STDMETHOD(GetUserType)(DWORD, LPSTR FAR*);
        STDMETHOD(SetExtent)(DWORD, LPSIZEL);
        STDMETHOD(GetExtent)(DWORD, LPSIZEL);
        STDMETHOD(Advise)(LPADVISESINK, LPDWORD);
        STDMETHOD(Unadvise)(DWORD);
        STDMETHOD(EnumAdvise)(LPENUMSTATDATA FAR*);
        STDMETHOD(GetMiscStatus)(DWORD, LPDWORD);
        STDMETHOD(SetColorScheme)(LPLOGPALETTE);
    END_INTERFACE_PART(OleObject)

    BEGIN_INTERFACE_PART(DataObject, IDataObject)
        STDMETHOD(GetData)(LPFORMATETC, LPSTGMEDIUM);
        STDMETHOD(GetDataHere)(LPFORMATETC, LPSTGMEDIUM);
        STDMETHOD(QueryGetData)(LPFORMATETC);
        STDMETHOD(GetCanonicalFormatEtc)(LPFORMATETC, LPFORMATETC);
        STDMETHOD(SetData)(LPFORMATETC, LPSTGMEDIUM, BOOL);
        STDMETHOD(EnumFormatEtc)(DWORD, LPENUMFORMATETC FAR*);
        STDMETHOD(DAdvise)(LPFORMATETC, DWORD, LPADVISESINK,
            LPDWORD);
        STDMETHOD(DUnadvise)(DWORD);
        STDMETHOD(EnumDAdvise)(LPENUMSTATDATA FAR*);
    END_INTERFACE_PART(DataObject)

    BEGIN_INTERFACE_PART(OleInPlaceObject, IOleInPlaceObject)
        STDMETHOD(GetWindow)(HWND FAR*);
        STDMETHOD(ContextSensitiveHelp)(BOOL);
        STDMETHOD(InPlaceDeactivate)();
        STDMETHOD(UIDeactivate)();
        STDMETHOD(SetObjectRects)(LPCRECT, LPCRECT);
        STDMETHOD(ReactivateAndUndo)();
    END_INTERFACE_PART(OleInPlaceObject)

    BEGIN_INTERFACE_PART(OleInPlaceActiveObject,
        IOleInPlaceActiveObject)
        STDMETHOD(GetWindow)(HWND FAR*);
        STDMETHOD(ContextSensitiveHelp)(BOOL);
```

```
        STDMETHOD(TranslateAccelerator)(LPMSG);
        STDMETHOD(OnFrameWindowActivate)(BOOL);
        STDMETHOD(OnDocWindowActivate)(BOOL);
        STDMETHOD(ResizeBorder)(LPCRECT, LPOLEINPLACEUIWINDOW,
            BOOL);
        STDMETHOD(EnableModeless)(BOOL);
    END_INTERFACE_PART(OleInPlaceActiveObject)

    DECLARE_INTERFACE_MAP()

    friend class COleServer;
    friend class COleServerItem;
};
```

The *COleServerItem* Class

The `COleServerItem` class implements the functionality of OLE compound document objects. You must do a bit more work in this class than in `COleServerDoc`.

`COleServerItem` provides the interface for activating embedded or linked objects. Therefore, you must provide the means to save and restore your object's native data. To do so, you override the `Serialize` method. This provides the container access to your data.

Usually, you also implement the `OnGetExtent` method, which returns to the container the object's natural extents.

Finally, you implement the `OnDraw` method. This method is used to draw the presentation data into a metafile that is then stored in the cache. The container uses this metafile to display your object when the server is not actived for visual editing.

Although drawing the metafile appears to be a simple task, it causes the most problems for developers when they first begin to develop an OLE server. Most of the confusion arises because OLE uses the HIMETRIC mapping system for drawing, and most developers seem to be used to the default MM_TEXT mode. You return to this problem in Chapters 6 and 7, which both cover OLE containers.

When used for linking, the `COleServerItem` class implements the `IDataObject` and `IOleObject` interfaces.

```
class COleServerItem : public CDocItem
{
    DECLARE_DYNAMIC(COleServerItem)
protected:
    // NOTE: many members in this class are protected, because
    // everything in this class is designed for implementing
    // an OLE server.
```

```
    // Requests come from OLE containers through non-C++ mechanisms,
    //   which results in this class' virtual functions being called.

// Constructors
    COleServerItem(COleServerDoc* pServerDoc, BOOL bAutoDelete);
        // If your COleServerItem is an integral part of your data,
        //  bAutoDelete should be FALSE. If your COleServerItem can be
        //  deleted when a link is released, it can be TRUE.

    COleDataSource* GetDataSource();
        // Use this data source to add conversion formats that your
        //  server should support. Usually such formats are
        //  added in the item's constructor.

// Public Attributes
public:
    COleServerDoc* GetDocument() const; // return server document

    // naming (for links only)
    const CString& GetItemName() const; // get name of linked item
    void SetItemName(const char* pszItemName);
                                        // set name of linked item

    // link state
    BOOL IsConnected() const;   // returns TRUE if item has a client
    BOOL IsLinkedItem() const;  // returns TRUE if item is not embedded

    // extents
    CSize m_sizeExtent;
        // HIMETRIC size -- the default implementation of OnSetExtent
        //  updates this member variable. This member tells the server
        //  how much of the object is visible in the container
        //  document.

// Operations
public:
    void NotifyChanged(DVASPECT nDrawAspect = DVASPECT_CONTENT);
        // call this after you change item
    void CopyToClipboard(BOOL bIncludeLink = FALSE);
        // helper for implementing server 'copy to clipboard'
    DROPEFFECT DoDragDrop(LPCRECT lpRectItem, CPoint ptOffset,
        BOOL bIncludeLink = FALSE,
        DWORD dwEffects = DROPEFFECT_COPY¦DROPEFFECT_MOVE,
        LPCRECT lpRectStartDrag = NULL);
    void GetClipboardData(COleDataSource* pDataSource,
        BOOL bIncludeLink = FALSE, LPPOINT lpOffset = NULL,
        LPSIZE lpSize = NULL);

// Overridables
    // you must implement overridables for yourself
    virtual BOOL OnDraw(CDC* pDC, CSize& rSize) = 0;
        // drawing for metafile format (return FALSE if not supported
        // or error) (called for DVASPECT_CONTENT only)
```

```
    // you may want to implement overridables yourself
    virtual void OnUpdate(COleServerItem* pSender,
        LPARAM lHint, CObject* pHint, DVASPECT nDrawAspect);
        // the default implementation always calls NotifyChanged

    virtual BOOL OnDrawEx(CDC* pDC, DVASPECT nDrawAspect,
          CSize& rSize);
        // advanced drawing -- called for DVASPECT
        // other than DVASPECT_CONTENT
    virtual BOOL OnSetExtent(DVASPECT nDrawAspect, const CSize& size);
    virtual BOOL OnGetExtent(DVASPECT nDrawAspect, CSize& rSize);
        // default implementation uses m_sizeExtent

    // you do not have to implement overridables
    virtual void OnDoVerb(LONG iVerb);
        // default routes to OnShow &/or OnOpen
    virtual BOOL OnSetColorScheme(const LOGPALETTE FAR* lpLogPalette);
        // default does nothing
    virtual COleDataSource* OnGetClipboardData(BOOL bIncludeLink,
        LPPOINT lpOffset, LPSIZE lpSize);
        // called for access to clipboard data
    virtual BOOL OnQueryUpdateItems();
        // called to determine if any out-of-date links are contained
    virtual void OnUpdateItems();
        // called to update any out-of-date links

protected:
    virtual void OnShow();
        // show item in the user interface (may edit in place)
    virtual void OnOpen();
        // show item in the user interface (must open fully)
    virtual void OnHide();
        // hide document (and sometimes the application)

    // very advanced overridables
public:
    virtual BOOL OnInitFromData(COleDataObject* pDataObject,
       BOOL bCreation);
    // initialize object from IDataObject

    // see COleDataSource for a description of these overridables
    virtual BOOL OnRenderGlobalData(LPFORMATETC lpFormatEtc,
       HGLOBAL* phGlobal);
    virtual BOOL OnRenderFileData(LPFORMATETC lpFormatEtc,
       CFile* pFile);
    virtual BOOL OnRenderData(LPFORMATETC lpFormatEtc,
       LPSTGMEDIUM lpStgMedium);
        // HGLOBAL version will be called first, then CFile* version

    virtual BOOL OnSetData(LPFORMATETC lpFormatEtc,
       LPSTGMEDIUM lpStgMedium);
        // Rare -- only if you support SetData (programmatic paste)

    // advanced helpers for CopyToClipboard
    void GetEmbedSourceData(LPSTGMEDIUM lpStgMedium);
```

```
    void AddOtherClipboardData(COleDataSource* pDataSource);
    BOOL GetLinkSourceData(LPSTGMEDIUM lpStgMedium);
    void GetObjectDescriptorData(LPPOINT lpOffset, LPSIZE lpSize,
        LPSTGMEDIUM lpStgMedium);

// Implementation
public:
    BOOL m_bNeedUnlock;  // if TRUE, need to pDoc->LockExternal(FALSE)
    BOOL m_bAutoDelete;  // if TRUE, OnRelease will 'delete this'

    // special version of OnFinalRelease to implement document locking
    virtual void OnFinalRelease();

protected:
    CString m_strItemName;          // simple item name

public:
    LPOLEADVISEHOLDER m_lpOleAdviseHolder;      // may be NULL
    LPDATAADVISEHOLDER m_lpDataAdviseHolder;    // may be NULL

    virtual ~COleServerItem();
#ifdef _DEBUG
    virtual void AssertValid() const;
    virtual void Dump(CDumpContext& dc) const;
#endif

    // implementation helpers
    void NotifyClient(OLE_NOTIFICATION wNotification, DWORD dwParam);
    LPDATAOBJECT GetDataObject();
    LPOLEOBJECT GetOleObject();

protected:
    virtual BOOL GetMetafileData(LPFORMATETC lpFormatEtc,
       LPSTGMEDIUM pmedium);
    // calls OnDraw or OnDrawEx
    virtual void OnSaveEmbedding(LPSTORAGE lpStorage);
    virtual BOOL IsBlank() const;

    // CItemDataSource implements OnRender reflections to
    // COleServerItem
    class CItemDataSource : public COleDataSource
    {
    protected:
        // the GetData and SetData interfaces forward to m_pItem
        virtual BOOL OnRenderGlobalData(LPFORMATETC lpFormatEtc,
            HGLOBAL* phGlobal);
        virtual BOOL OnRenderFileData(LPFORMATETC lpFormatEtc,
            CFile* pFile);
        virtual BOOL OnRenderData(LPFORMATETC lpFormatEtc,
            LPSTGMEDIUM lpStgMedium);
        virtual BOOL OnSetData(LPFORMATETC lpFormatEtc,
            LPSTGMEDIUM lpStgMedium);
    CItemDataSource m_dataSource;
        // data source used to implement IDataObject
```

```
// Interface Maps
//  (Note: these interface maps are used just for link implementation)
public:
    BEGIN_INTERFACE_PART(OleObject, IOleObject)
        STDMETHOD(SetClientSite)(LPOLECLIENTSITE);
        STDMETHOD(GetClientSite)(LPOLECLIENTSITE FAR*);
        STDMETHOD(SetHostNames)(LPCSTR, LPCSTR);
        STDMETHOD(Close)(DWORD);
        STDMETHOD(SetMoniker)(DWORD, LPMONIKER);
        STDMETHOD(GetMoniker)(DWORD, DWORD, LPMONIKER FAR*);
        STDMETHOD(InitFromData)(LPDATAOBJECT, BOOL, DWORD);
        STDMETHOD(GetClipboardData)(DWORD, LPDATAOBJECT FAR*);
        STDMETHOD(DoVerb)(LONG, LPMSG, LPOLECLIENTSITE, LONG,
            HWND, LPCRECT);
        STDMETHOD(EnumVerbs)(IEnumOLEVERB FAR* FAR*);
        STDMETHOD(Update)();
        STDMETHOD(IsUpToDate)();
        STDMETHOD(GetUserClassID)(CLSID FAR*);
        STDMETHOD(GetUserType)(DWORD, LPSTR FAR*);
        STDMETHOD(SetExtent)(DWORD, LPSIZEL);
        STDMETHOD(GetExtent)(DWORD, LPSIZEL);
        STDMETHOD(Advise)(LPADVISESINK, LPDWORD);
        STDMETHOD(Unadvise)(DWORD);
        STDMETHOD(EnumAdvise)(LPENUMSTATDATA FAR*);
        STDMETHOD(GetMiscStatus)(DWORD, LPDWORD);
        STDMETHOD(SetColorScheme)(LPLOGPALETTE);
    END_INTERFACE_PART(OleObject)

    BEGIN_INTERFACE_PART(DataObject, IDataObject)
        STDMETHOD(GetData)(LPFORMATETC, LPSTGMEDIUM);
        STDMETHOD(GetDataHere)(LPFORMATETC, LPSTGMEDIUM);
        STDMETHOD(QueryGetData)(LPFORMATETC);
        STDMETHOD(GetCanonicalFormatEtc)(LPFORMATETC,
            LPFORMATETC);
        STDMETHOD(SetData)(LPFORMATETC, LPSTGMEDIUM, BOOL);
        STDMETHOD(EnumFormatEtc)(DWORD, LPENUMFORMATETC FAR*);
        STDMETHOD(DAdvise)(LPFORMATETC, DWORD, LPADVISESINK,
            LPDWORD);
        STDMETHOD(DUnadvise)(DWORD);
        STDMETHOD(EnumDAdvise)(LPENUMSTATDATA FAR*);
    END_INTERFACE_PART(DataObject)

    DECLARE_INTERFACE_MAP()

    friend class CItemDataSource;
    friend class COleServerDoc;
    friend class COleLinkingDoc;
};
```

The *OleIPFrame* Class

The `OleIPFrame` class provides a base class for the application's in-place frame windows. The class sets up control bars and other adornments in the container's client area when the object is in-place active. The class also merges the menu with that of the host container during in-place activation.

```
class COleIPFrameWnd : public CFrameWnd
{
    DECLARE_DYNCREATE(COleIPFrameWnd)

// Constructors
public:
    COleIPFrameWnd();

// Overridables
public:
    virtual BOOL OnCreateControlBars(CWnd* pWndFrame, CWnd* pWndDoc);
        // create control bars on container windows (pWndDoc can be
        // NULL)
    void RepositionFrame(LPCRECT lpPosRect, LPCRECT lpClipRect);

// Implementation
public:
    BOOL m_bUIActive;   // TRUE if currently in UIactive state
    virtual BOOL LoadFrame(UINT nIDResource,
        DWORD dwDefaultStyle = WS_CHILD¦WS_BORDER¦WS_CLIPSIBLINGS,
        CWnd* pParentWnd = NULL,
        CCreateContext* pContext = NULL);
    virtual void RecalcLayout(BOOL bNotify = TRUE);
    virtual BOOL PreTranslateMessage(MSG* pMsg);
    virtual LRESULT OnSetMessageString(WPARAM wParam, LPARAM lParam);
    virtual ~COleIPFrameWnd();
#ifdef _DEBUG
    virtual void AssertValid() const;
    virtual void Dump(CDumpContext& dc) const;
#endif

protected:
    // in-place state
    OLEINPLACEFRAMEINFO m_frameInfo;
    LPOLEINPLACEFRAME m_lpFrame;
    LPOLEINPLACEUIWINDOW m_lpDocFrame;
    HWND m_hWndFrame;
    HWND m_hWndDocFrame;
    HMENU m_hSharedMenu;
    OLEMENUGROUPWIDTHS m_menuWidths;
    HOLEMENU m_hOleMenu;
    CRect m_rectPos;      // client area rectangle of the item
    CRect m_rectClip;     // area to which frame should be clipped
    BOOL m_bInsideRecalc;

    // in-place activation support
    BOOL BuildSharedMenu(COleServerDoc* pDoc);
    void DestroySharedMenu(COleServerDoc* pDoc);
    void UpdateControlBars(HWND hWnd);

protected:
    //{{AFX_MSG(COleIPFrameWnd)
    afx_msg void OnSize(UINT nType, int cx, int cy);
    afx_msg LRESULT OnRecalcParent(WPARAM wParam, LPARAM lParam);
    afx_msg LRESULT OnIdleUpdateCmdUI(WPARAM wParam, LPARAM lParam);
```

```
        afx_msg int OnCreate(LPCREATESTRUCT lpCreateStruct);
        afx_msg void OnDestroy();
        afx_msg LRESULT OnResizeChild(WPARAM wParam, LPARAM lParam);
        afx_msg void OnContextHelp();
        //}}AFX_MSG
        DECLARE_MESSAGE_MAP()

        friend class COleServerDoc;
};
```

The *COleResizeBar* Class

The `COleResizeBar` class, which is used with the `COleIPFrameWnd` class, is responsible for sizing active, in-place objects. Using a `CRectTracker` object, `COleResizeBar` places a hatched frame around the active object. Six sizing handles also appear on the frame. You do not need to use this class directly.

```
class COleResizeBar : public CControlBar
{
        DECLARE_DYNAMIC(COleResizeBar)

// Constructors
public:
        COleResizeBar();
        BOOL Create(CWnd* pParentWnd,
                DWORD dwStyle = WS_CHILD ¦ WS_VISIBLE,
                UINT nID = AFX_IDW_RESIZE_BAR);

// Implementation
public:
        virtual ~COleResizeBar();
        virtual void OnUpdateCmdUI(CFrameWnd* pTarget,
            BOOL bDisableIfNoHndler);
protected:
        CRectTracker m_tracker;     // implemented with a tracker
protected:
        //{{AFX_MSG(COleResizeBar)
        afx_msg BOOL OnEraseBkgnd(CDC* pDC);
        afx_msg void OnPaint();
        afx_msg void OnSize(UINT nType, int cx, int cy);
        afx_msg BOOL OnSetCursor(CWnd* pWnd, UINT nHitTest, UINT message);
        afx_msg void OnLButtonDown(UINT, CPoint point);
        afx_msg LRESULT OnSizeParent(WPARAM wParam, LPARAM lParam);
        //}}AFX_MSG
        DECLARE_MESSAGE_MAP()
};
```

Uniform Data Transfer Classes

MFC has four classes that handle the movement of data: `COleDropSource`, `COleDropTarget`, `COleDataSource`, and `COleDataObject`. You use these classes to implement drag-drop and clipboard-transfer operations. The following sections describe these classes.

The *COleDropSource* Class

The `COleDropSource` class is the object that controls the drag-drop operation. This class implements the COM interface `IDropSource` and provides feedback to the user during the operation. To use this class, you simply call its constructor.

```
class COleDropSource : public CCmdTarget
{
// Constructors
public:
     COleDropSource();

// Overridables
     virtual SCODE QueryContinueDrag(BOOL bEscapePressed,
         DWORD dwKeyState);
     virtual SCODE GiveFeedback(DROPEFFECT dropEffect);
     virtual BOOL OnBeginDrag(CWnd* pWnd);

// Implementation
public:
#ifdef _DEBUG
     virtual void Dump(CDumpContext& dc) const;
#endif

protected:
     BEGIN_INTERFACE_PART(DropSource, IDropSource)
          STDMETHOD(QueryContinueDrag)(BOOL, DWORD);
          STDMETHOD(GiveFeedback)(DWORD);
     END_INTERFACE_PART(DropSource)

     DECLARE_INTERFACE_MAP()

     CRect m_rectStartDrag;  // when mouse leaves this rect,
                             // drag-drop starts
     BOOL m_bDragStarted;    // has drag really started yet?

     // metrics for drag start determination
     static UINT nDragMinDist;   // min. amount mouse must move for drag
     static UINT nDragDelay;     // delay before drag starts

     friend class COleDataSource;
};
```

The *COleDropTarget* Class

`COleDropTarget` is the companion class for `COleDropSource`. The `COleDropTarget` class implements the functionality of a drag-drop target.

To use this class, you must create an instance of the class and call the `Register` method passing a pointer to the target window.

The `COleDropTarget` class implements the COM interface `IDropTarget`. Compare this implementation to the one that you developed in the section

"The `CDropTarget` Class," in Chapter 3, "A Sample C++ Application." Apart from the additional support for scrolling, both implementations are similar.

```
class COleDropTarget : public CCmdTarget
{
// Constructors
public:
     COleDropTarget();

// Operations
     BOOL Register(CWnd* pWnd);
     virtual void Revoke();  // virtual for implementation

// Overridables
     virtual DROPEFFECT OnDragEnter(CWnd* pWnd,
          COleDataObject* pDataObject, DWORD dwKeyState,
          CPoint point);
     virtual DROPEFFECT OnDragOver(CWnd* pWnd,
          COleDataObject* pDataObject, DWORD dwKeyState,
          CPoint point);
     virtual BOOL OnDrop(CWnd* pWnd, COleDataObject* pDataObject,
          DROPEFFECT dropEffect, CPoint point);
     virtual void OnDragLeave(CWnd* pWnd);
     virtual BOOL OnDragScroll(CWnd* pWnd, DWORD dwKeyState,
          CPoint point);

// Implementation
public:
     virtual ~COleDropTarget();
#ifdef _DEBUG
     virtual void AssertValid() const;
     virtual void Dump(CDumpContext& dc) const;
#endif

protected:
     HWND m_hWnd;            // HWND to which IDropTarget is attached
     LPDATAOBJECT m_lpDataObject;
                          // != NULL between OnDragEnter, OnDragLeave
     UINT m_nTimerID;     // != MAKEWORD(-1, -1) when in scroll area
     DWORD m_dwLastTick;  // valid only when m_nTimerID is valid
     UINT m_nScrollDelay; // time to next scroll

     // metrics for drag-scrolling
     static int nScrollInset;
     static UINT nScrollDelay;
     static UINT nScrollInterval;

     // implementation helpers
     void SetupTimer(CView* pView, UINT nTimerID);
     void CancelTimer(CWnd* pWnd);

// Interface Maps
protected:
```

```
    BEGIN_INTERFACE_PART(DropTarget, IDropTarget)
        STDMETHOD(DragEnter)(LPDATAOBJECT, DWORD, POINTL, LPDWORD);
        STDMETHOD(DragOver)(DWORD, POINTL, LPDWORD);
        STDMETHOD(DragLeave)();
        STDMETHOD(Drop)(LPDATAOBJECT, DWORD, POINTL pt, LPDWORD);
    END_INTERFACE_PART(DropTarget)

    DECLARE_INTERFACE_MAP()
};
```

The *COleDataSource* Class

The `COleDataSource` class creates an object that contains data to be used in a data transfer. The class implements the COM interface `IDataObject`.

A data transfer operation requires a data source and a data destination. When you are the data source, you must create an object of this class to transfer the data.

Normally, the sequence of events is as follows:

1. Your application's user selects data and either begins a drag-drop operation or places the data on the clipboard.
2. The application then creates an object of the type `COleDataSource`, and places the data in the object, using `CacheData` or `DelayRenderData` (for delayed rendering of the data).
3. The object that the application created is then passed to the `SetClipBoard` or `DoDragDrop` method.

You see this object in action in Chapter 7, "An MDI Linking Container."

```
class COleDataSource : public CCmdTarget
{
// Constructors
public:
    COleDataSource();

// Operations
    void Empty();   // empty cache (similar to ::EmptyClipboard)

    // CacheData & DelayRenderData operations
    // similar to ::SetClipboardData
    void CacheGlobalData(CLIPFORMAT cfFormat, HGLOBAL hGlobal,
        LPFORMATETC lpFormatEtc = NULL);    // for HGLOBAL-based data
    void DelayRenderFileData(CLIPFORMAT cfFormat,
        LPFORMATETC lpFormatEtc = NULL);
                                    // for CFile*-based delayed render
```

```
    // Clipboard and drag-drop access
    DROPEFFECT DoDragDrop(
         DWORD dwEffects =
         ➥DROPEFFECT_COPY¦DROPEFFECT_MOVE¦DROPEFFECT_LINK,
         LPCRECT lpRectStartDrag = NULL,
         COleDropSource* pDropSource = NULL);
    void SetClipboard();
    static void PASCAL FlushClipboard();
    static COleDataSource* PASCAL GetClipboardOwner();

    // Advanced: STGMEDIUM-based cached data
    void CacheData(CLIPFORMAT cfFormat, LPSTGMEDIUM lpStgMedium,
         LPFORMATETC lpFormatEtc = NULL);
                   // for LPSTGMEDIUM-based data
    // Advanced: STGMEDIUM- or HGLOBAL-based delayed render
    void DelayRenderData(CLIPFORMAT cfFormat,
        LPFORMATETC lpFormatEtc = NULL);
    // Advanced: support for SetData in COleServerItem
    //  (not generally useful for clipboard or drag-drop operations)
    void DelaySetData(CLIPFORMAT cfFormat,
        LPFORMATETC lpFormatEtc = NULL);
// Overridables
    virtual BOOL OnRenderGlobalData(LPFORMATETC lpFormatEtc,
        HGLOBAL* phGlobal);
    virtual BOOL OnRenderFileData(LPFORMATETC lpFormatEtc,
        CFile* pFile);
    virtual BOOL OnRenderData(LPFORMATETC lpFormatEtc,
        LPSTGMEDIUM lpStgMedium);
         // OnRenderFileData and OnRenderGlobalData are called by
         //  the default implementation of OnRenderData.

    virtual BOOL OnSetData(LPFORMATETC lpFormatEtc,
        LPSTGMEDIUM lpStgMedium);
         // used only in COleServerItem implementation

// Implementation
public:
    virtual ~COleDataSource();
#ifdef _DEBUG
    virtual void AssertValid() const;
    virtual void Dump(CDumpContext& dc) const;
#endif

protected:
    AFX_DATACACHE_ENTRY* m_pDataCache;  // data cache itself
    UINT m_nMaxSize;    // current allocated size
    UINT m_nSize;       // current size of the cache
    UINT m_nGrowBy;
         // number of cache elements to grow by for new allocs

    AFX_DATACACHE_ENTRY* Lookup(LPFORMATETC lpFormatEtc,
         DATADIR dataDir) const;
    AFX_DATACACHE_ENTRY* AllocSpace();

// Interface Maps
public:
    BEGIN_INTERFACE_PART(DataObject, IDataObject)
```

```
        STDMETHOD(GetData)(LPFORMATETC, LPSTGMEDIUM);
        STDMETHOD(GetDataHere)(LPFORMATETC, LPSTGMEDIUM);
        STDMETHOD(QueryGetData)(LPFORMATETC);
        STDMETHOD(GetCanonicalFormatEtc)(LPFORMATETC,
            LPFORMATETC);
        STDMETHOD(SetData)(LPFORMATETC, LPSTGMEDIUM, BOOL);
        STDMETHOD(EnumFormatEtc)(DWORD, LPENUMFORMATETC FAR*);
        STDMETHOD(DAdvise)(LPFORMATETC, DWORD, LPADVISESINK,
            LPDWORD);
        STDMETHOD(DUnadvise)(DWORD);
        STDMETHOD(EnumDAdvise)(LPENUMSTATDATA FAR*);
    END_INTERFACE_PART(DataObject)

    DECLARE_INTERFACE_MAP()

    friend class COleServerItem;
};
```

The *COleDataObject* Class

The `COleDataObject` class implements the receiving side of a data transfer. This class gives you full control over the type of data that is transferred to you. Usually, when transferring data, a data source offers the data in several formats. The availability of multiple formats makes the data accessible to more receivers.

For example, if a user drags some text from Microsoft Word to another application, Word offers the receiver the data in several formats, including Rich Text Format (RTF) and CF_TEXT. If the receiving application can accept RTF, the data is transferred in this format. The receiver receives all the formatting and font information, and the text appears as it did in Word. However, if the application cannot accept RTF, it can instead receive plain text without any formatting.

The `COleDataObject` class gives you control over these data formats. You also receive full control over the storage medium of the transfer data. You can receive the data into a global memory buffer, an OLE STGMEDIUM structure, or even a `CFile` object.

To use the class, you must attach a valid `COleDataSource` object to it after construction.

```
class COleDataObject

{
// Constructors
public:
    COleDataObject();

// Operations
    void Attach(LPDATAOBJECT lpDataObject, BOOL bAutoRelease = TRUE);
    LPDATAOBJECT Detach();
                // detach and get ownership of m_lpDataObject
    void Release(); // detach and release ownership of m_lpDataObject
    BOOL AttachClipboard(); // attach to current clipboard object
```

```
// Attributes
     void BeginEnumFormats();
     BOOL GetNextFormat(LPFORMATETC lpFormatEtc);
     CFile* GetFileData(CLIPFORMAT cfFormat,
          LPFORMATETC lpFormatEtc = NULL);
     HGLOBAL GetGlobalData(CLIPFORMAT cfFormat,
          LPFORMATETC lpFormatEtc = NULL);
     BOOL GetData(CLIPFORMAT cfFormat, LPSTGMEDIUM lpStgMedium,
          LPFORMATETC lpFormatEtc = NULL);
     BOOL IsDataAvailable(CLIPFORMAT cfFormat,
          LPFORMATETC lpFormatEtc = NULL);

// Implementation
public:
     LPDATAOBJECT m_lpDataObject;
     LPENUMFORMATETC m_lpEnumerator;
     ~COleDataObject();

protected:
     BOOL m_bAutoRelease;    // TRUE if destructor should call Release

private:
     // Disable the copy constructor and assignment by default
     //    so you get compiler errors rather than unexpected behavior
     //    if you pass objects by value or assign objects.
     COleDataObject(const COleDataObject&);  // no implementation
     void operator=(const COleDataObject&);  // no implementation
};
```

The OLE Dialog Classes

Seven MFC classes implement OLE user interface (UI) dialog boxes. Each of these dialog boxes follows Microsoft's user interface guidelines for OLE dialogs. For an OLE application developer, these dialog boxes are the OLE common dialogs.

All the OLE dialog classes use `COleDialog` as their base class. Many of these dialog classes are used together. For example, the standard Insert Object dialog box has a Change Icon command button. This button in turn invokes the Change Icon dialog box. The Insert Object dialog box also provides an option to create an object from a disk file.

The following sections describe these classes.

The *COleInsertDialog* Class

The `COleInsertDialog` class implements the Insert Object dialog box. You usually invoke this dialog box from your menu to insert an embedded or linked object in your container. A list of all registered servers is displayed to the user. You can choose to create the object with one of the listed servers or from a disk file.

```
class COleInsertDialog : public COleDialog
{
     DECLARE_DYNAMIC(COleInsertDialog)
// Attributes
public:
     OLEUIINSERTOBJECT m_io; // structure for OleUIInsertObject
// Constructors
     COleInsertDialog(DWORD dwFlags = IOF_SELECTCREATENEW,
          CWnd* pParentWnd = NULL);
// Operations
     virtual int DoModal();
     BOOL CreateItem(COleClientItem* pItem);
          // call after DoModal to create item based on dialog data
// Attributes (after DoModal returns IDOK)
     enum Selection { createNewItem, insertFromFile, linkToFile };
     UINT GetSelectionType() const;
          // return type of selection made
     CString GetPathName() const;  // return full path name
     REFCLSID GetClassID() const;  // get class ID of new item
     DVASPECT GetDrawAspect() const;
          // DVASPECT_CONTENT or DVASPECT_ICON
     HGLOBAL GetIconicMetafile() const;
          // returns HGLOBAL to METAFILEPICT struct with iconic data
// Implementation
public:
     virtual ~COleInsertDialog();
#ifdef _DEBUG
     virtual void Dump(CDumpContext& dc) const;
#endif
protected:
     char m_szFileName[OLEUI_CCHPATHMAX];
          // contains full path name after return
};
```


The *COleConvertDialog* Class

The `COleConvertDialog` class implements a dialog box that enables the user to change the type of an embedded or linked object. The dialog box offers the options of permanently changing the object from one type to another or simply activating the object as a different type.

Converting objects from one type to another is an important OLE concept, because it greatly increases the portability of compound documents. However, the concept has not as yet gathered much support from developers.

```
class COleConvertDialog : public COleDialog
{
     DECLARE_DYNAMIC(COleConvertDialog)
// Attributes
public:
     OLEUICONVERT m_cv;  // structure for OleUIConvert
// Constructors
     COleConvertDialog(COleClientItem* pItem,
```

```
            DWORD dwFlags = CF_SELECTCONVERTTO,
            CLSID FAR* pClassID = NULL,
            CWnd* pParentWnd = NULL);
// Operations
        virtual int DoModal();
            // just display the dialog and collect convert info
        BOOL DoConvert(COleClientItem* pItem);
            // do the conversion on pItem (after DoModal == IDOK)
// Attributes (after DoModal returns IDOK)
        enum Selection { noConversion, convertItem, activateAs };
        UINT GetSelectionType() const;
        HGLOBAL GetIconicMetafile() const;
                // returns NULL if same as before
        REFCLSID GetClassID() const;
        DVASPECT GetDrawAspect() const; // gets new draw aspect
// Implementation
public:
        virtual ~COleConvertDialog();
#ifdef _DEBUG
        virtual void Dump(CDumpContext& dc) const;
#endif
};
```

The *COleChangeIconDialog* Class

The `COleChangeIconDialog` class implements a dialog box that usually is used with the other dialog boxes to enable the user to associate any icon with an embedded or linked object.

```
class COleChangeIconDialog : public COleDialog
{
        DECLARE_DYNAMIC(COleChangeIconDialog)
// Attributes
public:
        OLEUICHANGEICON m_ci;   // structure for OleUIChangeIcon
// Constructors
        COleChangeIconDialog(COleClientItem* pItem,
            DWORD dwFlags = CIF_SELECTCURRENT,
            CWnd* pParentWnd = NULL);
// Operations
        virtual int DoModal();
        BOOL DoChangeIcon(COleClientItem* pItem);
// Attributes
        HGLOBAL GetIconicMetafile() const;
// Implementation
public:
        virtual ~COleChangeIconDialog();
#ifdef _DEBUG
        virtual void Dump(CDumpContext& dc) const;
#endif
};
```

The *COlePasteSpecialDialog* Class

The `COlePasteSpecialDialog` class implements the Paste Special dialog box, which enables users to control the type of object that is being inserted, embedded, or linked, and to select the type of data that the object is to contain.

```
class COlePasteSpecialDialog : public COleDialog
{
     DECLARE_DYNAMIC(COlePasteSpecialDialog)
// Attributes
public:
     OLEUIPASTESPECIAL m_ps; // structure for OleUIPasteSpecial
// Constructors
     COlePasteSpecialDialog(DWORD dwFlags = PSF_SELECTPASTE,
          COleDataObject* pDataObject = NULL, CWnd *pParentWnd = NULL);
// Operations
     OLEUIPASTEFLAG AddLinkEntry(UINT cf);
     void AddFormat(const FORMATETC& formatEtc, LPSTR lpstrFormat,
          LPSTR lpstrResult, DWORD flags);
     void AddFormat(UINT cf, DWORD tymed, UINT nFormatID,
          BOOL bEnableIcon, BOOL bLink);
     void AddStandardFormats(BOOL bEnableLink = TRUE);
     virtual int DoModal();
     BOOL CreateItem(COleClientItem *pNewItem);
          // creates a standard OLE item from selection data
// Attributes (after DoModal returns IDOK)
     int GetPasteIndex() const;      // resulting index to use for paste
     enum Selection { pasteLink = 1, pasteNormal = 2,
       pasteStatic = 3, pasteOther = 4};
     UINT GetSelectionType() const;
          // get selection type (pasteLink, pasteNormal, pasteStatic)
     DVASPECT GetDrawAspect() const;
          // DVASPECT_CONTENT or DVASPECT_ICON
     HGLOBAL GetIconicMetafile() const;
          // returns HGLOBAL to METAFILEPICT struct with iconic data
// Implementation
public:
     virtual ~COlePasteSpecialDialog();
#ifdef _DEBUG
     virtual void Dump(CDumpContext& dc) const;
     virtual void AssertValid() const;
#endif
     unsigned int m_arrLinkTypes[8];
          // size limit imposed by MFCOLEUI library
};
```

The *COleLinksDialog* Class

The `COleLinksDialog` class implements the Edit Links dialog box. This dialog box enables users to change the source of linked objects manually. As Chapter 1, "General Concepts," mentions, OLE now provides adaptive links. However, the Edit Links dialog box is still required in the current release of OLE because you can still break these links. This class implements the `IOleUILinkContainer` COM interface.

The need for this type of dialog box should disappear when a future version of Windows NT is released. This version should provide true link-tracking support from the operating system.

```
class COleLinksDialog : public COleDialog
{
     DECLARE_DYNAMIC(COleLinksDialog)
// Attributes
public:
     OLEUIEDITLINKS m_el;    // structure for OleUIEditLinks
// Constructors
     COleLinksDialog(COleDocument* pDoc, CView* pView,
          DWORD dwFlags = 0,
          CWnd* pParentWnd = NULL);
// Operations
     virtual int DoModal();  // display the dialog and edit links
// Implementation
public:
     virtual ~COleLinksDialog();
#ifdef _DEBUG
     virtual void Dump(CDumpContext& dc) const;
     virtual void AssertValid() const;
#endif
protected:
     COleDocument* m_pDocument;          // document being manipulated
     COleClientItem* m_pSelectedItem;
                                    // primary selected item in m_pDocument
     POSITION m_pos;                     // used during link enumeration
     BOOL m_bUpdateLinks;                // update links?
     BOOL m_bUpdateEmbeddings;           // update embeddings?
// Interface Maps
     BEGIN_INTERFACE_PART(OleUILinkContainer, IOleUILinkContainer)
          STDMETHOD_(DWORD,GetNextLink)(DWORD);
          STDMETHOD(SetLinkUpdateOptions)(DWORD, DWORD);
          STDMETHOD(GetLinkUpdateOptions)(DWORD, LPDWORD);
          STDMETHOD(SetLinkSource)(DWORD, LPSTR, ULONG, ULONG FAR*,
               BOOL);
          STDMETHOD(GetLinkSource)(DWORD, LPSTR FAR*, ULONG FAR*,
               LPSTR FAR*, LPSTR FAR*, BOOL FAR*, BOOL FAR*);
          STDMETHOD(OpenLinkSource)(DWORD);
          STDMETHOD(UpdateLink)(DWORD, BOOL, BOOL);
          STDMETHOD(CancelLink)(DWORD);
     END_INTERFACE_PART(OleUILinkContainer)
     DECLARE_INTERFACE_MAP()
};
```

The *COleUpdateDialog* Class

If a document that contains Automatic Links (links that are automatically updated when the document is opened) is opened, the dialog box created by the `COleUpdateDialog` class should appear. This dialog box displays a progress indicator that provides feedback to the user while the linked objects in the document are being updated. It also provides a Stop command button that enables the user to cancel the update process.

```
class COleUpdateDialog : public COleLinksDialog
{
     DECLARE_DYNAMIC(COleUpdateDialog)
// Constructors
public:
     COleUpdateDialog(COleDocument* pDoc,
          BOOL bUpdateLinks = TRUE, BOOL bUpdateEmbeddings = FALSE,
          CWnd* pParentWnd = NULL);
// Operations
     virtual int DoModal();
// Implementation
public:
     virtual ~COleUpdateDialog();
#ifdef _DEBUG
     virtual void Dump(CDumpContext& dc) const;
#endif
protected:
     CString m_strCaption;   // caption for the dialog box
};
```

The *COleBusyDialog* Class

If an OLE server does not respond to a request to update or open an object, the dialog box created by the `COleBusyDialog` class is usually displayed to the user. This class is usually used by the `COleMessageFiler` class.

```
class COleBusyDialog : public COleDialog
{
     DECLARE_DYNAMIC(COleBusyDialog)
// Attributes
public:
     OLEUIBUSY m_bz;
// Constructors
     COleBusyDialog(HTASK htaskBusy, BOOL bNotResponding = FALSE,
          DWORD dwFlags = 0, CWnd* pParentWnd = NULL);
// Operations
     virtual int DoModal();
     enum Selection { switchTo = 1, retry = 2, callUnblocked = 3 };
     UINT GetSelectionType() const;
// Implementation
public:
     ~COleBusyDialog();
#ifdef _DEBUG
     virtual void Dump(CDumpContext& dc) const;
#endif
protected:
     Selection m_selection;  // selection after DoModal returns IDOK
};
```

Miscellaneous Classes

The classes described in the following sections do not belong in any particular category. You seldom use any of these classes directly; in fact, the only one of these classes that you are likely to use is `CRectTracker`.

The *COleException* Class

The `COleException` class returns OLE errors in a container and a server application. Instead of creating an object of this class, you normally use the function call `AfxThrowOleException`.

The exceptions are just an extension of the normal MFC exception mechanism.

```
class COleException : public CException
{
     DECLARE_DYNAMIC(COleException)
public:
     SCODE m_sc;
     static SCODE PASCAL Process(const CException* pAnyException);
// Implementation (use AfxThrowOleException to create)
     COleException();
};
```

The *CRectTracker* Class

The `CRectTracker` class enables users to move and resize objects in containers. The class follows all the UI guidelines for embedded and linked objects. `CRectTracker` gives you full control over all aspects of the interface, from the type of border to the size and placement of the sizing handles.

Although you use this class primarily in OLE applications, you actually can use this class whenever you want to provide such an interface.

```
class CRectTracker
{
public:
// Constructors
     CRectTracker();
     CRectTracker(LPCRECT lpSrcRect, UINT nStyle);
// Style Flags
     enum StyleFlags
     {
          solidLine = 1, dottedLine = 2, hatchedBorder = 4,
          resizeInside = 8, resizeOutside = 16, hatchInside = 32,
     };
// Hit-Test codes
     enum TrackerHit
     {
          hitNothing = -1,
          hitTopLeft = 0, hitTopRight = 1,
          hitBottomRight = 2, hitBottomLeft = 3,
          hitTop = 4, hitRight = 5, hitBottom = 6,
          hitLeft = 7, hitMiddle = 8
     };
// Attributes
     UINT m_nStyle;      // current state
     CRect m_rect;       // current position (always in pixels)
```

```
    CSize m_sizeMin;    // minimum X and Y size during track operation
    int m_nHandleSize;
            // size of resize handles (default from WIN.INI)
// Operations
    void Draw(CDC* pDC) const;
    void GetTrueRect(LPRECT lpTrueRect) const;
    BOOL SetCursor(CWnd* pWnd, UINT nHitTest) const;
    BOOL Track(CWnd* pWnd, CPoint point, BOOL bAllowInvert = FALSE,
         CWnd* pWndClipTo = NULL);
    BOOL TrackRubberBand(CWnd* pWnd, CPoint point,
         BOOL bAllowInvert = TRUE);
    int HitTest(CPoint point) const;
    int NormalizeHit(int nHandle) const;
// Overridables
    virtual void DrawTrackerRect(LPCRECT lpRect, CWnd* pWndClipTo,
         CDC* pDC, CWnd* pWnd);
    virtual void AdjustRect(int nHandle, LPRECT lpRect);
    virtual void OnChangedRect(const CRect& rectOld);
// Implementation
public:
    virtual ~CRectTracker();
protected:
    BOOL m_bAllowInvert;    // flag passed to Track or TrackRubberBand
    // implementation helpers
    int HitTestHandles(CPoint point) const;
    UINT GetHandleMask() const;
    void GetHandleRect(int nHandle, CRect* pHandleRect) const;
    void GetModifyPointers(int nHandle, int**ppx, int**ppy,
         int* px, int*py);
    int GetHandleSize() const;
    BOOL TrackHandle(int nHandle, CWnd* pWnd, CPoint point,
         CWnd* pWndClipTo);
    void Construct();
};
```

The *COleStreamFile* Class

The `COleStreamFile` class implements the COM interface `IStream` and supports the compound file implementation in the framework. (Chapter 8, "OLE Compound Files," examines compound files in detail.) This class inherits from `CFile` and can be used just as you would use any object of the `CFile` type.

Before you can use this class, you must have a valid `IStorage` pointer.

```
class COleStreamFile : public CFile
{
    DECLARE_DYNAMIC(COleStreamFile)
// Constructors and Destructors
public:
    COleStreamFile(LPSTREAM lpStream = NULL);
// Operations
    // Note: OpenStream and CreateStream can accept either STGM_ flags
    //  or CFile::OpenFlags bits because common values are guaranteed
    //  to have the same semantics.
```

```
        BOOL OpenStream(LPSTORAGE lpStorage, LPCSTR lpszStreamName,
             DWORD nOpenFlags = modeReadWrite¦shareExclusive,
             CFileException* pError = NULL);
        BOOL CreateStream(LPSTORAGE lpStorage, LPCSTR lpszStreamName,
             DWORD nOpenFlags = modeReadWrite¦shareExclusive¦modeCreate,
             CFileException* pError = NULL);
        BOOL CreateMemoryStream(CFileException* pError = NULL);
        // attach and detach can be used when Open and Create functions
        // aren't adequate
        void Attach(LPSTREAM lpStream);
        LPSTREAM Detach();
   // Implementation
   public:
        LPSTREAM m_lpStream;
   #ifdef _DEBUG
        virtual void AssertValid() const;
        virtual void Dump(CDumpContext& dc) const;
   #endif
        virtual ~COleStreamFile();
        // attributes for implementation
        BOOL GetStatus(CFileStatus& rStatus) const;
        virtual DWORD GetPosition() const;
        // overrides for implementation
        virtual CFile* Duplicate() const;
        virtual LONG Seek(LONG lOff, UINT nFrom);
        virtual void SetLength(DWORD dwNewLen);
        virtual DWORD GetLength() const;
        virtual UINT Read(void FAR* lpBuf, UINT nCount);
        virtual void Write(const void FAR* lpBuf, UINT nCount);
        virtual void LockRange(DWORD dwPos, DWORD dwCount);
        virtual void UnlockRange(DWORD dwPos, DWORD dwCount);
        virtual void Abort();
        virtual void Flush();
        virtual void Close();
   };
```

The *COleDispatchException* Class

The `COleDispatchException` class implements exception handling for Automation exceptions. As with the `ColeException` class, you do not normally use the `COleDispatchException` class directly; instead, you call the `AfxThrowOleDispatchException` function.

```
class COleDispatchException : public CException
{
     DECLARE_DYNAMIC(COleDispatchException)
public:
// Attributes
     WORD m_wCode;
                  // error code (specific to IDispatch implementation)
     CString m_strDescription;
                  // human-readable description of the error
     DWORD m_dwHelpContext;     // help context for error
     // usualy empty in application that creates it (eg. servers)
     CString m_strHelpFile;
                  // help file to use with m_dwHelpContext
```

```
    CString m_strSource;        // source of the error (name of server)
// Implementation
public:
    COleDispatchException(LPCSTR lpszDescription,
        UINT nHelpID, WORD wCode);
    static void PASCAL Process(
        EXCEPINFO FAR* pInfo, const CException* pAnyException);
    SCODE m_scError;            // SCODE describing the error
};
```

The *COleMessageFilter* Class

You seldom need to use the `COleMessageFilter` class, which the framework normally creates when your application starts. You can retrieve a pointer to this object by calling `AfxOleGetMessageFilter`.

The `COleMessageFilter` class handles concurrency issues between OLE applications. You might use this object to place your application in a busy state while you are performing some lengthy operation.

After retrieving the `COleMessageFilter` object, you call `BeginBusyState`; when you are again ready to receive LPRC calls, you call `EndBusyState`.

This class implements the `IMessageFilter` interface.

```
class COleMessageFilter : public CCmdTarget
{
// Constructors
public:
    COleMessageFilter();
// Operations
    BOOL Register();
    void Revoke();
    // for controlling the busy state of the server application
    // (called app)
    virtual void BeginBusyState();
    virtual void EndBusyState();
    void SetBusyReply(SERVERCALL nBusyReply);
    // for controlling actions taken against rejected/retried calls
    void SetRetryReply(DWORD nRetryReply = 0);
        // used only when the "not responding" dialog is disabled
    void SetMessagePendingDelay(DWORD nTimeout = 5000);
        // used to determine amount of time before significant
        // message
    void EnableBusyDialog(BOOL bEnableBusy = TRUE);
    void EnableNotRespondingDialog(BOOL bEnableNotResponding = TRUE);
        // used to enable/disable the two types of busy dialogs
// Overridables
    virtual BOOL OnMessagePending(const MSG* pMsg);
        // return TRUE to eat the message (usually only if
        // processed)
// Implementation
```

```
public:
#ifdef _DEBUG
     virtual void AssertValid() const;
     virtual void Dump(CDumpContext& dc) const;
#endif
     virtual ~COleMessageFilter();
     virtual BOOL IsSignificantMessage(MSG* pMsg);
          // determine whether any significant messages
          // are present in the queue
     virtual int OnBusyDialog(HTASK htaskBusy);
     virtual int OnNotRespondingDialog(HTASK htaskBusy);
          // these functions display the busy dialog
protected:
     BOOL m_bRegistered;
     LONG m_nBusyCount;  // for BeginBusyState & EndBusyState
     BOOL m_bEnableBusy;
     BOOL m_bEnableNotResponding;
     BOOL m_bUnblocking;
     DWORD m_nRetryReply;
           // used only if m_bEnableNotResponding == FALSE
     DWORD m_nBusyReply;
     DWORD m_nTimeout;
// Interface Maps
protected:
     BEGIN_INTERFACE_PART(MessageFilter, IMessageFilter)
          STDMETHOD_(DWORD, HandleInComingCall)(DWORD, HTASK,
              DWORD, DWORD);
          STDMETHOD_(DWORD, RetryRejectedCall)(HTASK, DWORD, DWORD);
          STDMETHOD_(DWORD, MessagePending)(HTASK, DWORD, DWORD);
     END_INTERFACE_PART(MessageFilter)

     DECLARE_INTERFACE_MAP()
};
```

AppWizard Support for OLE

The AppWizard (fig. 5.3) provides all the support that you need to begin using these classes in your application. When initially creating your application, you can decide which feature of OLE you intend to support. You can select from a simple container, a mini server, a full server, or a container server.

The AppWizard generates the necessary class and provides default implementation of the required methods. It also generates a CLSID for your application. The AppWizard can also add full Automation support, and the ClassWizard provides additional support for Automation applications. Part III, "OLE Automation," discusses this support in greater detail.

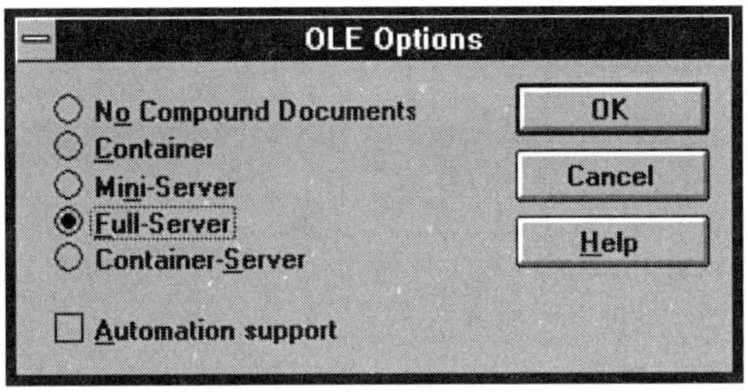

Fig. 5.3
The AppWizard in action.

From Here...

This chapter wrapped up the entire OLE API and all its interfaces in just a few C++ classes. As you learned in Chapter 3, "A Sample C++ Application," implementing COM interfaces is not that difficult when you are doing something like handling a drag-drop target, but when you begin to support visual editing, the details can become overwhelming.

However, the main reason for using MFC to implement OLE is not just to save a lot of work at the moment, but to save a lot of work in the future.

OLE is the foundation for Microsoft's future object-oriented operating systems. In a future release of the Windows operating system, Microsoft will expose all new operating system interfaces as COM interfaces. As with other new features of Windows, MFC makes it easier to implement these features in your application while still leaving you with the option of directly accessing the new APIs and interfaces.

Chapter 6

A Simple Container

In this chapter, you begin to develop an OLE container application using the Microsoft Foundation Classes (MFC). You first let the AppWizard create the application's skeleton code, and then you begin adding features.

The first version of the container supports the following actions:

- Inserting an object
- Sizing the embedded objects' presentation in the container
- Activating the object
- Saving and restoring the object
- Placing a context menu on the object

Creating the Skeleton with the AppWizard

After invoking the AppWizard, select the Container option from the OLE Options dialog box. This option enables the AppWizard to generate the minimum code necessary for OLE container support.

Although the code generated is sufficient to insert an object into the container, you still must write much code before you have a functional container. For example, the container provides no way to place the object by dragging it.

The next sections look at the code that the AppWizard generates and show you what you need add to provide the minimum support necessary.

The Application Module

The only code of interest in this module is in the `COleCntApp::InitInstance` method. The following sections examine each of the methods called in `InitInstance`.

The *AfxOleInit* Function

The first function of interest is `AfxOleInit`. This function is called to load and initialize the OLE libraries. This function checks the build numbers of the OLE libraries and compares them to the numbers used when compiling the application. These build numbers are not the same as the version numbers of the OLE libraries; instead, they are the internal build numbers of the OLE system. The build numbers are returned from the API call `OleBuildVersion`.

The rules for checking whether your application should run are simple. You can execute only against a major build version that is the same as that which you used while building your application. You can choose not to run against a different minor version, although you usually choose to do so.

After verifying the build numbers, you load the OLE libraries with a call to `OleInitialize`. If the current build is a debug build of your application, MFC also passes to OLE a pointer to a memory allocator. This allocator assists in debugging memory leaks.

The task memory allocator is then retrieved from OLE and stored internally. This allocator, which is cached to enhance performance, is used whenever buffers need to pass between the application and the OLE libraries.

Finally, a message filter is registered with OLE.

The *SetContainerInfo* Method

As you normally do with any MDI application, you create a document template object to manage the interface between your View, Frame, and Document classes. Because your application also is going to support visual editing or in-place activation, you must register a special resource that is used during in-place activation.

This resource consists of the menu and accelerator table that is to be used when an embedded object is in-place active. The method simply loads the resources and stores the handles internally:

```
void CDocTemplate::SetContainerInfo(UINT nIDOleInPlaceContainer)
{
     ASSERT(nIDOleInPlaceContainer != 0);
     // load menu to be used while in-place editing session
     // (as a container)
```

```
        HINSTANCE hInst = AfxFindResourceHandle(
             MAKEINTRESOURCE(nIDOleInPlaceContainer), RT_MENU);
        m_hMenuInPlace = ::LoadMenu(hInst,
             MAKEINTRESOURCE(nIDOleInPlaceContainer));
        m_hAccelInPlace = ::LoadAccelerators(hInst,
             MAKEINTRESOURCE(nIDOleInPlaceContainer));
   }
```

The remainder of this module's code creates and displays the frame window and handles the About dialog box code. Listing 6.1 shows the source code for the OLECNT.CPP module.

Listing 6.1 OLECNT.CPP

```
//-----------------------------------------------------------------
// olecnt.cpp : Defines the class behaviors for the application.
//

#include "stdafx.h"
#include "olecnt.h"

#include "mainfrm.h"
#include "olecndoc.h"
#include "olecnvw.h"

#ifdef _DEBUG
#undef THIS_FILE
static char BASED_CODE THIS_FILE[] = __FILE__;
#endif

/////////////////////////////////////////////////////////////////////
// COleCntApp

BEGIN_MESSAGE_MAP(COleCntApp, CWinApp)
     //{{AFX_MSG_MAP(COleCntApp)
     ON_COMMAND(ID_APP_ABOUT, OnAppAbout)
          // NOTE - the ClassWizard adds and removes mapping macros here.
          //    DO NOT EDIT what you see in these blocks of generated code!
     //}}AFX_MSG_MAP
     // Standard file-based document commands
     ON_COMMAND(ID_FILE_NEW, CWinApp::OnFileNew)
     ON_COMMAND(ID_FILE_OPEN, CWinApp::OnFileOpen)
     // Standard print setup command
     ON_COMMAND(ID_FILE_PRINT_SETUP, CWinApp::OnFilePrintSetup)
END_MESSAGE_MAP()
```

(continues)

Listing 6.1 Continued

```
/////////////////////////////////////////////////////////////////////////////
// COleCntApp construction

COleCntApp::COleCntApp()
{
     // TODO: add construction code here,
     // Place all significant initialization in InitInstance
}

/////////////////////////////////////////////////////////////////////////////
// The one and only COleCntApp object

COleCntApp NEAR theApp;

/////////////////////////////////////////////////////////////////////////////
// COleCntApp initialization

BOOL COleCntApp::InitInstance()
{
     // Initialize the OLE 2.0 libraries' OleBuildVersion
     if (!AfxOleInit())
     {
          AfxMessageBox(IDP_OLE_INIT_FAILED);
          return FALSE;
     }

     // Standard initialization
     // If you are not using these features and want to reduce the size
     // of your final executable, you should remove from the following
     // the specific initialization routines you do not need.

     SetDialogBkColor();        // Set dialog background color to gray
     LoadStdProfileSettings();
                     // Load standard INI file options (including MRU)

     // Register the application's document templates.
     // Document templates serve as the connection
     // between documents, frame windows, and views.

     CMultiDocTemplate* pDocTemplate;
     pDocTemplate = new CMultiDocTemplate(
          IDR_OLECNTTYPE,
          RUNTIME_CLASS(COleCntDoc),
          RUNTIME_CLASS(CMDIChildWnd),        // standard MDI child frame
          RUNTIME_CLASS(COleCntView));

     pDocTemplate->SetContainerInfo(IDR_OLECNTTYPE_CNTR_IP);
     AddDocTemplate(pDocTemplate);

     // create main MDI Frame window
     CMainFrame* pMainFrame = new CMainFrame;
     if (!pMainFrame->LoadFrame(IDR_MAINFRAME))
          return FALSE;
     m_pMainWnd = pMainFrame;
```

```
	// create a new (empty) document
	OnFileNew();

	if (m_lpCmdLine[0] != '\0')
	{
		// TODO: add command-line processing here
	}

	// The main window has been initialized, so show and update it.
	pMainFrame->ShowWindow(m_nCmdShow);
	pMainFrame->UpdateWindow();

	return TRUE;
}

/////////////////////////////////////////////////////////////////////////////
// CAboutDlg dialog used for App About
//
class CAboutDlg : public CDialog
{
public:
	CAboutDlg();

// Dialog Data
	//{{AFX_DATA(CAboutDlg)
	enum { IDD = IDD_ABOUTBOX };
	//}}AFX_DATA

// Implementation
protected:
	virtual void DoDataExchange(CDataExchange* pDX); // DDX/DDV support
	//{{AFX_MSG(CAboutDlg)
		// No message handlers
	//}}AFX_MSG
	DECLARE_MESSAGE_MAP()
};

CAboutDlg::CAboutDlg() : CDialog(CAboutDlg::IDD)
{
	//{{AFX_DATA_INIT(CAboutDlg)
	//}}AFX_DATA_INIT
}

void CAboutDlg::DoDataExchange(CDataExchange* pDX)
{
CDialog::DoDataExchange(pDX);
	//{{AFX_DATA_MAP(CAboutDlg)
	//}}AFX_DATA_MAP
}

BEGIN_MESSAGE_MAP(CAboutDlg, CDialog)
	//{{AFX_MSG_MAP(CAboutDlg)
		// No message handlers
	//}}AFX_MSG_MAP
END_MESSAGE_MAP()
```

(continues)

Listing 6.1 Continued

```
// App command to run the dialog
void COleCntApp::OnAppAbout()
{
     CAboutDlg aboutDlg;
     aboutDlg.DoModal();
}

//------------------------------------------------------------------
//------------------------------------------------------------------
```

The View Module

The View class contains all the code to create, display, and manipulate an embedded object. The following sections begin examining this code at the point that the user chooses Insert **O**bject from the **E**dit menu.

Inserting an Object

You begin by using the `ColeInsertDialog` class to create an OLE Insert Object dialog box. This class, which creates a dialog box that conforms totally to the OLE user interface (UI) guidelines, handles all the work of reading the registry for a list of available servers and enabling the user to select one.

When the user chooses which type of object to create, you create an object of the type `ColeCntCntrItem`. This class, which you define and implement, handles the interface between the container and the embedded or linked object. The class inherits from `COleClientItem` (a class that this chapter examines in detail later).

```
COleCntDoc* pDoc = GetDocument();
ASSERT_VALID(pDoc);
rc.SetRect(100,100,400,400);
pItem = new COleCntCntrItem(pDoc,rc);
ASSERT_VALID(pItem);

// Initialize the item from the dialog data.
if (!dlg.CreateItem(pItem))
{
     AfxThrowMemoryException();
}
ASSERT_VALID(pItem);

//------
// If the newly created object was created from the
// list of available servers, you activate the server
// to edit the object.
// If the object was created from a disk file, the
// presentation data is displayed.
if (dlg.GetSelectionType() == COleInsertDialog::createNewItem)
```

```
        pItem->DoVerb(OLEIVERB_SHOW, this);
    ASSERT_VALID(pItem);

    // Set the newly created object to be
    // the current object.
    m_pSelection = pItem;
    pDoc->UpdateAllViews(NULL);
```

The next step is to call `dlg.CreateItem` with a pointer to the newly created object. `dlg.CreateItem` calls the `Create` method appropriate for the type of OLE object that you are creating—a linked object from a disk file, an embedded object from a disk file, or a new object. If you are creating a new object, for example, `dlg.CreateItem` calls the method `COleClientItem::CreateNewItem`.

This method creates the new object by first calling `OleCreate` with the selected CLSID. The method then establishes a Data Advise Sink, to set up an asynchronous notification link for data changes, and a View Advise Sink, for notification of changes to the presentation data.

The method then calls `SetHostNames` to inform the object server of the container's name and the document in which the object is to be contained. The server uses these names in its Return To and Update menus.

When you initially create an object in this way, a strong reference lock is placed on the object. This lock is not suitable for a container, so `OleSetContainedObject` is then called to replace the strong lock with a weak one. A weak lock ensures that the container shuts down correctly when you close it.

At this point, you have created and loaded your object. If you are creating a new object from one of the servers listed in the Insert Object dialog box, you then activate the object to enable the user to create the initial data. If the data already exists, as in the case of a disk file, you skip the activation.

A pointer to the object is then stored in the `m_pSelection` class member and you call `UpdateAllViews` to refresh the display and show the object.

Drawing the Object

The `Draw` method is quite simple at this stage. You have only one object to draw and a tracker rectangle. To draw the object, you call its `Draw` method, passing a valid device context and a positioning rectangle.

The default implementation of `COleClientItem::Draw` queries the object for an `IViewObject` interface pointer. After the pointer is retrieved, you call the `IViewObject::Draw` method to draw the object. The default handler in OLE then plays the presentation metafile into the selected device.

Next, you draw a tracker rectangle around the object. Normally, you would draw the rectangle around a selected object only. However, as you currently have only one object and it is always selected, the tracker rectangle is always drawn.

The tracker rectangle enables the user to move and resize an object within the container. The rectangle also provides feedback to the user about the current state of the object. For example, objects that are opened in separate windows display a hatched pattern across the embedded object in the container.

Activating the Object

You can activate the object in two ways: by choosing it from the **E**dit menu or by double-clicking the object.

When an object is selected in a container, the framework adds the object's name to a cascaded submenu on the **E**dit menu. The submenu offers three options:

- *Edit the object.* This option activates the object in place.
- *Open the object.* This option is similar to the OLE 1.0 method of activating objects. The server is launched in a separate window.
- *Convert the object.* This option enables the user to convert the object from one type to another.

These three options are also available through a popup context menu that you activate by clicking the object with the right mouse button.

Double-clicking the object opens it in place. If you hold down the Ctrl key while double-clicking, you open the object in a separate window.

In your method for handling the mouse double-click, you first check for the status of the Ctrl keys and then call `COleClientItem::DoVerb` with the appropriate verb:

```
void COleCntView::OnLButtonDblClk(UINT, CPoint)
{
     //-------
     // Double-click activates the main verb
     // for the object.
     //
     if (m_pSelection != NULL)
     {
          BeginWaitCursor();

          LONG iVerb = OLEIVERB_PRIMARY;
          //----
```

```
            // If the Ctrl key is held down,
            // you activate in a separate
            // window.
            if (GetKeyState(VK_CONTROL) < 0)
            {
                iVerb = OLEIVERB_OPEN;
            }

            m_pSelection->DoVerb(iVerb, this);

            EndWaitCursor();
        }
    }
```

Activating an embedded object in place in a container is probably one of the more complex processes in OLE. The process requires a complicated interaction between the server owning the object and the container containing it. After you see what this process involves, you will forever be a convert to frameworks such as MFC.

The problem with this process isn't that the concepts are hard to grasp (after some initial mental wrestling, you will master them). Nor is the actual coding all that difficult (I know, because I've done it). The problem is that the process is loaded with details that you have to handle. You have to manage everything from routing accelerator keys to correctly placing the resized objects when they are in-place active. In other words, this is a perfect problem for a framework to solve.

Nevertheless, let's take a brief look at what is involved in this process. Normally, a container implements two COM interfaces specifically to support object embedding: `IOleClientSite` and `IAdviseSink`. To support in-place activation, the container also must implement `IOleInPlaceFrame`, `IOleInPlaceSite`, and `IOleInPlaceUIWindow`.

Object servers normally implement `IOleObject`, `IDataObject`, and `IPersistStorage`. To support in-place activation, the servers also must support `IOleInPlaceObject` and `IOleInPlaceActiveObject`.

The steps for activating an object in place are as follows:

1. The object first checks whether the container supports in-place activation, by calling `QueryInterface` for the `IOleInPlaceSite` interface. A container that supports this interface also supports in-place activation.

2. The object then calls `IOleInPlaceSite::CanInPlaceActivate` to check whether the container will allow this object to activate in place. Not all objects can be activated in place. For example, an object being displayed as an icon cannot be activated in place.

II

Using MFC

3. The object next retrieves pointers to the `IOleInPlaceUIWindow` and the `IOleInPlaceFrame` interfaces. These interfaces are implemented in separate objects, so the object does not use `QueryInterface` to retrieve them. Instead, the object retrieves both pointers by calling `IOleInPlaceSite::GetWindowContext`.

4. The `GetWindowContext` function also returns information about the position of the object within the container, whether the container is an MDI application, and the container's accelerator table. The object uses the positioning information to create an editing window for the object's data.

5. The object then changes the container's title bar to reflect the name of the object's server.

6. A hatched border is displayed around the object to indicate to the user that it is activated in place.

7. The next step, *menu merging,* merges the menu of the object with that of the container. (Chapter 1, "General Concepts," discusses menu merging.)

8. The object next negotiates with the container for border space for such frame adornments as toolbars. For objects like spreadsheets, these adornments also are placed around the object.

9. The object must now set in place special handling of keyboard accelerators. Although the object normally receives all keystrokes because it has the focus, accelerators are routed to the container's message pump. The container is responsible for passing these accelerators to the in-place active object.

10. If the container has a status bar, the container shares it with the object. Although the container maintains control of the status bar, the in-place object will send its status messages to it.

11. Finally, the container must handle any scrolling and resizing of the in-place object.

Okay, I lied—it *is* hard to code all this stuff. The only consolation is that once you have it working, you can reuse the code as necessary.

However, there is an easier way: use the framework. MFC is very successful at implementing this process and hiding its details from you. In fact, MFC performs all the preceding steps when you call `COleClientItem::DoVerb`.

Deactivating the Object

To deactivate the in-place object, you call the `COleClientItem::Close` method. You usually deactivate the object in response to the user pressing the Esc key or clicking with the mouse somewhere in the container outside of the active object.

```
        //-------
        // Close any in-place active item on this view.
        // The user pressed the Esc key.
        //
        COleClientItem* pActiveItem =
        ➥GetDocument()->GetInPlaceActiveItem(this);
        if (pActiveItem != NULL)
        {
             pActiveItem->Close();
        }
        ASSERT(GetDocument()->GetInPlaceActiveItem(this) == NULL);
    }
```

Besides deactivating the object, this method returns the container to its previous state. However, the method does not shut down the object server. This is actually an optimization trick to increase performance if an object is repeatedly activated and deactivated. The server is shut down only when the container closes.

Sizing the Object

You resize the container's object in two cases: when the object is not active, and when it is in-place active.

When the object is not active, the container normally displays a metafile that represents the object's contents. If the user selects the object and sizes the tracking rectangle that you have placed around it, you call the object's `Draw` method to redraw the metafile.

The OLE libraries' default handler actually performs the drawing. The presentation data is stored in a special stream within the object's storage. This combination of using the default handler to draw the object and storing the presentation data separately is done for performance reasons.

The important point is that the object server never has to be called to render the object to the screen or the printer.

The second case—when the object is in-place active and the user resizes the container or scrolls the container—is more complicated. In this case, you inform the object of the change in its surroundings by calling `COleClientItem::SetItemRects`. No parameters are passed, so the implementation uses the default clipping rectangle and positioning rectangle.

The implementation then calls `IOleInPlaceObject::SetObjectRects`. The following code shows the implementation of `IOleInPlaceObject::SetObjectRects`.

```
{
    ASSERT_VALID(this);
    ASSERT(m_lpObject != NULL);
    ASSERT(IsInPlaceActive());
    ASSERT(lpPosRect == NULL ||
        AfxIsValidAddress(lpPosRect, sizeof(RECT), FALSE));
    ASSERT(lpClipRect == NULL ||
        AfxIsValidAddress(lpClipRect, sizeof(RECT), FALSE));

    // get IOleInPlaceObject interface
    LPOLEINPLACEOBJECT lpInPlaceObject =
        _AFXQUERYINTERFACE(m_lpObject, IOleInPlaceObject);
    if (lpInPlaceObject == NULL)
        return FALSE;   // perhaps server crashed?

    // use OnGetPosRect if rectangle is not specified
    CRect rectPos;
    if (lpPosRect == NULL)
    {
        ASSERT(lpClipRect == NULL);
        OnGetItemPosition(rectPos);
        lpPosRect = &rectPos;
    }
    // use OnGetClipRect if clipping rectangle is not specified
    CRect rectClip;
    if (lpClipRect == NULL)
    {
        OnGetClipRect(rectClip);
        lpClipRect = &rectClip;
    }
    ASSERT(lpPosRect != NULL);
    ASSERT(lpClipRect != NULL);

    // notify the server of the new item rectangles
    m_scLast = GetScode(lpInPlaceObject->SetObjectRects(
        lpPosRect, lpClipRect));
    lpInPlaceObject->Release();

    // remember position rectangle as cached position
    return !FAILED(m_scLast);
}
```

As you can see, the framework handles most of the details for you. In this case, when the object is in-place active, the only method that you have to implement is `OnChangeItemPosition`. The following code is the implementation of `OnChangeItemPosition`:

```
BOOL COleCntCntrItem::OnChangeItemPosition(const CRect& rectPos)
{
    ASSERT_VALID(this);
```

```
    //---------------
    // During in-place activation,
    // COleCntCntrItem::OnChangeItemPosition()
    // is called by the server to change the position of the in-place
    // window. Usually this is as a result of the data in the server
    // document changing so that the extent has changed, or as a result
    // of in-place resizing.
    //
    // The default here is to call the base class, which calls
    // COleClientItem::SetItemRects to move the item
    // to the new position.

    if (rectPos != m_rc)
    {
        // invalidate old item
        Invalidate();
        // update to new rectangle
        m_rc = rectPos;

        GetDocument()->SetModifiedFlag();
        GetExtent(&m_ObjExt);

        // and invalidate new
        Invalidate();
    }
    if (!COleClientItem::OnChangeItemPosition(rectPos))
        return FALSE;

    return TRUE;
}
```


Assigning the Context Menu

The OLE UI guidelines require that you assign a context or popup menu to each object. This menu, which is usually accessed by the right mouse button, displays the verbs that can be used on the object. The menu also enables the user to delete the object, or copy or cut the object to the clipboard.

Each object has a unique set of verbs attached to it. These verbs are usually presented to the user in a cascaded menu that is placed on the popup menu or the container's Edit menu.

The framework places the verbs on the menu by implementing the method `COleDocument::OnUpdateObjectVerbMenu`.

The code in listings 6.2 and 6.3 is the implementation of the `CView` module.

Listing 6.2 OLECNVW.H

```
// Forward declarations
class COleCntView;
class COleCntCntrItem;
//----------------------------------------------------------------------
class CMyRectTracker : public CRectTracker
{
public:
     CMyRectTracker(COleCntView *pView) {this->pView = pView;}
     virtual ~CMyRectTracker() {};
     virtual void DrawTrackerRect( LPCRECT lpRect, CWnd* pWndClipTo,
         CDC* pDC, CWnd* pWnd );
private:
     COleCntView *pView;
};
//----------------------------------------------------------------------
class COleCntView : public CView
{
protected: // create from serialization only
     COleCntView();
     DECLARE_DYNCREATE(COleCntView)

// Attributes
public:
     COleCntDoc* GetDocument();
     // m_pSelection holds the selection to the current COleCntCntrItem.
     // For many applications, such a member variable isn't adequate to
     // represent a selection, such as a multiple selection or a selection
     // of objects that are not COleCntCntrItem objects. This selection
     // mechanism is provided just to help you get started.

     // TODO: replace this selection mechanism with one appropriate
     // to your application.
     COleCntCntrItem* m_pSelection;
     BOOL m_bInDrag;


// Operations
public:
     void SetupTracker(CMyRectTracker* pTracker,
         COleCntCntrItem* pItem,CRect* pTrueRect = NULL);
     void SetStatusText(LPCSTR lpcStr);
     COleCntCntrItem *GetSelection() const;
     COleCntCntrItem* GetHitItem(CPoint point);
// Implementation
public:
     virtual ~COleCntView();
     virtual void OnDraw(CDC* pDC);  // overridden to draw this view
#ifdef _DEBUG
     virtual void AssertValid() const;
     virtual void Dump(CDumpContext& dc) const;
#endif

protected:
     virtual void OnInitialUpdate(); // called first time after construct
```

```
    // Printing support
    virtual BOOL OnPreparePrinting(CPrintInfo* pInfo);
    virtual void OnBeginPrinting(CDC* pDC, CPrintInfo* pInfo);
    virtual void OnEndPrinting(CDC* pDC, CPrintInfo* pInfo);

    // OLE container support
    virtual BOOL IsSelected(const CObject* pDocItem) const;

// Generated message-map functions
protected:
    //{{AFX_MSG(COleCntView)
    afx_msg void OnSetFocus(CWnd* pOldWnd);
    afx_msg void OnSize(UINT nType, int cx, int cy);
    afx_msg void OnInsertObject();
    afx_msg void OnCancelEdit();
    afx_msg void OnLButtonDblClk(UINT nFlags, CPoint point);
    afx_msg void OnLButtonDown(UINT nFlags, CPoint point);
    afx_msg BOOL OnSetCursor(CWnd* pWnd, UINT nHitTest, UINT message);
    afx_msg void OnRButtonDown(UINT nFlags, CPoint point);
    //}}AFX_MSG
    DECLARE_MESSAGE_MAP()
};

#ifndef _DEBUG  // debug version in olecnvw.cpp
inline COleCntDoc* COleCntView::GetDocument()
   { return (COleCntDoc*)m_pDocument; }
#endif
```

Listing 6.3 OLECNVW.CPP

```
#include "stdafx.h"
#include "afxpriv.h"

#include "olecnt.h"

#include "olecndoc.h"
#include "cntritem.h"
#include "olecnvw.h"

#ifdef _DEBUG
#undef THIS_FILE
static char BASED_CODE THIS_FILE[] = __FILE__;
#endif

/////////////////////////////////////////////////////////////////////////////
// COleCntView

IMPLEMENT_DYNCREATE(COleCntView, CView)

BEGIN_MESSAGE_MAP(COleCntView, CView)
    //{{AFX_MSG_MAP(COleCntView)
    ON_WM_SETFOCUS()
```

(continues)

II

Using MFC

Listing 6.3 Continued

```
ON_WM_SIZE()
     ON_COMMAND(ID_OLE_INSERT_NEW, OnInsertObject)
     ON_COMMAND(ID_CANCEL_EDIT, OnCancelEdit)
     ON_WM_LBUTTONDBLCLK()
     ON_WM_LBUTTONDOWN()
     ON_WM_SETCURSOR()
     ON_WM_RBUTTONDOWN()
     //}}AFX_MSG_MAP
     // Standard printing commands
     ON_COMMAND(ID_FILE_PRINT, CView::OnFilePrint)
     ON_COMMAND(ID_FILE_PRINT_PREVIEW, CView::OnFilePrintPreview)
END_MESSAGE_MAP()

//--------------------------------------------------------------------
void CMyRectTracker::DrawTrackerRect( LPCRECT lpRect,
     CWnd* pWndClipTo, CDC* pDC, CWnd* pWnd )
{
     //-----------
     // This method is from the CrectTracker class.
     // You draw the focus rectangle and update the
     // status bar with the size of the currently
     // selected object.

     char szMsg[144];
     pDC->DrawFocusRect(lpRect);

     CString str;
     pView->GetSelection()->GetUserType(USERCLASSTYPE_FULL,str);
     wsprintf(szMsg,"%s %d  x  %d", (LPCSTR)str,lpRect->
     ➥right-lpRect->left,lpRect->bottom-lpRect->top);
     pView->SetStatusText(szMsg);
}
//--------------------------------------------------------------------

//////////////////////////////////////////////////////////////////////
// COleCntView construction/destruction
COleCntView::COleCntView()
{
     m_pSelection = NULL;
}
//--------------------------------------------------------------------
COleCntView::~COleCntView()
{
}
//--------------------------------------------------------------------
COleCntCntrItem *COleCntView::GetSelection() const
{
     //--------
     // Return the only object that you allow
     // in this simple container.
     //
     return m_pSelection;
}
```

```
//------------------------------------------------------------------
void COleCntView::SetupTracker(CMyRectTracker* pTracker,
    COleCntCntrItem* pItem, CRect* pTrueRect)
{
     //--------
     // Set up the tracker size and style.
     //
     ASSERT(pTracker != NULL);
     ASSERT(pItem != NULL);

     pTracker->m_rect = pItem->m_rc;

     // set minimum size for the OLE items
     pTracker->m_sizeMin.cx = 8;
     pTracker->m_sizeMin.cy = 8;

     pTracker->m_nStyle = 0;

     // set up resize handles if the item is selected
     if (pItem == m_pSelection)
     {
          pTracker->m_nStyle ¦= CMyRectTracker::resizeInside;
     }

     // put correct border, depending on item type
     if (pItem->GetType() == OT_LINK)
          pTracker->m_nStyle ¦= CMyRectTracker::dottedLine;
     else
          pTracker->m_nStyle ¦= CMyRectTracker::solidLine;

     // put hatching over the item if it is currently open
     if (pItem->GetItemState() == COleClientItem::openState ¦¦
          pItem->GetItemState() == COleClientItem::activeUIState)
     {
          pTracker->m_nStyle ¦= CMyRectTracker::hatchInside;
     }

     if (pTrueRect != NULL)
          pTracker->GetTrueRect(pTrueRect);
}
//------------------------------------------------------------------
void COleCntView::OnDraw(CDC* pDC)
{
     //--------
     // Central drawing method for screen and printer I/O.
     // You delegate the drawing of the object to the object
     // itself and then draw a tracker rectangle around it.
     COleCntDoc* pDoc = GetDocument();
     ASSERT_VALID(pDoc);

     if (m_pSelection == NULL)
     {
          POSITION pos = pDoc->GetStartPosition();
```

(continues)

Listing 6.3 Continued

```
        m_pSelection = (COleCntCntrItem*)pDoc->GetNextClientItem(pos);
    }

    if (m_pSelection != NULL)
    {
        if (m_pSelection->IsKindOf(RUNTIME_CLASS(COleCntCntrItem)))
        {
            m_pSelection->Draw(pDC, m_pSelection->m_rc);

            if (!pDC->IsPrinting() )
            {
                //------
                // Draw the tracker. You have only one object at this
                // stage of the container development and always draw
                // the tracker except if you are in print preview or
                // printing.
                CMyRectTracker tracker(this);
                CRect rectTrue;
                SetupTracker(&tracker, m_pSelection, &rectTrue);
                tracker.Draw(pDC);
            }
        }
    }
}
//----------------------------------------------------------------------
void COleCntView::OnInitialUpdate()
{
    CView::OnInitialUpdate();

    // TODO: remove this code when final selection model code is written
    m_pSelection = NULL;    // initialize selection

}
/////////////////////////////////////////////////////////////////////////////
// COleCntView printing
BOOL COleCntView::OnPreparePrinting(CPrintInfo* pInfo)
{
    // default preparation
    return DoPreparePrinting(pInfo);
}
//----------------------------------------------------------------------
void COleCntView::OnBeginPrinting(CDC* /*pDC*/, CPrintInfo* /*pInfo*/)
{
    // TODO: add extra initialization before printing
}
//----------------------------------------------------------------------
void COleCntView::OnEndPrinting(CDC* /*pDC*/, CPrintInfo* /*pInfo*/)
{
    // TODO: add cleanup after printing
}
/////////////////////////////////////////////////////////////////////////////
// OLE Client support and commands

BOOL COleCntView::IsSelected(const CObject* pDocItem) const
```

```
{
    // The following implementation is adequate if your selection
    // consists of only COleCntCntrItem objects. To handle different
    // selection mechanisms, you should replace this implementation.

    return pDocItem == m_pSelection;
}
//--------------------------------------------------------------------
void COleCntView::OnInsertObject()
{
    CRect rc;

    //----------
    // Invoke the standard Insert Object dialog box to obtain
    //  information for a new COleCntCntrItem object.
    //

    COleInsertDialog dlg;
    if (dlg.DoModal() != IDOK)
        return;

    BeginWaitCursor();

    COleCntCntrItem* pItem = NULL;
    TRY
    {
        // Create the new item connected to this document.
        COleCntDoc* pDoc = GetDocument();
        ASSERT_VALID(pDoc);
        rc.SetRect(100,100,400,400);
        pItem = new COleCntCntrItem(pDoc,rc);
        ASSERT_VALID(pItem);

        // Initialize the item from the dialog data.
        if (!dlg.CreateItem(pItem))
        {
            AfxThrowMemoryException();
        }
        ASSERT_VALID(pItem);

        //-------
        // If the newly created object was created from the
        // list of available servers, you activate the server
        // to edit the object.
        // If the object was created from a disk file,
        // you display the presentation data.
        if (dlg.GetSelectionType() ==COleInsertDialog::createNewItem)
            pItem->DoVerb(OLEIVERB_SHOW, this);

        ASSERT_VALID(pItem);

        // Set the newly created object
        // to be the current object.
```

(continues)

Listing 6.3 Continued

```
        m_pSelection = pItem;
            pDoc->UpdateAllViews(NULL);
        }
        CATCH(CException, e)
        {
            if (pItem != NULL)
            {
                ASSERT_VALID(pItem);
                pItem->Delete();
            }
            AfxMessageBox(IDP_FAILED_TO_CREATE);
        }
        END_CATCH

        EndWaitCursor();
    }
    //---------------------------------------------------------------------
    void COleCntView::OnCancelEdit()
    {
        //------
        // Close any in-place active item on this view.
        // The user pressed the Esc key.
        //
        COleClientItem* pActiveItem =
        ➥GetDocument()->GetInPlaceActiveItem(this);
        if (pActiveItem != NULL)
        {
            pActiveItem->Close();
        }
        ASSERT(GetDocument()->GetInPlaceActiveItem(this) == NULL);
    }
    //---------------------------------------------------------------------
    // Special handling of OnSetFocus and OnSize is required for a container
    // when an object is being edited in place.
    //
    void COleCntView::OnSetFocus(CWnd* pOldWnd)
    {
        COleClientItem* pActiveItem =
        ➥GetDocument()->GetInPlaceActiveItem(this);
        if (pActiveItem != NULL &&
            pActiveItem->GetItemState() == COleClientItem::activeUIState)
        {
            // need to set focus to this item if it is in the same view
            CWnd* pWnd = pActiveItem->GetInPlaceWindow();
            if (pWnd != NULL)
            {
                pWnd->SetFocus();   // don't call the base class
                return;
            }
        }

        CView::OnSetFocus(pOldWnd);
    }
```

```
//------------------------------------------------------------------
void COleCntView::OnSize(UINT nType, int cx, int cy)
{
     CView::OnSize(nType, cx, cy);
     COleClientItem* pActiveItem =
     ➥GetDocument()->GetInPlaceActiveItem(this);

     if (pActiveItem != NULL)
          pActiveItem->SetItemRects();
}
//------------------------------------------------------------------
void COleCntView::SetStatusText(LPCSTR lpcStr)
{
     ::SendMessage(AfxGetApp()->m_pMainWnd->m_hWnd,
         WM_SETMESSAGESTRING,0,(LONG)lpcStr);
}
////////////////////////////////////////////////////////////////////
// COleCntView diagnostics
#ifdef _DEBUG
void COleCntView::AssertValid() const
{
     CView::AssertValid();
}

void COleCntView::Dump(CDumpContext& dc) const
{
     CView::Dump(dc);
}
//------------------------------------------------------------------
COleCntDoc* COleCntView::GetDocument() // nondebug version is inline
{
     ASSERT(m_pDocument->IsKindOf(RUNTIME_CLASS(COleCntDoc)));
     return (COleCntDoc*)m_pDocument;
}
#endif //_DEBUG
//==================================================================
// Mouse handlers.
//
void COleCntView::OnLButtonDblClk(UINT, CPoint)
{
     //-------
     // Double-click activates the main verb
     // for the object.
     //
     if (m_pSelection != NULL)
     {
          BeginWaitCursor();

          LONG iVerb = OLEIVERB_PRIMARY;
          //----
          // If the Ctrl key is held down,
          // you activate in a separate window.
```

(continues)

II

Using MFC

Listing 6.3 Continued

```
            if (GetKeyState(VK_CONTROL) < 0)
            {
                 iVerb = OLEIVERB_OPEN;
            }

            // try to get initial presentation data
            //m_pSelection->UpdateLink();
            //m_pSelection->UpdateExtent();

            m_pSelection->DoVerb(iVerb, this);

            EndWaitCursor();
       }
}
//-----------------------------------------------------------------
void COleCntView::OnRButtonDown(UINT nFlags, CPoint point)
{
       //-------------
       // User pressed the right mouse button.
       // Show the object menu for the selected object.
       if (m_pSelection != NULL)
       {
            CMenu bar;
            if (bar.LoadMenu(ID_OBJECT_POPUP_MENU))
            {
                 CMenu& popup = *bar.GetSubMenu(0);
                 ASSERT(popup.m_hMenu != NULL);

                 ClientToScreen(&point);
                 popup.TrackPopupMenu(TPM_RIGHTBUTTON,point.x,
                     point.y,AfxGetMainWnd());
            }
       }
}
//-----------------------------------------------------------------
void COleCntView::OnLButtonDown(UINT nFlags, CPoint point)
{
       COleCntCntrItem* pItemHit = GetHitItem(point);


       if (pItemHit == NULL)
            return;

       //SetSelection(pItemHit);

       CRect rectLimit;
       GetClientRect(rectLimit);

       CMyRectTracker tracker(this);
       SetupTracker(&tracker, pItemHit);

       UpdateWindow(); // update before entering the tracker
```

```
    if (tracker.HitTest(point) == CMyRectTracker::hitMiddle)
                                                    // moving, not sizing
    {
        //------
        // Note: This code is not yet functional in Chapter 6.
        // You add the full OLE drag-drop support in Chapter 7.

        // determine mouse position offset from the item itself
        CRect rect = pItemHit->m_rc;
        CRect rect2 = rect;
        CPoint ptOffset(point.x - rect.left, point.y - rect.top);

        // determine sensitivity rectangle (determines when drag starts)
        CRect rectDrag(rect.left, rect.top, rect.left+1, rect.top+1);

        // execute the drag-drop operation
        m_bInDrag = TRUE;
        ClientToScreen(&rect);  // must be in screen coordinates
        ClientToScreen(&rectDrag);
        DROPEFFECT dropEffect = pItemHit->DoDragDrop(rect, ptOffset,
            TRUE, DROPEFFECT_COPY¦DROPEFFECT_MOVE, &rectDrag);
        if (m_bInDrag == FALSE) // move in same window
        {
            return;
        }
        m_bInDrag = FALSE;

        if (dropEffect == DROPEFFECT_MOVE)
        {
            // the item was moved (essentially a copy with delete)
            pItemHit->Invalidate();

            if (m_pSelection == pItemHit)
                m_pSelection = NULL;
            GetDocument()->DeleteItem(pItemHit);
        }
    }
    else if (tracker.Track(this, point))
    {
        pItemHit->Move(tracker.m_rect);
        GetDocument()->SetModifiedFlag();
    }
}
//-----------------------------------------------------------------
BOOL COleCntView::OnSetCursor(CWnd* pWnd, UINT nHitTest, UINT message)
{
    if (pWnd == this && m_pSelection != NULL)
    {
        CMyRectTracker tracker(this);
        SetupTracker(&tracker, m_pSelection);

        if (tracker.SetCursor(this, nHitTest))
```

(continues)

II

Using MFC

Listing 6.3 Continued

```
            return TRUE;
        }
        return CView::OnSetCursor(pWnd, nHitTest, message);
}
//-------------------------------------------------------------
COleCntCntrItem* COleCntView::GetHitItem(CPoint point)
{
        COleCntDoc* pDoc = GetDocument();
        COleCntCntrItem* pItemHit = NULL;

        // Find the item hit by the mouse
        POSITION pos = pDoc->GetStartPosition();
        if (pos != NULL)
        {
              COleCntCntrItem* pItem =
              ➥(COleCntCntrItem*)pDoc->GetNextItem(pos);
              if (pItem->IsKindOf(RUNTIME_CLASS(COleCntCntrItem)))
              {
                    CMyRectTracker tracker(this);
                    SetupTracker(&tracker, pItem);

                    if (tracker.HitTest(point) >= 0)
                    {
                          pItemHit = pItem;
                    }
              }
        }
        return pItemHit;
}
//-------------------------------------------------------------
//-------------------------------------------------------------
```

The Document Module

At this stage in the development of your container, you implement only one method of interest in the document module: `Serialize`. The call to `COleDocument::Serialize(ar)` ensures that your single object is saved and restored each time that you open the document.

You also implement the MAP entries that enable the clipboard to handle embedded and linked objects. You now delegate the clipboard input/output (I/O) to the framework. In Chapter 7, you complete the entire clipboard support.

Listings 6.4 and 6.5 show the source code for the implementation of your `CDocument` class.

Listing 6.4 OLECNDOC.H

```
// Forward declarations
class COleCntCntrItem;


class COleCntDoc : public COleDocument
{
protected: // create from serialization only
     COleCntDoc();
     DECLARE_DYNCREATE(COleCntDoc)

// Attributes
public:
// Operations
public:

// Implementation
public:
     virtual ~COleCntDoc();
     virtual void Serialize(CArchive& ar);  // overridden for document I/O
#ifdef _DEBUG
     virtual void AssertValid() const;
     virtual void Dump(CDumpContext& dc) const;
#endif
     void DeleteItem(COleCntCntrItem* pItem);
protected:
     virtual BOOL OnNewDocument();

// Generated message-map functions
protected:
     //{{AFX_MSG(COleCntDoc)
         // NOTE - the ClassWizard adds and removes member functions here.
         //    DO NOT EDIT what you see in these blocks of generated code!
     //}}AFX_MSG
     DECLARE_MESSAGE_MAP()
};
```

Listing 6.5 OLECNDOC.CPP

```
#include "stdafx.h"
#include "olecnt.h"

#include "cntritem.h"
#include "olecndoc.h"


#ifdef _DEBUG
#undef THIS_FILE
static char BASED_CODE THIS_FILE[] = __FILE__;
#endif
```

(continues)

Listing 6.5 Continued

```
/////////////////////////////////////////////////////////////////////////////
// COleCntDoc
//
IMPLEMENT_DYNCREATE(COleCntDoc, COleDocument)

BEGIN_MESSAGE_MAP(COleCntDoc, COleDocument)
    //{{AFX_MSG_MAP(COleCntDoc)
        // NOTE - the ClassWizard adds and removes mapping macros here.
        //    DO NOT EDIT what you see in these blocks of generated code!
    //}}AFX_MSG_MAP
    // Enable default OLE container implementation
    ON_UPDATE_COMMAND_UI(ID_EDIT_PASTE, COleDocument::OnUpdatePasteMenu)
    ON_UPDATE_COMMAND_UI(ID_EDIT_PASTE_LINK,
        COleDocument::OnUpdatePasteLinkMenu)
    ON_UPDATE_COMMAND_UI(ID_OLE_EDIT_LINKS,
        COleDocument::OnUpdateEditLinksMenu)
    ON_COMMAND(ID_OLE_EDIT_LINKS, COleDocument::OnEditLinks)
    ON_UPDATE_COMMAND_UI(ID_OLE_VERB_FIRST,
        COleDocument::OnUpdateObjectVerbMenu)
    ON_UPDATE_COMMAND_UI(ID_OLE_EDIT_CONVERT,
        COleDocument::OnUpdateObjectVerbMenu)
    ON_COMMAND(ID_OLE_EDIT_CONVERT, COleDocument::OnEditConvert)
END_MESSAGE_MAP()

/////////////////////////////////////////////////////////////////////////////
// COleCntDoc construction/destruction
//
COleCntDoc::COleCntDoc()
{
    // For most containers, using compound files is a good idea.
    EnableCompoundFile();

    // TODO: add one-time construction code here
}

COleCntDoc::~COleCntDoc()
{
}
//-------------------------------------------------------------------
void COleCntDoc::DeleteItem(COleCntCntrItem* pItem)
{
    ASSERT(pItem->GetDocument() == this);

    SetModifiedFlag();
    UpdateAllViews(NULL, 1, pItem); // pItem will be deleted
    pItem->Delete();
}
//-------------------------------------------------------------------
BOOL COleCntDoc::OnNewDocument()
{
    if (!COleDocument::OnNewDocument())
        return FALSE;
```

```
    // TODO: add reinitialization code here
    // (SDI documents will reuse this document)

    return TRUE;
}
//-------------------------------------------------------------------
/////////////////////////////////////////////////////////////////////
//
// COleCntDoc serialization

void COleCntDoc::Serialize(CArchive& ar)
{
    if (ar.IsStoring())
    {
        // TODO: add storing code here
    }
    else
    {
        // TODO: add loading code here
    }

    // Calling the base class COleDocument enables serialization
    //  of the container document's COleClientItem objects.
    COleDocument::Serialize(ar);
}
/////////////////////////////////////////////////////////////////////
//
// COleCntDoc diagnostics
#ifdef _DEBUG
void COleCntDoc::AssertValid() const
{
    COleDocument::AssertValid();
}

void COleCntDoc::Dump(CDumpContext& dc) const
{
    COleDocument::Dump(dc);
}
#endif //_DEBUG

/////////////////////////////////////////////////////////////////////
//
// COleCntDoc commands

//-------------------------------------------------------------------
//-------------------------------------------------------------------
```

The Object Interface Module

The `COleClientItem` class provides the interface between your container and the embedded or linked objects. The objects use these interfaces to inform the container of changes to the objects' size, position, state, and content.

You have to implement `COleClientItem::OnChange` and, if you want to support in-place activation, `COleClientItem::OnGetItemPosition`. You also implement four other methods: `OnChangeItemPosition`, `OnDeactivateUI`, `Move`, and `Serialize`.

The *OnChange* Method

The `OnChange` method is called whenever the user changes data in the in-place object. The method is also called when the user closes or saves data in the object.

Your first implementation of this method simply updates all open views in your application. In the next chapter, you add more code to this method.

The *OnChangeItemPosition* Method

The framework calls the `OnChangeItemPosition` method whenever the object changes its extents.

You check whether the object really has moved from its last position; if it has, you update the object by invalidating both its old and new positions. You then set the dirty bit on the document so that you remember to save the object's new position.

Finally, you pass the call to the base class. The default implementation calls `IOleInPlaceObject::SetObjectRects` to inform the server of the object's new position within the container. The container, which controls how much space is available to each object, can refuse to resize the object.

The *OnGetItemPosition* Method

The framework calls the `OnGetItemPosition` method when the object is about to be in-place activated. The method returns to the object server the object's current position.

Your implementation of this method is quite simple: you simply return the stored rectangle that you keep for each object.

The *OnDeactivateUI* Method

The `OnDeactivateUI` method is called when the user deactivates the in-place active object. The default implementation restores the merged menus and removes any toolbars, frame adornments, or object adornments. The object also removes its editing window.

You then call `COleClientItem::Deactivate` to release any reference counters on the object's in-place interfaces.

If you want to support the undo capability during in-place activation, you instead call `COleClientItem::DeactivateUI`. This method forces the object to hide its interface but to retain its undo buffer. You can then restore the last saved state by calling `COleClientItem::ReactivateAndUndo`.

The *Move* Method

You do not use the `Move` method until you implement the drag-drop capability in the next chapter. This method's purpose is to move the object to a new location within the container in response to the user selecting the object and dragging it.

If the object is in-place active during the move, you also call `SetItemRects` to inform the object server of the move.

The *Serialize* Method

To save and restore the object to your compound file, you must implement the `Serialize` method. You first call the base class implementation to enable the framework to save the object and its native data.

The base class implmentation begins by saving some version information and the framework-assigned name for the object. These names are in the form `Embedding` *nn*, where *nn* is a unique number assigned to the object. The object's display aspect is then saved. The display aspect specifies whether the object is currently displayed as an icon or whether the contents are displayed.

Next, you save the type of object. The object's type specifies whether the object is linked or embedded. Finally, the API function `OleSave` is called to save the actual contents to the open storage. You then save the current position and size of the object within the container.

Listings 6.6 and 6.7 show the source code for the implementation of your `COleClientItem` class.

Listing 6.6 CNTRITEM.H

```
class COleCntDoc;
class COleCntView;

class COleCntCntrItem : public COleClientItem
{
     DECLARE_SERIAL(COleCntCntrItem)

// Constructors
```

(continues)

Listing 6.6 Continued

```
public:
     COleCntCntrItem(COleCntDoc* pContainer,CRect& rc);
     COleCntCntrItem();

// Attributes
     CSize m_ObjExt;
     CRect m_rc;

public:
     COleCntDoc* GetDocument()
          { return (COleCntDoc*)COleClientItem::GetDocument(); }
     COleCntView* GetActiveView()
          { return (COleCntView*)COleClientItem::GetActiveView(); }

// Implementation
public:
     ~COleCntCntrItem();
#ifdef _DEBUG
     virtual void AssertValid() const;
     virtual void Dump(CDumpContext& dc) const;
#endif
     virtual void Serialize(CArchive& ar);
     virtual void OnGetItemPosition(CRect& rPosition);
     virtual void OnDeactivateUI(BOOL bUndoable);
     virtual void Invalidate(CView* pNotThisView = NULL);
     void Move(CRect &rc);
protected:
     virtual void OnChange(OLE_NOTIFICATION wNotification, DWORD dwParam);
     virtual BOOL OnChangeItemPosition(const CRect& rectPos);
};
```

Listing 6.7 OLECNT.CPP

```
#include "stdafx.h"
#include "olecnt.h"

#include "olecndoc.h"
#include "cntritem.h"

#ifdef _DEBUG
#undef THIS_FILE
static char BASED_CODE THIS_FILE[] = __FILE__;
#endif

/////////////////////////////////////////////////////////////////////////////
// COleCntCntrItem implementation

IMPLEMENT_SERIAL(COleCntCntrItem, COleClientItem, 0)
//---------------------------------------------------------------
COleCntCntrItem::COleCntCntrItem(COleCntDoc* pContainer, CRect& rc)
     : COleClientItem(pContainer)
```

```
{
     m_ObjExt.cx = 0;
     m_ObjExt.cy = 0;
     m_rc = rc;
}
//------------------------------------------------------------------
COleCntCntrItem::COleCntCntrItem()
{
     m_ObjExt.cx = 0;
     m_ObjExt.cy = 0;

     m_rc.SetRect(100, 100, 200,200);
}
//------------------------------------------------------------------
COleCntCntrItem::~COleCntCntrItem()
{

}
//------------------------------------------------------------------
void COleCntCntrItem::OnChange(OLE_NOTIFICATION nCode, DWORD dwParam)
{
     ASSERT_VALID(this);

     COleClientItem::OnChange(nCode, dwParam);

     // When an item is being edited (either in place or fully open),
     //  it sends OnChange notifications for changes in the state
     //  of the item or the visual appearance of its content.

     // TODO: invalidate the item by calling UpdateAllViews
     //  (with hints appropriate to your application)

     GetDocument()->UpdateAllViews(NULL);
          // for now, just update ALL views/no hints
}
//------------------------------------------------------------------
BOOL COleCntCntrItem::OnChangeItemPosition(const CRect& rectPos)
{
     ASSERT_VALID(this);

     //--------------
     // During in-place activation, COleCntCntrItem::OnChangeItemPosition
     // is called by the server to change the position of the in-place
     // window. Usually, this is a result of the data in the server
     // document changing so that the extent changes, or a result
     // of in-place resizing.
     //
     // The default is to call the base class, which calls
     // COleClientItem::SetItemRects to move the item
     // to the new position.
        SetObjectRects
     // First check whether you really have moved.
```

(continues)

II

Using MFC

Listing 6.7 Continued

```
    if (rectPos != m_rc)
     {
          Invalidate();
          m_rc = rectPos;
          Invalidate();
          // To force you to save the new position.
          GetDocument()->SetModifiedFlag();
     }

     if (!COleClientItem::OnChangeItemPosition(rectPos))
          return FALSE;

     return TRUE;
}
//---------------------------------------------------------------
void COleCntCntrItem::Invalidate(CView* pNotThisView)
{
     GetDocument()->UpdateAllViews(pNotThisView, 0, this);
}
//---------------------------------------------------------------
void COleCntCntrItem::OnGetItemPosition(CRect& rPosition)
{
     ASSERT_VALID(this);

     //--------
     //  During in-place activation, COleCntCntrItem::OnGetItemPosition
     //  is called to determine the location of this item. The default
     //  implementation created from AppWizard simply returns
     //  a hard-coded rectangle. Usually, this rectangle reflects
     //  the current position of the item relative to the view used
     //  for activation. You can obtain the view by calling
     //  COleCntCntrItem::GetActiveView.

     rPosition = m_rc;
}
//---------------------------------------------------------------
void COleCntCntrItem::OnDeactivateUI(BOOL bUndoable)
{
     COleClientItem::OnDeactivateUI(bUndoable);

     // Close an in-place active item whenever it removes the user
     //  interface. The action here should match as closely as possible
     //  the handling of the Esc key in the view.

     Deactivate();   // nothing fancy here -- just deactivate the object
}
//---------------------------------------------------------------
void COleCntCntrItem::Move(CRect &rc)
{
     // invalidate old rect
     Invalidate();
     // invalidate new
     m_rc = rc;
```

```
    Invalidate();

    // update item rect when in-place active
    if (IsInPlaceActive())
    {
        // You need to update the bounding
        // rectangle of the object if you are
        // in-place active.
        SetItemRects();
    }
}
//-----------------------------------------------------------------

void COleCntCntrItem::Serialize(CArchive& ar)
{
    ASSERT_VALID(this);

    //----------------------
    // Call the base class first to read in COleClientItem data.
    // Because this sets up the m_pDocument pointer returned from
    // COleCntCntrItem::GetDocument, it is a good idea to call
    // the base class Serialize first.
    COleClientItem::Serialize(ar);

    // now store/retrieve data specific to COleCntCntrItem
    if (ar.IsStoring())
    {
        WORD w = 0x5500;
        ar << w << m_rc << m_ObjExt;
    }
    else
    {
        WORD w;
        ar >> w >> m_rc >> m_ObjExt;
        if (w != 0x5500)
        {
           TRACE("Error restoring embedded object. Bad magic number\n");
           AfxThrowArchiveException(CArchiveException::generic);
        }
    }
}
//-----------------------------------------------------------------
/////////////////////////////////////////////////////////////////////////////
// COleCntCntrItem diagnostics

#ifdef _DEBUG
void COleCntCntrItem::AssertValid() const
{
    COleClientItem::AssertValid();
}
```

(continues)

Listing 6.7 Continued

```
void COleCntCntrItem::Dump(CDumpContext& dc) const
{
     COleClientItem::Dump(dc);
}
#endif
//-----------------------------------------------------------
//-----------------------------------------------------------
```

The Completed Container Skeleton

Figure 6.1 shows the OLE container that you have just created with MFC. An Excel 5.0 chart object is embedded in the container. By double-clicking this object, you activate the object in place.

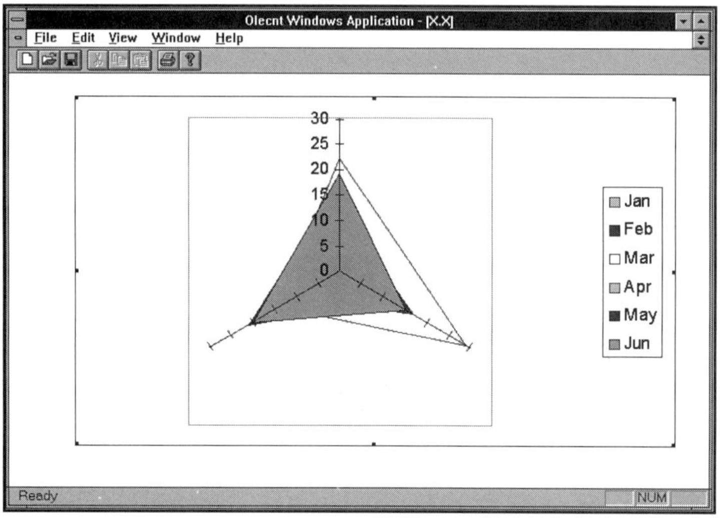

Fig. 6.1 The container with an embedded object.

From Here...

This concludes your look at the minimum requirements for implementing an OLE container in MFC. However, the container still lacks several features that you need to implement.

In the next chapter, you continue to develop this OLE container. You add support for multiple objects, a drag-drop capability, and full clipboard support.

Chapter 7

An MDI Linking Container

In this chapter, you continue to develop the OLE container that you began in the last chapter. You now concentrate on adding support for three important features:

- Full clipboard support
- Drag-drop support
- Linking support

COM Data Objects

In previous chapters, you saw how to define and use COM objects. As mentioned in Chapter 2, "The Component Object Model," one difference between a C++ object and a COM object is that you cannot directly access data in a COM object as you would in a C++ object. How do you access data that is stored in a COM object?

The answer is by using an interface known as `IDataObject`. Objects that support this interface are called *data objects*.

The `IDataObject` interface provides a rich and flexible means of transferring data between two processes. The key to its flexibility lies in the use of two new data structures: FORMATETC and STGMEDIUM.

In both standard clipboard input/output (I/O) and OLE 1.0, you transfer data by using global memory. Using global memory to store copies of large objects is very inefficient and degrades performance.

However, the introduction of these new FORMATETC and STGMEDIUM data structures gives an application a much wider choice of where the data resides and which type of data to transfer. The following sections examine both of these structures as well as the `IDataObject` interface.

The FORMATETC Structure

The FORMATETC structure is an enhancement to the standard clipboard formats. The structure is defined as follows:

```
typedef struct FARSTRUCT tagFORMATETC
{
    CLIPFORMAT          cfFormat;
    DVTARGETDEVICE FAR* ptd;
    DWORD               dwAspect;
    LONG                lindex;
    DWORD               tymed;
} FORMATETC, FAR* LPFORMATETC;
```

The following sections describe each of this structure's fields.

The *cfFormat* Field

The `cfFormat` field can contain a standard clipboard format, a private format that the application previously registered (with the Windows `RegisterClipboardFormat` API function), or one of the defined OLE formats. Table 7.1 describes the OLE formats.

Table 7.1 The Defined OLE Formats

OLE Format	Usage
Embedded source (CF_EMBEDSOURCE)	Creates an embedded object from an object application's native data
Link source (CF_LINKSOURCE)	Creates a new standard linked object
Custom link source (CF_CUSTOMLINKSOURCE)	Creates a new custom linked object
Embedded object (CF_EMBEDDEDOBJECT)	Creates an embedded or linked object from a container's existing embedded object
Object descriptor (CF_OBJECTDESCRIPTOR)	Describes the data being transferred and is made available with all transfers
Link source descriptor (CF_LINKSOURCEDESCRIPTOR)	Describes the link being transferred in the link source

The *ptd* Field

The `ptd` field is a pointer to a DVTARGETDEVICE data structure that contains information about the target device for which the data is being rendered. This field is usually used when the data is rendered for a specific printer, but it can, of course, apply to any device, including the screen. The structure is defined as follows:

```
typedef struct tagDVTARGETDEVICE
{
    DWORD tdSize;
    WORD  tdDriverNameOffset;
    WORD  tdDeviceNameOffset;
    WORD  tdPortNameOffset;
    WORD  tdExtDevmodeOffset;
    BYTE  tdData[1];
} DVTARGETDEVICE;
```

The structure is similar to a DEVNAMES structure. Each member is an offset to the actual data. See the *OLE Programmer's Reference* for a complete description of this data structure.

The *dwAspect* Field

The `dwAspect` field describes the level of detail and the type of view that is used for the data. The field can contain one entry from the following enumeration:

```
typedef enum tagDVASPECT
{
    DVASPECT_CONTENT        = 1,
    DVASPECT_THUMBNAIL      = 2,
    DVASPECT_ICON           = 4,
    DVASPECT_DOCPRINT       = 8,
} DVASPECT;
```

Table 7.2 (from the *OLE Programmer's Guide*) describes each of these values.

Table 7.2 Values for the *dwAspect* Field

Value	Meaning
DVASPECT_CONTENT	Provides a representation that enables the object to be displayed as an embedded object inside its container. This is the most common value for compound document objects. It is appropriate to use this value to get a presentation of the embedded object for rendering either on the screen or on a printer; DVASPECT_DOCPRINT, in contrast, indicates the look of the object as though it were printed.

(continues)

Table 7.2 Continued

Value	Meaning
DVASPECT_THUMBNAIL	Provides a thumbnail representation so that the object can be displayed in a browsing tool. This representation is an approximately 120-by-120-pixel, six-color, device-independent bitmap wrapped in a metafile.
DVASPECT_ICON	Provides an iconic representation of the object.
DVASPECT_DOCPRINT	Represents the object as though it were printed using the **P**rint command from the **F**ile menu. The described data represents a sequence of pages.

The *lindex* Field

If the `dwAspect` value is either DVASPECT_THUMBNAIL or DVASPECT_ICON, the value in the `lindex` member is ignored. However, if `dwAspect`'s value is DVASPECT_CONTENT or DVASPECT_DOCPRINT, the number should refer to the page that the caller is interested in.

Currently this field must be –1, indicating the entire object. However, a future release of OLE will support extended layout negotiation, which will enable you to specify other values for this field.

The *tymed* Field

The `tymed` field describes the type of medium in which the data is being transferred. Table 7.3 describes the possible values for this field.

Table 7.3 Values for the *tymed* Field

Value	Meaning	Release Mechanism
TYMED_HGLOBAL	Passes the data in a global memory handle, much like data is passed using DDE. All global handles must be allocated with the GMEM_SHARE flag.	`GlobalFree(hGlobal)`
TYMED_FILE	Passes the data in the contents of a file on the disk.	`OpenFile(lpszFile, &of, OF_DELETE)`
TYMED_ISTREAM	Passes the data using an instance of the `IStream` interface. The passed data is available through calls to `IStream::Read`.	`pStm->Release()`

Value	Meaning	Release Mechanism
TYMED_ISTORAGE	Passes the data using an instance of the `IStorage` interface; the passed data consists of the streams and storage objects nested under `IStorage`.	`pStg->Release()`
TYMED_GDI	Passes the data as a GDI object (bitmap).	`DeleteObject((HGDI) hGlobal)`
TYMED_MFPICT	Passes the data as a CF_METAFILEPICT, which contains a nested global handle.	`LPMETAFILEPICT pMF; pMF=GlobalLock-(hGlobal); DeleteMeta-File(pMF->hMF) GlobalUnlock(hGlobal); GlobalFree(hGlobal);`
TYMED_NULL	Indicates that no data is being passed. This value is not actually a medium.	

The STGMEDIUM Structure

The STGMEDIUM structure is used to describe the actual storage medium. The structure is defined as follows:

```
typedef struct tagSTGMEDIUM
{
    DWORD          tymed;

    union {
    HANDLE         hGlobal;
    LPSTR          lpszFileName;
    LPSTREAM       pstm;
    LPSTORAGE      pstg;
    };
   LPUNKNOWN       pUnkForRelease;
} STGMEDIUM;
```

The `tymed` members correspond to the `tymed` enumeration described for the FORMATETC structure. The `union` members point to the actual storage medium. This medium can be global memory, a disk file, an `IStream` object, or an `IStorage` object. If the `tymed` member is TYMED_NULL, the structure is considered to be set to NULL.

The `pUnkForRelease` member specifies who is responsible for freeing the resources associated with the medium. A NULL value in the member indicates that the receiving process should delete the resources. If the value contains a valid pointer, the originating process retains ownership of the medium.

The *IDataObject* Interface

The `IDataObject` interface is a standard COM interface that supports the `IUnknown` methods as well as various methods used to transfer data. The interface is defined as follows:

```
DECLARE_INTERFACE_(IDataObject, IUnknown)
{
        HRESULT QueryInterface (THIS_ REFIID riid, LPVOID FAR* ppvObj);
        ULONG AddRef (THIS) ;
        ULONG  Release (THIS);

        HRESULT GetData (THIS_ LPFORMATETC pFormatetc,
              LPSTGMEDIUM pmedium);
        HRESULT GetDataHere (THIS_ LPFORMATETC pFormatetc,
              LPSTGMEDIUM pmedium);
        HRESULT QueryGetData (THIS_ LPFORMATETC pFormatetc );
        HRESULT GetCanonicalFormatEtc (THIS_ LPFORMATETC pFormatetc,
              LPFORMATETC pFormatetcOut);
        HRESULT SetData (THIS_ LPFORMATETC pFormatetc,
              STGMEDIUM FAR * pmedium, BOOL fRelease);
        HRESULT EnumFormatEtc (THIS_ DWORD dwDirection,
              LPENUMFORMATETC FAR* ppenumFormatetc );
        HRESULT DAdvise (THIS_ FORMATETC FAR* pFormatetc, DWORD advf,
              LPADVISESINK pAdvise, DWORD FAR* pdwConnection);
        HRESULT DUnadvise (THIS_ DWORD dwConnection);
        HRESULT EnumDAdvise (THIS_ LPENUMSTATDATA FAR* ppenumAdvise );
};
```

The interface contains methods to send and receive data. There are also methods to enumerate the various FORMATETCs that a data object may support.

The `DAdvise` methods are used to establish an `IAdviseSink` notification mechanism between the data source and data consumer. These `AdviseSinks` are similar to dynamic data exchange (DDE) hot and warm links. After an `AdviseSink` is established, the data consumer can be notified of any changes to the data.

The `IDataObject` interface provides a standard means of transferring data. It does not matter which transfer method you use—the clipboard, drag-drop operations, or compound files. In each case, the same interface members are used.

MFC's *IDataObject* Support

The Microsoft Foundation Classes (MFC) library implements two classes to support `IDataObject`. The first class, `COleDataObject`, is used by the data consumer. If a user drops data on your application or performs a paste operation, you must create an instance of `COleDataObject`.

`COleDataObject` enables you to enumerate the data format offered, check whether a particular data format is available, and get the actual data. Table 7.4 describes the `COleDataObject` class members.

Table 7.4 The *COleDataObject* Class Members

Member	Description
`Attach`	Attaches the specified OLE data object to the `COleDataObject`
`AttachClipboard`	Attaches the data object that is on the clipboard
`BeginEnumFormats`	Prepares for one or more subsequent `GetNextFormat` calls
`Detach`	Detaches the associated `IDataObject` object
`GetData`	Copies data from the attached OLE data object in a specified format
`GetFileData`	Copies data from the attached OLE data object into a `CFile` pointer in the specified format
`GetGlobalData`	Copies data from the attached OLE data object into an HGLOBAL handle in the specified format
`GetNextFormat`	Returns the next data format available
`IsDataAvailable`	Checks whether data is available in a specified format
`Release`	Detaches and releases the associated `IDataObject` object

The second class implemented by MFC is `COleDataSource`. This class is used by data sources and acts as a cache in which to hold data that is being transferred. After you create an OLE object that needs to be transferred, you create an instance of `COleDataSource` and fill it with the data.

You can place the data into the data cache immediately or you can choose to use delayed rendering. With delayed rendering, you do not actually transfer the data until it is requested.

Table 7.5 describes the members of the `COleDataSource` class.

Table 7.5 The *COleDataSource* Class Members	
Member	**Description**
`CacheData`	Offers data in a specified format using a STGMEDIUM structure
`CacheGlobalData`	Offers data in a specified format using an HGLOBAL handle
`DelayRenderData`	Offers data in a specified format using delayed rendering
`DelayRenderFileData`	Offers data in a specified format in a `CFile` pointer
`DelaySetData`	Called for every format that is supported in `OnSetData`
`DoDragDrop`	Performs drag-drop operations with a data source
`Empty`	Empties the data from the `COleDataSource` object
`FlushClipboard`	Renders all data to the clipboard
`GetClipboardOwner`	Verifies that the data placed on the clipboard is still there
`OnRenderData`	Retrieves data as part of delayed rendering
`OnRenderFileData`	Retrieves data into a `CFile` as part of delayed rendering
`OnRenderGlobalData`	Retrieves data into an HGLOBAL handle as part of delayed rendering
`OnSetData`	Called to replace the data in the `COleDataSource` object
`SetClipboard`	Places a `COleDataSource` object on the clipboard

The Clipboard and OLE

The clipboard has been part of the PC computing world since the first release of Windows. Macintosh first popularized the concept of a system clipboard that can cut and paste data to and from a source. Although the clipboard has several limitations—most notably the fact that it can hold only one piece of data at a time—it is still the primary means of transferring data from one application to another.

OLE defines several new clipboard formats that support the transfer of OLE objects. Table 7.1 lists these formats. During a clipboard data transfer, the owner of the data object places one or more of these formats on the clipboard. The container can then paste one of these formats into the compound document.

The following sections examine how you can implement this clipboard support in an MFC application. You will use the container developed in the last chapter as an example.

The *OnEditPaste* Method

The framework calls the `OnEditPaste` method in response to the user selecting Paste from the Edit menu. Listing 7.1 is the code for the `OnEditPaste` method.

Listing 7.1 The *OnEditPaste* Method

```
//----------------------------------------------------------------
void COleCntView::OnEditPaste()
{
      OnPaste(FALSE,TRUE,NULL);
}
//----------------------------------------------------------------
BOOL COleCntView::OnPaste(BOOL fLink, BOOL fClipboard,
                          COleDataObject *pDO)
{
      BOOL fOK = TRUE;
      BeginWaitCursor();

      COleDataObject *pDataObject;
      //----
      // Begin by creating an empty item in which to store
      // the data.
      CRect rc;
      rc.SetRectEmpty();
      COleCntCntrItem* pItem = GetDocument()->CreateItem(rc);
      ASSERT_VALID(pItem);

      if(fClipboard)
      {
            COleDataObject CBData;
            CBData.AttachClipboard();
            pDataObject = &CBData;
      }
      else
            pDataObject = pDO;


      TRY
      {
            if(fLink)
```

(continues)

Listing 7.1 Continued

```
    {
        if (!pItem->CreateLinkFromData(pDataObject))
        {
            AfxThrowMemoryException();
        }
    }
    else
    {
        if (!pItem->CreateFromData(pDataObject) &&
                !pItem->CreateStaticFromData(pDataObject,
                    OLERENDER_DRAW))
        {
            AfxThrowMemoryException();
        }
    }

    //----
    // Prime the cache with the iconic representation
    // of the data.

    FORMATETC fmtetc;
    SETFORMATETC(fmtetc, CF_METAFILEPICT, DVASPECT_ICON, NULL,
                TYMED_MFPICT, -1);
    HGLOBAL hObj = pDataObject->GetGlobalData(CF_METAFILEPICT,
                &fmtetc);
    if (hObj != NULL)
    {
        pItem->SetIconicMetafile(hObj);

        STGMEDIUM stgMed;
        stgMed.tymed = TYMED_MFPICT;
        stgMed.hGlobal = hObj;
        ReleaseStgMedium(&stgMed);
    }


   //----
    // Set the current drawing aspect
    hObj = pDataObject->GetGlobalData(m_cfObjectDescriptor);
    if (hObj != NULL)
    {
        LPOBJECTDESCRIPTOR pObjDesc =
            (LPOBJECTDESCRIPTOR)GlobalLock(hObj);
        ASSERT(pObjDesc != NULL);
        pItem->SetDrawAspect(
             (DVASPECT)pObjDesc->dwDrawAspect);
        GlobalUnlock(hObj);
        GlobalFree(hObj);
    }

    pItem->UpdateExtents();
```

```
        }
        CATCH_ALL(e)
        {
              pItem->Delete();
              pItem = NULL;
              fOK = FALSE;
        }
        END_CATCH_ALL

//      SetSelection(pItem, TRUE);

        // Update the document and views
        GetDocument()->SetModifiedFlag();
        GetDocument()->UpdateAllViews(NULL, 0, pItem);

        EndWaitCursor();

        return fOK;

}
//----------------------------------------------------------------
//----------------------------------------------------------------
```

To handle the actual embedding of the object, you call the helper function `OnPaste`. `OnPaste` begins by creating a `COleCntCntrItem` object. The class that you implement derives from `COleClientItem`.

After creating the `COleCntCntrItem` object, you declare a `COleDataObject`. The `COleDataObject::AttachClipboard` method is then called to attach to `ColeDataObject` the data object that is on the clipboard.

You then call `CreateFromData` to create the embedded object. If this call fails, you try to create a static object. A static object contains only the presentation data (the metafile), but no native data. Therefore, you cannot activate static objects.

You have now successfully created an embedded object. By default, the OLE cache for each object contains only one data format, which usually is the metafile presentation format. To store other formats in the cache, you must do so explicitly by requesting the data and placing it in the cache.

Because you want to store other formats in your container application, you begin by initializing a FORMATETC data structure. You want an iconic representation of the object's data in a metafile. You then call `GetGlobalData` to retrieve this data format in a global memory block. If the call succeeds, you then call `SetIconicMetaFile` to stuff the icon into the embedded object's cache.

You then call `GetGlobalData` again to get the OBJECTDESCRIPTOR format for the object. From this structure, you extract the current aspect of the object and use the same aspect to initialize the embedded object that you want to display.

Finally, you call `UpdateExtents` to update the extents of the object and `UpdateAllViews` to force a repaint so that the object can be displayed in the application's client area. `UpdateExtents` is a member of your `COleClientItem` class.

The *OnEditPasteLink* Method

When the user chooses the **E**dit menu's Paste Link option, the framework calls the `OnEditPasteLink` method. As with the `OnEditPaste` method, you let the `OnPaste` helper method do all the work:

```
//-----------------------------------------------------------------
void COleCntView::OnEditPasteLink()
{
        OnPaste(TRUE,TRUE,NULL);
}
```

The only difference between the Paste and Paste Link methods is that the Paste Link method uses `CreateLinkFromData` to create a linked object rather than an embedded one:

```
if (!pItem->CreateLinkFromData(pDataObject))
{
        AfxThrowMemoryException();
}
```

The *OnEditPasteSpecial* Method

The Paste Special dialog box enables users to choose the format of data that they are transferring into the document. The user can choose from any of the formats offered by the data owner, and can also choose to embed or link the data. Listing 7.2 is the code for the `OnEditPasteSpecial` method that you use to present this dialog box.

Listing 7.2 The *OnEditPasteSpecial* Method

```
void COleCntView::OnEditPasteSpecial()
{
        COlePasteSpecialDialog dlg;

        dlg.AddStandardFormats();

        if (dlg.DoModal() != IDOK)
            return;
```

```
        COleCntCntrItem* pItem = NULL;
        TRY
        {
                CRect rc;
                rc.SetRectEmpty();

                pItem = GetDocument()->CreateItem(rc);
                if (!dlg.CreateItem(pItem))
                {
                        AfxThrowMemoryException();
                }

                // Try to get initial presentation data
                pItem->UpdateLink();

                // Try to get initial extent
                pItem->UpdateExtents();

                GetDocument()->SetModifiedFlag();
                GetDocument()->UpdateAllViews(NULL, 0, pItem);
        }
        CATCH_ALL(e)
        {
                if (pItem != NULL)
                        GetDocument()->DeleteItem(pItem);

                AfxMessageBox(_T("Failed to create item"));
                return;
        }
        END_CATCH_ALL
}
```


You begin by creating an object from the `COlePasteSpecialDialog` class. This class presents the standard Paste Special dialog box to the user. If the user chooses the OK button, you proceed to create an empty `COleCntCntrItem`. You then call `COlePasteSpecialDialog::CreateItem` to create the object in the selected format.

A call to `UpdateLink` ensures that you have the latest presentation data. The call to `UpdateExtents` ensures that you retrieve the extents from the object so that it can be displayed in the container.

As usual, the call to `UpdateAllView` invalidates the client area and ensures that the `Draw` method is called.

The *OnUpdatePaste* Method

The `OnUpdatePaste` method is a command handler that updates the entries on the **E**dit menu. This handler uses the command-routing map to route both the **P**aste and Paste Link options:

```
ON_UPDATE_COMMAND_UI(ID_EDIT_PASTE_LINK, OnUpdatePaste)
ON_UPDATE_COMMAND_UI(ID_EDIT_PASTE, OnUpdatePaste)
```

You begin by declaring a `COleDataObject` variable. You then call `COleDataObject::AttachClipboard` to attach to the data object any object on the clipboard. If the clipboard is empty, this method fails and can thus return FALSE. By returning FALSE, the method ensures that both menu items are displayed in a disabled state.

Even if you find data on the clipboard, you must be sure that you can create an embedded object from the data. If you can, the method returns TRUE, which enables both menu options.

The following is the code for the `OnUpdatePaste` method:

```
void COleCntView::OnUpdatePaste(CCmdUI* pCmdUI)
{
        //---
        // See whether any OLE objects
        // are on the clipboard.
        COleDataObject DataObject;
        BOOL fOK = FALSE;

        if(DataObject.AttachClipboard())
        {
                fOK = COleClientItem::CanCreateFromData(&DataObject);
        }

        pCmdUI->Enable(fOK);
}
```

The *OnEditCopy*, *OnEditCut*, and *OnEditClear* Methods

The next three methods are all very similar. `OnEditCopy` copies the currently selected item to the clipboard. To execute this action, you simply call `COleClientItem::CopyToClipboard`. `OnEditCut` is just a copy operation followed by a call to `COleDocument::DeleteItem`.

The `OnEditClear` method deletes the currently selected item. Listing 7.3 shows the method's code.

Listing 7.3 The *OnEditClear* Method

```
void COleCntView::OnEditClear
{
        ASSERT(m_pSelection != NULL);

        GetDocument()->DeleteItem(m_pSelection);
}
//-----------------------------------------------------------------
void COleCntView::OnEditCut()
{
        ASSERT(m_pSelection != NULL);
```

```
        TRY
        {
                m_pSelection->CopyToClipboard(TRUE);
                OnEditClear();
        }
        CATCH_ALL(e)
        {
                AfxMessageBox(_T("Error Failed to cut to clipboard"));
        }
        END_CATCH_ALL
}
//-----------------------------------------------------------------
void COleCntView::OnEditCopy()
{
        ASSERT(m_pSelection != NULL);
        TRY
        {
                m_pSelection->CopyToClipboard(TRUE);
        }
        CATCH_ALL(e)
        {
                AfxMessageBox(_T("Error Failed to copy to clipboard"));
        }
        END_CATCH_ALL
}
//-----------------------------------------------------------------
```


MFC Drag-drop Support

The next step is to add support for drag-drop operations. In Chapter 3, "A Sample C++ Application," you created a `CDropTarget` class to handle the dropping of objects onto your application's client area. In the sample container application, you use the MFC drag-drop support. You also enable the user to drag an object from the application and drop it into another OLE-compliant application.

Registering the Application

Before your application can accept objects from other applications, you must register the application as a drag-drop target. You should do this while creating the View class. The View class includes a `COleDropTarget` member called `m_dropTarget`. To register the container application, you call the `Register` method from that class:

```
int COleCntView::OnCreate(LPCREATESTRUCT lpCreateStruct)
{
        if (CView::OnCreate(lpCreateStruct) == -1)
                return -1;
```

```
        m_dropTarget.Register(this);

        return 0;
    }
```

The *OnDragEnter* Method

When the user drags an object to the client area, the framework calls the `OnDragEnter` method as the mouse cursor enters the client area.

This method is passed three parameters:

- A pointer to the object that is being dragged
- The current state of the keyboard modifer keys (Alt, Shift, and Ctrl)
- The current location of the mouse cursor

You normally use the `OnDragEnter` method to extract from the object information to be used during the drag-drop operation. In this case, you extract the object's extent so that you can provide the user with a feedback rectangle during the operation:

```
DROPEFFECT COleCntView::OnDragEnter(COleDataObject* pDataObject,
                                    DWORD grfKeyState, CPoint point)
{

      GetObjectInfo(pDataObject, &m_dragSize, &m_dragOffset);

      CClientDC dc(NULL);
      dc.HIMETRICtoDP(&m_dragSize);
      dc.HIMETRICtoDP(&m_dragOffset);

      return OnDragOver(pDataObject, grfKeyState, point);
}
```

You use the same method here as you used in Chapter 3 to extract the object's extents. Each object supports the OBJECTDESCRIPTOR clipboard format. This structure contains information about the object. Listing 7.4 demonstrates this method.

Listing 7.4 The *GetObjectInfo* Method

```
BOOL COleCntView::GetObjectInfo(COleDataObject* pDataObject,
                                CSize* pSize, CSize* pOffset)
{
      ASSERT(pSize != NULL);

    //----
      // Try to get the OBJECTDESCRIPTOR data
```

```
        HGLOBAL hObjDesc =
              pDataObject->GetGlobalData(m_cfObjectDescriptor);
        if (hObjDesc == NULL)
        {
              if (pOffset != NULL)
                    *pOffset = CSize(0, 0); // fill in defaults instead
              *pSize = CSize(0, 0);
              return FALSE;
        }
        ASSERT(hObjDesc != NULL);


        LPOBJECTDESCRIPTOR pObjDesc =
              (LPOBJECTDESCRIPTOR)GlobalLock(hObjDesc);
        ASSERT(pObjDesc != NULL);
        pSize->cx = (int)pObjDesc->sizel.cx;
        pSize->cy = (int)pObjDesc->sizel.cy;

        if (pOffset != NULL)
        {
              pOffset->cx = (int)pObjDesc->pointl.x;
              pOffset->cy = (int)pObjDesc->pointl.y;
        }

        GlobalUnlock(hObjDesc);
        GlobalFree(hObjDesc);


        return TRUE;
  }
```

The value that this method returns is an indicator of the type of drop action that would occur if the user dropped the object now. The effect can be either DROPEFFECT_NONE, which indicates that a drop would not be accepted at this location, or one of the values listed in table 7.6.

Table 7.6 Values Returned by the *OnDragEnter* Method

Value	Effect
DROPEFFECT_LINK for MK_CONTROL | MK_SHIFT	Creates a link between the object and its server
DROPEFFECT_COPY for MK_CONTROL	Creates a copy of the dropped object
DROPEFFECT_MOVE for MK_ALT	Creates a copy of the dropped object and deletes the original object

The *OnDragOver* Method

When the mouse cursor is within the client area, the framework calls the `OnDragOver` method continuously. Many calls are made to this method, so you shouldn't spend too much time in it.

The main function of `OnDragOver` is to provide the user with visual feedback during the drag-drop operation. To provide the ghost rectangle to the user, you use the `DrawFocusRect` method.

Finally, you return the DROPEFFECT result. This result ensures that the OLE libraries display the correct mouse cursor for that particular type of operation. OLE's User Interface Guidelines define these cursors, and the standard cursors supplied by the libraries conform to these guidelines.

Listing 7.5 is the code for the `OnDragOver` method.

Listing 7.5 The *OnDragOver* Method

```
DROPEFFECT COleCntView::OnDragOver(COleDataObject*,DWORD grfKeyState,
                                   CPoint point)
{
      point -= m_dragOffset;
                    // adjust target rect by original cursor offset


      DROPEFFECT DropEffect = DROPEFFECT_NONE;
      CRect rcClient;
      GetClientRect(&rcClient);

      if(rcClient.PtInRect(point))
      {
            if ((grfKeyState & (MK_CONTROL¦MK_SHIFT))
                 == (MK_CONTROL¦MK_SHIFT))
                  DropEffect = DROPEFFECT_LINK;
            else if ((grfKeyState & MK_CONTROL) == MK_CONTROL)
                  DropEffect = DROPEFFECT_COPY;
            else if ((grfKeyState & MK_ALT) == MK_ALT)
                  DropEffect = DROPEFFECT_MOVE;
            else
                  DropEffect = DROPEFFECT_MOVE;
      }

      if (point == m_dragPoint)
            return DropEffect;


      CClientDC dc(this);
      if (m_prevDropEffect != DROPEFFECT_NONE)
      {
            // Erase previous focus rect
            dc.DrawFocusRect(CRect(m_dragPoint, m_dragSize));
```

```
    }

    m_prevDropEffect = DropEffect;
    if (m_prevDropEffect != DROPEFFECT_NONE)
    {
          m_dragPoint = point;
          dc.DrawFocusRect(CRect(point, m_dragSize));
    }
    return DropEffect;
}
```

The *OnDrop* Method

The `OnDrop` method is called when the user releases the mouse button while the mouse cursor is over the client area. Listing 7.6 shows the code for this method.

Listing 7.6 The *OnDrop* Method

```
BOOL COleCntView::OnDrop(COleDataObject* pDataObject,
      DROPEFFECT dropEffect, CPoint point)
{
      ASSERT_VALID(this);


      OnDragLeave();

      // offset point as appropriate for dragging
      GetObjectInfo(pDataObject, &m_dragSize, &m_dragOffset);
      CClientDC dc(NULL);
      dc.HIMETRICtoDP(&m_dragSize);
      dc.HIMETRICtoDP(&m_dragOffset);
      point -= m_dragOffset;

      // if move is within the view
      if ((dropEffect & DROPEFFECT_MOVE) && m_bInDrag)
      {
            ASSERT(m_pSelection != NULL);
            m_bInDrag = FALSE;
                     // signal drag code that a move happened


            CRect rect = m_pSelection->m_rc;
            if (rect.TopLeft() != point)
            {
                  m_pSelection->Move(CRect(point,rect.Size()));
                  GetDocument()->SetModifiedFlag();
            }
      }

      // check and paste link
      else if ((dropEffect & DROPEFFECT_LINK) && OnPaste(TRUE,TRUE,
                pDataObject))
```

(continues)

Listing 7.6 Continued

```
            return TRUE;
        // paste embedding/static
        else if (OnPaste(FALSE,TRUE,pDataObject))
            return TRUE;

        return FALSE;
}
```

You begin by calling `DragLeave` to remove the ghost rectangle. You then prepare to handle three possibilities:

- If the user is simply dragging and dropping an object within your application, you call the object's move method to move the object to its new location.
- If the user is requesting a link operation, you call the `OnPaste` helper function with the `fLink` parameter set to TRUE.
- If you are creating a new embedded object, you call the helper function `OnPaste` with the `fLink` parameter set to FALSE.

The *OnDragLeave* Method

The `OnDragLeave` method is called when the user moves the mouse cursor away from the client area. You use this opportunity to erase the user-feedback rectangle from the screen. The code for this method follows:

```
void COleCntView::OnDragLeave()
{
        CClientDC dc(this);
        if (m_prevDropEffect != DROPEFFECT_NONE)
        {
                dc.DrawFocusRect(CRect(m_dragPoint,m_dragSize));
                m_prevDropEffect = DROPEFFECT_NONE;
        }
}
```

The *OnScrollBy* Method

You implement the `OnScrollBy` method to enable the user to drag an object to a section of the client area that is not currently visible. In the sample application, your `CView` class is actually a `CScrollView` class with a preset document size. You must use the `CScrollView` class to support scrolling.

During a drag operation, the user may place the mouse cursor in the drag-scroll hot area. If so, the framework calls this method. You remove any ghost rectangle, and let the framework perform the actual scrolling.

The code for the `OnScrollBy` method follows:

```
BOOL COleCntView::OnScrollBy(CSize sizeScroll, BOOL bDoScroll)
{

      if (bDoScroll && m_prevDropEffect != DROPEFFECT_NONE)
      {
            CClientDC dc(this);
            dc.DrawFocusRect(CRect(m_dragPoint, m_dragSize));
            m_prevDropEffect = DROPEFFECT_NONE;
      }

      // -----
      // Let the framework do the scrolling for you
      if (!CScrollView::OnScrollBy(sizeScroll, bDoScroll))
            return FALSE;

    //---
      // Update the position of any in-place active item
      if (bDoScroll)
      {
            UpdateWindow();
      }

      return TRUE;
}
```

You have now explored basically all that you need to do to support drag-drop operations in your application. You can see now what is meant by Uniform Data Transfer (UDT). Whether you are using the clipboard or the drag-drop method, you use to same code to move or copy the object.

Linking Support

A new feature of OLE 2.0 is the capability to link to embedded items. This feature is useful, for example, when you have a range of cells embedded in your application and you want to create a chart based on that data. Then, when the data is updated, the chart is automatically updated also.

Using MFC, adding support for linking to embedded items is not very difficult. The main issue that you must be aware of is that if your application contains an embedded item that has a external link connected to it, you must be prepared for your application to be launched by the application that contains the link.

To enable your application to be loaded programmatically, you must use the `COleTemplateServer` class. In `InitInstance`, you must connect your document template to the `COleTemplateServer` object. You then register your class objects by calling `COleTemplateServer::RegisterAll`.

The final step is to derive your Document class from the `COleLinkingDoc` class.

Listing 7.7 shows the source for the `CWinApp` module in which you add the support for linking just discussed.

Listing 7.7 The *CWinApp* Module

```
#include "stdafx.h"
#include "olecnt.h"

#include "mainfrm.h"
#include "olecndoc.h"
#include "olecnvw.h"

#ifdef _DEBUG
#undef THIS_FILE
static char BASED_CODE THIS_FILE[] = __FILE__;
#endif

static const GUID BASED_CODE clsid =
      { 0xB2A5B121, 0xA73B, 0x101B, {0x99, 0x48, 0x52, 0x41, 0x53,
        0x48, 0x00, 0x01}};


//////////////////////////////////////////////////////////////////////
// COleCntApp

BEGIN_MESSAGE_MAP(COleCntApp, CWinApp)
      //{{AFX_MSG_MAP(COleCntApp)
      ON_COMMAND(ID_APP_ABOUT, OnAppAbout)
        // NOTE - ClassWizard adds and removes mapping macros here.
        // DO NOT EDIT what you see in these blocks of generated code!
      //}}AFX_MSG_MAP
      // Standard file-based document commands
      ON_COMMAND(ID_FILE_NEW, CWinApp::OnFileNew)
      ON_COMMAND(ID_FILE_OPEN, CWinApp::OnFileOpen)
      // Standard print-setup command
      ON_COMMAND(ID_FILE_PRINT_SETUP, CWinApp::OnFilePrintSetup)
END_MESSAGE_MAP()

//////////////////////////////////////////////////////////////////////
// COleCntApp construction

COleCntApp::COleCntApp()
{
      // TODO: add construction code here,
      // Place all significant initialization in InitInstance
}
```

```
////////////////////////////////////////////////////////////////////
// The one and only COleCntApp object

COleCntApp NEAR theApp;

////////////////////////////////////////////////////////////////////
// COleCntApp initialization

BOOL COleCntApp::InitInstance()
{
      // Initialize OLE 2.0 libraries OleBuildVersion
      if (!AfxOleInit())
      {
            AfxMessageBox(IDP_OLE_INIT_FAILED);
            return FALSE;
      }

      // Standard initialization
      // If you are not using these features and want to reduce the
      // size of your final executable, you should remove from
      // the following the specific initialization routines
      // that you do not need.

      SetDialogBkColor();      // Set dialog background color to gray
      LoadStdProfileSettings();
                         // Load standard INI file options (including MRU)

      // Register the application's document templates.
      // Document templates serve as the connection
      // between documents, frame windows, and views.

      CMultiDocTemplate* pDocTemplate;
      pDocTemplate = new CMultiDocTemplate(
            IDR_OLECNTTYPE,
            RUNTIME_CLASS(COleCntDoc),
            RUNTIME_CLASS(CMDIChildWnd),  // standard MDI child frame
            RUNTIME_CLASS(COleCntView));

      pDocTemplate->SetContainerInfo(IDR_OLECNTTYPE_CNTR_IP);
      AddDocTemplate(pDocTemplate);

      // create main MDI Frame window
      CMainFrame* pMainFrame = new CMainFrame;
      if (!pMainFrame->LoadFrame(IDR_MAINFRAME))
            return FALSE;
      m_pMainWnd = pMainFrame;


      // connect the COleTemplate server to the document template
      m_server.ConnectTemplate(clsid, pDocTemplate, FALSE);
      COleTemplateServer::RegisterAll();

      if (RunEmbedded())
      {
           // application was run with /Embedding flag. Instead of
           // showing the window, the application waits to receive OLE
           // requests.
```

(continues)

Listing 7.7 Continued

```
            return TRUE;
        }
        // always update system registry when run nonembedded
        m_server.UpdateRegistry(OAT_CONTAINER);


        // create a new (empty) document
        OnFileNew();

        if (m_lpCmdLine[0] != '\0')
        {
        }

        // The main window has been initialized, so show and update it.
        pMainFrame->ShowWindow(m_nCmdShow);
        pMainFrame->UpdateWindow();

        return TRUE;
}
```

From Here...

You have now examined the various methods that you can use to create OLE objects in a compound document. Among the methods that you have seen are the clipboard, drag-drop operations, and the Insert Object dialog box. In the next chapter, you examine OLE's support for persistent storage of objects.

Chapter 8

OLE Compound Files

OLE 2.0 provides persistent storage for objects through the structured storage model. This chapter examines structured storage in detail, and also the current implementation of structured storage, compound files.

In this chapter, you do the following:

- Examine property sets in general and the Summary Information set in particular
- Develop an application that can display Summary Information property sets from applications such as Microsoft Word
- Examine how the Microsoft Foundation Classes (MFC) libraries use compound files

The Structured Storage Model

Before examining structured storage in detail, you must clearly understand the difference between structured storage and compound files. Structured storage is a *model* that describes a system that can be used to provide persistent storage to objects. Compound files are an *implementation* of structured storage. As you examine the structured storage interfaces more closely, you'll notice that compound files do not fully implement all these interfaces.

Structured storage was developed originally to solve the problems of saving compound documents and their objects to permanent storage. The model basically deals with the saving and retrieving of data.

The model describes a hierarchy system of storage and stream objects. The root of the hierarchy is a `LockBytes` object. Figure 8.1 illustrates this hierarchy.

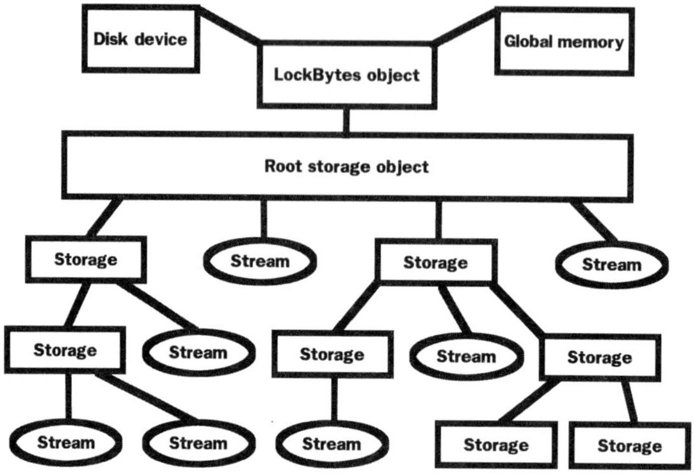

Fig. 8.1 Structured storage.

A primary goal of structured storage is to enable compound document objects to load and save themselves to storage without the object's container intervening. Each object has a stream exclusively for itself. However, because users are accustomed to thinking of a compound document as a single file, it was necessary to find a way to unify these multiple streams into a single unit.

The compound file implementation achieves this by providing what is essentially a file system within a file. As far as the operating system is concerned, a compound file is a single disk file. On the inside, the compound file is an entire file system complete with its own file allocation table (FAT), directories, and files.

Structured storage consists of three types of objects: a single `LockBytes` object, storage objects, and stream objects.

The *LockBytes* Object

A `LockBytes` object provides a layer between the root storage object and the actual storage medium. Because of this isolation from the storage device, you can implement structured storage on many types of devices without the object having any special knowledge of the model.

The compound file implementation supplied with OLE 2.0 manipulates a byte array that is an actual disk file.

Another implementation supplied with OLE 2.0 enables you to use global memory as a storage device, albeit a temporary one. Two API functions are available to manipulate this `LockBytes` implementation:

- `CreateILockBytesOnHGlobal` creates a `LockBytes` structure in global memory.
- `GetHGlobalFromILockBytes` returns the global memory handle that the memory `LockBytes` object uses.

You can of course write your own `ILockByte` implementation. The OLE 2.0 implementation of `ILockBytes` is complete, including the locking methods. Table 8.1 describes the methods of the `ILockBytes` interface.

Table 8.1 Methods of the *ILockBytes* Interface

Method	Description
`ReadAt`	Reads bytes from the byte array. The bytes are read from the specified position.
`WriteAt`	Writes bytes to a specified location in the byte array.
`Flush`	Flushes the internal buffers to the storage device.
`SetSize`	Changes the size of the byte array.
`LockRegion`	Locks a range of bytes on the byte array.
`UnlockRegion`	Unlocks a previously locked region.
`Stat`	Returns a STATSTG structure detailing information about the byte array.

Storages

Storages are the logical equivalent of directories. Like directories, storages can contain multiple streams and other storages. You access storages through the `IStorage` interface.

Storages can have access rights similar to streams. Therefore, you can restrict access to storages within a compound file. This, of course, is not possible with DOS directories.

After you have a pointer to an `IStorage` interface, you can create or open a stream object. You can move, copy, rename, delete, and enumerate objects within a particular storage.

You can also assign class IDs (CLSIDs) to storages. CLSIDs enable containers to find and load the object server that created the data.

To retrieve information about a storage, you call the `GetStat` method. Information returns in a STATSTG structure, which is defined as follows in STORAGE.H:

```
typedef struct tagSTATSTG{
     char FAR * pwcsName;
     DWORD type;
     ULARGE_INTEGER cbSize;
     FILETIME mtime;
     FILETIME ctime;
     FILETIME atime;
     DWORD grfMode;
     DWORD grfLocksSupported;
     CLSID clsid;
     DWORD grfStateBits;
     DWORD Reserved;
} STATSTG;
```

Table 8.2 describes the fields of this structure.

Table 8.2 The Fields of the STATSTG Structure

Field	Description
`lpszName`	The name of the element. The callee allocates this field, and the caller frees it. This field can be NULL on exit.
`type`	The type of the element. Legal values are STGTY_STORAGE, STGTY_STREAM, and STGTY_LOCKBYTES.
`cbSize`	The size of the element: the byte count for `IStream` and `ILockBytes`, and undefined for `IStorage` (0 is returned).
`mtime`	Time and date of modification.
`ctime`	Time and date of the creation of the element.
atime	Last access time.
grfMode	Mode in which the element was opened.
`grfLocksSupported`	Relevant only for `IStream` and `ILockBytes`. A group of Boolean flags indicates for each lock type whether a call to `LockRegion` is worthwhile. For each flag, a false (0) value indicates that a call to `LockRegion` with the corresponding lock type will always indicate that write locking is not currently supported. A true value indicates that such a call might be (but is not guaranteed to be) supported. These flags enable clients to determine up front whether locking is ever available on the stream or `LockBytes` object. Values for this group of flags are taken from the enumeration LOCKTYPE (see the *OLE Programmer's Reference).*

Field	Description
clsid	The class tag associated with the storage, if any; initially CLSID_NULL for newly created storages. This field is relevant for IStorages only.
grfStateBits	The value most recently set with IStorage::SetStateBits. This field is relevant for IStorages only.
reserved	Reserved for future use.

The current compound file implementation of IStorage is complete, unlike that of the IStream interface.

A storage object, which is the first storage created in a compound file, is known as the *root storage*. Root storage supports an additional interface, IRootStorage. The IRootStorage interface has just one member, SwitchToFile. This method switches the underlying disk file to which IStorage objects are being saved. You usually use this method when memory is low.

Table 8.3 describes each of the members of the IStorage interface.

Table 8.3 Members of the *IStorage* Interface

Method	Action
Release	Closes the storage. If the storage is opened in transacted mode, the last Release also implies a Revert. If the storage is opened with the STGM-DELETEONRELEASE flag, the storage is deleted here. The Release method is part of the IUnknown implementation.
CreateStream	Creates and opens a stream.
OpenStream	Opens a stream.
CreateStorage	Creates and opens a new substorage.
OpenStorage	Opens an existing storage.
CopyTo	Copies the entire contents from one storage into another.
Commit	Ensures that all changes made to the storage are reflected to the parent storage if the storage is opened in transacted mode. Committing a direct storage flushes all disk buffers.
Revert	Discards any changes made to the storage since the last Commit if the storage is opened in transacted mode.

(continues)

Table 8.3 Continued

Method	Action
`EnumElements`	Returns an `IEnumSTATSTG` object that enumerates the substorages and streams contained in the storage.
`MoveElementTo`	Copies or moves a substorage or a stream from one storage into another.
`DestroyElement`	Deletes a specified substorage or stream. If a substorage is destroyed, all elements contained within it are also destroyed.
`RenameElement`	Changes the name of a stream or substorage.
`SetElementTimes`	Sets the modification, last access, and creation date and time of a substorage or stream if supported by the underlying file system.
`SetClass`	Associates a CLSID with the storage. You can use `Stat` to retrieve the CLSID. Storages have the value CLSID_NULL when initially created.
`SetStateBits`	Enables you to store up to 32 bits of state information about the storage. Use `Stat` to retrieve the values. These bits are currently reserved.
`Stat`	Retrieves statistics for the storage. These statistics include name, create, modify, and access times. See table 8.2 for more information.

Enumerating Storages

The `IStorage::EnumElements` method returns an enumerator that you can use to enumerate over the storages in a compound file. The enumerator prototype is as follows:

```
DECLARE_INTERFACE_(IEnumSTATSTG, IUnknown)
{
...
  HRESULT Next (ULONG celt, STATSTG FAR * rgelt[], ULONG
*pceltFetched);
  HRESULT Skip (ULONG celt);
  HRESULT Reset ();
  HRESULT Clone (LPENUMSTATSTG FAR * ppenumStatStg);
};
```

The enumerator returns pointers to STATSTG structures.

Streams

As was previously mentioned, streams are analogous to files in a traditional file system. You expose streams through the `IStream` interface. Although you usually find streams in compound disk files, they can also be created in global memory.

Streams, like ordinary disk files, have a position pointer that you can use to search through the stream both forward and backward.

You can read and write data by calling `Read` and `Write`. Both of these methods enable you to read and write 2^{64} bytes in a single operation. The current implementation of compound files restricts this to 2^{32} bytes. As you can see from the definition of `IStream` in listing 8.1 (later in this chapter), range locking of bytes is supported. However, this range locking is not supported in the compound files implementation.

Transaction support is made available through the `Commit` and `Revert` methods. Again, compound files lack this functionality.

Streams have access rights and permissions. You can open streams in read-only mode, shared mode, and so on.

You also can marshal streams to other processes. If you join two processes together with shared memory, the custom marshaling features of OLE marshal the data through the shared memory area. This custom marshaling greatly increases the marshaling performance. The only drawback is that both processes share the same file pointer. However, you can avoid this problem by cloning the stream.

The `SetSize` method is handy for optimization. Calling this method when you create the stream enables you to preallocate a large block of contiguous data.

You close a stream like any Component Object Model (COM) object—by calling the `Release` method.

Table 8.4 describes the members of the `IStream` interface.

Table 8.4 Members of the *IStream* Interface

Method	Action
`Release`	Closes the stream. `IUnknown` implements this method. The usual reference-counting rules apply.
`Read`	Reads data from the current seek pointer into a buffer.
`Write`	Writes data from a buffer to the stream starting at the current seek pointer.

(continues)

Table 8.4 Continued

Method	Action
`Seek`	Moves the current seek pointer to a new location within the stream. This method follows the same semantics as the DOS SEEK function.
`SetSize`	Enables you to preallocate data space within the stream.
`CopyTo`	Copies the number of bytes from the current seek pointer in the stream to the current seek pointer in another stream.
`Commit`	Commits all changes to a transacted stream to its parent storage. If you open the stream in direct mode, the current file buffers are flushed. (This method is not available in the current implementation of compound files.)
`Revert`	Discards any changes made to the stream since the last `Commit`. (This method is not available in the current implementation of compound files.)
`LockRegion`	Locks a range of bytes in the stream. (This method is not available in the current implementation of compound files.)
`UnlockRegion`	Unlocks a locked region. (This method is not available in the current implementation of compound files.)
`Stat`	Retrieves a STATSTG structure containing information about the stream.
`Clone`	Creates a new stream object with a new seek pointer. Both seek pointers reference the same data, although you can move the pointers independently of each other.

Because `IStream` enables you to have streams that are 2^{64} bytes long, the `IStream::Seek` method requires an offset parameter that is 64 bits long. OLE defines a new data type, LARGE_INTEGER, for handling these large values. The data type is actually a data structure that consists of two members. Here is LARGE_INTEGER's prototype:

```
typedef struct  _LARGE_INTEGER
    {
    DWORD LowPart;
    LONG HighPart;
    }     LARGE_INTEGER;
```

A macro, `LISet32`, is supplied to initialize the structure:

```
#define LISet32(li, v) ((li).HighPart = (v) < 0 ? -1 : 0,
➥(li).LowPart = (v))
```

The macro takes care of sign-extending the high DWORD for you. There is also a ULARGE_INTEGER and corresponding `ULISet32` macro for signed values.

Compound Files

Compound files implement the structured storage supplied with OLE 2.0. This implementation provides you with several features that are useful to any type of application but especially useful when you are dealing with compound documents.

Creating a Compound File

Two API functions create compound files. The one that you choose depends on the storage medium that you intend to use.

`StgCreateDocFile` creates a new compound file on the file system. This function creates and opens a root storage object and returns an `IStorage` interface pointer to the object. If you want to open an existing compound file, you use the API function `StgOpenStorage`.

`StgCreateDocfileOnILockBytes` creates a compound file on the `ILockBytes` object. You use this function primarily when you do not want to use the supplied compound file implementation as your native storage. You can write a `LockBytes` implementation that understands your particular storage system and still creates a standard compound file. Then you can use streams and storages to access your data. The fact that the actual data is not being stored in a compound file would be totally transparent to your application.

After creating the initial file, you then create some substorages and streams. Creating the first storage is simple: using the `IStorage` interface pointer returned by the `StgCreateDocFile` function, you call `IStorage::CreateStorage`. This function creates and opens a new storage.

The process for creating streams is similar. This time you call `IStorage::CreateStream`. The following code fragment demonstrates how you open and create storages:

```
HRESULT hr;
IStorage  *pStorage, *pSubStorage;


// Create or open the docfile.
if (FAILED(StgIsStorageFile(STORAGE)))
{
     hr = StgCreateDocfile(STORAGE,
          STGM_READWRITE|STGM_SHARE_EXCLUSIVE,0,&pStorage);
}
```

II

Using MFC

```
else
{
     hr = StgOpenStorage(STORAGE,NULL,
          STGM_READWRITE¦STGM_SHARE_EXCLUSIVE,NULL,0,&pStorage);
}
// Create the storage for this object.
if (S_OK == hr)
{
     hr = pStorage->CreateStorage(SUBSTORAGE,
    STGM_CREATE¦STGM_READWRITE¦STGM_SHARE_EXCLUSIVE,0,0,&pSubStorage);
}
else
{
     AfxMessageBox("Error: Failed to create docfile");
     return;
}
```

Naming Conventions for Storages and Streams

The compound file implementation allows storages and streams to have names that are up to 32 characters long. The one exception to this rule is the name of the root storage. Because this storage's name is the same as that of the actual disk file, you must take into account the limitation of the underlying file system.

The naming scheme that you use must conform to the following rules:

- The names . and .. are reserved.
- Names cannot contain any of the following characters: . \ / : !

The namespace is also divided into two sections:

- Names beginning with \0x01 to \0x1f are reserved for use by the embedded object in a storage.
- Names beginning with \0x01 and \0x02 are reserved by the OLE libraries.
- Names beginning with \0x03 are used by the container in which the object is embedded.
- Names beginning with \0x04 are for the exclusive use of structured storage.
- Names beginning with \0x05 and \0x06 are reserved by the OLE libraries.
- All other names up to \0x1f are reserved for future use.

If you are already using a particular file format in your application, you can let OLE 2.0 convert that format to a compound file. If you pass the STGM_CONVERT flag to `StgOpenStorage`, OLE 2.0 creates a compound file with a single stream called CONTENTS. This stream contains your old file.

You can then use the `IStream` interface to work with the file. For a complete description of all the available flags, see the *OLE Programmer's Reference*.

One convenient feature of compound files is that the system automatically expands streams. This expansion is totally transparent to the application. The system allocates new data blocks for the stream as necessary. The only drawback to this approach is that compound files tend to become fragmented if the system constantly expands the streams.

If you delete a storage or stream in a compound file, the data is not actually removed. Instead, the object is marked as being deleted and the space is reused.

Access Modes

When accessing storages and streams, you can use six groups of flags. You can combine these flags by using the ¦ operator. However, you can use only one flag from each group.

When you use access mode with streams, keep in mind that the stream inherits its access mode from its storage. You can further restrict a stream's access mode, but you cannot give it more rights than its parent storage.

Table 8.5 describes the six groups of flags.

Table 8.5 Access Mode Flags

Flag	Description
Group 1	
STGM_READ	When applied to a stream, grants read access to the stream. When granted to storages, enables you to enumerate the storage and open any stream in read-only mode.
STGM_WRITE	Enables you to commit changes to a stream or storage.
STGM_READWRITE	Logically combines the two previous flags.
Group 2	
STGM_SHARE_DENY_NONE	Allows read and write access to the stream. This is the default sharing mode.
STGM_SHARE_DENY_READ	If successfully applied to a stream or storage, denies a request to open the storage or stream in read-only mode.

(continues)

Table 8.5 Continued

Flag	Description
Group 2	
STGM_SHARE_DENY_WRITE	If successfully applied to a stream or storage, denies a request to open the storage or stream in write-only mode.
STGM_SHARE_EXCLUSIVE	If successfully applied to a stream or storage, denies any requests to open the storage or stream.
Group 3	
STGM_DIRECT	Immediately writes to the storage device all writes to a stream.
STGM_TRANSACTED	Buffers all writes to a stream until a `Commit` is performed.
Group 4	
STGM_CREATE	Creates a new storage or stream, and removes one that already exists.
STGM_CONVERT	Converts noncompound files to a compound file that includes one stream called CONTENTS that contains the data from the original file.
STGM_FAILIFTHERE	Returns an error if a storage or stream already exists.
Group 5	
STGM_PRIORITY	Provides absolutely exclusive access to a storage. When a storage is opened in this mode, no "snapshot" of the data is taken, but no other process can access the file. This mode also denies access to a process that already has storages and streams opened in the file.
Group 6	
STGM_DELETEONRELEASE	Automatically deletes the storage or stream when the storage or stream is released.

The Transaction Model

Compound files support two distinct modes of access: direct and transacted.

Direct mode is what most developers are familiar with from dealing with traditional DOS file input/output (I/O). In direct mode, all changes are immediately and permanently written to the storage device.

In a compound document scenario, this mode can have disastrous effects from a user's perspective. For example, suppose that your document contains an embedded spreadsheet, and that you select the spreadsheet and activate it in place. When you finish changing the numbers, you return to the document. If you now quit from the word processor, you are prompted to save any changes. If you decide not to save any changes, you would assume that the changes made to the embedded spreadsheet object would also be discarded. However, with direct-mode access, the changes that you made to the spreadsheet object would have been made permanently when you deactivated the object.

One solution to this problem is transacted storage. When you open a storage in transacted mode, any changes that you make to the data are not updated until the storage is *committed*. You commit the data by calling `Commit` on the storage. The OLE 2.0 design specification describes committing a transaction on a storage as "publishing changes one more level outwards." In other words, nested storages publish transactions to their parents. The parents in turn publish their transactions to their parents. Finally, the root storage publishes transactions to the actual storage device. This is important to remember: the actual data on disk is not updated until the root storage is committed.

In fact, any operations that you perform on the members of a compound file—such as deleting storages, deleting streams, and renaming or moving elements—are not actually updated on the storage device until you commit the root storage.

Using transacted mode in your application is an easy way to provide an undo capability. Instead of calling `Commit` to make the changes permanent, you simply call `Revert` and discard the changes.

Lazy Reading of Streams

One way to bring Windows to its knees is to activate an OLE 1.0 video clip embedded in a Microsoft Word document. With OLE 1.0, you must load the entire object into memory before you can perform any operation.

Thus a design goal of structured storage was to enable objects to access their native data incrementally. The object reads only as much data as it needs at any given time.

Another feature of structured storage is that storages can be marshaled between processes. Therefore, if you are copying large objects between applications, you need only copy the `IStorage` pointer. The actual data remains on disk during the entire operation.

Special OLE Streams

Earlier you learned that OLE reserves some special streams for its own use. This section briefly examines each of these streams.

Currently, four streams are used. Table 8.6 describes these steams.

Table 8.6 OLE Special Streams

Stream Prefix	Description
\0x01...	Basic control streams (two at present)
\0x02...	OLE presentation formats (one per FORMATETC)
\0x03...	Used by the object's container
\0x04...	Used by the storage implementation to hold properties

Figure 8.2 shows a compound file with these streams visible.

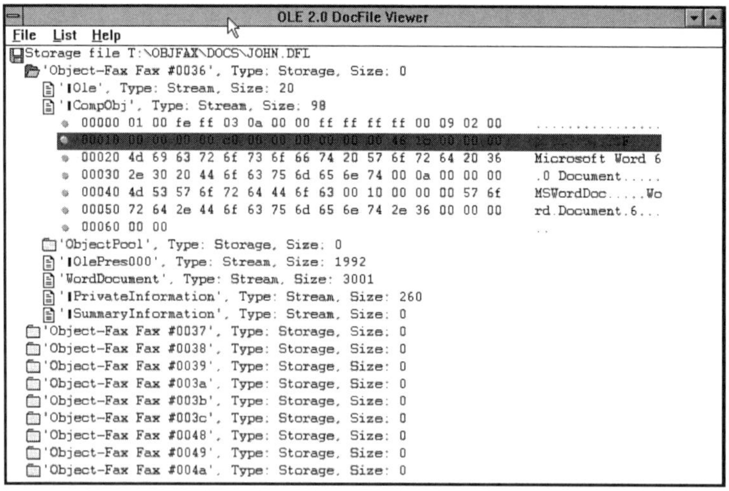

Fig. 8.2 The internals of a compound file.

The *CompObj* Stream

The `CompObj` stream, which also is called \1CompObj, contains information relating to the version of the object and its CLSID. Table 8.7 shows the layout of this stream.

Table 8.7 Layout of the *CompObj* Stream

Field	Length	Description
Byte order indicator	Word	Same byte order as Unicode (0xfffe)
Format version	Word	The version number of this stream
Operating system version	DWORD	The version of the operating system
Class name	–1 CLSID	–1 followed by the CLSID
Display name of class	Variable	User-readable name of the class
Format name	Variable	The data format, which is the same as the clipboard format

The OLE Stream

The OLE stream, or \1Ole, contains information specific to the management of OLE objects. Information stored in this stream indicates whether an object is linked or embedded. If the object is linked, the moniker is also stored. Table 8.8 shows the layout of this stream.

Table 8.8 Layout of the OLE Stream

Field	Length	Description
OLE version	DWORD	The high word contains the version of the OLE libraries; the low word is the version of this stream
Object flags	DWORD	Attribute flags for the object; when set, the low bit indicates a linked object
Update options	DWORD	Update option for a linked object
Reserved	DWORD	Reserved
Moniker	Variable	Moniker of the object relative to its container
Relative source moniker	Variable	Moniker of the source of the link, relative to the link object
Absolute source moniker	Variable	Absolute moniker of the link source
Last class	–1CLSID	CLSID of the object the last time it was bound

(continues)

Table 8.8 Continued

Field	Length	Description
Last display	Variable	Last display name given
`ltChange OfUpdate`	FILETIME	See `IOleObject::IsUpToDate` in the *OLE Programmer's Guide*
`ltKnown UpToDate`	FILETIME	See `IOleObject::IsUpToDate` in the *OLE Programmer's Guide*
`rtUpdate`	FILETIME	See `IOleObject::IsUpToDate` in the *OLE Programmer's Guide*

Monikers are prefixed with the length of the data. If the prefix is 0, no moniker exists.

The Presentation Stream

The presentation streams contain the presentation data used to display and print an object. They are usually metafiles, but can also be data-independent bitmaps (DIBs) or bitmaps. The stream is called `\2OlePres?`. Because an object can have multiple presentation formats, the number of the format must be appended to the name. Table 8.9 shows the layout of this stream.

Table 8.9 Layout of the Presentation Stream

Field	Length	Description
Clipboard format	Variable	The clipboard format of the data
Target device structure	Variable	A DVTARGETDEVICE structure; the field's length can be 4, to indicate a screen device context
Aspect	DWORD	Aspect for the presentation
LIndex	LONG	Used for extended object layout; should be –1 in OLE 2.0
Flags	DWORD	Advise flags for caching
Compression	DWORD	Must be 0 to indicate that no compression is being used
Width	Long	Must be in MM_HIMETRIC units
Size	Longs	Size of the data, in bytes
Presentation data	Variable	The actual data

The Downside of Compound Files

If you use transactioning in your compound files and intend to share these files among users on a network, performance may suffer.

If one user opens the file in read-write transacted mode and another user opens the file for reading, the current implementation of compound files will make a snapshot of the file for the second user. This snapshot involves making a *complete copy* of the file!

This copy is made to ensure that the user does not disturb the data that another user is reading when a commit is made. The only way to avoid the creation of the snapshot is for all users to open the files in read-only mode.

A future release of compound files may address this major limitation.

OLE's Use of Compound Files

Everything that you have seen so far about compound files now can be used as a separate technology apart from OLE 2.0. You can replace your file system with compound files and enjoy the benefits of transactional I/O, use long names on your streams and storages, perform lazy reading and writing of data, and store multiple streams and storages in a single file.

This chapter does not examine how OLE 2.0 uses compound files in Uniform Data Transfer and in compound documents.

When you embed or link objects in a compound document, the container and objects need a way to communicate regarding storage. The container is responsible for providing storage for embedded objects and for storing monikers for linked objects. OLE 2.0 defines four interfaces that are used for object storage: `IPersist`, `IPersistStorage`, `IPersistStream`, and `IPersistFile`.

The *IPersist* Interface

The base interface for `IPersistStorage`, `IPersistStream`, and `IPersistFile`, `IPersist` implements only one method apart from the `IUnknown` methods. `GetClassID` returns the object's CLSID:

```
DECLARE_INTERFACE_(IPersistStorage, IPersist)
{
    // *** IUnknown methods ***
  HRESULT QueryInterface (THIS_ REFIID riid, LPVOID FAR* ppvObj);
  ULONG AddRef (THIS);
  ULONG Release (THIS);

    // *** IPersist methods ***
```

```
    HRESULT GetClassID (THIS_ LPCLSID pclsid);
};
```

If you study the methods of each of these interfaces, you will see that they share much common functionality. The major difference among the interfaces is whether they are used on `IStorages`, monikers, or disk files.

The *IPersistStorage* Interface

All compound objects must support the `IPersistStorage` interface. The container uses this interface to communicate information about the storage allocated to the object.

After creating an object, a container must pass to the object a pointer to a valid storage. The container calls `IPersistStorage::InitNew` with a pointer to the storage. The object then calls `AddRef` for the pointer and keeps the pointer for the object's lifetime.

If an object already exists with a storage, the `IPersistStorage::Load` method is called with a pointer to the object's storage.

When the container saves the document, the object is instructed to save itself with a call to `IPersistStorage::Save`. If the container is doing an incremental save, the method is called with `fSameAsLoad` set to true. However, if the container is doing a full save, this parameter will be false and the storage pointer will point to a new storage. In this case, the object itself must perform a full save to the new storage.

During a full save, an object cannot fail because of low-memory conditions. The OLE design specification lists the methods that are guaranteed not to use memory. This list includes most of the `IStream` and `IStorage` methods except those that actually open something.

The implication for the object's implementor is clear. Your object may not fail because of a low-memory condition, but the methods that open storages and streams all use memory. The only solution is to open all your streams and storages when the object is first loaded. At this stage, you can fail to load because of low memory. After you have pointers to your open storages and streams, you can always fulfill your obligation to save your data successfully, even in a low-memory situation.

After the container calls `IPersistStorage::Save` to instruct the object to save itself, the object enters what is affectionately known as a "no-scribble" state. While in this state, the object cannot save any more data into the storage. The container is now responsible for committing the changes that the object saved. After committing the changes, the container calls

IPersistStorage::SaveCompleted. This method releases the object from the no-scribble state, again enabling the object to scribble in the storage.

During a full save, the application normally performs the full save to a temporary file, deletes the old original file, and renames the temporary file to the original name.

Due to the DOS file system's limitations—namely that you cannot delete or rename a file while it is open—this method does not work because all the objects in a compound document hold open storage pointers to various storages within the file. You can address this problem with the IPersistStorage::HandsOffStorage method.

The container calls this method to force the object to release its storage pointer. The object then enters the "hands-off" state. This state is similar to "no-scribble." After performing the full save, the container retrieves the storage pointers and returns them to the object during the IPesistStorage::SaveCompleted call. These storage pointers are guaranteed to be exactly the same as the storage pointer that you relinquished during the IPersistStorage::HandsOffStorage call.

Here is the code for the IPersistStorage interface:

```
DECLARE_INTERFACE_(IPersistStorage, IPersist)
{
    // *** IUnknown methods ***
  HRESULT QueryInterface (THIS_ REFIID riid, LPVOID FAR* ppvObj);
  ULONG AddRef (THIS);
  ULONG Release (THIS);

    // *** IPersist methods ***
  HRESULT GetClassID (THIS_ LPCLSID pclsid);

    // *** IPersistStorage methods ***
  HRESULT IsDirty (THIS);
  HRESULT InitNew (THIS_ LPSTORAGE pStg);
  HRESULT Load (THIS_ LPSTORAGE pStg);
  HRESULT Save (THIS_ LPSTORAGE pStgSave, BOOL fSameAsLoad);
  HRESULT SaveCompleted (THIS_ LPSTORAGE pStgNew);
  HRESULT HandsOffStorage (THIS);
};
```

The *IPersistStream* Interface

The IPersistStream interface is mainly used by monikers. The major difference between the IPersistStorage IStorage pointers and the IStream pointers of IPersistStream is that the IStream pointer is valid only during the method call. You cannot store such pointers as the IStorage pointers of IPersistStorage.

Compound document objects do not use this interface.

Here is the declaration for the `IPersistStream` interface:

```
DECLARE_INTERFACE_(IPersistStream, IPersist)
{
    // *** IUnknown methods ***
  HRESULT QueryInterface (THIS_ REFIID riid, LPVOID FAR* ppvObj);
  ULONG AddRef (THIS);
  ULONG Release (THIS);

    // *** IPersist methods ***
  HRESULT GetClassID (THIS_ LPCLSID pclsid);

    // *** IPersistStream methods ***
  HRESULT IsDirty (THIS);
  HRESULT Load (THIS_ LPSTREAM pStm);
  HRESULT Save (THIS_ LPSTREAM pStm, BOOL fClearDirty);
  HRESULT GetSizeMax (THIS_ ULARGE_INTEGER FAR * pcbSize);
};
```

The *IPersistFile* Interface

The `IPersistFile` interface loads and saves documents to the disk file rather than `IStorages`. You usually use `IPersistFile` to support linking to disk files.

With the `IPersistFile` interface, the object itself is responsible for opening the file.

The code for `IPersistFile` follows:

```
DECLARE_INTERFACE_(IPersistFile, IPersist)
{
    // *** IUnknown methods ***
  HRESULT QueryInterface (THIS_ REFIID riid, LPVOID FAR* ppvObj);
  ULONG AddRef (THIS);
  ULONG Release (THIS);

    // *** IPersist methods ***
  HRESULT GetClassID (THIS_ LPCLSID pclsid);

    // *** IPersistFile methods ***
  HRESULT IsDirty (THIS);
  HRESULT Load (THIS_ LPCSTR lpszFileName, DWORD grfMode);
  HRESULT Save (THIS_ LPCSTR lpszFileName, BOOL fRemember);
  HRESULT SaveCompleted (THIS_ LPCSTR lpszFileName);
  HRESULT GetCurFile (THIS_ LPSTR FAR * lplpszFileName);
};
```

Property Sets

Property sets are a standard means of storing data in a compound file. They define a structure or layout for data that other programs can read.

The OLE design specification defines property sets. The general idea behind property sets is that, by providing a standard means of storing data, other applications can also access the data. Perhaps the best example of this concept is shell-level browsing. In Windows 95, for example, the shell can search through a set of compound files for a set of keywords. This level of search is made possible by standard property sets. The OLE design specification defines one such standard property set: Summary Information.

This property set defines a standard set of fields that make up a Summary Information property set. You are probably familiar with the Summary Information dialog box in Word for Windows 6.0. This dialog box enables the user to store a set of attributes about the document. These attributes include such information as the author's name, the title, the subject of the document, and possibly a set of keywords that you can use to identify the document. Defining a standard mechanism for storing and retrieving this data enables applications such as the shell to search and browse documents.

A *property* is a piece of information that you can use to describe a particular piece of data. It consists of three parts: an identifier, a type indicator, and the actual value. Here is an example of a property:

Identifer	Type	Value
PID_AUTHOR	VT_LPSTR	"John Toohey"

The type indentifer field provides a rich and flexible means of storing various types of properties. As table 8.10 indicates, properties can consist of simple types like integers to complete storages.

Table 8.10 Type Indicator Values

Type Indicator	Code	Value Representation
VT_EMPTY	0	None. A property set with a type indicator of VT_EMPTY has no data associated with it (that is, the size of the type is 0).
VT_NULL	1	None. See VT_EMPTY. This type is like a pointer to NULL.
VT_I2	2	Two bytes representing a WORD value. This type is zero-padded to 32-bit boundary.
VT_I4	3	Four bytes representing a DWORD value.

(continues)

Table 8.10 Continued

Type Indicator	Code	Value Representation
VT_R4	4	Four bytes representing a 32-bit IEEE floating point value.
VT_R8	5	Eight bytes representing a 64-bit IEEE floating point value.
VT_CY	6	Eight-byte two's complement integer (scaled by 10,000). This type is commonly used for currency amounts.
VT_DATE	7	Time format used by many applications: a 64-bit floating point number representing the seconds since January 1, 1900. This value is stored in the same representation as VT_R8.
VT_BSTR	8	Counted, zero-terminated binary string, represented as a DWORD byte count (including the terminating null character) followed by the bytes of data.
VT_BOOL	11	Two bytes representing a Boolean (WORD) value containing 0 (false) or –1 (true). This value is zero-padded to a 32-bit boundary.
VT_VARIANT	12	A four-byte type indicator followed by the corresponding value. This value is used only with VT_VECTOR.
VT_I8	20	Eight bytes representing a signed integer.
VT_LPSTR	30	Same as VT_BSTR; this value is the representation of most strings.
VT_LPWSTR	31	A counted and zero-terminated Unicode string; a DWORD character count (where the count includes the terminating null character) followed by that many Unicode (16-bit) characters. Note that the count is not a byte count, but a WORD count.
VT_FILETIME	64	The 64-bit file time structure, FILETIME, as defined by 32-bit Windows.
VT_BLOB	65	DWORD count of bytes, followed by that many bytes of data. This type is similar to VT_BSTR but does not guarantee a null byte at the end of the data.

Type Indicator	Code	Value Representation
VT_STREAM	66	A VT_LPSTR (DWORD count of bytes followed by a zero-terminated string that many bytes long) that names the stream that contains the data. The real value for this property is stored in an `IStream` that is a sibling of the CONTENTS stream. This type is valid only for property sets that are stored in the CONTENTS stream of an `IStorage`.
VT_STORAGE	67	A VT_LPSTR (DWORD count of bytes followed by a zero-terminated string that many bytes long) that names the storage that contains the data. The real value is stored in an `IStorage` that contains the data that is a sibling of the CONTENTS stream that contains the property set. This type is valid only for property sets that are stored in the CONTENTS stream of an `IStorage`.
VT_STREAMED_OBJECT	68	Same as VT_STREAM, but indicates that the `IStream` named in this property contains a serialized object. A serialized object is a CLSID followed by initialization data for the class. The named `IStream` is a sibling to the CONTENTS stream that contains the property set. This type is valid only for property sets that are stored in the CONTENTS stream of an `IStorage`.
VT_STORED_OBJECT	69	Same as VT_STORAGE but indicates that the `IStorage` named in this property contains an object. This type is valid only for property sets stored in the CONTENTS stream of an `IStorage`.
VT_BLOB_OBJECT	70	A VT_LPSTR naming a stream that is a sibling to the CONTENTS stream. This stream contains a VT_BLOB value. The only significant difference between this type and VT_STREAMED_OBJECT is that this type does not have the system-level storage overhead that VT_STREAMED_OBJECT would have. This type, therefore, is more suitable for scenarios that involve many small objects.
VT_CF	71	A VT_BLOB containing a clipboard format identifier followed by the data in that format.
VT_CLSID	72	A class ID, which consists of a DWORD, two WORDs, and eight bytes.
VT_VECTOR	0x1000	If the type indicator is one of the preceding values with this bit on in addition, the value is a DWORD count of elements, followed by that many repetitions of the value. See the *OLE Programmer's Guide* for a detailed description.

Property sets can also have an optional dictionary that stores "human-readable" names describing each of the properties.

Property sets are stored as `IStorage` or `IStream` objects. The names of common property sets are prepended with 0x05. A `Storage` or `Stream` that contains a Summary Information property set, for example, would be called \005SummaryInformation. If you use a `Storage` to store property sets, you should store the main property set in a stream called CONTENTS. If a particular property has a VT_STREAM, VT_STORAGE, VT_BLOB_OBJECT, VT_STREAMED_OBJECT, or VT_STORED_OBJECT type, that stream or storage is stored as a sibling of the CONTENTS stream.

You can store the Summary Information property set only in an `IStream` object.

Like all OLE objects, the property set is identified by a globally unique identifier (GUID). The GUID used for property sets is a format ID.

The OLE design specification actually defines only one property set: the Summary Information property set. You must store this property set in an `IStream` object that exists off of the root storage. The format ID is F29F85E0-4FF9-1068-AB91-08002B27B3D9, and you must call the stream \005SummaryInformation. Table 8.11 shows the various properties defined for this property set.

Table 8.11 Summary Information Properties

Property Name	Property ID	Property ID Code	Type Indicator
Title	PID_TITLE	0x00000002	VT_LPSTR
Subject	PID_SUBJECT	0x00000003	VT_LPSTR
Author	PID_AUTHOR	0x00000004	VT_LPSTR
Keywords	PID_KEYWORDS	0x00000005	VT_LPSTR
Comments	PID_COMMENTS	0x00000006	VT_LPSTR
Template	PID_TEMPLATE	0x00000007	VT_LPSTR
Last saved by	PID_LASTAUTHOR	0x00000008	VT_LPSTR
Revision number	PID_REVNUMBER	0x00000009	VT_LPSTR
Total editing time	PID_EDITTIME	0x0000000A	VT_FILETIME

Property Name	Property ID	Property ID Code	Type Indicator
Last printed	PID_LASTPRINTED	0x0000000B	VT_FILETIME
Create time/date	PID_CREATE_DTM	0x0000000C	VT_FILETIME
Last saved time/date	PID_LASTSAVE_DTM	0x0000000D	VT_FILETIME
Number of pages	PID_PAGECOUNT	0x0000000E	VT_I4
Number of words	PID_WORDCOUNT	0x0000000F	VT_I4
Number of characters	PID_CHARCOUNT	0x00000010	VT_I4
Thumbnail	PID_THUMBNAIL	0x00000011	VT_CF
Name of creating application	PID_APPNAME	0x00000012	VT_LPSTR
Security	PID_SECURITY	0x00000013	VT_I4

The OLE Control Developer's SDK provides a C++ class, `CProperty`, that you can use to manipulate property sets. The sample application that you are about to build uses this class to read the Summary Information property set stored by Microsoft Word 6.0 in its documents. However, this application can read Summary Information property sets from any application that supports them.

The sample application's full source code is included on the companion disk. This chapter examines only the `CDocument` and `CSumInfo` modules.

When the user chooses **O**pen from the **F**ile menu, the framework calls the `OnOpenDocument` method. You first must determine whether the selected file is actually a compound file. To do so, you call the API function `StgIsStorageFile`. This function returns true if the file is in fact a compound file.

You then open the root storage for the compound file. After you have an initialed pointer to the `IStorage` interface for the root storage, you try to open the Summary Information stream. If this stream does not exist, you notify the user and return. If you get an `IStream` pointer to the property set, you store the pointer and return true. Listing 8.1 shows the code for the `CDocument` implementation.

Listing 8.1 The SUMMADOC.H and SUMMADOC.CPP Source Files

```
#include <tchar.h>

class CSummaryDoc : public CDocument
{
protected: // create from serialization only
     CSummaryDoc();
     DECLARE_DYNCREATE(CSummaryDoc)

// Attributes
public:
    TCHAR m_szStorage[_MAX_PATH];
     TCHAR m_szStream[_MAX_PATH];

     LPSTORAGE  m_pStorage;
     LPSTREAM m_pStream;

     BOOL m_fOpen;

// Operations
public:

// Overrides
     // ClassWizard-generated virtual function overrides
     //{{AFX_VIRTUAL(CSummaryDoc)
     public:
     virtual BOOL OnNewDocument();
     virtual BOOL OnOpenDocument(LPCTSTR lpszPathName);
     //}}AFX_VIRTUAL

// Implementation
public:
     virtual ~CSummaryDoc();
     virtual void Serialize(CArchive& ar);
#ifdef _DEBUG
     virtual void AssertValid() const;
     virtual void Dump(CDumpContext& dc) const;
#endif

protected:

// Generated message map functions
protected:
     //{{AFX_MSG(CSummaryDoc)
     // NOTE - ClassWizard adds and removes member functions here.
     //    DO NOT EDIT what you see in these blocks of generated code!
     //}}AFX_MSG
     DECLARE_MESSAGE_MAP()
};

/////////////////////////////////////////////////////////////////////////////

#include "stdafx.h"
#include "summary.h"
#include "summadoc.h"
```

```
#ifdef _DEBUG
#undef THIS_FILE
static char BASED_CODE THIS_FILE[] = __FILE__;
#endif

//////////////////////////////////////////////////////////////////////
//
// CSummaryDoc

IMPLEMENT_DYNCREATE(CSummaryDoc, CDocument)

BEGIN_MESSAGE_MAP(CSummaryDoc, CDocument)
     //{{AFX_MSG_MAP(CSummaryDoc)
     // NOTE - ClassWizard adds and removes mapping macros here.
     // DO NOT EDIT what you see in these blocks of generated code!
     //}}AFX_MSG_MAP
END_MESSAGE_MAP()

//////////////////////////////////////////////////////////////////////
// CSummaryDoc construction/destruction

CSummaryDoc::CSummaryDoc()
{
     m_pStorage = NULL;
     m_pStream = NULL;
     m_fOpen = FALSE;
}
//-------------------------------------------------------------------
CSummaryDoc::~CSummaryDoc()
{
     if(m_pStream)
          m_pStream->Release();

     if(m_pStorage)
          m_pStorage->Release();
}
//-------------------------------------------------------------------
BOOL CSummaryDoc::OnNewDocument()
{
     if (!CDocument::OnNewDocument())
          return FALSE;

     return TRUE;
}
//////////////////////////////////////////////////////////////////////
// CSummaryDoc serialization
//
void CSummaryDoc::Serialize(CArchive& ar)
{
     if (ar.IsStoring())
     {
     }
     else
     {
     }
}
```

(continues)

II

Using MFC

Listing 8.1 Continued

```
/////////////////////////////////////////////////////////////////////////////
// CSummaryDoc diagnostics
//
#ifdef _DEBUG
void CSummaryDoc::AssertValid() const
{
     CDocument::AssertValid();
}

void CSummaryDoc::Dump(CDumpContext& dc) const
{
     CDocument::Dump(dc);
}
#endif //_DEBUG

/////////////////////////////////////////////////////////////////////////////
// CSummaryDoc commands
BOOL CSummaryDoc::OnOpenDocument(LPCTSTR lpszPathName)
{
     SCODE sc;

     sc = StgIsStorageFile(lpszPathName);
     if (S_FALSE == sc)
     {
          AfxMessageBox(_T("Error : Not a compound file"));
          return FALSE;
     }
     else
     {
          sc = StgOpenStorage(lpszPathName,NULL,
           STGM_READWRITE¦STGM_SHARE_EXCLUSIVE,NULL,0,&m_pStorage);

          if(IS_ERROR(sc))
          {
               AfxMessageBox(AfxGetFullScodeString(sc));
               return FALSE;
          }
     }

     sc = m_pStorage->OpenStream(_T("\005SummaryInformation"),NULL,
               STGM_READWRITE¦STGM_SHARE_EXCLUSIVE,0L,&m_pStream);
     if(IS_ERROR(sc))
     {
          AfxMessageBox(_T("No Summary Stream"));
          m_pStorage->Release();
          m_pStorage = NULL;
          return FALSE;
     }

     m_fOpen = TRUE;
     return TRUE;
}
//---------------------------------------------------------------------------
//---------------------------------------------------------------------------
```

The next step is to extract the property set and display the fields. In the CFromView class, you read the property set from the IStream object into the member m_propset, which is an instance of the CProperty class.

Extracting the individual fields is simply a matter of calling CProperty::Get. You extract the fields in which you are interested and store them in class member variables.

The call to CWnd::Updatedata then moves the data from the member variables to the screen. Listing 8.2 shows the source code for the CFormView implementation.

Listing 8.2 The SUMINFO.CPP Module

```
#include "stdafx.h"
#include "summadoc.h"
#include "summary.h"
#include "suminfo.h"
#include "clsid.h"

#ifdef _DEBUG
#undef THIS_FILE
static char BASED_CODE THIS_FILE[] = __FILE__;
#endif


/////////////////////////////////////////////////////////////////////
// CSumInfo
//
IMPLEMENT_DYNCREATE(CSumInfo, CFormView)

CSumInfo::CSumInfo()
     : CFormView(CSumInfo::IDD)
{
     //{{AFX_DATA_INIT(CSumInfo)
     m_author = _T("");
     m_comment = _T("");
     m_keyword = _T("");
     m_subject = _T("");
     m_title = _T("");
     //}}AFX_DATA_INIT
}

CSumInfo::~CSumInfo()
{
}

void CSumInfo::DoDataExchange(CDataExchange* pDX)
{
     CFormView::DoDataExchange(pDX);
     //{{AFX_DATA_MAP(CSumInfo)
     DDX_Text(pDX, IDC_AUTHOR, m_author);
```

(continues)

Listing 8.2 Continued

```
	DDX_Text(pDX, IDC_COMMENTS, m_comment);
	DDX_Text(pDX, IDC_KEYWORDS, m_keyword);
	DDX_Text(pDX, IDC_SUBJECT, m_subject);
	DDX_Text(pDX, IDC_TITLE, m_title);
	//}}AFX_DATA_MAP
}


BEGIN_MESSAGE_MAP(CSumInfo, CFormView)
	//{{AFX_MSG_MAP(CSumInfo)
		// NOTE - ClassWizard adds and removes mapping macros here.
	//}}AFX_MSG_MAP
END_MESSAGE_MAP()


/////////////////////////////////////////////////////////////////////////////
// CSumInfo diagnostics

#ifdef _DEBUG
void CSumInfo::AssertValid() const
{
	CFormView::AssertValid();
}

void CSumInfo::Dump(CDumpContext& dc) const
{
	CFormView::Dump(dc);
}
#endif //_DEBUG

/////////////////////////////////////////////////////////////////////////////
// CSumInfo message handlers
void CSumInfo::OnInitialUpdate()
{
	CFormView::OnInitialUpdate();
	GetParentFrame()->RecalcLayout();
	ResizeParentToFit(FALSE);

	// Default argument is TRUE
	ResizeParentToFit(/*FALSE*/);
}
//---------------------------------------------------------------
#define PID_TITLE        0x00000002
#define PID_SUBJECT      0x00000003
#define PID_AUTHOR       0x00000004
#define PID_KEYWORDS     0x00000005
#define PID_COMMENTS     0x00000006

void CSumInfo::OnUpdate(CView* pSender, LPARAM lHint, CObject* pHint)
{
    CSummaryDoc* pDoc = (CSummaryDoc*)GetDocument();
	TCHAR test[144];
```

```
        if(pDoc->m_fOpen)
        {
            BOOL fOK = m_propset.ReadFromStream(pDoc->m_pStream);
            if(fOK)
            {
                DWORD cb;
                m_author = (LPSTR)m_propset.Get(
                        FormatID_SummaryInformation,PID_AUTHOR,&cb);
                m_title = (LPSTR)m_propset.Get(
                         FormatID_SummaryInformation,PID_TITLE,&cb);
                m_subject = (LPSTR)m_propset.Get(
                       FormatID_SummaryInformation,PID_SUBJECT,&cb);
                m_comment = (LPSTR)m_propset.Get(
                      FormatID_SummaryInformation,PID_COMMENTS,&cb);
                m_keyword = (LPSTR)m_propset.Get(
                      FormatID_SummaryInformation,PID_KEYWORDS,&cb);
            }
            UpdateData(FALSE);
        }
    }
    //-------------------------------------------------------------
    //-------------------------------------------------------------
```

Figure 8.3 shows the Summary Information application with the Microsoft Word document, OUTLINE.DOC, opened. Figure 8.4 shows the Microsoft Word Summary Information dialog box with the same document opened.

This section has looked briefly at property sets. Sections, dictionaries, extending property sets, or other uses for property sets have not been discussed. For a full discussion of these features, refer to the paper "OLE 2.0 Property Sets Exposed" by Charlie Kindel. This paper is available on CompuServe and the Microsoft Developer Network Library CD-ROM.

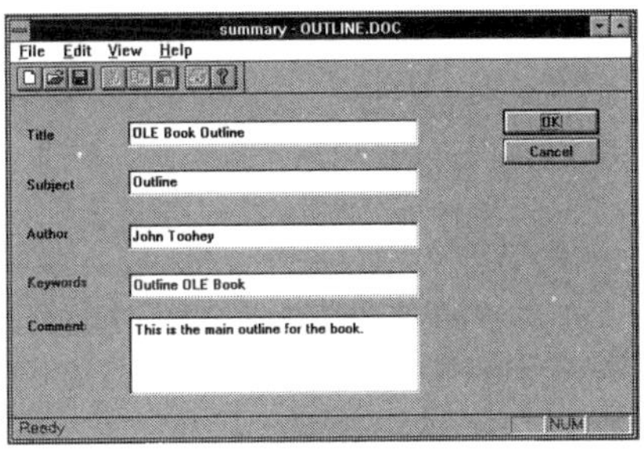

Fig. 8.3
The Summary Information application.

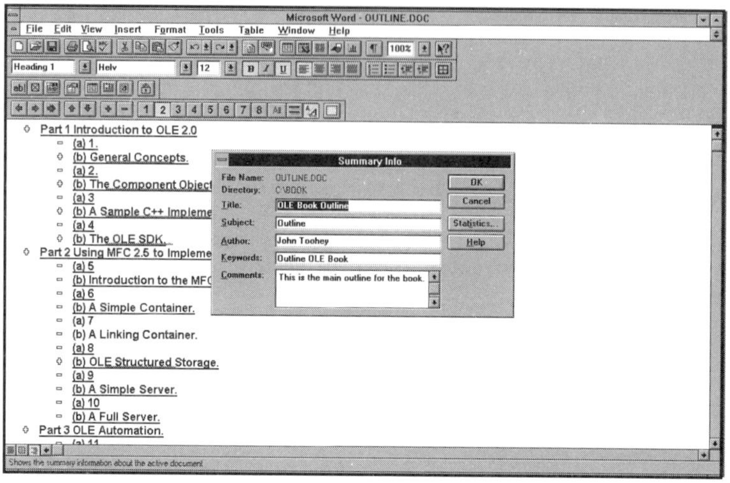

Fig. 8.4
Microsoft Word's Summary Information dialog box.

Also, for a thorough look at the `CProperty` class, you should read the source code supplied with the OLE Custom Control SDK.

MFC's Implementation of Compound Files

Support for compound files in the MFC framework comes in two forms. The first is almost transparent to the developer. By calling the `CDocument::EnableCompoundFile` method from your document's class constructor, you make it possible to use a compound file through the `CDocument::Serialize` method. The file attached to the `CArchive` object that is used in the `Serialize` method is in a compound file.

The second level of support comes in the form of a class for dealing with `IStream` objects. The class, `COleStreamFile`, which is also used internally within the framework, is available for you to use in your application. The class provides a thin wrapper on the `IStream` interface.

The `CDocument::EnableCompoundFile` works by simply setting the `m_bCompoundFile` flag. When the framework calls `OnOpenDocument` in response to the user selecting the **O**pen command, the selected file opens as a compound file. As you can see in listing 8.3, the file is opened in transacted mode and uses the share exclusive flag. Therefore, by default, nobody will be able to read or write this file while you have it open. If you want to share the file, you must duplicate the code in an override of `OnOpenDocument` and specify the attributes that you require.

Listing 8.3 The *OnOpenDocument* Method

```
BOOL COleDocument::OnOpenDocument(const char* pszPathName)
{
     ASSERT(pszPathName == NULL || AfxIsValidString(pszPathName));

     // just use default implementation if 'docfile' is not enabled
     if (!m_bCompoundFile && m_lpRootStg == NULL)
     {
          ASSERT(pszPathName != NULL);
          return CDocument::OnOpenDocument(pszPathName);
     }

     if (IsModified())
         TRACE0("Warning: OnOpenDocument replaces an unsaved
                 document\n");

     // abort changes to current docfile
     DeleteContents();
     if (m_bCompoundFile)
          _AfxRelease((LPUNKNOWN*)&m_lpRootStg);
     SetModifiedFlag(TRUE);  // dirty during deserialize

     BOOL bResult = FALSE;
     TRY
     {
          if (m_lpRootStg == NULL)
          {
               // open new storage file
               LPSTORAGE lpStorage;
               HRESULT hr = ::StgOpenStorage(pszPathName, NULL,
                              STGM_READWRITE|STGM_TRANSACTED|
                              STGM_SHARE_EXCLUSIVE,
                              0, 0, &lpStorage);
               if (hr != NOERROR)
                    AfxThrowOleException(hr);
               ASSERT(lpStorage != NULL);
               m_lpRootStg = lpStorage;
          }

          // use helper to read document from storage
          LoadFromStorage();

          SetModifiedFlag(FALSE); // start off with unmodified
          bResult = TRUE;
```

(continues)

Listing 8.3 Continued

```
        }
        CATCH_ALL(e)
        {
            DeleteContents();   // removed failed contents
            _AfxRelease((LPUNKNOWN*)&m_lpRootStg);

            // if not file-based load, return exceptions to the caller
            if (!m_bCompoundFile)
                THROW_LAST();

            TRY
                ReportSaveLoadException(pszPathName, e,
                    FALSE, AFX_IDP_FAILED_TO_OPEN_DOC);
            END_TRY
        }
        END_CATCH_ALL

        return bResult;
    }
```

As you learned earlier, opening the root storage in transacted mode bypasses the performance hit of having to take a snapshot of the entire file.

After you open the file, the interface pointer to the root storage is stored in the member variable `m_lpRootStg`. Then the helper function `LoadFromStorage` is called.

`LoadFromStorage` (listing 8.4) begins by declaring a `COleStreamFile` object. This MFC class reads and writes `IStreams`. It then tries to open the CONTENTS stream in exclusive mode. If you succeed in opening the stream, a `CArchive` object is created and the stream object is attached to it. The `Serialize` method is then called to read in the actual data.

Listing 8.4 The *LoadFromStorage* Method

```
void COleDocument::LoadFromStorage()
{
    ASSERT(m_lpRootStg != NULL);

    // open Contents stream
    COleStreamFile file;
    CFileException fe;
    if (!file.OpenStream(m_lpRootStg, szContents,
        CFile::modeReadWrite|CFile::shareExclusive, &fe))
    {
        AfxThrowFileException(fe.m_cause, fe.m_lOsError);
    }
```

```
        // load it with CArchive (loads from Contents stream)
            THROW_LAST();
        }
        END_CATCH_ALL
    }
```

To save a file with MFC, the framework calls `OnSaveDocument` (see listing 8.5). This method begins by checking whether you are using a file name other than that which you use when opening the file. If you are using a different file name, a new compound file is created. The helper method `SaveToStorage` is then called.

Listing 8.5 The *OnSaveDocument* Method

```
BOOL COleDocument::OnSaveDocument(const char* pszPathName)
{
    ASSERT(pszPathName == NULL || AfxIsValidString(pszPathName));

    // use default implementation if 'docfile' is not enabled
    if (!m_bCompoundFile && m_lpRootStg == NULL)
        return CDocument::OnSaveDocument(pszPathName);

    LPSTORAGE lpOrigStg = NULL;
    if (m_bCompoundFile)
        m_bSameAsLoad = (m_strPathName == pszPathName);

    BOOL bResult = FALSE;
    TRY
    {
        // open new root storage if necessary
        if (m_bCompoundFile && !m_bSameAsLoad)
        {
            // temporarily detach current storage
            lpOrigStg = m_lpRootStg;
            m_lpRootStg = NULL;

            LPSTORAGE lpStorage;
            HRESULT hr = ::StgCreateDocfile(pszPathName,
                        STGM_READWRITE|
                        STGM_TRANSACTED|STGM_SHARE_EXCLUSIVE|
                        STGM_CREATE, 0, &lpStorage);
            if (hr != NOERROR)
                AfxThrowOleException(hr);

            ASSERT(lpStorage != NULL);
            m_lpRootStg = lpStorage;
        }
        ASSERT(m_lpRootStg != NULL);

        // use helper to save to root storage
        SaveToStorage();
```

(continues)

Listing 8.5 Continued

```
        if (m_bCompoundFile)
        {
            // commit each of the items
            CommitItems(m_bRemember && !m_bSameAsLoad);

            // mark document as clean if remembering the storage
            if (m_bRemember)
                SetModifiedFlag(FALSE);

            // remember correct storage or
            // release save copy as storage
            if (!m_bSameAsLoad)
            {
                if (m_bRemember)
                {
                    // Save As case -- m_stgRoot is new storage,
                    //forget old storage
                    lpOrigStg->Release();
                }
                else
                {
                    // Save Copy As case.
                    // m_stgRoot should hook up to m_stgOrig.
                    m_lpRootStg->Release();
                    m_lpRootStg = lpOrigStg;
                }
            }
        }

        bResult = TRUE;
    }
    CATCH_ALL(e)
    {
        if (lpOrigStg != NULL)
        {
            // save as failed:
            //abort new storage, and reattach original
            _AfxRelease((LPUNKNOWN*)&m_lpRootStg);
            m_lpRootStg = lpOrigStg;
        }

        if (!m_bCompoundFile)
            THROW_LAST();

        TRY
            ReportSaveLoadException(pszPathName, e,
                TRUE, AFX_IDP_FAILED_TO_SAVE_DOC);
        END_TRY
    }
    END_CATCH_ALL
```

```
        // cleanup
        m_bSameAsLoad = TRUE;
        m_bRemember = TRUE;

        return bResult;
    }
```

The SaveToStorage method (see listing 8.6) begins by creating or opening the CONTENTS stream. If this succeeds, the stream is attached to a CArchive object and the Serialize method is called. This enables the objects to save their data into the archive. After the Serialize method finishes executing, the root storage is committed, ensuring that all changes are actually written to the file. (Remember, by default, MFC opens all compound files in transacted mode.)

Listing 8.6 The *SaveToStorage* Method

```
void COleDocument::SaveToStorage(CObject* pObject)
{
     ASSERT(m_lpRootStg != NULL);

     // create Contents stream
     COleStreamFile file;
     CFileException fe;
     if (!file.CreateStream(m_lpRootStg, szContents,
          CFile::modeWrite¦CFile::shareExclusive¦CFile::modeCreate, &fe))
     {
          AfxThrowFileException(fe.m_cause, fe.m_lOsError);
     }

     // save to Contents stream
     CArchive saveArchive(&file, CArchive::store ¦
     ➥CArchive::bNoFlushOnDelete);
     saveArchive.m_pDocument = this;
     saveArchive.m_bForceFlat = FALSE;

     TRY
     {
          // save the contents
          if (pObject != NULL)
               pObject->Serialize(saveArchive);
          else
               Serialize(saveArchive);
          saveArchive.Close();
          file.Close();

          // commit the root storage
          m_lpRootStg->Commit(STGC_ONLYIFCURRENT);
     }
```

(continues)

Listing 8.6 Continued

```
        CATCH_ALL(e)
        {
             file.Abort();       // will not throw an exception
             CommitItems(FALSE); // abort save in progress
             saveArchive.CArchive::~CArchive();

             THROW_LAST();
        }
        END_CATCH_ALL
    }
```

After returning from the `SaveToStorage` method, the sample application calls the `CommitItem` method for each object in the container. The `CommitItem` method calls `SaveCompleted` on the `IPersistStorage` interface for each object. As you saw earlier, calling the `IPersistStorage::SaveCompleted` method forces the object from the "no-scribble" state back into a normal "scribble" state.

Finally, the `m_lpRootStg` is released and the compound file is closed.

As you can see, support for compound files is provided primarily through the serialization mechanism. If you need more control over file sharing, creation of storages, property streams, and so on, you must go directly to the OLE API.

From Here...

In this chapter, you examined structured storage and compound files. In the next chapter, you develop your first COM object.

Chapter 9

A Simple MFC OLE Server

You now turn your attention to the job of creating an OLE object that you can insert into OLE containers.

In this chapter, you develop a *miniserver*—an object server that can create objects that you can insert into a container but that cannot exist outside of the container. Good examples of commercial miniservers are Microsoft WordArt and the Microsoft Equation Editor, which are both supplied with Microsoft Word. The server that you develop in this chapter enables the user to insert one of several bitmaps into a container. You also will enable the server to activate itself in place within the container.

You also will see the minimum that you need to do to write a functional miniserver with the Microsoft Foundation Classes (MFC).

The Server Architecture

Microsoft's AFX (Applications Frameworks) group added several new classes when it added OLE support to the standard Document/View architecture of MFC (see fig. 9.1). Two new classes, `COleDocument` and `COleServerDoc`, derive from `CDocument`. `COleDocument` provides most of the functionality for in-place editing, but the class that you are interested now is `COleServerDoc`.

The `COleServerDoc` class provides a collection call for `COleServerItems`. Instances of `COleServerItems` are the actual interfaces between the objects that you implement and the clients that use them. You could conceivably combine `COleServerDoc` and `COleServerItems` into a single class; however, to give server applications more flexibility, the more resource-intensive components were put into the `COleServerItem` class, making `COleServer` a much more lightweight class.

Fig. 9.1
The server document architecture.

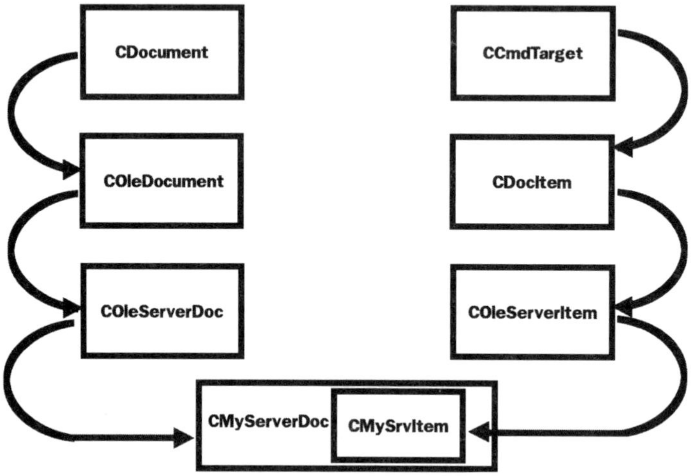

Five separate COM interfaces are implemented for use in the `COleServerDoc` class: `IPersistStorage`, `IOleObject`, `IDataObject`, `IOleInPlaceObject`, and `IOleInPlaceActiveObject`.

As always, the class libraries provide adequate default implementations for almost all the required methods. You implement `OnGetEmbeddItem` and `OnSetItemRects`.

If your object is an embedded object (rather than a linked object), you have only one `COleServerItem` object in your `COleServerDoc` class. This object is created in the `OnGetEmbeddItem` method. MFC calls this method when the framework needs to create and retrieve the pointer to your embedded object.

When a user moves or resizes the in-place frame on an active object, the framework calls `OnSetItemRects`. You use the position rectangle that is passed in this method call to reposition your object within the container.

`COleServerItem` encapsulates the interface between the OLE object and the container. You must implement two methods in this class:

- `GetExtent` is called by the framework to retrieve the object's *natural extents* (the size at which the object is normally viewed or printed).

- `Draw` renders the object into a metafile that is later used as the object's presentation data. The container displays this metafile when the object is not active.

GDI Mapping Modes

One of the most frustrating problems that you may encounter with OLE occurs when you use the HIMETRIC mapping mode while rendering your object's data into the presentation metafile.

In fact, this issue of mapping modes has nothing specifically to do with OLE. Mapping modes have existed in the Windows GDI since the first release of Windows. However, most developers manage to avoid mapping modes by using the default MM_TEXT mode in all of their applications. If your background is in the character-mode programming of MS-DOS, the MM_TEXT mode is exactly what you are used to: the origin is in the top-left corner, the X axis moves to the right, and the Y axis moves down.

In the OLE documentation and in this book, you'll notice that the units used when discussing OLE are HIMETRIC units. In the MM_HIMETRIC mapping mode (see fig. 9.2), each unit represents 0.001 of a centimeter. The default origin is the screen's top-left corner, but the Y axis decreases as it goes down. The fact that the Y axis is negative confuses many programmers who work with HIMETRIC units in OLE. HIMETRIC units in OLE are never negative numbers; instead, they are always represented as absolute values. So, when you implement a `GetExtent` method and return your object's extents, they are always positive numbers.

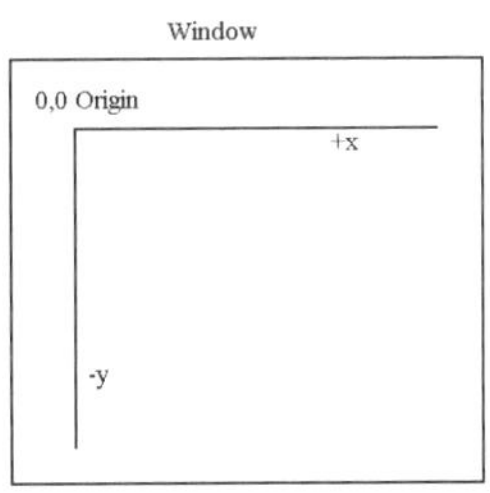

Fig. 9.2
The HIMETRIC mapping mode.

> **Note**
>
> The key to scaling a metafile is its extents. By themselves, extents have no meaning, but when expressed as a ratio, they become the scaling factor that GDI uses when translating logical units to device units. This translation of logical units to device units is what performs the actual scaling.

An OLE container's user interface must enable the user to move and scale the embedded and linked objects. These objects are represented by metafiles that the default handler in the OLE libraries played into the container's client area.

You create this metafile in the implementation of `COleServerItem::Draw`. In this method, you receive a device context to a metafile and then render your object onto this device context. This process sounds simple enough.

However, if you are using one of the constrained mapping modes—such as MM_TEXT, MM_LOMETRIC, MM_HIMETRIC, MM_LOENGLISH, MM_HIENGLISH, MM_TWIPS, or MM_ISOTROPIC—you run into problems. The cause of these problems is simple: the user expects to be able to resize your object's presentation data within a container. If you have used one of the constrained mapping modes, which are based on physical units, your object will not scale correctly.

Suppose, for example, that your application uses MM_HIMETRIC and your object is drawn at 3000×3000. This translates to a 3cm×3cm square. If the object is drawn into a metafile with that mapping mode and those extents, the user cannot scale the metafile because the sizes are hard-coded.

To create a metafile that scales correctly, you must use the unconstrained mapping mode MM_ANISOTROPIC. This particular mapping mode is based on arbitrary logical units rather than physical units of measure. To set these units, you call the Windows API functions `SetWindowExt` and `SetWindowOrg`.

For a complete discussion of mapping modes in Windows, see *Programming Windows* by Charles Petzold (Microsoft Press, 1988). Chapter 12 of Petzold's book explains each of the mapping modes and shows how you would use them in an application.

Metafiles

The presentation data for an OLE compound document object is stored as a metafile. This metafile is stored in a special stream in the container's compound file. When a user opens a compound document that contains embedded or linked OLE objects, the metafile is displayed. The default handler in the OLE libraries handles the drawing of the metafile. However, the object server actually creates the metafile.

A *metafile* is a file that contains a series of records. Each record represents a GDI function. When the metafile is "played back," each record is decoded, its parameters are placed on the stack, and the function call is executed. Metafiles provide a device-independent means of transferring images between applications.

When you create the metafile for your object's presentation data, you receive a metafile device context in `COleServerItem::Draw`. You then use this device context for all your drawing. However, you need to be aware of several limitations.

A metafile device context is not a real device context. Any GDI function that retrieves information from a device context cannot be used within a metafile. Such functions include `GetDeviceCaps`, `RectVisible`, and `GetTextMetrics`. (A complete list of all the functions that are not available for use within a metafile is in the *Windows SDK Programmer's Reference*, Volume 1.)

One particular function that you use in the sample application is `CreateCompatibleDC`. This function creates a memory device context that stores a device-dependent bitmap (DDB) in memory before it is moved to the screen. This function fails if you use it on a metafile device context. Later in this chapter, however, you will see how to work around this problem.

Examining the Code

In this section, you examine the steps required to develop a miniserver. Your sample OLE server will enable the user to embed one of three available bitmaps in an OLE container. You look at each of the source modules for the sample application.

You begin developing the sample application as usual, by having the Visual C++ AppWizard generate the initial skeleton code for your application. In the OLE Options dialog box, you choose the Mi**n**i-Server radio button (see fig. 9.3).

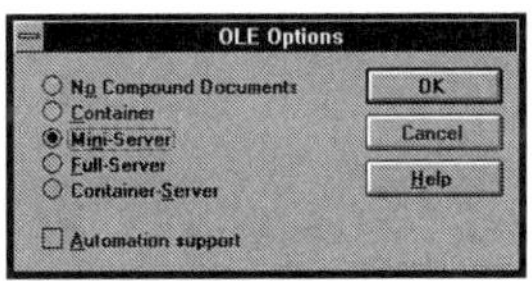

Fig. 9.3
Specifying a miniserver in the OLE Options dialog box.

The Window Application Class

The first module of interest is OLESERV.CPP. This module implements your `CWinApp` object and is responsible for initializing the OLE libraries.

The first thing that the AppWizard does is to call `CoCreateGuid` to generate a CLSID (class ID) for your object. As you learned in Chapter 2, "The Component Object Model," this globally unique identifier (GUID) is statistically guaranteed to be unique to your application.

Next, the AppWizard calls `AfxOleInit` to initialize the OLE libraries. All OLE applications—whether they are containers, object servers, or Automation applications—must call this function.

After you create the document template that ties your Document, View, and Frame classes together, you call `pDocTemplate->SetServerInfo`. This method identifies the resources that the object uses when it is activated in place and when it is opened in a separate window. In Chapter 2, you learned that objects and their containers merge their menus together during in-place activation. You use a separate menus resource for in-place activation and pass the handle to this menu in `SetServerInfo`. You also use a special frame window class during in-place activation, and also pass to `SetServerInfo` information about this class.

You parse the command line by calling the helper function `RunEmbedded`, which checks for the `/Embedding` parameter. If the application is launched with this parameter, you register your object's class factory and return. Internally, the framework calls `CoRegisterClassObject` to register the object class with the OLE libraries. If the object is not registered, the container cannot create objects of that class.

Because you are creating a miniserver—that is, you are not implementing a separate user interface—the application must fail to load if the `/Embedding` parameter is not on the command line. If the application cannot be loaded, it informs the user by using the standard framework message identified by IDP_USE_INSERT_OBJECT. Before you display this message to the user, you call `UpdateRegistry` to update the system registry with information about your server. The registration database can be corrupted, but a call to this function ensures that the server information is always stored in the database.

Listing 9.1 shows the code for the `CWinapp` implementation.

Listing 9.1 OLESRV.H and OLESRV.CPP—the Implementation Files for *CWinapp*

```
#ifndef __AFXWIN_H__
     #error include 'stdafx.h' before including this file for PCH
#endif
```

```
#include "resource.h"       // main symbols

/////////////////////////////////////////////////////////////////////////////
// COleservApp:
// See oleserv.cpp for the implementation of this class
//
class COleservApp : public CWinApp
{
public:
     COleservApp();

// Overrides
     virtual BOOL InitInstance();

// Implementation
     COleTemplateServer m_server;
     // Server object for document creation

     //{{AFX_MSG(COleservApp)
     afx_msg void OnAppAbout();
          // NOTE - ClassWizard adds and removes member functions here.
          //    DO NOT EDIT what you see in these blocks of generated code!
     //}}AFX_MSG
     DECLARE_MESSAGE_MAP()
};

//-------------------------------------------------------------------
#include "stdafx.h"
#include "oleserv.h"

#include "mainfrm.h"
#include "ipframe.h"
#include "olesedoc.h"
#include "olesevw.h"

#ifdef _DEBUG
#undef THIS_FILE
static char BASED_CODE THIS_FILE[] = __FILE__;
#endif

/////////////////////////////////////////////////////////////////////////////
// COleservApp

BEGIN_MESSAGE_MAP(COleservApp, CWinApp)
     //{{AFX_MSG_MAP(COleservApp)
     ON_COMMAND(ID_APP_ABOUT, OnAppAbout)
          // NOTE - ClassWizard adds and removes mapping macros here.
          //    DO NOT EDIT what you see in these blocks of generated code!
     //}}AFX_MSG_MAP
     // Standard file-based document commands
     ON_COMMAND(ID_FILE_NEW, CWinApp::OnFileNew)
     ON_COMMAND(ID_FILE_OPEN, CWinApp::OnFileOpen)
END_MESSAGE_MAP()
```

(continues)

II

Using MFC

Listing 9.1 Continued

```
/////////////////////////////////////////////////////////////////////////////
// COleservApp construction

COleservApp::COleservApp()
{
     // TODO: add construction code here,
     // Place all significant initialization in InitInstance
}

/////////////////////////////////////////////////////////////////////////////
// The one and only COleservApp object

COleservApp NEAR theApp;

// This identifier was generated to be statistically unique for your app.
// You may change it if you prefer to choose a specific identifier.
static const CLSID BASED_CODE clsid =
{ 0x8fe13520, 0x851b, 0x101b, { 0xbb, 0x57, 0x0, 0x60, 0x8c, 0xc0,
  0xba, 0x93 } };

/////////////////////////////////////////////////////////////////////////////
// COleservApp initialization

BOOL COleservApp::InitInstance()
{
     // Initialize OLE 2.0 libraries
     if (!AfxOleInit())
     {
          AfxMessageBox(IDP_OLE_INIT_FAILED);
          return FALSE;
     }

     // Standard initialization
     // If you are not using these features and want to reduce the size
     //  of your final executable, you should remove from the following
     //  the specific initialization routines you do not need.

     SetDialogBkColor();        // Set dialog background color to gray
     LoadStdProfileSettings();
                      // Load standard INI file options (including MRU)

     // Register the application's document templates.
     //  Document templates serve as the connection between
     //  documents, frame windows, and views.

     CSingleDocTemplate* pDocTemplate;
     pDocTemplate = new CSingleDocTemplate(
          IDR_MAINFRAME,
          RUNTIME_CLASS(COleservDoc),
          RUNTIME_CLASS(CMainFrame),     // main SDI frame window
          RUNTIME_CLASS(COleservView));
```

```
    pDocTemplate->SetServerInfo(
         IDR_SRVR_EMBEDDED, IDR_SRVR_INPLACE,
         RUNTIME_CLASS(CInPlaceFrame));
    AddDocTemplate(pDocTemplate);

    // Connect the COleTemplateServer to the document template.
    //  The COleTemplateServer creates new documents on behalf
    //  of requesting OLE containers by using information
    //  specified in the document template.
    m_server.ConnectTemplate(clsid, pDocTemplate, TRUE);
         // Note: SDI applications register server objects
         //    only if /Embedding or /Automation is present
         //    on the command line.

    // Parse the command line to see if launched as OLE server
    if (RunEmbedded())
    {
         // Register all OLE server (factories) as running.
         //   This enables the OLE 2.0 libraries to create objects
         //   from other applications.
         COleTemplateServer::RegisterAll();

         // Application was run with /Embedding or /Automation.
         //   Don't show the main window in this case.
         return TRUE;
    }

    // When a server application is launched stand-alone, you should
    //   update the system registry in case it has been damaged.
    m_server.UpdateRegistry(OAT_INPLACE_SERVER);

    // When a miniserver is run stand-alone, the registry is updated
    //  and the user is instructed to use the Insert Object dialog box
    //  in a container to use the server. Miniservers do not have
    //  stand-alone user interfaces.
    AfxMessageBox(IDP_USE_INSERT_OBJECT);
    return FALSE;
}

/////////////////////////////////////////////////////////////////////////////
// CAboutDlg dialog used for App About

class CAboutDlg : public CDialog
{
public:
    CAboutDlg();

// Dialog Data
    //{{AFX_DATA(CAboutDlg)
    enum { IDD = IDD_ABOUTBOX };
    //}}AFX_DATA

// Implementation
protected:
    virtual void DoDataExchange(CDataExchange* pDX);   // DDX/DDV support
```

(continues)

Listing 9.1 Continued

```
    //{{AFX_MSG(CAboutDlg)
        // No message handlers
    //}}AFX_MSG
    DECLARE_MESSAGE_MAP()
};

CAboutDlg::CAboutDlg() : CDialog(CAboutDlg::IDD)
{
    //{{AFX_DATA_INIT(CAboutDlg)
    //}}AFX_DATA_INIT
}

void CAboutDlg::DoDataExchange(CDataExchange* pDX)
{
    CDialog::DoDataExchange(pDX);
    //{{AFX_DATA_MAP(CAboutDlg)
    //}}AFX_DATA_MAP
}

BEGIN_MESSAGE_MAP(CAboutDlg, CDialog)
    //{{AFX_MSG_MAP(CAboutDlg)
        // No message handlers
    //}}AFX_MSG_MAP
END_MESSAGE_MAP()

// App command to run the dialog
void COleservApp::OnAppAbout()
{
    CAboutDlg aboutDlg;
    aboutDlg.DoModal();
}
```

The In-place Frame Class

In the preceding section, you saw that when you call `SetServerInfo` to inform the framework of the resources that you must use when you are active in place or in a separate window, you also pass the name of the class that is to be used to create your in-place frame window.

The `COleIPFrameWnd` class is responsible for the object's frame window when the object is in-place active. The class is also responsible for creating and positioning control bars within the container application's document window. Finally, `COleIPFrameWnd` handles notifications generated by an embedded `COleResizeBar` object when the user resizes the in-place editing window.

Your implementation of `CInPlaceFrame` derives from `COleIPFrameWnd`. The implementation contains a `COleResizeBar` member. This object is responsible for creating the tracker rectangle that surrounds your object when it is active in place. The `COleResizeBar` member implements the resizing handles and the hatch pattern that surrounds your object. Objects of `COleResizeBar` are usually used as embedded members of `COleIPFrameWnd` classes. All notifications that this member creates are sent to its parent, which in this case is the `COleIPFrameWnd` class.

If your object has a toolbar that needs to be visible during in-place activation, you also implement the `COleIPFrameWnd::OnCreateControlBars` method to create the toolbar.

Listing 9.2 shows the code for IPFRAME.CPP and IPFRAME.H.

Listing 9.2 IPFRAME.CPP and IPFRAME.H—the Implementation of the Frame Class

```
class CInPlaceFrame : public COleIPFrameWnd
{
     DECLARE_DYNCREATE(CInPlaceFrame)
public:
     CInPlaceFrame();

// Attributes
public:

// Operations
public:

// Implementation
public:
     virtual ~CInPlaceFrame();
#ifdef _DEBUG
     virtual void AssertValid() const;
     virtual void Dump(CDumpContext& dc) const;
#endif

protected:
     COleResizeBar   m_wndResizeBar;
     COleDropTarget  m_dropTarget;

// Generated message map functions
protected:
     //{{AFX_MSG(CInPlaceFrame)
     afx_msg int OnCreate(LPCREATESTRUCT lpCreateStruct);
          // NOTE - ClassWizard adds and removes member functions here.
          //    DO NOT EDIT what you see in these blocks of generated code!
     //}}AFX_MSG
     DECLARE_MESSAGE_MAP()
};

#include "stdafx.h"
#include "oleserv.h"
```

(continues)

Listing 9.2 Continued

```
#include "ipframe.h"

#ifdef _DEBUG
#undef THIS_FILE
static char BASED_CODE THIS_FILE[] = __FILE__;
#endif

//////////////////////////////////////////////////////////////////////
// CInPlaceFrame
//
IMPLEMENT_DYNCREATE(CInPlaceFrame, COleIPFrameWnd)

BEGIN_MESSAGE_MAP(CInPlaceFrame, COleIPFrameWnd)
     //{{AFX_MSG_MAP(CInPlaceFrame)
     ON_WM_CREATE()
     //}}AFX_MSG_MAP
END_MESSAGE_MAP()

//////////////////////////////////////////////////////////////////////
// CInPlaceFrame construction/destruction
//
CInPlaceFrame::CInPlaceFrame()
{
}
//-------------------------------------------------------------------
CInPlaceFrame::~CInPlaceFrame()
{
}
//-------------------------------------------------------------------
int CInPlaceFrame::OnCreate(LPCREATESTRUCT lpCreateStruct)
{
     if (COleIPFrameWnd::OnCreate(lpCreateStruct) == -1)
          return -1;

     // CResizeBar implements in-place resizing.
     if (!m_wndResizeBar.Create(this))
     {
          TRACE("Failed to create resize bar\n");
          return -1;      // fail to create
     }

     // By default, you should register a drop target that does
     // nothing with your frame window. This prevents drops from
     // "falling through" to a container that supports drag-drop.
     m_dropTarget.Register(this);

     return 0;
}

//////////////////////////////////////////////////////////////////////
// CInPlaceFrame diagnostics
//
#ifdef _DEBUG
```

```
void CInPlaceFrame::AssertValid() const
{
     COleIPFrameWnd::AssertValid();
}

void CInPlaceFrame::Dump(CDumpContext& dc) const
{
     COleIPFrameWnd::Dump(dc);
}
#endif //_DEBUG
//------------------------------------------------------------
//------------------------------------------------------------
```

The Document Class

The COleServerDoc class implements a container for embedded and linked objects. For applications such as the one that you are developing, which supports embedded items only, each Document class can support only one server item. That server item represents the entire document.

The Document class is also responsible for loading and saving the object to the IStorage object provided by the container.

The COleServerDoc defines one pure virtual member, OnGetEmbeddedItem, which creates and returns a pointer to the document's embedded object. You also implement OnSetItemRects to help the user scale the object when it is in-place active.

Listing 9.3 shows the complete code for the implementation of the Document class.

Listing 9.3 OLESEDOC.H and OLESEDOC.CPP—the Implementation of the Document Class

```
#include "cdib.h"

class COleservSrvrItem;

class COleservDoc : public COleServerDoc
{
protected: // create from serialization only
     COleservDoc();
     DECLARE_DYNCREATE(COleservDoc)

// Attributes
public:
     COleservSrvrItem* GetEmbeddedItem()
          { return (COleservSrvrItem*)COleServerDoc::GetEmbeddedItem(); }

     BITMAP m_bm;
     void FAR *lpBits;
     CSize m_size;
```

(continues)

Listing 9.3 Continued

```
     COLORREF m_crColor;
     CDib *m_DIB;
     CString m_FileName;
// Operations
public:
     CSize OnGetExtent();
     void OnSetExtent(CSize &rSize);
// Implementation
public:
     virtual ~COleservDoc();
     virtual void Serialize(CArchive& ar);
     virtual COleServerItem* OnGetEmbeddedItem();
#ifdef _DEBUG
     virtual void AssertValid() const;
     virtual void Dump(CDumpContext& dc) const;
#endif
     virtual BOOL OnOpenDocument(LPCSTR lpFileName);
protected:
     virtual BOOL OnNewDocument();
     virtual void OnSetItemRects(LPCRECT lpPosRect, LPCRECT lpClipRect);

// Generated message map functions
protected:
     //{{AFX_MSG(COleservDoc)
          // NOTE - ClassWizard adds and removes member functions here.
          //    DO NOT EDIT what you see in these blocks of generated code!
     //}}AFX_MSG
     DECLARE_MESSAGE_MAP()
};

/////////////////////////////////////////////////////////////////////////////


#include "stdafx.h"
#include "oleserv.h"

#include "olesedoc.h"
#include "srvritem.h"

#ifdef _DEBUG
#undef THIS_FILE
static char BASED_CODE THIS_FILE[] = __FILE__;
#endif

/////////////////////////////////////////////////////////////////////////////
// COleservDoc

IMPLEMENT_DYNCREATE(COleservDoc, COleServerDoc)

BEGIN_MESSAGE_MAP(COleservDoc, COleServerDoc)
     //{{AFX_MSG_MAP(COleservDoc)
```

```
    // NOTE - ClassWizard adds and removes mapping macros here.
    //    DO NOT EDIT what you see in these blocks of generated code!
    //}}AFX_MSG_MAP
END_MESSAGE_MAP()

/////////////////////////////////////////////////////////////////////////////
// COleservDoc construction/destruction
//
COleservDoc::COleservDoc()
{
    // Set the initial size to 3cm x 3cm
    m_size = CSize(3000,3000);
    m_crColor = RGB(192,192,192);
    m_DIB = NULL;
}
//-----------------------------------------------------------------
COleservDoc::~COleservDoc()
{

    if(m_DIB)
        delete m_DIB;
}
//-----------------------------------------------------------------
void COleservDoc::OnSetItemRects(LPCRECT lpPosRect, LPCRECT lpClipRect)
{
    //--------
    // The framework calls this method if the user
    // moves or resizes the active in-place object.
    // As you support scaling of your bitmaps, you use the
    // information in the pos rectangle to update your
    // object's extents.

    COleServerDoc::OnSetItemRects(lpPosRect,lpClipRect);

    TRACE("SetItemRect %d-%d %d-%d",
        lpPosRect->left,lpPosRect->top,
        lpPosRect->right,lpPosRect->bottom);

    POSITION pos = GetFirstViewPosition();
    CView* pFirstView = GetNextView(pos);

    CSize size(lpPosRect->right-lpPosRect->left,
            lpPosRect->bottom-lpPosRect->top);

    CClientDC dc(pFirstView);
    dc.DPtoHIMETRIC(&size);

    OnSetExtent(size);
}
//-----------------------------------------------------------------
BOOL COleservDoc::OnOpenDocument(LPCSTR lpFileName)
{
    TRY
    {
        if(m_DIB)
```

(continues)

Listing 9.3 Continued

```
                delete m_DIB;

            CFile  file((const char *)lpFileName,CFile::modeRead);
            m_DIB = new CDib;
            m_DIB->Create(&file);
        }
        CATCH_ALL(e)
        {
            AfxMessageBox("Error: Failed to open file");
            return FALSE;
        }
        END_CATCH_ALL

        m_FileName = lpFileName;
        return TRUE;
}
//--------------------------------------------------------------------
BOOL COleservDoc::OnNewDocument()
{
        if (!COleServerDoc::OnNewDocument())
            return FALSE;

        return TRUE;
}
///////////////////////////////////////////////////////////////////////
// COleservDoc server implementation
//
COleServerItem* COleservDoc::OnGetEmbeddedItem()
{
        //---------
        // The framework calls this function
        // to get the COleServerItem
        // that is associated with the document.
        // The function is called only when necessary.

        COleservSrvrItem* pItem = new COleservSrvrItem(this);
        ASSERT_VALID(pItem);
        return pItem;
}
//--------------------------------------------------------------------
void COleservDoc::OnSetExtent(CSize &rSize)
{
        //---------
        // Called by the framework to tell you how
        // much space is available in the client container.
        // You also call this method if the user moves or
        // resizes the active in-place object.
        m_size = rSize;
        UpdateAllViews(NULL);
}
```

```
//-------------------------------------------------------------
CSize COleservDoc::OnGetExtent()
{
     return m_size;
}
/////////////////////////////////////////////////////////////////////////////
// COleservDoc serialization
//
void COleservDoc::Serialize(CArchive& ar)
{
     DWORD dwSize;

     if (ar.IsStoring())
     {
          ar << m_size;

          dwSize = GlobalSize(m_DIB->m_hDIB);
          ar << dwSize;

          ar.Write(GlobalLock(m_DIB->m_hDIB),dwSize);
     }
     else
     {
          ar >> m_size;
          ar >> dwSize;

          m_DIB = new CDib();
          HANDLE hMem = GlobalAlloc(GHND,dwSize);
          LPSTR lpBuff = (LPSTR)GlobalLock(hMem);

          ar.Read(lpBuff,(UINT)dwSize);

          m_DIB->SetHandle(hMem);
     }
}

/////////////////////////////////////////////////////////////////////////////
// COleservDoc diagnostics
//
#ifdef _DEBUG
void COleservDoc::AssertValid() const
{
     COleServerDoc::AssertValid();
}

void COleservDoc::Dump(CDumpContext& dc) const
{
     COleServerDoc::Dump(dc);
}
#endif //_DEBUG
```

The following sections examine the code for the Document class in more detail.

The Document Constructor

You begin by initializing your object's variables. The initial size of your bitmap is set to 3cm by 3cm. You are using the MM_HIMETRIC mapping mode in your View class, so 3,000 units is equal to 3 centimeters. You set the object's default background to gray. Finally, you set the pointer to your bitmap class to 0. By using this pointer before you create a bitmap object, you prevent any general protection faults later in the code.

```
COleservDoc::COleservDoc()
{
        // Set your initial size to 3cm x 3cm
        m_size = CSize(3000,3000);
        m_crColor = RGB(192,192,192);
        m_DIB = NULL;
}
```

The *OnSetItemRects* Method

The framework calls the `OnSetItemRects` method if your object is moved or resized while it is in-place active. You receive two parameters. The first parameter is a pointer to a position rectangle. This rectangle tells you both the position and size of the object relative to the container's client area. The second parameter is a pointer to a clipping rectangle.

This method begins by calling the base class' implementation. You then convert the object's extents from device units to HIMETRIC units by calling `CDC::DPtoHIMETRIC`. To use the newly converted units when updating the object's size, you call `OnSetExtents`.

You need to know when the user wants to change the object's size because you support scaling of the object when it is in-place active.

```
void COleservDoc::OnSetItemRects(LPCRECT lpPosRect, LPCRECT lpClipRect)
{
        //--------
        // The framework calls this method if the user
        // moves or resizes the active in-place object.
        // Because you support scaling of your bitmaps,
        // you use the information in the pos rectangle
        // to update your object's extents.

        COleServerDoc::      OnSetItemRects(lpPosRect,lpClipRect);

        POSITION pos = GetFirstViewPosition();
        CView* pFirstView = GetNextView(pos);

        CSize size(lpPosRect->right-lpPosRect->left,
                   lpPosRect->bottom-lpPosRect->top);
```

```
        CClientDC dc(pFirstView);
        dc.DPtoHIMETRIC(&size);

        OnSetExtent(size);
    }
```

The *OnOpenDocument* Method

You call `OnOpenDocument` from your View class whenever the user wants to change the bitmap. You begin by creating a CDIB object. The `CDIB` class, which you examine in detail later, enables you to read device-independent bitmaps (DIB), display them, and save them to disk.

After you create the object, you call its `Create` method to read the bitmap into memory. The bitmap is now ready to be displayed.

```
BOOL COleservDoc::OnOpenDocument(LPCSTR lpFileName)
{
            TRY
        {
            if(m_DIB)
                delete m_DIB;

            CFile  file((const char *)lpFileName,CFile::modeRead);
            m_DIB = new CDib;
            m_DIB->Create(&file);
        }
        CATCH_ALL(e)
        {
            AfxMessageBox("Error: Failed to open file");
            return FALSE;
        }
        END_CATCH_ALL

        m_FileName = lpFileName;
        return TRUE;
}
```

The *OnGetEmbeddedItem* Method

The framework calls the `OnGetEmbeddedItem` method, which has no default implementation, to retrieve a pointer to a `COleServerItem` object. Your implementation is quite simple: you create the object and return a pointer to it.

```
COleServerItem* COleservDoc::OnGetEmbeddedItem()
{
        //----------
        // The framework calls OnGetEmbeddedItem to get
        // the COleServerItem that is associated with the document.
        // It is called only when necessary.
```

II

Using MFC

```
        COleservSrvrItem* pItem = new COleservSrvrItem(this);
        ASSERT_VALID(pItem);
        return pItem;
}
```

The *OnSetExtent* Method

The `OnSetExtent` method, which you define and implement in your Document class, is a parallel to a method of the same name in the `COleServerItem` class. You duplicate the method here because you want to keep all the information about the object in the Document class. Then the information can be accessed by both the View class and the Server Item class.

The framework calls this method in the `COleServerItem` class to tell the object how much space is initially available to it within the container. Your `ColeServerItem` implementation simply calls the `OnSetExtent` method in your Document class.

```
void COleservDoc::OnSetExtent(CSize &rSize)
{
        //----------
        // Called by the framework to tell you how
        // much space is available in the client container.
        // You also call this method if the user moves or
        // resizes the active in-place object.
        m_size = rSize;
        UpdateAllViews(NULL);
}
```

The *OnGetExtent* Method

The framework calls the `OnGetExtent` method to retrieve the object's size in HIMETRIC units. As with the `OnSetExtent` implementation, this method is in fact part of the `COleServerItem` class. You call this method from the implementation in `COleServerItem`.

```
CSize COleservDoc::OnGetExtent()
{
        return m_size;
}
```

The *Serialize* Method

Because you are developing a miniserver, you don't necessarily have to implement the `Serialize` method. You do not save any data to disk files as you would if you were implementing a full server.

However, when the user edits and updates your object, you call the `COleServeRItem::Serialize` method to enable the item to save itself to an archive. This archive is in fact connected to an `IStorage` interface pointer that is a part of the container's compound file.

Your miniserver supports only embedded objects, so you can simply delegate the `COleServerItem`'s `Serialize` call to your Document class.

In the code for the Document class, you save the current extents of the object so that you can recreate it with the same extents the next time that the object is edited. You then save the bitmap's size. You use this size variable to allocate a memory block that holds the bitmap when you reload it. Finally, you write the DIB to the container's storage.

```
void COleservDoc::Serialize(CArchive& ar)
{
        DWORD dwSize;

        if (ar.IsStoring())
        {
                ar << m_size;

                dwSize = GlobalSize(m_DIB->m_hDIB);
                ar << dwSize;

                ar.Write(GlobalLock(m_DIB->m_hDIB),dwSize);
        }
        else
        {
                ar >> m_size;
                ar >> dwSize;

                m_DIB = new CDib();
                HANDLE hMem = GlobalAlloc(GHND,dwSize);
                LPSTR lpBuff = (LPSTR)GlobalLock(hMem);

                ar.Read(lpBuff,(UINT)dwSize);

                m_DIB->SetHandle(hMem);
        }
}
```

The View Class

The View class displays the object when it is in-place active. Two methods are of interest here: the `OnDraw` method performs all the drawing while the object is in-place active, and the `OnEditBitmaps` method enables the user to select which of the three bitmaps to display.

Listing 9.4 shows the code for the View class implementation.

Listing 9.4 OLESEVW.H and OLESEVW.CPP—the Implementation of the View Class

```
class COleservView : public CView
{
protected: // create from serialization only
     COleservView();
     DECLARE_DYNCREATE(COleservView)

// Attributes
public:
     COleservDoc* GetDocument();

// Operations
public:

// Implementation
public:
     virtual ~COleservView();
     virtual void OnDraw(CDC* pDC);  // overridden to draw this view
#ifdef _DEBUG
     virtual void AssertValid() const;
     virtual void Dump(CDumpContext& dc) const;
#endif

protected:

// Generated message map functions
protected:
     //{{AFX_MSG(COleservView)
     afx_msg void OnEditBitmapsBitmap1();
     afx_msg void OnEditBitmapsBitmap2();
     afx_msg void OnEditBitmapsBitmap3();
     //}}AFX_MSG
     DECLARE_MESSAGE_MAP()
};

#ifndef _DEBUG  // debug version in olesevw.cpp
inline COleservDoc* COleservView::GetDocument()
   { return (COleservDoc*)m_pDocument; }
#endif

/////////////////////////////////////////////////////////////////////////////

#include "stdafx.h"
#include "oleserv.h"

#include "olesedoc.h"
#include "olesevw.h"

#ifdef _DEBUG
#undef THIS_FILE
static char BASED_CODE THIS_FILE[] = __FILE__;
#endif
```

```
///////////////////////////////////////////////////////////////////////////
// COleservView
//
IMPLEMENT_DYNCREATE(COleservView, CView)

BEGIN_MESSAGE_MAP(COleservView, CView)
     //{{AFX_MSG_MAP(COleservView)
     ON_COMMAND(ID_EDIT_BITMAPS_BITMAP1, OnEditBitmapsBitmap1)
     ON_COMMAND(ID_EDIT_BITMAPS_BITMAP2, OnEditBitmapsBitmap2)
     ON_COMMAND(ID_EDIT_BITMAPS_BITMAP3, OnEditBitmapsBitmap3)
     //}}AFX_MSG_MAP
END_MESSAGE_MAP()

///////////////////////////////////////////////////////////////////////////
// COleservView construction/destruction
//
COleservView::COleservView()
{
     // TODO: add construction code here
}
//-----------------------------------------------------------------------
COleservView::~COleservView()
{
}
///////////////////////////////////////////////////////////////////////////
// COleservView drawing
//
void COleservView::OnDraw(CDC* pDC)
{
     COleservDoc* pDoc = GetDocument();
     ASSERT_VALID(pDoc);

     CBrush br(pDoc->m_crColor);
     CSize size = pDoc->OnGetExtent();
     CPoint pt(0,0);
     CPen pen(PS_SOLID,2,RGB(0,0,0));


     pDC->SetMapMode(MM_HIMETRIC);
     size.cy = -size.cy;

     CRect rc(pt,size);

     CBrush *pOldBrush = pDC->SelectObject((CBrush*)&br);
     CPen *pOldPen = pDC->SelectObject((CPen *)&pen);

     pDC->Rectangle(rc);
     if(pDoc->m_DIB)
     {
          HBITMAP hbm = pDoc->m_DIB->BitmapFromDib();
          pDoc->m_DIB->StretchBitmap(pDC,rc.left,rc.top,rc.
                                     right,rc.bottom,hbm,SRCCOPY);
     }

}
```

(continues)

Listing 9.4 Continued

```
//////////////////////////////////////////////////////////////////////////
// COleservView diagnostics
//
#ifdef _DEBUG
void COleservView::AssertValid() const
{
     CView::AssertValid();
}
//-----------------------------------------------------------------
void COleservView::Dump(CDumpContext& dc) const
{
     CView::Dump(dc);
}
//-----------------------------------------------------------------
COleservDoc* COleservView::GetDocument() // nondebug version is inline
{
     ASSERT(m_pDocument->IsKindOf(RUNTIME_CLASS(COleservDoc)));
     return (COleservDoc*)m_pDocument;
}
#endif //_DEBUG
//////////////////////////////////////////////////////////////////////////
// COleservView message handlers
//
void COleservView::OnEditBitmapsBitmap1()
{
     COleservDoc* pDoc = GetDocument();
     ASSERT_VALID(pDoc);

     pDoc->OnOpenDocument("C:\\sean.bmp");
     Invalidate();
     pDoc->UpdateAllItems(NULL);
}
//-----------------------------------------------------------------
void COleservView::OnEditBitmapsBitmap2()
{
     COleservDoc* pDoc = GetDocument();
     ASSERT_VALID(pDoc);

     pDoc->OnOpenDocument("C:\\sean.bmp");
     Invalidate();
     pDoc->UpdateAllItems(NULL);

}
//-----------------------------------------------------------------
void COleservView::OnEditBitmapsBitmap3()
{
     COleservDoc* pDoc = GetDocument();
     ASSERT_VALID(pDoc);

     pDoc->OnOpenDocument("C:\\sean.bmp");
     Invalidate();
     pDoc->UpdateAllItems(NULL);
```

```
}
//----------------------------------------------------------------
//----------------------------------------------------------------
```

The following sections examine the code for the View class in more detail.

The *OnDraw* Method

When you initially create an object, a gray rectangle with a black border is drawn. If the user selected a bitmap from the **E**dit menu, that bitmap is then displayed in the rectangle.

To draw the object, you use the MM_HIMETRIC mapping mode. Because you support scaling of the bitmap while it is in-place active, the extents that you use are always retrieved from the Document class with a call to `OnGetExtent`. This method returns the object's extents in absolute HIMETRIC units. As you learned earlier in the "GDI Mapping Modes" section, the origin in this particular mapping mode is the top-left corner of the screen. The values on the X axis increase as you move to the right, but the values on the Y axis decrease as you move down the axis. Therefore, you must negate the `cy` value of the `CSize` variable that the `GetExtent` call returns.

If the user has already selected a bitmap, you invoke the `CDIB::StretchBitmap` method to draw the bitmap on the screen.

The *OnEditBitmaps* Method

The framework's command-routing mechanism calls the `OnEditBitmaps` method in response to the user selecting options from the **E**dit menu.

You begin by retrieving a pointer to the Document class and calling `OnOpenDocument` with the name of the bitmap file. You then invalidate your in-place frame window's client area to enable the framework to call the `OnDraw` method.

You then call `UpdateAllItems` to inform the Document class that the user has changed the data.

The Object Interface Class

The `COleServerItem` class is the interface between the server and the OLE libraries. You must implement the following two methods:

- The `OnDraw` method creates the metafile that your object uses as presentation data when it is not in-place activated.

- The `Serialize` method saves the object's native data into the container's compound file.

You also implement several other methods, including `OnSetExtent` and `OnGetExtent`.

Listing 9.5 shows the code for the Object Interface class implementation.

Listing 9.5 SRVRITEM.H and SRVRITEM.CPP—the Implementation of the Server Item Class

```
class COleservSrvrItem : public COleServerItem
{
     DECLARE_DYNAMIC(COleservSrvrItem)

// Constructors
public:
     COleservSrvrItem(COleservDoc* pContainerDoc);

// Attributes
     COleservDoc* GetDocument() const
          { return (COleservDoc*)COleServerItem::GetDocument(); }

// Implementation
public:
     ~COleservSrvrItem();
#ifdef _DEBUG
     virtual void AssertValid() const;
     virtual void Dump(CDumpContext& dc) const;
#endif
     virtual BOOL OnDraw(CDC* pDC, CSize& rSize);
     virtual BOOL OnGetExtent(DVASPECT dwDrawAspect, CSize& rSize);
     virtual BOOL OnSetExtent(DVASPECT dwDrawAspect, CSize& rSize);
protected:
     virtual void Serialize(CArchive& ar); // overridden for document I/O
};

#include "stdafx.h"
#include "oleserv.h"

#include "olesedoc.h"
#include "srvritem.h"

#ifdef _DEBUG
#undef THIS_FILE
static char BASED_CODE THIS_FILE[] = __FILE__;
#endif

/////////////////////////////////////////////////////////////////////////////
// COleservSrvrItem implementation

IMPLEMENT_DYNAMIC(COleservSrvrItem, COleServerItem)
```

```
COleservSrvrItem::COleservSrvrItem(COleservDoc* pContainerDoc)
     : COleServerItem(pContainerDoc, TRUE)
{
     // TODO: add one-time construction code here
     //  (for example, adding additional clipboard formats
     //  to the item's data source)
}
//-----------------------------------------------------------------
COleservSrvrItem::~COleservSrvrItem()
{
     // TODO: add cleanup code here
}
//-----------------------------------------------------------------
void COleservSrvrItem::Serialize(CArchive& ar)
{
     //---------
     //  The framework calls COleservSrvrItem::Serialize() if
     //  the item is copied to the clipboard. This can happen
     //  automatically through the OLE callback OnGetClipboardData().
     //  A good default for the embedded item is simply to delegate
     //  to the document's Serialize() function. If you support links,
     //  you will want to serialize just a portion of the document.

     if (!IsLinkedItem())
     {
          COleservDoc* pDoc = GetDocument();
          ASSERT_VALID(pDoc);
          pDoc->Serialize(ar);
     }
}
//-----------------------------------------------------------------
BOOL COleservSrvrItem::OnSetExtent(DVASPECT dwDrawAspect, CSize& rSize)
{
     COleservDoc* pDoc = GetDocument();
     ASSERT_VALID(pDoc);

     pDoc->OnSetExtent(rSize);
     return TRUE;
}
//-----------------------------------------------------------------
BOOL COleservSrvrItem::OnGetExtent(DVASPECT dwDrawAspect, CSize& rSize)
{
     //-----------
     //  Most applications, like this one, handle drawing only
     //  the content aspect of the item. If you want to support
     //  other aspects, such as DVASPECT_THUMBNAIL (by overriding
     //  OnDrawEx()), you should modify this implementation
     //  of OnGetExtent() to handle the additional aspects.

     if (dwDrawAspect != DVASPECT_CONTENT)
          return COleServerItem::OnGetExtent(dwDrawAspect, rSize);

     COleservDoc* pDoc = GetDocument();
     ASSERT_VALID(pDoc);
     rSize = pDoc->OnGetExtent();
```

(continues)

Listing 9.5 Continued

```
        return TRUE;
}
//-------------------------------------------------------------------
BOOL COleservSrvrItem::OnDraw(CDC* pDC, CSize& rSize)
{
        COleservDoc* pDoc = GetDocument();
        ASSERT_VALID(pDoc);

        CPoint pt(0,0);
        CBrush br(pDoc->m_crColor);

        rSize = pDoc->OnGetExtent();

        pDC->SetMapMode(MM_ANISOTROPIC);
        pDC->SetWindowOrg(0,0);
        pDC->SetWindowExt(rSize.cx,rSize.cy);

        CRect rc(pt,rSize);

        CBrush *pOldBrush = pDC->SelectObject((CBrush*)&br);

        pDC->Rectangle(rc);

        if(pDoc->m_DIB)
        {
                POSITION pos = pDoc->GetFirstViewPosition();
                CView* pFirstView = pDoc->GetNextView(pos);
                CClientDC dc(pFirstView);

                HBITMAP hbm = pDoc->m_DIB->BitmapFromDib();
                BOOL f = pDoc->m_DIB->StretchBitmap(pDC,rc.left,rc.
                                     top,rc.right,rc.bottom,hbm,SRCCOPY,&dc);
        }

        pDC->SelectObject((CBrush*)pOldBrush);

        return TRUE;
}
/////////////////////////////////////////////////////////////////////
// COleservSrvrItem diagnostics
//
#ifdef _DEBUG
void COleservSrvrItem::AssertValid() const
{
        COleServerItem::AssertValid();
}

void COleservSrvrItem::Dump(CDumpContext& dc) const
{
        COleServerItem::Dump(dc);
}
#endif

/////////////////////////////////////////////////////////////////////
```

The following sections examine the code for the Object Interface class in more detail.

The *Serialize* Method

When a user updates and saves the data within the object, the framework calls the `Serialize` method for each item within the object. If an object supports linking, several items can exist as selections within the object. For an embedded object, you need to consider only one item.

When you have only one item, the easiest implementation is to delegate to the Document class and let it take care of saving and loading the data. If you are dealing with multiple items, you would usually serialize each item in the `COleservSrvrItem::Serialize` method. In the case of single embedded items, it is easier to handle all the loading and saving in one place, using the `COleServerDoc::Serialize` method.

The *OnSetExtent* Method

The framework calls the `OnSetExtent` method to inform you of the amount of space available within the container for your object. You use this method to resize your object accordingly.

The *OnGetExtent* Method

The framework calls the `OnGetExtent` method to retrieve the object's natural extents. The container then uses these extents to size the object within the container.

Your Server Item implementation returns the object extents that are stored in the Document class. It does this by calling your own implementation of `GetExtent` in the Document class.

The *OnDraw* Method

The `OnDraw` method is called to render the object into a metafile that is later used as the object's presentation data. You receive two parameters: a pointer to a metafile device context, and the size, in HIMETRIC units, to draw the object.

The OLE User Interface Guidelines require, and users naturally expect, an object to be resizable within the container. When the user resizes the object, the object must scale itself accordingly.

To create a metafile capable of scaling, you must use the MM_ANISOTROPIC mode. This unconstrained mapping mode allows for arbitrary units in both the X and Y axis.

You begin by setting the mapping mode to MM_ANISOTROPIC and setting the window origin to 0,0. The next step is to set the window's extents to the size of the object. The extents are the key to the scaling of the metafile. Extents have no meaning by themselves, but when expressed as a ratio, they become the scaling factor that the GDI uses when translating logical units to device units.

You calculate the ratio by dividing the window extents by the viewport extents. The container sets the viewport extents, which are the actual device units. You must set the window extents, which are the logical units, to the object's size.

You then proceed to draw the rectangle and fill it with the gray background that you are using. These instructions are recorded in the metafile.

The final step is to draw the bitmap. The `CDIB::StretchBitmap` method that you use takes an extra parameter that is not used in the View class' `OnDraw` method. This parameter is a pointer to the client DC.

The reason for passing a DC as a parameter is that you must create a memory device context to store your bitmap before you move it to the screen. The usual technique for creating this device context is to call the `CreateCompatibleDC` function to create a memory device context that has the same attribute as the context that you will use to draw the bitmap.

However, the device context on which you are about to draw is a metafile device context, and you cannot call `CreateCompatibleDC` for a metafile device context. Therefore, you retrieve the device context for the View class and pass that context as a parameter to the `StretchBitmap` call.

The Bitmap Class

The CDIB class handles the loading, saving, and displaying of bitmaps in this application. The code for this class is based partially on some sample C code that ships with the Windows SDK.

Your version enables you to load a DIB from disk, convert it to a device-dependent bitmap (DDB), and display it on the screen.

The CDIB class also supports writing a DDB to metafile for use in OLE applications.

Listing 9.6 shows the complete implementation of the CDIB class.

Listing 9.6 CDIB.H and CDIB.CPP—the Implementation of the Bitmap Class

```
#define WIDTHBYTES(bits)    (((bits) + 31) / 32 * 4)

class CDib : public CObject
{
public:
     HANDLE m_hDIB;
     HPALETTE m_hPal;
     int m_nFileHandle;
public:
     CDib();
     virtual ~CDib();
     BOOL Create(CFile *pFile);
     BOOL Create(int nFileHandle);

     HANDLE ReadDibBitmapInfo (CFile *pFile);
     void DibInfo (LPBITMAPINFOHEADER lpbi);
     WORD DibNumColors (VOID FAR *pv);
     WORD PaletteSize (VOID FAR *pv);
     BOOL DibBlt (HDC hdc, int x0, int y0, int dx, int dy, int x1, int y1);
     BOOL WriteDIB (LPSTR szFile);
     HBITMAP BitmapFromDib ();
     BOOL DrawBitmap (CDC *pDC, int x, int y, HBITMAP hbm, DWORD rop);
     BOOL StretchBitmap (CDC *pDC, int x,
          int y, int cx, int cy, HBITMAP hbm, DWORD rop);
     BOOL StretchBitmap (CDC *pDC, int x,
          int y, int cx, int cy, HBITMAP hbm, DWORD rop,
          CClientDC *pClientDC);

     void SetHandle(HANDLE hMem) {m_hDIB = hMem;}
protected:
private:
};

#include "stdafx.h"
#include "cdib.h"


//-----------------------------------------------------------------
CDib::CDib()
{
}
//-----------------------------------------------------------------
CDib::~CDib()
{
     if(m_hDIB)
     {
          GlobalUnlock(m_hDIB);
          GlobalFree(m_hDIB);
     }
```

(continues)

II

Using MFC

Listing 9.6 Continued

```
}
//-----------------------------------------------------------------
BOOL CDib::Create(CFile *pFile)
{
     BITMAPINFOHEADER bi;
     LPBITMAPINFOHEADER lpbi;
     DWORD dwLen = 0;
     DWORD dwBits;
     HANDLE h;

     m_hDIB = ReadDibBitmapInfo(pFile);

     if(!m_hDIB)
          return FALSE;


     DibInfo(&bi);

     /* Calculate the memory needed to hold the DIB */
     dwBits = bi.biSizeImage;
     dwLen = bi.biSize + (DWORD)PaletteSize(&bi) + dwBits;

     /* Try to increase the size of the bitmap info buffer /*
     /* to hold the DIB */
     h = GlobalReAlloc(m_hDIB, dwLen, GHND);
     if (!h)
     {
          GlobalFree(m_hDIB);
          m_hDIB = NULL;
          return FALSE;
     }
     else
       m_hDIB = h;

     lpbi = (LPBITMAPINFOHEADER)GlobalLock(m_hDIB);
     UINT count;
     TRY
     {
          pFile->Seek(lpbi->biSize+PaletteSize(lpbi),SEEK_SET);
          count = pFile->Read((LPSTR)lpbi +
               (WORD)lpbi->biSize + PaletteSize(lpbi), dwBits);
     }
     CATCH_ALL(e)
     {
          GlobalUnlock(m_hDIB);
          GlobalFree(m_hDIB);
          return FALSE;
     }
     END_CATCH_ALL

     GlobalUnlock(m_hDIB);

     return TRUE;
}
```

```
//------------------------------------------------------------
BOOL CDib::Create(int nFileHandle)
{
     return FALSE;
}
//------------------------------------------------------------
HANDLE CDib::ReadDibBitmapInfo (CFile *pFile)
{
     DWORD off;
     HANDLE hbi = NULL;
     int size, i;
     WORD nNumColors;
     RGBQUAD FAR *pRgb;
     BITMAPINFOHEADER bi;
     BITMAPCOREHEADER bc;
     LPBITMAPINFOHEADER lpbi;
     BITMAPFILEHEADER bf;
     DWORD dwWidth = 0;
     DWORD dwHeight = 0;
     WORD wPlanes, wBitCount;

     // Reset file pointer and read file header
     pFile->SeekToBegin();
     if (sizeof(bf) != pFile->Read((LPSTR)&bf, sizeof(bf)))
          return NULL;

     if (sizeof(bi) != pFile->Read((LPSTR)&bi, sizeof(bi)))
          return NULL;

     nNumColors = DibNumColors(&bi);

     /* Check the nature (BITMAPINFO or BITMAPCORE) of the info block
     * and extract the field information accordingly. If a
     * BITMAPCOREHEADER, transfer its field information
     * to a BITMAPINFOHEADER-style block
     */
     switch (size = (int)bi.biSize)
     {
          case sizeof(BITMAPINFOHEADER):
                 break;

          case sizeof(BITMAPCOREHEADER):
               bc = *(BITMAPCOREHEADER *)&bi;
               dwWidth = (DWORD)bc.bcWidth;
               dwHeight = (DWORD)bc.bcHeight;
               wPlanes = bc.bcPlanes;
               wBitCount = bc.bcBitCount;
               bi.biSize = sizeof(BITMAPINFOHEADER);
               bi.biWidth = dwWidth;
               bi.biHeight = dwHeight;
               bi.biPlanes = wPlanes;
               bi.biBitCount = wBitCount;
               bi.biCompression = BI_RGB;
               bi.biSizeImage = 0;
               bi.biXPelsPerMeter = 0;
```

(continues)

Listing 9.6 Continued

```
            bi.biYPelsPerMeter = 0;
            bi.biClrUsed = nNumColors;
            bi.biClrImportant = nNumColors;
            pFile->Seek((LONG)
                 sizeof(BITMAPCOREHEADER) - sizeof(BITMAPINFOHEADER),
                  SEEK_CUR);
            break;
default:
  return NULL;
  }

if (bi.biSizeImage == 0)
{
     bi.biSizeImage =
     WIDTHBYTES ((DWORD)bi.biWidth * bi.biBitCount) * bi.biHeight;
}

if (bi.biClrUsed == 0)
     bi.biClrUsed = DibNumColors(&bi);

// Allocate for the BITMAPINFO structure and the color table.
hbi = GlobalAlloc(GHND,
                (LONG)bi.biSize + nNumColors * sizeof(RGBQUAD));
if (!hbi)
     return NULL;

lpbi = (LPBITMAPINFOHEADER)GlobalLock(hbi);
*lpbi = bi;

// Get a pointer to the color table
pRgb = (RGBQUAD FAR *)((LPSTR)lpbi + bi.biSize);
if (nNumColors)
{
       if (size == sizeof(BITMAPCOREHEADER))
       {
     /* Convert an old color table (3-byte RGBTRIPLEs) to a new
      * color table (4-byte RGBQUADs)
      */
          pFile->Read((LPSTR)pRgb, nNumColors * sizeof(RGBTRIPLE));
          for (i = nNumColors - 1; i >= 0; i--)
          {
             RGBQUAD rgb;

             rgb.rgbRed = ((RGBTRIPLE FAR *)pRgb)[i].rgbtRed;
             rgb.rgbBlue = ((RGBTRIPLE FAR *)pRgb)[i].rgbtBlue;
             rgb.rgbGreen = ((RGBTRIPLE FAR *)pRgb)[i].rgbtGreen;
             rgb.rgbReserved = (BYTE)0;
             pRgb[i] = rgb;
          }
       }
       else
          pFile->Read((LPSTR)pRgb, nNumColors * sizeof(RGBQUAD));
}
```

```
     if (bf.bfOffBits != 0L)
          pFile->Seek(off + bf.bfOffBits, SEEK_SET);

     GlobalUnlock(hbi);
     return hbi;
}
//-------------------------------------------------------------------
void CDib::DibInfo (LPBITMAPINFOHEADER lpbi)
{
     *lpbi = *(LPBITMAPINFOHEADER)GlobalLock(m_hDIB);

     if (lpbi->biSize != sizeof(BITMAPCOREHEADER))
     {
          if (lpbi->biSizeImage == 0L)
                lpbi->biSizeImage =
                ➥WIDTHBYTES(lpbi->biWidth*lpbi->biBitCount) * lpbi->biHeight;
           if (lpbi->biClrUsed == 0L)
              lpbi->biClrUsed = DibNumColors(lpbi);
     }

     GlobalUnlock(m_hDIB);
}
//-------------------------------------------------------------------
WORD CDib::DibNumColors (VOID FAR *pv)
{
     int bits;
     LPBITMAPINFOHEADER lpbi;
     LPBITMAPCOREHEADER lpbc;

     lpbi = ((LPBITMAPINFOHEADER)pv);
     lpbc = ((LPBITMAPCOREHEADER)pv);

     /*  With the BITMAPINFO format headers, the size of the palette
      *  is in biClrUsed, whereas in the BITMAPCORE-style headers, it
      *  is dependent on the bits per pixel ( = 2 raised to the power of
      *  bits/pixel).
      */
        if (lpbi->biSize != sizeof(BITMAPCOREHEADER))
        {
          if (lpbi->biClrUsed != 0)
             return (WORD)lpbi->biClrUsed;
           bits = lpbi->biBitCount;
        }
        else
           bits = lpbc->bcBitCount;


        switch (bits)
     {
             case 1:
                return 2;
             case 4:
                return 16;
```

(continues)

Listing 9.6 Continued

```
            case 8:
               return 256;
            default:
          return 0;
     }
}
//---------------------------------------------------------------------
WORD CDib::PaletteSize (VOID FAR *pv)
{
     LPBITMAPINFOHEADER lpbi;
     WORD NumColors;

     lpbi = (LPBITMAPINFOHEADER)pv;
     NumColors = DibNumColors(lpbi);

     if (lpbi->biSize == sizeof(BITMAPCOREHEADER))
          return NumColors * sizeof(RGBTRIPLE);
     else
            return NumColors * sizeof(RGBQUAD);
}
//---------------------------------------------------------------------
BOOL CDib::DibBlt (HDC hdc, int x0, int y0, int dx, int dy, int x1, int  y1)
{
     LPBITMAPINFOHEADER lpbi;
     LPSTR pBuf;

     lpbi = (LPBITMAPINFOHEADER)GlobalLock(m_hDIB);
     if (!lpbi)
       return FALSE;

     pBuf = (LPSTR)lpbi + (WORD)lpbi->biSize + PaletteSize(lpbi);
     int nRC = SetDIBitsToDevice(hdc, x0, y0, dx, dy, x1, y1, x1,
                  dy, pBuf, (LPBITMAPINFO) lpbi, DIB_RGB_COLORS);
     TRACE("After SetDI call\n");
     GlobalUnlock(m_hDIB);
     return TRUE;

}
//---------------------------------------------------------------------
BOOL CDib::WriteDIB (LPSTR szFile)
{
     BITMAPFILEHEADER hdr;
     LPBITMAPINFOHEADER lpbi;

     CFile file((const char *)szFile,CFile::modeCreate¦CFile::modeWrite);

     lpbi = (LPBITMAPINFOHEADER)GlobalLock(m_hDIB);

     hdr.bfType = 0x4d42;
     hdr.bfSize = GlobalSize(m_hDIB) + sizeof(BITMAPFILEHEADER);
     hdr.bfReserved1 = 0;
```

```
    hdr.bfReserved2 = 0;
    hdr.bfOffBits = (DWORD)sizeof(BITMAPFILEHEADER) + lpbi->biSize
    ➥+ PaletteSize(lpbi);

    file.Write((LPSTR)&hdr, sizeof(BITMAPFILEHEADER));

    file.Write((LPSTR)lpbi, GlobalSize(m_hDIB));

    GlobalUnlock(m_hDIB);

    return TRUE;
}
//---------------------------------------------------------------
HBITMAP CDib::BitmapFromDib ()
{
    LPBITMAPINFOHEADER lpbi;
    HDC hdc;
    HBITMAP hbm;

    lpbi = (LPBITMAPINFOHEADER)GlobalLock(m_hDIB);
    if (!lpbi)
      return NULL;

    hdc = GetDC(NULL);
    hbm = CreateDIBitmap(hdc, (LPBITMAPINFOHEADER)lpbi,
                         (LONG)CBM_INIT, (LPSTR)
                          lpbi + lpbi->biSize + PaletteSize(lpbi),
                          (LPBITMAPINFO) lpbi, DIB_RGB_COLORS);
    ReleaseDC(NULL, hdc);
    GlobalUnlock(m_hDIB);
    return hbm;
}
//---------------------------------------------------------------
BOOL CDib::DrawBitmap (CDC *pDC, int x, int y, HBITMAP hbm, DWORD rop)
{
    BITMAP bm;
    BOOL f;
    CDC dc;
    POINT pt, pt1;

    dc.CreateCompatibleDC(pDC);
    dc.SelectObject(hbm);
    dc.SetMapMode(pDC->GetMapMode());

    GetObject(hbm, sizeof(BITMAP), (LPSTR)&bm);
    pt.x = bm.bmWidth;
    pt.y = bm.bmHeight;
    pDC->DPtoLP(&pt);

    pt1.x = 0;
    pt1.y = 0;
    dc.DPtoLP(&pt1);

    f = pDC->BitBlt(x, y, pt.x, pt.y, &dc, pt1.x, pt1.y, rop);
```

(continues)

Listing 9.6 Continued

```
     dc.DeleteDC();
     return f;
}
//-------------------------------------------------------------------
BOOL CDib::StretchBitmap (CDC *pDC, int x, int y, int cx, int cy,
                          HBITMAP hbm, DWORD rop)
{
     BITMAP bm;
     BOOL f;
     CDC dc;
     POINT pt, pt1;
     int nMapMode;

     BOOL fOK = dc.CreateCompatibleDC(pDC);
     if(!fOK)
     {
          AfxMessageBox("Failed to create DC");
          return fOK;
     }

     dc.SelectObject(hbm);
     nMapMode = pDC->GetMapMode();
     if(0 == nMapMode)
     {
          //----------
          // Assume this is a metafile DC.
          // The metafile DC does not have an attribute DC
          // so you cannot use Get??? functions.
          // If it is a metafile, then you set
          // the mapping mode to MM_ANISOTROPIC
          nMapMode = MM_ANISOTROPIC;
     }

     dc.SetMapMode(nMapMode);

     GetObject(hbm, sizeof(BITMAP), (LPSTR)&bm);
     pt.x = bm.bmWidth;
     pt.y = bm.bmHeight;
     pDC->DPtoLP(&pt);

     pt1.x = 0;
     pt1.y = 0;
     dc.DPtoLP(&pt1);

     f = pDC->StretchBlt(x, y, cx, cy, &dc, pt1.x, pt1.y, pt.x, pt.y, rop);

     dc.DeleteDC();
     return f;
}
//-------------------------------------------------------------------
BOOL CDib::StretchBitmap (CDC *pDC, int x, int y, int cx, int cy,
                          HBITMAP hbm, DWORD rop, CClientDC *pClientDC)
```

```
{
     BITMAP bm;
     BOOL f;
     CDC dc;
     POINT pt, pt1;

     BOOL fOK = dc.CreateCompatibleDC(pClientDC);
     if(!fOK)
     {
          AfxMessageBox("Failed to create DC");
          return fOK;
     }
     dc.SelectObject(hbm);

     dc.SetMapMode(MM_ANISOTROPIC);

     GetObject(hbm, sizeof(BITMAP), (LPSTR)&bm);
     pt.x = bm.bmWidth;
     pt.y = bm.bmHeight;

     pt1.x = 0;
     pt1.y = 0;

     f = pDC->StretchBlt(x, y, cx, cy, &dc, pt1.x, pt1.y, pt.x, pt.y, rop);

     dc.DeleteDC();
     return f;
}
//------------------------------------------------------------------
//------------------------------------------------------------------
```


Understanding What Happened

To pull all this code together, you should examine the steps involved from the time a user selects Insert **O**bject from the **E**dit menu until the object is in-place active in the container and finally shut down again by the user:

1. When the user selects an object server, the container code calls `COleClientItem::CreateNewObject`, passing the CLSID of the server.

2. The OLE libraries locate the server from the registration database and start the server with the `-Embedding` or `/Embedding` command-line parameter.

3. The newly started server then calls `COleServer::Register` to register its object class with the OLE libraries.

4. `COleServer::OnCreateDoc` is then called to create a document object.

5. `COleServer::OnGetEmbeddedItem` is called to create and return an item.

6. `COleServerItem::OnShow` is then called to display the object.

7. When the user shuts down the object, the framework calls `COleServerDoc::NotifySaved`.

8. `COleServerItem::OnGetData` is called to retrieve the object's native data. This method in turn calls `COleServerItem::Serialize` to save the data to the container's storage.

9. `COleServerItem::OnGetData` is called again to retrieve the object's presentation data. This method in turn calls `COleServerItem::OnDraw` to render the object into the metafile.

10. `COleClientItem::OnChange` is called to notify the container that the server's data has changed.

11. `COleServer::BeginRevoke` is called to shut down the server.

12. `COleClientItem::OnChange` is called one last time to notify the container that the server has shut down.

When the object is edited again, the same basic steps are followed. The main difference is that `COleServerItem::OnSetData` is called to enable the object to retrieve its native data from the container's storage.

Testing the Server

You now need to test your server and check whether it is functioning correctly.

The first step is to register the object in the registration database so that it appears on the Insert Object dialog box of OLE container. The fastest way to do this is to try to execute the program as a stand-alone application.

Because the program is a miniserver and cannot be executed in this manner, it refuses to start. However, before the program returns, it registers itself in the registration database.

Now test the object by running any OLE container. Try Microsoft Word, for example. From the Insert Object dialog box, select the server called Oleser (see fig. 9.4).

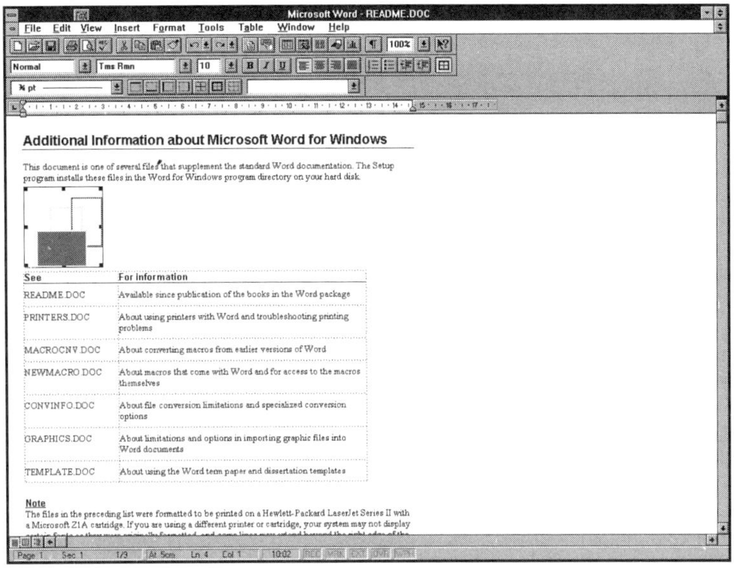

Fig. 9.4
The test server in action.

An empty, 3cm-by-3cm frame now appears in the Word client area. Note that the Word menu is merged with your menu. From the **E**dit menu, choose the **B**itmaps command and select a bitmap. The bitmap will then be drawn in the frame.

If you use the mouse to size the in-place frame, you will notice that the bitmap scales itself according to the size of the in-place frame.

If you click with the mouse in Word's client area, the server shuts down but the presentation data remains. If you now select and resize this object, the metafile is also resized because of the MM_ANISOTROPIC mapping mode that you recorded in the metafile.

From Here...

In this chapter, you learned how to create a miniserver. The next step is to create a full server, which is a server that can also run as a stand-alone.

Chapter 10

A Full OLE Server

In this chapter, you implement a full OLE server by converting the simple miniserver that you developed in Chapter 9, "A Simple MFC OLE Server."

The basic difference between full servers and miniservers is that a miniserver cannot exist outside of a container, because it has no user interface of its own. A miniserver does not save its data to disk files; rather, the data is usually saved in a container's compound file. An important limitation of miniservers is that they support only embedded items. Because miniservers cannot read and write from disk, they cannot support linking.

The full server, on the other hand, can run as a stand-alone application and is fully functional in this mode. It can read and write a file from disk. To support linking, the full server supports clipboard input/output (I/O). This enables the user to copy data to the clipboard and link it into a container.

All OLE servers must be capable of supporting multiple simultaneous connections. If the server is a miniserver or a full server Single Document Interface (SDI) application, it must support multiple instances of itself.

However, if the full server has a Multiple Document Interface (MDI), a new MDI child window is created for each connection. This approach requires only one instance of the application.

When the server application starts, it informs the OLE libraries of whichever approach it prefers. If the application is a miniserver or an SDI full server, a separate instance must be executed each time that the OLE libraries try to connect to an embedded or linked item. If the application is an MDI full server, the requests may be directed to the same instance of the application.

This chapter's sample application is an MDI application. The application, which can load and save device-independent bitmaps (DIBs), supports embedding the bitmaps and linking to bitmaps.

Your linking support is confined to simple file linking. In other words, your linked object manages only a simple file moniker. (See the section "A Closer Look at Linking," at the end of this chapter, for details on file monikers.)

The application supports the user giving a title to each bitmap that is stored. The application also demonstrates how to offer different data types during a clipboard transfer.

Examining the Code

In this section, you examine the source code that makes up the server application.

As usual, you begin by using the Visual C++ AppWizard to generate the initial skeleton code for your application. In the OLE Options dialog box, you choose the **F**ull-Server radio button (see fig. 10.1).

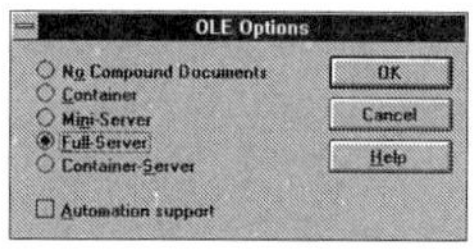

Fig. 10.1 Specifying a full server in the OLE Options dialog box.

The Window Application Class

The application's `CWinApp` object is located in the OLESRV2.CPP module. As with all MFC applications, this module is responsible for initializing and setting up the application.

In OLE applications, this module initializes the OLE libraries. For object and Automation servers, this module also initializes the CLSID that uniquely identifies the server.

The AppWizard generates the CLSID by calling `CoCreateGuid`. As you learned in Chapter 2, "The Component Object Model," this CLSID is statistically guaranteed to be unique to your application.

The next step is to call `AfxOleInit` to initialize the OLE libraries. All MFC OLE applications must call this function. Failure to do so results in undefined behavior in your application.

You then create the document template to tie your Document, View, and Frame classes together. Once you have a valid pointer to the document template, you call `pDocTemplate->SetServerInfo`. This method identifies the resources that the object uses when it is activated in place and when it is opened in a separate window. As mentioned in Chapter 2, objects and their containers merge their menus together during in-place activation. You use a separate menu resource for in-place activation, and pass the handle to this menu in `SetServerInfo`. You also use a special frame window class during in-place activation. Information about this class is also passed to `SetServerInfo`.

After you create the document template, you connect it to the `COleTemplateServer` object. The framework uses the `COleTemplateServer` object to create new document objects programmatically. The last parameter used in the `ConnectTemplate` call is interesting. An SDI server passes true as the last parameter, which tells the framework that the server supports multiple instances of the application. However, an MDI server passes false as the last parameter. You create a new MDI child window for each request.

The next step is to register all the application's class factories. Internally, the framework calls `CoRegisterClassObject` to register the object class with the OLE libraries. If the object is not registered, the container cannot create objects of the class. In Chapter 9, when you created the miniserver, you registered the object only if the application was launched with the `/Embedding` command line. For an MDI full server, however, you must always register your class factories, regardless of the command-line parameters.

You then call the helper function `RunEmbedded` to parse the command line. This function checks for the `/Embedding` parameters. If your application launches with the `/Embedding` parameters, it doesn't display its main window and simply returns. If your application wasn't launched to be embedded, you update the system registry and open your application's main window.

Listing 10.1 shows the code for your `CWinApp` implementation.

Listing 10.1 OLE2SRV.H and OLE2SRV.CPP—the Implementation Files for *CWinApp*

```
//-------------------------------------------------------------
// olesrv2.h : main header file for the OLESRV2 application
//

#ifndef __AFXWIN_H__
     #error include 'stdafx.h' before including this file for PCH
#endif

#include "resource.h"       // main symbols
```

(continues)

II

Using MFC

Listing 10.1 Continued

```
/////////////////////////////////////////////////////////////////////
// COleSrv2App:
// See olesrv2.cpp for the implementation of this class
//
class COleSrv2App : public CWinApp
{
public:
     COleSrv2App();

// Overrides
     virtual BOOL InitInstance();

// Implementation
     COleTemplateServer m_server;
          // Server object for document creation

     //{{AFX_MSG(COleSrv2App)
     afx_msg void OnAppAbout();
     // NOTE - ClassWizard adds and removes member functions here.
     //   DO NOT EDIT what you see in these blocks of generated code!
     //}}AFX_MSG
     DECLARE_MESSAGE_MAP()
};
/////////////////////////////////////////////////////////////////////


//-------------------------------------------------------------------
// olesrv2.cpp : Defines the class behaviors for the application.
//

#include "stdafx.h"
#include "olesrv2.h"

#include "mainfrm.h"
#include "ipframe.h"
#include "olesrdoc.h"
#include "olesrvw.h"

#ifdef _DEBUG
#undef THIS_FILE
static char BASED_CODE THIS_FILE[] = __FILE__;
#endif

/////////////////////////////////////////////////////////////////////
// COleSrv2App

BEGIN_MESSAGE_MAP(COleSrv2App, CWinApp)
```

```
    //{{AFX_MSG_MAP(COleSrv2App)
    ON_COMMAND(ID_APP_ABOUT, OnAppAbout)
        // NOTE - ClassWizard adds and removes mapping macros here.
        //    DO NOT EDIT what you see in these blocks of generated code!
    //}}AFX_MSG_MAP
    // Standard file-based document commands
    ON_COMMAND(ID_FILE_NEW, CWinApp::OnFileNew)
    ON_COMMAND(ID_FILE_OPEN, CWinApp::OnFileOpen)
    // Standard print setup command
    ON_COMMAND(ID_FILE_PRINT_SETUP, CWinApp::OnFilePrintSetup)
END_MESSAGE_MAP()

/////////////////////////////////////////////////////////////////////////////
// COleSrv2App construction

COleSrv2App::COleSrv2App()
{
    // TODO: add construction code here,
    // Place all significant initialization in InitInstance
}

/////////////////////////////////////////////////////////////////////////////
// The one and only COleSrv2App object

COleSrv2App NEAR theApp;

// This identifier was generated to be statistically unique for your app.
// You may change it if you prefer to choose a specific identifier.
static const CLSID BASED_CODE clsid =
{ 0x529e7ba0, 0x8b6a, 0x101b, { 0xbb, 0x57, 0x0, 0x60, 0x8c, 0xc0,
  0xba, 0x93 } };
/////////////////////////////////////////////////////////////////////////////
// COleSrv2App initialization

BOOL COleSrv2App::InitInstance()
{
    // Initialize OLE 2.0 libraries
    if (!AfxOleInit())
    {
        AfxMessageBox(IDP_OLE_INIT_FAILED);
        return FALSE;
    }

    // Standard initialization
    // If you are not using these features and want to reduce the size
    // of your final executable, you should remove from the following
    // the specific initialization routines you do not need.

    SetDialogBkColor();        // Set dialog background color to gray
    LoadStdProfileSettings();
                    // Load standard INI file options (including MRU)
```

(continues)

Listing 10.1 Continued

```
// Register the application's document templates.
// Document templates serve as the connection
// between documents, frame windows, and views.

CMultiDocTemplate* pDocTemplate;
pDocTemplate = new CMultiDocTemplate(
     IDR_OLESRVTYPE,
     RUNTIME_CLASS(COleSrv2Doc),
     RUNTIME_CLASS(CMDIChildWnd),      // standard MDI child frame
     RUNTIME_CLASS(COleSrv2View));

pDocTemplate->SetServerInfo(
     IDR_OLESRVTYPE_SRVR_EMB, IDR_OLESRVTYPE_SRVR_IP,
     RUNTIME_CLASS(CInPlaceFrame));
AddDocTemplate(pDocTemplate);

//------------
// Connect the COleTemplateServer to the document template.
// The COleTemplateServer creates new documents on behalf
// of requesting OLE containers by using information
// specified in the document template.
m_server.ConnectTemplate(clsid, pDocTemplate, FALSE);

//--------
// Register all OLE server factories as running. This enables the
// OLE 2.0 libraries to create objects from other applications.
COleTemplateServer::RegisterAll();

// Note: MDI applications register all server objects without regard
// to the /Embedding or /Automation on the command line.

// create main MDI Frame window
CMainFrame* pMainFrame = new CMainFrame;
if (!pMainFrame->LoadFrame(IDR_MAINFRAME))
     return FALSE;

m_pMainWnd = pMainFrame;

// Parse the command line to see if launched as OLE server
if (RunEmbedded() || RunAutomated())
{
     // Application was run with /Embedding or /Automation.
     //  Don't show the main window in this case.
     return TRUE;
}
```

```
    // When a server application is launched stand-alone, you should
    // update the system registry in case it has been damaged.
    m_server.UpdateRegistry(OAT_INPLACE_SERVER);


    if (m_lpCmdLine[0] == '\0')
    {
        // create a new (empty) document
        OnFileNew();
    }
    else
    {
        // open an existing document
        OpenDocumentFile(m_lpCmdLine);
    }

    // The main window has been initialized, so show and update it.
    pMainFrame->ShowWindow(m_nCmdShow);
    pMainFrame->UpdateWindow();

    return TRUE;
}

/////////////////////////////////////////////////////////////////////////////
// CAboutDlg dialog used for App About

class CAboutDlg : public CDialog
{
public:
    CAboutDlg();

// Dialog Data
    //{{AFX_DATA(CAboutDlg)
    enum { IDD = IDD_ABOUTBOX };
    //}}AFX_DATA

// Implementation
protected:
    virtual void DoDataExchange(CDataExchange* pDX);  // DDX/DDV support
    //{{AFX_MSG(CAboutDlg)
        // No message handlers
    //}}AFX_MSG
    DECLARE_MESSAGE_MAP()
};
```

(continues)

Listing 10.1 Continued

```
CAboutDlg::CAboutDlg() : CDialog(CAboutDlg::IDD)
{
     //{{AFX_DATA_INIT(CAboutDlg)
     //}}AFX_DATA_INIT
}

void CAboutDlg::DoDataExchange(CDataExchange* pDX)
{
     CDialog::DoDataExchange(pDX);
     //{{AFX_DATA_MAP(CAboutDlg)
     //}}AFX_DATA_MAP
}

BEGIN_MESSAGE_MAP(CAboutDlg, CDialog)
     //{{AFX_MSG_MAP(CAboutDlg)
          // No message handlers
     //}}AFX_MSG_MAP
END_MESSAGE_MAP()

// App command to run the dialog
void COleSrv2App::OnAppAbout()
{
     CAboutDlg aboutDlg;
     aboutDlg.DoModal();
}
////////////////////////////////////////////////////////////////////////
```

The In-place Frame Class

In the previous section, when you called `SetServerInfo` to inform the framework of the resources that you must use when you are active in place or in a separate window, you also passed the name of the class that creates your in-place frame window.

When an object is in-place active, the class responsible for the frame window is called `COleIPFrameWnd`. This class oversees the creating and positioning control bars within the container application's document window. Notifications generated by the embedded `COleResizeBar` during a move or resize operation are also handled by `COleIPFrameWnd`.

The implementation of `CInPlaceFrame` derives from `COleIPFrameWnd`. This class contains a `COleResizeBar` member that is responsible for creating the tracker rectangle that surrounds your object when it is active in place. The object implements the resizing handles and the hatch pattern surrounding the object. Objects of `COleResizeBar` are usually used as embedded members of `COleIPFrameWnd` classes. All notifications created by this member are sent to its parent, which in this case is the `COleIPFrameWnd` class.

Your object has a toolbar that must be visible during in-place activation, so you also must implement `COleIPFrameWnd::OnCreateControlBars`. The framework calls this method when the object is active in place.

The `CWnd` pointer that is passed in the first parameter is the container's frame window. You use this pointer to create toolbars and other controls. By using this pointer, you ensure that your tools are positioned correctly. However, using this pointer leaves you with a problem: if the container's frame window is the parent of your controls, all messages that those controls generate will be passed to the container. By calling `SetOwner` with a pointer to your `CInPlaceFrame` class, you ensure that all your controls' messages are routed correctly.

Listing 10.2 shows the code for the implementation of your In-place Frame class.

Listing 10.2 IPFRAME.CPP and IPFRAME.H—the Implementation of Your In-place Frame Class

```
//-----------------------------------------------------------------
// ipframe.h : interface of the CInPlaceFrame class
//

class CInPlaceFrame : public COleIPFrameWnd
{
     DECLARE_DYNCREATE(CInPlaceFrame)
public:
     CInPlaceFrame;

// Attributes
public:

// Operations
public:

// Implementation
public:
     virtual ~CInPlaceFrame();
#ifdef _DEBUG
     virtual void AssertValid() const;
     virtual void Dump(CDumpContext& dc) const;
#endif

     virtual BOOL OnCreateControlBars(CWnd* pWndFrame, CWnd* pWndDoc);

protected:
     CToolBar        m_wndToolBar;
     COleResizeBar   m_wndResizeBar;
     COleDropTarget  m_dropTarget;
```

(continues)

Listing 10.2 Continued

```
// Generated message map functions
protected:
	//{{AFX_MSG(CInPlaceFrame)
	afx_msg int OnCreate(LPCREATESTRUCT lpCreateStruct);
		// NOTE - ClassWizard adds and removes member functions here.
		//    DO NOT EDIT what you see in these blocks of generated code!
	//}}AFX_MSG
	DECLARE_MESSAGE_MAP()
};

/////////////////////////////////////////////////////////////////////////////
//-----------------------------------------------------------------------
// ipframe.cpp : implementation of the CInPlaceFrame class
//

#include "stdafx.h"
#include "olesrv2.h"

#include "ipframe.h"

#ifdef _DEBUG
#undef THIS_FILE
static char BASED_CODE THIS_FILE[] = __FILE__;
#endif

/////////////////////////////////////////////////////////////////////////////
// CInPlaceFrame

IMPLEMENT_DYNCREATE(CInPlaceFrame, COleIPFrameWnd)

BEGIN_MESSAGE_MAP(CInPlaceFrame, COleIPFrameWnd)
	//{{AFX_MSG_MAP(CInPlaceFrame)
	ON_WM_CREATE()
	//}}AFX_MSG_MAP
END_MESSAGE_MAP()

/////////////////////////////////////////////////////////////////////////////
// arrays of IDs used to initialize control bars

// toolbar buttons - IDs are command buttons
static UINT BASED_CODE buttons[] =
{
	// same order as in the bitmap 'itoolbar.bmp'
	ID_EDIT_CUT,
	ID_EDIT_COPY,
	ID_EDIT_PASTE,
	ID_SEPARATOR,
	ID_APP_ABOUT,
};
```

```
////////////////////////////////////////////////////////////////////////////
// CInPlaceFrame construction/destruction

CInPlaceFrame::CInPlaceFrame()
{
}

CInPlaceFrame::~CInPlaceFrame()
{
}

int CInPlaceFrame::OnCreate(LPCREATESTRUCT lpCreateStruct)
{
     if (COleIPFrameWnd::OnCreate(lpCreateStruct) == -1)
          return -1;

     // CResizeBar implements in-place resizing.
     if (!m_wndResizeBar.Create(this))
     {
          TRACE("Failed to create resize bar\n");
          return -1;      // fail to create
     }

     // By default, you should register a drop target that does
     //  nothing with your frame window. This prevents drops from
     //  "falling through" to a container that supports drag-drop.
     m_dropTarget.Register(this);

     return 0;
}

//-----------------------------------
// The framework calls OnCreateControlBars to create control bars
// on the container application's windows. pWndFrame is the
// top-level frame window of the container and is always non-NULL.
// pWndDoc is the doc-level frame window and is NULL when the container
// is an SDI application. A server application can place MFC control
// bars on either window.
BOOL CInPlaceFrame::OnCreateControlBars(CWnd* pWndFrame, CWnd* pWndDoc)
{
     // Create toolbar on client's frame window
     if (!m_wndToolBar.Create(pWndFrame) ||
          !m_wndToolBar.LoadBitmap(IDR_OLESRVTYPE_SRVR_IP) ||
          !m_wndToolBar.SetButtons(buttons, sizeof(buttons)/sizeof(UINT)))
     {
          TRACE("Failed to create toolbar\n");
          return FALSE;
     }
     // Set owner to this window, so messages are delivered to correct app
     m_wndToolBar.SetOwner(this);
```

(continues)

Listing 10.2 Continued

```
        return TRUE;
}

/////////////////////////////////////////////////////////////////////////////
// CInPlaceFrame diagnostics

#ifdef _DEBUG
void CInPlaceFrame::AssertValid() const
{
        COleIPFrameWnd::AssertValid();
}

void CInPlaceFrame::Dump(CDumpContext& dc) const
{
        COleIPFrameWnd::Dump(dc);
}
#endif //_DEBUG

/////////////////////////////////////////////////////////////////////////////
```

The Document Class

The `COleServerDoc` class implements a container for embedded and linked objects. For applications that support only embedded items, each Document class can support only one server item. Although your application supports linking, you have only one item for each Document class. If you were supporting linking to a part of your object (like Excel allows linking to a particular range of cells in a sheet), you would have to support more than one `COleServerItem` object.

The Document class is also responsible for loading and saving the object to the `IStorage` object provided by the container. Your application can also read and write files to disk, so you also provide support for those operations in this class.

Your application also supports the reading and writing of standard color bitmaps. These are files with the BMP extension. However, your application's native format is stored in files with the extension OLE. Normally, a user will read in a bitmap, add a title, and then save the bitmap as an OLE file.

To test your server's linking capabilities, you should place an OLE file on the clipboard, link it into a container, and then change the title in your server application. When you select Update Links from the container's **E**dit menu, you should see the title of the linked picture changing.

`COleServerDoc` defines one pure virtual member, `OnGetEmbeddedItem`, which creates and returns a pointer to the document's embedded object. You also implement `OnSetItemRects`, which helps the user scale the object when it is in-place active.

Listing 10.3 shows the complete code for the implementation of the Document class.

Listing 10.3 OLESRDOC.CPP and OLESRDOC.H—the Implementation of the Document Class

```
#include "cdib.h"
#if !defined (SRVDOC_H)
#define SRVDOC_H
// olesrdoc.h : interface of the COleSrv2Doc class
//
//////////////////////////////////////////////////////////////////

class COleSrv2SrvrItem;

class COleSrv2Doc : public COleServerDoc
{
protected: // create from serialization only
     COleSrv2Doc();
     DECLARE_DYNCREATE(COleSrv2Doc)

// Attributes
public:

     COleSrv2SrvrItem* GetEmbeddedItem()
          { return (COleSrv2SrvrItem*)COleServerDoc::GetEmbeddedItem(); }

     CSize m_size;
     CDib *m_DIB;
     CString m_FileName;
     COleSrv2SrvrItem* m_pItem;
     CString m_Title;
     COLORREF m_crColor;

// Operations
public:
     CSize OnGetExtent();
     void OnSetExtent(CSize &rSize);
     void SetTitle(LPCSTR lpTitle);
     void OnSetItemRects(LPCRECT lpPosRect, LPCRECT lpClipRect);
// Implementation
public:
     virtual ~COleSrv2Doc();
     virtual void Serialize(CArchive& ar);  // overridden for document I/O
     virtual COleServerItem* OnGetEmbeddedItem();
#ifdef _DEBUG
     virtual void AssertValid() const;
     virtual void Dump(CDumpContext& dc) const;
```

(continues)

II Using MFC

Listing 10.3 Continued

```
#endif
     virtual BOOL OnOpenDocument(const char *lpFileName);
     virtual BOOL OnSaveDocument(const char *lpPathName);
#if 0
     virtual BOOL OnRenderData(LPFORMATETC lpFormatEtc,
                               LPSTGMEDIUM lpStgMedium);
#endif
protected:
     virtual BOOL OnNewDocument();
// Generated message map functions
protected:
     //{{AFX_MSG(COleSrv2Doc)
          // NOTE - ClassWizard adds and removes member functions here.
          //   DO NOT EDIT what you see in these blocks of generated code!
     //}}AFX_MSG
     DECLARE_MESSAGE_MAP()
};
/////////////////////////////////////////////////////////////////////
#endif

//-----------------------------------------------------------------
// olesrdoc.cpp : implementation of the COleSrv2Doc class
//

#include "stdafx.h"
#include "olesrv2.h"

#include "olesrdoc.h"
#include "srvritem.h"

#ifdef _DEBUG
#undef THIS_FILE
static char BASED_CODE THIS_FILE[] = __FILE__;
#endif

/////////////////////////////////////////////////////////////////////
// COleSrv2Doc
//
IMPLEMENT_DYNCREATE(COleSrv2Doc, COleServerDoc)

BEGIN_MESSAGE_MAP(COleSrv2Doc, COleServerDoc)
     //{{AFX_MSG_MAP(COleSrv2Doc)
          // NOTE - ClassWizard adds and removes mapping macros here.
          //   DO NOT EDIT what you see in these blocks of generated code!
     //}}AFX_MSG_MAP
END_MESSAGE_MAP()
```

```
/////////////////////////////////////////////////////////////////////////////
// COleSrv2Doc construction/destruction
//
COleSrv2Doc::COleSrv2Doc()
{
     m_DIB = NULL;
     m_pItem = NULL;
     m_size = CSize(9000, 9000);
     m_Title = "Untitled";
     m_crColor = RGB(0,0,0);

}
//---------------------------------------------------------------
COleSrv2Doc::~COleSrv2Doc()
{
     if(m_DIB)
          delete m_DIB;
}
//---------------------------------------------------------------
BOOL COleSrv2Doc::OnSaveDocument(const char *lpPathName)
{
     CString str, ext;

     str = lpPathName;
     ext = str.Right(3);

     if(0 == ext.CompareNoCase("bmp"))
          return m_DIB->SaveDIB(lpPathName);
     else
          return COleServerDoc::OnSaveDocument(lpPathName);
}
//---------------------------------------------------------------
BOOL COleSrv2Doc::OnNewDocument()
{
     if (!COleServerDoc::OnNewDocument())
          return FALSE;

     // TODO: add reinitialization code here
     // (SDI documents will reuse this document)

     return TRUE;
}
//---------------------------------------------------------------
BOOL COleSrv2Doc::OnOpenDocument(const char *lpFileName)
{
     CString str, ext;
```

(continues)

II

Using MFC

Listing 10.3 Continued

```
        str = lpFileName;
        ext = str.Right(3);

        if(0 == ext.CompareNoCase("bmp"))
        {
             TRY
             {
                  if(m_DIB)
                       delete m_DIB;

                  CFile  file((const char *)lpFileName,CFile::modeRead);
                  m_DIB = new CDib;
                  m_DIB->Create(&file);
             }
             CATCH_ALL(e)
             {
                  AfxMessageBox("Error: Failed to open file");
                  return FALSE;
             }
             END_CATCH_ALL

             m_Title = m_FileName = lpFileName;
             return TRUE;
        }
        else
             return COleServerDoc::OnOpenDocument(lpFileName);
}
/////////////////////////////////////////////////////////////////////////////
// COleSrv2Doc server implementation
//
COleServerItem* COleSrv2Doc::OnGetEmbeddedItem()
{
        // The framework calls OnGetEmbeddedItem() to get
        // the COleServerItem that is associated with the document.
        // Call it only when necessary.

        if(NULL == m_pItem)
        {
             COleSrv2SrvrItem* pItem = new COleSrv2SrvrItem(this);
             ASSERT_VALID(pItem);
             m_pItem = pItem;
             return m_pItem;
        }
        else
             return m_pItem;
}
```

```
//--------------------------------------------------------------------
void COleSrv2Doc::OnSetItemRects(LPCRECT lpPosRect, LPCRECT lpClipRect)
{
     //--------
     // The framework calls this method if the user
     // moves or resizes the active in-place object.
     // Because you support scaling of your bitmaps,
     // you use the information in the pos rectangle
     // to update your object's extents.

     COleServerDoc::OnSetItemRects(lpPosRect,lpClipRect);

     TRACE("SetItemRect %d-%d %d-%d",
     lpPosRect->left,lpPosRect->top,lpPosRect->right,lpPosRect->bottom);

     POSITION pos = GetFirstViewPosition();
     CView* pFirstView = GetNextView(pos);

     CSize size(lpPosRect->right-lpPosRect->left,
                lpPosRect->bottom-lpPosRect->top);

     CClientDC dc(pFirstView);
     dc.DPtoHIMETRIC(&size);

     OnSetExtent(size);
}
//--------------------------------------------------------------------
void COleSrv2Doc::OnSetExtent(CSize &rSize)
{
     //----------
     // Called by the framework to tell you how
     // much space is available in the client container.
     // You also call this method if the user moves or
     // resizes the active in-place object.
     m_size = rSize;
     UpdateAllViews(NULL);
}
//--------------------------------------------------------------------
CSize COleSrv2Doc::OnGetExtent()
{
     return m_size;
}
//////////////////////////////////////////////////////////////////////
// COleSrv2Doc serialization
//
void COleSrv2Doc::Serialize(CArchive& ar)
{
     DWORD dwSize;

     if (ar.IsStoring())
     {
          ar << m_size;
```

(continues)

II

Using MFC

Listing 10.3 Continued

```
            dwSize = GlobalSize(m_DIB->m_hDIB);
            ar << dwSize;
            ar << m_Title;

            ar.Write(GlobalLock(m_DIB->m_hDIB),dwSize);
        }
        else
        {
            ar >> m_size;
            ar >> dwSize;
            ar >> m_Title;

            m_DIB = new CDib();
            HANDLE hMem = GlobalAlloc(GHND,dwSize);
            LPSTR lpBuff = (LPSTR)GlobalLock(hMem);

            ar.Read(lpBuff,(UINT)dwSize);

            m_DIB->SetHandle(hMem);
            COleServerDoc::SetTitle(m_Title);
        }
    }
    ///////////////////////////////////////////////////////////////////////////
    // COleSrv2Doc diagnostics
    //
    #ifdef _DEBUG
    void COleSrv2Doc::AssertValid() const
    {
        COleServerDoc::AssertValid();
    }

    void COleSrv2Doc::Dump(CDumpContext& dc) const
    {
        COleServerDoc::Dump(dc);
    }
    #endif //_DEBUG
    ///////////////////////////////////////////////////////////////////////////
    // COleSrv2Doc commands
    //
    void COleSrv2Doc::SetTitle(LPCSTR lpTitle)
    {
        m_Title = lpTitle;
        SetModifiedFlag(TRUE);

        COleServerDoc::SetTitle((const char *)lpTitle);
        OnGetEmbeddedItem()->NotifyChanged();
    }
    //-------------------------------------------------------------
    //-------------------------------------------------------------
```

The following sections examine the code of the Document class in more detail.

The Document Constructor

You begin by initializing your object's variables. The initial size of your bitmap is set to 9cm by 9cm. You use the MM_HIMETRIC mapping mode in your View class, so 9,000 units is equal to 9 centimeters. You set the title variable to "Untitled" and initialize your member pointers to NULL. You should always initialize all member variables in the object's constructor. This avoids the common bug of using uninitialized pointers.

The *OnSaveDocument* Method

The framework calls the `OnSaveDocument` method when the user selects the Save option from the menu or toolbar. If the file's extension is BMP, you call the `CDIB::SaveDIB` method to save it as a bitmap. However, if the extension is OLE, which is your application's default file type, you call the base class' implementation of `OnSaveDocument`. The default implementation eventually calls your `Serialize` method.

The *OnNewDocument* Method

For the `OnNewDocument` method, you simply defer to the base class' implementation.

The *OnOpenDocument* Method

The `OnOpenDocument` method is called in response to the user selecting the Open option on the menu or toolbar. You begin by checking the extension of the selected document. If the extension is BMP, you create an object of type `CDib` and pass a pointer to a `CFile` object to a `CDib` object.

Note

If the extension is not BMP, you assume that it is OLE. In a commercial application, such assumptions would be fatal. However, for the purpose of this sample application, you do not need to code extensive error-handling routines.

To open a file of type OLE, you defer to the base class' `OnOpenDocument` method. The default implementation eventually calls your `Serialize` method.

The *OnGetEmbeddedItem* Method

The framework usually calls the `OnGetEmbeddedItem` method to retrieve a pointer to your document's server item. You need access to the server item when you copy the object to the clipboard.

The first call to this method creates the server item. All subsequent calls return a pointer to this server item object.

The *OnSetItemRects* Method

The framework calls the `OnSetItemRects` method if your object is moved or resized while in-place active. You receive two parameters. The first parameter is a pointer to a position rectangle. This rectangle tells you both the position and size of the object relative to the container's client area. The second parameter is a pointer to a clipping rectangle.

When this method is called, you first call the base class' implementation. You then convert the object's extents from device units to HIMETRIC units by calling `CDC::DPtoHIMETRIC`. The `OnSetExtents` method uses the newly converted units when updating the object's size.

Because you support scaling of the object when it is in-place active, you need to know when the user wants to change the object's size. This applies only when the object is embedded in the container. As mentioned in Chapter 2, "The Component Object Model," only embedded objects can be activated in place. Linked objects are always edited in a separate editing window.

The *OnSetExtents* Method

The `OnSetExtents` method, which you define and implement in your Document class, is a parallel to a method of the same name in the `COleServerItem` class. You duplicate the method here to keep all the information about the object in the Document class so that both the View class and the `COleServerItem` class can access the information.

The framework calls this method in the `COleServerItem` class to tell the object how much space is initially available to it within the container. Your `ColeServerItem` implementation simply calls the `OnSetExtent` method in your Document class.

The *OnGetExtents* Method

The framework calls the `OnGetExtents` method to retrieve the object's size in HIMETRIC units. As with the `OnSetExtent` implementation, this method is in fact part of the `COleServerItem` class. You call this method from the implementation in `COleServerItem`.

The *Serialize* Method

The framework calls the `Serialize` method to save and restore your application's native data. This application's native data consists of a device-independent bitmap (DIB) and the bitmap's title and size.

The default implementations of `OnOpenDocument` and `OnSaveDocument` usually call this method. However, you override both these methods to ensure that you do not call the `Serialize` method when the user is loading or saving a plain bitmap. You use this method to load and save files only of type OLE.

The *OnSetTitle* Method

The `OnSetTitle` method is called whenever the user changes the picture's title. You first store the title in your class member variable. Then, to change the MDI window title, you call the base class' version. Finally, you call `OnNotifyChanged` to notify all open containers that contain links to your object that the object's data has changed.

The Title Class

A very simple `CDialog`-derived class, the Title class enables the user to change the title of the current picture. After retrieving the next picture title, the class calls the `COleSrv2Doc::SetTitle` method to update the title. Listing 10.4 shows this class' code, only in the interest of presenting to you the complete code for the full server application.

Listing 10.4 TITLE.CPP and TITLE.H—the Implementation of the *CTitle* Class

```
#include "olesrdoc.h"
/////////////////////////////////////////////////////////////////////////////
// CTitle dialog
//
class CTitle : public CDialog
{
// Construction
public:
     CTitle(COleSrv2Doc *pDoc,CWnd* pParent = NULL);

// Dialog Data
     //{{AFX_DATA(CTitle)
     enum { IDD = IDD_DIALOG1 };
     CString     m_Title;
     //}}AFX_DATA

     COleSrv2Doc *m_pDoc;
// Overrides
     // ClassWizard-generated virtual function overrides
     //{{AFX_VIRTUAL(CTitle)
     protected:
     virtual void DoDataExchange(CDataExchange* pDX);  // DDX/DDV support
     //}}AFX_VIRTUAL
```

(continues)

Listing 10.4 Continued

```
// Implementation
protected:

     // Generated message map functions
     //{{AFX_MSG(CTitle)
     virtual void OnOK();
     virtual void OnCancel();
     //}}AFX_MSG
     DECLARE_MESSAGE_MAP()
};
//-----------------------------------------------------------------
//-----------------------------------------------------------------
// title.cpp : implementation file
//

#include "stdafx.h"
#include "olesrv2.h"
#include "title.h"

#ifdef _DEBUG
#undef THIS_FILE
static char BASED_CODE THIS_FILE[] = __FILE__;
#endif

/////////////////////////////////////////////////////////////////////////////
// CTitle dialog
//
CTitle::CTitle(COleSrv2Doc *pDoc,CWnd* pParent /*=NULL*/)
     : CDialog(CTitle::IDD, pParent)
{
     m_pDoc = pDoc;
     //{{AFX_DATA_INIT(CTitle)
     m_Title = "";
     //}}AFX_DATA_INIT
}
//-----------------------------------------------------------------
void CTitle::DoDataExchange(CDataExchange* pDX)
{
     CDialog::DoDataExchange(pDX);
     //{{AFX_DATA_MAP(CTitle)
     DDX_Text(pDX, IDC_TITLE, m_Title);
     //}}AFX_DATA_MAP
}
//-----------------------------------------------------------------
BEGIN_MESSAGE_MAP(CTitle, CDialog)
     //{{AFX_MSG_MAP(CTitle)
     //}}AFX_MSG_MAP
END_MESSAGE_MAP()
/////////////////////////////////////////////////////////////////////////////
// CTitle message handlers
//
void CTitle::OnOK()
```

```
{
     UpdateData();
     m_pDoc->SetTitle(m_Title);

     CDialog::OnOK();
}
//-----------------------------------------------------------------
void CTitle::OnCancel()
{
     CDialog::OnCancel();
}
//-----------------------------------------------------------------
//-----------------------------------------------------------------
```

The View Class

As usual, the View class provides the interface between the user and the application. Your View class provides support for displaying the selected bitmaps both when an embedded object is active in place and when the application is running as a stand-alone application.

Listing 10.5 shows the implementation code for the View class.

Listing 10.5 OLESRVW.CPP and OLESRVW.H—the Implementation of the *CView* Class

```
//-----------------------------------------------------------------
// olesrvw.h : interface of the COleSrv2View class
//

class COleSrv2View : public CView
{
protected: // create from serialization only
     COleSrv2View();
     DECLARE_DYNCREATE(COleSrv2View)

// Attributes
public:
     COleSrv2Doc* GetDocument();

// Operations
public:

// Implementation
public:
     virtual ~COleSrv2View();
     virtual void OnDraw(CDC* pDC);  // overridden to draw this view
#ifdef _DEBUG
     virtual void AssertValid() const;
```

(continues)

Listing 10.5 Continued

```
    virtual void Dump(CDumpContext& dc) const;
#endif

protected:

    // Printing support
    virtual BOOL OnPreparePrinting(CPrintInfo* pInfo);
    virtual void OnBeginPrinting(CDC* pDC, CPrintInfo* pInfo);
    virtual void OnEndPrinting(CDC* pDC, CPrintInfo* pInfo);

// Generated message map functions
protected:
    //{{AFX_MSG(COleSrv2View)
    afx_msg void OnEditCopy();
    afx_msg void OnEditChangetitle();
    //}}AFX_MSG
    DECLARE_MESSAGE_MAP()
};

#ifndef _DEBUG  // debug version in olesrvw.cpp
inline ColeSrv2Doc* COleSrv2View::GetDocument()
   { return (COleSrv2Doc*)m_pDocument; }
#endif

/////////////////////////////////////////////////////////////////////

//-------------------------------------------------------------------
// olesrvw.cpp : implementation of the COleSrv2View class
//

#include "stdafx.h"
#include "olesrv2.h"

#include "olesrdoc.h"
#include "srvritem.h"
#include "olesrvw.h"
#include "title.h"

#ifdef _DEBUG
#undef THIS_FILE
static char BASED_CODE THIS_FILE[] = __FILE__;
#endif

/////////////////////////////////////////////////////////////////////
// COleSrv2View
//
IMPLEMENT_DYNCREATE(COleSrv2View, CView)
```

```
BEGIN_MESSAGE_MAP(COleSrv2View, CView)
     //{{AFX_MSG_MAP(COleSrv2View)
     ON_COMMAND(ID_EDIT_COPY, OnEditCopy)
     ON_COMMAND(ID_EDIT_CHANGETITLE, OnEditChangetitle)
     //}}AFX_MSG_MAP
     // Standard printing commands
     ON_COMMAND(ID_FILE_PRINT, CView::OnFilePrint)
     ON_COMMAND(ID_FILE_PRINT_PREVIEW, CView::OnFilePrintPreview)
END_MESSAGE_MAP()

/////////////////////////////////////////////////////////////////////
// COleSrv2View construction/destruction
//
COleSrv2View::COleSrv2View()
{
}
//-------------------------------------------------------------------
COleSrv2View::~COleSrv2View()
{
}

/////////////////////////////////////////////////////////////////////
// COleSrv2View drawing
//
void COleSrv2View::OnDraw(CDC* pDC)
{
     COleSrv2Doc* pDoc = GetDocument();
     ASSERT_VALID(pDoc);

     if(pDoc->m_DIB)
     {
          RECT rc;
          GetClientRect(&rc);
          HBITMAP hbm = pDoc->m_DIB->BitmapFromDib();
          pDoc->m_DIB->StretchBitmap(pDC,rc.left,rc.top,rc.right,
                                    rc.bottom,hbm,SRCCOPY);
          pDC->DrawText(pDoc->m_Title,-1,&rc,DT_CENTER);
     }

}
/////////////////////////////////////////////////////////////////////
// COleSrv2View printing

BOOL COleSrv2View::OnPreparePrinting(CPrintInfo* pInfo)
{
     // default preparation
     return DoPreparePrinting(pInfo);
}
```

(continues)

Listing 10.5 Continued

```
void COleSrv2View::OnBeginPrinting(CDC* /*pDC*/, CPrintInfo* /*pInfo*/)
{
     // TODO: add extra initialization before printing
}

void COleSrv2View::OnEndPrinting(CDC* /*pDC*/, CPrintInfo* /*pInfo*/)
{
     // TODO: add cleanup after printing
}
//////////////////////////////////////////////////////////////////////
// COleSrv2View diagnostics
//
#ifdef _DEBUG
void COleSrv2View::AssertValid() const
{
     CView::AssertValid();
}
//--------------------------------------------------------------------
void COleSrv2View::Dump(CDumpContext& dc) const
{
     CView::Dump(dc);
}
//--------------------------------------------------------------------
COleSrv2Doc* COleSrv2View::GetDocument()
{
     ASSERT(m_pDocument->IsKindOf(RUNTIME_CLASS(COleSrv2Doc)));
     return (COleSrv2Doc*)m_pDocument;
}
#endif //_DEBUG
//////////////////////////////////////////////////////////////////////
// COleSrv2View message handlers
//
void COleSrv2View::OnEditCopy()
{
     COleSrv2Doc* pDoc = GetDocument();
     ASSERT_VALID(pDoc);

     COleSrv2SrvrItem *pItem  =
     ➥(COleSrv2SrvrItem *)pDoc->OnGetEmbeddedItem();
     pItem->CopyToClipboard(TRUE);
}
//--------------------------------------------------------------------
void COleSrv2View::OnEditChangetitle()
{

     COleSrv2Doc* pDoc = GetDocument();
     ASSERT_VALID(pDoc);
```

```
        CTitle dlg(pDoc);
        dlg.DoModal();
    }
    //-----------------------------------------------------------
    //-----------------------------------------------------------
```

The following sections examine the code of the View class in more detail.

The *OnDraw* Method

The `OnDraw` method takes care of drawing the bitmap in the MDI child window's client area. The `CDib` class does the actual drawing.

The method also draws the picture's selected title, centered over the picture.

The *OnEditCopy* Method

The `OnEditCopy` method is responsible for copying the current object to the clipboard. You use the `COleServerItem:CopyToClipboard` method to do the actual copying. You pass true as the parameter to this method, which indicates that you support linking to the object.

This method call hides an enormous amount of code. It begins by calling `COleServerItem::OnGetClipboardData`. This method creates a `COleDataSource` object and then calls `COleServerItem::GetClipboardData`. The default implementation of this method caches at least four types of data for your object:

- CF_EMBEDDEDOBJECT
- CF_OBJECTDESCRIPTOR
- CF_LINKSOURCE
- CF_LINKSOURCEDESCRIPTOR

Any user-defined types are also cached. The example application also supports CF_TEXT.

Let's examine one of these types in detail. To cache CF_EMBEDDEDOBJECT data, the method calls `GetEmbeddedSourceData`. This method begins by using global memory to create an `ILockBytes` object. If the object is created successfully, the method calls the OLE API function `StgCreateDocfileOnILockBytes` to create an `IStorage` interface from the `ILockBytes` object. This `IStorage` interface pointer is then passed to the `OnSaveEmbedding` method.

`OnSaveEmbedding` eventually calls your server item's `Serialize` method. When saving the object's native data, the `Serialize` method does not know that it is actually saving the data to a global memory block. This block of memory is then copied to the clipboard.

The *OnEditChangeTitle* Method

The `OnEditChangeTitle` method is called when the user chooses Change **T**itle from the **E**dit menu. You create an object of type `CTitle` that prompts the user for a new title for the picture.

The Object Interface Class

The `COleServerItem` class is the interface between the server and the OLE libraries. Listing 10.6 shows the complete code for the implementation of the Object Interface class.

Listing 10.6 SRVRITEM.CPP and SRVRITEM.H—the Implementation of the Object Interface Class

```
//-----------------------------------------------------------------
// srvritem.h : interface of the COleSrv2SrvrItem class
//

class COleSrv2SrvrItem : public COleServerItem
{
     DECLARE_DYNAMIC(COleSrv2SrvrItem)

// Constructors
public:
     COleSrv2SrvrItem(COleSrv2Doc* pContainerDoc);

// Attributes
     COleSrv2Doc* GetDocument() const
          { return (COleSrv2Doc*)COleServerItem::GetDocument(); }

// Implementation
public:
     ~COleSrv2SrvrItem();
#ifdef _DEBUG
     virtual void AssertValid() const;
     virtual void Dump(CDumpContext& dc) const;
#endif
     virtual BOOL OnDraw(CDC* pDC, CSize& rSize);
     virtual BOOL OnGetExtent(DVASPECT dwDrawAspect, CSize& rSize);
     virtual BOOL OnSetExtent(DVASPECT dwDrawAspect, CSize& rSize);
     virtual BOOL OnRenderGlobalData(LPFORMATETC lpFormatEtc,
                                     HGLOBAL* phGlobal);
```

```
protected:
     virtual void Serialize(CArchive& ar);
                    // overridden for document I/O
};

/////////////////////////////////////////////////////////////////////
//-----------------------------------------------------------------
// srvritem.cpp : implementation of the COleSrv2SrvrItem class
//

#include "stdafx.h"
#include "olesrv2.h"

#include "olesrdoc.h"
#include "srvritem.h"

#ifdef _DEBUG
#undef THIS_FILE
static char BASED_CODE THIS_FILE[] = __FILE__;
#endif

/////////////////////////////////////////////////////////////////////
// COleSrv2SrvrItem implementation
//
IMPLEMENT_DYNAMIC(COleSrv2SrvrItem, COleServerItem)

COleSrv2SrvrItem::COleSrv2SrvrItem(COleSrv2Doc* pContainerDoc)
     : COleServerItem(pContainerDoc, TRUE)
{
     GetDataSource()->DelayRenderData(CF_TEXT);
}
//-------------------------------------------------------------------
COleSrv2SrvrItem::~COleSrv2SrvrItem()
{

}
//-------------------------------------------------------------------
void COleSrv2SrvrItem::Serialize(CArchive& ar)
{
     //------------
     //  The framework calls COleSrv2SrvrItem::Serialize() if
     //  the item is copied to the clipboard. This can happen
     //  automatically through the OLE callback OnGetClipboardData().

     COleSrv2Doc* pDoc = GetDocument();
     ASSERT_VALID(pDoc);
     pDoc->Serialize(ar);
}
//-------------------------------------------------------------------
BOOL COleSrv2SrvrItem::OnSetExtent(DVASPECT dwDrawAspect, CSize& rSize)
{
     COleSrv2Doc* pDoc = GetDocument();
     ASSERT_VALID(pDoc);
```

(continues)

Listing 10.6 Continued

```
        pDoc->OnSetExtent(rSize);
        return TRUE;
}
//------------------------------------------------------------------
BOOL COleSrv2SrvrItem::OnGetExtent(DVASPECT dwDrawAspect, CSize& rSize)
{
        //-------------
        //  Most applications, including this one, handle drawing only
        //  the content aspect of the item. If you want to support
        //  other aspects, such as DVASPECT_THUMBNAIL (by overriding
        //  OnDrawEx), you should modify the implementation of
        //  OnGetExtent() to handle the additional aspect(s).

        if (dwDrawAspect != DVASPECT_CONTENT)
             return COleServerItem::OnGetExtent(dwDrawAspect, rSize);

        //----------
        // COleSrv2SrvrItem::OnGetExtent() is called to get the extent,
        // in HIMETRIC units, of the entire item.

        COleSrv2Doc* pDoc = GetDocument();
        ASSERT_VALID(pDoc);

        rSize = pDoc->OnGetExtent();

        return TRUE;
}
//------------------------------------------------------------------
BOOL COleSrv2SrvrItem::OnDraw(CDC* pDC, CSize& rSize)
{
        COleSrv2Doc* pDoc = GetDocument();
        ASSERT_VALID(pDoc);


        CPoint pt(0,0);
        CBrush br(pDoc->m_crColor);

        rSize = pDoc->OnGetExtent();

        pDC->SetMapMode(MM_ANISOTROPIC);
        pDC->SetWindowOrg(0,0);
        pDC->SetWindowExt(rSize.cx,rSize.cy);

        CRect rc(pt,rSize);

        CBrush *pOldBrush = pDC->SelectObject((CBrush*)&br);

        pDC->Rectangle(rc);

        if(pDoc->m_DIB)
        {
```

```
        POSITION pos = pDoc->GetFirstViewPosition();
        CView* pFirstView = pDoc->GetNextView(pos);
        CClientDC dc(pFirstView);

        HBITMAP hbm = pDoc->m_DIB->BitmapFromDib();
        BOOL f = pDoc->m_DIB->StretchBitmap(pDC, rc.left, rc.top,
            rc.right, rc.bottom, hbm, SRCCOPY, &dc);
        pDC->DrawText(pDoc->m_Title,-1,&rc,DT_CENTER);
    }

    pDC->SelectObject((CBrush*)pOldBrush);

    return TRUE;
}
//-----------------------------------------------------------------
BOOL COleSrv2SrvrItem::OnRenderGlobalData(LPFORMATETC lpFormatEtc,
                                          HGLOBAL* phGlobal)
{
    ASSERT(lpFormatEtc != NULL);

    COleSrv2Doc* pDoc = GetDocument();
    ASSERT_VALID(pDoc);

    if (lpFormatEtc->cfFormat != CF_TEXT)
        return COleServerItem::OnRenderGlobalData(lpFormatEtc,phGlobal);

    if(NULL == *phGlobal)
    {
        TRACE("::OnRenderGlobalData : Handle is NULL\n");
        *phGlobal = GlobalAlloc(GHND,256);
        LPSTR lp = (LPSTR)GlobalLock(*phGlobal);
        lstrcpy(lp,pDoc->m_Title);
        GlobalUnlock(*phGlobal);
        return TRUE;
    }
    else
    {
        LPSTR lp = (LPSTR)GlobalLock(*phGlobal);
        lstrcpy(lp,pDoc->m_Title);
        GlobalUnlock(*phGlobal);
        return TRUE;
    }
}
/////////////////////////////////////////////////////////////////////
// COleSrv2SrvrItem diagnostics
//
#ifdef _DEBUG
void COleSrv2SrvrItem::AssertValid() const
{
    COleServerItem::AssertValid();
}
```

(continues)

Listing 10.6 Continued

```
void COleSrv2SrvrItem::Dump(CDumpContext& dc) const
{
    COleServerItem::Dump(dc);
}
#endif
//-----------------------------------------------------------
//-----------------------------------------------------------
```

The following sections examine the code of the Object Interface class in more detail.

The Object Interface Constructor

The class begins by getting the `CDataSource` object associated with your object. During clipboard I/O, you offer CF_TEXT data in addition to the standard OLE formats.

You then call `CDataSource::DelayRenderData` to inform the object of the type of data that you will be offering. You call this method because you do not want to render the data immediately. If you want to render data immediately, you call `CacheGlobalData` instead.

When the data is required, the framework calls `OnRenderGlobalData`.

Although you are using global memory to pass the data, you also can use a file to pass data. This technique is particularly useful if you are handling large amounts of data. When using files to transfer data, you use the `DelayRenderFileData` and `OnRenderFileData` methods.

The *Serialize* Method

When data is copied to the clipboard, the framework calls your `Serialize` method to create the data for CF_EMBEDDEDOBJECT. You defer to your Document class' `Serialize` method, because you offer the entire item.

In a server that supports linking, you normally would enable the user to link to just a portion of the data. In this case, you would serialize the selected portion in this method. The sample application supports only file monikers, to keep things simple.

The *OnSetExtent* Method

The framework calls the `OnSetExtent` method to tell you how much space is available within the container for your object. You use this method to resize your object accordingly.

The *OnGetExtent* Method

The framework calls the `OnGetExtent` method to retrieve the object's natural extents. The container uses these extents to size the object within the container.

Your implementation returns the object's extents, which are stored in the Document class. To receive these extents, you call your own implementation of `GetExtent` in the Document class.

The *OnDraw* Method

The `OnDraw` method is called to render the object into a metafile that is used later as the object's presentation data. You receive two parameters: a pointer to a device context that is actually a metafile device context, and the size, in HIMETRIC units, to draw the object.

The OLE User Interface Guidelines require, and users naturally expect, an object to be resizable within the container. When the user resizes the object, the object must scale itself accordingly.

To create a metafile that is capable of scaling, you must use the MM_ANISOTROPIC mode. This unconstrained mapping mode allows arbitrary units in both the X and Y axes.

You begin by setting the mapping mode to MM_ANISOTROPIC and setting the window origin to 0,0. The next step is to set the window's extents to the size of the object.

> **Note**
>
> Remember that the extents are the key to the scaling of the metafile. By themselves, extents have no meaning. However, when expressed as a ratio, extents become the scaling factor that the GDI uses when translating logical units to device units.

You calculate the ratio by dividing the window extents by the viewport extents. The container sets the viewport extents, which are the actual device units. You have set the window extents, which are the logical units, to the object's size.

You then draw the bitmap into the prepared metafile. This metafile then contains a bitmap that can be sized and scaled.

The *OnRenderGlobalData* Method

When the frameworkrequires additional data that you provide through data transfer operations such as a copy or paste, the `OnRenderGlobalData` is called.

You first check the type of data that the framework requires. If the data type is not CF_TEXT, you call the base class.

If you can supply the requested data type, you then must check whether the memory for the data is already allocated. If not, you have to allocate enough memory to hold the data. You then copy the data into the memory block. For the full server application, you offer only a simple text string—the title of the bitmap.

If you want to offer data either through the clipboard or during a drag-drop operation, you use this method in a similar manner.

Testing the Server

After starting the application, load and open a bitmap file. The bitmap is then displayed in the MDI child window's client area. If you choose Change **T**itle from the **E**dit menu, you can add a descriptive name to the picture. You can then choose **C**opy from the **E**dit menu to place on the clipboard a copy of the object. If you now execute the `IDataObject` viewer utility that comes with the OLE SDK, you can view the object on the clipboard.

Figure 10.2 shows the available data formats. A total of six formats are available. You use the Embed Source format if you want to embed the object in a container. The Object Descriptor format describes the object in detail.

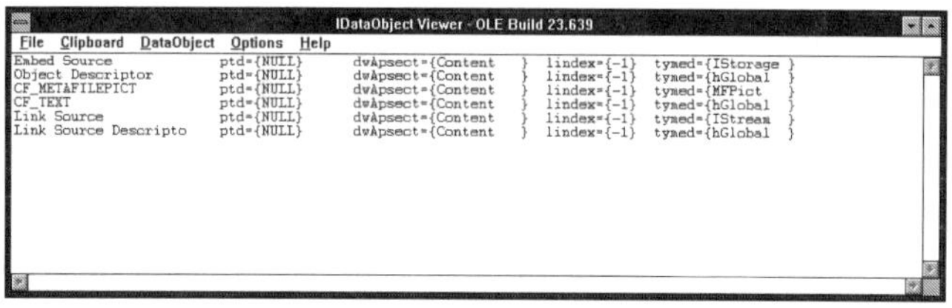

Fig. 10.2
The *IDataObject* viewer.

CF_METAFILEPICT is the metafile that contains the object's presentation data. This data is used if the user chooses to paste a picture of the data rather than the object itself. CF_TEXT is the additional format that you placed on the clipboard during the `OnRenderGlobalData` method.

Next is the Link Source format that you use during linking. This format is a simple file moniker that contains information about the location of your data files. Figure 10.3 shows the available information.

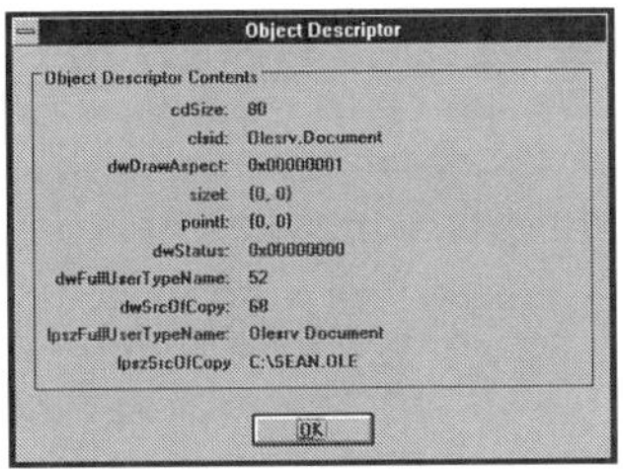

Fig. 10.3
The Link Source Descriptor.

If you now start Word for Windows and choose Paste **S**pecial from the **E**dit menu, you see the Paste Special dialog box shown in figure 10.4. You can choose to link the actual object, the title string, or the metafile.

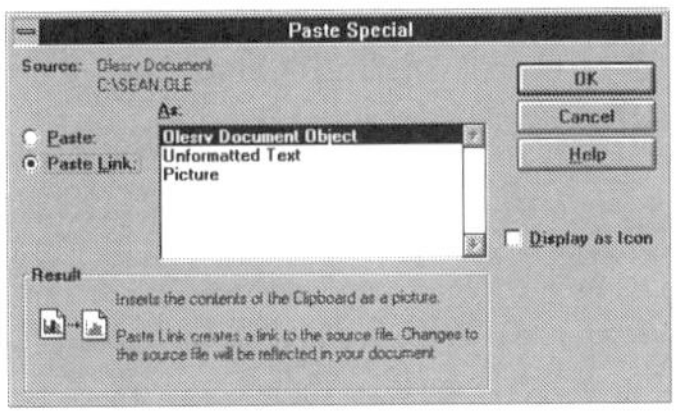

Fig. 10.4
The Paste Special dialog box of Word for Windows.

Figure 10.5 shows the results of linking the object in Word for Windows. If you now change the picture's title in your application, Word for Windows is automatically updated.

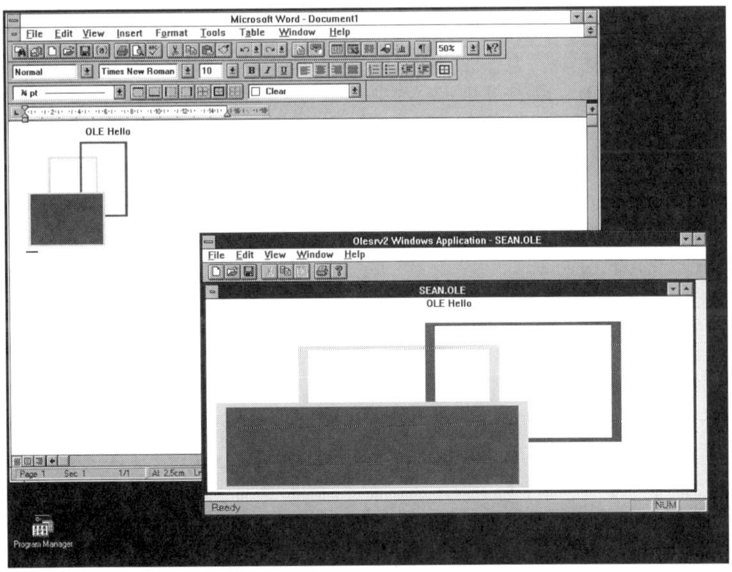

Fig. 10.5
The test application in action.

A Closer Look at Linking

The basic difference between embedded and linked objects is that embedded objects store both their native data and presentation data in the object's container. Linked objects store the presentation data within the container, but save their native data elsewhere.

The primary advantage of linked objects is that another user can update the data and the changes are then reflected in the container.

Now examine how you implement the linking. OLE 2.0 introduces a new type of object, called a *moniker*, to handle linking. Monikers are component objects that support `IUnknown` and `IMoniker` interfaces. These objects contain the name that is used to locate the source of the data. In the case of a simple file moniker, this name is the full path to the data file. Monikers also include the code to start and reconnect to the object server responsible for the data, a process known as *binding*. The method that performs binding is `IMoniker::BindToObject`. (Chapter 1, "General Concepts," discusses the various types of monikers.)

What happens when a container binds to a linked object? In the following example, you examine only the steps required to bind to a simple file moniker.

The process begins with the default handler calling `GetClassFile`. If the linked source is a compound file, the function call can extract the CLSID of the object server that created the object. If the source is not a compound file, the `GetClassFile` function tries to find the object server by searching the registration database.

After the function locates the server, it is executed with the `/Embedding` command-line parameter. The server then creates and registers a class factory.

You next ask the class factory to create an object. This newly created object is then queried for an `IPersistFile` interface. The `IPersistFile::Load` method is then called to load the file.

At this stage, the server is loaded with the file but still hidden. (Remember, your application does not display its windows when started with the `/Embedding` parameter.) The handler now uses `QueryInterface` to query the `IPersistFile` interface pointer for an `IOleObject` pointer.

Because the linked object contains all of your data, the object must support `IDataObject`, `IOleObject`, `IPersistStorage`, `IPersistFile`, and of course

`IUnknown`. After retrieving the `IOleObject` interface pointer, the default handler can call `IOleObject::DoVerb` to open the server application and edit the object.

If the object server is already running, the handler searches the running object table (ROT) for the object. All link sources are required to register a moniker in the ROT when they start up. If an object is running, the handler can retrieve an interface pointer by calling `IRunningObjectTable::GetObject`.

The OLE libraries use the ROT when a container loads a compound document that contains linked objects. As the container loads each object, the default handler checks whether a moniker for the object is registered in the ROT. If the handler finds such a moniker, the object's data is automatically updated.

As you learned in Chapter 1, the OLE specification defines an alert object table (AOT) that is used if a server starts up when a container that contains a linked object is already running. In this case, the container has already registered the linked objects in the AOT, and the server can automatically update them when it starts. However, the AOT is not implemented in the current release of OLE. Perhaps this deficiency will be resolved in a future release of OLE.

From Here...

This chapter concludes Part III's examination of MFC and component objects. In Part IV, you begin examining OLE Automation.

Part III

OLE Automation

11 General Concepts of OLE Automation

12 Creating a Simple Automation Controller

13 Creating a Simple Automation Server

14 MFC and Automation

15 An MFC Automation Client

16 An MFC Automation Server

Windows Application - Ole

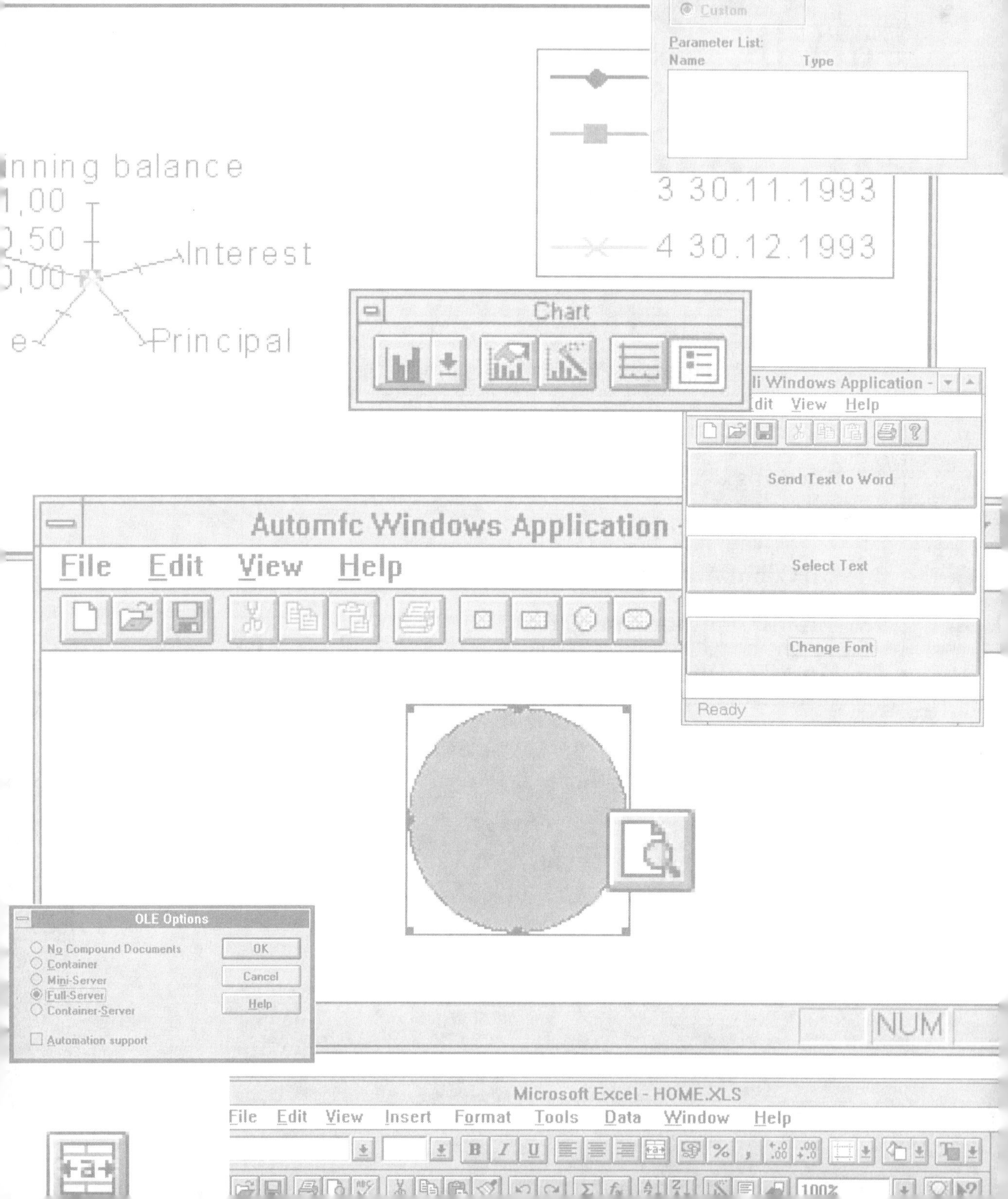

Chapter 11

General Concepts of OLE Automation

OLE Automation enables developers to expose (make available) their application's functions or methods. Users and other developers can then access these functions or methods, which usually are grouped into objects.

In this chapter, you look at the architecture of OLE Automation and see how to apply it toward building custom software. In particular, you examine the following:

- The recommended and required objects, and the methods that the application should support.
- The support for multiple national languages included with OLE Automation.
- The type libraries. You see how they are created and how object browsers and Automation controllers subsequently use them.

Background

For several years, application developers have recognized the need to enable users to customize their applications. The first applications to provide user customization were spreadsheets. These applications provided this capability with macro languages. Eventually, these macro languages grew into powerful programming languages. Today, users can use products such as Microsoft Excel and Microsoft Word to create powerful vertical applications.

However, providing this capability through macro languages causes several problems. No two macro languages are the same, not even when the applications come from the same software vendor. Because of these languages' complexity, you must invest considerable time and effort to gain proficiency with them. Also, because no common macro language exists, you cannot draw on your expertise with one language when you move on to another application's language.

Although today's macro languages provide full control of the application, they provide little or no support for controlling the application from another application. Allowing an external application (one written in a high-level language such as C or C++) access to this control is important, because although the macro language provides full control of all aspects of its application, the language is usually interpreted and thus may execute very slowly. The lack of development tools is also a major drawback. In some applications, laying out a custom dialog box is a painstaking process of hand-coding field coordinates and field lengths. Also, when you develop vertical applications with these macro languages, you have to ship the source code with the application.

The first attempt to address the cross-application issue was dynamic data exchange (DDE). DDE enables the developer to open a channel between applications and send commands from a client application to a server application. Even for experienced developers, working with DDE can be a nightmare. It is slow and provides no support for remote access of servers. Fortunately, OLE Automation, which enables clients to access server methods as if they were an intregal part of the client, has effectively made DDE obsolete.

The promise of OLE Automation is simply to provide a standard way for all applications to expose some or all of their functionality and to let any other application access this functionality. Automation opens the door for cross-application macro languages. One of the first examples is Visual Basic for Applications (VBA), which currently ships with Microsoft Excel 5.0 and Microsoft Project 4.0. (Microsoft Access 2.0 has a similar version of BASIC, AccessBasic, but it does not currently use the VBA engine.) Although this proprietary language is used solely by Microsoft products, it is nonetheless a cross-application macro language that is driven by Automation.

Component objects are the basis of component software, and the building blocks for tomorrow's applications. OLE Automation provides the glue that binds these objects together, and the means to control the objects' programmatically. However, not all component objects are Automation objects, and vice versa. In the future, more developers will probably add Automation support to their component objects. In fact, OLE controls are component objects with Automation interfaces.

Although the main reason for implementing Automation in your application is to enable other applications to exploit your application's functionality, your application can also use Automation internally. With this feature of Automation, you can break down your monolithic applications into smaller, self-contained units and control the interaction between the units.

Before continuing, you need to be familiar with some OLE Automation terminology:

Term	Meaning
Automation object or server	Any object that can be programatically controlled through the `IDispatch` interface.
Automation controller	Any application that can control Automation objects. Good examples include Visual Basic 3.0 and Visual Basic for Applications.
Method	A function that an Automation object exposes and that can be called by an Automation controller.
Property	An attribute or variable that can be set or read through Automation.

Automation Objects

OLE Automation provides developers with a standard way to expose their application's functionality. It also provides a standard for controlling exposed objects.

What is an Automation object? Chapter 1, "General Concepts," defined a component object as an object that supports at least one interface, `IUnknown`. An Automation object supports `IUnknown` and another interface, `IDispatch`. This new interface is the primary means by which applications expose their functionality (see fig. 11.1).

Of course, an Automation object must always provide a means by which it can be created initially. Therefore, every application that supports Automation also implements an object that supports the `IClassFactory` interface. As usual, the class factory object is responsible for creating the server object.

An object may also support several optional interfaces. Among these interfaces may be one that allows access to more than one instance of the object. Such an interface is called a *collection*. Objects that support a collection expose an interface called `IEnumVARIANT`.

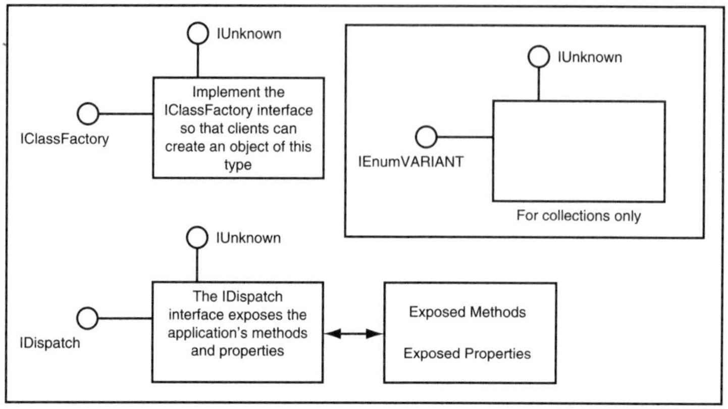

Fig. 11.1
An Automation object.

Finally, objects need a way to communicate information about the methods and properties that they expose. Objects also need information about the number and types of parameters that each method can accept. This information is made available through `ITypelib` and `ITypeInfo`.

The *IDispatch* Interface

Each Automation object implements the `IDispatch` interface, which all Automation controllers use when accessing the object. The interface provides the basic communication channel between the two processes.

The `IDispatch` interface is defined as follows:

```
DECLARE_INTERFACE_(IDispatch, IUnknown)
{
    BEGIN_INTERFACE

    /* IUnknown methods */
    STDMETHOD(QueryInterface)(THIS_ REFIID riid,
        void FAR* FAR* ppvObj) PURE;
    STDMETHOD_(unsigned long, AddRef)(THIS) PURE;
    STDMETHOD_(unsigned long, Release)(THIS) PURE;

    /* IDispatch methods */
    STDMETHOD(GetTypeInfoCount)(THIS_ unsigned int FAR* pctinfo) PURE;
    STDMETHOD(GetTypeInfo)(
      THIS_
      unsigned int itinfo,
      LCID lcid,
      ITypeInfo FAR* FAR* pptinfo) PURE;

    STDMETHOD(GetIDsOfNames)(
      THIS_
      REFIID riid,
      TCHAR FAR* FAR* rgszNames,
```

```
        unsigned int cNames,
        LCID lcid,
        DISPID FAR* rgdispid) PURE;

    STDMETHOD(Invoke)(
        THIS_
        DISPID dispidMember,
        REFIID riid,
        LCID lcid,
        unsigned short wFlags,
        DISPPARAMS FAR* pdispparams,
        VARIANT FAR* pvarResult,
        EXCEPINFO FAR* pexcepinfo,
        unsigned int FAR* puArgErr) PURE;
};
```

OLE Automation uses the same object programming model as the rest of OLE—the Component Object Model (COM). Like all COM objects, each Automation object must support the `IUnknown` interface.

The first three methods in `IDispatch` are `QueryInterface`, `AddRef`, and `Release`. The interface defines four other virtual methods that must be implemented. The first two, `GetTypeInfoCount` and `GetTypeInfo`, retrieve type information from the object.

`GetTypeInfoCount` retrieves the number (currently either 1 or 0) of the type of interface that an object supports. Objects that do not support any `ITypeInfo` interfaces return 0. Although Automation can still control such objects, an object browser cannot extract information about the methods and properties that these objects support.

`GetTypeInfo` retrieves a pointer to an `ITypeInfo` interface. This interface extracts detailed information about each method and property that the object exposes. The interface is defined as follows:

```
DECLARE_INTERFACE_(ITypeInfo, IUnknown)
{
    BEGIN_INTERFACE

    /* IUnknown methods */
    STDMETHOD(QueryInterface)(THIS_ REFIID riid,
        void FAR* FAR* ppvObj) PURE;
    STDMETHOD_(unsigned long, AddRef)(THIS) PURE;
    STDMETHOD_(unsigned long, Release)(THIS) PURE;

    /* ITypeInfo methods */
    STDMETHOD(GetTypeAttr)(THIS_ TYPEATTR FAR* FAR* pptypeattr) PURE;
    STDMETHOD(GetTypeComp)(THIS_ ITypeComp FAR* FAR* pptcomp) PURE;
    STDMETHOD(GetFuncDesc)(THIS_ unsigned int index,
        FUNCDESC FAR* FAR* ppfuncdesc) PURE;

    STDMETHOD(GetVarDesc)(THIS_unsigned int index,
        VARDESC FAR* FAR* ppvardesc) PURE;
```

```
    STDMETHOD(GetNames)(THIS_MEMBERID memid,BSTR FAR* rgbstrNames,
        unsigned int cMaxNames, unsigned int FAR* pcNames) PURE;

    STDMETHOD(GetRefTypeOfImplType)(THIS_unsigned int index,
        HREFTYPE FAR* phreftype) PURE;

    STDMETHOD(GetImplTypeFlags)(THIS_unsigned int index,
        int FAR* pimpltypeflags) PURE;

    STDMETHOD(GetIDsOfNames)(THIS_TCHAR FAR* FAR* rgszNames,
        unsigned int cNames, MEMBERID FAR* rgmemid) PURE;

    STDMETHOD(Invoke)(THIS_void FAR* pvInstance,
        MEMBERID memid,unsigned short wFlags,
        DISPPARAMS FAR *pdispparams, VARIANT FAR *pvarResult,
        EXCEPINFO FAR *pexcepinfo, unsigned int FAR *puArgErr) PURE;

    STDMETHOD(GetDocumentation)(THIS_MEMBERID memid,BSTR FAR* pbstrName,
        BSTR FAR* pbstrDocString, unsigned long FAR* pdwHelpContext,
        BSTR FAR* pbstrHelpFile) PURE;

    STDMETHOD(GetDllEntry)(THIS_MEMBERID memid,INVOKEKIND invkind,
        BSTR FAR* pbstrDllName, BSTR FAR* pbstrName,
        unsigned short FAR* pwOrdinal) PURE;

    STDMETHOD(GetRefTypeInfo)(THIS_HREFTYPE hreftype,
        ITypeInfo FAR* FAR* pptinfo) PURE;

    STDMETHOD(AddressOfMember)(THIS_MEMBERID memid,
        INVOKEKIND invkind, void FAR* FAR* ppv) PURE;

    STDMETHOD(CreateInstance)(THIS_IUnknown FAR* punkOuter,REFIID riid,
        void FAR* FAR* ppvObj) PURE;

    STDMETHOD(GetMops)(THIS_ MEMBERID memid, BSTR FAR* pbstrMops) PURE;

    STDMETHOD(GetContainingTypeLib)(THIS_ITypeLib FAR* FAR* pptlib,
        unsigned int FAR* pindex) PURE;

    STDMETHOD_(void, ReleaseTypeAttr)(THIS_ TYPEATTR FAR* ptypeattr)PURE;
    STDMETHOD_(void, ReleaseFuncDesc)(THIS_ FUNCDESC FAR* pfuncdesc)PURE;
    STDMETHOD_(void, ReleaseVarDesc)(THIS_ VARDESC FAR* pvardesc) PURE;
};
```

As you can see, many methods must be implemented to support this interface. Fortunately, you do not normally implement this interface manually. Usually, you describe all the methods and properties in a type library and then use the `ITypeLib::GetTypeInfoOfGuid` method to create an `ITypeInfo` pointer. Type libraries and the type information interfaces are discussed in greater detail later in this chapter.

The next method defined by `IDispatch` is `GetIDsOFNames`. This method maps the names of exposed methods and properties to DISPIDs. A *DISPID* (dispatch ID) is a 32-bit number that represents a method or property name. You use a DISPID to reduce expensive string table lookup functions. When you access a method or property, you always identify it by using its DISPID. You also use DISPIDs to identify the types of arguments passed to the `IDispatch::Invoke` method. Table 11.1 lists five DISPIDs that have special meanings.

Table 11.1 DISPIDs with Special Meanings

DISPID	Description
DISPID_VALUE	The default member for the object. This member is the property or method that is invoked if you use the object name from an OLE Automation controller without specifying a property or method.
DISPID_NEWENUM	A special, restricted method required for collection objects. The method returns the collection object and should have the flag FUNCFLAG_FRESTRICTED.

DISPID_EVALUATE	The method that is implicitly invoked when the OLE Automation controller encloses the arguments in square brackets. For example, the following two lines are equivalent:
	`x.[A1:C1].value = 10x`
	`Evaluate("A1:C1").value = 10`
	In the preceding example, the `Evaluate` method has the dispatch ID DISPID_EVALUATF.

DISPID_PROPERTYPUT	An indication of the parameter that receives the value of an assignment when a property is being updated.
DISPID_UNKNOWN	The value returned by `IDispatch::GetIDsOfNames` to indicate that a member or parameter name was not found.

Normally, an application calls the `GetIDsOFNames` function once for each method or property that it intends to use. The application then caches the DISPIDs that are returned. This technique speeds up the process of invoking methods later.

Automation objects can implement the `IDispatch` interface in three ways, each of which is discussed in the following sections.

Using *CreateStdDispatch* To Implement *IDispatch*

`CreateStdDispatch` is an API function implemented by the OLE libraries. The function creates a standard implementation of the `IDispatch` interface. The function takes four parameters:

```
HRESULT CreateStdDispatch (punkOuter, pvThis, ptinfo, ppunkStdDisp)
IUnknown FAR* punkOuter
void FAR* pvThis
ITypeInfo FAR* ptinfo
IUnknown FAR* FAR* ppunkStdDisp
```

The first parameter, `punkOuter`, is a pointer to a controlling unknown. The interface delegates to this pointer for its `IUnknown` implementation. The second parameter, `pvThis`, is a pointer to the object to be exposed. The third parameter, `ptInfo`, is a pointer to an `ITypeInfo` interface that describes the object's type information. The last parameter, `ppunkStdDisp`, passes a pointer to the location to which you want the `IDispatch` pointer to return. If the function call succeeds, the interface pointer is valid when it returns.

Creating the *ITypeInfo* Pointer. From where do you get the `ITypeInfo` interface pointer? You can create this pointer in two ways.

If you are using type libraries, the following code segment (from the application developed in Chapter 13, "Creating a Simple Automation Server") gives you the initial pointer:

```
HRESULT hResult;
    ITypeLib FAR * pTypeLib;
    ITypeInfo FAR * pTypeInfo;
    IUnknown FAR * punkStdDisp;

    // Load the the type library.
    // LoadRegType uses information in the registration database
    // to locate and load the type library.
    hResult = LoadRegTypeLib(LIBID_AUTOSRVTLB,1,0,0x0409,&pTypeLib);
    if (NOERROR != hResult)
     {
         if((hResult = LoadTypeLib("autosrv.tlb",&pTypeLib)) != NOERROR)
```

```
            return NULL;
    }

    // Get Dispatch TypeInfo from the type library.
    hResult = pTypeLib->GetTypeInfoOfGuid(IID_IAutoSrv,&pTypeInfo);
    if (NOERROR != hResult)
          return NULL;
```

You begin by loading your type library from disk, using the `LoadTypeLib` or `LoadRegTypeLib` API functions. If this call succeeds, you receive a valid pointer to an `ITypeLib` interface. Using this pointer, you then call `ITypLib::GetTypeInfoOfGuid`. This method returns a valid pointer to an `ITypeInfo` interface for a particular GUID.

The second way to create the `ITypeInfo` interface is to use the API call `CreateDispTypeInfo`, as follows:

```
HRESULT CreateDispTypeInfo (pinterfacedata, lcid, pptinfo)
INTERFACEDATA pinterfacedata
LCID lcid
ITypeInfo FAR* FAR* pptinfo
```

This function takes three parameters. The first parameter is a pointer to an INTERFACEDATA structure. This structure consists of the following:

```
typedef struct FARSTRUCT tagPARAMDATA
{
    TCHAR FAR* szName;          // parameter name
    VARTYPE vt;                 // parameter type
} PARAMDATA, FAR* LPPARAMDATA;

typedef struct FARSTRUCT tagMETHODDATA
{
    TCHAR FAR* szName;          // method name
    PARAMDATA FAR* ppdata;      // pointer to an array of PARAMDATAs
    DISPID dispid;              // method ID
    unsigned int iMeth;         // method index
    CALLCONV cc;                // calling convention
    unsigned int cArgs;         // count of arguments
    unsigned short wFlags;      // same wFlags as on IDispatch::Invoke
    VARTYPE vtReturn;
} METHODDATA, FAR* LPMETHODDATA;

typedef struct FARSTRUCT tagINTERFACEDATA
{
    METHODDATA FAR* pmethdata; // pointer to an array of METHODDATAs
    unsigned int cMembers;     // count of members
} INTERFACEDATA, FAR* LPINTERFACEDATA;
```

The calling function must fill out this structure completely. As you can imagine, this process can be tedious and error prone. The pointer returned from this call does not even provide a complete description of the data. In fact, this API call is actually intended to automate the implementation of the `IDispatch` interface.

Therefore, you should use type libraries to create an `ITypeInfo` interface pointer, as described earlier in this section. The OLE SDK's DISPCALC program also provides many examples of the implementation of this technique.

Problems with *CreateStdDispatch*. You can see how easy it is to implement IDispatch by using `CreateStdDispatch`. However, this technique has some limitations.

`CreateStdDispatch` supports only one national language. However, if you plan to sell your applications in Europe, for example, having your application support multiple national languages is a definite commercial advantage. In this situation, you must use one of the other two methods to create an `IDispatch` interface.

Another limitation is that `CreateStdDispatch` supports only the standard dispatch exception codes. If you want more control over reporting errors and raising exceptions, this API function will not satisfy your needs.

Delegating the *IDispatch* Calls

To delegate a call, you implement the `IDispatch::Invoke` method but call the API function `DispInvoke`. This helper function is prototyped as follows:

```
HRESULT DispInvoke(_this, ptinfo, dispidMember, wFlags, pparams,
pvarResult, pexcepinfo, puArgErr)
void FAR* _this
ITypeInfo FAR* ptinfo
LONG dispidMember
unsigned short wFlags
DISPPARAMS FAR* pparams
VARIANT FAR* pvarResult
EXCEPINFO     pexcepinfo
unsigned int FAR* puArgErr
```

The first parameter, `_this`, is a pointer to the exposed object. The second parameter, `ptinfo`, is a pointer to the object's `ITypeInfo` implementation. The other parameters are the same as those passed to `IDispatch::Invoke`.

This function gives you full control both before and after the dispatch call. With this call, you can support multiple national languages and create application-specific exceptions to return to the dispatch caller.

The way that this function implements the dispatch call is interesting. The function actually creates a stack frame, extracts the parameters and their types from the DISPARAMS structure, and pushes them on to the stack. Finally, the function calls the correct object method through the object's virtual dispatch table. The function's first parameter is a pointer to the object.

The OLE SDK's CPOLY demo is an example of a program that uses this method to create an `IDispatch` pointer.

You can implement `IDispatch::GetIDsOfNames` by calling the API helper function `DispGetIDsOfNames`. This function uses the type information, passed as an `ITypeInfo` interface pointer in the first parameter, to map the set of names to equivalent DISPIDs. The other parameters are the same as those passed during the `IDispatch::GetIDsOfNames` call. The function prototype is as follows:

```
HRESULT DispGetIDsOfNames (ptinfo, rgszNames, cNames, rgdispid)
ITypeInfo * ptinfo
char FAR* FAR* rgszNames
unsigned int    cNames
DISPID FAR* rgdispid
```

Of the three methods for enabling Automation objects to implement the `IDispatch` interface, this method is the simplest to implement and gives the user the most control. It requires the least work on the developer's part while providing full control of national languages and exception codes.

Implementing the Dispatch Methods Directly

The last method for implementing the `IDispatch` interface is to implement all the dispatch functions yourself. This method gives you complete control at all times, which may be a useful advantage if your application has special needs.

To implement `IDispatch::GetIDsOfNames`, you must match what is passed in the parameter names to the local DISPID for each parameter. The best way to do this is to use a table lookup algorithm. The CPOLY demo application provides an example of how you can implement a table lookup method. The table lookup function itself is implemented in the MISC.CPP module in the SPOLY directory.

To implement the `IDispatch::Invoke` method, you must parse the DISPARAMS parameter (by filling in the VARIANT return code structure and casing the `dispidMember` parameter) and then call the correct function. You must also fill in the EXCEPINFO structure in case an exception occurs.

Unless you have a good reason to implement the dispatch interface like this, you should use the type libraries and type information interfaces, because doing so requires less work.

Automation Controllers

Automation controllers are the applications that use Automation objects. There are two categories of Automation controllers: script languages and C++ controllers. The next chapter shows an example of a simple C++ Automation controller that you can use to insert text into a Microsoft Word document. An example of using a script language is to write an Excel macro in Visual Basic for Applications to control Word.

Script Languages

The first category is script or macro languages. These tools are primarily used by users and system integrators to build custom solutions that incorporate the best features of many different applications. One of the promises of OLE Automation is to enable users to use applications in ways not originally conceived by the applications' designers. OLE Automation fulfills this promise with Automation controllers. Good examples of Automation controllers are Visual Basic (VB) 3.0 and Visual Basic for Applications. The DISPTEST utility included with the OLE SDK is a stripped-down version of Visual Basic and is an excellent utility for testing Automation objects.

Using script languages is usually straightforward and easy. The general sequence of a command is for the user to declare an object-type variable. This variable is then assigned the return value from some `CreateObject` functions. If the function returns successfully, the variable can be used to access any method or property exposed by the object.

In DISPTEST or VB, the following code segment can access an Automation object:

```
Dim MyObj As Object
Set MyObj = CreateObject("ProgID.ObjectName");
MyObj.InvokeSomeMethod
```

Note that the user does not have to learn anything new (except how to declare and create the object). The user continues to use the same syntax as before. Also, the user is accessing external Automation objects, but is unaware of them. The user doesn't need to know anything about OLE, object models, object interfaces, and so on. This feature alone should ensure that users will accept this new technology.

To make this code sequence work, DISPTEST and VB do a lot of work behind the scenes. The next section describes what is required to access an Automation object from C++.

C++ Controllers

Accessing Automation objects from within your application requires a little more work than using a tool such as Visual Basic. Remember that the COM programming model is the basis for OLE Automation. In other words, the process of creating Automation objects is the same as creating component objects. The same rules regarding interfaces and reference counting apply.

You should already be familar with most of the steps for accessing Automation objects from within your application:

1. Initialize the OLE libraries by calling `OleInitialize`.
2. Call `CoCreateInstance` to create an instance of the object.
3. Query the return interface pointer for `IDispatch`. All Automation objects support this interface for exposing objects.
4. Use `GetIDsOfNames` to map method and property names to appropriate DISPIDs.
5. Call the `IDispatch::Invoke` method to call the exposed method or to access the exposed property.
6. Release the dispatch pointer when you are finished using it.
7. Release the OLE libraries by calling `OleUninitialize`.

Chapter 12, "Creating a Simple Automation Controller," includes an example that shows how to use this method to access Microsoft Word 6.0.

As you can see, accessing Automation objects in this way is not that complicated. However, an even easier technique is available that is almost as easy for programmers as using VB is for users. This technique involves using type libraries and the Microsoft Foundation Class (MFC) ClassWizard. Chapter 15, "An MFC Automation Client," shows how easily you can control Microsoft Excel 5.0 with Automation and a little help from the ClassWizard.

Object Browsers

Object browsers are a class of Automation applications that enable the user to browse and read information for type libraries and also information from the exposed `ITypeInfo` interfaces. Browsers serve several purposes for both the user and the developer. This section examines two browsers: Ole2View and the Excel 5.0 Object Browser.

Ole2View

Chapter 4, "The OLE SDK," introduced the object viewer utility Ole2View, which provides the interface viewer for COM interfaces. The SDK ships with several interface viewers, one of which is a viewer for the `IDispatch`, `ITypeLib`, and `ITypeInfo` interfaces. Figure 11.2 shows the screen that is displayed when you select the `IDispatch` interface from Microsoft Word 6.0.

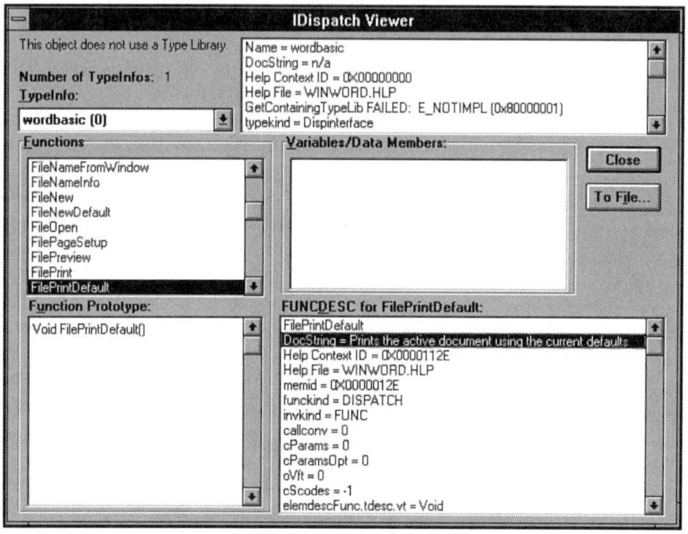

Fig. 11.2
Viewing the Word 6.0 *IDispatch* interface.

The interface viewer is implemented so that it actually views only `ITypeInfo` interfaces. When presented with an `ITypeLib` interface, the viewer calls `ITypeLib::GetTypeInfo` to retrieve the `ITypeInfo` pointer; if called with an `IDispatch` interface pointer, the viewer calls `IDispatch::GetTypeInfo` to retrieve the pointer.

The top-left corner of the screen indicates that Word supports only one `ITypeInfo` interface. This is normal for applications that do not use type libraries, and Microsoft Word 6.0 ships without a type library.

The **F**unctions list box displays all the methods that Word exposes. This list is created by a combination of `ITypeInfo::GetFuncDesc` and `ITypeInfo::GetNames`. The FUNC**D**ESC list box displays complete information about the selected method. This information contains everything from the calling convention of the function to the help ID string that the application uses to describe the method. The F**u**nction Prototype information is built by the interface viewer code from information obtained from `ITypeInfo`.

All the information displayed by the interface viewer is obtained by querying the `ITypeInfo` and `ITypeLib` interfaces.

As you can see, a tool such as Ole2View is very important to developers. It is useful as a learning tool and invaluable as a debugging aid. As an bonus, Microsoft has included the source code for the interface viewer with the OLE SDK. This code is a fine example of how to create an object browser and access type libraries.

The Excel 5.0 Object Browser

You find a different type of object browser in Excel 5.0. The Excel Object Browser (fig. 11.3) is intended for the user who is writing Excel macros.

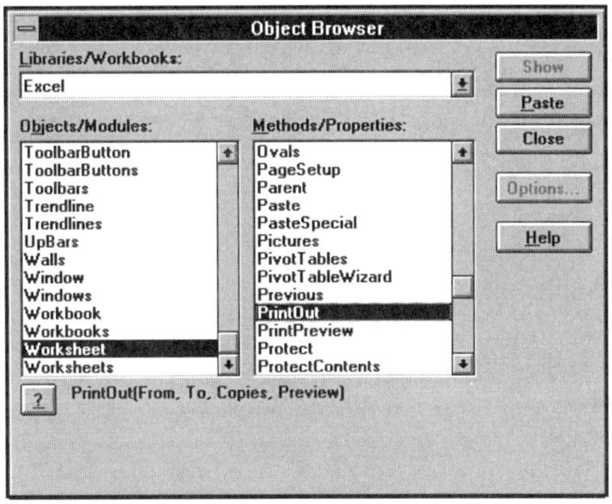

Fig. 11.3 The Excel Object Browser.

To extract the information displayed in figure 11.3, Excel uses its own type library. The O**b**jects/Modules list box displays all the objects exposed by Excel 5.0. The **M**ethods/Properties list box shows the properties and methods exposed by the object currently selected in the O**b**jects/Modules list box. After selecting the correct object and method, the user can choose the **P**aste button to paste the function call into a macrosheet. By choosing the **H**elp button, the user invokes the help file and help topic described by the `ITypeInfo` interface for the object.

This use of type libraries will become increasingly common as application developers begin to add Automation support to their applications. The technique is an excellent way to provide the user with access to the many objects and their associated methods. As cross-application macro languages become common, these object browsers will provide a common access point to all the objects that are available to each application. Because the interfaces necessary to develop these browsers are standard COM interfaces, developers will also be able to write their own browsers.

In fact, both the Excel Object Browser and the browser implemented by the Ole2View utility use exactly the same techniques to present the user with the information that they provide. Both browsers use the `ITypeInfo` and `ITypeLib` COM interfaces to extract the information about the exposed objects, methods, and properties that are available in the type library.

Exposing Objects in Your Application

As you continue working with OLE Automation, you must define some standard objects and methods. As an application exposes more objects, you must be able to thread your way through this network of objects. By defining a set of standard objects, you can ensure that, given an arbitrary dispatch interface pointer, you can access the application's root object and some basic methods, such as printing the object. Part of your standards for objects must include naming guidelines.

Microsoft defines several objects that each application should support in addition to the objects specific to the application. Table 11.2 lists these standard objects. These objects all assume a document-oriented application.

Table 11.2 Microsoft's Standard Objects

Object	Description
`Application`	The root object
`Document`	The object that supports printing, saving, opening, and so on
`Documents`	The collection object that is used to iterate over multiple document objects (collection objects enable you to loop over each object in the collection)
`Characters`	The text-formatting object
`Font`	The object that describes the font used in the document
`Window`	The application's display
`Windows`	The collection object for `Window` objects
`MenuBar`	The menu bar object

Object	Description
MenuBars	The collection object for MenuBar
Menu	The menu object
Menus	The collection object for Menu objects
File	The object for handing file access
Files	The collection object for File objects

Also, all objects should support the following two properties:

- The Application property, which returns the Application object, VT_DISPATCH
- The Parent property, which returns the creator of the object, VT_DISPATCH

The following sections examine some of these objects and their methods and properties. For complete details for all these objects, refer to the OLE documentation.

The *Application* Object

The Application object is the root of the object tree. All applications must support this object. The object has several required properties and one required method, as table 11.3 indicates. Each of the properties provides read-only access.

Table 11.3 Required Properties and Methods for *Application* Objects

Property or Method Name	Return Type	Description
Application	VT_DISPATCH	This property returns the Application object.
FullName	VT_BSTR	This property returns the file specification for the application, including the path.

(continues)

Table 11.3 Continued

Property or Method Name	Return Type	Description
`Name`	VT_BSTR	This property returns the application's name, such as "Microsoft Excel." The `Name` property is the default member (DISPID_VALUE) for the `Application` object.
`Parent`	VT_DISPATCH	This property returns the `Application` object.
`Quit`	VT_EMPTY	This method exits the application and closes all open documents

Several optional methods and properties can also be implemented. The OLE documentation covers all these methods and properties.

You should implement two of these optional properties: `ActiveDocument` and `Documents`. The `ActiveDocument` property should return a dispatch pointer to the currently open document, if one is open. The `Documents` property returns a collection pointer that can be used to iterate over all the open documents in an MDI application.

The *Document* Object

The `Document` object should support, at a minimum, the properties and methods listed in tables 11.4 and 11.5. Each of the properties provides read-only access.

Table 11.4 Properties That the *Document* Object Should Support

Property Name	Return Type	Description
`Application`	VT_DISPATCH	Returns the `Application` object.
`FullName`	VT_BSTR	Returns the file specification of the document, including the path.
`Name`	VT_BSTR	Returns the file name of the document, not including the file's path specification.

Property Name	Return Type	Description
`Parent`	VT_DISPATCH	Returns the parent of the `Document` object.
`Path`	VT_BSTR	Returns the document's path specification, not including the file name or file name extension.
`Saved`	VT_BOOL	Returns true if the document has never been saved, but has not changed since its creation. Returns true if the document has been saved and has not changed since the last save. Returns false if the document has never been saved and has changed since its creation, or if it was saved, but has changed since the last save.

Table 11.5 Methods That the *Document* Object Should Support

Method Name	Return Type	Description
`Activate`	VT_EMPTY	Activates the first window associated with a given document.
`Close`	VT_EMPTY	Closes all the windows associated with a given document and removes the document from the `Documents` collection. This method takes two optional arguments: `saveChanges (VT_BOOL)` and `fileName (VT_BSTR)`. The `fileName` argument specifies the name of the file in which to save the document.
`Print`	VT_EMPTY	Prints the document. This method takes three optional arguments: `from (VT_I2)`, `to (VT_I2)`, and `copies (VT_I2)`. The `from` and `to` arguments specify the page range to print.
`Save`	VT_EMPTY	Saves changes to the file specified in the document's `FullName` property.

(continues)

Table 11.5 Continued

Method Name	Return Type	Description
SaveAs	VT_EMPTY	Saves changes to a file. This property takes one optional argument: filename (VT_BSTR). The filename argument can include a path specification.

The *Documents* Collection

The Documents collection object is used to access one or more Document objects. Tables 11.6 and 11.7 list the properties and methods that you should implement for this object. Each of the properties provides read-only access.

Table 11.6 Properties That the *Documents* Object Should Support

Property Name	Return Type	Description
Application	VT_DISPATCH	Returns the Application object
Count	VT_I4	Returns the number of items in the collection
Parent	VT_DISPATCH	Returns the parent of the Documents collection object

Table 11.7 Methods That the *Documents* Object Should Support

Method Name	Return Type	Description
Add	VT_DISPATCH	Creates a new document, adds it to the collection, and returns the created document.
Close	VT_EMPTY	Closes all documents in the collection.

Method Name	Return Type	Description
Item	VT_DISPATCH or VT_EMPTY	Returns a Document object from the collection or VT_EMPTY if the document does not exist. This method takes an optional argument, index, that may take a string (VT_BSTR) indicating the document name, a number (VT_I4) indicating the ordered position within the collection, or either (VT_VARIANT). If you omit the index argument, this method returns the Documents collection. This method is the default member (DISPID_VALUE).
Open	VT_DISPATCH or VT_EMPTY	Opens an existing document, adds it to the collection, and returns the document that was opened or VT_EMPTY if the object could not be opened. This method takes one required argument, filename, and one optional argument, password. Both arguments have the type VT_BSTR.
_NewEnum	VT_DISPATCH	Returns an object that implements IEnumVARIANT.

The *Font* Object

The Font object should support the properties listed in table 11.8.

Table 11.8 Properties That the *Font* Object Should Support

Property Name	Return Type	Description	Access
Application	VT_DISPATCH	Returns the Application object	Read-only
Bold	VT_BOOL	Sets or returns whether the font is boldface	Read-write
Italic	VT_BOOL	Sets or returns whether the font is italic	Read-write
Parent	VT_DISPATCH	Returns the parent of the Font object	Read-only

(continues)

Table 11.8 Continued

Property Name	Return Type	Description	Access
`Shadow`	VT_BOOL	Sets or returns whether the font appears with a shadow	Read-write
`Size`	VT_R4	Sets or returns the size of the font in points	Read-write

A Real-World Example

In this section, you examine an actual application that supports OLE Automation and see how the application implements its object hierarchy. You also see just how closely it follows the preceding guidelines.

Excel 5.0, the first major commercial application to ship with full Automation support, has 128 programmable objects. Figures 11.4 and 11.5 show the object hierarchy of the Excel 5.0 exposed objects.

Excel supports the `Application` object as the root object to its object tree. The object supports all the global attributes and methods for Excel, including over a hundred properties and methods. If you use Excel's Object Browser, you find that Excel supports the recommended methods and properties for an `Application` object.

Excel does not have a document object because spreadsheets do not deal with documents. Instead, Excel provides a `Worksheet` object. Excel supports both a `Worksheet` object and a `Worksheets` collection object.

If you examine other recommended objects, such as `Window` and `Menus`, you discover that Excel fully implements these objects as recommended.

Excel has naturally added many objects, methods, and properties that apply specifically to Excel. This combination of private objects and standard objects demonstrates how you should design and expose an object hierarchy through Automation. If you examine the `Worksheets` collection object that is a property of the `Application` object, you see how you can begin to thread your way through the hierarchy. You begin by creating an `Excel.Application` object and acquiring a dispatch interface for that object. Through that single dispatch pointer, your application can access all the functionality of Excel.

The type library supplied with Excel 5.0 exports all its methods, properties, and return values as VARIANTs. However, the OLE specifications do not recommend this behavior. When you expose objects through Automation, you should explicitly define each parameter and return type according to its type. In other words, if your method takes an integer as a parameter, you should define and accept a VT_I2 parameter type.

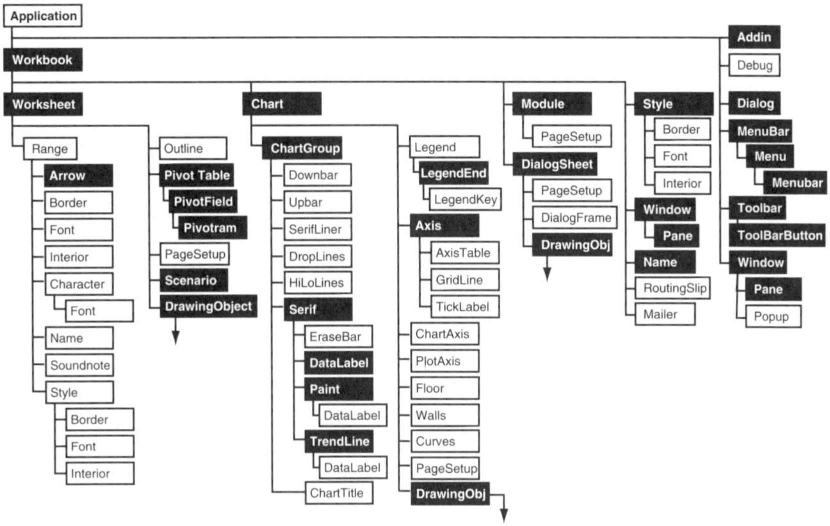

Fig. 11.4
The Excel 5.0 object hierarchy (objects displayed in black are also collections).

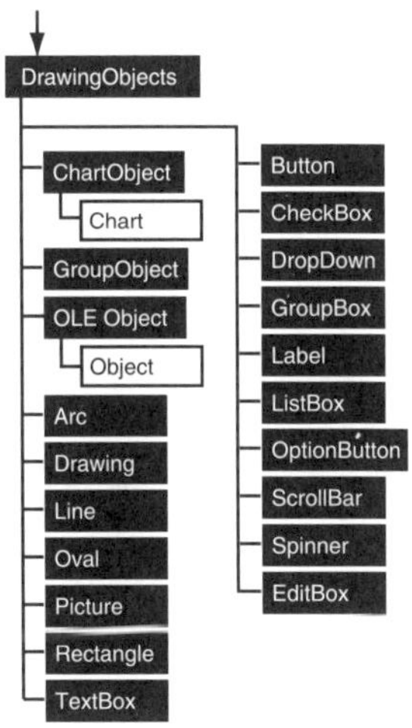

Fig. 11.5
The Excel 5.0 object hierarchy (continued).

Restricting Access to Objects

When you begin to design an object hierarchy, the issue of security and restricting access to objects and methods naturally arises. One way to prevent an object browser from seeing a particular object or method is to use the `restricted` keyword in the ODL file when you create the type library. However, the best way is to implement a `Security` object that acts as a gateway to a subtree of the object hierarchy. To access any objects on this subtree, the user must first retrieve a pointer from the `Security` object, which requires a password before it returns the object pointer.

The issue of object restriction becomes particularly critical in a network environment in which licensing issues are important. In a distributed environment, where thousands of users may be accessing your object, you must keep track of the number of active users. Distributed OLE, which will be available in a future release of Windows NT, will address this important issue.

National Language Support

As was mentioned earlier, a major goal of Automation is to enable users to build custom solutions that incorporate the functionality of today's applications. Although developers from all over the world are accustomed to using English-based names for API calls—for example, the function name `CreateWindow` is the same wherever you are programming—this is not the case for users.

Users naturally prefer to use their native language, so when writing macros or scripts, they expect object, method, and property names to be localized. The formatting of dates and currency are similar issues. For example, although Americans present the month first in a date string, Europeans use the day as the first field.

Automation supports national languages with a set of API functions that compare strings and convert cases. Automation also introduces a locale ID (LCID) that conveys information about the user's environment (the user's national language, date formatting, and so on). All the `IDispatch` methods (except `IDispatch::GetTypeInfoCount`) take an LCID as a parameter.

An LCID is a 32-bit DWORD value. The first 16 bits contain the language ID (LANGID) and the top 16 bits are reserved. The LANGID word consists of a primary and sublanguage ID. The sublanguage ID differentiates between versions of the same language, such as French and Canadian French. The operating system presets two LCIDs, LOCALE_SYSTEM_DEFAULT and LOCALE_USER_DEFAULT.

During an `IDispatch::Invoke` call, an application developer can check the LCID before calling the method. During an `IDispatch::GetIDsOfNames` call, you have the opportunity to map the localized method and property names to the correct DISPIDs. Application developers have several choices when supporting locales:

- You can accept any LCID during a method call and simply ignore the LCID. For object and method names, you can simply force the user to use English. However, when interpreting formatting information, this choice can be dangerous. For example, date formats can be easily misinterpreted.
- You can fail the call if an unsupported LCID is passed. This option prevents users from selecting locales that your objects do not support.
- You can support an LCID for all national language versions of your application. To use this option, you must load a different type library for each LCID. This solution is not the best. Although your application will be acceptable to more users throughout the world, they also may write code to access your Automation objects in one language but run the code unchanged in a different locale.

Using Type Libraries

Using type libraries is the best way to expose type information about objects and methods. Type libraries are written in Object Description Language (ODL) and compiled with the MkTypLib compiler. They can be stored as substorage in a compound file, or bound into a DLL as a resource or as a stand-alone compound file. If stored as resources, type libraries must have an ID of 1 and be of the type `typelib`. Substorages in a compound file must be called `\006typelib`.

Type libraries offer the developer the same advantage as resource files. Specifically, you do not have to write the code in your application to support `ITypeInfo` interfaces. You describe your object, methods, and properties using ODL and then create a type library. ODL is a rich language for describing objects and methods. The language's structure is similar to that of the Interface Description Language (IDL), which is used to describe remote procedure call (RPC) interfaces. In later chapters, you use ODL to build your own type libraries.

Type libraries, like OLE objects, should be registered in the system registry. You should place these libraries under the top level key (`TypeLib`) and include the information listed in table 11.9.

Table 11.9 Information To Specify for Type Libraries

Field	Description
`libUUID`	The UUID for the library.
`DIR`	Location of the type library.
`VERSION`	Major and minor version number of the type library and the full name of the application.
`HELPDIR`	Location of the help file for the type library.
`LCID`	The locale ID and name of the corresponding type library. If an application supports many type libraries, all are placed with the `LCID` key.

As was previously mentioned, one of the best features of type libraries for MFC programmers is the Automation ClassWizard that ships with Visual C++ 1.5. The Wizard can read type libraries directly and generate the necessary C++ code to access all the methods and properties exposed by the type library.

From Here...

In this chapter, you looked at the background and architecture of OLE Automation. In Chapter 12, you begin to apply Automation to develop an application and see how Automation works in practice.

Creating a Simple Automation Controller

In this chapter, you develop a simple Automation controller, using Microsoft Word 6.0 as your server. The goal of this chapter is to show you what you need, at a minimum, to control an application such as Microsoft Word 6.0.

In this chapter, you learn how to do the following:

- Create an object
- Get a pointer to an `IDispatch` interface
- Call exposed methods through the `IDispatch` interface

A Simple Automation Controller

The application that you will develop is a simple Automation controller. The controller uses Microsoft Word 6.0 as its server, but you can use any suitable server if you modify the controller's code accordingly.

When the application starts up, it creates an instance of Word. The controller then presents three push buttons:

- The first button creates a new, empty document in Word and inserts some text into it.
- The second button selects the text.
- The third button changes the default font to 24-point Arial and deselects the text.

The code was developed in Microsoft Visual C++ and using the Microsoft Foundation Classes (MFC) framework. However, to implement to Automation code, you do not use any of the OLE classes from MFC. The reason that you will implement your own code is to show exactly what is required at a code level to control a server such as Microsoft Word 6.0.

Figure 12.1 shows you what the application looks like after you send the text to Word and change the font.

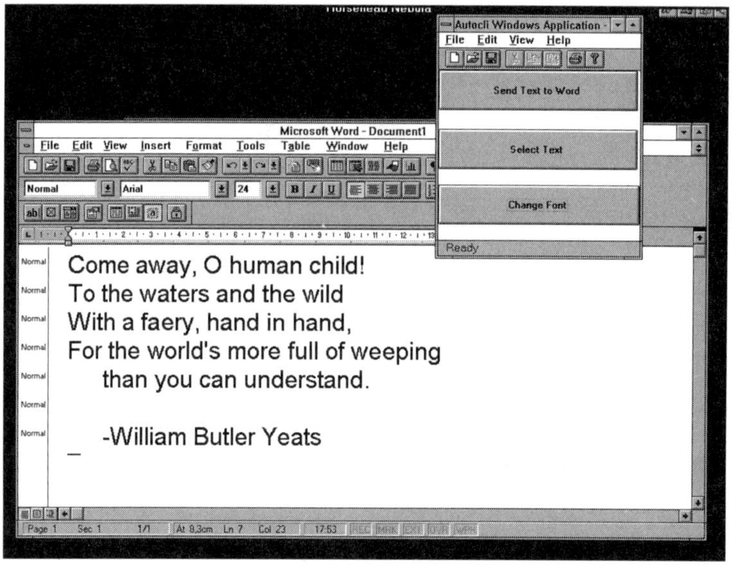

Fig. 12.1
The Automation controller.

Initializing the OLE Libraries

In the constructor for the application's `CWinApp` object, `CAutoCliApp`, you enlarge the message queue to 96. You should do so for all OLE applications, because of the amount of message traffic generated by the LRPC (lightweight remote procedure call) mechanism. However, if you use MFC in your application development, you can omit this step because MFC performs it automatically.

> **Caution**
>
> Always call the `SetMessageQueue` function before you do anything else in your application. This function destroys the existing message queue. Calling `SetMessageQueue` after messages have been generated can result in some strange behavior in your application.

In the `CAutoCliApp::InitInstance` function, you check for the version number of the OLE libraries. You compare the build numbers to that which you used to build your application. The OLE2VER.H header file defines the external variables `rmm` and `rup`. If the major version of the libraries in memory differs from the libraries that you used, or if the minor number is less than what you used, you simply exit the application.

After verifying the library's build numbers, you call `OleInitialize` to initialize the libraries, passing in NULL so that the application can use the default memory allocator.

After you successfully load the OLE libraries, you continue creating the application's main window. After you create the window, you move it to the screen's top-left corner so that it does not obstruct your view of Word.

Now let's see what happens when you call `FileNew`. Listing 12.1 shows AUTOCLI.CPP, which implements the `CWinApp` class.

Listing 12.1 AUTOCLI.CPP

```
#include "stdafx.h"
#include "autocli.h"

#include "mainfrm.h"
#include "autocdoc.h"
#include "autocvw.h"

#ifdef _DEBUG
#undef THIS_FILE
static char BASED_CODE THIS_FILE[] = __FILE__;
#endif

/////////////////////////////////////////////////////////////////////
// CAutoCliApp

BEGIN_MESSAGE_MAP(CAutoCliApp, CWinApp)
     //{{AFX_MSG_MAP(CAutoCliApp)
     ON_COMMAND(ID_APP_ABOUT, OnAppAbout)
     //}}AFX_MSG_MAP
     // Standard file based document commands
     ON_COMMAND(ID_FILE_NEW, CWinApp::OnFileNew)
     ON_COMMAND(ID_FILE_OPEN, CWinApp::OnFileOpen)
     // Standard print setup command
     ON_COMMAND(ID_FILE_PRINT_SETUP, CWinApp::OnFilePrintSetup)
END_MESSAGE_MAP()

/////////////////////////////////////////////////////////////////////
// CAutoCliApp construction
CAutoCliApp::CAutoCliApp()
```

(continues)

Listing 12.1 Continued

```
{
     // This is a requirement of OLE. This is
     // due to the amount of traffic that the LRPC
     // protocol can generate.
     // NOTE: This call is NOT necessary in MFC 2.5
     // and higher applications. MFC automatically sets
     // the message queue. The code is shown here to illustrate
     // that OLE applications should increase the message
     // queue size to 96.
     SetMessageQueue(96);
}

/////////////////////////////////////////////////////////////////////
// The one and only CAutoCliApp object
CAutoCliApp NEAR theApp;
/////////////////////////////////////////////////////////////////////
// CAutoCliApp shutdown
int CAutoCliApp::ExitInstance()
{
     // Shut down the OLE libraries.
     // NOTE: If you were using the MFC OLE support, you would
     // not need to do this, because the framework uninitializes
     // OLE if AfxOleInit() has been called.

     OleUninitialize();
     return 0;
}
/////////////////////////////////////////////////////////////////////
// CAutoCliApp initialization
BOOL CAutoCliApp::InitInstance()
{
     HRESULT hResult;
     DWORD dwVersion;

     //-----------
     // Always check that the version of the OLE libraries
     // is compatible with the libraries that you used to build
     // your application.
     // NOTE: This is not necessary if you are using the MFC
     // OLE support. In that case, you would call the AfxOleInit()
     // API, which replaces the following code, up to and including
     // the OleInitialize() call.
     dwVersion  = OleBuildVersion();
     if (HIWORD(dwVersion) != rmm || LOWORD(dwVersion) < rup)
     {
          AfxMessageBox("Error: Incompatible OLE libraries");
          // Any error code will do
          hResult = ResultFromScode(E_FAIL);
          return FALSE;
     }
```

```
    // Initialize the OLE libraries
   if((hResult = OleInitialize(NULL)) != NOERROR)
        return FALSE;


    SetDialogBkColor();
    LoadStdProfileSettings();


    CSingleDocTemplate* pDocTemplate;
    pDocTemplate = new CSingleDocTemplate(
                   IDR_MAINFRAME,
                   RUNTIME_CLASS(CAutoCliDoc),
                   RUNTIME_CLASS(CMainFrame), // main SDI frame window
                   RUNTIME_CLASS(CAutoCliView));
    AddDocTemplate(pDocTemplate);

    OnFileNew();

    // Just move it to the top-left corner
    // so you can see what you are doing with Word.
    DWORD dw = ::GetDialogBaseUnits();
    int nWidth = (130 * LOWORD(dw)) / 4;
    int nHeight = (150 * HIWORD(dw)) / 8;

    HWND hWnd = m_pMainWnd->m_hWnd;
    ::MoveWindow(hWnd,0,0,nWidth,nHeight,TRUE);


    return TRUE;
}

/////////////////////////////////////////////////////////////////
// CAboutDlg dialog used for App About

class CAboutDlg : public CDialog
{
public:
    CAboutDlg();

// Dialog Data
    //{{AFX_DATA(CAboutDlg)
    enum { IDD = IDD_ABOUTBOX };
    //}}AFX_DATA

// Implementation
protected:
    virtual void DoDataExchange(CDataExchange* pDX); // DDX/DDV support
    //{{AFX_MSG(CAboutDlg)
         // No message handlers
    //}}AFX_MSG
```

(continues)

Listing 12.1 Continued

```
     DECLARE_MESSAGE_MAP()
    };

    CAboutDlg::CAboutDlg() : CDialog(CAboutDlg::IDD)
    {
         //{{AFX_DATA_INIT(CAboutDlg)
         //}}AFX_DATA_INIT
    }

    void CAboutDlg::DoDataExchange(CDataExchange* pDX)
    {
         CDialog::DoDataExchange(pDX);
         //{{AFX_DATA_MAP(CAboutDlg)
         //}}AFX_DATA_MAP
    }

    BEGIN_MESSAGE_MAP(CAboutDlg, CDialog)
         //{{AFX_MSG_MAP(CAboutDlg)
              // No message handlers
         //}}AFX_MSG_MAP
    END_MESSAGE_MAP()

    // App command to run the dialog
    void CAutoCliApp::OnAppAbout()
    {
         CAboutDlg aboutDlg;
         aboutDlg.DoModal();
}
```

Creating an Instance of a Word Object

Microsoft Word 6.0 exposes only one object through Automation. That object, however, is `Wordbasic`, so through that one pointer you gain complete access to all the functionality of Microsoft Word 6.0.

To create an instance of a Word Basic object, you begin by getting the CLSID (class ID) of the `Wordbasic` object. Note in the registration database that the ProgID for `Wordbasic` is `Word.basic`. You pass this name to the `CLSIDFromProgID` API call, which looks in the registry for the ProgID that you pass and finds the associated CLSID. If the call succeeds, you are returned the CLSID in the `clsid` variable.

Next, you call `CoGetClassObject` to get a pointer to the object's class factory object. The class factory object is responsible for creating the actual COM objects. The first parameter is the object's `clsid` variable. The function returns a pointer to the object's class factory interface.

> **Note**
>
> You could have simply used `CoCreateInstance` here and bypassed the calls to `CoGetClassObject` and `pCF->CreateInstance`, but I want to show you the exact steps required to create an object.

Using the class factory pointer, you now create an instance of the class by calling `pCF->CreateInstance`. You ask to be returned a pointer to the `IUnknown` interface of the newly created object by passing `IID_Unknown` as the REFIID parameter.

You can now query the `IUnknown` interface pointer for a pointer to `IDispatch`. If the object supports this interface (as Word does), you store the dispatch pointer and release the class factory and unknown pointers. Throughout its lifetime, the application keeps the dispatch pointer.

Alternatively, you could simply ask for an `IDispatch` pointer in the original `CreateInstance` call. However, to demonstrate the use of `QueryInterface`, I chose to retrieve the pointer by calling `QueryInterface` on the `IUnknown` pointer.

During the destructor call for the document class, you release the dispatch pointer on Word. This closes Word immediately. You then call `CoFreeUnusedLibraries`.

You should call this function after you release the last copy of an interface pointer. The reason for using `CoFreeUnusedLibraries` is that Windows implements in-process servers as DLLs. OLE loads these DLLs into memory by calling `LoadLibrary` and unloads them by calling `FreeLibrary`. Although an object removes itself from memory when its reference count drops to zero, the DLL remains in memory. Calling `CoFreeUnusedLibraries` periodically enables the OLE libraries to unload DLLs that are not currently in use. For example, if `AfxOleInit` has been called, the MFC `CWinApp` class calls `CoFreeUnusedLibraries` in `CWinApp::OnIdle`. `OnIdle` is called whenever the application is idle (that is, when no user commands are pending).

At this stage, the application is initialized and awaiting user input. Word should also be open on the screen, awaiting input through the `IDispatch` pointer. (This behavior, however, is a bug in Word. The Automation server should remain hidden until you explictly open it by invoking some `DisplayWindow` function.)

Error Reporting

As Chapter 2, "The Component Object Module," explained, all OLE calls return an HRESULT as a return code. While you develop an OLE application, displaying these return codes is often useful. The function `HRESULTtoString` takes an HRESULT code and returns a pointer to a string that contains the actual code, a description of the code, the module name, and the call's line number. I have included a macro call, REPORT_ERROR, that calls this function with the necessary parameters. The macro is defined as follows:

```
#define REPORT_ERROR(hr)     AfxMessageBox(
    HRESULTtoString(hr,__FILE__,__LINE__))
```

This macro uses the MFC `MessageBox` function to display the results on the screen, but you can easily redirect the output to a debugging monitor by replacing the function with a call to `OutputDebugString`.

The debug version of the MFC libraries supplies several functions that produce readable formats for the OLE error codes. This macro uses the `AfxGetFullScodeString` function.

You can redefine the macro REPORT_ERROR in a release build of your application. Listings 12.2 and 12.3 show you the `CDocument` class implementation.

Listing 12.2 AUTOCDOC.H

```
#include <windows.h>
#include <ole2.h>
#include <ole2ver.h>
#ifndef WIN32
#include <olenls.h>
#endif
#include <dispatch.h>

//---------------------------------------------------------------
// OLE HRESULT Error reporting routines
extern "C" LPSTR HRESULTtoString(HRESULT hr, LPSTR lpModule, int
nLine);

#define REPORT_ERROR(hr)
     AfxMessageBox(HRESULTtoString(hr,__FILE__,__LINE__))
//---------------------------------------------------------------

class CAutoCliDoc : public CDocument
{
protected: // create from serialization only
     CAutoCliDoc();
     DECLARE_DYNCREATE(CAutoCliDoc)
```

```
// Attributes
public:
// Operations
public:
     LPUNKNOWN m_punk;
     LPDISPATCH m_pDisp;
     LPCLASSFACTORY m_pCF;
     LPSTR m_lpQuote;
// Implementation
public:
     virtual ~CAutoCliDoc();
     virtual void Serialize(CArchive& ar); // overridden for document I/O
#ifdef _DEBUG
     virtual void AssertValid() const;
     virtual void Dump(CDumpContext& dc) const;
#endif

protected:
     virtual BOOL OnNewDocument();

// Generated message map functions
protected:
     //{{AFX_MSG(CAutoCliDoc)
          // NOTE - the ClassWizard will add and remove
          // member functions here.
          // DO NOT EDIT what you see in these blocks of generated code!
     //}}AFX_MSG
     DECLARE_MESSAGE_MAP()
};
```

Listing 12.3 AUTOCDOC.CPP

```
#include "stdafx.h"
#include "autocli.h"

#include "autocdoc.h"

#ifdef _DEBUG
#undef THIS_FILE
static char BASED_CODE THIS_FILE[] = __FILE__;
#endif

/////////////////////////////////////////////////////////////////
// CAutoCliDoc
IMPLEMENT_DYNCREATE(CAutoCliDoc, CDocument)

BEGIN_MESSAGE_MAP(CAutoCliDoc, CDocument)
     //{{AFX_MSG_MAP(CAutoCliDoc)
        // NOTE - the ClassWizard will add and remove mapping macros here.
```

(continues)

Listing 12.3 Continued

```
// DO NOT EDIT what you see in these blocks of generated code!
     //}}AFX_MSG_MAP
END_MESSAGE_MAP()
/////////////////////////////////////////////////////////////////////////////
// CAutoCliDoc construction/destruction
CAutoCliDoc::CAutoCliDoc()
{
     lpQuote = new char[512];

     lstrcpy(lpQuote,
"Come away, O human child!\n\
To the waters and the wild\n\
With a faery, hand in hand,\n\
For the world's more full of weeping\n\
     than you can understand.\n\n\
     -William Butler Yeats");
}
//---------------------------------------------------------------------------
CAutoCliDoc::~CAutoCliDoc()
{
     // Release your interface pointers
     if (m_pDisp != NULL
        m_pDisp->Release();

     // This function currently does nothing
     // but you should call it.
     CoFreeUnusedLibraries();
}
//---------------------------------------------------------------------------
BOOL CAutoCliDoc::OnNewDocument()
{
     BOOL fStatus = FALSE;

     if (!CDocument::OnNewDocument())
          return fStatus;

     // Here you try to create an instance of Word 6.0
     CLSID clsid;

     // This is the ProgID for Word Basic
     HRESULT hr = CLSIDFromProgID("Word.basic", &clsid);
     if(S_OK == hr)
     {
          // Get a class factory for the Word Basic object
          hr = CoGetClassObject(clsid,CLSCTX_SERVER,NULL,
              IID_IClassFactory,(LPVOID FAR *)&m_pCF);
          if(SUCCEEDED(hr))
          {
               // Now create an instance of this object
               hr = m_pCF->CreateInstance(NULL,IID_IUnknown,
                   (LPVOID FAR *)&punk);
```

```
                if(S_OK == hr)
                {
                    // Now query for the IDispatch interface
                    // If you get it, you store it for later use;
                    // otherwise you simply fail the function
                    hr = punk->QueryInterface(IID_IDispatch,
                        (LPVOID FAR *)&pDisp);
                    if(S_OK == hr)
                    {
                        fStatus = TRUE;
                    }
                    else
                    {
                        REPORT_ERROR(hr);
                    }
                    m_punk->Release();
                    m_punk = NULL ;
                }
                m_pCF->Release();
                m_pCF->Release() ;
            }
            else
            {
                REPORT_ERROR(hr);
            }
        }
        else
            REPORT_ERROR(hr);

        return fStatus;
}
//////////////////////////////////////////////////////////////////////////
// CAutoCliDoc serialization
void CAutoCliDoc::Serialize(CArchive& ar)
{
        if (ar.IsStoring())
        {
            // TODO: add storing code here
        }
        else
        {
            // TODO: add loading code here
        }
}
//////////////////////////////////////////////////////////////////////////
// CAutoCliDoc diagnostics
#ifdef _DEBUG
void CAutoCliDoc::AssertValid() const
{
        CDocument::AssertValid();
}

void CAutoCliDoc::Dump(CDumpContext& dc) const
{
```

(continues)

Listing 12.3 Continued

```
 CDocument::Dump(dc);
}
#endif //_DEBUG
//--------------------------------------------------------------------
extern "C" LPSTR HRESULTtoString(HRESULT hr, LPSTR lpModule, int nLine)

#ifdef   DEBUG
     wsprintf(sz,"%s-%d [%s] (0x%lx)",(LPSTR)lpModule,
         nLine,(LPSTR) AfxGetFullScodeString(sc),sc);
#else
     wsprintf(sz,"OLE error in module %s, line %d (0x%lx)",(LPSTR)
         lpModule,nLine,sc);
#endif

     return (LPSTR)sz ;
}
//--------------------------------------------------------------------
//--------------------------------------------------------------------
```

Accessing the Automation Methods

When you click the Send Text button, the framework calls the `OnSendtext` handler. The code begins by retrieving the dispatch pointer that you saved while creating the document.

First, you need to create an empty document in Word by using the Word Basic command `FileNew`. You must get this method's DISPID from Word. A DISPID is simply a number that represents a particular method. The `IDispatch` interface supports a method, `GetIDsOfNames`, that returns a DISPID from a member name.

Note

Ordinarily you would use an application's type library to map the member names to corresponding DISPIDs. However, some OLE Automation servers, including Word 6.0, do not ship with type libraries. Besides, it is useful to see how to do this mapping without using type libraries.

The `GetIDsOfNames` method is called with five parameters:

- The first parameter is reserved and should be `IID_Null`.
- The second parameter is a pointer to an array of names that must be mapped.
- The third parameter is the number of names in the name array.

- The fourth parameter is the locale ID to use when interpreting the names.
- The final parameter is a pointer to an array of DISPIDs.

If more than one name is passed in the first name of the name array, the member name and subsequent names represent parameters. The names are case insensitive.

You call `GetIDsOfNames` with `FileNew` as the member name. You pass 1 as the number of names because you are not going to pass any parameters with this call.

If `GetIDsOfNames` returns S_OK, you can call the `Invoke` method on the `IDispatch` interface pointer. This method takes eight parameters:

- The first parameter is the DISPID that the `GetIDsOfNames` call returned.
- The second parameter is reserved and should be `IID_Null`.
- The third parameter is the locale context that is used when interpreting the arguments.
- The fourth parameter is a set of flags that describe the context of the `Invoke` call. The following are the possible context values for `IDispatch::Invoke`:

DISPATCH_METHOD	The member was accessed as a method. If a property of the same name exists, both this value and the DISPATCH_PROPERTYGET flag may be set.
DISPATCH_PROPERTYGET	The member is being retrieved as a property or data member.
DISPATCH_PROPERTYPUT	The member is being changed as a property or data member.
DISPATCH_PROPERTYPUTREF	The member is being changed by a reference assignment rather than a value assignment. This value is valid only when the property accepts a reference to an object.

While calling a method, you pass DISPATCH_METHOD.

- The fifth parameter is a pointer to a DISPPARAMS structure. This structure, which describes the arguments being passed, is defined in DISPATCH.H as follows:

```
typedef struct FARSTRUCT tagDISPPARAMS{
    VARIANTARG FAR* rgvarg;
    DISPID FAR* rgdispidNamedArgs;
    unsigned int cArgs;
    unsigned int cNamedArgs;
} DISPPARAMS;
```

The first member is a pointer to a VARIANTARG structure. This structure, which describes the type of each parameter, is defined as follows:

```
typedef struct FARSTRUCT tagVARIANT VARIANTARG;
typedef struct tagVARIANT  {
     VARTYPE vt;
     unsigned short wReserved1;
     unsigned short wReserved2;
     unsigned short wReserved3;
     union {
          short        iVal;              /* VT_I2               */
          long         lVal;              /* VT_I4               */
          float        fltVal;            /* VT_R4               */
          double       dblVal;            /* VT_R8               */
          VARIANT_BOOL bool;              /* VT_BOOL             */
          SCODE        scode;             /* VT_ERROR            */
          CY           cyVal;             /* VT_CY               */
          DATE         date;              /* VT_DATE             */
          BSTR         bstrVal;           /* VT_BSTR             */
          IUnknown     FAR* punkVal;      /* VT_UNKNOWN          */
          IDispatch    FAR* pdispVal;     /* VT_DISPATCH         */
          short        FAR* piVal;        /* VT_BYREF|VT_I2      */
          long         FAR* plVal;        /* VT_BYREF|VT_I4      */
          float        FAR* pfltVal;      /* VT_BYREF|VT_R4      */
          double       FAR* pdblVal;      /* VT_BYREF|VT_R8      */
          VARIANT_BOOL FAR* pbool;        /* VT_BYREF|VT_BOOL    */
          SCODE        FAR* pscode;       /* VT_BYREF|VT_ERROR   */
          CY           FAR* pcyVal;       /* VT_BYREF|VT_CY      */
          DATE         FAR* pdate;        /* VT_BYREF|VT_DATE    */
          BSTR         FAR* pbstrVal;     /* VT_BYREF|VT_BSTR    */
          IUnknown FAR* FAR* ppunkVal;    /* VT_BYREF|VT_UNKNOWN */
          IDispatch FAR* FAR* ppdispVal;  /* VT_BYREF|VT_DISPATCH */
          SAFEARRAY    FAR* parray;       /* VT_ARRAY|*          */
          VARIANT      FAR* pvarVal;      /* VT_BYREF|VT_VARIANT */
          void         FAR* byref;        /* Generic ByRef       */
     };
} ;
```

The VT type tells you the type of the arguments. The following table (which is from the *OLE Programmer's Guide*) describes each of these types. You use several of these functions when dealing with VARIANTARG variables. Although you can manipulate VARIANTs directly, using the VARIANT manipulating functions supplied with the OLE libraries is preferable and also easier.

VT_EMPTY	No value was specified. If an argument is left blank, you should not return VT_EMPTY for the argument. Instead, you should return the VT_ERROR: DISP_E_MEMBERNOTFOUND.
VT_EMPTY | VT_BYREF	Illegal.
VT_I2	A two-byte integer was specified; its value is in `iVal`.
VT_I2 | VT_BYREF	A reference to a two-byte integer was passed; a pointer to the value is in `piVal`.
VT_I4	A four-byte integer was specified; its value is in `lVal`.
VT_I4 | VT_BYREF	A reference to a four-byte integer was passed; a pointer to the value is in `plVal`.
VT_R4	An IEEE four-byte real is stored in `fltVal`.
VT_R4 | VT_BYREF	A reference to an IEEE four-byte real was passed; a pointer to the value is in `pfltVal`.
VT_R8	An eight-byte IEEE real was specified; its value is in `dblVal`.
VT_R8 | VT_BYREF	A reference to an eight-byte IEEE real was passed; a pointer to its value is in `pdblVal`.
VT_CY	A currency value was specified. A currency number is stored as an eight-byte, two's complement integer, scaled by 10,000 to give a fixed-point number with 15 digits to the left of the decimal point and four digits to the right. The value is in `cyVal`.
VT_CY | VT_BYREF	A reference to a currency value was passed; a pointer to the value is in `pcyVal`.
VT_BSTR	A string was passed. The string is stored in `bstrVal`. You must use the BSTR functions to obtain or free this pointer.

VT_BSTR | VT_BYREF	A reference to a string was passed. A BSTR* that points to a BSTR function is in `pbstrVal`. You must use the BSTR functions to obtain or free the referenced pointer.
VT_NULL	A propagating NULL value was specified. (Don't confuse this value with the NULL pointer.) The NULL value is used for tristate logic, as with SQL.
VT_NULL | VT_BYREF	Illegal.
VT_ERROR	A SCODE was specified. The error type is specified in the SCODE. Operations on error values usually should raise an exception or propagate the error to the return value, as appropriate.
VT_ERROR | VT_BYREF	A reference to a SCODE was passed. A pointer to the value is in `pscode`.
VT_BOOL	A Boolean (true or false) value was specified. A value of 0xFFFF (all bits 1) indicates true, a value of 0 (all bits 0) indicates false. No other values of `bool` are legal.
VT_BOOL | VT_BYREF	A reference to a Boolean value. A pointer to the Boolean value is in `pbool`.
VT_DATE	A value denoting a date and time was specified. Dates are represented as double-precision numbers, where midnight, January 1, 1900 is 2.0, January 2, 1900 is 3.0, and so on. The value is passed in `date`.
VT_DATE | VT_BYREF	A reference to a date was passed. A pointer to the value is in `pdate`.
VT_DISPATCH	A pointer to an object was specified. The pointer is in `pdispVal`. This object is known only to implement `IDispatch`; to determine whether the object supports any other desired interface, call `QueryInterface` on the object. Objects that do not implement `IDispatch` should be passed with VT_UNKNOWN.

VT_DISPATCH | VT_BYREF	A pointer to a pointer to an object was specified. The pointer to the object is stored in the location referred to by `ppdispVal`.
VT_VARIANT	Illegal. VARIANTARGs must be passed by reference.
VT_VARIANT | VT_BYREF	A pointer to another VARIANTARG is passed in `pvarVal`. This referenced VARIANTARG will never have the VT_BYREF bit set in the VT, so only one level of indirection can ever be present. You can use this value to support languages that enable variables passed by reference to have their types changed by the called function.
VT_UNKNOWN	A pointer to an object that implements the `IUnknown` interface is passed in `punkVal`.
VT_UNKNOWN | VT_BYREF	A pointer to a pointer to the `IUnknown` interface is passed in `ppunkVal`. The pointer to the interface is stored in the location referred to by `ppunkVal`.
VT_ARRAY | <anything>	An array of that data type was passed. (VT_EMPTY and VT_NULL are illegal types to combine with VT_ARRAY.) The pointer in `pByrefVal` points to an array descriptor, which describes the dimen sions, size, and in-memory location of the array. The array descriptor is never accessed directly, but instead is read and modified by the VARIANT manipulation function described in the *OLE Programmer's Guide.*

The method that you are currently calling does not take any parameters, so you simply pass a zeroed-out structure.

- The sixth parameter is a pointer to a VARIANT that holds the return error code. If you do not want a return code, this parameter should be NULL.

- The seventh parameter is a pointer to an EXCEPTINFO data structure. This pointer is used if the `IDispatch:Invoke` method raises an exception.
- The eighth and final parameter is the index into the argument table that tells you which argument has caused a type mismatch. This parameter is filled in if the result is DISP_E_TYPEMISMATCH. If more than one argument has an error, this parameter should contain the number of the first argument that has an error.

If the call succeeded, you now have a new, empty document opened in Word. You then insert some text in the open document.

Follow the same steps as before. Get the DISPID of the member `Insert` by calling `GetIDsOfNames`. This time, the method that you are about to call takes one parameter, which is a pointer to the text that you want to insert.

In this case, you must fill out the DISPPARAMS structure. You begin by setting the first field to point to your VARIANT structure, and then proceed to fill in the VARIANT structure.

The first field is the type of the argument. You are passing in a string, so the type is VT_BSTR. The value of the string is a pointer to a shared copy of the data. You use the API function `SysAllocString` to allocate the memory for the data. Next is the DISPID of the method that you are about to call. You are not using named arguments in this call, so you set this field to 0. Finally, you set the number-of-arguments field (`cArgs`) to 1, which is the number of arguments that you are passing.

After you call `Invoke`, the chorus of *The Stolen Child* by William Butler Yeats appears in your document.

Clicking the Select Text button selects all the text in the current document. You use the same type of code that you used here when you created the empty document.

The Change Font button changes the font used in the text to a 24-point Arial font and then deselects the text. The only interesting part of this code is the use of VT_I2, which passes an integer rather than a string.

Listings 12.4 and 12.5 are the implementation of the View class.

Listing 12.4 AUTOCVW.H

```
class CAutoCliView : public CFormView
{
protected: // create from serialization only
     CAutoCliView();
     DECLARE_DYNCREATE(CAutoCliView)

public:
     //{{AFX_DATA(CAutoCliView)
     enum{ IDD = IDD_AUTOCLI_FORM };
          // NOTE: the ClassWizard will add data members here
     //}}AFX_DATA

// Attributes
public:
     CAutoCliDoc* GetDocument();

// Operations
public:

// Implementation
public:
     virtual ~CAutoCliView();
#ifdef _DEBUG
     virtual void AssertValid() const;
     virtual void Dump(CDumpContext& dc) const;
#endif

protected:
     virtual void DoDataExchange(CDataExchange* pDX);  // DDX/DDV support

     // Printing support
     virtual BOOL OnPreparePrinting(CPrintInfo* pInfo);
     virtual void OnBeginPrinting(CDC* pDC, CPrintInfo* pInfo);
     virtual void OnEndPrinting(CDC* pDC, CPrintInfo* pInfo);
     virtual void OnPrint(CDC* pDC, CPrintInfo*);

     HRESULT GetProperty(LPSTR lpszPropName,LCID lcid,
         LPDISPATCH pdisp,VARIANTARG *vargResult);
// Generated message map functions
protected:
     //{{AFX_MSG(CAutoCliView)
     afx_msg void OnFont();
     afx_msg void OnSelectText();
     afx_msg void OnSendText();
     //}}AFX_MSG
     DECLARE_MESSAGE_MAP()
};

#ifndef _DEBUG  // debug version in autocvw.cpp
inline CAutoCliDoc* CAutoCliView::GetDocument()
   { return (CAutoCliDoc*)m_pDocument; }
#endif
```

Listing 12.5 AUTOCVW.CPP

```
#include "stdafx.h"
#include "autocli.h"
#include "autocdoc.h"
#include "autocvw.h"
#ifdef _DEBUG
#undef THIS_FILE
static char BASED_CODE THIS_FILE[] = __FILE__;
#endif
/////////////////////////////////////////////////////////////////////////////
// CAutoCliView

IMPLEMENT_DYNCREATE(CAutoCliView, CFormView)

BEGIN_MESSAGE_MAP(CAutoCliView, CFormView)
     //{{AFX_MSG_MAP(CAutoCliView)
     ON_BN_CLICKED(IDC_FONT, OnFont)
     ON_BN_CLICKED(IDC_SELECTTEXT, OnSelectText)
     ON_BN_CLICKED(IDC_SENDTEXT, OnSendText)
     //}}AFX_MSG_MAP
     // Standard printing commands
     ON_COMMAND(ID_FILE_PRINT, CFormView::OnFilePrint)
     ON_COMMAND(ID_FILE_PRINT_PREVIEW, CFormView::OnFilePrintPreview)
END_MESSAGE_MAP()

/////////////////////////////////////////////////////////////////////////////
// CAutoCliView construction/destruction

CAutoCliView::CAutoCliView()
     : CFormView(CAutoCliView::IDD)
{
     //{{AFX_DATA_INIT(CAutoCliView)
          // NOTE: the ClassWizard will add member initialization here
     //}}AFX_DATA_INIT
     // TODO: add construction code here
}

CAutoCliView::~CAutoCliView()
{
}

void CAutoCliView::DoDataExchange(CDataExchange* pDX)
{
     CFormView::DoDataExchange(pDX);
     //{{AFX_DATA_MAP(CAutoCliView)
          // NOTE: the ClassWizard will add DDX and DDV calls here
     //}}AFX_DATA_MAP
}

/////////////////////////////////////////////////////////////////////////////
// CAutoCliView diagnostics

#ifdef _DEBUG
```

```
void CAutoCliView::AssertValid() const
{
     CFormView::AssertValid();
}

void CAutoCliView::Dump(CDumpContext& dc) const
{
     CFormView::Dump(dc);
}

CAutoCliDoc* CAutoCliView::GetDocument() // nondebug version is inline
{
     ASSERT(m_pDocument->IsKindOf(RUNTIME_CLASS(CAutoCliDoc)));
     return (CAutoCliDoc*)m_pDocument;
}
#endif //_DEBUG

/////////////////////////////////////////////////////////////////////////////
// CAutoCliView message handlers
void CAutoCliView::OnFont()
{
     HRESULT hRC;
     LPDISPATCH lpDisp = GetDocument()->pDisp;

     //-------
     // Now change the font to 16-point Arial.
     //
     DISPID dispid[2];
     DISPPARAMS dispParam;
     VARIANTARG varg[1];
     DISPPARAMS FAR *pDispParam;

     char far *szMemberFont = "Font";
     char far *szMemberFontSize = "FontSize";
     char far *szMemberMove = "CharRight";

     hRC = lpDisp->GetIDsOfNames(IID_NULL,&szMemberFont,1,
         LOCALE_SYSTEM_DEFAULT,dispid);
     if(hRC == S_OK)
     {
          dispParam.rgvarg = &varg[0];
          dispParam.rgvarg[0].vt  = VT_BSTR;
          dispParam.rgvarg[0].bstrVal  = SysAllocString("Arial");
          dispParam.rgdispidNamedArgs = &dispid[0];
          dispParam.cNamedArgs = 0;
          dispParam.cArgs = 1;
          pDispParam = &dispParam;
          hRC = lpDisp->Invoke(dispid[0],
              IID_NULL,LOCALE_SYSTEM_DEFAULT,
              DISPATCH_METHOD,pDispParam,NULL,NULL,NULL);
```

(continues)

Listing 12.5 Continued

```
if(FAILED(hRC))
               REPORT_ERROR(hRC);
     }
     else
          REPORT_ERROR(hRC);

     //-------
     // Change the point size
     hRC = lpDisp->GetIDsOfNames(IID_NULL,
         &szMemberFontSize,1,LOCALE_SYSTEM_DEFAULT,dispid);
     if(hRC == S_OK)
     {
          dispParam.rgvarg = &varg[0];
          dispParam.rgvarg[0].vt  = VT_I2;
          dispParam.rgvarg[0].iVal  = 24;
          dispParam.rgdispidNamedArgs = &dispid[0];
          dispParam.cNamedArgs = 0;
          dispParam.cArgs = 1;
          pDispParam = &dispParam;
          hRC = lpDisp->Invoke(dispid[0],
              IID_NULL, LOCALE_SYSTEM_DEFAULT,DISPATCH_METHOD,
              pDispParam,NULL,NULL,NULL);
          if(FAILED(hRC))
               REPORT_ERROR(hRC);
     }
     else
          REPORT_ERROR(hRC);

     //-------
     // Deselect the current selection
     hRC = lpDisp->GetIDsOfNames(IID_NULL,
         &szMemberMove,1,LOCALE_SYSTEM_DEFAULT,dispid);
     if(hRC == S_OK)
     {
          dispParam.rgvarg = &varg[0];
          dispParam.rgvarg[0].vt  = VT_I2;
          dispParam.rgvarg[0].iVal  = 1;
          dispParam.rgdispidNamedArgs = &dispid[0];
          dispParam.cNamedArgs = 0;
          dispParam.cArgs = 1;
          pDispParam = &dispParam;
          hRC = lpDisp->Invoke(dispid[0],IID_NULL,
              LOCALE_SYSTEM_DEFAULT,DISPATCH_METHOD,
              pDispParam,NULL,NULL,NULL);
          if(FAILED(hRC))
               REPORT_ERROR(hRC);
     }
     else
          REPORT_ERROR(hRC);


}
//------------------------------------------------------------------
void CAutoCliView::OnSelectText()
```

```
{
    HRESULT hRC;
    LPDISPATCH lpDisp = GetDocument()->pDisp;

    //-----------
    // Select all the text in the document.
    DISPID dispid1;
    DISPPARAMS disparamNoArgs = {NULL,NULL,0,0};
    char far *szMemberSelect = "EditSelectAll";

    hRC = lpDisp->GetIDsOfNames(IID_NULL,&szMemberSelect,1,LOCALE_SYSTEM_DEFAULT,&dispid1);
    if(hRC == S_OK)
    {
        hRC = lpDisp->Invoke(dispid1,IID_NULL,LOCALE_SYSTEM_DEFAULT,
            DISPATCH_METHOD,&disparamNoArgs,NULL,NULL,NULL);
        if(FAILED(hRC))
            REPORT_ERROR(hRC);
    }
    else
        REPORT_ERROR(hRC);
}
//----------------------------------------------------------------------
void CAutoCliView::OnSendText()
{
    HRESULT hRC;
    LPDISPATCH lpDisp = GetDocument()->pDisp;

    //-----------
    // Begin by asking Word to open a new document.
    DISPID dispid1;
    DISPPARAMS disparamNoArgs = {NULL,NULL,0,0};
    char far *szMemberFileNew = "FileNew";

    hRC = lpDisp->GetIDsOfNames(IID_NULL,
        &szMemberFileNew,1,LOCALE_SYSTEM_DEFAULT,&dispid1);
    if(hRC == S_OK)
    {
        hRC = lpDisp->Invoke(dispid1,IID_NULL, LOCALE_SYSTEM_DEFAULT,
            DISPATCH_METHOD,&disparamNoArgs,NULL,NULL,NULL);
        if(FAILED(hRC))
            REPORT_ERROR(hRC);
    }
    else
        REPORT_ERROR(hRC);

    //-------
    // Now insert the text into the newly
    // created document.
    DISPID dispid[2];
    DISPPARAMS dispParam;
    VARIANTARG varg[1];
    DISPPARAMS FAR *pDispParam;
```

(continues)

III

OLE Automation

Listing 12.5 Continued

```
    char far *szMemberInsert = "Insert";

        hRC = lpDisp->GetIDsOfNames(IID_NULL,
            &szMemberInsert,1,LOCALE_SYSTEM_DEFAULT,dispid);
        if(hRC == S_OK)
        {
             dispParam.rgvarg = &varg[0];
             dispParam.rgvarg[0].vt  = VT_BSTR;
             dispParam.rgvarg[0].bstrVal =
                       SysAllocString(GetDocument()->lpQuote);

     dispParam.rgdispidNamedArgs = &dispid[1];
             dispParam.cNamedArgs = 0;
             dispParam.cArgs = 1;
             pDispParam = &dispParam;
             hRC = lpDisp->Invoke(dispid[0],IID_NULL,
                 LOCALE_SYSTEM_DEFAULT,DISPATCH_METHOD,pDispParam,
                 NULL,NULL,NULL);
             if(FAILED(hRC))
                  REPORT_ERROR(hRC);
        }
        else
             REPORT_ERROR(hRC);
}
//-----------------------------------------------------------------
HRESULT CAutoCliView::GetProperty(LPSTR lpszPropName,
     LCID lcid,LPDISPATCH pdisp,VARIANTARG *vargResult)
{
      DISPPARAMS disp;
      HRESULT hr;
      EXCEPINFO excepInfo;
      unsigned int uArgErr;
      DISPID dispidProperty;

      // Initialize the variant that will hold the return value
      VariantInit(vargResult);

      // Specify information about the parameters that the
      // property takes. This property takes no parameters.
      disp.rgvarg = NULL;
      disp.rgdispidNamedArgs = NULL;
      disp.cArgs = 0;
      disp.cNamedArgs = 0;

      // Get the dispid of the property
      hr = pdisp->GetIDsOfNames(IID_NULL,
          &lpszPropName, 1, lcid, &dispidProperty);
      if(FAILED(hr))
      {
           REPORT_ERROR(hr);
           goto error;
      }
```

```
        // Get the value of the property
        hr = pdisp->Invoke(dispidProperty,
            IID_NULL, lcid, DISPATCH_PROPERTYGET, &disp,
            vargResult, &excepInfo, &uArgErr);
        if(FAILED(hr))
        {
             REPORT_ERROR(hr);
             goto error;
        }

        return NOERROR;

error:
        // Free any resources contained in the variant
        VariantClear(vargResult);
        return hr;
}
//------------------------------------------------------------
```

From Here...

This concludes your look at the minimum requirements for creating an Automation controller. You saw how to create an object and retrieve its `IDispatch` interface pointer. You also saw how to get the DISPIDs for your server's methods and how to invoke the exposed method. In Chapter 15, "An MFC Automation Client," you see how to use type libraries to simplify this process of retrieving the DISPIDs and also how to get and set properties through `IDispatch`.

Chapter 13

Creating a Simple Automation Server

In this chapter, you develop your first OLE Automation server. Although you will write the code in C++, you won't use the Microsoft Foundation Classes (MFC) library (because you are learning how an Automation server is structured and using MFC would only confuse the issue). This is one instance in which you do not want to hide the details.

In this chapter, you accomplish the following:

- Develop a server that exposes only one single-method object. This lone object should suffice for the purpose of this lesson.
- Examine the `DispTest` tool that is provided with the OLE SDK. You will use the tool to test your server.
- Discover another tool, MkTypLib, that creates type libraries from ODL (Object Description Language) files.

A Simple Automation Server

The application that you are about to develop is a simple server that provides its clients a famous (or sometimes not-so-famous) quote. The object stores the quotes internally. To access them, you use the exposed method `GetQuote`. The object uses a simple random-number generator to return a different quote each time that the application is asked to provide one.

The application consists of three objects:

- CObject is the object that provides the exposed Automation methods. CObject inherits from _IAutoSrv, which is the machine-generated interface definition for the exposed object.
- CAutoSrv, the application's main object, is responsible for the objects' data. The object inherits from IUnknown and provides the implementation for this interface.
- CAutoSrvCF is the class factory for CAutoSrv. This object is responsible for creating objects of the type CAutoSrv. CAutoSrvCF inherits from IClassFactory and provides the implementation for this interface.

The application's initialization code is in MAIN.CPP. In this code, you register the window class, initialize the OLE libraries and objects, and finally enter the standard message pump.

The Initialization Code

You first register the window class for the application. Then you call the InitOle function. You begin by checking the build versions of the currently loaded OLE libraries and comparing these versions to the build number that you use while building the application. The rule is simple: Your application can run only if the major version number of the OLE libraries is the same as the major version number of the OLE libraries that you used when building the application. Normally the minor version number does not cause any problems. However, if your application uses specific features that you know may change between minor revisions of the libraries, you must also check that the application can run only against the major version of the libraries with which you compiled but can run against any minor version. The numbers returned by the OleBuildVersion API call are not the product's version numbers (that is, they do not return 2.0 or 2.01); instead, they are the internal build numbers of the code itself.

OleInitialize is called to initialize the OLE libraries so that they can be used. You must always call this function before any other OLE function except OleBuildVersion. You also must pair this OleInitialize call with an OleUninitialize call. Chapter 2, "The Component Object Module," when discussing OLE memory allocators, mentioned that you can use a user-defined memory allocator for local memory management. To do so, you pass a pointer to an IMalloc interface during the OleInitialize call. If you do not intend to use a special memory allocator, simply pass NULL; OLE then uses a default task memory allocator.

To create the application object, `CAutoSrv`, you call the create method. The class definition defines the create method as static. You soon will see what happens when an object is created.

After you have an instance of `CAutoSrv`, you create an instance of `CAutoSrvCF`, which is the class factory interface for creating objects of the type `CAutoSrv`. When a client application wants to create a `CAutoSrv` object, OLE uses this interface to create the object. This implementation is quite simple because the application has only one object and you have already created an instance of it.

Before OLE can use the class factory object to create class objects, you must register the factory's `IClassFactory` interface.

To register your class factory, you call the API function `CoRegisterClassObject()`. This function takes five parameters. The first parameter is the class ID of the object that you are registering. In this case, the object name is `CLSID_CAutoSrv`, which is the class ID defined for the GUID. (GUID.C defines all the application's GUIDs.)

The second parameter is a pointer to the class factory object's `IClassFactory` interface. You then define the object's context. The following contexts are available:

CLSCTX_INPROC_SERVER	An in-process server implemented in a DLL
CLSCTX_INPROC_HANDLER	A DLL handler
CLSCTX_LOCAL_SERVER	An .EXE server

This application's object is an .EXE server, so you pass the type CLSCTX_LOCAL_SERVER.

The third parameter is a flag that defines the type of connection that the object can have. You want to connect only one client at a time to your application.

Finally, you pass a parameter to the variable that holds a pointer to the registered class. You use this variable later when you unregister the class factory object.

You then release the reference count on the class factory and return. You have now correctly initialized the application's OLE section.

Shutting Down

The only other function of interest in MAIN.CPP is the `ExitOle` function. While shutting down the application, you reverse the process that you started in `InitOle`.

You first remove your object from the running object table (ROT). To do so, you call `CoRevokeClassObject`, passing in the object ID that you received during the `CoRegisterClassObject` function call. You then release the pointer on the object by calling the `Release` method of the object's `IUnknown` interface. Finally, you shut down the OLE libraries by calling `OleUninitialize`.

The MAIN.CPP module (listing 13.1) contains the code for registering and creating the application's window and for initializing and shutting down the OLE libraries.

Listing 13.1 MAIN.CPP

```
#include "resource.h"
#include "autosrv.h"

#include <stdlib.h>
#include <string.h>


//---------------------------------------------------------------//
// Globals
DWORD g_dwCAutoSrvCF = 0;
CAutoSrv FAR* g_pAutoSrv = NULL;
char g_szAppName[] = "AutoSrv";

//---------------------------------------------------------------//
// Prototypes
HRESULT InitOle(void);
void ExitOle(void);
BOOL InitApplication(HANDLE);
BOOL InitInstance(HANDLE, int);

extern "C"
{
long FAR PASCAL WndProc(HWND, UINT, WPARAM, LPARAM);
int PASCAL WinMain(HANDLE, HANDLE, LPSTR, int);
}


//---------------------------------------------------------------
extern "C" int PASCAL WinMain(HANDLE hinst,
➥HANDLE hPrevInstance,LPSTR lpCmdLine,int nCmdShow)
{
```

```
    //-------------------------------------------
    // WinMain.
    // Initialize the application and OLE, and then
    // pump messages until the application shuts down.
    //
    //
    MSG msg;

    SetMessageQueue(96) ;
    // Init the application. Register the window class, etc.
        if(!hPrevInstance)
         if(!InitApplication(hinst))
              return FALSE;

    // Load and init the OLE libraries
        if(NOERROR != InitOle())
         return FALSE;

        if(!InitInstance(hinst,nCmdShow))
        {
         ExitOle();
         return FALSE;
        }


        while(GetMessage(&msg, NULL, NULL, NULL))
        {
         TranslateMessage(&msg);
         DispatchMessage(&msg);
        }

        ExitOle();

        return msg.wParam;
}
//--------------------------------------------------------------//
BOOL InitApplication(HANDLE hInst)
{
   //-------------------------------------------
     // InitApplication
     // Register the window class with windows
     //
     //
         WNDCLASS  wc;

         wc.style            = CS_HREDRAW ¦ CS_VREDRAW;
         wc.lpfnWndProc      = WndProc;
         wc.cbClsExtra       = 0;
         wc.cbWndExtra       = DLGWINDOWEXTRA;
         wc.hInstance        = hInst;
         wc.hIcon            = LoadIcon(hInst,MAKEINTRESOURCE(101));
         wc.hCursor          = LoadCursor(NULL, IDC_ARROW);
         wc.hbrBackground    = (HBRUSH) (COLOR_APPWORKSPACE+1);
         wc.lpszMenuName     = NULL;
         wc.lpszClassName    = g_szAppName;
```

(continues)

Listing 13.1 Continued

```
     if(!RegisterClass(&wc))
          return FALSE;

         return TRUE;
}
//--------------------------------------------------------------------//
BOOL InitInstance(HANDLE hInst, int nCmdShow)
{
     //-----------------------------------------------
     // InitInstance
     // Create the window and minimize it.
     HWND hWnd = CreateWindow(g_szAppName,"Quote Server",
         WS_OVERLAPPEDWINDOW,
         0,0,CW_USEDEFAULT,CW_USEDEFAULT,NULL,NULL,hInst,NULL);
         ShowWindow(hWnd,SW_MINIMIZE);
         g_pAutoSrv->m_hWnd = hWnd;

         return TRUE;
}
//--------------------------------------------------------------------//
extern "C" long FAR PASCAL _export
➥WndProc(HWND hwnd,UINT message,WPARAM wParam,LPARAM lParam)
{
     //-----------------------------------------------
     // WndProc.
     // Main message switch.
     //
     // The only thing of concern here is
     // to refuse to open the icon to a window.
     //
     switch(message)
     {
          case WM_QUERYOPEN:
               return 0L;
          case WM_DESTROY:
               PostQuitMessage(0);
               return 0;
    }
    return DefWindowProc(hwnd, message, wParam, lParam);
}
//--------------------------------------------------------------------//
HRESULT InitOle()
{
     //-----------------------------------------------
     // InitOle
     // Initialize the OLE libraries and create instances
     // of the object and object class factory.
     //
     //
     HRESULT hResult;
         IClassFactory FAR* pcf;
         DWORD dwVersion;
```

```
    //---------
    // Always check that the version of the OLE libraries
    // is compatible with the libraries that you used to build
    // your application.
    dwVersion  = OleBuildVersion();
        if (HIWORD(dwVersion) != rmm || LOWORD(dwVersion) < rup)
        {
             MessageBox(GetFocus(),"Error: Incompatible OLE libraries",
             ➥"Error",0);
             // Any error code will do
             hResult = ResultFromScode(E_FAIL);
             return hResult;
        }

    // Initialize the OLE libraries
        if((hResult = OleInitialize(NULL)) != NOERROR)
         return hResult;

    // Create the object.
        if((g_pAutoSrv = CAutoSrv::Create()) == NULL)
        {
         hResult = ResultFromScode(E_OUTOFMEMORY);
         return hResult;
        }

        // Create a class factory for the object
        pcf = CAutoSrvCF::Create();
        if (NULL == pcf)
        {
         ExitOle();
         return hResult;
        }

        // Register the class factory.
        hResult = CoRegisterClassObject(CLSID_CAutoSrv,pcf,
        ➥CLSCTX_LOCAL_SERVER,REGCLS_SINGLEUSE,&g_dwCAutoSrvCF);
        if (NOERROR != hResult)
        {
         pcf->Release();
         ExitOle();
         return hResult;
        }

        pcf->Release();

        return NOERROR;
}
//------------------------------------------------------------//
void ExitOle()
{
     //----------------------------------------------
     // ExitOle
     // Shut down the object and close the OLE libraries
     //
```

(continues)

Listing 13.1 Continued

```
    //

            // If a class factory was successfully created earlier,
            // tell OLE that the object is no longer available.
            if(g_dwCAutoSrvCF != 0)
             CoRevokeClassObject(g_dwCAutoSrvCF);

            // Cause the remaining typeinfo to be released
            if (g_pAutoSrv != NULL)
             g_pAutoSrv->Release();

            // Release the OLE libraries
            OleUninitialize();
    }
  //-----------------------------------------------------------//
```

Creating Objects

You create this application object with `OleInit`. Like the MFC framework, I always use a two-step method for creating objects: First I use the constructor only to initialize any internal variable, and then I call a create function. Using this method, you can return an error code from the creation function if an error occurs. Listing 13.1, which defines a static create function to create the object, demonstrates a variation of this method. Because the function is static, it exists outside of the object's lifetime.

The constructor initializes the quote table. Note the use of `SysAllocString` to allocate memory for each string. Each of these calls is paired with a `SysFreeString` in the object's destructor. The constructor also creates an instance of the object `CObject`. This object defines the methods that the application exposes through Automation. You examine this object in more detail later.

Next, you call `AddRef` for the newly created object. (Chapter 2, "The Component Object Model," discusses reference counting.)

You then call the helper function `CreateDispatchInterface`. The first step is to load the type library for the application, initially by calling `LoadRegTypeLib`. This function uses information in the registration database to load the type library.

The first parameter is the GUID of the type library. (GUID.C defines the GUIDs.) The next two parameters refer to the library's minor and major version numbers. The third parameter is the national language code of the library. Finally, you pass a pointer to a pointer to an `ITypeInfo` interface. The returned interface pointer is stored in this variable.

If the `LoadRegTypeLib` function call fails, the user probably has not registered the application's type library. The application then tries to load the library from disk, by calling `LoadTypeLib`. If this function also fails, the application has problems and simply returns.

After you load the type library, you next load the type information for the `IAutoSrv` interface. The variable `pTypeInfo` returns the pointer to this interface. You then release the reference counter on the actual type library.

You now have all the information that you need to create an `IDispatch` interface pointer for the object. This sample code uses `CreateStdDispatch` to create a standard implementation. This function greatly simplifies the creation of an `IDispatch` interface.

However, `CreateStdDispatch` has two limitations: the function supports only one national language type, and supports only dispatch-defined exception codes from the `Invoke` method. For this server, these limitations are of no real concern. However, if you intend to sell your application in Europe, you would need to support national languages, so this method would not be useful to you.

Now that you are finished with the interface pointer on `IAutoSrv`, you release it. You then return the `IDispatch` pointer to the caller. On returning, you store the dispatch pointer in the member variable `m_Disp`.

IUnknown Implementation

As Chapter 2, "The Component Object Model," discussed, each object must implement `IUnknown` to qualify as a Windows object. This sample application's object supports four interfaces: `IID_Unknown`, `IID_Dispatch`, `IID_DAutoSrv`, and `IID_IAutoSrv`.

When queried for `IID_Unknown`, the application simply calls `AddRef` and returns a pointer to `this`. The application forwards the interfaces `IID_Dispatch` and `IID_DAutoSrv` to the dispatch pointer that you created with `CreateStdDispatch`. The `CObject` class implements the interface `IID_IAutoSrv`, which is the Automation-exposed interface to the `GetQuote` method. From this method, you return a pointer to `CObject`. The application then calls

AddRef for all returned pointers and returns E_NOINTERFACE for all unknown interfaces.

The AddRef function increases the reference count and returns it for debugging purposes. Although the specification does not require that all objects do so, most OLE objects return the current reference count during AddRef and Release calls. This count can help tremendously when you are debugging reference count problems.

If the reference count drops to 0 during a Release call, you release the dispatch pointer, post a quit message to the application pump, and finally delete the object.

IClassFactory Implementation

Every OLE object registered in the system registry with a CLSID requires a class factory object. The class factory object, which OLE uses to create class objects, typically supports only IUnknown and IClassFactory. In other words, each object registered in the registry has two COM objects associated with it: a class factory object and a class object. OLE uses the IClassFactory interface to create instances of your class objects. The class factory implementation is rather simple, consisting of only one class object (CAutoSrv) that you have already created (by calling CAutoSrv::Create in InitOle). OLE uses this interface to create objects.

So, during a CreateInstance call, you simply return a CAutoSrv::QueryInterface call. This call returns the correct interface pointer to the caller (g_pAutoSrv).

Again, as with all objects, you implement the IUnknown interface. During a QueryInterface call, you support just two interfaces: IUnknown and IClassFactory. The application's AddRef and Release functions are similar to CAutoSrv::AddRef and CAutoSrv::Release.

Note

Although not implemented in this application, the LockServer function can be useful. This function locks a server in memory. A client who does not want to reload the server from disk each time its reference count hits 0 can use this function as an optimization tool. Each call to LockServer(TRUE) must be paired with a call to LockServer(FALSE).

Listing 13.2 contains the definition of the class factory object and `CAutoSrv` object, and listing 13.3 contains the actual implementation of the objects.

Listing 13.2 AUTOSRV.H

```
#include <windows.h>
#include <ole2.h>
#include <ole2ver.h>
#ifndef WIN32
#include <olenls.h>
#endif
#include <dispatch.h>

#include "clsid.h"
#include "object.h"

#pragma warning(disable:4355)

#define MAXQUOTES     10

//-----------------------------------------------------------------//
// The CAutoSrv object
class FAR CAutoSrv : public IUnknown
{
public:
         CAutoSrv();
         ~CAutoSrv();
         static CAutoSrv FAR * Create();

     // Implementation of IUnknown
         STDMETHOD(QueryInterface)(REFIID riid, void FAR* FAR* ppv);
         STDMETHOD_(ULONG, AddRef)(void);
         STDMETHOD_(ULONG, Release)(void);

         HWND m_hWnd;
         BSTR m_bstrQuotes[MAXQUOTES];
private:
         ULONG m_refs;          // Reference count.
         IUnknown FAR* m_Disp; // Pointer to the standard dispatch object.
         CObject FAR* m_ExternInterface; // Exposed interface
};
//-----------------------------------------------------------------//
// The CAutoSrv class factory
class FAR CAutoSrvCF : public IClassFactory
{
public:
         CAutoSrvCF();
         static IClassFactory FAR* Create();

     // Implementation of IUnknown
         STDMETHOD(QueryInterface)(REFIID riid, void FAR* FAR* ppv);
```

(continues)

Listing 13.2 Continued

```
        STDMETHOD_(ULONG, AddRef)(void);
        STDMETHOD_(ULONG, Release)(void);

        // IClassFactory methods
        STDMETHOD(CreateInstance)(IUnknown FAR*
        ➥punkOuter,REFIID riid,void FAR* FAR* ppv);
        STDMETHOD(LockServer)(BOOL fLock);

private:
        ULONG m_refs;
};
//-----------------------------------------------------------//
```

Listing 13.3 AUTOSRV.CPP

```
// Include files and macro definitions
#include "resource.h"
#include "autosrv.h"


//-----------------------------------------------------------
IUnknown FAR * CreateDispatchInterface(IUnknown FAR* punkController,
                                       void FAR* pProgInterface)
{
    HRESULT hResult;
    ITypeLib FAR * pTypeLib;
    ITypeInfo FAR * pTypeInfo;
    IUnknown FAR * punkStdDisp;

    // Load the the type library.
    // LoadRegType uses information in the registration database
    // to locate and load the type library.
    hResult = LoadRegTypeLib(LIBID_AUTOSRVTLB,1,0,0x0409,&pTypeLib);
    if (NOERROR != hResult)
     {
          if((hResult = LoadTypeLib("autosrv.tlb",&pTypeLib)) != NOERROR)
               return NULL;
    }

    // Get Dispatch TypeInfo from the type library.
    hResult = pTypeLib->GetTypeInfoOfGuid(IID_IAutoSrv,&pTypeInfo);
    if (NOERROR != hResult)
          return NULL;

    // Release the reference counter.
    pTypeLib->Release();
```

```
    // Create a standard dispatch object.

    hResult = CreateStdDispatch(punkController,
                               pProgInterface,pTypeInfo,&punkStdDisp);
    // Release the pointer to the previously created TypeInfo.
    pTypeInfo->Release();

    if (NOERROR != hResult)
          return NULL;

    return punkStdDisp;
}
//-----------------------------------------------------------------
CAutoSrv::CAutoSrv()
{
    m_refs = 0;
    m_Disp = NULL;

    // m_ExternInterface is the exposed interface
    // to this object.
    m_ExternInterface = new CObject;
    m_ExternInterface->m_pAutoSrv = this;

     // Set up the famous quotes table
        m_bstrQuotes[0] = SysAllocString(
        ➥"Study art and logic - learn to draw your own conclusions.");
        m_bstrQuotes[1] = SysAllocString("When a finger points
        ➥at the moon, the imbecile looks at the finger.");
        m_bstrQuotes[2] = SysAllocString(
        ➥"Negative slack tends to increase.");
        m_bstrQuotes[3] = SysAllocString("Information travels more surely
        ➥to those with a lesser need to know.");
        m_bstrQuotes[4] = SysAllocString("Always yield to temptation -
        ➥it may never pass your way again.");
        m_bstrQuotes[5] = SysAllocString(
        ➥"Reality is for people who cannot cope with science fiction.");
        m_bstrQuotes[6] = SysAllocString("When faced with two evils,
        ➥I like to do the one I've never tried before. - Mae West");
        m_bstrQuotes[7] = SysAllocString(
        ➥"Anything free is worth what you pay for it.");
        m_bstrQuotes[8] = SysAllocString(
        ➥"What you can not avoid, welcome.");
        m_bstrQuotes[9] = SysAllocString(
        ➥"Walk softly but carry a big stick.");
}
//-----------------------------------------------------------------
CAutoSrv::~CAutoSrv()
{
     // Release the quotes table
```

(continues)

Listing 13.3 Continued

```
 for(int i = 0; i < MAXQUOTES;i++)
        SysFreeString(m_bstrQuotes[i]);

    delete m_ExternInterface;
    m_ExternalInterface = NULL ;    //for safety's sake
}
//------------------------------------------------------------------
CAutoSrv FAR * CAutoSrv::Create()
{
    CAutoSrv FAR* pObj;
    IUnknown FAR* punkStdDisp;


    pObj = new FAR CAutoSrv();
    if(NULL == pObj)
          return NULL;

    pObj->AddRef();

    punkStdDisp = CreateDispatchInterface((IUnknown
    ➥FAR*) pObj,pObj->m_ExternInterface);
    if (NULL == punkStdDisp)
    {
      pObj->Release();
      return NULL;
    }

    pObj->m_Disp = punkStdDisp;
    return pObj;
}
//------------------------------------------------------------------
STDMETHODIMP CAutoSrv::QueryInterface(REFIID riid, void FAR* FAR* ppv)
{

    if (riid == IID_IUnknown)
    {
          *ppv = this;
    }
    else if (riid == IID_IDispatch ¦¦ riid == IID_DAutoSrv)
    {
         return m_Disp->QueryInterface(IID_IDispatch, ppv);
    }
    else if (riid == IID_IAutoSrv)
    {
          *ppv = &m_ExternInterface;
    }
    else
    {
            *ppv = NULL;
          return ResultFromScode(E_NOINTERFACE);
    }
    AddRef();
```

```
    return NOERROR;
}
//----------------------------------------------------------------
STDMETHODIMP_(ULONG) CAutoSrv::AddRef()
{
    // Return reference counts for debugging.
    return ++m_refs;
}
//----------------------------------------------------------------
STDMETHODIMP_(ULONG) CAutoSrv::Release()
{
    // When the reference count reaches 0,
    // destroy the object and kill the
    // application.
    if(—m_refs == 0)
    {
     if(NULL != m_Disp)
          m_Disp->Release();

      PostQuitMessage(0);
      delete this;
      return 0;
    }
    // Return reference counts for debugging.
    return m_refs;
}
//----------------------------------------------------------------
//----------------------------------------------------------------
// This is the ClassFactory implementation
// for the application's only object.
//
CAutoSrvCF::CAutoSrvCF()
{
    m_refs = 1;
}
//----------------------------------------------------------------
IClassFactory FAR* CAutoSrvCF::Create()
{
    return new FAR CAutoSrvCF();
}
//----------------------------------------------------------------
STDMETHODIMP CAutoSrvCF::QueryInterface(REFIID riid, void FAR* FAR* ppv)
{
    // Support just two interfaces: the ubiquitous IUnknown
    // and, of course, IClassFactory.
    if(riid == IID_IUnknown ¦¦ riid == IID_IClassFactory)
    {
     AddRef();
          *ppv = this;
          return NOERROR;
    }
    *ppv = NULL;
    return ResultFromScode(E_NOINTERFACE);
}
//----------------------------------------------------------------
```

(continues)

Listing 13.3 Continued

```
STDMETHODIMP_(ULONG) CAutoSrvCF::AddRef()
{
    // Increase the reference count and return
    // the current reference count for debugging purposes

    return ++m_refs;
}
//-------------------------------------------------------------------
STDMETHODIMP_(ULONG) CAutoSrvCF::Release()
{
    // Count down to 0 and then
    // self-destruct
    if(—m_refs == 0)
    {
       delete this;
       return 0;
    }
    // Return the current reference count
    // for debugging purposes
    return m_refs;
}
//------------------------------------------------------------------
STDMETHODIMP CAutoSrvCF::CreateInstance(
➥IUnknown FAR* punkOuter,REFIID riid, void FAR* FAR* ppv)
{
    extern CAutoSrv FAR* g_pAutoSrv;

    // You have already created the only instance of
    // this object, so simply return a QueryInterface
    // on the object.
    return g_pAutoSrv->QueryInterface(riid, ppv);
}
//-------------------------------------------------------------------
STDMETHODIMP CAutoSrvCF::LockServer(BOOL fLock)
{
    return NOERROR;
}
//------------------------------------------------------------------
//------------------------------------------------------------------
```

The *CObject* Implementation

The `CObject` class is the object that exposes the `GetQuote` method through Automation. As usual, you implement the `IUnknown` interface. All the `IUnknown` methods defer to the `CAutoSrv` `IUnknown` interface.

The `GetQuote` method returns a random string from the `CAutoSrv` object. The private method `GetNextQuoteID` simply returns a random number that is used as an index into the quote table.

Listings 13.4 and 13.5 show both the definition and implementation of the object that you are exposing through Automation.

Listing 13.4 OBJECT.H

```
class FAR CAutoSrv;

#include "iautosrv.h"

class FAR CObject : public _IAutoSrv
{
public:
    // Your implementation of IUnknown
    STDMETHOD(QueryInterface)(THIS_ REFIID riid, LPVOID FAR * ppvObj);
    STDMETHOD_(ULONG, AddRef)(THIS);
    STDMETHOD_(ULONG, Release)(THIS);

    // This is the method that you are exposing
    STDMETHOD_(BSTR, GetQuote)(THIS);
private:
    // Returns a random index into the quote table
    int GetNextQuoteID(void);
public:
    CAutoSrv FAR* m_pAutoSrv;
};
```

Listing 13.5 OBJECT.CPP

```
#include <stdlib.h>
#include <time.h>

#include "resource.h"
#include "autosrv.h"

//------------------------------------------------------------------
int CObject::GetNextQuoteID(void)
{
     int n;

     srand((unsigned)time(NULL));

     n = rand() % MAXQUOTES;
     return n;
}
//------------------------------------------------------------------
STDMETHODIMP_(BSTR) CObject::GetQuote()
{
     // This is the method that returns
     // the quote
```

(continues)

Listing 13.5 Continued

```
    return SysAllocString(m_pAutoSrv->m_bstrQuotes[GetNextQuoteID()]);
}
//--------------------------------------------------------------
STDMETHODIMP CObject::QueryInterface(REFIID riid, void FAR* FAR* ppv)
{
     // Defer to the controlling unknown
     return m_pAutoSrv->QueryInterface(riid, ppv);
}
//--------------------------------------------------------------
STDMETHODIMP_(ULONG) CObject::AddRef()
{
     // Defer to the controlling unknown
     return m_pAutoSrv->AddRef();
}
//--------------------------------------------------------------
STDMETHODIMP_(ULONG) CObject::Release()
{
     // Defer to the controlling unknown
     return m_pAutoSrv->Release();
}
//--------------------------------------------------------------
//--------------------------------------------------------------
```

The Type Library

You have already implemented the various objects in this sample application, so now you need to tie all these objects together. You need an `IDispatch` interface to expose the `GetQuote` method, but where can you find it?

In the `CAutoSrv` module, you used the API function `CreateStdDispatch` to create an `IDispatch` pointer that the application returns during a `QueryInterface` call on the object. The third parameter that you passed to this function is a pointer to an interface that describes the methods that you are exposing.

This type description information is critical when you use OLE Automation. The reason is quite simple. Suppose that you have a Visual Basic program that must call a method in a C++ application. Before calling this method, VB must know which parameters the method requires and the type of each parameter. VB also needs to know whether the method returns data, and if so, the type of that data. So from where does this information come?

The answer lies in the OLE *type libraries*. Type libraries enable applications to describe the objects that they expose through Automation. The objects' methods and properties are also described.

To create a type library, you write an object description script. The language that you use is ODL (Object Description Language). Obviously, the ODL file that you create for this sample application is very simple. Later in this chapter, you use more complicated scripts.

In the ODL file that you create for this application, the first section of the script consists of the library attributes. In an ODL file, you always place attributes within a pair of square brackets.

The first attribute is the library's UUID, which uniquely identifies the library. The next attribute is the helpstring. This attribute is used primarily by type library browsers to display descriptive information about the library. To retrieve a helpstring's value, you use the `GetDocumentation` functions. The LCID attribute is the locale ID for the library. Finally, the last attribute provides the version number for the type library.

The `library` keyword gives the name of the library. Between the braces are the library contents. These contents can include data type information such as aliases, enumerations, structures, or unions, as well as the module, interface, `IDispatch` interface, and component object class type.

The first statement that you use in the ODL script is `importlib`, which imports another type library into this one. You are importing STDOLE.TLB. This library, which ships with the OLE libraries, is required for the `IDispatch` interface.

You now describe the interface that you are exposing, `_IAutoSrv`. You inherit this interface in `CObject`, and that object also implements the interface. Within the square brackets, you list the interface's attributes. The attribute `odl` identifies the interface as an ODL interface. The CLSID for the interface is followed by the helpstring.

You then describe the interface itself. As you have already seen, you expose only one method in this application. That method is defined at this point in the ODL script.

While compiling the ODL file, the MyTypLib program generates the interface description for `_IAutoSrv`. The program also generates a header file that you include in OBJECT.H.

The `dispinterface` statement defines a set of properties and methods on which you can call `IDispatch::Invoke`. For the sample application, you list the `_IAutoSrv` interface. The interface `_DAutoSrv`, which inherits from `IDispatch`, is machine-generated by the MkTypLib program.

Finally, you describe the attributes for the sample application's object, `CAutoSrv`. The attributes include the CLSID and the helpstring. The `coclass` statement tells the MkTypLib program that you are describing a Component Object Model (COM) interface. The description includes the `IDispatch` interface and the interface for the exposed object.

You generate the type library by running the MkTypLib program with the following parameters:

```
mktyplib /nocpp /h iautosrv.h /o autosrv.log /tlb autosrv.tlb
autosrv.odl
```

The program generates a type library called AUTOSRV.TLB and a header file called IAUTOSRV.H. As you have already seen, this header file includes the definition for the `_IAutoSrv` and `_DAutoSrv` interfaces.

Note

If you execute MkTypLib from the DOS command line, you must run the WX server in Windows. For a full description of the parameters that this program takes, refer to the OLE 2.0 SDK's documentation.

You now have a type library that can be used by any Automation controller such as Visual Basic. Your next step is to register the type library.

Listing 13.6 is the Object Definition Language (ODL) file for the application.

Listing 13.6 The ODL File

```
[
     uuid(82D56580-591B-101B-BB57-00608CC0BA93),
     helpstring("Creating OLE Applications Simple Automation server"),
     lcid(0x0409),
     version(1.0)
]
library AutoSrv
{
    importlib("stdole.tlb");

    [
          // The UUID for the interface IID_IObject.
```

```
        odl,
        uuid(8B0D9560-591B-101B-BB57-00608CC0BA93),
        helpstring("Automation Quote Server")
    ]

    interface _IAutoSrv : IUnknown
    {
        BSTR GetQuote(void);
    }


    [
        uuid(910B1780-591B-101B-BB57-00608CC0BA93),
        helpstring("Automation Quote Server DispInterface")
    ]

    dispinterface _DAutoSrv
    {
        interface _IAutoSrv;
    }


    [
        // This is the UUID for the object class
        uuid(72B15100-591B-101B-BB57-00608CC0BA93),
        helpstring("Automation Quote Server")
    ]
    coclass AutoSrv
    {
        dispinterface _DAutoSrv;
        interface _IAutoSrv;
    }
};
```

Listing 13.7 is the code that the ODL compiler generates. This code is the class definition for the `IAutoSrv` interface.

Listing 13.7 IAUTOSRV.H

```
/* This header file is machine-generated by mktyplib.exe */
/* Interface to type library: AutoSrv */

#ifndef _AutoSrv_H_
#define _AutoSrv_H_

/* Definition of interface: _IAutoSrv */
DECLARE_INTERFACE_(_IAutoSrv, IUnknown)
{
    /* IUnknown methods */
    STDMETHOD(QueryInterface)(THIS_ REFIID riid, LPVOID FAR* ppvObj) PURE;
    STDMETHOD_(ULONG, AddRef)(THIS) PURE;
```

(continues)

Listing 13.7 Continued

```
 STDMETHOD_(ULONG, Release)(THIS) PURE;

    /* _IAutoSrv methods */
    STDMETHOD_(BSTR, GetQuote)(THIS) PURE;
};

/* Definition of dispatch interface: _DAutoSrv */
DECLARE_INTERFACE_(_DAutoSrv, IDispatch)
{
    /* IUnknown methods */
    STDMETHOD(QueryInterface)(THIS_ REFIID riid, LPVOID FAR* ppvObj) PURE;
    STDMETHOD_(ULONG, AddRef)(THIS) PURE;
    STDMETHOD_(ULONG, Release)(THIS) PURE;

    /* IDispatch methods */
    STDMETHOD(GetTypeInfoCount)(THIS_ UINT FAR* pctinfo) PURE;

    STDMETHOD(GetTypeInfo)(
      THIS_
      UINT itinfo,
      LCID lcid,
      ITypeInfo FAR* FAR* pptinfo) PURE;

    STDMETHOD(GetIDsOfNames)(
      THIS_
      REFIID riid,
      char FAR* FAR* rgszNames,
      UINT cNames,
      LCID lcid,
      DISPID FAR* rgdispid) PURE;

    STDMETHOD(Invoke)(
      THIS_
      DISPID dispidMember,
      REFIID riid,
      LCID lcid,
      WORD wFlags,
      DISPPARAMS FAR* pdispparams,
      VARIANT FAR* pvarResult,
      EXCEPINFO FAR* pexcepinfo,
      UINT FAR* puArgErr) PURE;

/* Capable of dispatching all the methods of interface _IAutoSrv */
};

#endif
```

Registering the Object and the Type Information

Before you can use the type library, you must register it in the registration database. To do so, you create an AUTOSRV.REG file that contains the information that you need to register. The format of this text file is as follows:

```
REGEDIT


HKEY_CLASSES_ROOT\AutoSrv.Application =
➥Using OLE 2.X in Application Development Simple Automation Object
HKEY_CLASSES_ROOT\AutoSrv.Application\Clsid =
➥{72B15100-591B-101B-BB57-00608CC0BA93}

;;;;;;;;;;;;;;;;;;;;;;;;;;;;;;;;;;;;;;;;;;;;;
; registration info AutoSrv.Application.1

HKEY_CLASSES_ROOT\AutoSrv.Application.1 =
➥Using OLE 2.X in Application Development Simple Automation Object
HKEY_CLASSES_ROOT\AutoSrv.Application.1\Clsid =
➥{72B15100-591B-101B-BB57-00608CC0BA93}


;;;;;;;;;;;;;;;;;;;;;;;;;;;;;;;;;
; registration info AutoSrv 1.0

HKEY_CLASSES_ROOT\CLSID\{72B15100-591B-101B-BB57-00608CC0BA93}
➥= IDispatch AutoSrv Example
HKEY_CLASSES_ROOT\CLSID\{72B15100-591B-101B-BB57-00608CC0BA93}\ProgID
➥= AutoSrv.Application.1
HKEY_CLASSES_ROOT\CLSID\{72B15100-591B-101B-BB57-00608CC0BA93}
➥\VersionIndependentProgID = AutoSrv.Application
HKEY_CLASSES_ROOT\CLSID\{72B15100-591B-101B-BB57-00608CC0BA93}
➥\LocalServer = autosrv.exe /Automation


;;;;;;;;;;;;;;;;;;;;;;;;;;;;;;;;;;;;;
; registration info AutoSrv TypeLib

HKEY_CLASSES_ROOT\TypeLib\{82D56580-591B-101B-BB57-00608CC0BA93}
HKEY_CLASSES_ROOT\TypeLib\{82D56580-591B-101B-BB57-00608CC0BA93}\1.0 =
➥Using OLE 2.X in Application Development Simple Automation
➥Object Type Library
HKEY_CLASSES_ROOT\TypeLib\{82D56580-591B-101B-BB57-00608CC0BA93}
➥\1.0\HELPDIR =
HKEY_CLASSES_ROOT\TypeLib\{82D56580-591B-101B-BB57-00608CC0BA93}
➥\1.0\409\win16 = autosrv.tlb
```

```
HKEY_CLASSES_ROOT\Interface\{910B1780-591B-101B-BB57-00608CC0BA93}
➥= _DAutoSrv
HKEY_CLASSES_ROOT\Interface\{910B1780-591B-101B-BB57-00608CC0BA93}
➥\ProxyStubClsid = {00020420-0000-0000-C000-000000000046}
HKEY_CLASSES_ROOT\Interface\{910B1780-591B-101B-BB57-00608CC0BA93}
➥\NumMethod = 7
HKEY_CLASSES_ROOT\Interface\{910B1780-591B-101B-BB57-00608CC0BA93}
➥\BaseInterface = {00020400-0000-0000-C000-000000000046}
```

You begin by setting up information about the `AutoSrv` application. Under the HKEY_CLASSES_ROOT, you set the name of the application and the CLSID. Under the CLSID subkey, you register your application's `ProcID`, `LocalServer` name, and `VersionIndependentProgID`. (Chapter 2, "The Component Object Models," describes these keys in detail.)

You then register information about the type library under the `TypeLib` key. You give the actual library's name and location and, of course, the CLSID.

After the file is read, the application executes it from the File Manager and merges the information into the registration database.

Generating the CLSIDs

To generate the CLSIDs for this application, you use the GUIDGEN.EXE program supplied with the OLE SDK. This program generates unique UUIDs and places them on the clipboard, in the following form:

```
72B15100-591B-101B-BB57-00608CC0BA93
DEFINE_GUID(varNameHere, 0x72B15100L, 0x591B, 0x101B, 0xBB,
            0x57, 0x00, 0x60,0x8C, 0xC0, 0xBA, 0x93);
```

You can then use the CLSID directly in your code. The DEFINE_GUID macro is important because it binds your class interface names to the GUID. To use this macro, you must include the header file INITGUID.H before you use the macro. You include the file only once in the build process.

Listing 13.8 contains the code that generates the CLSIDs that you use in this application. You use four CLSIDs, which this code generates with the DEFINE_GUID macro.

Listing 13.8 CLSID.C and CLSID.H

```
/*     clsid.c
 *
 *  This file allocates and initializes the CLSIDs.
 *
 */
// initguid.h requires this.
//
#include <compobj.h>

// This redefines the DEFINE_GUID() macro to do allocation.
//
#include <initguid.h>

// Due to the previous header, including this causes the DEFINE_GUID
// definitions in the following header(s) to actually allocate data.
//
#include "clsid.h"

/*  clsid.h
 *
 *  This file defines the CLSIDs for the class that you
 *  will register with OLE.
 *
 */

DEFINE_GUID(CLSID_CAutoSrv,0x72B15100L, 0x591B, 0x101B, 0xBB,
            0x57, 0x00, 0x60,0x8C, 0xC0, 0xBA, 0x93);

DEFINE_GUID(IID_IAutoSrv, 0x8B0D9560L, 0x591B, 0x101B, 0xBB,
            0x57, 0x00, 0x60,0x8C, 0xC0, 0xBA, 0x93);

DEFINE_GUID(IID_DAutoSrv, 0x910B1780L, 0x591B, 0x101B, 0xBB,
            0x57, 0x00, 0x60,0x8C, 0xC0, 0xBA, 0x93);

DEFINE_GUID(LIBID_AUTOSRVTLB,0x82D56580L, 0x591B, 0x101B, 0xBB,
            0x57, 0x00, 0x60,0x8C, 0xC0, 0xBA, 0x93);
```

Testing the Object

You can now begin building the application. From within the Visual C++ environment, you open the AutoSrv project. When building an OLE application, you must link with the OLE import libraries (see fig. 13.1). For OLE applications that do not support Automation, it suffices to link with OLE2.LIB and COMPOBJ.LIB. OLE2DISP.LIB and TYPELIB.LIB are also required for Automation support.

After you successfully build the application, you can execute it. The application runs as an icon. However, at this point, the application is not very useful. Because it is a server, you must now develop a client that can talk to it.

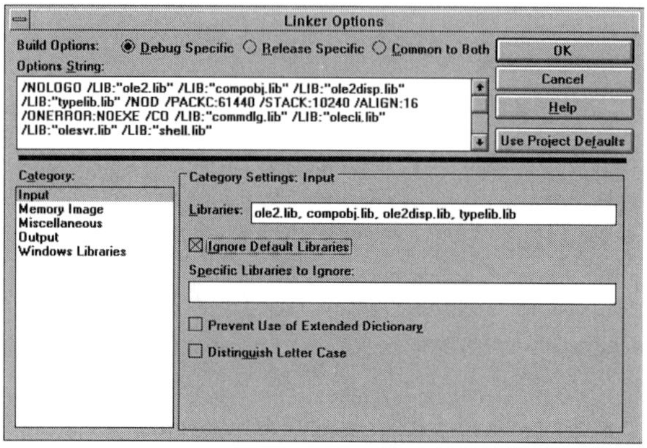

Fig. 13.1
Linking with the OLE libraries.

The OLE SDK includes a useful tool, DISPTEST, which actually is a scaled-down version of Visual Basic. This tool enables you to write scripts to test Automation servers. I have written a sample script that you can use to test the server. The sample script and its accompanying form are included on the companion disk. The DISPTEST make file, AUTOSRV.MAK, is in the directory CH13.

When you open AUTOSRV.MAK, you see the form that you use to test the server. The form (see fig. 13.2) consists of a button and an output window. Pressing the button invokes the `GetQuote` method in the server application and displays the returned quote in the output window.

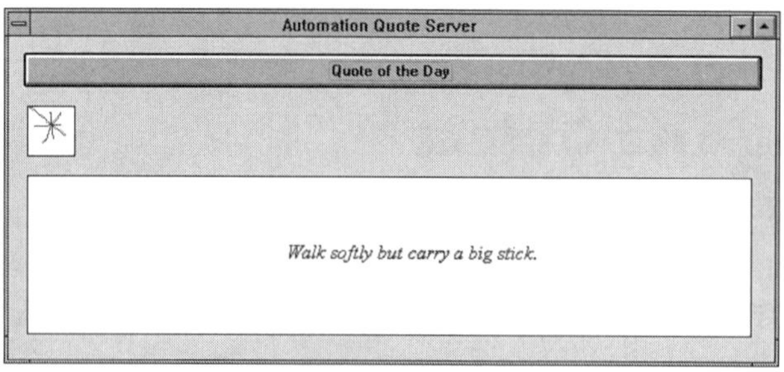

Fig. 13.2
The Automation Quote Server screen.

The script begins by defining the variable `MyObj` as an object. You then call

```
Set MyObj = CreateObject ("autosrv.application")
```

to initialize the object to point at the `IDispatch` interface. When you click the Quote of the Day button, the following code is executed to retrieve the quote:

```
Sub btnQuote_Click ()

    display.Cls

    nWidth = 6975
    nHeight = 1935

    Msg = MyObj.GetQuote

    nOffset = (TextWidth(Msg) / 2) ' Text in center.
    nHeight = TextHeight(Msg)
    display.CurrentX = (display.Width / 2) - nOffset
    display.CurrentY = (display.Height / 2) - nHeight

    display.Print Msg

End Sub
```

Note the call to `MyObj.GetQuote`, which is the method call on the exposed object.

You can now use this script to test your Automation server.

From Here...

The server that you have just developed is as simple a server as you are likely to see. However, you have seen how to create component objects and implement the class factory interface. You also examined the `CreateStdDispatch` function call and saw how to use it to simplify the creation of an `IDispatch` interface pointer. Finally, you have examined type libraries and briefly looked at the ODL language.

In Chapter 15, "An MFC Automation Client," you witness the power of type libraries as you use the MFC Wizards and the Excel type library to generate method calls for Microsoft Excel 5.0.

Chapter 14

MFC and Automation

The Microsoft Foundation Classes (MFC) framework provides an enormous amount of "canned" functionality. To develop OLE Automation applications, you do not need a deep understanding of how MFC implements this functionality. However, such an understanding comes in handy when you are debugging your application, and helps give you the bigger picture of OLE and MFC interaction.

In this chapter, you do not develop a specific application; instead, you take a look behind the scenes at some of the work that MFC does for you. In particular, you learn about the following:

- The OLE Automation support that Microsoft added to the MFC class libraries
- The new Automation Wizard introduced with Visual C++ 1.5
- The implementation details of the Automation support for both clients and servers

Creating an Application with the AppWizard

The first step to acquiring OLE Automation support in your MFC application is to select the **A**utomation Support check box in the OLE Options dialog box (see fig. 14.1). The AppWizard then generates some generic OLE code and code specific to supporting Automation.

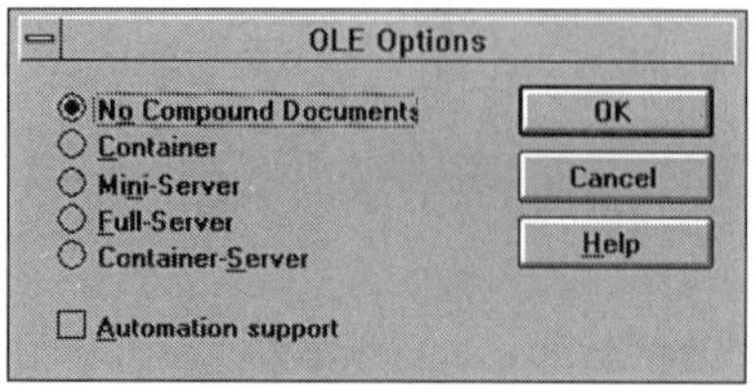

Fig. 14.1
Selecting Automation Support.

The first MFC function called is `AfxOleInit`. This function checks the build information for the OLE libraries and initializes them if they are the correct version. If you are creating a debug build of your application, MFC also passes a debug memory allocator to the `OleInitialize` function (see Chapter 2, "The Component Object Model," for a complete discussion of memory allocators). MFC then retrieves and caches the default task memory allocator for later use. Finally, MFC creates and registers a message filter object that implements the `IMessageFilter` interface.

Next you need to connect your document template class to the `COleTemplateServer` member, `m_server`. This class, which derives from `COleObjectFactory`, implements the `IClassFactory` interface. All your class factories are then registered with the OLE libraries.

OLE relies extensively on the system registry for information regarding OLE servers and clients. Applications must register themselves when they start up, to save the user from having to use REGEDIT.EXE and REG files. To do this in an MFC application, you call the `UpdateRegistery` method of your `COleTemplateServer` member.

In your application's document constructor, the AppWizard adds a call to `EnableAutomation`. This method is a member of `CCmdTarget`. In the MFC architecture, the `CCmdTarget` mechanism routes to various targets all commands, menu commands, keyboard accelerators, toolbar buttons, and so on. Therefore, all objects that receive commands must derive from the `CCmdTarget` class. Microsoft has extended this command-handling architecture to support OLE Automation, so that any class that exposes methods through Automation using the MFC Automation support also must derive from `CCmdTarget`.

The `EnableAutomation` method tells MFC to turn on the `IDispatch` interface for your application.

Finally, a call to `AfxOleLockApp` is made. Chapter 2 discussed how the Component Object Model (COM) tracks an object's lifetime with `IUnknown::AddRef` and `IUnknown::Release`. Each time that an object is used, that object's reference count increases. After finishing with an object, a client decreases the reference count. When an object's reference drops to zero, the framework calls `CCmdTarget::OnFinalRelease`. The default implementation deletes the object. This method is useful for the final cleanup and the release of resources.

MFC also maintains, through `AfxOleLockApp` and `AfxOleUnlockApp`, another count for additional control. This is a count of active objects. If the user quits an application that has an active object count greater than zero, MFC does not exit the application; instead, the framework simply hides the main window until all the application's clients release it. An application can query the active object count by calling `AfxOleCanExitApp`. This function returns true if the application has no outstanding reference counts.

This function call concludes the AppWizard-generated code for OLE Automation support. The next step is to invoke the ClassWizard to create programmable objects.

Supporting Automation with the ClassWizard

You use the ClassWizard to generate code for your programmable classes, methods, and properties. The ClassWizard supplied with Visual C++ 1.5 and 2.0 includes the new tabbed dialog box interface also provided with Microsoft Word 6.0 and Microsoft Excel 5.0. OLE Automation provides its own tab (see fig. 14.2). This new interface widget, which is also a standard control in Windows 95, enables the user to view and edit information selectively in what would otherwise be a large and complex dialog box.

Creating the Class

The first command button is Add Class. By choosing this button, you create an object that can be exposed through Automation. The Add Class dialog box (fig. 14.3) enables you to select the new class name and the names of the implementation files.

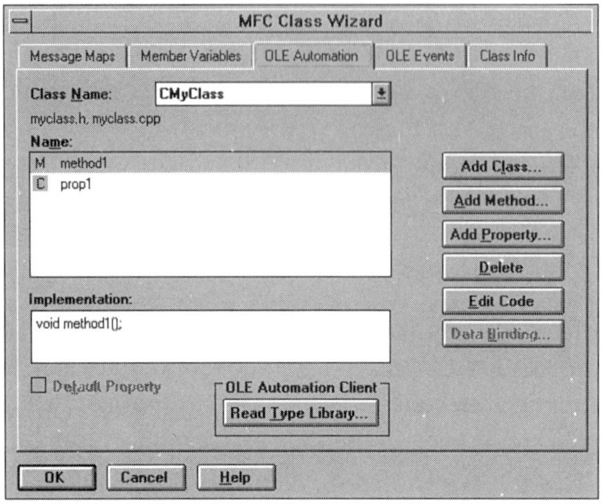

Fig. 14.2
The MFC ClassWizard.

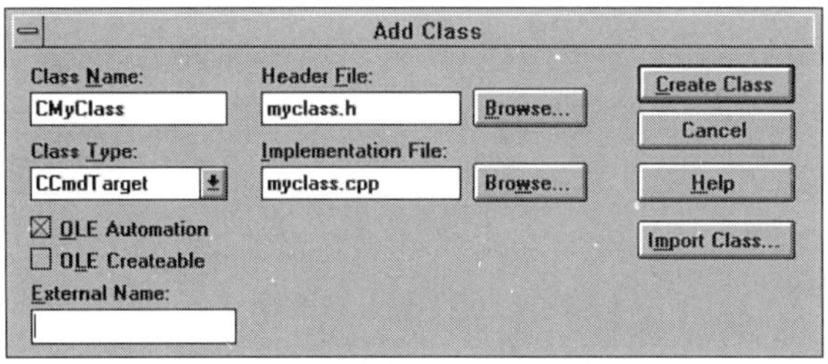

Fig. 14.3
The Add Class dialog box.

Also in the Add Class dialog box, you can choose the class type in the Class **T**ype scroll list. In figure 14.3, the class `CCmdTarget` is selected. You then select the **O**LE Automation check box and provide the class with an external name in the **E**xternal Name text box. The external name is the name that Automation controllers use when accessing objects of this type. Select the O**L**E Creatable check box if you want to enable Automation controllers to create objects of this class. Then select the **C**reate Class button to create your new class.

Adding a Method

You now add a method to your class. Choose the ClassWizard's **A**dd Method command button, which invokes the Add Method dialog box shown in figure 14.4.

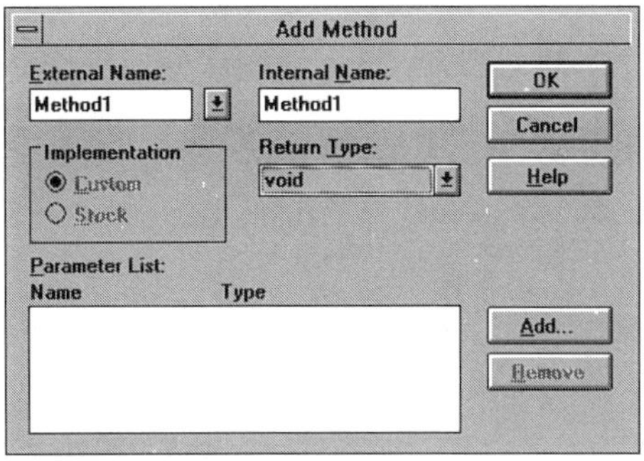

Fig. 14.4
The Add Method dialog box.

Again, you select an internal and external name. The internal name is the method name used in your code, and the external name is the exposed method name used by Automation controllers. Although both names can be the same, keep in mind that your methods and properties will be used by people who may not be familiar with Hungarian notation. Therefore, choose user-friendly names for your external names.

You select the method's return type in the Return **T**ype combo box. You can select from 13 different types, including scalar types, pointers, and `IDispatch` interface pointers.

Finally, in the **P**arameter List, you select the parameters that your method can accept. Note that all return and parameter return types are machine-independent: there are no `int` types. The reason for this independence is to ensure that all methods can be called from a remote computer. If you are making a remote method call from a 16-bit version of Windows to a remote Windows NT machine, and the call uses `int` parameters, converting the parameters is a problem. Using a machine-independent `short` type, however, eliminates this type of problem.

You can expose properties or member variables in two ways. The first is to expose the variable itself. This method is analogous to declaring a variable `public` in a class definition. The second method is to expose it through a pair of `Get` and `Set` methods. This method is similar to the C++ technique of declaring a variable `private` and providing two `public` methods to access it.

The sample code that you examine later in this chapter creates two properties: one is accessed through `Get` and `Set` methods, and the other is accessed directly.

The Add Property dialog box (see fig. 14.5) also enables you to declare a notification function that is called each time the member variable is changed. You access this dialog box by choosing the ClassWizard's Add **P**roperty button.

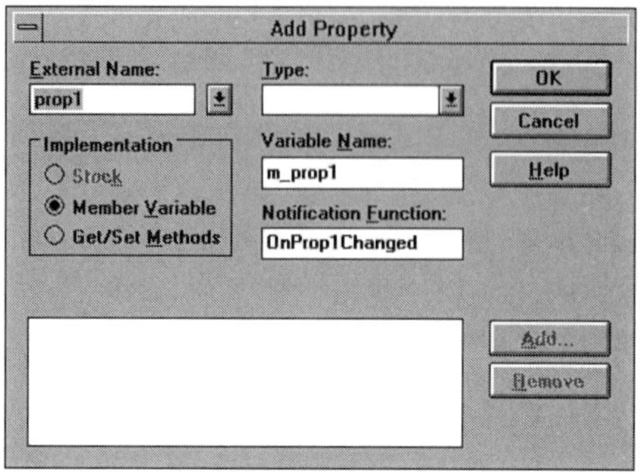

Fig. 14.5
The Add Property dialog box.

Supporting Automation Clients

The options that you have examined so far are for creating an OLE Automation server—an application that exposes objects through Automation. To create an Automation client or controller, you must access exposed objects in another application. In Chapter 12, "Creating a Simple Automation Controller," you wrote code for accessing methods exposed by Microsoft Word 6.0. Using type libraries and the ClassWizard, you can completely automate this process.

By choosing the ClassWizard's Read **T**ype Library command button, you invoke a dialog box from which you can select a type library. For the sample code, you select the type library that ships with Microsoft Excel 5.0 (XLEN50.OLB).

> **Note**
>
> A major problem with the current implementation of this option is that it is an all-or-nothing proposition. You cannot selectively decide which methods or properties to include in your code. The ClassWizard generates code for each defined method and property in the type library. Therefore, the type library for an application such as Microsoft Excel 5.0 can result in a lot of code. Perhaps a future version of the ClassWizard will include an object browser that enables you to select the specific methods in which you are interested.

You examine this option and Automation client support in greater detail in the section "Automation Client Support Revisited," later in this chapter.

Examining the Code

Listing 14.1 shows the code that the ClassWizard generates for you.

Listing 14.1 MYCLASS.H

```
// CMyClass command target
class CMyClass : public CCmdTarget
{
     DECLARE_DYNCREATE(CMyClass)
protected:
     CMyClass();          // protected constructor used by dynamic creation

// Attributes
public:

// Operations
public:

// Overrides
     // ClassWizard generate virtual function overrides
     //{{AFX_VIRTUAL(CMyClass)
         // NOTE - the ClassWizard adds and removes member functions here.
     //}}AFX_VIRTUAL

// Implementation
protected:
     virtual ~CMyClass();

     // Generated message map functions
     //{{AFX_MSG(CMyClass)
         // NOTE - the ClassWizard adds and removes member functions here.
     //}}AFX_MSG
     DECLARE_MESSAGE_MAP()
     DECLARE_OLECREATE(CMyClass2)
     // Generated OLE dispatch map functions
     //{{AFX_DISPATCH(CMyClass)
     short m_prop1;
     afx_msg void OnProp1Changed();
     afx_msg short GetProp2();
     afx_msg void SetProp2(short nNewValue);
     afx_msg void method1();
     //}}AFX_DISPATCH
     DECLARE_DISPATCH_MAP()
};
```

The OLECREATE Macro

In MYCLASS.H, the first macro related to Automation is DECLARE_OLECREATE. This macro declares a `COleObjectFactory` member and a CLSID member in the class. The macro expands as follows:

```
protected: \
     static COleObjectFactory NEAR factory; \
     static const GUID CDECL BASED_CODE guid;
```

The first variable declares the class factory object for the object. The second variable is the object's CLSID.

The DECLARE_DISPATCH_MAP Macro

Next in the code are the declarations for the exposed methods and properties. You have four methods and one property. These declarations are followed by the DECLARE_DISPATCH_MAP macro, which expands as follows:

```
private: \
     static AFX_DISPMAP_ENTRY BASED_CODE _dispatchEntries[]; \
protected: \
     static AFX_DISPMAP BASED_CODE dispatchMap; \
     virtual AFX_DISPMAP FAR* GetDispatchMap() const;
```

This macro declares a member `dispatchMap`, which is an AFX_DISPMAP structure. This structure contains a pointer to the base class' dispatch map and a pointer to a structure that contains information about each of the exposed methods and properties. The pointer to the base class' dispatch table is the mechanism that the framework uses to thread the dispatch tables together. If an object does not implement a method call, the framework can route the call to the base class. This mechanism is similar to that used for message maps (see fig. 14.6). The framework traverses this list of dispatch maps, looking for a particular method or property during an `IDispatch::Invoke` call.

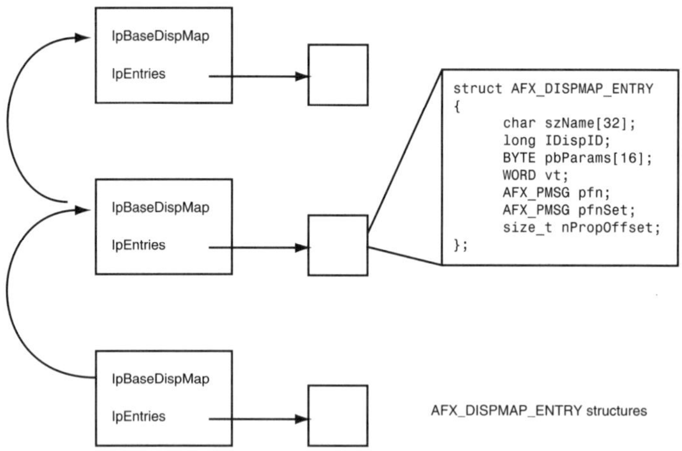

Fig. 14.6 Dispatch maps.

The AFX_DISPMAP and AFX_DISPMAP_ENTRY structures are declared as follows:

```
struct AFX_DISPMAP
{
     AFX_DISPMAP FAR* lpBaseDispMap;
```

```
        AFX_DISPMAP_ENTRY FAR* lpEntries;
};
struct AFX_DISPMAP_ENTRY
{
        char szName[32];    // member/property name
        long lDispID;       // DISPID (may be DISPID_UNKNOWN)
        BYTE pbParams[16]; // member parameter description
        WORD vt;            // return value type or type of property
        AFX_PMSG pfn;       // normal member On<membercall> or OnGet<property>
        AFX_PMSG pfnSet;    // special member for OnSet<property>
        size_t nPropOffset;// property offset
};
```

The CPP file includes the following definition for the dispatch map table:

```
BEGIN_DISPATCH_MAP(CMyClass, CCmdTarget)
        //{{AFX_DISPATCH_MAP(CMyClass)
        DISP_PROPERTY_NOTIFY(CMyClass, "prop1", m_prop1,
            OnProp1Changed, VT_I2)
        DISP_PROPERTY_EX(CMyClass, "prop2", GetProp2, SetProp2, VT_I2)
        DISP_FUNCTION(CMyClass, "method1", method1, VT_EMPTY,
                        VTS_NONE)
        //}}AFX_DISPATCH_MAP
END_DISPATCH_MAP()
```

The following sections examine each of the macros included in this file.

The BEGIN_DISPATCH_MAP Macro. You begin with the BEGIN_DISPATCH_MAP macro, which takes two parameters: the name of the class, and the name of the base class. The macro expands as follows:

```
AFX_DISPMAP FAR* CMyClass::GetDispatchMap() const \
        { return &CMyClass::dispatchMap; } \
AFX_DISPMAP BASED_CODE CMyClass::dispatchMap = \
        { &(CCmdTarget::dispatchMap), CMyClass::_dispatchEntries }; \
AFX_DISPMAP_ENTRY BASED_CODE CMyClass::_dispatchEntries[] = \
{
```

This macro implements the `GetDispatchMap` function that the DECLARE_DISPATCH_MAP macro declared. This function returns a pointer to the dispatch map table.

The `dispatchMap` member is then initialized with the address of the base class (in this case, `CCMdTarget`), the dispatch table, and a pointer to the dispatch table.

The final line in the macro is also the opening line in the initialization of your dispatch table.

The DISP_XXXX Macros. The next macro, DISP_PROPERTY_NOTIFY, takes five parameters and is used to fill in the first entry in the AFX_DISPMAP_ENTRY structure:

```
DISP_PROPERTY_NOTIFY(CMyClass,     // Class name
              "prop1",             // Property's external name
              m_prop1,             // Property's internal name
              OnProp1Changed,      // Notify function
              VT_I2)               // Property's type
```

The macro expands as follows:

```
{ prop1, DISPID_UNKNOWN, "", VT_I2, (AFX_PMSG)0, \
    (AFX_PMSG)(void (MyClass::*)(void))OnProp1Changed, \
    offsetof(MyClass, m_prop1) }, \
```

This macro sets up your notification function so that it is called whenever the property `m_prop1` changes.

MFC 2.5 defines five macros to define methods and properties:

```
DISP_FUNCTION(theClass, szExternalName, pfnMember, vtRetVal,
     vtsParams)
DISP_PROPERTY(theClass, szExternalName, memberName, vtPropType)
DISP_PROPERTY_NOTIFY(theClass, szExternalName, memberName,
     pfnAfterSet, vtPropType)
DISP_PROPERTY_EX(theClass, szExternalName, pfnGet, pfnSet,
     vtPropType)
DISP_PROPERTY_PARAM(theClass, szExternalName, pfnGet, pfnSet,
     vtPropType, vtsParams)
```

Generating the DISPIDs. Note that all these macros define the DISPID for the method or property to be DISPID_UNKNOWN. As Chapter 12, "Creating a Simple Automation Controller," mentioned, when you call the methods exposed by Microsoft Word 6.0, you use DISPID parameters during the `IDispatch::Invoke` call. DISPIDs are 32-bit numbers that represent the user-readable names for methods and properties. You use DISPIDs because string table lookups can be expensive. You can think of DISPIDs as hash values that are similar to the ATOM table in Windows.

Within an OLE Automation server's implementation, the implementor must decide how to define all DISPIDS (except for negative-valued DISPIDs, which are reserved).

Which DISPIDs are used for the methods and properties that you are declaring with these macros? Initially, the DISPIDs are assigned the value DISPID_UNKNOWN. During a call to `IDispatch::GetIDsofNames`, the framework generates a DISPID for each method or property in the dispatch table.

The framework splits the 32-bit DISPID into two 16-bit components. The entry's distance from the top of the dispatch table is placed in the first component, the DISPID's LOWORD. The first entry in the table is assigned the value 1, the next 2, and so on. The HIWORD is assigned the distance from the topmost derived class.

In listing 14.1, the property `m_prop` is assigned the DISPID (DISPID) 0x00000001. The property is defined in this class so that the HIWORD is 0x0000 and the first entry in the table, so the LOWORD is 0x0001. For example, suppose a class derives from your class and has the following dispatch map:

```
BEGIN_DISPATCH_MAP(CMyClassDerv, CMyClass)
     DISP_PROPERTY(CMyClassDerv,prop3,m_prop3,VT_I2)
END_DISPATCH_MAP()
```

The DISPID in the class `CMyClassDerv` for the property `m_prop3` would be (DISPID) 0x00000001, but the DISPID for the inherited property `m_prop1` would be (DISPID) 0x00010001.

If you want to generate your own DISPIDs, MFC provides a set of macros that enable you to choose the DISPID for each method or property. These macros are defined as follows:

```
DISP_FUNCTION_ID(theClass, szExternalName, dispid, pfnMember,
    vtRetVal, vtsParams)
DISP_PROPERTY_ID(theClass, szExternalName, dispid, memberName,
    vtPropType)
DISP_PROPERTY_NOTIFY_ID(theClass, szExternalName, dispid,
    memberName, pfnAfterSet, vtPropType)
DISP_PROPERTY_EX_ID(theClass, szExternalName, dispid, pfnGet,
    pfnSet, vtPropType)
DISP_PROPERTY_PARAM_ID(theClass, szExternalName, dispid, pfnGet,
    pfnSet, vtPropType, vtsParams)
```

Each of these macros takes a DISPID as a parameter. They have the same names as the other macros, except that _ID is appended to each name. These macros are useful if you need to maintain compatibility with older versions of your software that already have assigned DISPIDs.

The END_DISPATCH_MAP Macro. The END_DISPATCH_MAP macro terminates the dispatch map. This macro expands as follows:

```
{ VTS_NONE, DISPID_UNKNOWN, VTS_NONE, VT_VOID, \
     (AFX_PMSG)NULL, (AFX_PMSG)NULL, (size_t)-1 } }; \
```

All the macro does is add a zeroed entry to the end of the AFX_DISPMAP_ENTRY array. The entry is a marker to indicate to the framework that it has reached the end of the dispatch table.

The IMPLEMENT_OLECREATE Macro

The DECLARE_OLECREATE macro, which is inserted into the header file, declares the `COleObjectFactory` member and CLSID member. The IMPLEMENT_OLECREATE macro defines both of these members. The macro is defined and expanded as follows:

```
IMPLEMENT_OLECREATE(CMyClass, "myclass", 0x6ddef3a0, 0x68cd,
    0x101b, 0x99, 0x48, 0x7e, 0xf9, 0xe6, 0xaf, 0x22, 0x43)
```

The macro uses token pasting to generate a unique name to pass to the constructor for `COleObjectFactory`:

```
static const char BASED_CODE _szProgIDCMyClass[] = myclass; \
COleObjectFactory NEAR CMyClass::factory(CMyClass::guid, \
     RUNTIME_CLASS(CMyClass), FALSE, _szProgIDCMyClass); \
const GUID CDECL BASED_CODE CMyClass::guid = \
     { 0x6ddef3a0, 0x68cd, 0x101b, { 0x99, 0x48, 0x7e, 0xf9,
      0xe6, 0xaf, 0x22, 0x43 } };
```

You now have a class factory that can dynamically create objects of the type `CMyClass`, and you have an initialized CLSID.

Moving on to the Next Steps

The ClassWizard has also generated some method stubs. The next step is to fill in these stubs with real code and build the application. After you have a clean build, you use DISPTEST or Visual Basic 3.0 to create a simple script to access the exposed object. This concludes your look at MFC's Automation support for servers.

Automation Client Support Revisited

An Automation client is a program that uses objects exposed by Automation servers. These programs are also known as Automation controllers. Chapter 12, "Creating a Simple Automation Controller," mentioned that you would use a type library to create an Automation client. In this section, you see how using type libraries in combination with the ClassWizard can greatly simplify the process.

For this example, you use the type library from the DispCalc2 sample application supplied with the OLE 2.0 SDK.

Reading the Type Library

From the ClassWizard dialog box, you select the Read **T**ype Library command button. You then choose the type library DSPCALC2.TLB. The Confirm Classes dialog box then appears, as shown in figure 14.7. The ClassWizard has read the type information about the exposed objects from DSPCALC2.TLB. One class, `_DCalculator`, is available. The ClassWizard then generates the code necessary to access this object.

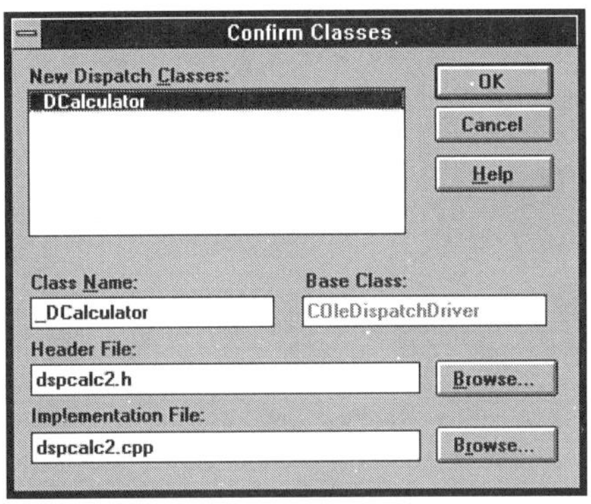

Fig. 14.7
The Confirm Classes dialog box.

The ClassWizard generates a class, `_DCalculator`, which derives from `COleDispatchDriver`. `_COleDispatchDriver` is the main MFC class for driving Automation servers and the wrapper class for the `IDispatch` interface. You usually do not use this class alone but as a base class for Automation clients.

Using `_DCalculator`, you can create a dispatch interface in two ways:

- You can call the `CreateDispatch` method with either a CLSID or the ProgID of the Automation server.
- If you already have a valid `IDispatch` interface pointer, you can simply attach the pointer to the class using the `AttachDispatch` method.

The code in listing 14.2 shows the definition of thc `COleDispatchDriver` and `_DCalculator` classes.

Listing 14.2 The *CDispatchDriver* definition and DSPCALC2.H

```
class COleDispatchDriver
{
// Constructors
public:
     COleDispatchDriver();
```

(continues)

Listing 14.2 Continued

```
// Operations
     BOOL CreateDispatch(REFCLSID clsid, COleException* pError = NULL);
     BOOL CreateDispatch(LPCSTR lpszProgID, COleException* pError = NULL);

     void AttachDispatch(LPDISPATCH lpDispatch, BOOL bAutoRelease = TRUE);
     LPDISPATCH DetachDispatch();
          // detach and get ownership of m_lpDispatch
     void ReleaseDispatch();

     // helpers for IDispatch::Invoke
     void InvokeHelper(DISPID dwDispID, WORD wFlags,
          VARTYPE vtRet, void* pvRet, const BYTE FAR* pbParamInfo, ...);
     void SetProperty(DISPID dwDispID, VARTYPE vtProp, ...);
     void GetProperty(DISPID dwDispID,
         VARTYPE vtProp, void* pvProp) const;
// Implementation
public:
     LPDISPATCH m_lpDispatch;

     ~COleDispatchDriver();
     void InvokeHelperV(DISPID dwDispID, WORD wFlags, VARTYPE vtRet,
          void* pvRet, const BYTE FAR* pbParamInfo, va_list argList);

protected:
     BOOL m_bAutoRelease;    // TRUE if destructor should call Release

private:
     // Disable the copy constructor and assignment by default
     //   so that you get compiler errors rather than unexpected
     //   behavior if you pass objects by value or assign objects.
     COleDispatchDriver(const COleDispatchDriver&);  // no implementation
     void operator=(const COleDispatchDriver&);      // no implementation
};
Dispcalc2.h
// Machine-generated IDispatch driver class(es)
// created with MFCDSPWZ tool.

/////////////////////////////////////////////////////////////////////////
// _DCalculator wrapper class

class _DCalculator : public COleDispatchDriver
{
// Attributes
public:

// Operations
public:
     void SetAccum(long nNewValue);
     long GetAccum();
     void SetOpnd(long nNewValue);
     long GetOpnd();
```

```
        void SetOp(short nNewValue);
        short GetOp();
        BOOL Eval();
        void Clear();
        void Display();
        void Quit();
        BOOL Button(const char* Button);
};
```

Creating the Dispatch Pointer

To use the newly created class, you create an instance of the class `_DCalculator`. You then call the `CreateDispatch` method, giving either the CLSID or the ProgID of the DispCalc server.

```
BOOL CMyApp::CreateDisp()
{

     // Create the calculator object you will drive through OLE Automation
     // The m_calc member is a class of type _DCalculator
     COleException e;
     if (!m_calc.CreateDispatch("Dspcalc2.Application", &e))
     {
          AfxMessageBox(IDP_UNABLE_TO_CREATE);
          AfxThrowUserException();
     }

     return TRUE;
}
```

The first step in the `CreateDispatch` call is a `CoCreateInstance` call that creates a component object and retrieves the first interface pointer, which is a pointer to the `IUnknown` interface. If this call succeeds, the object is placed in the running state.

The final step is a `QueryInterface` for an `IDispatch` pointer. If this call succeeds, you release the `IUnknown` pointer and return.

If either of these steps fails, the SCODE returned from the function call returns in the `COleException` parameter.

You now have a valid `IDispatch` interface pointer stored in the `m_lpDispatch` member of your class.

Invoking the Exposed Methods

To call an exposed object, you simply call the generated class' method, using the necessary parameters. Listing 14.3 shows what happens when you call the `::SetAcum` method.

Listing 14.3 DSPCALC2.CPP

```
// Machine-generated IDispatch driver class(es)
// created with MFCDSPWZ tool.

#include "stdafx.h"
#include "dspcalc2.h"

/////////////////////////////////////////////////////////////////////////////
// _DCalculator properties

/////////////////////////////////////////////////////////////////////////////
// _DCalculator operations

void _DCalculator::SetAccum(long nNewValue)
{
     static BYTE BASED_CODE parms[] =
          VTS_I4;
     InvokeHelper(0x60010016, DISPATCH_PROPERTYPUT, VT_EMPTY, NULL, parms,
           nNewValue);
}

long _DCalculator::GetAccum()
{
     long result;
     InvokeHelper(0x60010016, DISPATCH_PROPERTYGET, VT_I4,
         (void*)&result, NULL);
     return result;
}

void _DCalculator::SetOpnd(long nNewValue)
{
     static BYTE BASED_CODE parms[] =
          VTS_I4;
     InvokeHelper(0x60010046, DISPATCH_PROPERTYPUT, VT_EMPTY, NULL, parms,
           nNewValue);
}

long _DCalculator::GetOpnd()
{
     long result;
     InvokeHelper(0x60010046, DISPATCH_PROPERTYGET, VT_I4,
         (void*)&result, NULL);
     return result;
}

void _DCalculator::SetOp(short nNewValue)
{
     static BYTE BASED_CODE parms[] =
          VTS_I2;
     InvokeHelper(0x60010076, DISPATCH_PROPERTYPUT, VT_EMPTY, NULL, parms,
           nNewValue);
}

short _DCalculator::GetOp()
```

```
{
     short result;
     InvokeHelper(0x60010076, DISPATCH_PROPERTYGET, VT_I2,
         (void*)&result, NULL);
     return result;
}

BOOL _DCalculator::Eval()
{
     BOOL result;
     InvokeHelper(0x600100ae, DISPATCH_METHOD, VT_BOOL,
         (void*)&result, NULL);
     return result;
}

void _DCalculator::Clear()
{
     InvokeHelper(0x600100c4, DISPATCH_METHOD, VT_EMPTY, NULL, NULL);
}

void _DCalculator::Display()
{
     InvokeHelper(0x600100da, DISPATCH_METHOD, VT_EMPTY, NULL, NULL);
}

void _DCalculator::Quit()
{
     InvokeHelper(0x600100f0, DISPATCH_METHOD, VT_EMPTY, NULL, NULL);
}

BOOL _DCalculator::Button(const char* Button)
{
     BOOL result;
     static BYTE BASED_CODE parms[] =
          VTS_BSTR;
     InvokeHelper(0x60010106, DISPATCH_METHOD, VT_BOOL,
         (void*)&result, parms, Button);
     return result;
}
```

The `_DCalculator::SetAcum` method calls the inherited method `InvokeHelper`. This method takes a variable number of parameters and handles all the details of calling `IDispatch::Invoke`.

The first parameter is the DISPID of the method or property that you are calling. The ClassWizard extracts this information from the type library.

The second parameter describes the call's context. The value of this parameter can be one of the following:

Value	Description
DISPATCH_METHOD	The member is being accessed as a method. If there is a property of the same name, both this flag and the DISPATCH_PROPERTYGET flag may be set.
DISPATCH_PROPERTYGET	The member is being retrieved as a property or data member.
DISPATCH_PROPERTYPUT	The member is being changed as a property or data member.
DISPATCH_PROPERTYPUTREF	The member is being changed by a reference assignment rather than a value assignment. This value is valid only when the property accepts a reference to an object.

In the `SetAcum` method, you set a value into an exposed property, so you pass DISPATCH_PROPERTYPUT as your context.

The third parameter describes the return type from the method call. The type can be any of the following values:

Symbol	Return Type
VT_EMPTY	`void`
VT_I2	`short`
VT_I4	`long`
VT_R4	`float`
VT_R8	`double`
VT_CY	`CY`
VT_DATE	`DATE`
VT_BSTR	`BSTR`
VT_DISPATCH	`LPDISPATCH`
VT_ERROR	`SCODE`
VT_BOOL	`BOOL`
VT_VARIANT	`VARIANT`
VT_UNKNOWN	`LPUNKNOWN`

You do not expect any return value, and the method returns void, so you pass VT_EMPTY as the return parameter type.

The fourth parameter is a pointer to the return type variable. This type must be the same as that described in the previous parameters. For this example, you pass NULL.

The fifth parameter is a pointer to a space-separated list of parameter types. Each of these types represents a variable in the variable parameter list that follows this list. The following are the possible values:

Symbol	Parameter Type
VTS_I2	`short`
VTS_I4	`long`
VTS_R4	`float`
VTS_R8	`double`
VTS_CY	`const CY*`
VTS_DATE	`DATE`
VTS_BSTR	`const char*`
VTS_DISPATCH	`LPDISPATCH`
VTS_SCODE	`SCODE`
VTS_BOOL	`BOOL`
VTS_VARIANT	`const VARIANT*`
VTS_UNKNOWN	`LPUNKNOWN`
VTS_PI2	`short*`
VTS_PI4	`long*`
VTS_PR4	`float*`
VTS_PR8	`double*`
VTS_PCY	`CY*`
VTS_PDATE	`DATE*`
VTS_PBSTR	`BSTR*`

(continues)

Symbol	Parameter Type
VTS_PDISPATCH	LPDISPATCH*
VTS_PSCODE	SCODE*
VTS_PBOOL	BOOL*
VTS_PVARIANT	VARIANT*
VTS_PUNKNOWN	LPUNKNOWN*

The property that you are setting is a `long` value, so you pass VTS_I4. The method takes only one parameter, so you are finished. If there are more parameters, you place their type in the ASCIIZ string, separated by spaces.

The last parameter is the `long` value that you are setting in the property.

The `InvokeHelper` method parses your parameter list and correctly fills in the DISPPARAMS structure. Filling in this structure correctly is a tedious operation, as you learned in Chapter 12, "Creating a Simple Automation Controller." The `InvokeHelper` method then calls the `IDispatch::Invoke` method from your `m_lpDispatch` member. Any return values are then retrieved and placed in the return variables. Any errors cause `InvokeHelper` to throw an exception.

Getting and Setting Property Values

Finally, two helper methods get and set property values:

- The `SetProperty` method takes a DISPID as its first parameter. The next parameter is the type VARTYPE, and the last property is a variable parameter list. In fact, this method takes only one parameter in the variable parameter list: the property that you are setting.
- The `GetProperty` method takes three parameters: the DISPID, the VARTYPE, and a pointer to the return value.

Both of these methods are simple wrappers for an `InvokeHelper` call.

From Here...

As you have seen, adding OLE Automation client support to your application is a simple process. The only caveat is that, to use the ClassWizard effectively, you must have access to a type library. This normally is not a problem, because most vendors who expose Automation objects ship a type library with their application. However, there are exceptions. Microsoft Word 6.0, for example, ships without a type library.

Adding server support takes a little more work, but with the aid of the Automation ClassWizard, the task is relatively painless.

In the next chapter, you use the ClassWizard to read the type library shipped with Excel 5.0 and develop an application that can control Excel through Automation.

Chapter 15

An MFC Automation Client

This chapter examines the support that the Microsoft Foundation Classes (MFC) and Visual C++ provide for creating an OLE Automation client. You will use the type library supplied with Microsoft Excel 5.0 and the Visual C++ ClassWizard to generate the code for the methods and properties exposed by Excel.

In this chapter, you learn about the following:

- The Excel object model, which closely follows the OLE Automation guidelines
- How to use OLE Automation to leverage Excel's charting capabilities into your applications
- How to develop an MFC application that accesses Excel's methods and properties

The Excel Object Model

Microsoft Excel 5.0 was the first major commercial application designed as a set of objects with each object being exposed through OLE Automation. The object model closely follows the guidelines set down in the OLE Automation design specification.

Excel exposes over 128 objects. These objects provide access to hundreds of methods and properties that encompass every area of Excel functionality. Figure 15.1 is an overview of the objects exposed by Excel.

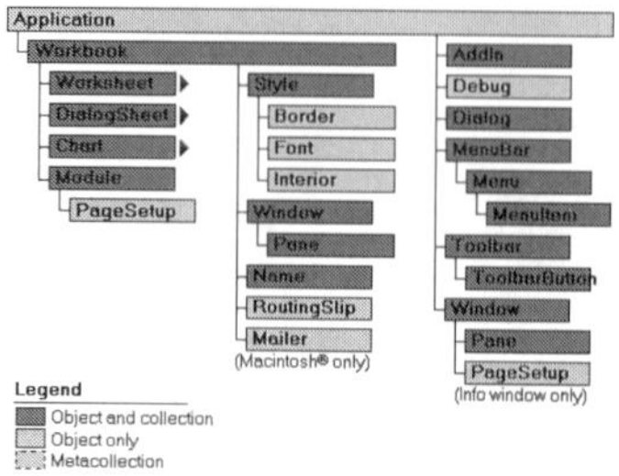

Fig. 15.1
The Excel object hierarchy.

Access to the Excel object system is provided through the `Application` object. After you successfully retrieve an `IDispatch` interface pointer to the `Application` object, you can thread your way through the hierarchy retrieving `IDispatch` pointers to other objects and collections.

Excel supports several `Automation` collections that are used to enumerate such objects as workbooks, worksheets, and charts.

You can use the extremely powerful functionality exposed by Excel to create custom applications such as financial systems and enterprise information systems. This functionality is available to any application that supports OLE Automation. Visual Basic is perhaps the best example of an OLE Automation controller that you can use to control Excel. Later in this chapter, you will see how you can access Excel from a C++ application.

By breaking Excel into objects and exposing them through OLE Automation, Microsoft is in fact giving you access to the Excel code. Excel is just one demonstration of the power of component object software. Because of this model, you can leverage the charting capabilities of Excel into your application.

The Test Application

The test application that you are about to develop enables you to start and shut down Excel programmatically. The application also enables you to change some of Excel's default appearance and finally to create or open an Excel workbook.

The application is not very useful, but does clearly demonstrate how to access from an MFC application the methods and properties exposed by Excel.

As usual, you use the AppWizard to create the initial template for your application. You select the OLE Automation option and let the AppWizard create a Single Document Interface (SDI) template for you.

The first thing that you do is use the AppStudio to create a dialog template. After you create the template, you use the ClassWizard to generate a new class that inherits from `CFormView`. The form view will represent your user interface for this application. You then place in your application template this new class, `CExcel`, which replaces the view module that the AppWizard generated for you.

The code for the dialog template follows:

```
CSingleDocTemplate* pDocTemplate;
pDocTemplate = new CSingleDocTemplate(
     IDR_MAINFRAME,
     RUNTIME_CLASS(CXclientDoc),
     RUNTIME_CLASS(CMainFrame),
     RUNTIME_CLASS(CExcel));
AddDocTemplate(pDocTemplate);
```

This technique of using a dialog template as the main interface for an application is extremely useful, particularly for writing quick utilities and test programs such as this one. This technique was first demonstrated by Charles Petzold in *Programming Windows*, way back in 1988.

After your main application is working, you use the ClassWizard to read the Excel type library. Listing 15.1 shows the code for the main application object.

Listing 15.1 XCLIENT.CPP

```
#include "stdafx.h"
#include "xclient.h"

#include "mainfrm.h"
#include "xcliedoc.h"
#include "excel.h"
#include "ctl3d.h"

#ifdef _DEBUG
#undef THIS_FILE
static char BASED_CODE THIS_FILE[] = __FILE__;
#endif

/////////////////////////////////////////////////////////////////////////////
// CXclientApp

BEGIN_MESSAGE_MAP(CXclientApp, CWinApp)
     //{{AFX_MSG_MAP(CXclientApp)
     ON_COMMAND(ID_APP_ABOUT, OnAppAbout)
          // NOTE - ClassWizard adds and removes mapping macros here.
          //    DO NOT EDIT what you see in these blocks of generated code!
     //}}AFX_MSG_MAP
```

(continues)

Listing 15.1 Continued

```
    // Standard file-based document commands
    ON_COMMAND(ID_FILE_NEW, CWinApp::OnFileNew)
    ON_COMMAND(ID_FILE_OPEN, CWinApp::OnFileOpen)
END_MESSAGE_MAP()

/////////////////////////////////////////////////////////////////////////////
// CXclientApp construction

CXclientApp::CXclientApp()
{
    // TODO: add construction code here,
    // Place all significant initialization in InitInstance
}

/////////////////////////////////////////////////////////////////////////////
// The one and only CXclientApp object

CXclientApp NEAR theApp;

// This identifier was generated to be statistically unique for your app.
// You can change it if you prefer to choose a specific identifier.
static const CLSID BASED_CODE clsid =
{ 0x8d83bac0, 0xa4a4, 0x101b, { 0x99, 0x48, 0x52, 0x41, 0x53, 0x48,
                                0x0, 0x1 } };
/////////////////////////////////////////////////////////////////////////////
// CXclientApp initialization
//
int CXclientApp::ExitInstance()
{
    Ctl3dUnregister(AfxGetInstanceHandle());
    return CWinApp::ExitInstance();
}
//-----------------------------------------------------------------
BOOL CXclientApp::InitInstance()
{

    Ctl3dRegister(AfxGetInstanceHandle());
    Ctl3dAutoSubclass(AfxGetInstanceHandle());

    // Initialize OLE 2.0 libraries
    if (!AfxOleInit())
    {
        AfxMessageBox(IDP_OLE_INIT_FAILED);
        return FALSE;
    }
    // Standard initialization
    // If you are not using these features and want to reduce the size
    // of your final executable, you should remove from the following
    // the specific initialization routines you do not need.

    SetDialogBkColor();        // Set dialog background color to gray
```

```
    LoadStdProfileSettings();
                    // Load standard INI file options (including MRU)

    // Register the application's document templates.
    // Document templates serve as the connection
    // between documents, frame windows, and views.

    CSingleDocTemplate* pDocTemplate;
    pDocTemplate = new CSingleDocTemplate(
         IDR_MAINFRAME,
         RUNTIME_CLASS(CXclientDoc),
         RUNTIME_CLASS(CMainFrame),
         RUNTIME_CLASS(CExcel));
    AddDocTemplate(pDocTemplate);

    // Connect the COleTemplateServer to the document template.
    //  The COleTemplateServer creates new documents on behalf
    //  of requesting OLE containers by using information
    //  specified in the document template.
    m_server.ConnectTemplate(clsid, pDocTemplate, TRUE);


    // Parse the command line to see if launched as OLE server
    if (RunEmbedded() || RunAutomated())
    {
         // Register all OLE server (factories) as running.
         // This enables the OLE 2.0 libraries to create objects
         // from other applications.
         COleTemplateServer::RegisterAll();

         // Application was run with /Embedding or /Automation.
         // Don't show the main window in this case.
         return TRUE;
    }

    // When a server application is launched stand-alone,
    // you should update the system registry in case
    // it has been damaged.
    m_server.UpdateRegistry(OAT_DISPATCH_OBJECT);
    COleObjectFactory::UpdateRegistryAll();

    // create a new (empty) document
    OnFileNew();

    if (m_lpCmdLine[0] != '\0')
    {
         // TODO: add command-line processing here
    }


    return TRUE;
}
```

(continues)

Listing 15.1 Continued

```
///////////////////////////////////////////////////////////////////////////
// CAboutDlg dialog used for App About

class CAboutDlg : public CDialog
{
public:
     CAboutDlg();

// Dialog Data
     //{{AFX_DATA(CAboutDlg)
     enum { IDD = IDD_ABOUTBOX };
     //}}AFX_DATA

// Implementation
protected:
     virtual void DoDataExchange(CDataExchange* pDX);  // DDX/DDV support
     //{{AFX_MSG(CAboutDlg)
          // No message handlers
     //}}AFX_MSG
     DECLARE_MESSAGE_MAP()
};

CAboutDlg::CAboutDlg() : CDialog(CAboutDlg::IDD)
{
     //{{AFX_DATA_INIT(CAboutDlg)
     //}}AFX_DATA_INIT
}

void CAboutDlg::DoDataExchange(CDataExchange* pDX)
{
     CDialog::DoDataExchange(pDX);
     //{{AFX_DATA_MAP(CAboutDlg)
     //}}AFX_DATA_MAP
}

BEGIN_MESSAGE_MAP(CAboutDlg, CDialog)
     //{{AFX_MSG_MAP(CAboutDlg)
          // No message handlers
     //}}AFX_MSG_MAP
END_MESSAGE_MAP()

// App command to run the dialog
void CXclientApp::OnAppAbout()
{
     CAboutDlg aboutDlg;
     aboutDlg.DoModal();
}
```

Reading the Type Library

The Excel type library is called XLEN50.OLB. The OLB extension stands for *object library* but is in fact an ordinary OLE type library.

To use the type library in your application, you start the ClassWizard and select the Automation tab and select the Read Type Library command button. You then see the screen shown in figure 15.2.

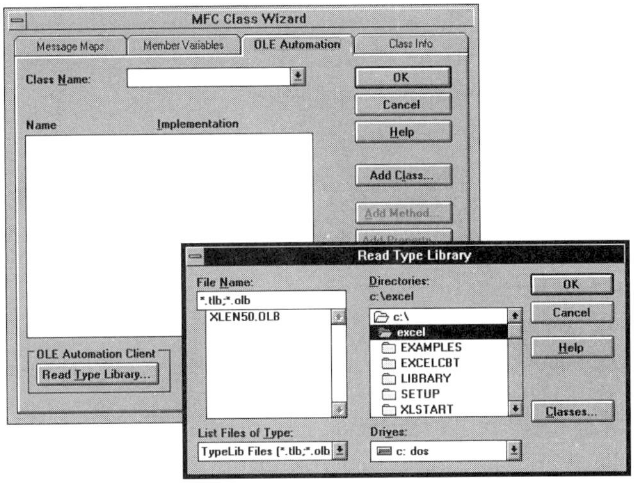

Fig. 15.2 The Automation MFC Class Wizard dialog box.

When the MFC Class Wizard dialog box opens the type library, you see a list of all the objects that are available through the type library. For the sample application, you use the `Application` and `Workbook` objects. You also tell the ClassWizard to save the generated code in XLEN50.CPP and XLEN50.H. (See fig. 15.3.)

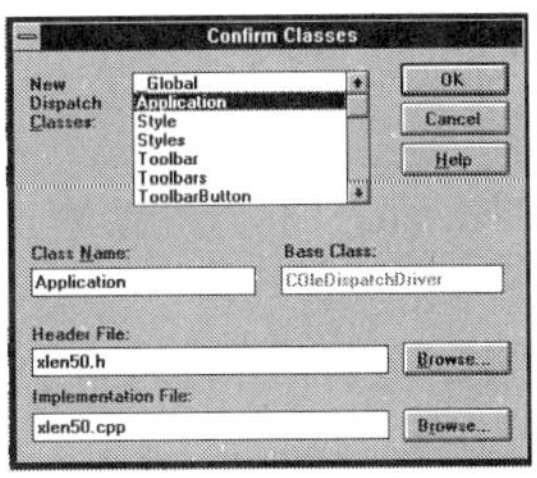

Fig. 15.3 Selecting the objects from the type library.

Changing the Generated Code

The first time I used the Excel type library to generate the code for an OLE Automation controller, I was excited by the prospect of getting all that functionality in my code with almost no effort. Imagine my surprise when I examined the code generated.

Listing 15.2 shows the generated code for the `Worksheet` class definition. Every method that returns something returns it in a VARIANT, and each argument to each method is also a VARIANT. Although this approach works, it definitely is *not* the way to write a type library. Microsoft recommends that if you design a type library, you use appropriate types rather than VARIANTs for your method parameters and return values.

Listing 15.2 The *Worksheet* Class Definition

```
class Worksheet : public COleDispatchDriver
{
// Attributes
public:
     VARIANT GetAutoFilterMode();
     void SetAutoFilterMode(const VARIANT&);
     VARIANT GetCircularReference();
     void SetCircularReference(const VARIANT&);
     VARIANT GetConsolidationFunction();
     void SetConsolidationFunction(const VARIANT&);
     VARIANT GetConsolidationOptions();
     void SetConsolidationOptions(const VARIANT&);
     VARIANT GetConsolidationSources();
     void SetConsolidationSources(const VARIANT&);
     VARIANT GetCreator();
     void SetCreator(const VARIANT&);
     VARIANT GetDisplayAutomaticPageBreaks();
     void SetDisplayAutomaticPageBreaks(const VARIANT&);
     VARIANT GetFilterMode();
     void SetFilterMode(const VARIANT&);
     VARIANT GetIndex();
     void SetIndex(const VARIANT&);
     VARIANT GetName();
     void SetName(const VARIANT&);
     VARIANT GetNext();
     void SetNext(const VARIANT&);
     VARIANT GetOnCalculate();
     void SetOnCalculate(const VARIANT&);
     VARIANT GetOnData();
     void SetOnData(const VARIANT&);
     VARIANT GetOnDoubleClick();
     void SetOnDoubleClick(const VARIANT&);
     VARIANT GetOnEntry();
     void SetOnEntry(const VARIANT&);
     VARIANT GetOnSheetActivate();
```

```
     void SetOnSheetActivate(const VARIANT&);
     VARIANT GetOnSheetDeactivate();
     void SetOnSheetDeactivate(const VARIANT&);
     VARIANT GetOutline();
     void SetOutline(const VARIANT&);
     VARIANT GetPageSetup();
     void SetPageSetup(const VARIANT&);
     VARIANT GetParent();
     void SetParent(const VARIANT&);
     VARIANT GetPrevious();
     void SetPrevious(const VARIANT&);
     VARIANT GetProtectContents();
     void SetProtectContents(const VARIANT&);
     VARIANT GetProtectDrawingObjects();
     void SetProtectDrawingObjects(const VARIANT&);
     VARIANT GetProtectScenarios();
     void SetProtectScenarios(const VARIANT&);
     VARIANT GetStandardHeight();
     void SetStandardHeight(const VARIANT&);
     VARIANT GetStandardWidth();
     void SetStandardWidth(const VARIANT&);
     VARIANT GetTransitionExpEval();
     void SetTransitionExpEval(const VARIANT&);
     VARIANT GetTransitionFormEntry();
     void SetTransitionFormEntry(const VARIANT&);
     VARIANT GetType();
     void SetType(const VARIANT&);
     VARIANT GetUsedRange();
     void SetUsedRange(const VARIANT&);
     VARIANT GetVisible();
     void SetVisible(const VARIANT&);

// Operations
public:
     VARIANT Activate();
     VARIANT Application();
     VARIANT Arcs(const VARIANT& Index);
     VARIANT Buttons(const VARIANT& Index);
     VARIANT Calculate();
     VARIANT Cells(const VARIANT& RowIndex, const VARIANT&
ColumnIndex);
     VARIANT ChartObjects(const VARIANT& Index);
     VARIANT CheckBoxes(const VARIANT& Index);
     VARIANT CheckSpelling(const VARIANT& CustomDictionary,
          const VARIANT& IgnoreUppercase, const VARIANT&
AlwaysSuggest);
     VARIANT ClearArrows();
     VARIANT Columns(const VARIANT& Index);
     VARIANT Copy(const VARIANT& Before, const VARIANT& After);
     VARIANT Delete();
     VARIANT DrawingObjects(const VARIANT& Index);
     VARIANT Drawings(const VARIANT& Index);
     VARIANT DropDowns(const VARIANT& Index);
     VARIANT _Evaluate(const VARIANT& Name);
     VARIANT Evaluate(const VARIANT& Name);
     VARIANT GroupBoxes(const VARIANT& Index);
```

(continues)

Listing 15.2 Continued

```
        VARIANT GroupObjects(const VARIANT& Index);
        VARIANT Labels(const VARIANT& Index);
        VARIANT Lines(const VARIANT& Index);
        VARIANT ListBoxes(const VARIANT& Index);
        VARIANT Move(const VARIANT& Before, const VARIANT& After);
        VARIANT OLEObjects(const VARIANT& Index);
        VARIANT OptionButtons(const VARIANT& Index);
        VARIANT Ovals(const VARIANT& Index);
        VARIANT Paste(const VARIANT& Destination, const VARIANT& Link);
        VARIANT PasteSpecial(const VARIANT& Format, const VARIANT& Link,
               const VARIANT& DisplayAsIcon, const VARIANT& IconFileName,
               const VARIANT& IconIndex, const VARIANT& IconLabel);
        VARIANT Pictures(const VARIANT& Index);
        VARIANT PivotTables(const VARIANT& Index);
        VARIANT PivotTableWizard(const VARIANT& SourceType,
             const VARIANT& SourceData, const VARIANT& TableDestination,
             const VARIANT& TableName, const VARIANT& RowGrand,
             const VARIANT& ColumnGrand, const VARIANT& SaveData,
             const VARIANT& HasAutoFormat, const VARIANT& AutoPage);
        VARIANT PrintOut(const VARIANT& From, const VARIANT& To,
             const VARIANT& Copies, const VARIANT& Preview);
        VARIANT PrintPreview();
        VARIANT Protect(const VARIANT& Password,
             const VARIANT& DrawingObjects, const VARIANT& Contents,
             const VARIANT& Scenarios);
        VARIANT Range(const VARIANT& Cell1, const VARIANT& Cell2);
        VARIANT Rectangles(const VARIANT& Index);
        VARIANT Rows(const VARIANT& Index);
        VARIANT SaveAs(const VARIANT& Filename, const VARIANT& FileFormat,
             const VARIANT& Password, const VARIANT& WriteResPassword,
             const VARIANT& ReadOnlyRecommended,
             const VARIANT& CreateBackup);
        VARIANT Scenarios(const VARIANT& Index);
        VARIANT ScrollBars(const VARIANT& Index);
        VARIANT Select(const VARIANT& Replace);
        VARIANT ShowAllData();
        VARIANT ShowDataForm();
        VARIANT Spinners(const VARIANT& Index);
        VARIANT TextBoxes(const VARIANT& Index);
        VARIANT Unprotect(const VARIANT& Password);
};
```

Instead of making direct calls to the methods that you want to access, you must first package the method arguments into VARIANTs, invoke the method, and then unpack the returned VARIANT. Perhaps a future release of the type library will address this problem.

To make some of the methods a little easier to call, you can change the code generated by the ClassWizard. In the following example, you change the methods that return a pointer to an `IDispatch` interface for the first entry in the collection `Workbooks`:

```
LPDISPATCH Application::Workbooks(const VARIANT& Index)
{
     LPDISPATCH result;
     InvokeHelper(0x23c, DISPATCH_METHOD, VT_DISPATCH,
               (void*)&result,NULL);
     return result;
}
```

Such changes do not take too much time to make, but they can greatly simplify the code required to invoke these methods from your application code.

Each of these classes derives from `COleDispatchDriver` (see listing 15.3). This class, which is usually used as the base class for classes generated from type libraries, implements the client side of OLE Automation. The class provides methods to access and update properties and to invoke exposed methods.

Listing 15.3 The *COleDispatchDriver* Class

```
class COleDispatchDriver
{
// Constructors
public:
     COleDispatchDriver();
// Operations
     BOOL CreateDispatch(REFCLSID clsid, COleException* pError = NULL);
     BOOL CreateDispatch(LPCSTR lpszProgID, COleException* pError = NULL);
     void AttachDispatch(LPDISPATCH lpDispatch, BOOL bAutoRelease = TRUE);
     LPDISPATCH DetachDispatch();
          // detach and get ownership of m_lpDispatch
     void ReleaseDispatch();

     // helpers for IDispatch::Invoke
     void InvokeHelper(DISPID dwDispID, WORD wFlags,
          VARTYPE vtRet, void* pvRet, const BYTE FAR* pbParamInfo, ...);
     void SetProperty(DISPID dwDispID, VARTYPE vtProp, ...);
     void GetProperty(DISPID dwDispID, VARTYPE vtProp,
                    void* pvProp) const;
// Implementation
public:
     LPDISPATCH m_lpDispatch;

     ~COleDispatchDriver();
```

(continues)

Listing 15.3 Continued

```
     void InvokeHelperV(DISPID dwDispID, WORD wFlags, VARTYPE vtRet,
          void* pvRet, const BYTE FAR* pbParamInfo, va_list argList);
protected:
     BOOL m_bAutoRelease;    // TRUE if destructor should call Release
private:
     // Disable the copy constructor and assignment by default
     // so you will get compiler errors rather than unexpected
     // behavior if you pass objects by value or assign objects.
     COleDispatchDriver(const COleDispatchDriver&);  // no implementation
     void operator=(const COleDispatchDriver&);      // no implementation
};
```

Accessing Excel

The next step in creating your test application is to connect to Excel. The `OnStart` command handler is responsible for locating and starting Excel.

You begin by getting the CLSID for Excel. To retrieve the CLSID, you use the API function `CLSIDFromProgID`. You then call `GetActiveObject`. If Excel is already running, you connect to its class object through this method. If this call succeeds, you then call `QueryInterface` for the `IDispatch` interface. Once you have a valid `IDispatch` pointer, you can initialize the Excel `Application` object by attaching the `IDispatch` pointer to it.

If you cannot find a running version of Excel, you call `CreateDispatch` to start and connect to a copy of Excel.

Now that you have a pointer to the Excel `Application` object, you can use that pointer to access all the methods defined by the `Application` class and to read and write the properties defined by the class. Listing 15.4 shows the extent of the functionality available from this class.

Listing 15.4 The *Application* Class

```
/////////////////////////////////////////////////////////////////////
// Application wrapper class

class Application : public COleDispatchDriver
{
// Attributes
public:
```

```
VARIANT GetActiveCell();
void SetActiveCell(const VARIANT&);
VARIANT GetActiveChart();
void SetActiveChart(const VARIANT&);
VARIANT GetActiveDialog();
void SetActiveDialog(const VARIANT&);
VARIANT GetActiveMenuBar();
void SetActiveMenuBar(const VARIANT&);
VARIANT GetActivePrinter();
void SetActivePrinter(const VARIANT&);
VARIANT GetActiveSheet();
void SetActiveSheet(const VARIANT&);
VARIANT GetActiveWindow();
void SetActiveWindow(const VARIANT&);
VARIANT GetActiveWorkbook();
void SetActiveWorkbook(const VARIANT&);
VARIANT GetAlertBeforeOverwriting();
void SetAlertBeforeOverwriting(const VARIANT&);
VARIANT GetAltStartupPath();
void SetAltStartupPath(const VARIANT&);
VARIANT GetAskToUpdateLinks();
void SetAskToUpdateLinks(const VARIANT&);
VARIANT GetBuild();
void SetBuild(const VARIANT&);
VARIANT GetCalculateBeforeSave();
void SetCalculateBeforeSave(const VARIANT&);
VARIANT GetCalculation();
void SetCalculation(const VARIANT&);
VARIANT GetCaller();
void SetCaller(const VARIANT&);
VARIANT GetCanPlaySounds();
void SetCanPlaySounds(const VARIANT&);
VARIANT GetCanRecordSounds();
void SetCanRecordSounds(const VARIANT&);
VARIANT GetCaption();
void SetCaption(const VARIANT&);
VARIANT GetCellDragAndDrop();
void SetCellDragAndDrop(const VARIANT&);
VARIANT GetClipboardFormats();
void SetClipboardFormats(const VARIANT&);
VARIANT GetColorButtons();
void SetColorButtons(const VARIANT&);
VARIANT GetCommandUnderlines();
void SetCommandUnderlines(const VARIANT&);
VARIANT GetConstrainNumeric();
void SetConstrainNumeric(const VARIANT&);
VARIANT GetCopyObjectsWithCells();
void SetCopyObjectsWithCells(const VARIANT&);
VARIANT GetCreator();
void SetCreator(const VARIANT&);
VARIANT GetCustomListCount();
void SetCustomListCount(const VARIANT&);
VARIANT GetCutCopyMode();
void SetCutCopyMode(const VARIANT&);
```

(continues)

Listing 15.4 Continued

```
VARIANT GetDataEntryMode();
void SetDataEntryMode(const VARIANT&);
VARIANT GetDDEAppReturnCode();
void SetDDEAppReturnCode(const VARIANT&);
VARIANT GetDefaultFilePath();
void SetDefaultFilePath(const VARIANT&);
VARIANT GetDisplayAlerts();
void SetDisplayAlerts(const VARIANT&);
VARIANT GetDisplayClipboardWindow();
void SetDisplayClipboardWindow(const VARIANT&);
VARIANT GetDisplayExcel4Menus();
void SetDisplayExcel4Menus(const VARIANT&);
VARIANT GetDisplayFormulaBar();
void SetDisplayFormulaBar(const VARIANT&);
VARIANT GetDisplayFullScreen();
void SetDisplayFullScreen(const VARIANT&);
VARIANT GetDisplayInfoWindow();
void SetDisplayInfoWindow(const VARIANT&);
VARIANT GetDisplayNoteIndicator();
void SetDisplayNoteIndicator(const VARIANT&);
VARIANT GetDisplayRecentFiles();
void SetDisplayRecentFiles(const VARIANT&);
VARIANT GetDisplayScrollBars();
void SetDisplayScrollBars(const VARIANT&);
VARIANT GetDisplayStatusBar();
void SetDisplayStatusBar(const VARIANT&);
VARIANT GetEditDirectlyInCell();
void SetEditDirectlyInCell(const VARIANT&);
VARIANT GetEnableCancelKey();
void SetEnableCancelKey(const VARIANT&);
VARIANT GetEnableTipWizard();
void SetEnableTipWizard(const VARIANT&);
VARIANT GetFileConverters();
void SetFileConverters(const VARIANT&);
VARIANT GetFixedDecimal();
void SetFixedDecimal(const VARIANT&);
VARIANT GetFixedDecimalPlaces();
void SetFixedDecimalPlaces(const VARIANT&);
VARIANT GetHeight();
void SetHeight(const VARIANT&);
VARIANT GetIgnoreRemoteRequests();
void SetIgnoreRemoteRequests(const VARIANT&);
VARIANT GetInteractive();
void SetInteractive(const VARIANT&);
VARIANT GetInternational();
void SetInternational(const VARIANT&);
VARIANT GetIteration();
void SetIteration(const VARIANT&);
VARIANT GetLargeButtons();
void SetLargeButtons(const VARIANT&);
VARIANT GetLeft();
void SetLeft(const VARIANT&);
VARIANT GetLibraryPath();
```

```
void SetLibraryPath(const VARIANT&);
VARIANT GetMailSession();
void SetMailSession(const VARIANT&);
VARIANT GetMailSystem();
void SetMailSystem(const VARIANT&);
VARIANT GetMathCoprocessorAvailable();
void SetMathCoprocessorAvailable(const VARIANT&);
VARIANT GetMaxChange();
void SetMaxChange(const VARIANT&);
VARIANT GetMaxIterations();
void SetMaxIterations(const VARIANT&);
VARIANT GetMemoryFree();
void SetMemoryFree(const VARIANT&);
VARIANT GetMemoryTotal();
void SetMemoryTotal(const VARIANT&);
VARIANT GetMemoryUsed();
void SetMemoryUsed(const VARIANT&);
VARIANT GetMouseAvailable();
void SetMouseAvailable(const VARIANT&);
VARIANT GetMoveAfterReturn();
void SetMoveAfterReturn(const VARIANT&);
VARIANT GetName();
void SetName(const VARIANT&);
VARIANT GetOnCalculate();
void SetOnCalculate(const VARIANT&);
VARIANT GetOnData();
void SetOnData(const VARIANT&);
VARIANT GetOnDoubleClick();
void SetOnDoubleClick(const VARIANT&);
VARIANT GetOnEntry();
void SetOnEntry(const VARIANT&);
VARIANT GetOnSheetActivate();
void SetOnSheetActivate(const VARIANT&);
VARIANT GetOnSheetDeactivate();
void SetOnSheetDeactivate(const VARIANT&);
VARIANT GetOnWindow();
void SetOnWindow(const VARIANT&);
VARIANT GetOperatingSystem();
void SetOperatingSystem(const VARIANT&);
VARIANT GetOrganizationName();
void SetOrganizationName(const VARIANT&);
VARIANT GetParent();
void SetParent(const VARIANT&);
VARIANT GetPath();
void SetPath(const VARIANT&);
VARIANT GetPathSeparator();
void SetPathSeparator(const VARIANT&);
VARIANT GetPreviousSelections();
void SetPreviousSelections(const VARIANT&);
VARIANT GetPromptForSummaryInfo();
void SetPromptForSummaryInfo(const VARIANT&);
VARIANT GetRecordRelative();
void SetRecordRelative(const VARIANT&);
VARIANT GetReferenceStyle();
void SetReferenceStyle(const VARIANT&);
```

(continues)

Listing 15.4 Continued

```
        VARIANT GetRegisteredFunctions();
        void SetRegisteredFunctions(const VARIANT&);
        VARIANT GetScreenUpdating();
        void SetScreenUpdating(const VARIANT&);
        VARIANT GetSelection();
        void SetSelection(const VARIANT&);
        VARIANT GetSheetsInNewWorkbook();
        void SetSheetsInNewWorkbook(const VARIANT&);
        VARIANT GetShowToolTips();
        void SetShowToolTips(const VARIANT&);
        VARIANT GetStandardFont();
        void SetStandardFont(const VARIANT&);
        VARIANT GetStandardFontSize();
        void SetStandardFontSize(const VARIANT&);
        VARIANT GetStartupPath();
        void SetStartupPath(const VARIANT&);
        VARIANT GetStatusBar();
        void SetStatusBar(const VARIANT&);
        VARIANT GetThisWorkbook();
        void SetThisWorkbook(const VARIANT&);
        VARIANT GetTop();
        void SetTop(const VARIANT&);
        VARIANT GetTransitionMenuKey();
        void SetTransitionMenuKey(const VARIANT&);
        VARIANT GetTransitionMenuKeyAction();
        void SetTransitionMenuKeyAction(const VARIANT&);
        VARIANT GetTransitionNavigKeys();
        void SetTransitionNavigKeys(const VARIANT&);
        VARIANT GetUsableHeight();
        void SetUsableHeight(const VARIANT&);
        VARIANT GetUsableWidth();
        void SetUsableWidth(const VARIANT&);
        VARIANT GetUserName();
        void SetUserName(const VARIANT&);
        VARIANT GetValue();
        void SetValue(const VARIANT&);
        VARIANT GetVersion();
        void SetVersion(const VARIANT&);
        VARIANT GetVisible();
        void SetVisible(const VARIANT&);
        VARIANT GetWidth();
        void SetWidth(const VARIANT&);
        VARIANT GetWindowsForPens();
        void SetWindowsForPens(const VARIANT&);
        VARIANT GetWindowState();
        void SetWindowState(const VARIANT&);

// Operations
public:
        VARIANT _WSFunction(const VARIANT& Range, const VARIANT& Arg1,
                            const VARIANT& Arg2, const VARIANT& Arg3,
                            const VARIANT& Arg4, const VARIANT& Arg5,
```

```
                    const VARIANT& Arg6, const VARIANT& Arg7,
                    const VARIANT& Arg8, const VARIANT& Arg9,
                    const VARIANT& Arg10, const VARIANT& Arg11,
                    const VARIANT& Arg12, const VARIANT& Arg13,
                    const VARIANT& Arg14, const VARIANT& Arg15,
                    const VARIANT& Arg16, const VARIANT& Arg17,
                    const VARIANT& Arg18, const VARIANT& Arg19,
                    const VARIANT& Arg20, const VARIANT& Arg21,
                    const VARIANT& Arg22, const VARIANT& Arg23,
                    const VARIANT& Arg24, const VARIANT& Arg25,
                    const VARIANT& Arg26, const VARIANT& Arg27,
                    const VARIANT& Arg28, const VARIANT& Arg29,
                    const VARIANT& Arg30);
VARIANT Acos();
VARIANT Acosh();
VARIANT ActivateMicrosoftApp(const VARIANT& Index);
VARIANT AddChartAutoFormat(const VARIANT& Chart,
                           const VARIANT& Name,
                           const VARIANT& Description);
VARIANT AddCustomList(const VARIANT& ListArray,
                      const VARIANT& ByRow);
VARIANT AddIns(const VARIANT& Index);
VARIANT And();
VARIANT Application_();
VARIANT Asin();
VARIANT Asinh();
VARIANT Atan2();
VARIANT Atanh();
VARIANT AveDev();
VARIANT Average();
VARIANT BetaDist();
VARIANT BetaInv();
VARIANT BinomDist();
VARIANT Calculate();
VARIANT Ceiling();
VARIANT Cells(const VARIANT& RowIndex, const VARIANT& ColumnIndex);
VARIANT CentimetersToPoints(const VARIANT& Centimeters);
VARIANT Charts(const VARIANT& Index);
VARIANT CheckSpelling(const VARIANT& Word,
                      const VARIANT& CustomDictionary,
                      const VARIANT& IgnoreUppercase);
VARIANT ChiDist();
VARIANT ChiInv();
VARIANT ChiTest();
VARIANT Choose();
VARIANT Clean();
VARIANT Columns(const VARIANT& Index);
VARIANT Combin();
VARIANT Confidence();
VARIANT ConvertFormula(const VARIANT& Formula,
                       const VARIANT& FromReferenceStyle,
                       const VARIANT& ToReferenceStyle,
                       const VARIANT& ToAbsolute,
                       const VARIANT& RelativeTo);
```

(continues)

Listing 15.4 Continued

```
VARIANT Correl();
VARIANT Cosh();
VARIANT Count();
VARIANT CountA();
VARIANT CountBlank();
VARIANT CountIf();
VARIANT Covar();
VARIANT CritBinom();
VARIANT DAverage();
VARIANT Days360();
VARIANT Db();
VARIANT DCount();
VARIANT DCountA();
VARIANT Ddb();
VARIANT DDEExecute(const VARIANT& Channel, const VARIANT& String);
VARIANT DDEInitiate(const VARIANT& App, const VARIANT& Topic);
VARIANT DDEPoke(const VARIANT& Channel, const VARIANT& Item,
                const VARIANT& Data);
VARIANT DDERequest(const VARIANT& Channel, const VARIANT& Item);
VARIANT DDETerminate(const VARIANT& Channel);
VARIANT Degrees();
VARIANT DeleteChartAutoFormat(const VARIANT& Name);
VARIANT DeleteCustomList(const VARIANT& ListNum);
VARIANT DevSq();
VARIANT DGet();
VARIANT Dialogs(const VARIANT& Index);
VARIANT DialogSheets(const VARIANT& Index);
VARIANT DMax();
VARIANT DMin();
VARIANT Dollar();
VARIANT DoubleClick();
VARIANT DProduct();
VARIANT DStdDev();
VARIANT DStdDevP();
VARIANT DSum();
VARIANT DVar();
VARIANT DVarP();
VARIANT _Evaluate(const VARIANT& Name);
VARIANT Evaluate(const VARIANT& Name);
VARIANT Even();
VARIANT Excel4IntlMacroSheets(const VARIANT& Index);
VARIANT Excel4MacroSheets(const VARIANT& Index);
VARIANT ExecuteExcel4Macro(const VARIANT& String);
VARIANT ExponDist();
VARIANT Fact();
VARIANT FDist();
VARIANT Find();
VARIANT FindB();
VARIANT FindFile();
```

```
VARIANT FInv();
VARIANT Fisher();
VARIANT FisherInv();
VARIANT Fixed();
VARIANT Floor();
VARIANT Forecast();
VARIANT Frequency();
VARIANT FTest();
VARIANT Fv();
VARIANT GammaDist();
VARIANT GammaInv();
VARIANT GammaLn();
VARIANT GeoMean();
VARIANT GetCustomListContents(const VARIANT& ListNum);
VARIANT GetCustomListNum(const VARIANT& ListArray);
VARIANT GetOpenFilename(const VARIANT& FileFilter,
                        const VARIANT& FilterIndex, const NT& Title,
                        const VARIANT& ButtonText);
VARIANT GetSaveAsFilename(const VARIANT& InitialFilename,
                          const VARIANT& FileFilter,
                          const VARIANT& FilterIndex,
                          const VARIANT& Title,
                          const VARIANT& ButtonText);
VARIANT Goto(const VARIANT& Reference, const VARIANT& Scroll);
VARIANT Growth();
VARIANT HarMean();
VARIANT Help(const VARIANT& HelpFile, const VARIANT& HelpContextID);
VARIANT HLookup();
VARIANT HypGeomDist();
VARIANT InchesToPoints(const VARIANT& Inches);
VARIANT Index();
VARIANT InputBox(const VARIANT& Prompt, const VARIANT& Title,
                 const VARIANT& Default, const VARIANT& Left,
                 const VARIANT& Top, const VARIANT& HelpFile,
                 const VARIANT& HelpContextID, const VARIANT& Type);
VARIANT Intercept();
VARIANT Intersect(const VARIANT& Arg1, const VARIANT& Arg2,
                  const VARIANT& Arg3, const VARIANT& Arg4,
                  const VARIANT& Arg5, const VARIANT& Arg6,
                  const VARIANT& Arg7, const VARIANT& Arg8,
                  const VARIANT& Arg9, const VARIANT& Arg10,
                  const VARIANT& Arg11, const VARIANT& Arg12,
                  const VARIANT& Arg13, const VARIANT& Arg14,
                  const VARIANT& Arg15, const VARIANT& Arg16,
                  const VARIANT& Arg17, const VARIANT& Arg18,
                  const VARIANT& Arg19, const VARIANT& Arg20,
                  const VARIANT& Arg21, const VARIANT& Arg22,
                  const VARIANT& Arg23, const VARIANT& Arg24,
                  const VARIANT& Arg25, const VARIANT& Arg26,
                  const VARIANT& Arg27, const VARIANT& Arg28,
                  const VARIANT& Arg29, const VARIANT& Arg30,
                  const VARIANT& Arg31);
```

(continues)

Listing 15.4 Continued

```
        VARIANT Ipmt();
        VARIANT Irr();
        VARIANT IsErr();
        VARIANT IsError();
        VARIANT IsLogical();
        VARIANT IsNA();
        VARIANT IsNonText();
        VARIANT IsNumber();
        VARIANT Ispmt();
        VARIANT IsText();
        VARIANT Kurt();
        VARIANT Large();
        VARIANT LinEst();
        VARIANT Ln();
        VARIANT Log();
        VARIANT Log10();
        VARIANT LogEst();
        VARIANT LogInv();
        VARIANT LogNormDist();
        VARIANT Lookup();
        VARIANT MacroOptions(const VARIANT& Macro,
                             const VARIANT& Description,
                             const VARIANT& HasMenu,
                             const VARIANT& MenuText,
                             const VARIANT& HasShortcutKey,
                             const VARIANT& ShortcutKey,
                             const VARIANT& Category,
                             const VARIANT& StatusBar,
                             const VARIANT& HelpContextID,
                             const VARIANT& HelpFile);
        VARIANT MailLogoff();
        VARIANT MailLogon(const VARIANT& Name,
             const VARIANT& Password, const VARIANT& DownloadNewMail);
        VARIANT Match();
        VARIANT Max();
        VARIANT MDeterm();
        VARIANT Median();
        VARIANT MenuBars(const VARIANT& Index);
        VARIANT Min();
        VARIANT MInverse();
        VARIANT MIrr();
        VARIANT MMult();
        VARIANT Mode();
        VARIANT Modules(const VARIANT& Index);
        VARIANT Names(const VARIANT& Index, const VARIANT& IndexLocal,
                 const VARIANT& RefersTo);
        VARIANT NegBinomDist();
        VARIANT NextLetter();
        VARIANT NormDist();
        VARIANT NormInv();
```

```
VARIANT NormSDist();
VARIANT NormSInv();
VARIANT NPer();
VARIANT Npv();
VARIANT Odd();
VARIANT OnKey(const VARIANT& Key, const VARIANT& Procedure);
VARIANT OnRepeat(const VARIANT& Text, const VARIANT& Procedure);
VARIANT OnTime(const VARIANT& EarliestTime,
        const VARIANT& Procedure, const VARIANT& LatestTime,
        const VARIANT& Schedule);
VARIANT OnUndo(const VARIANT& Text, const VARIANT& Procedure);
VARIANT Or();
VARIANT Pearson();
VARIANT Percentile();
VARIANT PercentRank();
VARIANT Permut();
VARIANT Pi();
VARIANT Pmt();
VARIANT Poisson();
VARIANT Power();
VARIANT Ppmt();
VARIANT Prob();
VARIANT Product();
VARIANT Proper();
VARIANT Pv();
VARIANT Quartile();
VARIANT Quit();
VARIANT Radians();
VARIANT Range(const VARIANT& Cell1, const VARIANT& Cell2);
VARIANT Rank();
VARIANT Rate();
VARIANT RecordMacro(const VARIANT& BasicCode,
                    const VARIANT& XlmCode);
VARIANT RegisterXLL(const VARIANT& Filename);
VARIANT Repeat();
VARIANT Replace();
VARIANT ReplaceB();
VARIANT Rept();
VARIANT ResetTipWizard();
VARIANT Roman();
VARIANT Round();
VARIANT RoundDown();
VARIANT RoundUp();
VARIANT Rows(const VARIANT& Index);
VARIANT RSq();
VARIANT Run(const VARIANT& Macro, const VARIANT& Arg1,
        const VARIANT& Arg2, const VARIANT& Arg3,
        const VARIANT& Arg4, const VARIANT& Arg5,
        const VARIANT& Arg6, const VARIANT& Arg7,
        const VARIANT& Arg8, const VARIANT& Arg9,
        const VARIANT& Arg10, const VARIANT& Arg11,
```

(continues)

Listing 15.4 Continued

```
                 const VARIANT& Arg12, const VARIANT& Arg13,
                 const VARIANT& Arg14, const VARIANT& Arg15,
                 const VARIANT& Arg16, const VARIANT& Arg17,
                 const VARIANT& Arg18, const VARIANT& Arg19,
                 const VARIANT& Arg20, const VARIANT& Arg21,
                 const VARIANT& Arg22, const VARIANT& Arg23,
                 const VARIANT& Arg24, const VARIANT& Arg25,
                 const VARIANT& Arg26, const VARIANT& Arg27,
                 const VARIANT& Arg28, const VARIANT& Arg29,
                 const VARIANT& Arg30);
        VARIANT Save(const VARIANT& Filename);
        VARIANT Search();
        VARIANT SearchB();
        VARIANT SendKeys(const VARIANT& Keys, const VARIANT& Wait);
        VARIANT SetDefaultChart(const VARIANT& FormatName);
        VARIANT Sheets(const VARIANT& Index);
        VARIANT ShortcutMenus(const VARIANT& Index);
        VARIANT Sinh();
        VARIANT Skew();
        VARIANT Sln();
        VARIANT Slope();
        VARIANT Small();
        VARIANT Standardize();
        VARIANT StDev();
        VARIANT StDevP();
        VARIANT StEyx();
        VARIANT Substitute();
        VARIANT Subtotal();
        VARIANT Sum();
        VARIANT SumIf();
        VARIANT SumProduct();
        VARIANT SumSq();
        VARIANT SumX2MY2();
        VARIANT SumX2PY2();
        VARIANT SumXMY2();
        VARIANT Syd();
        VARIANT Tanh();
        VARIANT TDist();
        VARIANT Text();
        VARIANT TInv();
        VARIANT Toolbars(const VARIANT& Index);
        VARIANT Transpose();
        VARIANT Trend();
        VARIANT Trim();
        VARIANT TrimMean();
        VARIANT TTest();
        VARIANT Undo();
```

```
    VARIANT Union(const VARIANT& Arg1, const VARIANT& Arg2,
                  const VARIANT& Arg3, const VARIANT& Arg4,
                  const VARIANT& Arg5, const VARIANT& Arg6,
                  const VARIANT& Arg7, const VARIANT& Arg8,
                  const VARIANT& Arg9, const VARIANT& Arg10,
                  const VARIANT& Arg11, const VARIANT& Arg12,
                  const VARIANT& Arg13, const VARIANT& Arg14,
                  const VARIANT& Arg15, const VARIANT& Arg16,
                  const VARIANT& Arg17, const VARIANT& Arg18,
                  const VARIANT& Arg19, const VARIANT& Arg20,
                  const VARIANT& Arg21, const VARIANT& Arg22,
                  const VARIANT& Arg23, const VARIANT& Arg24,
                  const VARIANT& Arg25, const VARIANT& Arg26,
                  const VARIANT& Arg27, const VARIANT& Arg28,
                  const VARIANT& Arg29, const VARIANT& Arg30,
                  const VARIANT& Arg31);
    VARIANT USDollar();
    VARIANT Var();
    VARIANT VarP();
    VARIANT Vdb();
    VARIANT VLookup();
    VARIANT Volatile(const VARIANT& Volatile);
    VARIANT Wait(const VARIANT& Time);
    VARIANT Weekday();
    VARIANT Weibull();
    VARIANT Windows(const VARIANT& Index);
    LPDISPATCH Workbooks(const VARIANT& Index);
    LPDISPATCH Worksheets(const VARIANT& Index);
    VARIANT ZTest();
};
```

When Excel first starts, it is invisible. Therefore, the first property that you set is the `Visible` property. You set this property by calling the `SetVisible` method with the parameter set to true. To pass the parameter, you must first pack it into a VARIANT.

In the `OnStart` method, you first initialize VARIANT by calling `VariantInit(&v)` with the address of the VARIANT variable. The argument for `SetVisible` is a Boolean data type. You set the VARIANT type to VT_BOOL and the value to true.

Listing 15.5 shows the complete source code for your `CView` module. The `CView` code for controlling Excel uses the code generated from the type library.

Listing 15.5 EXCEL.H and EXCEL.CPP

```
//////////////////////////////////////////////////////////////////////////////
// CExcel form view
//
#ifndef __AFXEXT_H__
#include <afxext.h>
#endif

#include "xlen50.h"

class CExcel : public CFormView
{
     DECLARE_DYNCREATE(CExcel)
protected:
     CExcel();

// Form Data
public:
     //{{AFX_DATA(CExcel)
     enum { IDD = IDD_DIALOG1 };
     CButton     m_createws;
     CButton     m_ok;
     CButton     m_cancel;
     CButton     m_stop;
     CButton     m_start;
     CString     m_wsname;
     //}}AFX_DATA

// Attributes
public:
     Application m_ExcelApp;
     Workbooks m_ExcelWorkBooks;

     BOOL m_fOK;
// Operations
public:
     void OnInitialUpdate();
// Implementation
protected:
     virtual ~CExcel();
     virtual void DoDataExchange(CDataExchange* pDX);
     // Generated message map functions
     //{{AFX_MSG(CExcel)
     afx_msg void OnStart();
     afx_msg void OnStop();
     virtual void OnCancel();
     virtual void OnOK();
     afx_msg void OnCreateWS();
     afx_msg void OnChangeWSname();
     //}}AFX_MSG
     DECLARE_MESSAGE_MAP()
```

```
    // Generated OLE dispatch map functions
    //{{AFX_DISPATCH(CExcel)
    // NOTE - ClassWizard adds and removes member functions here.
    //}}AFX_DISPATCH
    DECLARE_DISPATCH_MAP()
};

/////////////////////////////////////////////////////////////////////////////

#include "stdafx.h"
#include "xclient.h"
#include "excel.h"
#include "ctl3d.h"

#ifdef _DEBUG
#undef THIS_FILE
static char BASED_CODE THIS_FILE[] = __FILE__;
#endif

/////////////////////////////////////////////////////////////////////////////
// CExcel
//
IMPLEMENT_DYNCREATE(CExcel, CFormView)

CExcel::CExcel()
    : CFormView(CExcel::IDD)
{
    EnableAutomation();

    //{{AFX_DATA_INIT(CExcel)
    m_wsname = "";
    //}}AFX_DATA_INIT

}
//-----------------------------------------------------------------
CExcel::~CExcel()
{
}
//-----------------------------------------------------------------
void CExcel::DoDataExchange(CDataExchange* pDX)
{
    CFormView::DoDataExchange(pDX);
    //{{AFX_DATA_MAP(CExcel)
    DDX_Control(pDX, IDC_CREATEWS, m_createws);
    DDX_Control(pDX, IDOK, m_ok);
    DDX_Control(pDX, IDCANCEL, m_cancel);
    DDX_Control(pDX, IDC_STOP, m_stop);
    DDX_Control(pDX, IDC_START, m_start);
    DDX_Text(pDX, IDC_WHNAME, m_wsname);
    //}}AFX_DATA_MAP
}
//-----------------------------------------------------------------
```

(continues)

Listing 15.5 Continued

```
BEGIN_MESSAGE_MAP(CExcel, CFormView)
     //{{AFX_MSG_MAP(CExcel)
     ON_BN_CLICKED(IDC_START, OnStart)
     ON_BN_CLICKED(IDC_STOP, OnStop)
     ON_BN_CLICKED(IDC_CREATEWS, OnCreateWS)
     ON_EN_CHANGE(IDC_WHNAME, OnChangeWSname)
     //}}AFX_MSG_MAP
END_MESSAGE_MAP()

BEGIN_DISPATCH_MAP(CExcel, CFormView)
     //{{AFX_DISPATCH_MAP(CExcel)
          // NOTE - ClassWizard adds and removes mapping macros here.
     //}}AFX_DISPATCH_MAP
END_DISPATCH_MAP()

//-----------------------------------------------------------------
void CExcel::OnInitialUpdate()
{
     Ctl3dSubclassDlg(m_hWnd,CTL3D_ALL);

     CFormView::OnInitialUpdate();
     GetParentFrame()->RecalcLayout();
     ResizeParentToFit(FALSE);
     // Default argument is TRUE
     ResizeParentToFit(/*FALSE*/);

     CButton *b = (CButton *)GetDlgItem(IDC_CREATEWS);
     b->EnableWindow(FALSE);

}
//-----------------------------------------------------------------

/////////////////////////////////////////////////////////////////////
// CExcel message handlers
void CExcel::OnStart()
{

    CLSID clsid;
    LPUNKNOWN pUnk = NULL;
    LPDISPATCH pDisp = NULL;
    VARIANT v;

    m_fOK = TRUE;
    VariantInit(&v);
    //----
    // Check whether Excel is already running.
     if (S_OK == CLSIDFromProgID("Excel.Application",&clsid))
     {
          if (S_OK == GetActiveObject((const CLSID &)clsid, NULL,
              &pUnk))
          {
```

```
                if (NOERROR == pUnk->QueryInterface(IID_IDispatch,
                   (LPVOID FAR *)&pDisp))
                {
                  m_ExcelApp.m_lpDispatch = (LPDISPATCH)pDisp;
#ifdef _DEBUG
                  AfxMessageBox("Excel was running. IDispatch
                                  retrieved");
#endif
                }
                else
                {
#ifdef _DEBUG
                  AfxMessageBox(    "Error: Unable to retrieve
                                  the IDispatch pointer from Excel");
#endif
                  m_fOK = FALSE;
                }

                return;
            }

      }

      COleException e;
      if (!m_ExcelApp.CreateDispatch("Excel.Application.5", &e))
      {
           AfxMessageBox("Unable to Create Dispatch Object");
           return;
      }

      V_VT(&v) = VT_BOOL;
      V_BOOL(&v) = TRUE;
      m_ExcelApp.SetVisible(v);

      //----
      // Set Excel to display large buttons.
      m_ExcelApp.SetLargeButtons(v);

      //----
      // Change the caption.
      CString s = "Using OLE 2.x in Application Development";
      V_VT(&v) = VT_BSTR;
      V_BSTR(&v) = s.AllocSysString();

      m_ExcelApp.SetCaption(v);

      VariantClear(&v);
}
//------------------------------------------------------------
```

(continues)

Listing 15.5 Continued

```
void CExcel::OnStop()
{
     //------
     // Shut down Excel
     if (m_ExcelApp.m_lpDispatch != NULL)
     {
          m_ExcelApp.Quit();
     }


     //----
     // Release the dispatch pointer.
     if (m_ExcelApp.m_lpDispatch != NULL)
     {
          m_ExcelApp.ReleaseDispatch();
          m_ExcelApp.m_lpDispatch = NULL;
     }

}
//-------------------------------------------------------------------
void CExcel::OnCancel()
{
}
//-------------------------------------------------------------------
void CExcel::OnOK()
{
}
//-------------------------------------------------------------------
void CExcel::OnCreateWS()
{
    VARIANT v;
    VARIANT vDummy;
    VARIANT vIndex;
    LPDISPATCH pDisp;
    LPDISPATCH pDispWorkBook;

    VariantInit(&v);
    VariantInit(&vDummy);
    VariantInit(&vIndex);

    //----
    // Pass for empty arguments
    V_VT(&vDummy) = VT_ERROR;
    V_ERROR(&vDummy) = DISP_E_PARAMNOTFOUND;


     TRY
     {
          V_VT(&vIndex) = VT_I2;
```

```
            V_I2(&vIndex) = 0;

            pDisp =     m_ExcelApp.Workbooks(vIndex);
            m_ExcelWorkBooks.AttachDispatch(pDisp);
        }
        CATCH(COleDispatchException,e)
        {
            AfxMessageBox("Error: Unable to initialize WorkBook member");
            return;
        }
        END_CATCH

        V_VT(&v) = VT_BSTR;
        V_BSTR(&v) = m_wsname.AllocSysString();


        TRY
        {
            pDispWorkBook = m_ExcelWorkBooks.Open(v, vDummy, vDummy,
                vDummy, vDummy, vDummy, vDummy, vDummy, vDummy,
                vDummy, vDummy, vDummy);
        }
        CATCH(COleDispatchException,e)
        {
            AfxMessageBox(
                      "Error: Unable to open WorkBook. Creating a new
                       one");
            pDispWorkBook = m_ExcelWorkBooks.Add(vDummy);

        }
        END_CATCH

        pDispWorkBook->Release();

        VariantClear(&v);
        VariantClear(&vDummy);
}
//-------------------------------------------------------------
void CExcel::OnChangeWSname()
{
        CEdit *e = (CEdit *) GetDlgItem(IDC_WHNAME);
        CButton *b = (CButton *)GetDlgItem(IDC_CREATEWS);

        if(0 == e->LineLength())
            b->EnableWindow(FALSE);
        else
            b->EnableWindow(TRUE);

}
//-------------------------------------------------------------
//-------------------------------------------------------------
```

Once Excel is visible, you ask Excel to display large buttons in its toolbars. To do so, you set the `largebuttons` property with the call to `SetLargeButtons`. Again, this method takes a Boolean as a parameter, so you reuse the VARIANT from the previous call.

Finally, you set the caption to the title of this book by calling `SetCaption`. This property takes a BSTR as its parameter type. You use the `CString::AllocSysString` to return a BSTR type from a `CString` object.

Shutting down Excel is simply a matter of calling the `Quit` method. After you call this method, you release the `IDispatch` pointer by calling `Release`.

Now that Excel is up and running, you need to create a workbook. The `Application` object has a collection object that enumerates or creates new workbooks. As you can see in figure 15.4, the `Application` object contains a collection of workbooks. Each workbook in turn contains collections of worksheets.

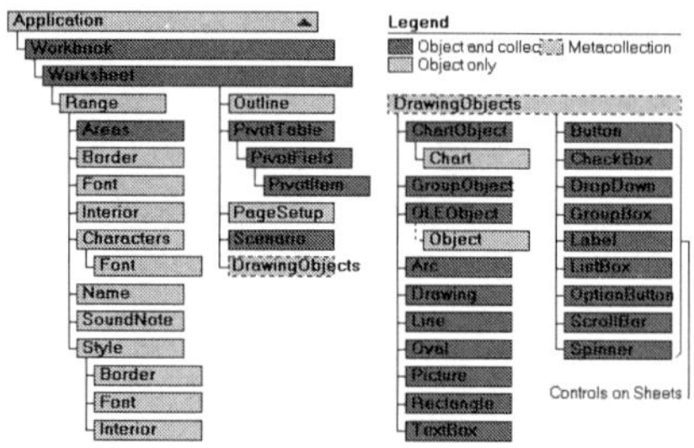

Fig. 15.4
The Excel *Workbook* object.

To access the `Workbooks` collection, you access the `Workbooks` property to get an `IDispatch` pointer. You then use this `IDispatch` pointer to initialize the `m_ExcelWorkbooks` member variable. Notice that the call to `m_ExcelApp.Workbooks` returns an `IDispatch` pointer. In the original code, generated by the ClassWizard from the Excel type library, this method returned a VARIANT. You change the generated code to return a straight `IDispatch` pointer.

With the newly initialized member, `m_ExcelWorkbooks`, you can now open an existing workbook or create a new one.

As you can see, accessing Excel's methods and properties is quite simple. If you have a pointer to an object, you can access the members directly. If the object that you want to access is contained by an object, you must retrieve an `IDispatch` pointer before accessing it. Each object can always return an `IDispatch` pointer to the main `Application` class, so returning to base is simply a matter of retrieving from the object the `Application IDispatch` pointer.

Using the techniques presented in this section, you can create just about any type of custom application with Excel. In fact, if not for the additional effort required to use VARIANTs, it is almost as if you have access to a class library that fully implements the functionality of Excel. This is what programmable objects and component software are all about. Currently, the only drawback to this application is the amount of resources required to start Excel each time you want to use a particular function. In the future, when major software applications such as Excel ship with each object coded as a separate in-process or EXE server, you will no longer need this overhead.

Running the Application

Figure 15.5 shows the test application up and running. Notice the caption in Excel and the large buttons on the toolbar. The figure shows the screen just after you create the workbook.

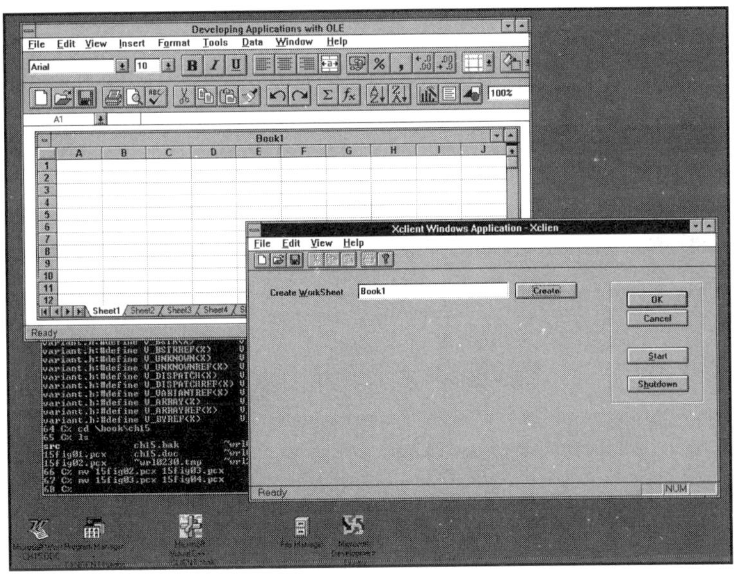

Fig. 15.5
The test application.

From Here...

In this chapter, you have used MFC to control an OLE Automation server. The process is pretty straightforward when you have the support of a type library. However, because of the Excel library's use of VARIANTs, you had to make some changes to the generated code.

In the next chapter, you turn the tables and use MFC to create an OLE Automation server that Visual Basic can control.

Chapter 16

An MFC Automation Server

In this chapter, you develop a Microsoft Foundation Classes (MFC) Windows application that you can control through OLE Automation. As you develop the application, you also learn how to do the following:

- Use the ClassWizard to add Automation support to the application
- Use MFC to expose methods and properties
- Implement a simple collection object that demonstrates what is required to expose a collection of objects through Automation
- Implement OLE interfaces that are not directly supported by the framework
- Write a script that uses DISPTEST to drive the server

The Test Application

The sample application that you develop in this chapter enables the user to perform three actions:

- Draw on the screen a shape that the user can move and size
- Choose one of four shapes: a square, a circle, a rectangle, or a rounded rectangle
- Change the current shape's color

The user can perform each of these actions with a mouse. However, the application also enables an Automation controller to control these actions. As you will see, adding Automation support to an MFC application requires very little effort.

The Initialization Code

You begin by using the AppWizard to generate the skeleton code. To add the initial Automation support, you select the **A**utomation Support check box in the OLE Options dialog box.

The AppWizard first generates a CLSID by calling `CoCreateGUID`. (Chapter 2, "The Component Object Model," discusses CLSIDs in detail.) The Automation controllers use this CLSID to refer to the application.

The `InitApp` method first calls `AfxOleInit` to initialize the OLE libraries and ensure that you are running against the correct version of the libraries. You then connect the document template to the application's class factory implementation.

The command line is parsed to see whether the application was executed with the `/Automation` switch. If so, you register the object in the running object table (ROT) and return. This action effectively starts the application, even though its main window remains hidden. This behavior is required for applications such as spell checkers that implement "hidden" objects. However, if your application must display its main window, you have two choices: you can implement a `DisplayWindow` method and expose it through Automation, or you can create and display your main window before you return.

Finally, the AppWizard generates code to register the application in the system registry. Most programs let their installation program register their OLE objects for them. However, the registration database can be corrupted or deleted. You shouldn't burden your user with having to merge registration files into the registry. Instead, you should always update the registry from within your application when it starts up. Incurring this small piece of overhead when your application loads more than pays for itself in reduced support calls.

Listing 16.1 shows the code for the implementation of the `CWinApp` derived object.

Listing 16.1 AUTOMFC.CPP

```
#include "stdafx.h"
#include "automfc.h"

#include "mainfrm.h"
#include "automdoc.h"
#include "automvw.h"

#ifdef _DEBUG
#undef THIS_FILE
static char BASED_CODE THIS_FILE[] = __FILE__;
#endif

/////////////////////////////////////////////////////////////////////////////
// CAutoApp
BEGIN_MESSAGE_MAP(CAutoApp, CWinApp)
     //{{AFX_MSG_MAP(CAutoApp)
     ON_COMMAND(ID_APP_ABOUT, OnAppAbout)
     //}}AFX_MSG_MAP
     // Standard file-based document commands
     ON_COMMAND(ID_FILE_NEW, CWinApp::OnFileNew)
     ON_COMMAND(ID_FILE_OPEN, CWinApp::OnFileOpen)
END_MESSAGE_MAP()

/////////////////////////////////////////////////////////////////////////////
// CAutoApp construction
CAutoApp::CAutoApp()
{
}
/////////////////////////////////////////////////////////////////////////////
// The one and only CAutoApp object
CAutoApp NEAR theApp;

// This identifier is generated to be statistically unique for your app.
// You can change it if you prefer to choose a specific identifier.
static const CLSID BASED_CODE clsid =
{ 0x83a3f4a1, 0x5fb4, 0x101b, { 0x99, 0x48, 0x7e, 0xf9, 0xe6, 0xaf, \
  0x22, 0x43 } };
/////////////////////////////////////////////////////////////////////////////
// CAutoApp initialization
BOOL CAutoApp::InitInstance()
{
     // Initialize OLE 2.0 libraries
     if (!AfxOleInit())
     {
          AfxMessageBox(IDP_OLE_INIT_FAILED);
          return FALSE;
     }

     //  Register the application's document templates.
     //  Document templates serve as the connection between
     //  documents, frame windows, and views.
```

(continues)

III

OLE Automation

Listing 16.1 Continued

```
        CSingleDocTemplate* pDocTemplate;
        pDocTemplate = new CSingleDocTemplate(
             IDR_MAINFRAME,
             RUNTIME_CLASS(CAutoDoc),
             RUNTIME_CLASS(CMainFrame),      // main SDI frame window
             RUNTIME_CLASS(CAutoView));
        AddDocTemplate(pDocTemplate);

        //  Connect the COleTemplateServer to the document template.
        //  The COleTemplateServer creates new documents on behalf
        //  of the requesting OLE containers by using information
        //  specified in the document template.
        m_server.ConnectTemplate(clsid, pDocTemplate, TRUE);

        if (RunEmbedded() || RunAutomated())
        {
             // Register all OLE server (factories) as running.
             //  This enables the OLE 2.0 libraries to create objects
             //  from other applications.
             COleTemplateServer::RegisterAll();

             // The fact that you return TRUE here means that the main
             // window is not opened. Therefore, the Automation client
             // must call a method to open it; also, the application
             // must implement such a method.
             return TRUE;
        }

        // When a server application is launched stand-alone, you should
        // update the system registry in case it has been damaged.
        m_server.UpdateRegistry(OAT_DISPATCH_OBJECT);
        COleObjectFactory::UpdateRegistryAll();

        if (m_lpCmdLine[0] == '\0')
        {
             OnFileNew();
        }
        else
        {
             OpenDocumentFile(m_lpCmdLine);
        }

        return TRUE;
}
////////////////////////////////////////////////////////////////////////////
// CAboutDlg dialog used for App About
class CAboutDlg : public CDialog
{
public:
        CAboutDlg();

        //{{AFX_DATA(CAboutDlg)
        enum { IDD = IDD_ABOUTBOX };
        //}}AFX_DATA
```

```
// Implementation
protected:
     virtual void DoDataExchange(CDataExchange* pDX);  // DDX/DDV support
     //{{AFX_MSG(CAboutDlg)
          // No message handlers
     //}}AFX_MSG
     DECLARE_MESSAGE_MAP()
};
//------------------------------------------------------------
CAboutDlg::CAboutDlg() : CDialog(CAboutDlg::IDD)
{
     //{{AFX_DATA_INIT(CAboutDlg)
     //}}AFX_DATA_INIT
}
//------------------------------------------------------------
void CAboutDlg::DoDataExchange(CDataExchange* pDX)
{
     CDialog::DoDataExchange(pDX);
     //{{AFX_DATA_MAP(CAboutDlg)
     //}}AFX_DATA_MAP
}
//------------------------------------------------------------
BEGIN_MESSAGE_MAP(CAboutDlg, CDialog)
     //{{AFX_MSG_MAP(CAboutDlg)
          // No message handlers
     //}}AFX_MSG_MAP
END_MESSAGE_MAP()
//------------------------------------------------------------
void CAutoApp::OnAppAbout()
{
     CAboutDlg aboutDlg;
     aboutDlg.DoModal();
}
//------------------------------------------------------------
//------------------------------------------------------------
```

The View Class

The View class implementation consists of pretty standard MFC stuff. You begin by setting up the command-routing maps for the command handlers.

In the View class' constructor, you initialize the tracker rectangle. The `CRectTracker` class is one of the gems of the MFC framework. Although originally intended to be used to support embedded OLE objects, `CRectTracker` can actually be used to frame any object. The tracker rectangle enables you to move and resize any object. A set of sizing handles automatically appears and handles all of the user's sizing interaction. You have complete control over the object's border, the size of the sizing handles, and their placement inside, outside, or on the border. You also can overlay the object with a hatched pattern, as described in the OLE UI guidelines. In the sample application, you use the tracker to enable the user to move and resize the current shape.

The rest of the code in this module displays the currently selected shape and changes the shape and the default color.

The `OnDraw` method draws the currently selected shape using the size of the tracker rectangle and the currently selected fill color.

Each of the toolbar and menu command handlers updates the relevant data member in the Document class and calls the document method, `RefreshWindow`. You write the code this way because these methods are also exposed through Automation. You are exposing the Automation methods in the Document class; therefore, instead of duplicating the code in both the View and Document class, you simply place it in the Document class.

Listing 16.2 shows the definition of the View class and its implementation.

Listing 16.2 AUTOMVW.H

```
//-----------------------------------------------------------//

class CAutoView : public CView
{
protected:
      CAutoView();
      DECLARE_DYNCREATE(CAutoView)

// Attributes
      CBrush m_bkBrush;
      CRectTracker m_tracker;
      BOOL m_ViewCircle;
      BOOL m_ViewSquare;
      BOOL m_ViewRectangle;
      BOOL m_ViewRRectangle;
public:
      CAutoDoc* GetDocument();


// Operations
public:

// Implementation
public:
      virtual ~CAutoView();
      virtual void OnDraw(CDC* pDC);  // overridden to draw this view
#ifdef _DEBUG
      virtual void AssertValid() const;
      virtual void Dump(CDumpContext& dc) const;
#endif

protected:
```

```
// Generated message map functions
protected:
      //{{AFX_MSG(CAutoView)
      afx_msg void OnViewCircle();
      afx_msg void OnViewRectangle();
      afx_msg void OnViewSquare();
      afx_msg void OnViewRoundedrectangle();
      afx_msg void OnEditColor();
      afx_msg void OnUpdateEditColor(CCmdUI* pCmdUI);
      afx_msg void OnLButtonDown(UINT nFlags, CPoint point);
      afx_msg BOOL OnSetCursor(CWnd* pWnd, UINT nHitTest, UINT message);
      //}}AFX_MSG
      DECLARE_MESSAGE_MAP()
};

#ifndef _DEBUG  // debug version in automvw.cpp
inline CAutoDoc* CAutoView::GetDocument()
   { return (CAutoDoc*)m_pDocument; }
#endif

/////////////////////////////////////////////////////////////////////

#include "stdafx.h"
#include "automfc.h"

#include "automdoc.h"
#include "automvw.h"

#ifdef _DEBUG
#undef THIS_FILE
static char BASED_CODE THIS_FILE[] = __FILE__;
#endif

/////////////////////////////////////////////////////////////////////
// CAutoView
IMPLEMENT_DYNCREATE(CAutoView, CView)

BEGIN_MESSAGE_MAP(CAutoView, CView)
      //{{AFX_MSG_MAP(CAutoView)
      ON_COMMAND(ID_VIEW_CIRCLE, OnViewCircle)
      ON_COMMAND(ID_VIEW_RECTANGLE, OnViewRectangle)
      ON_COMMAND(ID_VIEW_SQUARE, OnViewSquare)
      ON_COMMAND(ID_VIEW_ROUNDEDRECTANGLE, OnViewRoundedrectangle)
      ON_COMMAND(ID_EDIT_COLOR, OnEditColor)
      ON_UPDATE_COMMAND_UI(ID_EDIT_COLOR, OnUpdateEditColor)
      ON_WM_LBUTTONDOWN()
      ON_WM_SETCURSOR()
      //}}AFX_MSG_MAP
END_MESSAGE_MAP()
```

(continues)

Listing 16.2 Continued

```
//////////////////////////////////////////////////////////////////////
// CAutoView construction/destruction
CAutoView::CAutoView()
{

      m_tracker.m_rect.SetRect(0,0,100,100);
      m_tracker.m_nStyle |= CRectTracker::resizeInside;
      m_tracker.m_nStyle |= CRectTracker::solidLine;
}
//--------------------------------------------------------------------
CAutoView::~CAutoView()
{
}
//////////////////////////////////////////////////////////////////////
// CAutoView drawing
void CAutoView::OnDraw(CDC* pDC)
{
      CAutoDoc* pDoc = GetDocument();

      ASSERT_VALID(pDoc);

      m_bkBrush.CreateSolidBrush(pDoc->m_currShape->GetColor());
      CBrush *pOldBrush = pDC->SelectObject(&m_bkBrush);

      pDoc->m_currShape->OnDraw(pDC,&m_tracker.m_rect);
      m_tracker.Draw(pDC);

      pDC->SelectObject(pOldBrush);
      m_bkBrush.DeleteObject();
}
//////////////////////////////////////////////////////////////////////
// CAutoView diagnostics
#ifdef _DEBUG
void CAutoView::AssertValid() const
{
      CView::AssertValid();
}

void CAutoView::Dump(CDumpContext& dc) const
{
      CView::Dump(dc);
}
//--------------------------------------------------------------------
CAutoDoc* CAutoView::GetDocument()
{
      ASSERT(m_pDocument->IsKindOf(RUNTIME_CLASS(CAutoDoc)));
      return (CAutoDoc*)m_pDocument;
}
#endif //_DEBUG
```

```
///////////////////////////////////////////////////////////////////
// CAutoView message handlers
//
void CAutoView::OnViewCircle()
{
      CAutoDoc* pDoc = GetDocument();
      pDoc->OnSetShape(CIRCLE);
      pDoc->m_currShape->OnGetDesc();
      pDoc->RefreshWindow();
}
//-----------------------------------------------------------------
void CAutoView::OnViewRectangle()
{
      CAutoDoc* pDoc = GetDocument();
      pDoc->OnSetShape(RECTANGLE);
      pDoc->m_currShape->OnGetDesc();
      pDoc->RefreshWindow();
}
//-----------------------------------------------------------------
void CAutoView::OnViewSquare()
{
      CAutoDoc* pDoc = GetDocument();
      pDoc->OnSetShape(SQUARE);
      pDoc->m_currShape->OnGetDesc();
      pDoc->RefreshWindow();
}
//-----------------------------------------------------------------
void CAutoView::OnViewRoundedrectangle()
{
      CAutoDoc* pDoc = GetDocument();
      pDoc->OnSetShape(RRECTANGLE);
      pDoc->m_currShape->OnGetDesc();
      pDoc->RefreshWindow();
}
//-----------------------------------------------------------------
void CAutoView::OnEditColor()
{
      CAutoDoc* pDoc = GetDocument();
      CColorDialog dlg;
      if (dlg.DoModal() != IDOK)
            return;
      pDoc->m_currShape->SetColor(dlg.GetColor());
      pDoc->RefreshWindow();
}
//-----------------------------------------------------------------
void CAutoView::OnUpdateEditColor(CCmdUI* pCmdUI)
{
}
//-----------------------------------------------------------------
void CAutoView::OnLButtonDown(UINT nFlags, CPoint point)
{
      CAutoDoc* pDoc = GetDocument();
```

(continues)

Listing 16.2 Continued

```
        m_tracker.Track(this,point,FALSE);
        pDoc->RefreshWindow();
        CView::OnLButtonDown(nFlags, point);
}
//-------------------------------------------------------------
BOOL CAutoView::OnSetCursor(CWnd* pWnd, UINT nHitTest, UINT message)
{
        if (pWnd == this && m_tracker.SetCursor(this, nHitTest))
              return TRUE;

        return CView::OnSetCursor(pWnd, nHitTest, message);
}
//-------------------------------------------------------------
```

The Document Class

The Document class is where you expose the Automation methods and properties. This section shows you how to enable a class for Automation support and how to use the ClassWizard to add methods and properties to the class.

Initializing the Document Class

The Component Object Model (COM) interface that drives Automation is `IDispatch`. So where is the `IDispatch` implementation? The answer lies in the `EnableAutomation` method call. This method, which is a member of `CCmdTarget`, implements the dispatch code for the user and wires the code through the dispatch map table to the methods. (Because this crucial method call is a member of the `CCmdTarget` class, all Automation objects must ultimately derive from `CCmdTarget`.)

The `AfxOleLockApp` function increases an internal reference counter in the framework. MFC keeps a count of all active objects contained within the application. If a user closes the application while an active object still exists, the framework simply hides the application's main window. You don't let the application terminate until all active objects are released. You pair this function call with the `AfxOleUnLockApp` call in your document's destructor.

In the document's constructor, you call both `EnableAutomation` and `AfxOleLockApp`. You also initialize the array of shapes. Later in this chapter, you expose this array as a simple collection.

Adding Methods with the ClassWizard

The ClassWizard generates the first method. As was mentioned at the beginning of this chapter, when you start an application with the `/Automation` command-line parameter, you hide the application's main window. The sample application must display a main window, so the first method that you need to implement is a `DisplayWindow` method.

From the ClassWizard, you choose the **A**dd Method command button. In the Add Method dialog box, you can then select the method's external and internal name. The external name is the name exposed to the user. This name should be a user-friendly, descriptive name for the method. For your internal name, however, you can use Hungarian notation. For the sample application, you use `DispayWnd` for both names (see fig 16.1). `DisplayWnd` is the first method that you must call from the Visual Basic script to open the main window.

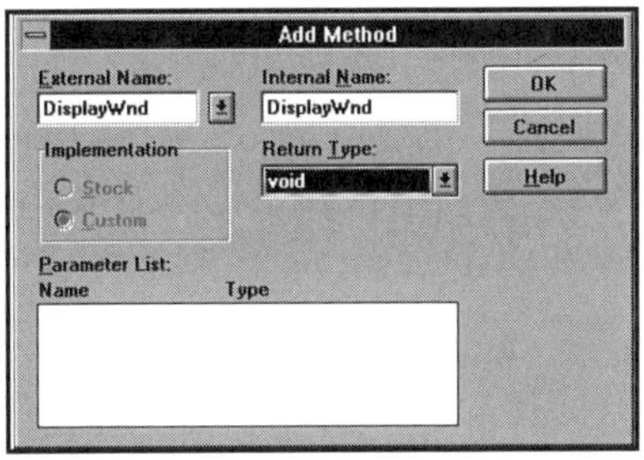

Fig. 16.1
Specifying internal and external names with the ClassWizard.

The ClassWizard adds a DISP_FUNCTION macro to the dispatch map table:

```
DISP_FUNCTION(CAutoDoc, "RefreshWindow", RefreshWindow, VT_EMPTY,
     VTS_NONE)
```

You can see from the macro that the method returns a VT_EMPTY value and takes a VTS_NONE parameter. In other words, the method returns a void and does not take any parameters.

Next, you add four more methods with the ClassWizard:

- The `GetShape` method returns a dispatch pointer to the currently selected shape. The technique that this method employs is the same as that which you will use to enable the user to navigate through your object hierarchy. In other words, you let the user create the initial `Application` object and then return dispatch pointers to the various objects in your hierarchy through this initial object.

- The `SetShape` method accepts a VT_I2 parameter, which is used to change the current shape. The shapes available are part of the enumeration SHAPEs declared in CAUTODOC.H (see listing 16.5).
- The `RefreshWindow` method is used by the controller to update the display after the controller changes one of the object's properties.
- The `GetShapeCount` method returns the number of shapes available. All collection objects must implement a `Count` method to return the collection's size. Notice that although the implementation of this method is called `GetShapeCount`, the name that you expose to the Automation controller is `Count`.

Implementing the *CShape* Object

The sample application handles the `CShape` object. The user cannot create this object. Instead, you expose this object to the user through the Document object's `GetShape` method.

The `CShape` object is actually the base class for each of the four shapes. Through this base class, you expose one method and one property.

The property is the color of the shape. Using ClassWizard, you create the paired `Get` and `Set` methods to manipulate this property. The DISP_PROPERTY_EX macro registers these methods in the dispatch map.

The method that you expose returns a description of the shape. In this method, the ClassWizard inserts the standard DISP_FUNCTION macro. The method returns a BSTR to the caller. The variable that stores the description within the class is a `CString`. Therefore, when you return the description, you must change from a `CString` type to a BSTR type. To do so, you use the `CString` method, `AllocSysString`. Another method, `SetSysString`, sets an existing BSTR variable with the contents of a `CString` object.

Listings 16.3 and 16.4 show the code for the `CShape` definition and implementation.

Listing 16.3 SHAPE.H

```
#ifndef SHAPE_H
#define SHAPE_H
```

```
/////////////////////////////////////////////////////////////////////////////
CShape command target
//
class CShape : public CCmdTarget
{
     DECLARE_DYNCREATE(CShape)
protected:
     CShape();       // protected constructor used by dynamic creation

// Attributes
public:
     COLORREF      m_crBkColor;          // Current color
     CString      *m_type;               // Type of shape
// Operations
public:
// Overrides

     // ClassWizard generated virtual-function overrides
     //{{AFX_VIRTUAL(CShape)
         // NOTE - the ClassWizard adds and removes member functions here.
     //}}AFX_VIRTUAL

     virtual void OnDraw(CDC *pDC, CRect *rc);
     virtual void OnFinalRelease();
// Implementation
public:
     virtual ~CShape();

     // Generated message map functions
     //{{AFX_MSG(CShape)
         // NOTE - the ClassWizard adds and removes member functions here.
     //}}AFX_MSG
     DECLARE_MESSAGE_MAP()
public:
     // Generated OLE dispatch map functions
     //{{AFX_DISPATCH(CShape)
     afx_msg long GetColor();
     afx_msg void SetColor(long nNewValue);
     afx_msg BSTR OnGetDesc();
     //}}AFX_DISPATCH
     DECLARE_DISPATCH_MAP()
};
/////////////////////////////////////////////////////////////////////////////
class CSquare : public CShape
{
public:
     CSquare();
     virtual ~CSquare();
     void OnDraw(CDC *pDC, CRect *rc);
};
/////////////////////////////////////////////////////////////////////////////
class CCircle : public CShape
{
public:
```

(continues)

Listing 16.3 Continued

```
    CCircle();
    virtual ~CCircle();
    void OnDraw(CDC *pDC, CRect *rc);
};
////////////////////////////////////////////////////////////////////
class CRectangle : public CShape
{
public:
    CRectangle();
    virtual ~CRectangle();
    void OnDraw(CDC *pDC, CRect *rc);
};
////////////////////////////////////////////////////////////////////
class CRrectangle : public CShape
{
public:
    CRrectangle();
    virtual ~CRrectangle();
    void OnDraw(CDC *pDC, CRect *rc);
};
#endif
////////////////////////////////////////////////////////////////////
////////////////////////////////////////////////////////////////////
```

Listing 16.4 SHAPE.CPP

```
#include "stdafx.h"
#include "automfc.h"
#include "shape.h"

#ifdef _DEBUG
#undef THIS_FILE
static char BASED_CODE THIS_FILE[] = __FILE__;
#endif

////////////////////////////////////////////////////////////////////
// CShape
//
IMPLEMENT_DYNCREATE(CShape, CCmdTarget)
//------------------------------------------------------------------
CShape::CShape()
{
    EnableAutomation();
    AfxOleLockApp();
    m_crBkColor = RGB(255,0,0);
}
//------------------------------------------------------------------
```

```
CShape::~CShape()
{
     AfxOleUnlockApp();
}
//-----------------------------------------------------------------
void CShape::OnFinalRelease()
{
}
//-----------------------------------------------------------------
BEGIN_MESSAGE_MAP(CShape, CCmdTarget)
     //{{AFX_MSG_MAP(CShape)
          // NOTE - the ClassWizard adds and removes mapping macros here.
     //}}AFX_MSG_MAP
END_MESSAGE_MAP()

BEGIN_DISPATCH_MAP(CShape, CCmdTarget)
     //{{AFX_DISPATCH_MAP(CShape)
     DISP_PROPERTY_EX(CShape, "color", GetColor, SetColor, VT_I4)
     DISP_FUNCTION(CShape, "Description", OnGetDesc, VT_BSTR, VTS_NONE)
     //}}AFX_DISPATCH_MAP
END_DISPATCH_MAP()

///////////////////////////////////////////////////////////////////
CShape message handlers
long CShape::GetColor()
{
     //-----------
     // GetColor: Returns the currently selected
     // background color. This is one of the methods
     // that you will expose through Automation.
     //
     return m_crBkColor;
}
//-----------------------------------------------------------------
void CShape::SetColor(long nNewValue)
{
     //-------
     // SetColor: Set the current background color.
     // This is one of the methods that you expose
     // through Automation.
     //
     m_crBkColor = nNewValue;

}
//-----------------------------------------------------------------
void CShape::OnDraw(CDC *pDC, CRect *rc)
{
     AfxMessageBox("CShape::OnDraw");
}
//-----------------------------------------------------------------
BSTR CShape::OnGetDesc()
```

(continues)

Listing 16.4 Continued

```
{
     ASSERT(m_type != NULL);
     return m_type->AllocSysString();
}
//-----------------------------------------------------------------
// These are the virtual draw members
// for each of the shapes.
//
CSquare::CSquare()
{
     m_type = new CString("Square");
}
//-----------------------------------------------------------------
CSquare::~CSquare()
{
     delete m_type;
}
//-----------------------------------------------------------------
void CSquare::OnDraw(CDC *pDC, CRect *rc)
{
     pDC->Rectangle(rc);
}
//-----------------------------------------------------------------
CCircle::CCircle()
{
     m_type = new CString("Circle");
}
//-----------------------------------------------------------------
CCircle::~CCircle()
{
     delete m_type;
}
//-----------------------------------------------------------------
void CCircle::OnDraw(CDC *pDC, CRect *rc)
{
     pDC->Ellipse(rc);
}
//-----------------------------------------------------------------
CRectangle::CRectangle()
{
     m_type = new CString("Rectangle");
}
//-----------------------------------------------------------------
CRectangle::~CRectangle()
{
     delete m_type;
}
//-----------------------------------------------------------------
void CRectangle::OnDraw(CDC *pDC, CRect *rc)
{
     pDC->Rectangle(rc);
}
//-----------------------------------------------------------------
CRrectangle::CRrectangle()
```

```
{
     m_type = new CString("Rounded Rectangle");
}
//------------------------------------------------------------
CRrectangle::~CRrectangle()
{
     delete m_type;
}
//------------------------------------------------------------
void CRrectangle::OnDraw(CDC *pDC, CRect *rc)
{
     CPoint pt(40,80);

     pDC->RoundRect(rc,pt);
}
//------------------------------------------------------------
//------------------------------------------------------------
```

Implementing the Collection Object

A collection is defined in the OLE documentation as being "a grouping of exposed objects." The purpose of a collection is to enable the user to iterate over the collection. OLE does not define a specific collection type. Instead, collection objects are standard Automation objects that support several redefined methods and one predefined property.

All collections must support the `Count` property. In addition, all collection objects have four methods defined for them. Table 16.1 describes the `Count` property and each of the methods supported by collections.

Table 16.1 The Property and Methods Supported by Collections

Property or Method Name	Return Type	Description
`Count`	VT_I4	Returns the number of items in a collection. This property is read-only.
Add	VT_DISPATCH or VT_EMPTY	Adds an item to a collection, and returns VT_DISPATCH if the object is created (the object cannot exist outside the collection) or VT_EMPTY if no object is created (the object can exist outside the collection).

(continues)

Table 16.1 Continued

Property or Method Name	Return Type	Description
`Item`	Varies with type of collection	Returns the indicated item in the collection. `Item` can take one or more arguments to indicate which element within the collection to return. `Item` is the default member (DISPID_VALUE) for the collection object.
`_NewEnum`	VT_DISPATCH	Returns an object that implements `IEnumVARIANT`. Automation controllers use this method to implement features like Visual Basic for Applications' `For...Each` construct.
`Remove`	VT_EMPTY	Removes an item from a collection, using indexing arguments in the same way as the `Item` method.

Two of these methods, `Remove` and `Add`, are optional. The sample code does not implement either of these methods. However, the application implements both the `Item` and `_NewEnum` methods, which are required.

When you declare the `_NewEnum` and `Item` methods in the dispatch map table, they are outside the //AFX_DISPATCH_MAP comments, because you hand-code these map entries. The ClassWizard supplied with Visual C++ 1.5 cannot create dispatch map entries with user-defined DISPIDs. Microsoft should correct this shortcoming in a future release of Visual C++.

Chapter 2, "The Component Object Model," discussed COM enumerators and provided an example of a string enumerator. The sample code requires a VARIANT enumerator. To retrieve the enumerator object, the controller calls the predefined method `_NewEnum`. This method has a special DISPID, DISPID_NEWENUM. Because you are using a special DISPID for the method, you use the DISP_FUNCTION_ID macro to declare the map. This macro enables you to select the DISPID. To return a dispatch pointer to Automation objects below the `Application` object, you use the same technique that you use to return the dispatch interface. The `GetIDispatch` method returns the dispatch pointer from an MFC object that calls the `EnableAutomation` method.

The _NewEnum function is required so that OLE Automation controller languages, such as Visual Basic for Applications, can implement collection iteration constructs. Because collections do not necessarily have contiguous item indices (for example, item(0), item(1), and item(3) may exist, but item(2) may not), controllers must be capable of iterating over a collection without relying on contiguous indices. For example, using the For n/Next n construct in Visual Basic, you can try to iterate over a collection as follows:

```
For n = 1 To collect.Count
     MsgBox collect(n).Text
Next n
```

However, this code is not guaranteed to work with collections that do not support contiguous indices (or collections that do not support integer indices). The _NewEnum method enables Visual Basic to support the For...Each construct instead:

```
For Each x In collect
     MsgBox x.Text
Next x
```

The second method that you declare in this manner is Item. Item is the collection's default method. Again, this method uses a predefined DISPID, which in this case is DISPID_VALUE. Your implementation of Item takes an index into the collection as a parameter and returns a dispatch pointer to the selected object.

The Item method's return value varies according to the type of collection. This method may take one or more parameters, which can be numbers, strings, or any other types. Again, the type of parameter depends on the type of collection that you are handling. Although your collection allows indexing only with the array index, most collections allow indexing with more than one type of parameter.

Listing 16.5 shows the definition of the CAutoDoc class. The class is implemented in listing 16.6.

Listing 16.5 CAUTODOC.H

```
#include "shape.h"

enum SHAPE {SQUARE,RECTANGLE,CIRCLE,RRECTANGLE};

class CAutoDoc : public CDocument
{
```

(continues)

Listing 16.5 Continued

```
protected:
     CAutoDoc();
     DECLARE_DYNCREATE(CAutoDoc)

// Attributes
public:
     CObArray  m_shapes;
     CShape *m_currShape;
// Operations
public:
     void OnFinalRelease();
// Implementation
public:
     virtual ~CAutoDoc();
     virtual void Serialize(CArchive& ar);
#ifdef _DEBUG
     virtual void AssertValid() const;
     virtual void Dump(CDumpContext& dc) const;
#endif
protected:
     virtual BOOL OnNewDocument();
     //{{AFX_MSG(CAutoDoc)
     //}}AFX_MSG
     DECLARE_MESSAGE_MAP()

     //DECLARE_OLECREATE(CAutoDoc)
public:
     // Generated OLE dispatch map functions
     //{{AFX_DISPATCH(CAutoDoc)
     afx_msg void RefreshWindow();
     afx_msg void DisplayWnd();
     afx_msg short GetShapeCount();
     afx_msg LPDISPATCH _NewEnum();
     afx_msg LPDISPATCH Item(short nPos);
     afx_msg void OnSetShape(short shape);
     afx_msg LPDISPATCH GetShape();
     //}}AFX_DISPATCH
     DECLARE_DISPATCH_MAP()
};
//-----------------------------------------------------------------
```

Listing 16.6 CAUTODOC.CPP

```
#include "stdafx.h"
#include "automfc.h"

#include "automdoc.h"
#include "varenum.h"
#include "shape.h"
```

```
#ifdef _DEBUG
#undef THIS_FILE
static char BASED_CODE THIS_FILE[] = __FILE__;
#endif

/////////////////////////////////////////////////////////////////////
// CAutoDoc

IMPLEMENT_DYNCREATE(CAutoDoc, CDocument)

BEGIN_MESSAGE_MAP(CAutoDoc, CDocument)
     //{{AFX_MSG_MAP(CAutoDoc)
     //}}AFX_MSG_MAP
END_MESSAGE_MAP()

BEGIN_DISPATCH_MAP(CAutoDoc, CDocument)
     //{{AFX_DISPATCH_MAP(CAutoDoc)
     DISP_FUNCTION(CAutoDoc, "RefreshWindow", RefreshWindow,
         VT_EMPTY, VTS_NONE)
     DISP_FUNCTION(CAutoDoc, "DisplayWnd", DisplayWnd, VT_EMPTY, VTS_NONE)
     DISP_FUNCTION(CAutoDoc, "Count", GetShapeCount, VT_I2, VTS_NONE)
     DISP_FUNCTION(CAutoDoc, "SetShape", OnSetShape, VT_EMPTY, VTS_I2)
     DISP_FUNCTION(CAutoDoc, "GetShape", GetShape, VT_DISPATCH, VTS_NONE)
     //}}AFX_DISPATCH_MAP
     //------------------
    // You need to use the XXX_ID macro here because the DISPID
    // for the IEnumVARIANT method must use the predefined DISPID.
    DISP_FUNCTION_ID(CAutoDoc, "_NewEnum", DISPID_NEWENUM,
        _NewEnum, VT_DISPATCH, VTS_NONE)
    DISP_FUNCTION_ID(CAutoDoc, "Item", DISPID_VALUE, Item, \
        VT_DISPATCH, VTS_I2)
END_DISPATCH_MAP()

//IMPLEMENT_OLECREATE(CAutoDoc, "Document", 0x6ddef3a0, 0x68cd, \
     0x101b, 0x99, 0x48, 0x7e, 0xf9, 0xe6, 0xaf, 0x22, 0x44)

/////////////////////////////////////////////////////////////////////
// CAutoDoc construction/destruction
CAutoDoc::CAutoDoc()
{
     //------
     // Enable Automation support for this object.
     // This method sets up the IDispatch interface.
     EnableAutomation();

     m_shapes.Add(new CSquare);
     m_shapes.Add(new CRectangle);
     m_shapes.Add(new CCircle);
     m_shapes.Add(new CRrectangle);
```

(continues)

Listing 16.6 Continued

```
        // Set the default shape to be a square
        m_currShape = (CShape *)m_shapes.GetAt(0);

        // Place a strong lock on the object.
        AfxOleLockApp();
}
//---------------------------------------------------------------------
CAutoDoc::~CAutoDoc()
{
        //--------------
        // Delete each of the shape objects
        // and release the object lock.
        CShape *s;
        int nMax = m_shapes.GetSize();
        for (int i = 0; i < nMax; i++)
        {
                s = (CShape *)m_shapes.GetAt(i);
                delete s;
        }
        m_shapes.RemoveAll();
        AfxOleUnlockApp();
}
//---------------------------------------------------------------------
void CAutoDoc::OnFinalRelease()
{
        //------
        // Delete the object because the last client
        // has released the object.
    delete this;
}
//---------------------------------------------------------------------
BOOL CAutoDoc::OnNewDocument()
{
        if (!CDocument::OnNewDocument())
                return FALSE;


        return TRUE;
}
/////////////////////////////////////////////////////////////////////
// CAutoDoc serialization
void CAutoDoc::Serialize(CArchive& ar)
{
        if (ar.IsStoring())
        {
        }
        else
        {
        }
}
/////////////////////////////////////////////////////////////////////
```

```
// CAutoDoc diagnostics
#ifdef _DEBUG
void CAutoDoc::AssertValid() const
{
     CDocument::AssertValid();
}
//-----------------------------------------------------------------
void CAutoDoc::Dump(CDumpContext& dc) const
{
     CDocument::Dump(dc);
}
#endif //_DEBUG
//-----------------------------------------------------------------
// These are the methods that you are exposing through Automation.
//
//
void CAutoDoc::OnSetShape(short shape)
{
     m_currShape = (CShape *)m_shapes.GetAt(shape);
}
//-----------------------------------------------------------------
void CAutoDoc::RefreshWindow()
{
     //----------
     // RefreshWindow: Invalidates the main window's client area.
     // You expose this method through Automation also.
     //
     UpdateAllViews(NULL);
     SetModifiedFlag(FALSE);
}
//-----------------------------------------------------------------
void CAutoDoc::DisplayWnd()
{
     //-------
     // DisplayWnd: Called to display the
     // main window.
     POSITION pos = GetFirstViewPosition();
     CView* pView = GetNextView(pos);
     if (pView != NULL)
     {
          CFrameWnd* pFrameWnd = pView->GetParentFrame();
          pFrameWnd->ActivateFrame(SW_SHOW);
          pFrameWnd = pFrameWnd->GetParentFrame();
          if (pFrameWnd != NULL)
               pFrameWnd->ActivateFrame(SW_SHOW);
     }
}
//-----------------------------------------------------------------
short CAutoDoc::GetShapeCount()
{
     //-------
     // GetShapeCount: Returns the number of shapes
     // available.
```

(continues)

Listing 16.6 Continued

```
     return m_shapes.GetSize();
}
//-----------------------------------------------------------------
LPDISPATCH CAutoDoc::_NewEnum()
{
     //----------
     // _NewEnum: Return a pointer to an IEnumVARIANT
     // enumerator for the collection object.

    CVarEnum *pEnum = new CVarEnum(&m_shapes);
    return pEnum->GetIDispatch(FALSE);
}
//-----------------------------------------------------------------
LPDISPATCH CAutoDoc::Item(short nPos)
{
     //----------
     // Item: Predefined method to return a specified
     // item from the collection.

     ASSERT(nPos > 0);

    if (nPos >= m_shapes.GetSize())
    {
        AfxThrowOleDispatchException(0, "Requested shape not found");
    }

    CShape *s = (CShape *)m_shapes[nPos];
    LPDISPATCH lpResult = s->GetIDispatch(FALSE);

     return lpResult;
}
//-----------------------------------------------------------------
LPDISPATCH CAutoDoc::GetShape()
{
     //----------
     // Return a pointer to the dispatch
     // interface pointer to the currently
     // selected shape.
     LPDISPATCH lpResult = m_currShape->GetIDispatch(FALSE);
     ASSERT(lpResult != NULL);

     return lpResult;
}
//-----------------------------------------------------------------
//-----------------------------------------------------------------
```

The *IEnumVARIANT* Implementation

IEnumVARIANT is the enumerator that you use to iterate over collections. Listing 16.7 shows how the OLE headers define the IEnumVARIANT interface.

Listing 16.7 The Definition of *IEnumVARIANT*

```
DECLARE_INTERFACE_(IEnumVARIANT, IUnknown)
{
    BEGIN_INTERFACE

    /* IUnknown methods */
    STDMETHOD(QueryInterface)(THIS_ REFIID riid,
        void FAR* FAR* ppvObj) PURE;
    STDMETHOD_(unsigned long, AddRef)(THIS) PURE;
    STDMETHOD_(unsigned long, Release)(THIS) PURE;

    /* IEnumVARIANT methods */
    STDMETHOD(Next)(
      THIS_ unsigned long celt, VARIANT FAR* rgvar,
          unsigned long FAR* pceltFetched) PURE;
    STDMETHOD(Skip)(THIS_ unsigned long celt) PURE;
    STDMETHOD(Reset)(THIS) PURE;
    STDMETHOD(Clone)(THIS_ IEnumVARIANT FAR* FAR* ppenum) PURE;
};
```

Note that you have a problem: MFC does not implement the `IEnumVARIANT` interface for you, so you must implement this interface yourself. This implementation initially seems like a difficult task; however, by examining the MFC source code, you can easily determine how the framework implements COM interfaces.

The enumerator that you implement is `CVarEnum`. This class, which derives from `CCmdTarget`, implements the four required `IEnumVARIANT` methods:

- The `Next` method retrieves one or more elements from the collection.
- The `Skip` method moves the current object pointer in the collection list.
- The `Reset` method resets the current pointer to the first member of the collection.
- The `Clone` method copies the current state of the collection.

The sample code derives the `CVarEnum` class from `CCmdTarget` and implements the COM interfaces as nested classes. The process consists of five steps:

1. Derive your class from `CCmdTarget`. This ensures that the class inherits the `IUnknown` implementation.
2. Use the DECLARE_INTERFACE_MAP macro, which expands as follows to set up the interface map entries:

```
private: \
static AFX_INTERFACEMAP_ENTRY BASED_CODE _interfaceEntries[];      \
```

```
protected: \
        static AFX_INTERFACEMAP BASED_CODE interfaceMap; \
        virtual AFX_INTERFACEMAP FAR* GetInterfaceMap() const;
```

3. Use the BEGIN_INTERFACE_PART and END_INTERFACE_PART macros to bracket the IEnumVARIANT declarations. These macros expand as follows for this implementation.

```
class FAR XEnumVar : public IEnumVARIANT \
{ \
public: \
     STDMETHOD_(ULONG, AddRef)(); \
     STDMETHOD_(ULONG, Release)(); \
     STDMETHOD(QueryInterface)(REFIID iid, LPVOID far* ppvObj); \
```

Note the declarations of both the nested class, XEnumVar, and of the IUnknown implementation.

The END_INTERFACE_PART macro closes the nested class declaration and declares the nested class as a friend of the main class:

```
} m_xVarEnum; \
friend class XVarEnum; \
```

4. Use the BEGIN_INTERFACE_MAP and END_INTERFACE_MAP macros in the CPP file. The macros expand as follows:

```
AFX_INTERFACEMAP FAR* VarEnum::GetInterfaceMap() const \
     { return &VarEnum::interfaceMap; } \
AFX_INTERFACEMAP BASED_CODE VarEnum::interfaceMap = \
     { &(CCmdTarget::interfaceMap), VarEnum::_interfaceEntries, }; \
AFX_INTERFACEMAP_ENTRY BASED_CODE VarEnum::_interfaceEntries[] = \
{

          { NULL, (size_t)-1 } \
     }; \
```

These macros fill in the interface entries array with the offset within the class and the IID (interface ID) names of each interface that you declare with the INTERFACE_PART macro. CCmdTarget's QueryInterface implementation uses these entries. The QueryInterface method threads its way through the linked interface maps looking for an object that supports the requested interface.

5. Implement each of the IEnumVariant interface's methods. In each of the implemented methods, you use the macro METHOD_PROLOGUE. This macro initializes the pThis class pointer to point to the parent class. You are calling this macro from within the nested class, so pThis should now point to CVarEnum:

```
CVarEnum* pThis = ((CVarEnum*)((char*)_AfxGetPtrFromFarPtr(this) - \
    offsetof(CVarEnum, m_xVarEnum))); \
```

The *IUnknown* and *IEnumVARIANT* Methods

For each of the `IUnknown` methods, you delegate to the `CCmdTarget` implementation. For each of the `IEnumVARIANT` methods, you delegate to the implementation of the parent class.

The *CVarEnum* Methods

The `CVarEnum` methods consist of the following:

- The `OnNext` method returns objects from the collection. The method takes three parameters: the first parameter is the number of objects to return, the second is a pointer to an array of VARIANTs to hold the returned objects, and the last is the actual number of objects returned.

  The method begins by calling the `VariantInit` function to set the VARIANT array to zero. Next, you loop for each object to be retrieved. Beginning at the current position in the collection, you extract the dispatch interface pointer for each object and place the pointer in the VARIANT array. If you overrun the array, you simply break out of the loop. The method, therefore, does not always return the number of requested objects, which is one of the reasons that the last parameter returns the number of actual objects retrieved.

- The `OnRest` method simply resets the current object number to zero. The controller then can begin to iterate over the collection again from the start.

- The `OnSkip` method moves the current collection position pointer by the amount requested.

- The `OnClone` method copies the collection's current state, returns a pointer to a new enumerator, and sets the collection's current position to be the same in the new enumerator.

This wraps up your implementation of `IEnumVARIANT` with a custom interface that MFC does not support. The techniques used here can be applied to any COM interface that is not implemented by MFC. Listing 16.8 defines the `CVarEnum` class, and listing 16.9 implements the class.

Listing 16.8 VARENUM.H

```
#if !defined(VARENUM_H)
#define VARENUM_H

class CVarEnum : public CCmdTarget
{
     DECLARE_DYNCREATE(CVarEnum)
protected:
     CVarEnum();      // protected constructor used by dynamic creation
public:
     CVarEnum(CObArray *pShapes);
     void virtual OnFinalRelease();

// Attributes
public:
     CObArray     *m_pShapes;
     short         m_CurrentPos;
// Operations
public:
// Overrides

// Implementation
protected:
     virtual ~CVarEnum();

    virtual HRESULT OnNext(unsigned long ulQty,
        VARIANT FAR* paVariant, unsigned long FAR* pulQtyFetched);
    virtual HRESULT OnSkip(unsigned long ulQty);
    virtual HRESULT OnReset();
    virtual CVarEnum *OnClone();

public:

    DECLARE_INTERFACE_MAP()

    BEGIN_INTERFACE_PART(VarEnum, IEnumVARIANT)
        STDMETHOD(Next)(unsigned long celt, VARIANT FAR* rgvar,
            unsigned long FAR* pceltFetched);
        STDMETHOD(Skip)(unsigned long celt);
        STDMETHOD(Reset)(void);
        STDMETHOD(Clone)(IEnumVARIANT FAR* FAR* ppenum);
    END_INTERFACE_PART(VarEnum)
};
#endif
```

Listing 16.9 VARENUM.CPP

```
#include "stdafx.h"
#include "automfc.h"
#include "varenum.h"
#include "shape.h"
```

```
#ifdef _DEBUG
#undef THIS_FILE
static char BASED_CODE THIS_FILE[] = __FILE__;
#endif

#ifdef NDEBUG
#define XTRACE(str) OutputDebugString(str);
#endif

/////////////////////////////////////////////////////////////////////////////
// CVarEnum

IMPLEMENT_DYNCREATE(CVarEnum, CCmdTarget)


BEGIN_INTERFACE_MAP(CVarEnum, CCmdTarget)
    INTERFACE_PART(CVarEnum, IID_IEnumVARIANT, VarEnum)
END_INTERFACE_MAP()


//-------------------------------------------------------------------
// The following are the methods of the nested class XVarEnum
//
STDMETHODIMP_(ULONG) CVarEnum::XVarEnum::AddRef()
{
    METHOD_PROLOGUE(CVarEnum, VarEnum)
    return pThis->ExternalAddRef();
}
//-------------------------------------------------------------------
STDMETHODIMP_(ULONG) CVarEnum::XVarEnum::Release()
{
    METHOD_PROLOGUE(CVarEnum, VarEnum)
    return pThis->ExternalRelease();
}
//-------------------------------------------------------------------
STDMETHODIMP CVarEnum::XVarEnum::QueryInterface(REFIID iid,
    LPVOID far *pvvObj)
{
    METHOD_PROLOGUE(CVarEnum, VarEnum)
    return (HRESULT) pThis->ExternalQueryInterface(&iid, pvvObj);
}
//-------------------------------------------------------------------
STDMETHODIMP CVarEnum::XVarEnum::Next(unsigned long celt,
    VARIANT FAR* rgvar, unsigned long FAR* pceltFetched)
{
    METHOD_PROLOGUE(CVarEnum, VarEnum)
    return pThis->OnNext(celt, rgvar, pceltFetched);
}
//-------------------------------------------------------------------
STDMETHODIMP CVarEnum::XVarEnum::Skip(unsigned long celt)
{
    METHOD_PROLOGUE(CVarEnum, VarEnum)
    return pThis->OnSkip(celt);
```

(continues)

Listing 16.9 Continued

```
}
//-----------------------------------------------------------------
STDMETHODIMP CVarEnum::XVarEnum::Reset(void)
{
    METHOD_PROLOGUE(CVarEnum, VarEnum)
    return pThis->OnReset();
}
//-----------------------------------------------------------------
STDMETHODIMP CVarEnum::XVarEnum::Clone(IEnumVARIANT FAR* FAR* ppenum)
{
     return NULL;
}
//-----------------------------------------------------------------
// This is where you actually implement the VarEnumIANT methods
//
CVarEnum::CVarEnum()
{
     EnableAutomation();
     m_CurrentPos = 0;
     m_pShapes = NULL;
}
//-----------------------------------------------------------------
CVarEnum::CVarEnum(CObArray *pShapes)
{
     EnableAutomation();
     m_CurrentPos = 0;
     m_pShapes = pShapes;
}
//-----------------------------------------------------------------
CVarEnum::~CVarEnum()
{
}
//-----------------------------------------------------------------
void CVarEnum::OnFinalRelease()
{
    delete this;
}
//-----------------------------------------------------------------
#if 0
BEGIN_DISPATCH_MAP(CVarEnum, CCmdTarget)
     //{{AFX_DISPATCH_MAP(CVarEnum)
          // NOTE - the ClassWizard adds and removes mapping macros here.
     //}}AFX_DISPATCH_MAP
END_DISPATCH_MAP()
#endif
//-----------------------------------------------------------------
// This is the implementation of the IVarEnumIANT interface
HRESULT CVarEnum::OnNext(unsigned long ulQty, VARIANT FAR* paVariant,
    unsigned long FAR* pulQtyFetched)
{
    unsigned long n;
    short nSize = m_pShapes->GetSize();
```

```
    CShape *pShape;
    LPDISPATCH lpDisp;

    XTRACE("CVarEnum::OnNext\n");

     // Call VariantInit to clear each member
     // of the array in which you are to return
     // your objects.
    for(n = 0; n < ulQty; n++)
    {
        VariantInit(&(paVariant[n]));
    }


    for (n = 0; n < ulQty; n++)
    {
         // Fallen off the edge?
        if (m_CurrentPos >= nSize)
        {
             return ResultFromScode(S_FALSE);
        }

        VARIANT FAR *ptVar = &(paVariant[n]);
        V_VT(ptVar) = VT_DISPATCH;
        pShape  = (CShape *)m_pShapes->GetAt(m_CurrentPos++);
        lpDisp = pShape->GetIDispatch(FALSE);
        V_DISPATCH(ptVar) = lpDisp;
    }

    *pulQtyFetched = n;
    return ResultFromScode(S_OK);
}
//------------------------------------------------------------------
HRESULT CVarEnum::OnReset()
{
     XTRACE("CVarEnum::OnReset\n");
    m_CurrentPos = 0;
    return ResultFromScode(S_OK);
}
//------------------------------------------------------------------
HRESULT CVarEnum::OnSkip(unsigned long ulQty)
{
    unsigned long ulPos = 0;
    short nSize = m_pShapes->GetSize();

     XTRACE("CVarEnum::OnSkip\n");
    for (ulPos = 0; ulPos < ulQty; ulPos++)
    {
        if (m_CurrentPos >= nSize)
        {
            return ResultFromScode(S_FALSE);
        }
        m_CurrentPos++;
    }
```

(continues)

Listing 16.9 Continued

```
    return ResultFromScode(S_OK);
}
//------------------------------------------------------------
CVarEnum *CVarEnum::OnClone()
{
     XTRACE("CVarEnum::OnClone\n");
    CVarEnum *pEnum = new CVarEnum(m_pShapes);
    pEnum->m_CurrentPos = m_CurrentPos;
    return pEnum;
}
//------------------------------------------------------------
//------------------------------------------------------------
```

The Test Script

To test the MFC server and collection object, you can use the program shown in listing 16.10. The program, Form_load, is a small, Visual Basic 3.0 script. Figure 16.2 shows the program's main screen.

Listing 16.10 Form_Load from the Visual Basic Test Script

```
Sub Form_Load ()
    Set MyObj = CreateObject("Auto16.Document")
    MyObj.DisplayWnd

    Dim Nr As Integer
    Dim index As Integer
    Dim X As String

    Nr = MyObj.Count()
    For index = 1 To Nr
        Set MyShape = MyObj(index - 1)
        Shapes.AddItem MyShape.Description
        Set MyShape = Nothing
    Next


    Set MyShape = MyObj.GetShape
End Sub
```

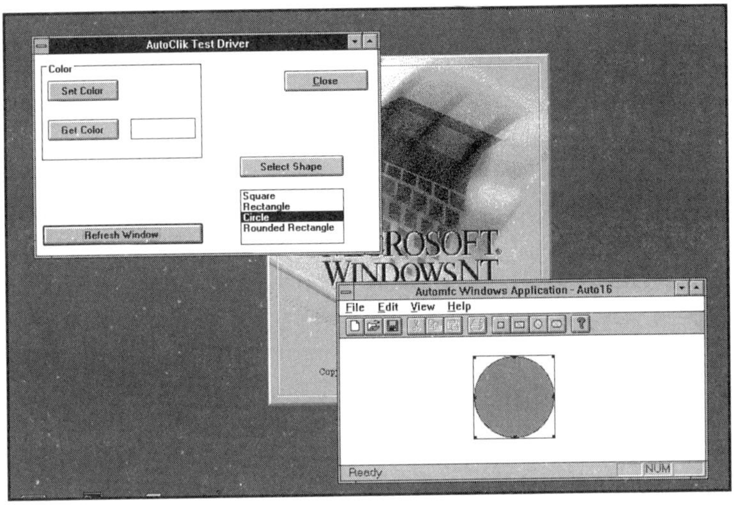

Fig. 16.2
The main screen of the test application.

The test application begins by creating an object of type `Auto16.Document`. After creating the object, you call the `DisplayWnd` method to display the main window.

Next, you find out how many objects the application supports by getting the `Count` property. You then loop and extract the object description information from each object. Notice that you use the default `Item` method for this looping and extracting. Because `Item` is the object's default method, you do not have to call the `Item` method explicitly.

You implement the `IEnumVARIANT` enumerator, so why don't you use it to iterate through the objects? The answer is simple: neither Visual Basic 3.0 nor the DISPTEST application supports the `For...Each` construct that you normally use to invoke the enumerator.

However, Visual Basic for Applications, which ships with Excel 5.0, does support this construct. Listing 16.11 shows a simple test macro, written in VBA, that calls your object's enumerator. You should run this macro in debug mode to see the objects' descriptions being printed to the Debug window.

Listing 16.11 The Visual Basic for Applications Test Macro

```
Sub ForEach()
    Dim MyObj As Object
    Dim MyShape As Object
    Set MyObj = CreateObject("Auto16.document")
```

(continues)

Listing 16.11 Continued

```
        For Each MyShape In MyObj
            Debug.Print MyShape.Description
        Next
        Set MyObj = Nothing
    End Sub
```

The rest of the Visual Basic test application enables you to select the color of the current shape and to switch between shapes. You must call the `RefreshWnd` method each time that you change one of the objects' properties.

Finally, to quit the application, you release the dispatch pointers by setting the object variable to `Nothing`.

From Here...

This chapter concludes your look at OLE Automation. In the next chapter, you begin to examine some of the more advanced features of OLE and look at the direction that OLE is heading.

Part IV

Beyond OLE 2.0

17 OLE Custom Interfaces

18 Thirty-two-bit OLE

19 Distributed Objects

20 The Future of OLE

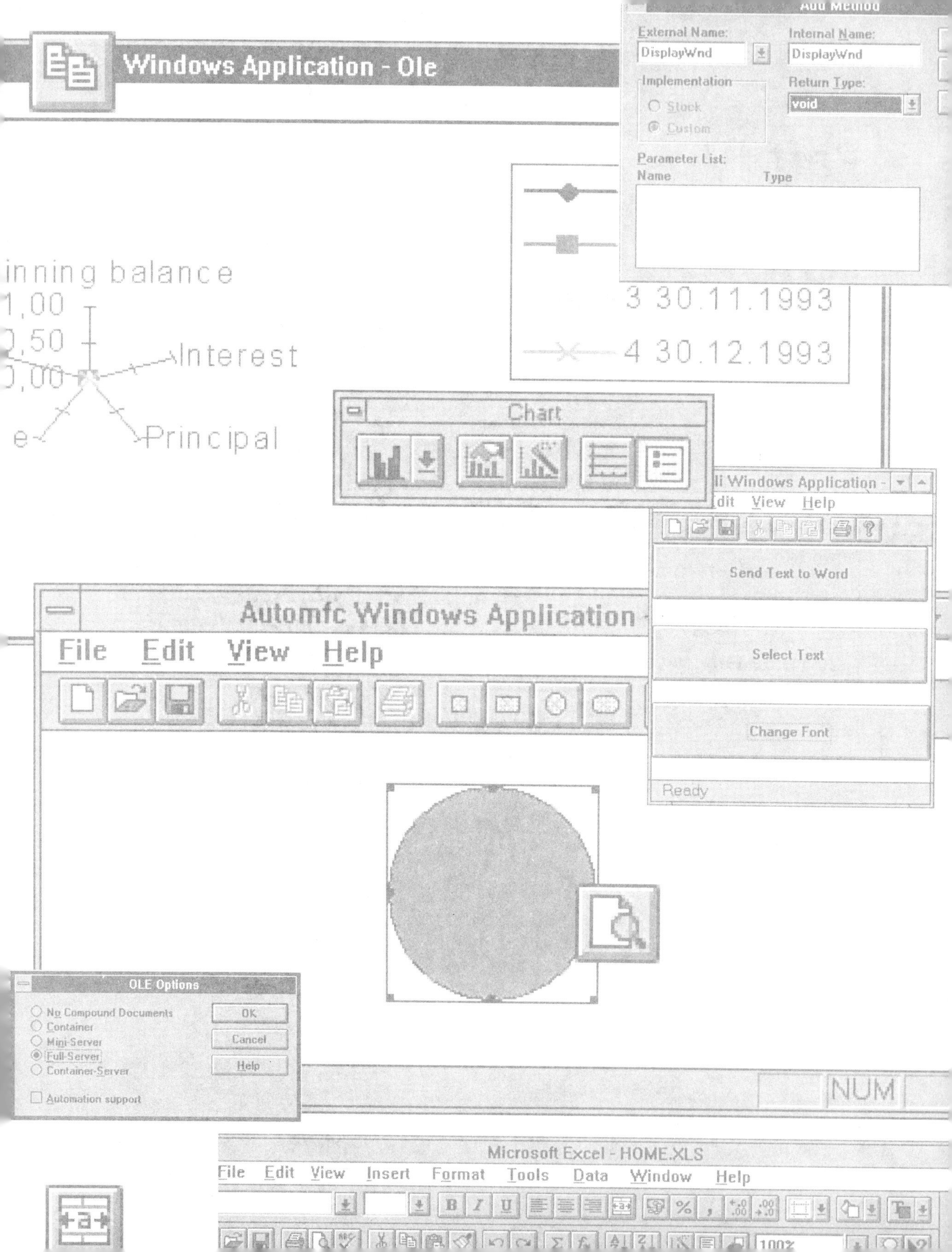

Windows Application - Ole
Add Method
External Name:
DisplayWnd
Internal Name:
DisplayWnd
Implementation
Stock
Custom
Return Type:
void
Parameter List:
Name
Type
inning balance
Interest
Principal
3 30.11.1993
4 30.12.1993
Chart
li Windows Application -
Edit View Help
Send Text to Word
Select Text
Change Font
Ready
Automfc Windows Application
File Edit View Help
OLE Options
No Compound Documents
Container
Mini-Server
Full-Server
Container-Server
Automation support
OK
Cancel
Help
NUM
Microsoft Excel - HOME.XLS
File Edit View Insert Format Tools Data Window Help

Chapter 17

OLE Custom Interfaces

OLE custom interfaces are one of the most exciting aspects of OLE. Custom interfaces enable you to extend the functionality of the Component Object Model (COM) by adding new interfaces. These new interfaces have the same features as the standard COM interfaces. In other words, you can remote calls to custom interfaces across process boundaries and, with Distributed OLE, across networks.

Custom interfaces provide many advantages over using OLE Automation. Because custom interfaces are in fact COM interfaces, the same notion of a contract exists. If you get a pointer to a custom interface, you are guaranteed that the interface will support all its published methods. This is not the case with OLE Automation. Also, although custom interfaces provide type checking of all parameters, OLE Automation may not. Finally, using OLE Automation is usually slower than using custom interfaces. On the other hand, OLE Automation does provide scriptability through products such as Visual Basic and Visual Basic for Applications. OLE Automation also provides automatic type coercion.

In the chapter, you do the following:

- Examine the architecture of custom interfaces
- Explore the tools available for creating custom interface proxies and stubs
- Modify the OLE Automation quote server that you developed in Chapter 13, "Creating a Simple Automation Server," by adding a custom interface that you can use in place of OLE Automation to retrieve the quotes

Custom Interface Architecture

Before you look at the architecture of custom interfaces, the following section briefly examines how you implement standard COM interfaces.

First, however, you need to be familiar with two terms:

- A *proxy* is a piece of code that is responsible for packaging interface parameters into a message buffer and passing that buffer to a channel that is responsible for transferring the data to another process.
- A *stub* is a piece of code that retrieves data for a channel, unpackages the parameters from the buffer, and calls the client code using the parameters.

Because of the architecture of proxies and stubs, the location of servers and clients are transparent.

Standard Interfaces

When you call `CoGetClassObject` in your code, the default handler in OLE tries to locate the object server by looking up its CLSID in the system registry. (If the server is already running, this step is bypassed.)

The object server's first task is to create and register its class object. The OLE Stub Manager then creates a stub for this class object.

On the client side, the OLE Proxy Manager creates an interface proxy for `IClassFactory` and returns to your application a pointer to this proxy.

When you call `IClassFactory::CreateInstance`, you are actually calling an implementation of `IClassFactory::CreateInstance` in the proxy, which marshals the parameters into the remote procedure call (RPC) channel. The data is then sent across the wire to the object server's class object stub. The stub then unmarshals the parameters and calls the *real* implementation of `IClassFactory::CreateInstance` as implemented by the object server.

The process of creating and using proxies and stubs is used for all COM interfaces except those implemented in in-process handlers. Figure 17.1 shows how the proxies and stubs work together.

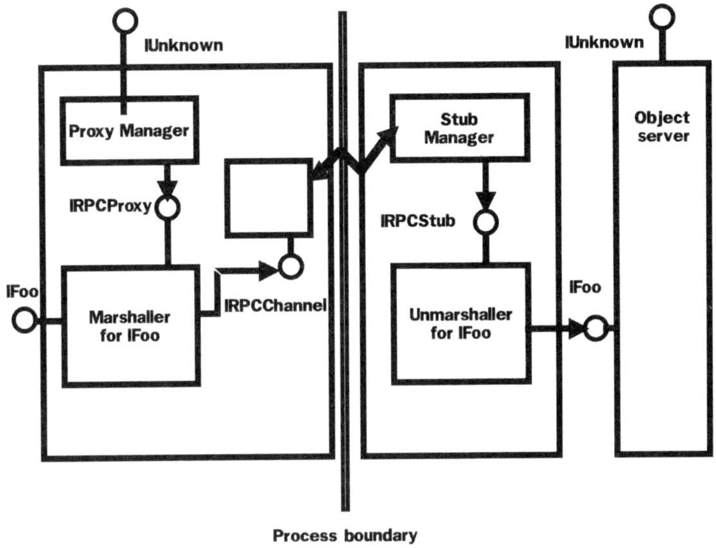

Fig. 17.1
Proxies and stubs.

The main point that you need to understand is that whenever you call a COM interface pointer, you are not actually calling the object server. Instead, you are calling the OLE-generated proxy for that particular interface. This proxy in turn calls a stub (through RPC) that calls the actual server code.

For any particular object, OLE creates an object proxy. This object proxy consists of a Proxy Manager and one or more interface proxies. For each interface that an object supports, OLE creates an interface proxy. The reason that OLE creates a special proxy for each interface is that the interface proxy is responsible for marshaling the interface parameters. This marshaling requires intimate knowledge of the interface definition.

Interfaces are remoted in this manner to enable objects to exist in different processes. (Because interfaces must enable objects to exist in different processes, common function calls cannot work.) The other major benefit of this architecture is transparency. Clients and servers are unaware that they in fact exist in separate processes. This transparency is crucial because it lays the foundation for OLE to add distributed support without requiring changes to the objects.

Marshaling

Marshaling is the process of packaging data for transmission to a remote process and unpackaging the data at the remote process. To implement marshaling support, you create separate functions that support each possible data type. If a pointer to a data buffer is to be marshaled, you must copy the data pointer to another buffer, transmit the buffer, have the receiving stub allocate a new buffer, and finally copy the data into the remote buffer. To marshal a scalar type such as an integer, you simply copy it into the message buffer.

OLE supports two types of marshaling: custom and standard. Standard marshaling of standard COM interfaces is done by proxies and stubs supplied by OLE. Standard marshaling of custom interfaces is done by user-supplied proxies and stubs. These proxies and stubs are supplied as separate DLLs. All proxy and stub components are registered in the system registry under the Interfaces key. Each proxy and stub DLL has an entry in this Interfaces section named `ProxyStubClsid`.

Custom marshaling, on the other hand, is achieved by proxies and stubs implemented by the object server. One example of custom marshaling is the shared memory mechanism used by compound files in 32-bit Windows. Custom marshaling implements both `IStorage` and `IStream`. Developers often use custom marshaling to avoid the context switching of standard marshaling, which adversely affects performance. Custom marshaling is more complex to implement than standard marshaling and requires that the server implement the `IMarshal` interface. The code that you develop later in this chapter uses only standard marshaling.

Custom Interfaces

To implement a custom interface, you define and register an interface ID (IID). Clients then use this IID when they create objects of that type. This is the easy part of implementing custom interfaces.

As you may have surmised, you must also implement marshaling for your custom interface. The OLE libraries can marshal only the standard COM interfaces.

When OLE 2.0 was first released, developers had to hand-code the proxy and stub for each interface that they wanted to implement. With the release of 32-bit OLE, Microsoft has released a new tool for generating the proxy and stub for a custom interface. This tool is a new version of the Microsoft Interface Description Language (MIDL 2.0) compiler. Instead of writing the code to implement proxies and stubs, you use the Interface Description Language

(IDL) to describe the interface. You compile the IDL file with the MIDL compiler. The output from the compiler is the C++ header and implementation files for the proxy and stub. Building the proxy and stub DLL is simply a matter of compiling these files and linking with some libraries supplied with the SDK. After you build the DLL, you must register the new proxy and stub in the system registery.

You can still build custom interfaces for 16-bit OLE, but you must implement the marshaling code manually. Another approach is to use the MIDL compiler to generate 32-bit proxies and stubs and port them to Win16.

Later in this chapter, you use the new MIDL compiler to develop your custom interface. First, however, you must examine proxies, stubs, and the Service Control Manager in more detail.

The Service Control Manager

The Service Control Manager (SCM) is a new component of 32-bit OLE. The SCM is responsible for locating and loading OLE servers. Originally, you could simply look up the name of an in-process DLL or local server in the system registry. However, to support OLE's potential capability to locate remote object servers, Microsoft developed the SCM.

You still use the system registry to hold information about each object, and the SCM caches this information. If a client application attempts to create an object from an in-process object server, the SCM passes the request to the OLE libraries. The SCM locates and loads the server, whether it is local or remote. If the server is already running, the SCM connects to it.

The process for locating and connecting to a remote object server consists of the following steps if your application calls `BindToObject` with a file moniker:

1. The application calls the `BindToObject` API.
2. `BindToObject` then invokes the SCM, passing the CLSID for the object.
3. The SCM then connects to or creates the server process.
4. The object server then creates and registers its class object. The object is registered with the SCM.
5. The SCM then activates the object. In this case, this activation requires a call to `IClassFactory::CreateInstance` followed by a call to `IPersistFile::Load`.

6. The marshaled interface pointer returns to the SCM.
7. SCM will then return the marshaled pointer to the client.
8. `BindToObject` uses this marshaled information to connect directly to the server object.
9. Finally, `BindToObject` converts the marshaled information into a `vtable` pointer that is returned to the client application.

The client then uses the `vtable` pointer to call methods on the object. The process for connecting to remote objects is similar. However, regardless of whether the server is remote, local, or in process, the client always receives a `vtable` pointer.

The Proxy

The proxy is the server substitute located on the client side of the process boundary. The proxy is responsible for marshaling the interface parameters and placing them in the RPC channel. This channel is responsible for actually transporting the data. You implement proxies as aggregate objects that consist of a Proxy Manager and an interface proxy for each interface supported.

The Proxy Manager implements the controlling unknown for the aggregate. Each interface proxy supports the `IRPCProxyBuffer` interface. When you call one of the implemented interfaces, the interface proxy begins by getting a marshaling package from the RPC channel. The `IRpcChannel::GetStream` method is then used to retrieve the package. The interface proxy then marshals the parameters to the stream by calling `IStream::Write` for each parameter. After all the parameters are placed in the channel, the proxy calls `IRpcChannel::Call` to send the data to the remote stub. When this function call returns, the returned parameters are retrieved from the channel and unmarshaled. The proxy then closes the stream and returns the data to the caller. Figure 17.2 shows the structure of the proxy.

The RPC run-time library handles the actual transport of the data. The version of RPC developed by Microsoft is fully compatible with the Open Software Foundation's Distributed Computing Environment (OSF DCE). You can configure RPC to use different network transports. Transports are available for NetBIOS, IPX/SPX,and TCP/IP networks. RPC also provides the name service that is used to locate object servers on the network. Finally, RPC provides a security service that restricts the access of objects.

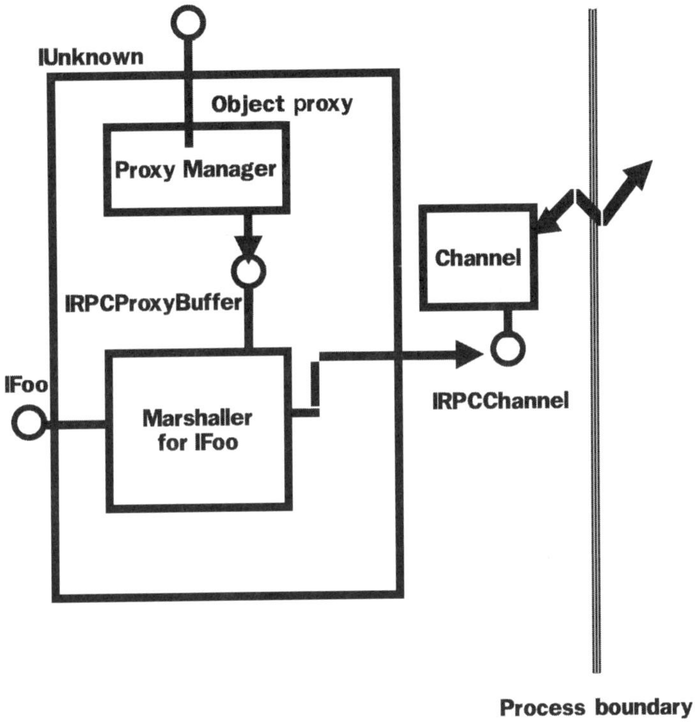

Fig. 17.2
The proxy.

The Stub

After the receiving channel receives the marshaled data, it is passed to the interface stub. The stub then unmarshals the data and makes the actual call on the server interface. Stubs are not implemented as aggregates and each stub supports the `IRPCStubBuffer` interface.

Both stubs and proxies use the `IRPCChannelBuffer` to talk to the underlying RPC run-time library.

Figure 17.3 shows the structure of the stub.

A Sample Custom Interface Implementation

In this section, you develop your own custom interface. For this example, you modify the OLE Automation quote server that you developed in Chapter 13, "Creating a Simple Automation Server," by implementing the server with a custom interface rather than with `IDispatch`.

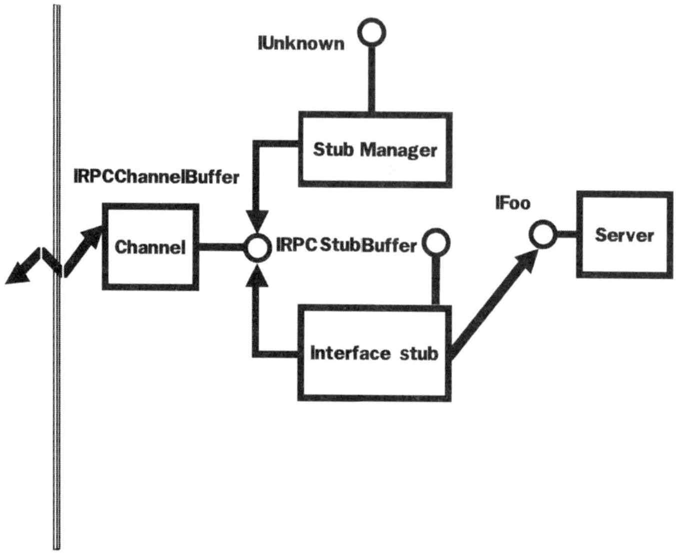

Fig. 17.3
The stub.

The application consists of three parts. The first is the proxy and stub implementation. You implement this part as an in-process DLL. You then develop the server application that exposes the custom interface. Finally, you develop a simple client application that accesses this custom interface.

Creating the Proxy and Stub

The first step is to create the in-process server that serves as your proxy and stub implementation for the custom interface. To generate the code that you use to build the DLL, you use the MIDL 2.0 compiler that ships with the 32-bit Windows SDK (the 1994 version of the 32-bit Windows SDK, which supports development with Windows 95 and Windows NT 3.5). You also use the UUIDGEN tool to generate the IID for your interface.

To build the IDL file that contains the description of your interface, you use the IDL language. You used this language in Part III, "OLE Automation," when you developed type libraries.

Designing the Interface

Before you begin designing the interface, you need to be aware of some guidelines. Microsoft specifies these guidelines to help ensure that the custom interfaces that you design today continue to work when support for distributed objects becomes available.

The first rule is that you should avoid using data types that are dependent on the hardware on which you are running. For example, if you specify an `int` data type on an Intel I386 machine running Windows NT, you may not be able to recreate the data on a machine that does not use 32-bit `int`s. To ensure that your data can be recreated in the remote machine's address space, you must use unambiguous data types. In fact, the MIDL compiler does not even accept the type `int`. You must explicitly declare your integers to be short or long.

Likewise, you cannot use void pointers. Instead, you must explicitly declare the data type so that the receiving stub can reproduce it. In your custom interface, you have to tell the MIDL compiler the exact length of your pointer to an array of characters. Simply describing the data type as `char *` is not enough; this description is too vague and would be interpreted as a pointer to a single character.

You must initialize all pointers, including those contained as members in structures. If the pointers do not currently point to any data, you must set them to NULL.

Finally, be careful if you want to let pointers point to the same piece of memory. If you want to do so, you should declare the pointers as aliases in the IDL file. If a pointer is not declared as an alias, you should never let it point to the same memory area as another pointer.

The IDL File

Again, your custom interface is quite simple. It contains only one method, `GetString`, which takes two parameters. The first parameter is an index to the array of quotes that your server makes available. The second parameter is a pointer to a character buffer that holds the returned string.

Listing 17.1 shows the IDL file for your custom interface, `IMyCInterface`. The IDL file consists of two parts: the header and the body.

Listing 17.1 The IDL File

```
//-----------------------------------------------------------//
// IDL file to create the proxy/stub code for your custom interface
//-----------------------------------------------------------//

[
    object,
     uuid(9dffb854-9e7d-101b-97c9-524153480001),
    pointer_default(unique)
```

(continues)

Listing 17.1 Continued

```
]

interface IMyCInterface : IUnknown
{
    import "unknwn.idl";

    HRESULT GetString( [in] short nIndex,
                       [out, string, size_is(81)] OLECHAR *psz);
}
```

The first part is the interface header, which describes the interface as a whole. The header begins with the keyword `object`, which indicates that the interface is a COM interface. The `object` keyword is followed by the interface ID (IID) for your interface. To generate this IID, you use the UUIDGEN tool supplied with the SDK. The `pointer_default` keyword specifies the default attribute for all pointers except those specified in parameter lists. The `pointer_default` keyword may contain one of the following values: `Unique`, `Ref`, or `Ptr`. The *RPC Programmer's Guide* fully describes each of these pointer attributes.

The body of the IDL file contains the data members used in this interface and the function prototypes. You can also include statements for the C++ preprocessor, as you will see when you examine the UNKNWN.IDL file. The first statement is the name of the interface. For this example, the name is `IMyCInterface`. Because this is to be a COM interface, you naturally have it inherit from `IUnknown`. The next statement imports the IDL description for `IUnknown`. You examine this file in the next section.

The prototype for the lone member function is worth examining in detail. As you can see in listing 17.1, the function, `GetString`, returns an HRESULT. The function takes two parameters. The first parameter is an index into the array of quotes that the server has stored. Note that you use the `short` keyword to tell the compiler that the variable is a 16-bit value. The `in` keyword tells the MIDL compiler that this parameter is filled in when you call the function.

The second parameter is a pointer to a character array. Because this declaration is too vague for MIDL, you qualify the declaration with the `string` keyword and the `size_is` keyword. These keywords tell the compiler that the array is a character array that is 81 characters long. When you call this function, this parameter is not filled. Instead, it is filled in when the function returns. Therefore, you prefix the function with the `out` keyword.

Listing 17.2 shows the IDL file for the `IUnknown` interface. The `local` keyword at the beginning of the interface header tells the MIDL compiler to generate header files only and not stubs.

Listing 17.2 The *IUnknown* IDL File

```
[
  local,
  object,
  uuid(00000000-0000-0000-C000-000000000046),
  pointer_default(unique)
]

interface IUnknown
{
    import "wtypes.idl";

    typedef [unique] IUnknown *LPUNKNOWN;

    HRESULT QueryInterface([in] REFIID riid,
                           [out, iid_is(riid)] void **ppvObject);

    ULONG AddRef(void);

    ULONG Release(void);
     cpp_quote("#if defined(__cplusplus) && !defined(CINTERFACE)")
     cpp_quote("extern \"C\" {")
     cpp_quote("#endif")

     cpp_quote("void STDAPICALLTYPE MIDL_GetMarshalSizeMax(
              RPC_MESSAGE *pMessage, REFIID riid,IUnknown *punk);")
     cpp_quote("void STDAPICALLTYPE MIDL_MarshalInterface(
              RPC_MESSAGE *pMessage, REFIID riid, void *pv);")
     cpp_quote("void STDAPICALLTYPE MIDL_UnmarshalInterface(
              RPC_MESSAGE *pMessage, REFIID riid, void **ppv);")

     cpp_quote("#if defined(__cplusplus) && !defined(CINTERFACE)")
     cpp_quote("}")
     cpp_quote("#endif")
}
```

The interface body consists of the standard `IUnknown` functions: `QueryInterface`, `AddRef`, and `Release`.

The `cpp_quote` keyword instructs MIDL to emit the specified string, without the quotation marks, into the generated header file. Note that the header file declares three additional functions.

Building the DLL

When you run the MIDL compiler against the IDL files, you generate four files. The first file, BPS_P.CXX, includes the proxy and stub code. This code will be used to generate the proxy and stub DLL. The file also contains the code for the proxy and stub factory interface that creates the proxy and stub. Listing 17.3 shows the code generated for your interface's proxy and stub.

Listing 17.3 BPS_P.CXX and BPS_X.HXX

```
#ifndef __BPS_X_H__
#define __BPS_X_H__

#include "stdrpc.hxx"
#include ".\bps.h"
#include "wtypes.h"
#include "unknwn.h"
#ifdef __cplusplus

class CProxyIMyCInterface : public CProxyIUnknown
{
public:
    CProxyIMyCInterface(IUnknown *punkOuter, REFIID riid) :
        CProxyIUnknown(punkOuter, riid)
    {};

    virtual HRESULT STDMETHODCALLTYPE GetString
    (
     short nIndex,
     OLECHAR *psz
    );

};

class CPSFactoryBufferIMyCInterface : public CStdPSFactoryBuffer
{
public:
    CPSFactoryBufferIMyCInterface();

    virtual HRESULT STDMETHODCALLTYPE CreateProxy
    (
        IUnknown *pUnkOuter,
        REFIID riid,
        IRpcProxyBuffer **ppProxy,
        void **ppv
    );

    virtual HRESULT STDMETHODCALLTYPE CreateStub
    (
        REFIID riid,
        IUnknown *punkServer,
        IRpcStubBuffer **ppStub

    );
```

```
};

class CStubIMyCInterface : public CStubIUnknown
{
public:
    CStubIMyCInterface(REFIID riid) : CStubIUnknown(riid){};
    virtual HRESULT STDMETHODCALLTYPE Invoke(RPCOLEMESSAGE *_prpcmsg,
                                     IRpcChannelBuffer *_pRpcChannel);
    HRESULT STDMETHODCALLTYPE CStubGetString(MIDLMESSAGE * _prpcmsg);

};
extern "C" {
#endif


#define IMyCInterface_GetString_OPNUM 0
#ifdef __cplusplus
}
#endif
#endif //__BPS_X_H__


#include "stdrpc.hxx"
#pragma hdrstop
#include ".\bps_x.h"

#pragma code_seg("PSFBctor")
CPSFactoryBufferIMyCInterface _gPSFactoryBufferIMyCInterface;

CPSFactoryBufferIMyCInterface::CPSFactoryBufferIMyCInterface() :
➥CStdPSFactoryBuffer(IID_IMyCInterface)
{
}

#pragma code_seg()


HRESULT STDMETHODCALLTYPE CPSFactoryBufferIMyCInterface::CreateProxy
(
    IUnknown *punkOuter,
    REFIID riid,
    IRpcProxyBuffer **ppProxy,
    void **ppv
)
{
    HRESULT hr = E_OUTOFMEMORY;
    CProxyIMyCInterface *pProxy;

    pProxy = new CProxyIMyCInterface(punkOuter, riid);
    *ppv = pProxy;
    if(pProxy)
    {

        *ppProxy = new CStdProxyBuffer(pProxy);
        if(*ppProxy)
        {
```

(continues)

Listing 17.3 Continued

```
                hr = S_OK;
            }
            else
            {
                delete pProxy;
                *ppv = 0;
            }

        }
        return hr;
    }

    HRESULT STDMETHODCALLTYPE CPSFactoryBufferIMyCInterface::CreateStub
    (
        REFIID riid,
        IUnknown *punkServer,
        IRpcStubBuffer **ppStub

    )
    {
        HRESULT hr = E_OUTOFMEMORY;

        *ppStub = new CStubIMyCInterface(riid);
        if(*ppStub)
        {
            hr = S_OK;
            if(punkServer)
                hr = (*ppStub)->Connect(punkServer);
        }
        return hr;
    }

    #pragma code_seg(".ORPC")
    HRESULT STDMETHODCALLTYPE CStubIMyCInterface::Invoke(
              RPCOLEMESSAGE *pMessage, IRpcChannelBuffer *pRpcChannel)
    {
        MIDLMESSAGE message;
        HRESULT hResult = S_OK;

        memcpy(&message, pMessage, sizeof(*pMessage));
        message.pRpcChannel = pRpcChannel;
        message.packet = message.Buffer;
        switch(message.iMethod)
        {
        case IMyCInterface_GetString_OPNUM:
            hResult = CStubGetString(&message);
            break;
        default:
            hResult = RPC_E_INVALIDMETHOD;
            break;
        }
        pMessage->cbBuffer = (unsigned char *)message.Buffer -
                      (unsigned char *)message.packet;
```

```
    pMessage->Buffer = message.packet;
    return hResult;
}


HRESULT STDMETHODCALLTYPE CProxyIMyCInterface::GetString
(
     short nIndex,
     OLECHAR *psz
)
{
    MIDLMESSAGE _message;
    PRPC_MESSAGE _prpcmsg = (PRPC_MESSAGE) &_message;

    HRESULT  _ret_value;
    unsigned long _valid_total;
    unsigned long _alloc_bound;
    unsigned long _alloc_total;
    unsigned long _valid_lower;

    unsigned char *_tempbuf;
    unsigned char *_savebuf;
    void *_buffer;
    void *_treebuf;


    //Initialize [out] parameters
    memset((void *) psz, 0, (81 * sizeof(wchar_t)));
    _try
    {

        //Calculate size of message buffer
        RpcInitMessage(&_message, _pRpcChannel);
                _prpcmsg->BufferLength = 2;


        //Get RPC message
        _message.iMethod = IMyCInterface_GetString_OPNUM;
        RpcGetBuffer(&_message, _iid);


        //Marshal [in] and [in,out] parameters
                /* send data from nIndex */
        (*(unsigned long FAR *)&_prpcmsg->Buffer) ++;
        *(unsigned long FAR *)&_prpcmsg->Buffer &= 0xfffffffe;
        *(*(short FAR *FAR *)&_prpcmsg->Buffer)++ = (short)nIndex;



        //Send the request message, then receive the result message.
        RpcSendReceive(&_message);
                //Unmarshal parameters and return value
                _tempbuf = (unsigned char FAR *)_prpcmsg->Buffer;
        _treebuf = 0;
        if (psz ==0)
     RpcRaiseException(RPC_X_NULL_REF_POINTER);
```

(continues)

Listing 17.3 Continued

```
        // recv total number of elements
          long_from_ndr((PRPC_MESSAGE)_prpcmsg, &_alloc_total);
          data_from_ndr((PRPC_MESSAGE)_prpcmsg,
                        (void __RPC_FAR *) (psz), "s2", 1);
          /* receive data into &_ret_value */
          long_from_ndr((PRPC_MESSAGE)_prpcmsg,
                        (unsigned long FAR *)&_ret_value);

          RpcFreeBuffer(&_message);
      }
      _except(EXCEPTION_EXECUTE_HANDLER)
      {
          RpcClientErrorHandler(&_message, GetExceptionCode(),
                                &_ret_value, 0, 0);
      }
      return _ret_value;

}

HRESULT STDMETHODCALLTYPE CStubIMyCInterface::CStubGetString(
                                          MIDLMESSAGE * _pMessage)
{
    HRESULT _hResult = S_OK;

        short nIndex;

        OLECHAR *psz = 0;

    HRESULT  _ret_value;
    unsigned long _alloc_total;
    unsigned char  *_savebuf;
    unsigned char *_tempbuf;
    PRPC_MESSAGE _prpcmsg = (PRPC_MESSAGE) _pMessage;
    //Initialize [in] and [in, out] parameters

    _try
    {
        //Unmarshal [in] and [in,out] parameters
                /* receive data into &nIndex */
        short_from_ndr((PRPC_MESSAGE)_prpcmsg,
                       (unsigned short FAR *)&nIndex);

        //Initialize [out] parameters
                _alloc_total = 81;
        psz = (OLECHAR *)MIDL_user_allocate ((size_t)
                      (_alloc_total * sizeof(OLECHAR)));

        memset((void *) psz, 0, (81 * sizeof(wchar_t)));
        _ret_value = ((IMyCInterface *)_pInterface)->GetString(
                      (short )nIndex, (OLECHAR *)psz);
        RpcCheckHRESULT(_ret_value);
                //Calculate size of message buffer
                _prpcmsg->BufferLength = 16;
```

```
        if (psz ==0)
    RpcRaiseException(RPC_X_NULL_REF_POINTER);
        if (81)
          {
          if (((MIDL_wchar_strlen((wchar_t __RPC_FAR  *  )(psz))+1)) >
               (size_t) (81)) RpcRaiseException(RPC_X_INVALID_BOUND);
          }
        else
          {
          if (((MIDL_wchar_strlen((wchar_t __RPC_FAR  *  )(psz))+1)) !=
               (size_t) (81)) RpcRaiseException(RPC_X_INVALID_BOUND);
          }
        _prpcmsg->BufferLength += 3;
        _prpcmsg->BufferLength &= (unsigned int)0xfffffffc;
        _prpcmsg->BufferLength += 4;
        data_size_ndr((void __RPC_FAR *)psz, (PRPC_MESSAGE)_prpcmsg,
                      "s2", 1);

        //Get RPC message buffer
        RpcGetBuffer(_pMessage, _iid);

        //Marshal [out] and [in,out] parameters
                // send total number of elements
        *(unsigned long FAR *)&_prpcmsg->Buffer += 3;
        *(unsigned long FAR *)&_prpcmsg->Buffer &= 0xfffffffc;
        *(*(long FAR *FAR *)&_prpcmsg->Buffer)++ = 81;
        data_into_ndr((void __RPC_FAR *)psz, (PRPC_MESSAGE)_prpcmsg,
                      "s2", 1);
        /* send data from _ret_value */
        *(unsigned long FAR *)&_prpcmsg->Buffer += 3;
        *(unsigned long FAR *)&_prpcmsg->Buffer &= 0xfffffffc;
        *(*(long FAR *FAR *)&_prpcmsg->Buffer)++ = (long)_ret_value;

    }
    _except(EXCEPTION_EXECUTE_HANDLER)
    {
        _hResult = GetExceptionCode();

    }
    //Clean up local variables
        MIDL_user_free((void FAR  *)(psz));
return _hResult;
}

#pragma code_seg()
```

Notice the proxy code that marshals the `GetString` parameters and the stub code that unmarshals them on the other side. Note also the use of structured exception handling to handle errors.

The BPS.H header file in listing 17.4 contains the definition for your interface. Both C and C++ compilers can use the generated code.

Listing 17.4 BPS.H

```
#include <windows.h>
#ifndef __IMyCInterface__
#define __IMyCInterface__

#include "basetyps.h"
/* Forward declaration */
typedef interface IMyCInterface IMyCInterface;

#include "wtypes.h"
#include "unknwn.h"

#ifndef _ERROR_STATUS_T_DEFINED
typedef unsigned long error_status_t;
#define _ERROR_STATUS_T_DEFINED
#endif


#ifndef _WCHAR_T_DEFINED
typedef unsigned short wchar_t;
#define _WCHAR_T_DEFINED
#endif


#if defined(__cplusplus) && !defined(CINTERFACE)

/* C++ Language Binding */
extern "C" const IID IID_IMyCInterface;

interface IMyCInterface : public IUnknown
{
public:
    virtual HRESULT STDMETHODCALLTYPE GetString
    (
     short nIndex,
     OLECHAR *psz
    ) = 0;

};

#else

/* C Language Binding */
extern const IID IID_IMyCInterface;

typedef struct IMyCInterfaceVtbl
{

    HRESULT (STDMETHODCALLTYPE FAR *QueryInterface)
    (
        IMyCInterface FAR *this,
     REFIID riid,
     void **ppvObject
    );
```

```
    ULONG (STDMETHODCALLTYPE FAR *AddRef)
    (
        IMyCInterface FAR *this
    );

    ULONG (STDMETHODCALLTYPE FAR *Release)
    (
        IMyCInterface FAR *this
    );

    HRESULT (STDMETHODCALLTYPE FAR *GetString)
    (
        IMyCInterface FAR *this,
     short nIndex,
     OLECHAR *psz
    );

} IMyCInterfaceVtbl;

interface IMyCInterface
{
    IMyCInterfaceVtbl FAR *lpVtbl;
} ;

#ifdef COBJMACROS

#define IMyCInterface_QueryInterface(pI, riid, ppvObject) \
    (*(pI)->lpVtbl->QueryInterface)((pI), riid, ppvObject)

#define IMyCInterface_AddRef(pI) \
    (*(pI)->lpVtbl->AddRef)((pI))

#define IMyCInterface_Release(pI) \
    (*(pI)->lpVtbl->Release)((pI))

#define IMyCInterface_GetString(pI, nIndex, psz) \
    (*(pI)->lpVtbl->GetString)((pI), nIndex, psz)
#endif /* COBJMACROS */

#endif

#endif /*__IMyCInterface__*/
```

Finally, listing 17.5 is BPS_I.C, the interface identifier file. This file defines the IID for your interface.

Listing 17.5 BPS_I.C

```
typedef struct _IID
{
    unsigned long x;
    unsigned short s1;
```

(continues)

Listing 17.5 Continued

```
    unsigned short s2;
    unsigned char  c[8];
} IID;

const IID IID_IMyCInterface = {0x9dffb854,0x9e7d,0x101b,
                           {0x97,0xc9,0x52,0x41,0x53,0x48,0x00,0x01}};
```

To build your proxy and stub DLL, you must link in some helper files in addition to BPS_I.C. These helper files include helper functions for the marshaling code and also the standard DLL entry point, `DLLGetClassObject`. Figure 17.4 shows the entire build process for your proxy and stub DLL.

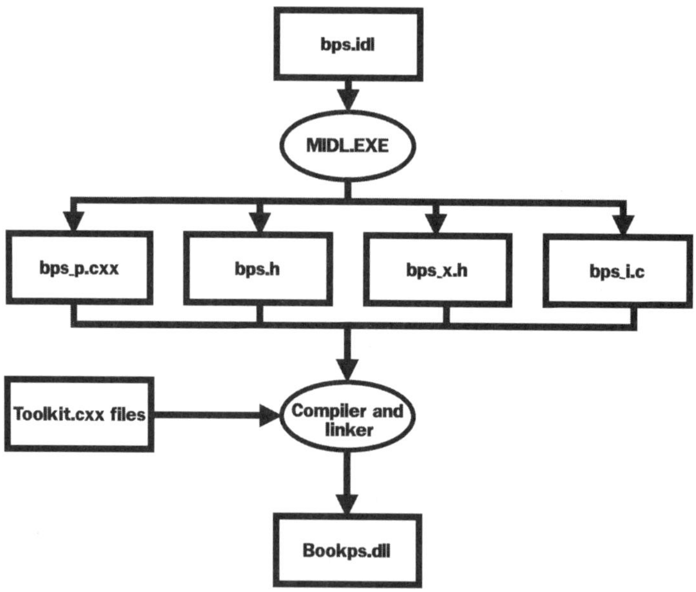

Fig. 17.4
The build process for the proxy and stub DLL.

Listing 17.6 shows the make file that you use to build the DLL.

Listing 17.6 The Make File for the Proxy and Stub DLL

```
#-----------------------------------------------------------------
# Make file to build the proxy/stub DLL
#-----------------------------------------------------------------

!include <ntwin32.mak>
```

```
MFLAGS     = /ms_ext /c_ext /cpp_cmd$(cc)
OLEFLAGS = -DUNICODE -DINC_OLE2 -I ..\bookps

all: bookps.dll

unknwn.h: unknwn.idl
    cmidl $(MFLAGS) unknwn.idl

bps_i.c, bps_p.cxx: bps.idl unknwn.h
    cmidl $(MFLAGS) bps.idl

bps_i.obj: bps_i.c
    $(cc) $(cvars) $(cflags) $(cdebug) $(OLEFLAGS) bps_i.c

bps_p.obj: bps_p.cxx
    $(cc) $(cvars) $(cflags) $(cdebug) $(OLEFLAGS) bps_p.cxx

stdrpc.obj: stdrpc.cxx stdrpc.hxx
    $(cc) $(cvars) $(cflags) $(cdebug) $(OLEFLAGS) stdrpc.cxx

stdclass.obj: stdclass.cxx stdclass.hxx
    $(cc) $(cvars) $(cflags) $(cdebug) $(OLEFLAGS) stdclass.cxx

bookps.dll: bps_p.obj stdclass.obj bookps.def stdrpc.obj bps_i.obj
    $(implib) -DEF:bookps.def -MACHINE:$(CPU)\
    -OUT:proxstba.lib bps_p.obj stdclass.obj stdrpc.obj
    $(implib) -MACHINE:$(CPU) -OUT:bookps.lib proxstba.lib bps_i.obj
    $(link) $(linkdebug) -subsystem:console $(ole2libsdll)\
      rpcrt4.lib rpcndr.lib -DLL -OUT:bookps.dll \
    bps_p.obj bps_i.obj stdclass.obj stdrpc.obj bookps.lib
proxstba.exp
```

The Server Code

After successfully building the proxy and stub DLL for your custom interface, you create the object server that implements your interface. As mentioned earlier, this server is basically the same one that you created in Chapter 13, "Creating a Simple Automation Server." The main difference is that this code is fully Unicode-compatible and does not use OLE Automation.

The MAIN.CPP File

After creating your application's main window, you check the build versions of the OLE libraries. You then initialize the libraries and proceed to create your object.

This application has only one COM object, so you create it when the server starts. Normally, you would not create the object until your `IClassFactory::CreateInstance` method was called.

After creating the object itself, you create your class object and register it with the OLE libraries. When you register the class object with OLE, you create the object's stub. The proxy for your client application links to this stub when the client creates an object from this server. Listing 17.7 shows the code for MAIN.CPP (the sample application's main module). Notice the use of the TEXT macro to enable all the text strings to be compiled for Unicode.

Listing 17.7 MAIN.CPP

```
#include "autosrv.h"

#include <stdlib.h>
#include <string.h>


//---------------------------------------------------------------//
// Globals
DWORD g_dwCAutoSrvCF = 0;
CAutoSrv FAR* g_pAutoSrv = NULL;
TCHAR g_szAppName[] = TEXT("AutoSrv");

//---------------------------------------------------------------//
// Prototypes
HRESULT InitOle(void);
void ExitOle(void);
BOOL InitApplication(HANDLE);
BOOL InitInstance(HANDLE, int);

extern "C"
{
long FAR PASCAL WndProc(HWND, UINT, WPARAM, LPARAM);
int PASCAL WinMain(HANDLE, HANDLE, LPSTR, int);
}


//---------------------------------------------------------------
extern "C" int PASCAL WinMain(HANDLE hinst,
                   HANDLE hPrevInstance,LPSTR lpCmdLine,int
nCmdShow)
{
     //------------------------------------------
     // WinMain.
     // Initialize your application and OLE
     // and then pump messages until the application shuts down.
     //
     //
    MSG msg;

     // Init the application. Register the window class, etc.
    if(!hPrevInstance)
          if(!InitApplication(hinst))
               return FALSE;
```

```
    // Load and init the OLE libraries
    if(NOERROR != InitOle())
          return FALSE;

    if(!InitInstance(hinst,nCmdShow))
    {
          ExitOle();
          return FALSE;
    }


    while(GetMessage(&msg, NULL, NULL, NULL))
    {
          TranslateMessage(&msg);
          DispatchMessage(&msg);
    }

    ExitOle();

    return msg.wParam;
}
//---------------------------------------------------------------//
BOOL InitApplication(HANDLE hInst)
{
     //---------------------------------------------
     // InitApplication
     // Register your window class with Windows
     //
     //
    WNDCLASS  wc;

    wc.style            = CS_HREDRAW ¦ CS_VREDRAW;
    wc.lpfnWndProc      = WndProc;
    wc.cbClsExtra       = 0;
    wc.cbWndExtra       = DLGWINDOWEXTRA;
    wc.hInstance        = hInst;
    wc.hIcon            = LoadIcon(hInst,MAKEINTRESOURCE(101));
    wc.hCursor          = LoadCursor(NULL, IDC_ARROW);
    wc.hbrBackground    = (HBRUSH) (COLOR_APPWORKSPACE+1);
    wc.lpszMenuName     = NULL;
    wc.lpszClassName    = g_szAppName;

     if(!RegisterClass(&wc))
          return FALSE;

    return TRUE;
}
//---------------------------------------------------------------//
BOOL InitInstance(HANDLE hInst, int nCmdShow)
{
     //---------------------------------------------
     // InitInstance
     // Create your window and minimize it.
```

(continues)

Listing 17.7 Continued

```
      HWND hWnd = CreateWindow(g_szAppName,TEXT("Quote Server"),
                              WS_OVERLAPPEDWINDOW, 0,0,CW_USEDEFAULT,
                              CW_USEDEFAULT,NULL,NULL,hInst,NULL);
    ShowWindow(hWnd,SW_MINIMIZE);
    g_pAutoSrv->m_hWnd = hWnd;

    return TRUE;
}
//-----------------------------------------------------------//
extern "C" long CALLBACK WndProc(HWND hwnd,UINT message,
                                 WPARAM wParam,LPARAM lParam)
{
     //-----------------------------------------
     // WndProc.
     // Main message switch.
     //
     // The only thing that really concerns you here is
     // to refuse to open the icon to a window.
     //
     switch(message)
     {
          case WM_QUERYOPEN:
               return 0L;
          case WM_DESTROY:
               PostQuitMessage(0);
               return 0;
    }
    return DefWindowProc(hwnd, message, wParam, lParam);
}
//-----------------------------------------------------------//
HRESULT InitOle()
{
     //-----------------------------------------
     // InitOle
     // Initialize the OLE libraries and create instances
     // of your object and object class factory.
     //
     //
    HRESULT hResult;
    IClassFactory FAR* pcf;
    DWORD dwVersion;

     //---------
     // Always check that the version of the OLE libraries
     // is compatible with the libraries you used to build
     // your application.
     dwVersion  = OleBuildVersion();
    if (HIWORD(dwVersion) != rmm || LOWORD(dwVersion) < rup)
    {
         MessageBox(GetFocus(),TEXT("Error: Incompatible OLE
                                    libraries"),TEXT("Error"),0);
         // Any error code will do
         hResult = ResultFromScode(E_FAIL);
```

```
        return hResult;
    }

     // Initialize the OLE libraries
    if((hResult = OleInitialize(NULL)) != NOERROR)
          return hResult;

     // Create your object.
    if((g_pAutoSrv = CAutoSrv::Create()) == NULL)
    {
          hResult = ResultFromScode(E_OUTOFMEMORY);
          return hResult;
    }

    // Create a class factory for your object
    pcf = CAutoSrvCF::Create();
    if (NULL == pcf)
    {
          ExitOle();
          return hResult;
    }

    // Register the class factory.

     CLSID clsid;

     LPOLESTR lp = TEXT("{d0ae2f60-9ea0-101b-97ca-524153480001}");
     CLSIDFromString(lp,&clsid);

    hResult = CoRegisterClassObject(clsid,pcf,
          CLSCTX_LOCAL_SERVER,REGCLS_MULTIPLEUSE,&g_dwCAutoSrvCF);
    if (NOERROR != hResult)
    {
          pcf->Release();
          ExitOle();
          return hResult;
    }

    pcf->Release();

    return NOERROR;
}
//-----------------------------------------------------------------//
void ExitOle()
{
     //-----------------------------------------------
     // ExitOle
     // Shut down your object and close the OLE libraries
     //
     //

    // If a class factory was successfully created earlier,
    // tell OLE that the object is no longer available.
    if(g_dwCAutoSrvCF != 0)
          CoRevokeClassObject(g_dwCAutoSrvCF);
```

(continues)

Listing 17.7 Continued

```
    // cause the remaining typeinfo to be released
    if (g_pAutoSrv != NULL)
          g_pAutoSrv->Release();

    // Release the OLE libraries
    OleUninitialize();
}
//-----------------------------------------------------------------//
```

The AUTOSRV.CPP Module

The AUTOSRV.CPP module (listing 17.8) implements your object's class factory. The class factory implementation is pretty basic. (Chapter 13, "Creating a Simple Automation Server," discusses the `IClassFactory` implementation in detail.) You acknowledge `QueryInterface` for `IUnknown` and `IClassFactory`. During the `CreateInstance` call, you return a pointer to your main object. The MAIN.CPP module creates this object when it starts.

Listing 17.8 AUTOSRV.H and AUTOSRV.CPP

```
#include <windows.h>
#include <tchar.h>

#include <ole2ver.h>


#pragma warning(disable:4355)

#define MAXQUOTES     10

//-----------------------------------------------------------------//
// The CAutoSrv object
class FAR CAutoSrv : public IUnknown
{
public:
    CAutoSrv();
    ~CAutoSrv();
    static CAutoSrv FAR * Create();

     // Implementation of IUnknown
    STDMETHOD(QueryInterface)(REFIID riid, void FAR* FAR* ppv);
    STDMETHOD_(ULONG, AddRef)(void);
    STDMETHOD_(ULONG, Release)(void);

    HWND m_hWnd;
    TCHAR m_lpQuotes[MAXQUOTES][256];
     STDMETHOD(GetString)(short nID, LPTSTR lpMsg);
public:
    ULONG m_refs;                            // Reference count.
```

```
};
//---------------------------------------------------------------//
// The CAutoSrv class factory
class FAR CAutoSrvCF : public IClassFactory
{
public:
    CAutoSrvCF();
    static IClassFactory FAR* Create();

     // Implementation of IUnknown
    STDMETHOD(QueryInterface)(REFIID riid, void FAR* FAR* ppv);
    STDMETHOD_(ULONG, AddRef)(void);
    STDMETHOD_(ULONG, Release)(void);

    // IClassFactory methods
    STDMETHOD(CreateInstance)(IUnknown FAR* punkOuter,REFIID riid,
              void FAR* FAR* ppv);
    STDMETHOD(LockServer)(BOOL fLock);

private:
    ULONG m_refs;
};
//---------------------------------------------------------------//
//---------------------------------------------------------------//

// Include files and macro definitions
#include "autosrv.h"
#include "..\bookps\bps.h"


//-----------------------------------------------------------------
CAutoSrv::CAutoSrv()
{
     m_refs = 0;

     // Set up your famous quotes table
        _tcscpy(m_lpQuotes[0],
          TEXT("Study art and logic - \
               learn to draw your own conclusions."));
        _tcscpy(m_lpQuotes[1],
          TEXT("When a finger points at the moon, \
               the imbecile looks at the finger."));
        _tcscpy(m_lpQuotes[2],
          TEXT("Negative slack tends to increase."));
        _tcscpy(m_lpQuotes[3],
          TEXT("Information travels more surely to those \
               with a lesser need to know."));
        _tcscpy(m_lpQuotes[4],
          TEXT("Always yield to temptation - \
               it may never pass your way again."));
        _tcscpy(m_lpQuotes[5],
          TEXT("Reality is for people who cannot cope \
               with science fiction."));
```

(continues)

Listing 17.8 Continued

```
     _tcscpy(m_lpQuotes[6],
          TEXT("When faced with two evils I like to do the one \
             I've never tried before. - Mae West"));
     _tcscpy(m_lpQuotes[7], TEXT("Anything free is worth \
                                  what you pay for it."));
     _tcscpy(m_lpQuotes[8], TEXT("What you cannot avoid, welcome."));
     _tcscpy(m_lpQuotes[9], TEXT("Walk softly but carry a big stick."));
}
//---------------------------------------------------------------------
CAutoSrv::~CAutoSrv()
{
}
//---------------------------------------------------------------------
CAutoSrv FAR * CAutoSrv::Create()
{
     CAutoSrv FAR* pObj;

     pObj = new FAR CAutoSrv();
     if(NULL == pObj)
          return NULL;

     pObj->AddRef();

     return pObj;
}
//---------------------------------------------------------------------
STDMETHODIMP CAutoSrv::GetString(short nID, LPTSTR lpMsg)
{
     _tcscpy(lpMsg,m_lpQuotes[nID]);
     return (S_OK);
}
//---------------------------------------------------------------------
STDMETHODIMP CAutoSrv::QueryInterface(REFIID riid, void FAR* FAR* ppv)
{
     if (riid == IID_IUnknown)
     {
          *ppv = this;
     }
     else if (riid == IID_IMyCInterface)
     {
          *ppv = this;
     }
     else
     {
          *ppv = NULL;
          return ResultFromScode(E_NOINTERFACE);
     }
     AddRef();
     return NOERROR;
}
//---------------------------------------------------------------------
STDMETHODIMP_(ULONG) CAutoSrv::AddRef()
{
     // Return ref counts for debugging.
     return ++m_refs;
}
```

```
//------------------------------------------------------------
STDMETHODIMP_(ULONG) CAutoSrv::Release()
{
     // When your ref count reaches zero,
     // you destroy the object and kill the
     // application.
     if(—m_refs == 0)
     {
          PostQuitMessage(0);
          delete this;
          return 0;
     }
     // Return ref counts for debugging.
     return m_refs;
}
//------------------------------------------------------------
//------------------------------------------------------------
// This is the ClassFactory implementation for your one
// and only object.
//
CAutoSrvCF::CAutoSrvCF()
{
     m_refs = 1;
}
//------------------------------------------------------------
IClassFactory FAR* CAutoSrvCF::Create()
{
     return new FAR CAutoSrvCF();
}
//------------------------------------------------------------
STDMETHODIMP CAutoSrvCF::QueryInterface(REFIID riid, void FAR* FAR* ppv)
{
     // You support just two interfaces: the ubiquitous IUnknown
     // and, of course, IClassFactory.
     if(riid == IID_IUnknown ¦¦ riid == IID_IClassFactory)
     {
     AddRef();
     *ppv = this;
     return NOERROR;
     }
     *ppv = NULL;
     return ResultFromScode(E_NOINTERFACE);
}
//------------------------------------------------------------
STDMETHODIMP_(ULONG) CAutoSrvCF::AddRef()
{
     // Increase your ref count and return
     // the current ref count for debugging purposes

     return ++m_refs;
}
```

(continues)

Listing 17.8 Continued

```
//-----------------------------------------------------------------
STDMETHODIMP_(ULONG) CAutoSrvCF::Release()
{
     // You count down to zero and then
     // self-destruct
     if(—m_refs == 0)
     {
     delete this;
     return 0;
     }
     // You return the current ref count
     // for debugging purposes
     return m_refs;
}
//-----------------------------------------------------------------
STDMETHODIMP CAutoSrvCF::CreateInstance(IUnknown FAR* punkOuter,
               REFIID riid, void FAR* FAR* ppv)
{
     extern CAutoSrv FAR* g_pAutoSrv;

     // You have already created your only instance of
     // this object, so you simply return a QueryInterface
     // on your object.
     return g_pAutoSrv->QueryInterface(riid, ppv);
}
//-----------------------------------------------------------------
STDMETHODIMP CAutoSrvCF::LockServer(BOOL fLock)
{
     return NOERROR;
}
//-----------------------------------------------------------------
//-----------------------------------------------------------------
```

In the `QueryInterface` method for your main class, you acknowledge `IUnknown` and `IMyCInterface`. Finally, you implement the actual `GetString` function, which copies the text from the requested array element into the passed character buffer. You use the portable sting-manipulation functions from TCHAR.H because you need to support Unicode.

That wraps up the server's implementation. As you can see, it is a basic OLE object server. The fact that you are using a custom interface has not had any impact on the code. In fact, the only real change to the code is the addition of Unicode support.

The Client Code

You implement the client test code as a simple Windows NT Console application. Console applications, which you write with the Console API, provide a fast way to create simple test applications without the overhead of writing a

GUI application. Console applications have full access to the Win32 API, and, as you can see from this test program, full access to OLE.

You begin by initializing the OLE libraries. If the initialization succeeds, you then call the `CallServer` function.

`CallServer` starts by creating a class object, using your server's CLSID. You ask `CoGetClassObject` to return a pointer to an `IClassFactory` interface. If the call succeeds, you use the `IClassFactory` pointer to create an instance of your server's main object. This call returns a pointer to your custom interface.

With the custom interface pointer, you can now call the only method that that interface supports, `GetString`. Listing 17.9 shows the code for the client application.

Listing 17.9 The Client Application

```
#include <windows.h>
#include <tchar.h>
#include <stdio.h>
#include <bps.h>

//-----------------------------------------------------------------
void CallServer()
{
    HRESULT hr;
    WCHAR wszObject[128];
    IUnknown *pIUnk = NULL;
    IMyCInterface *pIMyCInterface = NULL;
     IClassFactory *pCF;
     CLSID clsid;
     LPOLESTR lp = TEXT("{d0ae2f60-9ea0-101b-97ca-524153480001}");

     // Get a handle to the console
     DWORD dwWrite;
     HANDLE hCon = GetStdHandle(STD_OUTPUT_HANDLE);

     printf("About to call server\n");
     hr = CLSIDFromString(lp,&clsid);
     if(SUCCEEDED(hr))
     {
          // Get a class factory for the server
          hr = CoGetClassObject(clsid,CLSCTX_SERVER,NULL,
                                IID_IClassFactory,(LPVOID FAR *)&pCF);
          if(SUCCEEDED(hr))
          {
               // Now create an instance of this object
               hr = pCF->CreateInstance(NULL,IID_IMyCInterface,
                          (LPVOID FAR *)&pIMyCInterface);
               if(S_OK == hr)
               {
                    for(UINT n = 0; n < 10 ; n++)
```

(continues)

Listing 17.9 Continued

```
                    {
                         pIMyCInterface->GetString(n,wszObject);
                         _tcscat(wszObject,TEXT("\n"));
                         WriteConsole(hCon,wszObject,_
                                   tcslen(wszObject),
                                   &dwWrite,NULL);
                    }
               }

               pCF->Release();
          }
          else
          {
               printf("Error: Failed to create object (%x)\n",hr);
          }
     }
     else
     {
          printf("Error: Failed to get CLSID (%x)\n",hr);
     }

     return;
}
//------------------------------------------------------------------
void _cdecl main()
{
     HRESULT hr = S_OK;

     printf("\nClient: Begin Server Test\n");

     //———
     // As usual, you initialize the OLE libraries
     // before calling any other function.

     hr = CoInitializeEx(NULL, COINIT_MULTITHREADED);

     if( FAILED(hr))
     {
          printf("Error: CoInitializeEx failed (%x)\n",hr);
      return;
     }

      CallServer();

     CoUninitialize();

     printf("Client: End Server Test\n");
     return;
}
//------------------------------------------------------------------
//------------------------------------------------------------------
```

Registering the Server, Proxy, and Stub

Before you can actually use your new server with its custom interface, you must register both the server and the custom interface with the system registry.

You register the actual object server in the normal way. The only interesting key is the `ActivateAtBits` key. If this key is set to N, you cannot activate the server from a remote client.

The second step is to register the custom interface. You register the IID for the interface, as well as the CLSID for the `Proxy/Stub` DLL. You then register the DLL as an in-process DLL.

The following is the complete information contained in the REGEDIT file:

```
REGEDIT

HKEY_CLASSES_ROOT\CLSID\{d0ae2f60-9ea0-101b-97ca-524153480001} =
➥OLE Book Custom Interface Server
HKEY_CLASSES_ROOT\CLSID\{d0ae2f60-9ea0-101b-97ca-524153480001}
➥\LocalServer32 = booksrvr.exe
HKEY_CLASSES_ROOT\BookServer = OLE Book Server
HKEY_CLASSES_ROOT\BookServer\CLSID =
➥{d0ae2f60-9ea0-101b-97ca-524153480001}
HKEY_CLASSES_ROOT\CLSID\{d0ae2f60-9ea0-101b-97ca-524153480001}
➥\ActivateAtBits = N

HKEY_CLASSES_ROOT\Interface\{9dffb854-9e7d-101b-97c9-524153480001}
➥= IMyCInterface
HKEY_CLASSES_ROOT\Interface\{9dffb854-9e7d-101b-97c9-524153480001}
➥\ProxyStubClsid32 = {9dffb854-9e7d-101b-97c9-524153480001}
HKEY_CLASSES_ROOT\CLSID\{9dffb854-9e7d-101b-97c9-524153480001} =
➥IMyCInterface_PSFactory
HKEY_CLASSES_ROOT\CLSID\{9dffb854-9e7d-101b-97c9-524153480001}
➥\InprocServer32 = bookps.dll
```

Testing the Application

After you build the three components—the client application, the server application, and the proxy and stub DLL—you should copy them to a directory on your search path. Make sure that you register the object and the custom interface in the system registry.

Running the client application invokes the Service Control Manager. The SCM in turn locates and starts your server. The SCM eventually returns, in COMPOB32.DLL, a marshaled interface pointer to the client application.

After retrieving the interface pointer to your custom interface, you loop and print all the quotations from the server database. Figure 17.5 shows a sample session with the client application. You can see the quote server running as an icon and the output from the client application in the shell window.

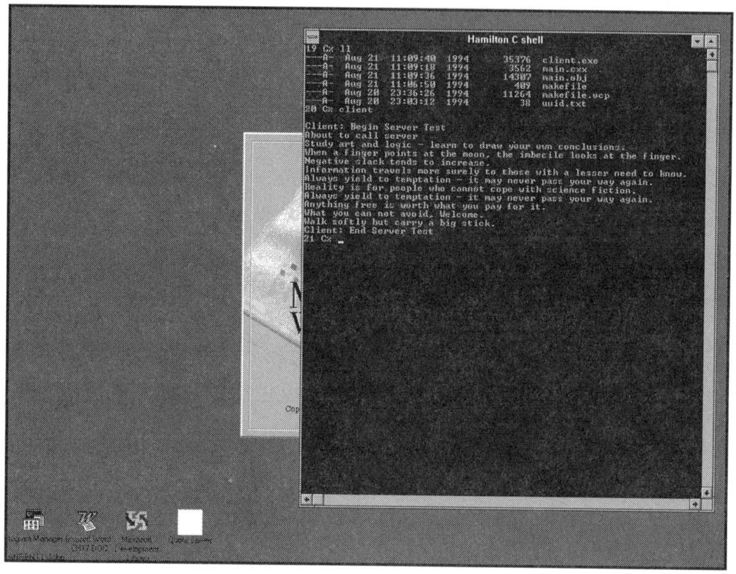

Fig. 17.5
A sample session with the client application.

From Here...

In this chapter, you wrote a custom COM interface. You learned that custom COM interfaces are a powerful feature and that, thanks to the new version of the MIDL compiler, implementing them is a reasonably straightforward process. In the next chapter, you explore Distributed OLE.

Chapter 18

Thirty-two-bit OLE

The release of Microsoft's Windows NT marked a significant event in the history of Windows. Windows NT was the first completely 32-bit operating system released by Microsoft.

Windows NT was also significant for another reason. The API that is used to program Windows NT, Win32, is a 32-bit API. The Win32 API, not the current Win16 with which most developers are familiar, is the future of Windows programming. In fact, to underscore this fact, Microsoft has released a version of Win32 known as Win32s that runs under Windows 3.1. The *s* in Win32s stands for *subset*, and this API is in fact a subset of the full Win32 API available in Windows NT. Win32s does not support threads, security, or Unicode. In early 1995, Microsoft is planning to release another version of Windows, called Windows 95, which also will support Win32. This version provides full support for threads but not security or Unicode.

In this chapter, you do the following:

- Examine the Win32 API to see what is involved in 32-bit programming. Most of the issues involved with 32-bit OLE are also Win32 issues.
- Examine the changes that Microsoft made to OLE in the move to 32 bits.
- Convert the simple drag-drop application that you developed in Chapter 3, "A Sample C++ Application," to use 32-bit OLE.

Background to Win32

When the Windows NT developers designed the API that was to be used on their platform, one of the design goals was to retain as much compatibility with the Win16 API as possible. To a large extent, the developers achieved this goal.

Win32 is a superset of the Win16 API. The old Win16 functions have been expanded to support 32 bits, and several new functions have been added. Win32 provides full support for a flat 32-bit addressing mode, multitasking, threads, security, and structured exception handling. Win32 also provides source code portability to other non-Intel platforms such as RISC (Reduced Instruction Set CPU) processors and the Digital Alpha processor. In fact, with the release of Visual C++ 2.0, Microsoft is even providing support for the Macintosh (68K and PowerPC) through the Win32 API. Win32 is a true cross-platform API.

The Flat Memory Model

Win32 deals exclusively with a virtual memory model. Under this scheme, memory addresses are never represented by actual physical addresses. Each memory address is part of a four-gigabyte virtual address space (see fig. 18.1). Unlike the segmented memory architecture of Win16, virtual memory under Win32 is implemented in a flat memory address space. This address space is divided into *pages*. Each memory page is 4K. (On a DEC Alpha machine, the page size is 8K.)

Fig. 18.1
Win32 memory map.

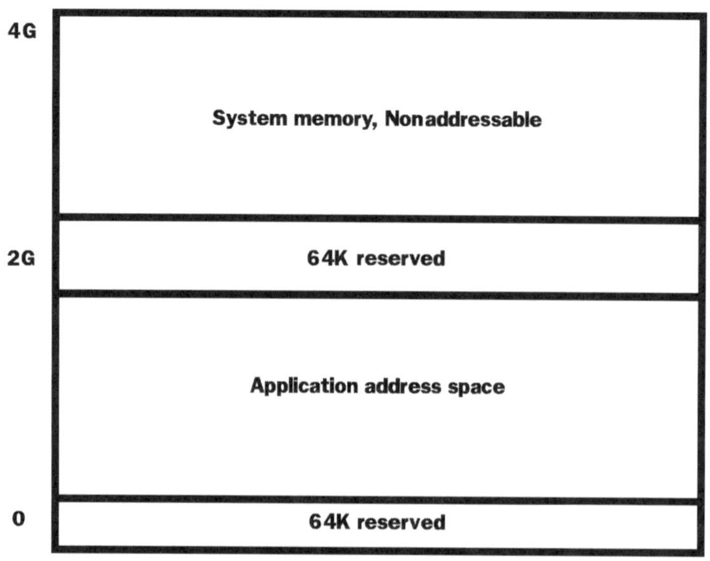

The Virtual Memory Manager (VMM) is responsible for organizing and controlling the virtual memory system. The VMM is in charge of mapping pages in and out of physical memory. The machine's disk stores pages that are not currently in use. The use of disk space as an extension to physical memory greatly increases the system's capacity. When an application accesses a memory location that is in fact stored in a swap file, a page fault is generated. The VMM then reloads the page and maps it back into memory. All of this activity is, of course, transparent to the application. In fact, memory management for applications is greatly simplified under Win32.

Because of Win32's use of 32-bit registers, an application can address any memory location with a single pointer. This is similar to the tiny memory model used by many of the first DOS programs, except that Win32 programs are not constrained to a single 64K segment. In Win32, the concepts of global and local memory do not exist, because all memory is allocated from the application's private address space—all two gigabytes of it!

This private virtual address space for each application also means that the current limitation of graphic device interface (GDI) resources in Win16 will also disappear.

Under Win32, memory leaks and unfreed resources are a thing of the past, because when an application terminates, the system removes its entire private address space, automatically freeing anything that the application has left behind.

The Asynchronous Input Model

Win16 had one system message queue. All hardware events, such as mouse messages and keyboard messages, were placed in this queue. Each application was then responsible for retrieving the message from its message pump.

The problem with this approach was that if one application retrieved a message from the system queue and then entered a time-intensive task or simply hung, no other application could access the system queue. In other words, the entire system would hang.

Win32 solves this problem by deserializing the input model. Each process under Win32 is assigned its own message queue. The system creates a single thread that is responsible for queuing hardware messages. This thread is called the raw input thread (RIT). Each time that an event occurs, such as the user pressing the mouse button, the thread creates the appropriate WM_LMOUSE* messages and sends the message to the process whose window is currently under the mouse cursor.

The asynchronous input model (see fig. 18.2) ensures that the system can never hang when one application is tying up the message queue.

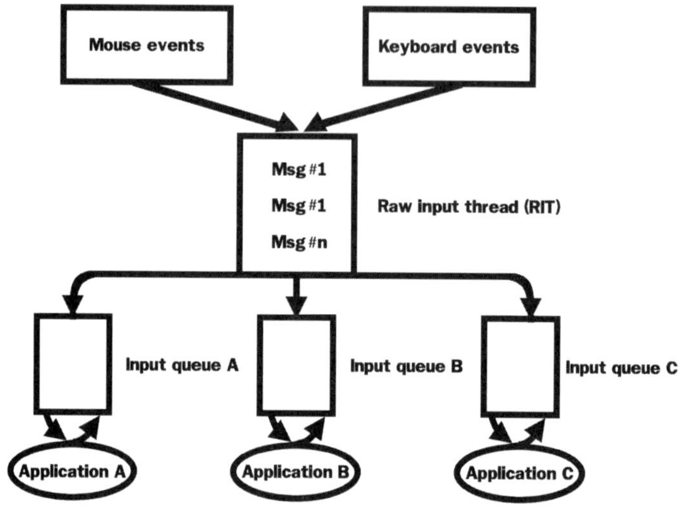

Fig. 18.2
The asynchronous input model.

In your code, be careful of assumptions regarding synchronous input. Under Win16, an application that captured the mouse was guaranteed to receive all mouse messages generated by the system. That guarantee no longer exists. Under Win32, more than one application can capture the mouse.

Threads

In both Windows NT and Windows 95, a thread is the basic unit of execution. All applications or processes have at least one thread. The operating system achieves multitasking by preemptively switching between threads.

Threads are undoubtedly one of the most powerful features of Win32. They are also the least understood. When asked how they would implement threads in their applications, some programmers answer that they would implement background printing. This might seem an obvious choice, but on closer inspection, it might not be such a simple task. For example, what do you do if the user changes some text in your document while you are performing a background print? The user does not want or expect that the data that appears on the hard copy will contain the changes that he or she just made. In this case, you have to copy the document to a temporary file and print that file.

There is a time and place for everything, and threads are no exception to this rule.

One good use of threads is to provide a responsive user interface while performing a CPU- or disk-intensive task. In this case, one thread would handle the user interface while another thread would handle the background task. This ensures that the user interface can still respond to user input while the background task is working.

Any tasks that you performed with timers in a Win16 environment are good candidates to be created as separate threads.

One of the best models is to create one thread for the entire user interface and then create worker threads as required by the application. Threads greatly enhance an application, but you should use them sparingly. The next section deals with some of the problems and issues that you must deal with when using threads.

Thread Synchronization

For all the power that threads bring to your application, they also bring a whole new set of problems. The problems fall into two main categories:

- *Protecting variables and resources from corruption.* Win32 provides preemptive switching between threads. Therefore, at the end of the time slice allocated to a particular thread, the operating system switches to another thread. If this other thread is running in the same process as the first thread, it will have access to all the same resources. In fact, in a multiprocessor machine, both of these threads could be running simultaneously.

- *Serializing access to resources.* One thread must wait for another to complete an operation before it can continue. For example, if a thread requires the result of a calculation to create a chart, that thread must wait for a calculation thread to complete its processing.

Critical Sections

Critical sections are the easiest synchronization method to use and are perhaps the easiest to understand. The concept is simple: when you enter a block of code that must be protected, you declare a critical section.

After a thread enters a critical section, the system suspends any other thread that attempts to enter that section. Only when the first thread completes its task and leaves the critical section will the second thread be awakened and allowed to resume.

Win32 provides four functions for dealing with critical sections:

- `InitializeCriticalSection` initializes a CRITICAL_SECTION data structure. You use this structure when entering and leaving a critical section.
- `EnterCriticalSection` is called to enter the critical section.
- `LeaveCriticalSection` is called when you leave a critical section. If this function is not called, all threads that are blocking on this critical section remain suspended.
- `DeleteCriticalSection` is called to release any resource owned by the critical section.

You can use critical sections to protect threads only within a single process. One common use for critical sections is to protect GDI objects. Multiple threads cannot access GDI objects simultaneously. Therefore, if your application has a font that is globally shared among threads, you would use a critical section to ensure that only one thread at a time was using it.

Synchronization Objects

Synchronization objects exist in one of two states: signaled or unsignaled. You use these objects to control access to threads. When dealing with these objects, you primarily use two API functions: `WaitForSingleObject` and `WaitForMultipleObject`. When you use either of these functions and the object that you are waiting for is not signaled, the system automatically blocks the calling thread. Threads blocked by the system are put to sleep, so they consume no CPU cycles.

Several different types of synchronization objects exist, including mutexes, semaphores, and events. These objects are used exclusively to synchronize access to threads. Another set of objects, *waitable objects*, includes file objects, threads, and processes. All of these objects can be used to signal events. In fact, synchronization objects are a subset of waitable objects.

Mutexes. A mutex is similar to a critical section, except that multiple processes can use mutexes. If a thread in process A needs to wait for a thread in process B to complete before continuing its work, you can use a mutex to synchronize the threads.

When process B starts, it creates a mutex called, for example, `mymutex`. Process A also attempts to create a mutex with the same name. The system, seeing that the mutex already exists, returns a handle to the original mutex.

When process B begins to execute, it sets, or *signals*, the mutex. Process A calls `WaitForSingleObject` before entering the code that needs to be synchronized. If the mutex is signaled, the system suspends the thread in process A. The thread in process A is awakened and allowed to continue only when process B resets the mutex.

Semaphores. Semaphores differ from mutexes in two respects:

- No ownership is associated with a semaphore. Therefore, any thread can clear the semaphore. Only the owner can reset a mutex.
- Semaphores have a reference count associated with them.

When you create a semaphore, you specify the maximum number of threads that can simultaneously access a certain resource. The system blocks any thread that attempts to own a semaphore that has reached its limit, until one of the other threads releases the semaphore.

An example of the use of semaphores is a network application that restricts the number of users who can use a particular server concurrently.

Events. Events enable one thread to signal another thread or group of threads that a specific event has occurred. For example, when your application is reading a file from disk, all the threads that normally operate on that data should be blocked. When the thread responsible for loading the disk file completes the load, that thread signals the waiting threads by setting an event.

There are two types of events:

- *Auto-reset* events, as the name suggests, are automatically reset to the nonsignaled state by the `WaitForSingleObject` and `WaitForMultipleObject` functions. This ensures that only one waiting thread is reawakened.
- *Manual-reset* events, on the other hand, enable more than one waiting thread to be awakened. Neither `WaitForSingleObject` nor `WaitForMultipleObject` automatically resets these events. The application must manually reset the events by calling `ResetEvent`.

Memory Mapped Files

Win32 provides a full set of file manipulation functions. DOS is no longer used to perform disk input/output (I/O). Win32 provides a consistent naming scheme for the file APIs. `OpenFile` is called to open a file, and `ReadFile` and

WriteFile are called for reading and writing. Finally, CloseFile is called to close the file. CopyFile and DeleteFile are also available for moving and copying files.

The ability to use virtual memory to read and write to files is extremely powerful. With memory-mapped files, the entire file is read into memory and the application accesses the file in memory. This frees the application from buffering the data and from performing file I/O for each read and write to the file.

You can load mapped files into any address in the application's process space. In fact, memory-mapped files can be created entirely in memory and shared among other processes. This usage is similar to creating named shared memory, as is available under OS/2

Issues in 32-bit Programming

Apart from all the new and exciting features that Win32 brings to application programmers, it also bring some problems. This section briefly examines some of these issues.

The most obvious difference between Win16 and Win32 programming is that all pointers, handles, and coordinates are now 32 bits wide. Pointers are no longer near or far; they are simply pointers.

Under Win16, programmers have often used int, WORD, short, and UINT interchangeably. This did not really matter, because these are all 16-bit values. However, under Win32, UINT and int are 32-bit values, while WORD and short are still 16-bit values. Be very careful casting values from one type to another. For example, the following code, which casts an HWND to a WORD, does not work correctly under Win32:

```
hWnd = (WORD) SendMessage( hWnd, WM_GETMDIACTIVATE, 0, 0 );
```

In the following example, the code incorrectly checks for an error from the SendMessage function:

```
WORD wCurSel = (WORD) SendMessage(hList,LB_GETSEL,0,0L);
if(LB_ERR != wCurSel)
{
        // This code always executes.
}
else
{
        // Nothing selected so return.
}
```

The problem here is that LB_ERR is defined as –1, which is a 32-bit integer under Win32. The comparison with the WORD variable is always incorrect.

A good rule of thumb is to use WORD for values that should be 16 bits wide, and UINT for values that should be 16 bits wide in Win16 and 32 bits wide under Win32. Whenever you are dealing with a GDI or USER handle, use the appropriate type and not the generic type HANDLE. For example, a handle to a pen should be HPEN, and a handle to a window should be an HWND. If you code exclusively for Win32, you should stop using WORD.

Message Parameters

Under Win16, callback procedures typically take four parameters. The last two parameters pass information to the procedure. The first of these parameters is a 16-bit variable called `wParam` and the other is a 32-bit parameter known as `lParam`.

Because all handles are 16 bits wide under Win16, the `lParam` is often used to pack two 16-bit values. This technique is commonly used with WM_COMMAND messages. When a menu or control sends a WM_COMMAND message to its parent, the notification code and the window handle are both packed into the `lParam`. The control ID is sent in the 16-bit `wParam`.

As all handles under Win32 are now 32 bits wide, this technique will obviously not work anymore. Microsoft's solution is to set the window handle, which is now 32 bits wide, in the `lParam` parameter, and pack the two 16-bit values into the 32-bit `wParam`.

In your code, you must create conditional define statements and code for both environments, as in the following example:

```
case WM_COMMAND:
#ifdef WIN32
       hWndCtl = (HWND)lParam;
       wCode = HIWORD(wParam);
       wID = LOWORD(wParam);
#else
       hWndCtl = (HWND)(LOWORD)lParam;
       wCode = HIWORD(lParam);
       wID = wParam;
#endif
```

The WM_CTLCOLOR message has been replaced by seven separate messages. Table 18.1 shows the other messages that have changed for Win32. The Win32 SDK provides a complete description of each of these messages.

Table 18.1 Messages Changed for Win32

Message	*wParam*	*lParam*
WM_ACTIVATE	LOWORD = `fActive`	
HIWORD = `fMinimized`	Handle of the window being activated	
WM_CHARTOITEM	LOWORD = caret	
HIWORD = character code	List box window handle	
WM_HSCROLL	LOWORD = scrollbar	
HIWORD = thumb position	Handle of the parent control	
WM_VSCROLL	LOWORD = scrollbar	
HIWORD = thumb position	Handle of the parent control	
WM_MDIACTIVATE	Handle of the child window to be activated or deactivated	0 or the handle of the child window being activated
WM_MDISETMENU	Handle of the frame menu	Handle of the window popup menu
WM_MENUCHAR	LOWORD = character code HIWORD = menu flag	Handle of the popup menu
WM_MENUSELECT	LOWORD = 0 or menu item HIWORD = menu flag	Handle of the popup menu
WM_PARENTNOTIFY	LOWORD = event	
HIWORD = child window ID	Handle of the child window or the packed cursor position	
WM_VKEYTOITEM	LOWORD = character code, HIWORD = caret location	Handle of the list box
EM_GETSEL	Returns the selection start position	Returns the selection end position
EM_SETSEL	Specifies beginning of the selection	Specifies end of the selection
EM_LINESCROLL	Characters to scroll horizontally	Characters to scroll vertically

The DDE messages have also changed. Again, refer to the Win32 SDK for more information about these changes.

The Graphic Device Interface

All coordinates passed and returned by GDI functions now use 32-bit values. These functions fall into two categories.

The first category consists of the GDI functions that change the current coordinates. In Win16, these functions return the current coordinates as a 32-bit value. This value consists of the 16-bit X position and the 16-bit Y position packed into a 32-bit variable. This is not possible under Win32 because each coordinate is a 32-bit value.

The solution is to use the new versions of each of these functions (see table 18.2). The functions that have the same name as their Win16 counterparts have *Ex* appended to the name. Each of these functions takes a new parameter that is a pointer to a 32-bit POINT structure. This structure returns the current GDI coordinates. If you do not want to process the returned coordinates, pass NULL as the last parameter.

Table 18.2 The Set Coordinate GDI Functions

Win16 Function	Win32 Version
`MoveTo`	`MoveToEx`
`OffsetViewportOrg`	`OffsetViewportOrgEx`
`OffsetWindowOrg`	`OffsetWindowOrgEx`
`ScaleViewportExt`	`ScaleViewportExtEx`
`ScaleWindowExt`	`ScaleWindowExtEx`
`SetBitmapDimension`	`SetBitmapDimensionEx`
`SetMetaFileBits`	`SetMetaFileBitsEx`
`SetViewportExt`	`SetViewportExtEx`
`SetWindowExt`	`SetWindowExtEx`
`SetWindowOrg`	`SetWindowOrgEx`

The second category consists of the GDI functions that return information about the current coordinates (see table 18.3). Like the the Set functions in table 18.2, each of these Get functions takes an extra parameter that is a pointer to a POINT or SIZE structure.

Table 18.3 The Get Coordinate GDI Functions

Win16 Function	Win32 Version
`GetAspectRatioFilter`	`GetAspectRatioFilterEx`
`GetBitmapDimension`	`GetBitmapDimensionEx`
`GetBrushOrg`	`GetBrushOrgEx`
`GetCurrentPosition`	`GetCurrentPositionEx`
`GetTextExtent`	`GetTextExtentPoint`
`GetTextExtentEx`	`GetTextExtentExPoint`
`GetViewportExt`	`GetViewportExtEx`
`GetViewportOrg`	`GetViewportOrgEx`
`GetWindowExt`	`GetWindowExtEx`
`GetWindowOrg`	`GetWindowOrgEx`

None of the original Win16 versions of these functions are available under Win32. If you attempt to use any of these functions, you get errors linking your application. The *Ex* versions are, however, available under both platforms. For this reason, these versions are sometimes called *portable* versions.

Structure Alignments

All data structures should be aligned on an eight-byte boundary. Each individual memory should be aligned on an address that is natural for that data type. For example, integers should be aligned on 32-bit boundaries and shorts should be aligned on 16-bit boundaries. Misaligning structures can harm your application's performance. On a MIPS processor, a misaligned data member generates a hardware exception fault. The system handles the exception automatically, but your application will pay in clock cycles.

The Application's Command Line

In a Win16 environment, the command line passed to the application on startup points to the first parameter on the command line. You can take advantage of this in the code that parses the command line looking for `/Embedded` or `/Automation`. In a Win32 environment, the first parameter on the command line is always the name of the application.

Checking for Multiple Instances of an Application

The `hPrevInstance` parameter passed to `WinMain` on start up does not contain the handle of a previous instance of the application under Win32. If you want to check for multiple instances of your application, you should use the `FindWindow` function, as in the following example:

```
HWND hWnd;
if(NULL != (hWnd = FindWindow("MyClassName",NULL)))
{
       // hWnd contains the handle to another instance of the app.
       HWND hWndChild = GetLastActivePopup(hWnd);
       // Bring Windows to the top of the z-order
      BringWindowToTop(hWnd);
       // If a popup window is active, you bring it to the top also.
      if(hWnd != hWndChild)
      BringWindowToTop(hWndChild);
      return FALSE;
}
else
       // This app is not already running.
```

Your application can also use a named object to identify a previous instance.

Unicode

A future release of Windows NT will include distributed object support. An issue that arises from this support is the transferring of data objects across a global network. For example, a data object whose data was created using a European character set will not be readable on a machine running a Japanese code page.

Background

Unicode is one solution to this Tower of Babel. The Win32 SDK defines Unicode as a "16-bit, fixed-width character encoding standard that encompasses virtually all of the characters commonly used on computers today." In the Unicode system, each character is 16 bits wide. This allows a total of 65,536 characters in the character set. This total is a huge improvement over the 256 characters currently allowed by code pages. Unicode has the backing of almost all the major software companies, including Microsoft, Lotus, Adobe, Taligent, NeXT, UniSys, Aldus, Borland, IBM, Hewlett-Packard, Digital, and WordPerfect. The complete Unicode standard is published in a two-volume book called *The Unicode Standard Version 1.0*, published by Addison-Wesley.

To retain compatibility with the current system, the first 256 characters in Unicode are mapped to the ANSI/ISO character set.

The base character set for Windows NT is Unicode. All files and directory names under the NTFS file system are Unicode. As you have seen, however, NT client applications can choose to support either Unicode or ANSI character sets.

Interestingly, Novell NetWare 4.0's directory services operate in Unicode. NetWare provides a mapping layer to map OEM code page data from the network client to Unicode for storing.

Using Unicode in Your Application

You might want to support Unicode in your applications for two reasons:

- *Portability*. By supporting Unicode, your application does not have to worry about multiple code pages and locales.
- *Performance*. Because Windows NT uses Unicode as its base character set, all function calls made to the Win32 subsystem using ANSI strings are first converted to Unicode, acted on, and then converted back to ANSI before they are returned to the calling application. You can improve an application's performance significantly by supporting Unicode at the application level and bypassing this conversion.

Changing Your Code

Supporting Unicode in your application is not a major task. Thanks to some clever macros defined in the Win32 SDK header files, you can do most of the conversions with your editor's search-and-replace feature.

There are now two functions for every API function that deals with text. For example, the `TextOut` API function is now replaced with `TextOutA` and `TextOutW`. The *A* functions deal with ANSI text, and the *W* functions deal with wide-character or Unicode text. (Fortunately, the macros hide this difference.) The `TextOut` macro now expands to `TextOutW` if Unicode is defined, and to `TextOutA` if not. These macros enable developers to maintain a single code base for both Win16 and Win32. They also enable legacy code to be successfully compiled.

Note

Most programmers are guilty of using character arrays for storing both text and binary data. As you convert your code to support both Unicode and ANSI, it is worthwhile to begin to differentiate between these two types. You should store all text strings in TCHAR arrays and store all byte data in BYTE arrays. You should use the `str` family of functions only on TCHAR data. To manipulate BYTE data, use `memcpy`, `memmove`, and so on.

Using these semantics greatly increases your code's readability.

Note

The Win32 SDK includes the file TCHAR.H, which provides macros that make it easy for you to create source code that can be compiled for both Unicode and ANSI environments. For example, this file defines the TCHAR macro as well as a set of string manipulation functions (for example, _tcstr) that map between the ANSI and Unicode C run-time functions.

To create a body of code that can be compiled for both Win32 and Win16, you must begin to use the portable type definitions when declaring variables. Each of these types expands differently depending on whether UNICODE is defined. Table 18.4 shows the definitions that you need to change.

Table 18.4 Portable Type Definitions

Win16 Definition	Portable Version
CHAR	TCHAR
LPSTR	LPTSTR
LPCH	LPTCH
NPSTR	LPTSTR
PSTR	LPTSTR
char	TCHAR
LPTSTR (const char *)	LPCTSTR

You should prefix all literal strings in your application with *L*. The TEXT macro supplied with the Win32 SDK provides a portable way to do this prefixing. (The MFC include files provide an easier-to-use _T macro that performs the same prefixing.) If Unicode is defined, the macro prefixes the string with *L*; otherwise, the macro skips the string. For example, the following code snippet shows how you can use the macro:

```
MessageBox(hWnd,TEXT("Hello World"),TEXT("MyApplication"),MB_OK);
```

Of course, all of your application's strings should be stored in a string table in your resource files.

Table 18.5 Windows and C Run-Time Functions and Their Unicode Equivalents

ANSI	Unicode
AnsiNext	CharNext
AnsiPrev	CharPrev
AnsiUpper/ AnsiUpperBuff	CharUpper/CharUpperBuff
AnsiLower/AnsiLowerBuff	CharLower/CharLowerBuff
AnsiToOem/AnsiToOemBuff	CharToOem/CharToOemBuff
OemToAnsi/OemToAnsiBuff	OemtoChar/OemtoCharBuff
atoi/atof/atol/atold	wcstombs
OpenFile	CreateFile/CreateFileEx
_lclose	CloseHandle
_lread	ReadFile

One consequence of working with Unicode is that all character buffers are now twice the size that they are under ANSI. To count the number of characters in a buffer, you must divide the length of the buffer by `sizeof(TCHAR)`. If you want to allocate a memory buffer based on the string's length, you must multiply the string length by `sizeof(TCHAR)`.

Table 18.5, taken from the Win32 SDK, shows the Windows and C run-time functions that manipulate strings and their Unicode equivalents.

Functionality	Byte or Character Based
Moves to the next character in a string.	Character-based
Moves to the previous character in a string.	Character-based
Converts a character or character string to uppercase.	N/A
Converts a character or character string to lowercase.	N/A
Translates a string to OEM characters.	Character-based
Translates an OEM string.	Character-based
Converts a character string to an integer. Use `wcstombs` to convert the wide-character string to a multibyte string before calling `atoi`.	N/A
Opens a file. `OpenFile` is not Unicode; use `CreateFile` or `CreateFileEx` instead.	N/A
Closes an open file. Use `CloseHandle` to close a file created by a `CreateFile` or `CreateFileEx` call.	N/A
Reads a file.	Byte-based

(continues)

Table 18.5 Continued

ANSI	Unicode
_lwrite	WriteFile
memset	wcsset
strcat	lstrcat or wcscat
strchr	wcschr
strcmp	lstrcmp or wcscmp
strcmpi	lstrcmpi or wcscmpi
strcoll	wcscoll
strcpy	lstrcpy or wcscpy
strcspn	wcscspn
strdup	wcsdup
strftime	wcsftime
stricmp	wcsicmp
strlen	lstrlen or wcslen

Functionality	Byte or Character Based
Writes a file.	Byte-based
Sets a buffer to the specified character. Use this for binary buffers.	Byte-based
Concatenates two strings.	N/A
Finds the first occurrence of a character in a string.	N/A
Compares two strings. Note that `lstrcmp` is not equivalent to `wcscmp: lstrcmp` uses the collating tables that are built into the code page/locale, while `wcscmp` does a lexicographical comparison (by value only).	N/A
Compares two strings regardless of case. Note that `lstrcmpi` is not equivalent to `wcscmpi: lstrcmpi` uses the collating tables that are built into the code page/locale, while `wcscmpi` does a lexicographical comparison (by value only).	N/A
Compares two strings based on the current locale.	N/A
Copies a string into the given buffer.	N/A
Returns the index of the substring in the first string.	Character-based
Duplicates the given string, allocates space for it, and returns the string's address.	N/A
Formats the current time (`tm`) structure and converts it to a string.	N/A
Compares two strings regardless of case.	N/A
Returns the length of the specified string in bytes.	Byte-based

(continues)

Table 18.5 Continued

ANSI	Unicode
strlwr	wcslwr
strncat	wcsncat
strncmp	wcsncmp
strncpy	wcsncpy
strnicmp	wcsnicmp
strnset	wcsnset
strpbrk	wcspbrk
strrchr	wcsrchr
strrev	wcsrev
strset	wcsset
strspn	wcsspn
strstr	wcsstr
strtod	wcstod

Functionality	Byte or Character Based
Converts uppercase characters in the given string to lowercase.	N/A
Appends the specified number of characters in the second string to the first string specified.	Character-based
Compares the first *n* characters in two given strings.	Character-based
Copies the first *n* characters in the second string to the first string.	Character-based
Compares the first *n* characters in two strings regardless of case.	Character-based
Sets the first *n* characters in the specified string.	Character-based
Finds the first occurrence of `string1` in `string2`.	N/A
Finds the last occurrence of the given character in the specified string.	N/A
Reverses the order of the characters in the specified string.	N/A
Sets all the characters in the specified string to the given character.	N/A
Returns the index of the first character in `string1` that does not belong to the set of characters specified in `string2`.	Character-based
Returns a pointer to the first occurrence of `string1` in `string2`.	N/A
Converts the given string to a double precision value.	N/A

(continues)

Table 18.5 Continued

ANSI	Unicode
strtok	wcstok
strtol	wcstol
stroul	wcstoul
strxform	wcsxfrm
strupr	wcsupr
sprintf	wsprintf
vsprintf	vswprintf

Functionality	Byte or Character Based
Finds the next token in a string.	N/A
Converts the given string to a long integer value.	N/A
Converts the given string to an unsigned long integer value.	N/A
Transforms the strings specified by *string2* based on the current locale, and stores the result in *string1*.	Character-based
Converts lowercase characters in the given string to uppercase.	N/A
Formats and stores a series of characters and values in the given buffer. Note that `wsprintf` does not return an accurate count of characters printed for Unicode strings. Instead, it returns the count of individual Unicode characters. Because some Unicode characters (for example, in the Japanese version of Windows NT) take two columns to display, column alignment is difficult.	N/A
Similar to `sprintf` except that it takes a variable argument list. Note that `vswprintf` does not return an accurate count of characters printed for Unicode strings. Instead, it returns the count of individual Unicode characters. Because some Unicode characters (for example, in the Japanese version of Windows NT) take two columns to display, column alignment is difficult.	N/A

Finally, reading and writing files can be a problem. If you intend to read and write files only in a Unicode environment, there is no problem. However, if your files must also be accessible to Win16 applications, you must convert the data to ANSI as you write it to disk. Win32 provides two functions to assist you in this process: `MultiByteToWideChar` converts a data buffer from ANSI to Unicode; `WideCharToMultiByte` converts from Unicode to ANSI.

Unicode Font Support

Unicode support has one slight problem. Although your application fully supports Unicode characters, not all these characters can be displayed, simply because not all fonts have been upgraded to support the Unicode character set. Literally thousands of Unicode characters are available, so perhaps this incomplete support is unsurprising.

Windows NT provides a Lucida Sans Serif TrueType font, L_10646.TTF, that has over 1,300 Unicode characters. In the future, as more type foundries begin to support Unicode in their font families, Unicode font support should become less of an issue.

Structured Exception Handling

Structured exception handling (SEH) enables you to divide the main body of your code from the error-checking part. The feature provides a robust means of trapping both hardware and software errors or exceptions in your code. SEH is language- and platform-independent.

SEH works by registering an exception handle on each stack frame during a nested function call. When an exception is raised, the system can unwind the stack to find an exception handler that handles that particular exception.

The following code segment demonstrates a simple use of SEH:

```
LPTSTR lpUserName = NULL;

GetUserName(lpUserName);

LPTSR GetUserName(LPTSTR lpBuffer)
{
        try
        {
                strcpy(lpBuffer,_TEXT("This is not going to work"));
                return lpBuffer;
        }
        except(GetException() == EXCEPTION_ACCESS_VIOLATION ?
                                EXCEPTION_EXECUTE_HANDLER :
                                EXCEPTION_CONTINUE_SEARCH)
```

```
        {
                MessageBox(NULL,"Invalid buffer pointer","Error",MB_OK);
                return NULL;
        }
}
```

In the preceding example, you call the `GetUserName` function with a NULL pointer. Normally this call would cause a general protection (GP) fault. However, by using the `try`/`except` syntax, you can trap all errors that occur in the `try` section and handle them gracefully in the `except` section.

Another part of SEH is known as termination handling. In the sample code, the code within the `except` section executes when an exception is raised. A *termination handler* is code that always executes, regardless of whether an exception is raised. The keyword `finally` is used to define a block of code as a termination handler.

Termination handlers provide you with the means of performing function-level cleanup in one place. You can close all open files, free allocated memory blocks, and more. The following code provides an example of a termination handler:

```
BOOL ConvertFile()
{
        try
        {
                LPTSTR lp = new TCHAR[1024];
                if(!lp)
                        return FALSE;

                OFSTRUCT of;
                HFILE hFile = OpenFile(_TEXT("MyFile.dat"),&of,OF_READ);
                if(HFILE_ERROR == hFile)
                        return FALSE;

                // read the file
                // do something with the data
                // return a pointer to the data
                return TRUE;
        }
        finally
        {
                if(lp)
                        delete lpl
                if(hFile)
                        CloseFile(hFile);
        }
}
```

SEH provides a powerful debugging framework for your application. The exception handlers can display debugging information and solicit input from users during an exception. If you cannot or do not want to handle a particular exception, you can pass the exception back to the previous handler.

You should watch out for the following when dealing with SEH:

- If you do not process an exception, you must call the previous exception handler. Swallowing an exception defeats the whole purpose of exception handling.
- Be careful of generating an error in the termination handler. Always check all pointers, handles, and so on, before you free them in the termination handler.

The real power of exception handing, however, is in the filter routines. You can call these routines from the `except` statement. The filter routine has full access to all the exception information and can even access local variables. The following code shows an example of a filter routine:

```
DWORD MyFilter(LPEXCEPTION_POINTERS ep)
{
      LPVOID lpAddress = ep->ExceptionRecord->ExceptionAddress;
      DWORD dwCode = GetExceptionCode();
      TCHAR msg[81];
      wsprintf(msg,"Code = %x Address = %x",dwCode,lpAddress);
      MessageBox(NULL,msg,"Debug",MB_OK);
      return EXCEPTION_EXECUTE_HANDLER;
}
try
{
      BadFunction();
}
except(MyFilter(GetExceptionInformation())
{
      ExitThread(GetExceptionCode());
}
```

For a complete description of SEH, see Chapter 10 of *Advanced Windows NT* by Jeffery Richter.

OLE in a 32-bit Environment

Windows NT 3.5 and Windows 95 ship with the 32-bit OLE libraries as part of the system (OLE is no longer provided as part of applications). Thirty-two-bit OLE is pure OLE. It provides the same functionality as 16-bit OLE 2.01. In fact, most of the differences involve Win32. This section explores the differences between 16-bit and 32-bit OLE.

The first major change from 16-bit OLE is the use of remote procedure call (RPC) as the interprocess calling (IPC) mechanism. The old lightweight remote procedure call (LRPC, which was based on the Windows messaging system) has been replaced with a version that uses true DCE (Distributed Computing Environment) RPC. The use of RPC is the first step toward a distributed version of OLE.

Sixteen-bit OLE made a clear distinction between HRESULT and SCODE function return codes. Chapter 2, "The Component Object Model," discussed the API functions and macros that are available to convert from one type to another. With 32-bit OLE, this distinction no longer exists. SCODE is now the preferred type to use for return codes. HRESULT is retained for backward compatibility with old code.

Under 32-bit OLE, the internal workings of antimonikers have undergone some minor changes. In 16-bit OLE, two antimonikers joined together form a third antimoniker with an internal count of two. With 32-bit OLE, these two antimonikers form a composite moniker. The only difference is that `GetClassID` returns a `CLSID_CompositeMoniker` instead of a `CLSID_AntiMoniker`.

You can no longer use `IPersist` to retrieve the handler's CLSID. The only way to retrieve the CLSID is to call `IStdMarshallInfo::GetClassForHandler`.

Finally, the only types of storage mediums that you can pass to `IDateObject::GetDataHere` (but not `::GetData`) are `IStream`, `IStorage`, or HGLOBAL. You cannot pass a metafile, GDI object, or bitmap.

Interoperability

There is complete interoperability between 16-bit OLE 2.01 applications and 32-bit OLE applications. When you provide support for 16-bit OLE and 32-bit OLE, the only potential problem occurs if you support in-process server DLLs. To provide interoperability, you must supply both a 16-bit DLL and a 32-bit DLL. You must register both DLLs separately as `InProcServer32` for the 32-bit DLL and `InProcServer` for the 16-bit DLL. (This applies to 16 bit clients only; 32-bit clients can access a 16-bit controls directly.)

Long File Names

OLE monikers now support long file names on both Windows 95 and Windows NT.

Compound Files

When saving data to compound files, you may find that the data differs between Win16 and Win32 platforms. If you must support both platforms, save the 32-bit data into a separate stream. If you do so, you must also use a separate CLSID for each stream.

Another problem involves accessing the compound file simultaneously from multiple threads. A single semphore controls all access to a compound file, so only one thread at a time can access the file.

Security Issues

OLE for Win32 does not provide any security support. Distributed OLE will address this omission. However, you should still be aware of security when you are accessing files and linked objects. Although OLE does not support security, access control lists (ACLs) may be in place on some files. Security violations are likely to result in `Access Denied` or `File Not Found` error messages.

Shared Memory

OLE uses shared memory to maintain information about objects and also to read and write compound files.

Enhanced Metafiles

Thirty-two-bit OLE now supports the new enhanced metafile available under Win32. The new format provides many improvements over the old format.

Probably the most important feature is device independence. The Win32 SDK states that when an application creates a 2-by-4-inch picture on a VGA display and stores that picture in a metafile, the picture maintains those dimensions when you print it on a 300-dpi laser printer or display it in another application running on an 8514/A video display. You could not easily achieve this device independence with the old metafile formats.

The new format achieves this device independence by using a *reference device context*. When you create the metafile, information about the current device context (DC) is stored within the metafile header. The HORZSIZE and VERTSIZE of the current DC are stored in the `szlMillimeters` field, and the HORZRES and VERTRES values are stored in the `szlDevice` field. (See listing 18.1.) The bounding rectangle of the metafile is stored in the `rclFrame` field. You can use this information to recreate a similar DC when the metafile is played back.

Listing 18.1 The New Metafile Header

```
typedef struct tagENHMETAHEADER
{
  DWORD   iType;            // Record type EMR_HEADER.
  DWORD   nSize;            // Record size in bytes. This may be greater
                            // than the sizeof(ENHMETAHEADER).
  RECTL   rclBounds;        // Inclusive-inclusive bounds in device units.
  RECTL   rclFrame;         // Inclusive-inclusive Picture Frame of
                            // metafile in .01 mm units.
  DWORD   dSignature;       // Signature. Must be ENHMETA_SIGNATURE.
  DWORD   nVersion;         // Version number.
  DWORD   nBytes;           // Size of the metafile in bytes.
  DWORD   nRecords;         // Number of records in the metafile.
  WORD    nHandles;         // Number of handles in the handle table.
                            // Handle index zero is reserved.
  WORD    sReserved;        // Reserved. Must be zero.
  DWORD   nDescription;     // Number of chars in the Unicode
                            // description string. This is 0 if there
                            // is no description string.
  DWORD   offDescription;   // Offset to the metafile description record.
                            // This is 0 if there is no description string.
  DWORD   nPalEntries;      // Number of entries in the metafile palette.
  SIZEL   szlDevice;        // Size of the reference device in pixels.
  SIZEL   szlMillimeters;   // Size of the reference device in millimeters.
} ENHMETAHEADER;
```

The new metafile format also enables you to store the current GDI palette within the metafile. Figure 18.3 shows the differences between the old metafile format and the new format.

Under 32-bit OLE, the metafiles are the same as 16-bit OLE with the addition of a tagged record that contains the new metafile format. If you play the metafile under 16-bit OLE, this record is skipped. Under 32-bit OLE, however, the record is recognized and played.

OLE and Unicode

Thirty-two-bit OLE is fully Unicode, so if you are porting 16-bit code from OLE 2.x, you must deal with the Unicode issue. Depending on your application's size and the amount of time that you have, you can choose from one of three ways to implement Unicode in your application.

The cleanest solution is simply to port your application to Unicode, following the guidelines outlined in the previous sections. As you have seen, this task is not complex. If you use the portable type definitions in your source code, you can maintain a common source base for both ANSI and Unicode versions

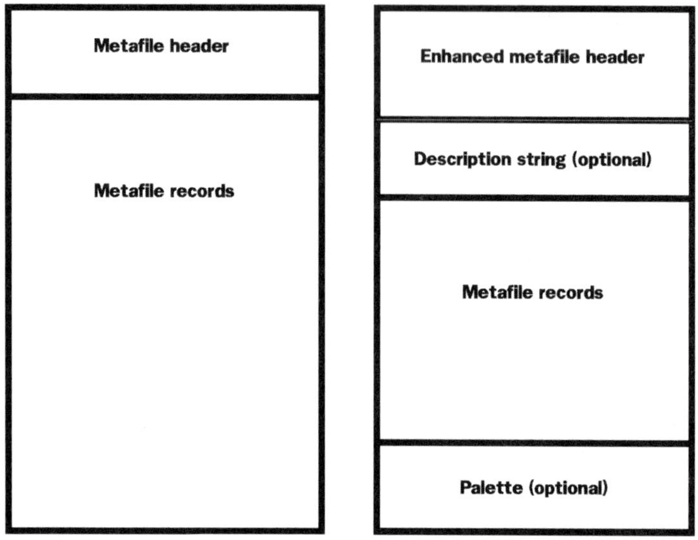

Fig. 18.3
The new and old metafile formats.

of your code. Unfortunately, unless you target Windows NT exclusively, you cannot use a common binary for all Win32 platforms, because Windows 95 does not support Unicode.

The second solution is to leave your code in ANSI and convert to Unicode before you call OLE. This solution works in a Windows NT environment. Under Windows 95, you would simply skip the conversion routines. The flip side of the technique is to convert your code to Unicode internally and convert it to ANSI before calling any Win32 routines that do not support Unicode.

Finally, you can use the ANSIOLE *thunk*. The OLE SDK contains source code that you can use to build a thunk that can automatically convert from ANSI to Unicode. This translation "thunking layer" sits between your application and the OLE libraries. When you use this approach, most applications don't require any source code changes. For a large application, this approach enables you to have your application up and running quickly with Unicode support. The downside is that this extra mapping layer affects your application's performance.

The Registry

Because 32-bit OLE is now a part of the operating system, the installation program takes care of installing the DLLs and updating the registry correctly.

Developers no longer have to ship the OLE libraries with their applications.

In addition, a new set of keys, described in table 18.6, has been added for 32-bit support.

Table 18.6 New Keys for 32-bit Support

Key	Description
`LocalServer32`	A 32-bit server EXE
`InProcServer32`	A 32-bit in-process server DLL
`InProcHandler32`	A 32-bit handler DLL
`ProxyStubClsid32`	Maps an IID to a CLSID in a 32-bit proxy DLL

A Win32 key has also been added to support 32-bit type libraries.

Examining the Code

In this section, you examine the code for the drag-drop target that you originally developed in Chapter 3, "A Sample C++ Application." You then examine each of the modules in turn and see the changes that were necessary to port this rather simple application to 32-bit OLE.

The OLE1.CPP File

When you developed this application for 16-bit OLE, you learned that you had to enlarge the application's message queue, because Win16's default message queue size, eight, is too small to handle large amounts of LRPC traffic. Under Win32, the system enlarges the message queue dynamically. The `SetMessageQueue` function is essentially an NOP (an instruction that does nothing) on Win32. However, you should always include this call in your code if you want to target Win32s. The second change in this module is the use of the TEXT macro, which converts the error messages to Unicode if Unicode is defined, and to ANSI if not.

Listing 18.2 shows OLE1.CPP with the changes.

Listing 18.2 The Modified OLE1.CPP

```
#include "stdafx.h"
#include "ole1.h"

#include "mainfrm.h"
#include "oledoc.h"
#include "oleview.h"
#include "iodnd.h"

#ifdef _DEBUG
#undef THIS_FILE
static char BASED_CODE THIS_FILE[] = __FILE__;
#endif

//////////////////////////////////////////////////////////////////////
// COleApp

BEGIN_MESSAGE_MAP(COleApp, CWinApp)
       //{{AFX_MSG_MAP(COleApp)
       ON_COMMAND(ID_APP_ABOUT, OnAppAbout)
           // NOTE - ClassWizard adds and removes mapping macros here.
           //  DO NOT EDIT what you see in these blocks of generated code!
       //}}AFX_MSG_MAP
       // Standard file-based document commands
       ON_COMMAND(ID_FILE_NEW, CWinApp::OnFileNew)
       ON_COMMAND(ID_FILE_OPEN, CWinApp::OnFileOpen)
END_MESSAGE_MAP()

//////////////////////////////////////////////////////////////////////
// COleApp construction

COleApp::COleApp()
{
       // This is a requirement of OLE due to the amount
       // of traffic that the LRPC protocol can generate.
       SetMessageQueue(96);
}

//////////////////////////////////////////////////////////////////////
// The one and only COleApp object

COleApp NEAR theApp;

//////////////////////////////////////////////////////////////////////
// COleApp initialization
int COleApp::ExitInstance()
{

       // Shut down the OLE libraries
       OleUninitialize();

       return CWinApp::ExitInstance();
}
```

```
//------------------------------------------------------------------
BOOL COleApp::InitInstance()
{
    DWORD dwVersion;

       //----------
       // Always check that the version of the OLE libraries
       // is compatible with the libraries that you used
       // to build your application.
       dwVersion  = OleBuildVersion();
    if (HIWORD(dwVersion) != rmm ¦¦ LOWORD(dwVersion) < rup)
    {
           AfxMessageBox(TEXT("Error: Incompatible OLE libraries"));
           return FALSE;
    }

       // Initialize the OLE libraries
    if((hResult = OleInitialize(NULL)) != NOERROR)
              return FALSE;


       // Register the application's document templates.
       // Document templates serve as the connection
       // among documents, frame windows, and views.

       CSingleDocTemplate* pDocTemplate;
       pDocTemplate = new CSingleDocTemplate(
              IDR_MAINFRAME,
              RUNTIME_CLASS(COleDoc),
              RUNTIME_CLASS(CMainFrame),     // main SDI frame window
              RUNTIME_CLASS(COleView));

       AddDocTemplate(pDocTemplate);

       OnFileNew();

       return TRUE;
}

/////////////////////////////////////////////////////////////////////
// CAboutDlg dialog used for App About

class CAboutDlg : public CDialog
{
public:
       CAboutDlg();

// Dialog Data
       //{{AFX_DATA(CAboutDlg)
       enum { IDD = IDD_ABOUTBOX };
       //}}AFX_DATA

// Implementation
protected:
       virtual void DoDataExchange(CDataExchange* pDX); // DDX/DDV support
```

(continues)

Listing 18.2 Continued

```
        //{{AFX_MSG(CAboutDlg)
                // No message handlers
        //}}AFX_MSG
        DECLARE_MESSAGE_MAP()
};

CAboutDlg::CAboutDlg() : CDialog(CAboutDlg::IDD)
{
        //{{AFX_DATA_INIT(CAboutDlg)
        //}}AFX_DATA_INIT
}

void CAboutDlg::DoDataExchange(CDataExchange* pDX)
{
        CDialog::DoDataExchange(pDX);
        //{{AFX_DATA_MAP(CAboutDlg)
        //}}AFX_DATA_MAP
}

BEGIN_MESSAGE_MAP(CAboutDlg, CDialog)
        //{{AFX_MSG_MAP(CAboutDlg)
                // No message handlers
        //}}AFX_MSG_MAP
END_MESSAGE_MAP()

// App command to run the dialog
void COleApp::OnAppAbout()
{
        CAboutDlg aboutDlg;
        aboutDlg.DoModal();
}
```

The OLEDOC.CPP

The changes to the document module involve declaring the storage and stream names as class members. You begin by including TCHAR.H. This header file contains all the macros used to provide the portable type definitions.

Notice that both the arrays are now declared to be of type TCHAR. If Unicode is defined, the type resolves to `wchar_t`; otherwise, the type simply resolves to `char`. Listing 18.3 shows the code for OLEDOC.H.

Listing 18.3 OLEDOC.H

```
#if !defined( _OLEDOC_H_ )
#define _OLEDOC_H_
```

```
#include <tchar.h>

// oledoc.h : interface of the COleDoc class
//
//////////////////////////////////////////////////////////////////////
// Forward reference
interface CDropTarget;

class COleDoc : public CDocument
{
protected: // create from serialization only
        COleDoc();
        DECLARE_DYNCREATE(COleDoc)

// Attributes
public:
        CDropTarget FAR *m_pCDropTarget;
        HWND m_TargetWnd;
        LPOLEOBJECT m_lpOleObj;

        TCHAR m_szStorage[_MAX_PATH];
        TCHAR m_szStream[_MAX_PATH];
// Operations
public:
        void SaveObject(LPDATAOBJECT lpDataObj);
        void DrawObject(CDC *pDC, LPRECT lprc);
// Implementation
public:
        virtual ~COleDoc();
        virtual void Serialize(CArchive& ar);
                                        // overridden for document I/O
#ifdef _DEBUG
        virtual void AssertValid() const;
        virtual void Dump(CDumpContext& dc) const;
#endif

protected:
        virtual BOOL OnNewDocument();

// Generated message map functions
protected:
        //{{AFX_MSG(COleDoc)
          // NOTE - ClassWizard adds and removes member functions here.
          //    DO NOT EDIT what you see in these blocks of generated code!
        //}}AFX_MSG
        DECLARE_MESSAGE_MAP()
};

//////////////////////////////////////////////////////////////////////
   #endif
```

In the constructor, you initialize the storage and stream name members. Note again the use of the TEXT macro to ensure that the code is portable. When Unicode is defined, the strings are Unicode strings and you cannot use the standard `strcpy` function. The function `_tcscpy` is a portable version of strcpy. When Unicode is defined, _tcscpy evaluates to wcscpy, which is the wide-character version of strcpy. When Unicode is not defined, _tcscpy evaluates to strcpy.

The remainder of the code remains the same as it was for the 16-bit implementation. Listing 18.4 shows the complete code for the OLEDOC.CPP module.

Listing 18.4 OLEDOC.CPP

```
#include "stdafx.h"
#include "ole1.h"

#include "oledoc.h"

#ifdef _DEBUG
#undef THIS_FILE
static char BASED_CODE THIS_FILE[] = __FILE__;
#endif

/////////////////////////////////////////////////////////////////////////////
// COleDoc

IMPLEMENT_DYNCREATE(COleDoc, CDocument)

BEGIN_MESSAGE_MAP(COleDoc, CDocument)
       //{{AFX_MSG_MAP(COleDoc)
         // NOTE - ClassWizard adds and removes mapping macros here.
         //    DO NOT EDIT what you see in these blocks of generated
code!
       //}}AFX_MSG_MAP
END_MESSAGE_MAP()

/////////////////////////////////////////////////////////////////////////////
// COleDoc construction/destruction

COleDoc::COleDoc()
{
       m_lpOleObj = NULL;

       _tcscpy(m_szStorage,TEXT("\\mydoc.dfl"));
       _tcscpy(m_szStream,TEXT("mystream"));
}
//---------------------------------------------------------------------------
COleDoc::~COleDoc()
{
}
//---------------------------------------------------------------------------
BOOL COleDoc::OnNewDocument()
{
       if (!CDocument::OnNewDocument())
              return FALSE;

       return TRUE;
}
```

```
/////////////////////////////////////////////////////////////////////////////
// COleDoc serialization

void COleDoc::Serialize(CArchive& ar)
{
        if (ar.IsStoring())
        {
                // TODO: add storing code here
        }
        else
        {
                // TODO: add loading code here
        }
}

/////////////////////////////////////////////////////////////////////////////
// COleDoc diagnostics

#ifdef _DEBUG
void COleDoc::AssertValid() const
{
        CDocument::AssertValid();
}

void COleDoc::Dump(CDumpContext& dc) const
{
        CDocument::Dump(dc);
}
#endif //_DEBUG

/////////////////////////////////////////////////////////////////////////////
// COleDoc commands
void COleDoc::DrawObject(CDC *pDC, LPRECT lprc)
{
        HRESULT hr;
        IStorage  *pStorage, *pSubStorage;
        IUnknown *punk;

        // Open your compound file and the substorage
        // containing the embedded object.
        hr = StgOpenStorage(m_szStorage,NULL,
                STGM_READWRITE¦STGM_SHARE_EXCLUSIVE,NULL,0,&pStorage);
        hr = pStorage->OpenStorage(m_szStream,NULL,
                STGM_READWRITE¦STGM_SHARE_EXCLUSIVE,0,0,&pSubStorage);

        // Load the object into memory
        hr = OleLoad(pSubStorage,IID_IUnknown,NULL,(LPVOID FAR *) &punk);
        // Draw the presentation data
        hr = OleDraw(punk,DVASPECT_CONTENT,pDC->m_hDC,lprc);

        // Release the storage refs
        pSubStorage->Release();
```

(continues)

Listing 18.4 Continued

```
        pStorage->Release();
        // Release the object
        punk->Release();
}
//------------------------------------------------------------------
void COleDoc::SaveObject(LPDATAOBJECT lpDataObj)
{
        //----------
        // Create an OLE compound file and save the
        // data transfer object as an embedded object.
        //

        HRESULT hr;
        IStorage  *pStorage, *pSubStorage;


        // Create or open the docfile.
        if (FAILED(StgIsStorageFile(m_szStorage)))
        {
                hr = StgCreateDocfile(m_szStorage,
                        STGM_READWRITE¦STGM_SHARE_EXCLUSIVE,0,&pStorage);
        }
        else
        {
                hr = StgOpenStorage(m_szStorage,NULL,
                        STGM_READWRITE¦STGM_SHARE_EXCLUSIVE,NULL,
                        0,&pStorage);
        }
        // Create the storage for this object.
        if (S_OK == hr)
        {
                hr = pStorage->CreateStorage(m_szStream,
                       STGM_CREATE¦STGM_READWRITE¦STGM_SHARE_EXCLUSIVE,
                       0,0,&pSubStorage);
        }
        else
        {
                AfxMessageBox(TEXT("Error: Failed to create docfile"));
                return;
        }

        if (S_OK == hr)
        {
                IPersistStorage *pps;
                // ------
                // Here you create the embedded object
                // from the data transfer object.
                hr = OleCreateFromData( lpDataObj, IID_IOleObject,
                     OLERENDER_DRAW, NULL, NULL, pSubStorage,
                     (LPVOID FAR *)&m_lpOleObj);
                if (S_OK == hr)
                {
                        hr = m_lpOleObj->QueryInterface(
                                IID_IPersistStorage,
```

```
                            (LPVOID FAR *)&pps);
                    if (S_OK == hr)
                    {
                           // Save the object in your newly
                           // created stream.
                           hr = OleSave(pps,pSubStorage,TRUE);
                           pps->SaveCompleted(NULL);
                           pps->Release();
                    }

             }
             m_lpOleObj->Release();
             pSubStorage->Release();
      }
      // Releasing the reference counter will close the file.
      pStorage->Release();
}
//-----------------------------------------------------------------
//-----------------------------------------------------------------
```

Linking the Application

The remainder of the code modules remains the same as the original Win16 version. Building the application requires some changes to the make file and also a change in compilers. Because you are developing a 32-bit application, you want to use a 32-bit compiler to generate the code. The compiler I used was a beta version of Visual C++ 2.0. Visual C++ 2.0 is a 32-bit-only compiler that can target Win32 and 68K and PowerPC Macintosh. It also has one of the most impressive development environments that I have ever seen.

Preprocessor Definitions. The first changes involve defining the constants UNICODE (for Win32 Unicode support), _UNICODE (for C run-time Unicode support), INC_OLE2, and WIN32.

The Unicode `#define` statements are used for the portable type definitions and macros for TCHAR.H. The C run-time libraries use the _UNICODE manifest constant. You use the INC_OLE2 manifest constant to pull in the OLE headers. Finally, you define WIN32 because that is the platform that you are targeting.

Figure 18.4 shows the Project Settings dialog box with these options selected.

The Import Libraries. To use 32-bit OLE, you must link two libraries. The first library is OLE32.LIB, which is the main import library for the OLE APIs. If your application supports OLE Automation, you must also link with OLEAUT32.LIB. Finally, you must link the UUID.LIB import library.

Figure 18.5 shows these options selected in the Project Settings dialog box.

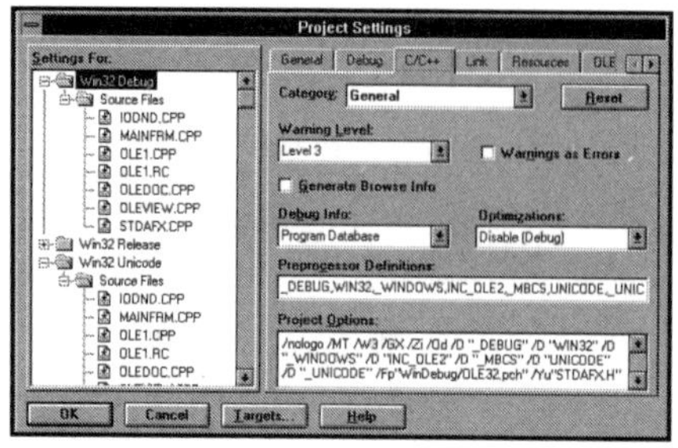

Fig. 18.4
The preprocessor definitions selected in the Project Settings dialog box.

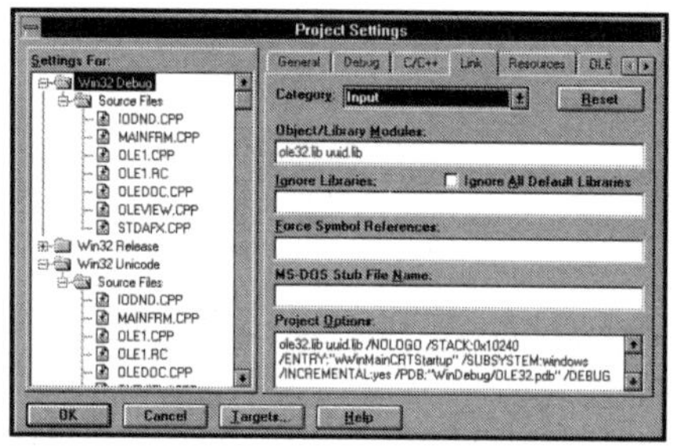

Fig. 18.5
The import libraries selected in the Project Settings dialog box.

The Program Entry Point. Most programmers are used to having `WinMain` as their application entry point. The startup code calls the function after the initialization of some global variables and the application stack and heap.

Your application's entry point will be `wWinMainCRTStartup`. The initial *w* refers to the Unicode (wide-character) support available in this function. Basically, the initial indicates that the command line will be in Unicode when you receive it.

You call the `WinMain` function if Unicode is not defined. Otherwise, you call the `wWinMain` family.

Figure 18.5 shows these options selected in the Project Settings dialog box.

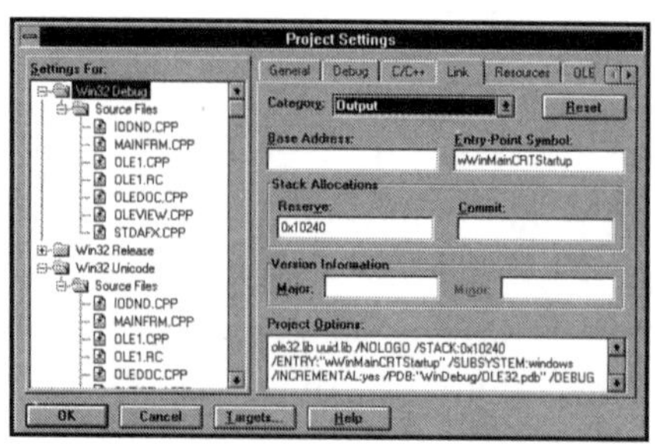

Fig. 18.6
Setting the program entry point in the Project Settings dialog box.

From Here...

In this chapter, you examined Win32 and 32-bit OLE. While examining the main features of Win32, this chapter is not an in-depth or comprehensive examination of Win32. Jeffery Richter's *Advanced Windows NT* provides an in-depth look at Win32 from a developer's perspective, and Helen Custer's *Inside Windows NT* provides an architectural overview of Win32. Both of these books are published by Microsoft Press.

In the next chapter, you take a look at distributed objects and Distributed OLE.

Chapter 19

Distributed Objects

Distributed computing and distributed objects promise to be among the most exciting developments in computing in the coming years. In this chapter, you explore some of the developments so far and see where OLE will fit into this brave new world. You also look at some of the pieces that make distributed computing work.

In this chapter, you learn about the following:

- The Distributed Computing Environment (DCE) specification that facilitates the development and use of distributed systems
- The Common Object Request Broker Architecture (CORBA) specification, which deals with distributed objects in a similar environment
- The Common Object Model (COM), an open architecture that enables interoperation between Microsoft's and Digital's technology
- Distributed OLE, the technology that will enable objects to connect to each other across an enterprise

The Promise of Distributed Objects

Simply stated, the distributed objects concept is the application of object technology in a distributed computing environment.

The key to this technology's success is transparency. Andrew Tanenbaum, in his book *Computer Networks* (Prentice Hall, 1988), describes a distributed system as one in which "the existence of multiple autonomous computers is transparent." Neither programmers nor users should be aware of any difference between local and remote objects. Apart from such issues as security, the underlying object system should handle connections to a local server, an in-proc server, or a remote server. In fact, the only real issue for programmers to handle is the inherent latency in distributed systems. For example, network traffic can slow response time for remote object servers.

The entire system of remote and local objects should be presented to the user as a single entity. Everything from network printers to remote volumes becomes objects. All are joined together into one unified namespace.

This scenario enables developers to develop distributed applications without changing their programming model. The fact that parts of the application are running on remote PCs on the network is completely transparent.

The primary goal of distributed objects is information sharing. The concept provides the foundation for true workgroup computing by providing access to all the data within an organization.

From a business perspective, distributed objects will lower the cost of computing by fully utilizing all the resources of the network. Processor-intensive tasks can be executed on high-end hardware, while the result can return transparently to low-end PCs.

The Distributed Computing Environment

The Open Software Foundation (OSF), an international consortium of all the major software and hardware vendors, has developed a model known as the Distributed Computing Environment (DCE). DCE provides a set of operating system and network services that facilitate the development and use of distributed systems. These services are network-, platform-, and vendor-independent. DCE currently defines seven services, including threads, RPC (remote procedure call), directory services, time services, security services, distributed file system (DSF), and diskless support. The DSF and diskless support builds on the other services.

The DCE (see fig. 19.1) is a layered architecture similar to the Open Systems Interconnection (OSI) model. The bottom layer provides the transport services, the next layer is the thread layer, followed by the RPC layer, and so on. Each layer builds on features from the previous layer.

A thorough discussion of the OSF DCE is beyond the scope of this book. However, the following sections briefly examine each of the layers.

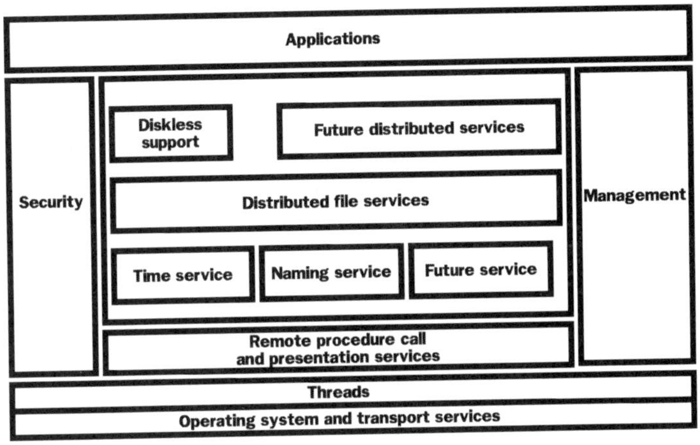

Fig. 19.1
The Distributed Computing Environment (DCE).

Threads

A *thread* is basically a unit of execution. In modern multitasking operating systems, threads are the basic entity for which CPU time is allocated. The operating system divides its time among all the active threads in the system. Although a single processor can execute only one thread at a time, you can achieve the illusion of running more than one program simultaneously by allocating a small "slice" of time to each thread.

Threads are very important in applications that use RPC because of its inherent synchronous nature. Applications that are waiting for RPC calls to return can continue to execute other threads of execution.

For systems that do not support threads, DCE provides a threads package. This library of routines enables such systems to participate in distributed environments.

Remote Procedure Call (RPC)

All programmers are familiar with the procedural programming model RPC. In this model, large tasks are broken into smaller procedures. These smaller procedures are often grouped together and stored in programming libraries.

These libraries are usually linked directly into the application or, in the case of environments such as Windows or OS/2, in dynamic linked libraries (DLLs). With RPC, these libraries can exist on remote computers but are accessed as if they were stored locally. This is similar to the client-server model of computing.

In the client-server model, applications are usually split into two parts: a front end that handles user interaction and displaying data, and a back end that stores and retrieves the data. Novell NetWare and LAN Manager networks are examples of client-server environments. In these networks, the file server provides storage and security services to the client workstation.

Writing an application that works in a client-server environment usually requires knowledge of network protocols and interprocess communications (IPC) mechanisms. In a Novell environment, you use the IPX/SPX protocols to talk to the file server. In an Advanced NT Server network, you use named pipes or mail slots. In a heterogeneous network environment, things get even more complicated, because you have to contend with incompatible protocols.

RPC provides you with a network-independent IPC mechanism. RPC handles the details relating to network protocols and transport mechanisms. It also provides the code necessary to handle time-outs, lost connections, and network failures.

Using RPC, you simply call procedures and functions as you would using standard libraries or DLLs. The programming model used with RPC is exactly the same as the local procedure model.

To achieve interoperability with systems written by different vendors, OSF defined the core protocol, which cannot be modified. Various vendors, including Microsoft, have added extensions to the core protocol, but all implementations support this core.

OSF defines the following as being the most important properties of a remote procedure call:

- *Simplicity.* An RPC follows the local procedure model.
- *Transparency.* An RPC is independent of network protocols.
- *Performance.* The RPC mechanism should not result in any performance degradation.

Directory Services

As was previously mentioned, everything in a distributed environment is an object, including printers, users, and file servers. The OSF DCE directory services are responsible for locating and tracking all these objects throughout the enterprise.

For performance reasons, these services are split into two distinct types: the Cell Directory Service and the Global Directory Service.

The Cell Directory Service (CDS) is responsible for providing directory services with a predefined group, such as a local area network (LAN), a workgroup, or a domain. In OSF DCE parlance, this grouping is called a *cell*. Most requests for name services are for objects that reside within the cell, so these service providers can be optimized for speed.

If the request is for an object that is outside the LAN, workgroup, or domain, the request is sent through the Global Directory Agent (GDA). The GDA acts as a directory service gateway for the cell. The GDA passes the request to another CDS or to the Global Directory Service (GDS). The GDS is based on the CCITT X.500 standard.

Security Services

DCE uses the Kerberos authentication system as the basis for its security services. Developed at MIT, the Kerberos system is named after the three-headed dog who guards the gates of Hades in Greek mythology.

In the Kerberos system, the Kerberos Authentication Server grants each user a "ticket" that consists of the user's name, the server name, the user's network address, and a timestamp. The ticket also includes an encrypted session key. To access remote servers, the user presents this key to a Ticket Granting Server (TGS), which then grants a ticket for that particular server. To encrypt tickets, Kerberos uses private key encryption.

Kerberos uses three levels of security:

- The lowest level of security clearance requires that the user's access rights be verified when he or she connects to the remote resource. After the initial connection, no more checking is performed.
- The second level requires that Kerberos verify each network package.
- The highest level provides the second level's security plus encryption of each network package.

Kerberos also can check a user's authorization to use a particular resource. Checks such as the Access Control Lists (ACLs) found on Windows NT are also available.

The Distributed File System

A Distributed File System (DFS) is necessary to enable users to access files and data in heterogeneous environments. The files should have the same names regardless of the environments in which they are actually located. A DFS needs to provide security, reliability, and availability at all times.

The DFS used by DCE is based on the Andrew File System (AFS), a high-performance file system that supports directory and file replication. The implementation of the DFS uses the lower layers in the OSF DCE model. The directory services provide a uniform naming system for all files. Security services using ACLs regulate access to files, and RPC is used to transfer data across the network.

Time Services

Time services are provided by special servers known as Distributed Time Service (DTS) servers. File servers within the enterprise use these servers to synchronize the server time clocks. The time server provides a consistent timestamp that DFS can use. The DTS uses the Coordinated Universal Time (UTC), which is the international standard.

Diskless Support Services

The diskless support services describe how DCE can be loaded on diskless workstations or PCs.

OMG CORBA

The Common Object Request Broker Architecture (CORBA) is a specification produced by the Object Management Group (OMG). The OMG, like the OSF, is a consortium of computer vendors including companies such as Microsoft, Hewlett-Packard, IBM, Digital, and Sun Microsystems. OMG's purpose is to develop specifications to integrate object technology with distributed computing.

While the OSF DCE deals with distributed computing on heterogeneous networks, CORBA deals with distributed objects in a similar environment.

CORBA is concerned with two main entities: the Interface Repository (IR) and the Object Request Broker (ORB).

While the Interface Definition Language (IDL) that DCE RPC deals with is procedural function calls, the CORBA IDL deals with class definitions. IR keeps track of these interface definitions and provides run-time access to all information contained in the original IDL files.

The ORB is a type of object server that handles requests from client applications to objects and returns the objects' responses. These objects can exist anywhere on a distributed network. The object user has no idea of where the actual object resides or even whether the object has used other remote objects to perform the requested action.

ORBs are used to locate and activate objects in heterogeneous environments. The objects can be running on any operating system or hardware.

To invoke a method on a remote object, the client software calls an object proxy. This object proxy then calls a proxy stub on the object server. The ORB is then responsible for locating the actual object on the network, marshaling the method call to the object, and returning the results to the client.

CORBA systems support a function-dispatch mechanism called the Dynamic Invocation Interface (DII). This mechanism enables a method to be invoked by its name rather than by a reference to the method. This enables developers to make run-time decisions about which method to invoke. A similar feature is available in SmallTalk and Objective-C.

In theory, any CORBA-compliant system, such as IBM's Distributed System Object Model (DSOM), should be able to interoperate with any ORG. Unfortunately, this is not the case. The actual interoperability standard from OMG is not yet finished. So, although applications developed with DSOM can interoperate with other applications developed with DSOM, they cannot work with Digital's ObjectBroker. However, as the next section describes, the Common Object Model addresses some of these interoperability problems.

The Common Object Model

The Common Object Model (COM) is an open architecture, jointly developed by Microsoft and Digital, that enables interoperation between OLE and Digital's ObjectBroker technology. Built on a core subset of OLE and a communication protocol based on DCE RPC, the Common Object Model is the first step toward making OLE a true multiplatform object system.

COM enables applications that use ObjectBroker to cooperate and communicate with OLE applications. This interoperability is completely transparent to the OLE applications.

ObjectBroker is one of the first fully compliant CORBA applications. Applications that use ObjectBroker are provided with transparent access to objects and resources on a variety of platforms, including OSF/1, OpenVMS, ULTRIX, HP-UX, and SunOS.

COM allows OLE applications running under Windows NT to access objects, through the ObjectBroker technology, existing anywhere on the enterprise.

These links are totally transparent to both the object server and the clients.

At the Win32 Developers Conference held in Anaheim, California in December 1993, Microsoft demonstrated an OSF/1 server running a stock quote server being linked to a copy of Excel running on Windows NT (see fig. 19.2). The Excel application contained a spreadsheet that was being constantly updated by data being sent from the OSF/1 server. Neither Excel nor the OSF/1 application knew anything about each other. This once again demonstrates the strength and scalability of the Common Object Model.

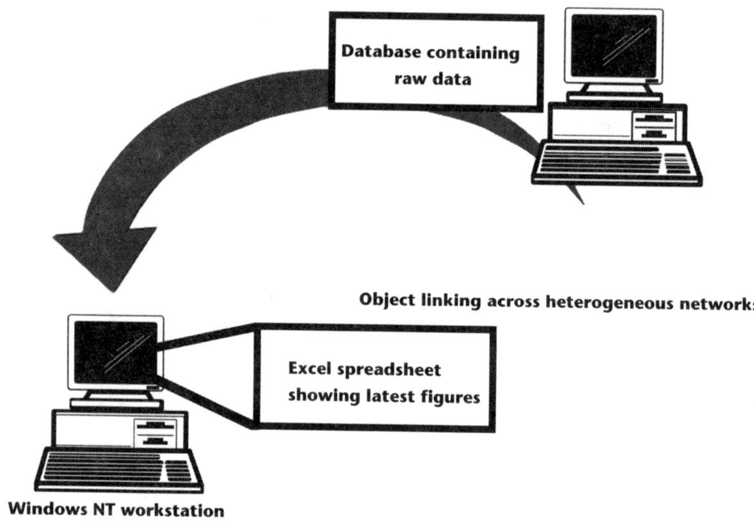

Fig. 19.2
The Common Object Model.

Distributed OLE

Adding distributed capabilities to OLE is the next obvious step. These capabilities will enable objects to connect to each other across an enterprise. The next major release of Windows NT will be the first Windows platform to support Distributed OLE.

Distributed OLE is 100-percent compatible with OLE. Any application that can access local objects today will also be capable of accessing remote objects without recompiling or changing the code.

The key architectural feature of OLE that makes this compatibility possible is the interprocess communications (IPC) mechanism designed by the OLE architects. You can replace lightweight remote procedure calls (LRPC), which handle the marshaling and unmarshaling of interfaces between local objects, with true remote procedure calls (RPC). Microsoft RPC enables objects to connect across networks. In fact, in both Windows 95 and Windows NT 3.5, Microsoft replaces the LRPC mechanism with RPC.

OLE achieves this compatibility by using proxies and stubs. The proxy, which is interface-specific, is responsible for packing or marshaling the interface parameters and passing them to the transport channel. This channel is in fact the RPC layer. On the receiving end, the stub, which is also interface-specific, unmarshals the incoming parameters and calls the actual object. The object's return codes and such are then passed back, using the same mechanism (see fig. 19.3). Because the proxy and stub are interface-specific, a proxy and stub pair must exist for each standard COM interface. Therefore, when developing custom interfaces, you must write your own marshaling code for each interface.

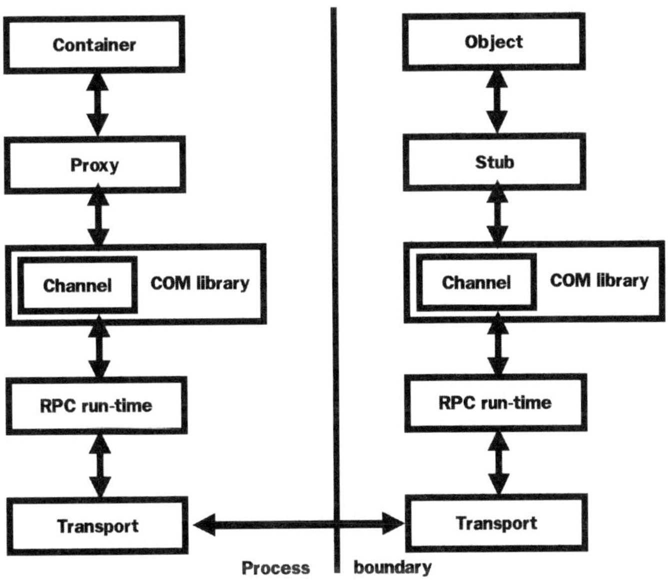

Fig. 19.3
The distributed objects architecture.

To locate remote servers, Distributed OLE introduces a new component called the Service Control Manager (SCM).

When a client tries to connect to an object, the SCM attempts to locate it from a database of class information. If the object is local, the name is passed to the OLE libraries. However, if the object server is remote, the SCM connects to the SCM on the remote computer. The SCM on the remote computer then starts the object server. When the server registers its class factory interface, this interface pointer is returned to the client.

All the standard services built into RPC, such as security and user authentication, automatically become a part of OLE. Each application that uses OLE gets these features, without any changes to the application's code. Applications that are unaware of security, including all current OLE applications, get a default level of security. Object servers that are non-security-aware cannot be run on remote computers. Such servers are always loaded into their clients' process space.

There is, however, one limitation: Windows APIs cannot run on remote computers, because window handles (HWNDs) and device contexts (DCs) make no sense to a remote process; they make sense only in the context in which they were created. However, this limitation is minor. For most applications, you want to keep the user interface on one PC while remoting data processing or collection objects.

From Here...

In this chapter, you briefly examined distributed computing and objects. The next chapter examines some of the future directions of OLE.

Chapter 20
The Future of OLE

For the last 19 chapters, you have explored OLE as it is today. You have seen how OLE evolved from DDE to OLE 1.0 and finally to the current version.

You have seen how OLE grew from being a specification and implementation for creating compound documents in the Microsoft Windows environment to a system that not only includes compound documents but an object model that provides the foundation and infrastructure for the next generation of operating systems from Microsoft.

OLE provides a binary standard for objects that is independent of programming languages. It gives you a robust and scaleable object system and the promise of new and exciting features in coming releases.

In short, OLE is an advanced system that brings the power of object technology to both developers and users. But that is just one side of the story. OLE provides, through the Component Object Model (COM), the means to build applications for tomorrow's object-based operating systems. This, however, is just the beginning. This chapter explores what might lie ahead in OLE's future.

In this chapter, you explore the potential for the following future technologies:

- Property inheritance
- Extended object layout
- Object tunneling
- Support for irregularly shaped objects
- In-place editing of linked objects
- Shared toolbars
- Cross-platform interoperability

- Custom controls
- Distributed objects
- True link tracking
- Document objects
- Extensions for real-time market data

Property Inheritance

Property inheritance is a container's capability to export property information to embedded or linked objects.

To understand the problem that this feature is intended to solve, consider the following example. Suppose that your spreadsheet has a group of cells that represent the company's sales figures for the current fiscal year. The columns and rows have headers that contain information about each of the numbers. The font that your spreadsheet uses for text is Times Roman Italic. You also have written a report with your word processor. To move the sales figures into your report, you select the table in the spreadsheet and drag it to your word processor. Unfortunately, the font that your word processor report uses is Century Schoolbook. To restore the document's appearance, you must activate the object and change the font.

With property inheritance, the container informs the object, before the drop, of the font that is currently in use. The object can then change its font and transform its appearance to match that of the text in the document.

A similar problem also arises if you decide to change the font used in a report that contains OLE objects. Again, you need a mechanism by which the container can inform the objects of the change. These smart objects save you time by automatically adjusting themselves to their environment.

Property inheritance was originally planned to be part of the OLE specification, but was dropped. Perhaps future releases of OLE will finally incorporate this feature.

Extended Object Layout

Any future release of OLE will undoubtedly add an object placement system that facilitates large objects that cross page boundaries.

Such object placement problems occur, for example, when you insert a large spreadsheet object into a compound document. The object's adornments for column headers are always placed on the first page, so you have to page back and forth when reading the data.

Another example occurs when a word processor repaginates and an object lies on the page break. In the current release of OLE, the object must always be forced to the next page, leaving a gap in the page on which you actually placed the object.

With an extended object layout feature, the OLE libraries would break the object into separate parts for each page. That way, the column heading appears on each page (see fig. 20.1).

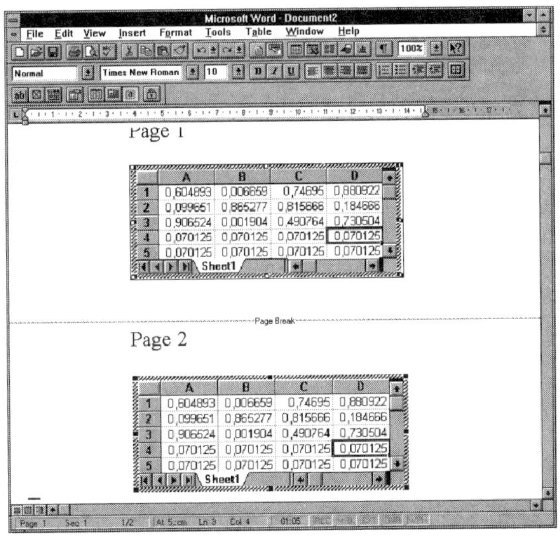

Fig. 20.1 The extended object layout feature.

In effect, what you see is similar to the MFC Document/View architecture, in which you have multiple views of the same data object.

Object Tunneling

One important feature of OLE is that in a compound document scenario, metafiles that represent the contents of the embedded and linked objects are cached and stored separately to facilitate fast rendering on various output devices by the default or a custom handler.

But what happens if you try to search the document for an occurrence of a particular word? Today's containers treat the contained objects simply as graphic objects and skip over them. So much for the concept of a unifying container that treats all objects as a single entity.

What is needed is a mechanism for the container to activate and tunnel (search or spell-check the actual data contained within the object) into each of the objects while performing its search. The same feature is also required by spelling and grammar checkers.

To implement this feature, Microsoft will probably have to add a new interface to OLE. This interface would be supported by both containers and objects. When a container wants to search or spell-check an object, the container and object would pass raw, unformatted text between them to enable the container to work with the data. The container would always be responsible for performing the actual work on the data, to ensure that data is handled uniformly throughout the document.

Currently, even if this solution were possible, activating each object would impose a significant performance penalty. As the industry gets closer to the achievement of true compound documents that are composed of OLE custom controls or objects with in-process (in-proc) handlers, more objects will support the "inside-out" method of activation—that is, the objects will always be active but not user-interface (UI) active. This method will exact almost no performance loss when "tunneling" through objects.

Support for Irregularly Shaped Objects

Although the support for irregularly shaped objects is a relatively minor issue, such a feature could prove useful in certain situations. Currently, all OLE objects are rectangular, so when you place an object within a body of text, for example, the text wraps around the smallest rectangle that encompasses the object.

This feature would enable the text to flow around the actual object itself. For example, if you insert an embedded pie chart into a report, the text would flow around the actual sides of the pie chart, not the smallest rectangle that the pie chart fits in.

When OLE adds support for irregularly shaped objects, this feature will probably also provide support for overlapping and transparent objects.

OpenDoc's specification claims to support irregular objects, so Microsoft probably will include this support in a future release of OLE.

In-place Editing of Linked Objects

Although users are frequently confused by the fact that OLE does not enable them to edit a linked object in place, this deficiency has sound technical causes (chiefly the fact that the container does not store the object's data). Not only does the object's server start in a separate window (like an embedded object that is opened), a different set of UI guidelines exists for linked objects. For example, an object that is opened in a separate window normally uses a hatched pattern to cover the object's site within the container. For a linked object, however, this hatched pattern is removed. Users notice these apparent inconsistencies, which needlessly complicate users' understanding of the compound document paradigm.

According to the OLE User Interface Guidelines, a linked object should be thought of as an "updating image of another piece of data residing at another point in the same document or within a different document altogether." Such subtlety is lost on the user. Instead of trying to justify something that is obviously wrong (from the user's point of view), this particular distinction between embedded and linked objects should simply be eliminated.

Shared Toolbars

As you'll recall from this book's discussion of visual editing, an important part of visual editing's user interface is the merging of the container's and object's main menus. So far, no standard for toolbars exists among applications, so you cannot merge toolbars.

Because of the popularity of the Microsoft Foundation Classes (MFC), more applications are beginning to use Microsoft's style for toolbars. When Microsoft releases Windows 95, toolbars and status bars will become standard controls supplied by the operating system. As applications begin to adopt these new common controls, developers will produce extensions to the visual editing COM interfaces that enable you to merge toolbars.

Cross-platform Interoperability

OLE's cross-platform support comes in two forms. The first form is the sharing of files between applications running under different operating systems. If, for example, you e-mail from a Windows workstation to a Macintosh user a compound file that contains a report, you must ensure that the Macintosh user can open and read the document.

The second form, of course, is to have the same programming model on each platform. You should be concerned about only platform-specific issues such as byte ordering.

Interoperability and the Macintosh

OLE for System 7, which Microsoft released in July of 1994, supports the same functionality as its 16-bit Windows cousin and also enables compound documents to be freely exchanged between Windows and Macintosh workstations.

When you view compound documents in the Macintosh environment, the default handler handles such issues as byte ordering and automatic conversion between Windows bitmaps, device-dependent bitmaps (DDBs) and device-independent bitmaps (DIBs), and the Macintosh PICT file format. Object conversion will enable automatic conversion between bitmaps to the Macintosh PICT format.

Future releases of OLE for Macintosh may make available remote Automation and Uniform Data Transfer (UDT) between Macintosh and Windows clients.

Interoperability and Windows NT

Windows NT 3.5 includes 32-bit OLE, which will bring OLE to native NT applications. The 32-bit OLE offers exactly the same functionality as its 16-bit counterpart. Being a Windows NT implementation, 32-bit OLE also fully supports Unicode.

Windows NT 3.5 will also deliver full 16- and 32-bit interoperability. This feature enables 16-bit OLE applications, such as the 16-bit version of Word for Windows 6.x, to exchange data with 32-bit OLE applications. This interoperability is vital, because most current OLE applications are of the 16-bit variety. If you try to drag an object from one 16-bit application (such as Word for Windows) to another application, the drag-drop functionality ceases to work when the cursor leaves the first application. This occurs because the applications reside in separate address spaces and also because of NT's security features.

After Microsoft releases Windows 95, 32-bit OLE should quickly replace 16-bit OLE. Likewise, 32-bit Windows will become the standard API for developing applications for the Windows family of operating systems.

OLE Controls

Most developers are familiar with Visual Basic custom controls, or VBXs as they are more commonly known. VBXs, which were the first real examples of component software, have become increasingly popular over the last couple of years. In fact, a whole new industry has sprung up around the development of such controls, most of which have been aimed at the corporate or solution developer.

Unfortunately, VBXs are closely tied to the Visual Basic environment. Even though MFC supports VBXs, only version 1.0 controls are supported through the VBX emulation process. Visual Basic controls are built on a 16-bit architecture and are not portable to other platforms—not even to the 32-bit Windows platform.

Microsoft's solution to these problems, OLE Controls, combines the best features of VBX architecture with OLE objects. In fact, OLE Controls are in-place document objects that can be programmatically controlled through OLE Automation. In other words, all OLE Controls support `IDispatch`.

OLE Controls expose properties and respond to external events. Events are handled through a new connection architecture that enables objects to support *outgoing interfaces*. Although objects normally support incoming interfaces, outgoing interfaces enable them to call implementations in other objects.

Containers that support these new objects will implement a new COM interface called `IOleControlSite`. The control itself will implement `IOleControl`. Here again, you see the extensibility of the Component Object Model demonstrated. These interfaces, like all COM interfaces, support `IUnknown` and behave like all other interfaces.

Another major difference between OLE Controls and standard OLE objects is that the controls all support *inside-out* activation. This means that when the controls are in view or are selected by a single mouse click, they will be in-place active, but not UI active.

For property editing, OLE Controls provide standard dialog boxes for both containers and controls. A licensing mechanism similar to that supplied with current VBXs is also available. Once OLE is available on the Macintosh, OLE Controls for that platform should also begin to appear.

Distributed Objects

Currently, OLE supports two kinds of object servers: in-process (`InProc`) servers that are implemented as DLLs, and local servers that are implemented as EXEs. Both kinds of servers enable users to access and integrate objects on the PC.

The next logical step is to support remote servers, enabling users to access objects across an enterprise. Distributed OLE will in fact provide communication between objects across heterogeneous networks.

Distributed OLE promises to be one of the most exciting advances in OLE in the coming years. Developers will be able to split their applications into multiple components and execute the individual components on different machines. This will enable the applications to offload CPU-intensive tasks to more powerful PCs and keep the UI-intensive objects local. Yet all of this will be completely transparent to the user. Although the user will have the impression that all the relevant objects are located locally, in fact the user will be leveraging the resources of the entire network.

Because of the COM's unique architecture, these remote features will also be transparent to developers. The current implementation of lightweight remote procedure calls (LRPC) will simply be replaced with remote procedure calls (RPC). Microsoft's RPC, which is compatible with the RPC specification of the Open Software Foundation's Distributed Computing Environment (OSF DCE), adds features that enable OLE to transfer data between remote applications. Some of these new features enable COM interfaces to be marshaled across the network. The standard proxies and stubs are replaced with RPC proxies and stubs to package the data and transport it across the wire (see fig. 20.2).

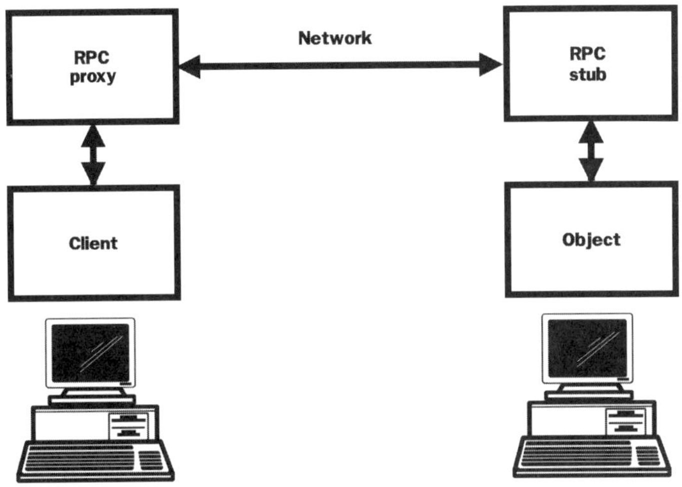

Fig. 20.2
Distributed OLE.

True Link Tracking

The current implementation of OLE has two major problems regarding object linking. The first problem is the "broken link" issue. Although the industry has come a long way from the simplistic link management of OLE 1.0, there is still a long way to go.

Further support for link tracking has to come from the operating system. With the upcoming release of the new version of Windows NT and its object file system (OFS), this support will finally be in place.

The OFS file system will support the same interface as the current structured storage, so applications that you write now will be fully compatible with OFS. Each object stored in an OFS file system will be assigned a GUID from the operating system to assist in tracking the object. The new version of Windows NT will automatically index all objects, which will assist in rapidly searching both property sets and contents. This version of Windows NT will support a fully distributed object system and present this to the user in one unified namespace. Also, this version of Windows NT will make no distinctions among network volumes, local disk drives, or remote systems.

Document Objects

As more developers begin the move toward the next versions of Windows and Windows NT, you will see a more document-centered approach to the user interface. Multiple Document Interface (MDI), which was so popular in the Windows 3.x environment, will begin to decline.

Developers will begin to break applications into collections of OLE components held together in special containers. These containers or document objects will be capable of containing OLE Controls and creating objects specific to that particular type of document object.

A word-processing document object will automatically create objects such as text formatters, spell checkers, and search objects. When the user chooses File New menu options, the document object will create and activate in place an OLE rich text editor. When the user requests that the document be spell-checked, the document object will use the interfaces of the spell-checker object and the `IDataObject` interface of the rich text editor to spell-check the document.

When you save data, the application will store it with the document object's CLSID. Then when you open the data object, the document object will load and the data stream will be passed to the rich text control.

Slowly, the old concept of applications and data files will disappear, to be replaced by the notion of data objects and service objects. The primary focus for the user will become the document, not the application. This is the core concept of the document-centered paradigm.

The Windows Open Services Architecture Extensions for Real-time Market Data

Real-time access to data is the lifeblood of the financial and securities industries. Currently, you usually access this information through proprietary systems that are both expensive and incompatible with one another.

To provide a standard for accessing and supplying real-time information, Microsoft and the Open Market Data Council for Windows have jointly developed a specification called the Windows Open Services Architecture Extensions for Real-time Market Data (WOSA/XRT).

In developing the XRT specification, the group had two goals:

- To provide seamless access to any real-time data source from any Windows-based application.

- To provide developers with a flexible infrastructure that facilitates the development of high-end, custom solutions.

The group chose OLE as the key object technology required to meet these goals. OLE Automation and Uniform Data Transfer (UDT) are the two technologies used by WOSA/XRT. OLE's UDT mechanism provides the means for transferring real-time data between applications. OLE Automation enables developers to build custom applications that consist of multiple OLE component objects.

The WOSA/XRT specification defines data objects and data users. *Data objects* support the COM interfaces `IDispatch` and `IDataObject`. *Data users* support `IAdviseSink`. The XRT does not define any new COM interfaces or APIs; these three standard COM interfaces implement the entire architecture. In fact, the specification is mainly concerned with defining the programmability interface that is used between the data object and the data user.

Using OLE to develop real-time applications enables developers to leverage their experience with OLE and to access such tools as MFC and Visual C++.

The WOSA/XRT standard is further proof that OLE is much more than a compound document object technology.

Windows 95 File Viewers

If you select any file object on a Windows 95 system, you will notice a Quick View option on the context menu. If you select this option, the system's shell uses the CLSID registered for that file object to invoke a specific viewer for that file type. These file viewers provide a fast way for the user to view and possibly print the contents of a file object.

These file viewers are in fact OLE component objects. The viewers implement the `IPersistFile` interface and a new COM interface called `IFileViewer`. Because they are implemented as OLE component objects, the viewers are extensible and extremely powerful. They not only provide a basic viewing functionality, but can also behave as OLE containers and support in-place activation of embedded objects.

Users can also select part of the document from within the viewer and drag and drop it to another container.

The Windows 95 Shell

One of the more interesting features of the Windows 95 shell, the Explorer, is its capability to extend the shell by writing shell extension handlers. These handlers are similar to OLE in-proc servers.

The shell currently supports five types of handlers:

Handler	Purpose
Context menu handler	Adds options to the context menu for an object
Icon handler	Adds icons to file objects
Drag-drop handler	Adds a context menu that is used when an object is dropped on the desktop
Property sheet handler	Adds pages to a property sheet for a file object
Copy handlers	Called when a file object is being copied, moved, deleted, or renamed

To implement a shell extension, the handler implements a class factory for `IShellExtInt` and, depending on the type of handler, `IContextMenu`, `IShellPropSheetExt`, or `IExtractIcon`. If a handler supports `IExtractIcon`, it must also support `IPersistFile`.

The handler also supports the exported functions `DllGetClassObject` and `DllCanUnloadNow`. These are exactly the same functions that are implemented by a standard in-proc server.

Again, it is obvious that OLE in general and the COM in particular are far more than simply a compound document architecture. They form the foundation and infrastructure for all object extensions to the operating system, the file system, and the shell.

Index

Symbols

\1Ole streams (Special OLE stream), 239-240
\2OlePres? (Special OLE stream), 240-262
16-bit variables (32-bit conversion), 557
1CLSID.C (listing 13.8), 421
1CLSID.H (listing 13.8), 421
32-bit OLE applications, 556-561, 576-579

A

access (object restricting), 368-370
accessing
- Automation
  - methods, 382-395
  - objects, 357
- Excel 5.0, 458-477
- structured storage, 25-26

ACL (Access Control List), 595
ActivateAtBits key, 547
active object menus, 18
active objects
- counting, 427, 488
- frame windows, 272-275
- moving, 280-281
- resources, 268
- sizing, 148, 280-281

Add Class dialog box, 427-428
Add Method dialog box, 428-429, 489
Add Property dialog box, 429
adding methods to classes, 428-429
AddRef function, 406
AddRef function (IUnknown interface), 36
***Advanced Windows NT*, 574, 589**
AFS (Andrew File System), 596
AFX (Applications Frameworks), 263
AfxOleInit function, 168, 426
AfxOleLockApp function, 488
aligning data structures (Win32), 560
ANSIOLE thunks, 578
antimonikers, 22, 575
AOT (alert object table), 97, 341
API function, 44
application objects, 404-405
Application class (listing 15.4), 458-469
application container submenu, 174
applications, 425-427
- 16 and 32-bit OLE interoperability, 575
- 32-bit OLE applications, 576
- Automation controllers, 356-357
- Automation server, 397-398
- class (windows), 306-312
- code conversions, 562-572
- command lines (Win32), 560
- concurrency handling, 163
- Console applications, 544
- containers
  - creating, 167-200
  - saving documents, 242
  - submenus, 176
- customizing, 345-347
- debugging, 426, 574
- drag-drop, 98, 215-216
- entry points, 588
- exposing objects, 360-368
- file I/O (input/output), 119-120
- frameworks, 117-118
- international, 368-369
- linking, 587-589
- MkTypLib, 416
- modules, 168-200
- multiple instances, 561
- objects, 361-362
- prefixing strings, 564-570
- shutdown, 54
- standard objects, 360-361
- structures (fields), 69-70
- test application (Excel 5.0 object model), 448-452
- threads, 552-553
- units conversions, 72
- using Unicode, 562-572
- UUIDGEN.EXE, 38
- Windows (executing from DOS boxes), 112
- WXSRVR program, 112-113

AppWizard, 167-200, 306
- applications, 425-427
- OLE support, 164
- templates, 448-449

architecture (custom interfaces), 516-519
archives, 283
assigning
- CLSID (class IDs) to structured storage, 227
- context menus to embedded objects, 179-190

asynchronous input model (Win32), 551-552
AUTOCLI.CPP (listing 12.1), 373-376

AUTOCVW.CPP (listing 12.5), 390-395
AUTOCVW.H (listing 12.4), 389
AUTODOC.CPP (listing 12.3), 379-382
AUTODOC.H (listing 12.2), 378-379
Automation, 345-370
- C++ controllers, 349
- clients, 447-477
- controllers, 356-357, 436-444
- Excel 5.0, 366-367
- exceptions, 162-163
- method accessing, 382-395
- objects, 347-357
- servers, 93-94, 398-399, 479-512

Automation support (ClassWizard), 427-436
AUTOMFC.CPP (listing 16.1), 481
AUTOMVW.H (listing 16.2), 484-488
AutoSrv interface, 417-418
AUTOSRV.REG file, 419-420
AUTOSRV.CPP (listing 13.3), 408-412
AUTOSRV.CPP (listing 17.8), 540-547
AUTOSRV.H (listing 13.2), 407-408
AUTOSRV.H (listing 17.8), 540-547
auxiliary user types, 41

B

binding (monikers), 340-341
Bitmap class, 292-303
bitmaps, 281
- displaying, 327-332
- metafiles, 337

blocking Win32 threads, 554
borders (objects), 483
BPS.H (listing 17.4), 532-533
BPS_I.C (listing 17.5), 533-534
BPS_P.CXX (listing 17.3), 526-531
BPS_X.HXX (listing 17.3), 526-531
browsers, 112, 357-360
Busy dialog box, 159

C

C run-time functions, 564-570
C++ controllers (Auto mation controllers), 357
CAUTODOC.CPP (listing 16.6), 498-502
CAUTODOC.H (listing 16.5), 497-498
CAutoSrv (Automation server), 398-399
CDIB.CPP (listing 9.6), 293-303
CDIB.H (listing 9.6), 293-303
CDispatchDriver definition (listing 14.2), 437-439
CDocItem class, 123
CDocTemplate class, 121
CDocument class, 119-120
CDropTarget class, 53-89
- DragEnter method, 72-74
- DragLeave method, 75
- DragOver method, 74-75
- Drop operation, 75
- GetDrag method, 71-72
- IDropTarget interface, 58-69
- implementing, 69-75
- initializing, 53-54

CDS (Cell Directory Service), 595
CExcel class, 449
CF_TEXT data format, 153
cfFormat field (FORMATETC data structure), 202
Change Title command (Edit menu), 338
Change Type dialog box, 40
class factories
- full server application, 307
- implementing, 540-548
- objects, 407-408
- registering, 399

classes
- adding methods, 428-429
- Bitmap class, 292-303
- CDocItem class, 123
- CDocTemplate class, 121
- CDocument class, 119-120
- CDropTarget class (IDropTarget interface), 58-69
- CExcel class, 449
- CMainFrame class, 118
- CObject class, 412-414
- COleBusyDialog class, 159
- COleChangeIconDialog class, 156
- COleClient Item class, 129-135
- COleCntCntrItem class, 172-173
- COleConvertDialog class, 155-156
- COleDataObject class, 153-154
- COleDataSource class, 151-153, 208
- COleDialog class, 122-123
- COleDispatchDriver class, 124
- COleDispatchException class, 162-163
- COleDocument class, 124-127
- COleDropSource class, 149
- COleDropTarget class, 149-151
- COleException class, 160
- COleInsertDialog class, 154-155
- ColeInsertDialog class, 172
- COleIPFrameWnd class, 312
- COleLinkingDoc class, 127-129
- COleLinksDialog class, 157-158
- COleMessageFilter class, 163-165
- COleObjectFactory class, 136-137
- COlePasteSpecialDialog class, 157
- COleResizeBar class, 148
- COleServerDoc class, 316
- COleServerItem class, 142-146
- COleStreamFile class, 161-162
- COleTemplateServer class, 137-142
- COleUpdateDialog class, 158-159

ClassWizard, 357
- Add Property button, 429
- adding methods, 489-495
- Automation support, 427-436
- method stubs, 436

Client Application (listing 17.9), 545-547

client codes, 544-546
client-server environments, 594
clipboard, 208-215, 331-332
closing streams (structured storage), 231
CLSID (class IDs), 38, 420-421
assigning to storages, 227
generator, 96-97
CLSIDFromProgID function, 458
CMainFrame class, 118
CNTRITEM.H (listing 6.6), 195-196
CObject (Automation server), 398
CObject class, 412-414
CoCreateGUID function, 37
code field (SCODE), 43
codes
client codes, 544-546
miniservers code summary, 301-302
portable codes, 60
return codes, 378
CoGetClassObject function, 38
CoGetMalloc function, 45
COleBusyDialog class, 159
COleChangeIconDialog class, 156
COleClient Item class, 129-135
COleCntCntrItem class, 172-173
COleConvertDialog class, 155-156
COleDataObject class, 153-154, 207
COleDataSource class, 151-153, 208
COleDialog class, 122-123
COleDispatchDriver class, 124
COleDispatchDriver class (listing 15.3), 457-458
COleDispatchException class, 162-163
COleDocument class, 124-127
COleDropSource class, 149
COleDropTarget class, 149-151
COleException class, 160
COleInsertDialog class, 154-155, 172
COleIPFrameWnd class, 312
COleLinkingDoc class, 127-129
COleLinksDialog class, 157-158
COleMessageFilter class, 163-165
COleObjectFactory class, 136-137
COlePasteSpecialDialog class, 157
COleResizeBar class, 148
COleServerDoc class, 316
COleServerItem class, 142-146
COleStreamFile class, 161-162
COleTemplateServer class, 137-142
COleUpdateDialog class, 158-159
CoLockObjectExternal function, 67-68
COM (Component Object Model), 12, 33-51, 597-598
interfaces, 264
Memory Allocator, 44-45
command lines (Win32 applications), 560
commands
DataObject menu
Enumerate FormatEtc, 95
GetDataObject, 95
Show Link Source Descriptor, 96
Edit menu
Change Title, 338
Insert Object, 172
Paste, 209
Paste Link, 212
Paste Special, 339
File menu
Open, 119-120
Run the Registry Editor, 100
Objects menu, 100
compiling interface files, 519
CompObj streams (special OLE streams), 238-239
Container classes, 127-135
creating, 427-428
CRectTracker class, 160-161
CView class, 120-121
Document class, 275-283, 316-325, 488-490
In-Place Frame class, 272-275
initializing, 488
MFC base classes, 122-127
MFC OLE classes, 121-164
nested, 503-505
Object Interface class, 287-292, 332-341
OLE Dialog classes, 154-159
OleIPFrame class, 146-148
server classes, 136-148
Title class, 325-327
UDT (Uniform Data Transfer) class, 148-154
View class, 172-190, 283-287, 483-488
Window Application class, 267-272
component objects, 34
activating, 174-176
aggregating, 47-49
default verb, 41
delegating, 46-50
drawing, 173-190
dropped
displaying, 75, 82-89
storing, 76-82
external locks, 67-68
finding, 37-42
inheriting, 46-47
interfaces (support), 35
loading, 37
local servers, 40
locking, 67-68
marshaling, 50-51
monikers, 340
reference counting, 36-37
return codes, 42-44
searching, 37-42
status information, 41-42
strong locks, 67-68
tracker rectangles, 174
weak locks, 68
component software, 15-16
composite monikers, 575
compound document objects, 142-146
compound documents, 11
compound files, 13, 24-27, 233-241, 256-262
access mode flags, 235-236
converting formats, 234
creating, 76
defining, 249
displaying, 92-93
OLE (Object Linking and Embedding), 241-244
saving, 259
storing data, 244-256
transacted storage, 237
Win32 applications, 576
***Computer Networks*, 591**
concurrency handling applications, 163

Confirm Classes dialog box, 437
Console applications, 544
Constructor (CDropTarget class), 69-70
container applications, 167-200, 242
Container classes, 127-135
Container option (Options dialog box), 167
containers
- binding to linked objects, 340-341
- creating, 127-129
- frame windows, 312-316
- implementing, 275-283
- memory space, 282, 291, 336
- property inheritance, 602
- objects, 160
- returning errors, 160
- source codes, 167

context field (SCODE), 43
context menus, 179-190
control bars, 272-275
Control key (Insert Control dialog box), 42
controls (OLE Controls), 607-608
Conversion field, 40
converting
- applications
  - codes, 562-572
  - units, 72
- data (ANSI to Unicode), 572
- formats to compound files, 234

Coordinated Universal Time, *see* UTC
copying framework data, 338
CORBA (Common Object Request Broker Architecture), 596-597
CoRegisterClassObject function, 399
counting
- active objects, 427, 488
- reference counts, 68

CPP file macros, 433-436
Create class button, 428
Create method (CDropTarget class), 70
CreateILockBytesOnHGlobal function, 227
CreateStdDispatch function, 352-354
CRectTracker class, 160-161
Critical sections (thread synchronization), 553-554
cross-platform interoperability, 606-607
CShape objects, 490-510
currently defined facilities, 43
Custer, Helen, 589
custom interfaces, 515-548
- implementing, 518-519, 521-548
- testing, 547-548

custom marshaling, 50, 518
customizing applications, 345-347
CVarEnum enumerator, 503-505
CVarEnum methods, 505-512
CView class, 120-121
CWinApp (full server object), 306-312
CWinApp Module (listing 7.7), 222-224
CWnd pointer, 313

D

data
- compound file storage, 244-256
- conversion (ANSI to Unicode), 572
- formats (full server), 338-339
- frameworks, 338
- marshaling, 518
- properties, 245
- Real-time market data, 610-611
- unmarshaling, 521
- viewing, 120-121

Data Advise Sink (data changes), 173
data formats
- CF_TEXT, 153
- enumerating, 95
- listing, 100
- RTF (Rich Text Format), 153-155
- viewing, 95-96

data sinks, 173
data structures
- alignments (Win32), 560
- FORMATETC data structure, 71, 202-205
- INTERFACEDATA structure, 353
- STATSTG structure, 228
- STGMEDIUM data structure, 205-208

data transfer, 153-155, 201-215
data transfer objects, 151-153
data types
- defaults, 41

DataFormats field, 41
DataObject menu commands, 95-96
DC (device context), 576
DCE (Distributed Computing Environment), 37, 575, 592-596
DCs (device contexts), 600
DDB (device-dependent bitmap), 267, 292
DDE (dynamic data exchange), 10, 346
DDE messages (Win32), 558
deactivating embedded objects, 177
debugging
- applications, 426, 574
- objects, 113
- streams, 99
- structured storage, 92

Debugging Handler, 113
DECLARE_DISPATCH_MAP macro, 432-436
DefaultFile key (DataFormats field), 41
DefaultIcon field, 41
defaults
- collection methods, 497
- component object verb, 41
- data types, 41
- handlers, 41
- OLE2.DLL, 40

delegating
- component objects, 46-50
- IDispatch calls, 354-355

DeleteCriticalSection function, 554
designing interfaces, 522-523
destructor (CDropTarget class), 70
device contexts, *see* DCs
device-independent bitmaps, *see* DIBs
DFS (Distributed File System), 595-596
dialog boxes, *see* individual listings
DIB (device-independent bitmaps), 281, 305

dictionary property sets, 248
DII (Dynamic Invocation Interface), 597
direct access tocompound files, 237
direct storage, 25
directory services, 594-595
diskless support services, 596
DISP_FUNCTION macro, 489
DispGetIDsofNames function, 355
DISPIDs (dipatch IDs), 351, 434-435
DispInvoke function, 354-355
displaying
- bitmaps, 292-303, 327-332
- compound files, 92-93
- dropped component objects, 82-89
- dropped objects, 75
- fields, 253-255

DISPTEST utility (Automation servers), 93-94, 356, 422
Distributed Computing Environment, *see* DCE
Distributed File System, *see* DFS
distributed objects, 591-600, 608
Distributed OLE, 598-600, 608
Distributed System Object Model, *see* DSOM
Distributed Time Service, *see* DTS
DLLs (dynamic linked libraries), 593
- creating, 526-535
- storing, 377
- unloading, 99

DocFile Viewer, 92-93
Document class, 84-89, 275-283, 316-325, 488-490
Document constructor, 280, 323
Document View architecture, 118-121
documenting embedded object changes, 193-200
documents
- compound documents, 11
- modules, 190-193
- objects, 362-365, 609-610
- saving container applications, 242
- templates, 306-312

Documents collection object, 364-365
DOE (Distributed Objects Everywhere), 49
DOI (Document-Oriented Interface), 15
drag-drop, 149
- applications, 98
- feedback, 218-219
- support, 215-221
- targets, 149-151

drag-drop support, 29-30
DragEnter method (CDropTarget class), 72-74
DragLeave method (CDropTarget class), 75
DragOver method (CDropTarget class), 74-75
Draw method (component objects), 173
DrawGhostRect method (View class), 84
drawing
- component objects, 173-190
- objects, 287

Drop operation (CDropTarget class), 75
dropped objects, 75
DSOM (Distributed System Object Model), 16, 597
DSPCALC2.H (listing 14.2), 437-439
DSPCALCW.CPP (listing 14.3), 440-441
DTS (Distributed Time Service), 596
dwAspect field (FORMATETC data structure), 203-204
Dynamic Data Exchange, *see* DDE
Dynamic Invocation Interface, *see* DII
Dynamic Linked Libraries, *see* DLLs

E

Edit Links dialog box, 157-158
Edit menu, 174
Edit menu commands
- Change Title, 338
- Insert Object, 172
- Paste, 209
- Paste Link, 212
- Paste Special, 339

embedded objects, 340-341
- activating, 175-176, 200
- assigning context menus, 179-190
- changing, 155-156
- copying to clipboard, 331-332
- creating, 211-212
- deactivating, 177
- documenting changes, 193-200
- hands-off state, 243
- linking to, 221-224
- Move method (COleClientItem class), 195
- no-scribble state, 242
- OnChange method (COleClientItem class), 194
- OnChangeItemPosition method (COleClientItem class), 194
- OnDeactivateUI method (COleClientItem class), 194-195
- OnGetItemPosition method (COleClientItem class), 194
- pointers, 264
- retrieving size, 324
- saving, 190-195
- scaling, 324
- Serialize method (COleClientItem class), 195
- sizing, 177-179, 337
- storage, 241-243
- visual editing, 17-31

Embedding parameters, 268
EnableAutomation method (AppWizard), 426, 488
enlarging message queues, 53, 372
EnterCriticalSection function, 554
entry points (applications), 588
Enumerate FormatEtc command (DataObject menu), 95
enumerating data formats, 95
enumerators, 73
- CVarEnum, 503-505
- functions, 45-46
- IEnumVARIANT, 502-505
- objects, 46
- storages, 230

errors
codes
HRESULT (handle to a result code), 42
SCODE (status code), 42, 44
reporting, 378-382
returning to containers/ applications, 160
events (synchronization objects), 555
Excel 5.0
accessing, 458-477
Object Browser, 359-360
object model, 447-448
OLE Automation, 366-367
quitting, 448-452
starting, 448-452
test application, 477
toolbar buttons, 476
type libraries, 453-477
workbooks, 476-477
EXCEL.CPP (listing 15.5), 470-475
EXCEL.H (listing 15.5), 470-475
exception handlers, 574
executing Windows applications from DOS boxes, 112
ExitOle function, 400
expanding
interfaces, 59-60
streams (compound files), 235
exposed methods, 439-444
exposing objects in applications, 360-368
extended object layout, 602-603
external locks, 67-68

F

facilities (currently defined), 43
facility field (SCODE) field, 43
FAT (file allocation table), 226
fields
application structures, 69-70
AuxUserType, 41
cfFormat field (FORMATETC data structure), 202
code field (SCODE), 43
context field (SCODE), 43
Conversion, 40
DataFormats, 41
DefaultIcon, 41
displaying, 253-255
dwAspect field (FORMATETC data structure), 203-204
facility field (SCODE), 43
InProcHandler, 40
InProcServer, 40
lindex field (FORMATETC data structure), 204
LocalServer, 40
MiscStatus, 41-42
Object Descriptor fields, 95-96
ProgID, 40
ptd field (FORMATETC data structure), 203
severity field (SCODE), 42
SIZEL, 72
STATSTG structure, 228-229
tymed field (FORMATETC data structure), 204-205
type identifier field, 245-247
Verb, 40-41
VersionIndependentProgID, 39-40
file I/O (input/output), 119-120
File menu commands
Open, 119-120
Run the Registry Editor, 100
files
AUTOSRV. REG file, 419-420
compound files, 13, 24-27
creating, 76
data storage, 244-256
defining, 249
displaying, 92-93
OLE (Object Linking and Embedding), 241-244
saving, 259
sharing, 256-262
Win32 applications, 576
IDL files, 522
interface files, 519
memory-mapped files (Win32), 555-556
metafiles, 177, 266-267, 337
in 32-bit OLE applications, 576-577
reference device context, 576
REGEDIT file, 547
filter routines, 574
FindWindow function, 561
flags (compound file access modes), 235-236
flat memory model (Win32), 550-551
Font objects, 365-366
fonts (Unicode), 572
foreign languages, 368-369
Form_Load from the Visual Basic test script (listing 16.10), 510
FORMATETC data structure, 28, 71-73, 202-205
formats
AUTOSRV.REG file, 419
converting to compound files, 234
data (full server), 338-339
data formats
CF_TEXT, 153
RTF (Rich Text Format), 153-155
metafiles, 576-577
OLE formats, 202
frame windows (containers), 312-316
frameworks
applications, 117-118
data, 338
Free Module utility, 99-100
full servers, 305-306
data formats, 338-339
source code, 306-338
testing, 338-339
Full-Server radio button (Options dialog box), 306
functions
AddRef function, 406
AddRef function (IUnknown interface), 36
AfxOleInit function, 168, 426
AfxOleLockApp function, 488
API function, 44
C run-time functions, 564-570
CLSIDFromProgID function, 458
CoCreateGUID, 37
CoGetClassObject, 38
CoGetMalloc, 45
CoLockObjectExternal, 67-68
CoRegisterClassObject function, 399
CreateILockBytesOnHGlobal function, 227

CreateStdDispatch function, 352-354
DeleteCriticalSection function, 554
DispGetIDsofNames function, 355
DispInvoke function, 354-355
EnterCriticalSection function, 554
enumerator functions, 45-46
ExitOle function, 400
FindWindow function, 561
GDI (graphic device interface) functions, 266, 559-560
GetHGlobalFromILockBytes function, 227
InitializeCriticalSection function, 554
InitOle function, 398
LeaveCriticalSection function, 554
LockServer function, 406
OleCreateFromData, 77
OleInitialize, 168, 398
OleLoad, 84-85
OleQueryCreateFromData, 72
OleQueryLinkFromData, 72
OleSave, 77
OleUninitialize, 54
RegisterDragDrop, 67, 83
Release function (IUnknown interface), 36
ReleaseStgMedium, 72
RevokeDragDrop, 83
RunEmbedded function, 268, 307
SetMessageQueue, 53
SetMessageQueue function, 372, 579
StgCreateDocFile function, 233
StgCreateDocFileOnILockBytes function, 233
StglsCreatDocFile, 76
StglsStorageDocFile, 76
StglsStorageFile function, 249
StgOpenStorage, 76
SysAllocString function, 388
UpdateAllViews, 75
WriteClassStg, 78

Functions list box, 358
future development of OLE, 601-612

G

GDA (Global Directory Agent), 595
GDI (graphic device interface), 559-560
functions, 266
mapping modes, 265-266
resources, 551
GDS (Global Directory Service), 595
generators
CLSID (class ID) generator, 96-97
Type Library Generator, 111-112
GetDataObject command (DataObject menu), 95
GetDrag method (CDropTarget class), 71-72
GetHGlobalFromILockBytes function, 227
GetIDsOFNames method
Automation, 382-383
IDispatch interface, 351
GetObjectInfo Method (listing 7.4), 216-220
GetProperty method (property values), 444
GetQuote method (CObject class), 412
GetSet key (DataFormats field), 41
GetShape method, 489
GetShapeCount method, 490
GetTypeInfo method (IDispatch interface), 349
GetTypeInfoCount method (IDispatch interface), 349
graphic device interface, *see* GDI
GUID (globally unique identifier), 37, 248

H

handlers
Debugging Handler, 113
defaults, 41
exception handlers, 574
OnStart command handler, 458
termination handlers, 573
handles
HWNDs (window handles), 600
sizing, 148, 483
handling (Automation exceptions), 162
hands-off state (embedded objects), 243
headers
interfaces, 524
macros, 59-60
HIMETRIC units, 265, 282
HRESULT (handle to a result code), 42

I

IAdviseSinks interface, 206
IAUTOSRV.H (listing 13.7), 417-418
icons (dialog boxes), 156
IClassFactory interface, 399, 406-412
IDataObject interface, 151-153, 201-208
IDataObject Viewer, 95-96
identifiers
CLSID (class identifiers), 38
DISPIDs (dipatch IDs), 351, 434-435
GUIDs (globally unique identifiers), 37, 248
IID (Interface ID), 524
IIDs (interface identifiers), 38
LANGID (language ID), 368
LCID (locale ID), 368
UUIDs (universally unique identifiers), 38, 96
identifying component objects (local servers), 40
IDispatch interface, 347-355
calls, 354-355
pointers, 439, 476
viewer, 101
IDropTarget interface, 58-69
IDL (Interface Description Language), 369, 519, 596
IDL files (listing 17.1), 522-524
IDropSource interface, 149
IDropTarget interface, 98, 149-151

IEnumVARIANT interface, 347
- enumerator, 502-505
- listing 16.7, 503
- methods, 503-505

IID (interface ID), 38, 524
ILockBytes interface, 227
IMalloc interface, 45
IMessageFilter interface, 163-165, 426
IMPLEMENT_OLECREATE macro, 436
implementation files
- AUTOCLI.CPP, 373-376
- AUTOCVW.CPP, 390-395
- AUTODOC.CPP, 379-382
- AUTOMFC.CPP, 481
- AUTOMVW.H, 484-488
- AUTOSRV.CPP, 408-412, 540-547
- CAUTODOC.CPP, 498-502
- CDIB.CPP, 293-303
- DSPCALCW.CPP, 440-441
- EXCEL.CPP, 470-475
- IODND.CPP, 62-67
- IPFRAME.CPP, 273-280, 313-316
- IRUNOBJ.CPP, 104-110
- MAIN.CPP, 400-404
- modified OLE 1.CPP, 579
- modified OLE1.CPP, 579-582
- OBJECT.CPP, 413-414
- OLE1.CPP, 55-58
- OLE2SRV.CPP, 307-312
- OLECNDOC.CPP, 191-193
- OLECNT.CPP, 169-172, 196-200
- OLECNVW.CPP, 181-190
- OLEDOC.CPP, 79-82, 584-587
- OLESEDOC.CPP, 275-280
- OLESERV.CPP, 268-280
- OLESEVW.CPP, 284-303
- OLESRDOC.CPP, 317-322
- OLESRVW.CPP, 327-331
- OLEVIEW.CPP, 87-89
- SHAPE.CPP, 492-495
- SRVRITEM.CPP, 288-303, 332-336
- SUMINFO.CPP Module, 253-255
- SUMMADOC.CPP, 250-252
- TITLE.CPP, 325-327
- VARENUM.CPP, 506-510
- XCLIENT.CPP, 449-452

import libraries, 421-423, 587
in-proc (in-process) servers, 40, 50
In-place Frame class, 272-275
in-place frame windows, 146
in-place objects
- editing, 605
- sizing, 148

indices (object collections), 497
inheriting component objects, 46-47
InitializeCriticalSection function, 554
initializing
- Automation server, 398-399
- CDropTarget class, 53-54
- classes, 488
- libraries, 54, 168, 268, 306, 372-376, 400-404
- object variables, 323
- objects, 93

InitOle function, 398
InprocHandler field, 40
InProcServer field, 40
input (synchronous), 552
Insert Object command (Edit menu), 172
Insert Object dialog box, 154-155, 172
Insertable key (Insert Object dialog box), 42
inserting text (Word files), 388
***Inside Windows NT*, 589**
Interface Description Language, *see* IDL
INTERFACEDATA structure, 353
interfaces, 33-34
- AutoSrv interface, 417-418
- collection interfaces, 347
- COM interfaces, 264
- custom interfaces, 515-548
- designing, 522-523
- expanding, 59-60
- files, 519
- headers, 524
- IAdviseSinks interface, 206
- IDataObject interface, 151-153, 201-208
- IDispatch interface, 348-356
- IDropSource interface, 149
- IDropTarget interface, 58-69, 98, 149-151
- IClassFactory interface, 399
- IEnumVARIANT interface, 347
- ILockBytes interface, 227
- IMalloc, 45
- IMessageFilter interface, 163-165, 426
- IPersist interface, 241-242
- IPersistFile interface, 244-262
- IPersistStorage interface, 242-243
- IPersistStream interface, 243-244
- IRootStorage interface, 229
- IStorage interface, 227-230
- IStream interface, 231-232
- ITypeInfo interface, 349-350
- IUnknown, 34-36, 48
- IUnknown interface, 347
- IStream interface, 161
- marshaling parameters, 520
- pointers, 36-37, 48, 61, 76
- responsive user interface, 553
- standard interfaces, 516-517
- static, 36
- string enumerators, 46
- stubs, 521
- supporting component objects, 35
- viewers, 100-110

international applications, 368-369
interoperability (between 16 and 32-bit OLE applications), 575
Invoke method (IDispatch interface pointer), 383-388
IODND.CPP (listing 3.4), 62-67
IODND.H (listing 3.3), 60-61
IOleInPlaceObject interface, 178
IPC (interprocess calling), 575
IPC (interprocess communications), 594, 598
IPersist interface, 241-262
IPFRAME.CPP (listing 10.2), 313-316
IPFRAME.CPP (listing 9.2), 273-280
IPFRAME.H (listing 10.2), 313-316
IPFRAME.H (listing 9.2), 273-280
IR (interface repository), 596
IRootStorage interface, 229
IRUNOBJ.CPP (listing 4.2), 104-110
IRUNOBJ.H (listing 4.1), 103-114

IStorage interface, 227-230, 283
IStream interface, 161, 231-232
ISVs (independent software vendors), 11
Item method (collections), 497
ITypeInfo interface, 349-354
IUnknown interface, 34-36, 48, 68-69, 347, 405-406
IDL file (listing 17.2), 525-547
methods, 505

K

keys
32-bit OLE applications, 579
ActivateAtBits key, 547
Control key (Insert Control dialog box), 42
DefaultFile key (DataFormats field), 41
GetSet key (DataFormats field), 41
Insertable key (Inser Object dialog box), 42
Readable key, 40
Readwritable key, 40

L

LAN (local area network), 595
LANGID (language ID), 368
LCID (locale ID), 368
LeaveCriticalSection function, 554
libraries, 11
import libraries, 587
initializing, 54, 168, 268, 306, 372-376, 400-404
loading, 168
OLB (object library), 453
quitting, 400-404
type libraries, 369-370, 414-418
lindex field (FORMATETC data structure), 204
linked objects, 340-341
changing, 155-156
in-place editing, 605
monikers, 21-23
tracking, 19-23
linking
applications, 587-589
import libraries, 421-423
linking containers, 137
list boxes, 359
listings
3.1 OLE 1.H, 54-55
3.2 OLE1.CPP, 55-58
3.3 IODND.H, 60-61
3.4 IODND.CPP, 62-67
3.5 OLEDOC.H, 78-79
3.6 OLEDOC.CPP, 79-82
3.7 OLEVIEW.H, 86-87
3.8 OLEVIEW.CPP, 87-89
4.1 IRUNOBJ.H, 103-114
4.2 IRUNOBJ.CPP, 104-110
6.1 OLECNT.CPP, 169-172
6.2 OLECNVW.H, 180-181
6.3 OLECNVW.CPP, 181-190
6.4 OLECNDOC.H, 191
6.5 OLECNDOC.CPP, 191-193
6.6 CNTRITEM.H, 195-196
6.7 OLECNT.CPP, 196-200
7.1 OnEditPaste method, 209-212
7.2 OnEditPasteSpecial method, 212-213
7.3 OnEditClear method, 214-215
7.4 GetObjectInfo method, 216-220
7.5 OnDragOver method, 218-220
7.6 OnDrop method, 219-220
7.7 CWinApp Module, 222-224, 224
8.1 SUMMADOC.CPP, 250-252
8.1 SUMMADOC.H, 250-252
8.2 SUMINFO.CPP module, 253-255
8.3 OnOpenDocument method, 257-258
8.4 LoadFromStorage method, 258-259
8.5 OnSaveDocument method, 259-261
8.6 SaveToStorage method, 261-262
9.1 OLESERV.CPP, 268-280
9.1 OLESERV.H, 268-280
9.2 IPFRAME.CPP, 273-280
9.2 IPFRAME.H, 273-280
9.3 OLESEDOC.CPP, 275-280
9.3 OLESEDOC.H, 275-280
9.4 OLESEVW.CPP, 284-303
9.4 OLESEVW.H, 284-303
9.5 SRVRITEM.CPP, 288-303
9.5 SRVRITEM.H, 288-303
9.6 CDIB.CPP, 293-303
9.6 CDIB.H, 293-303
10.1 OLE2SRV.CPP, 307-312
10.1 OLE2SRV.H, 307-312
10.2 IPFRAME.CPP, 313-316
10.2 IPFRAME.H, 313-316
10.3 OLESRDOC.CPP, 317-322
10.3 OLESRDOC.H, 317-322
10.4 TITLE.CPP, 325-327
10.4 TITLE.H, 325-327
10.5 OLESRVW.CPP, 327-331
10.5 OLESRVW.H, 327-331
10.6 SRVRITEM.CPP, 332-336
10.6 SRVRITEM.H, 332-336
12.1 AUTOCLI.CPP, 373-376
12.2 AUTODOC.H, 378-379
12.3 AUTODOC.CPP, 379-382
12.4 AUTOCVW.H, 389
12.5 AUTOCVW.CPP, 390-395
13.1 MAIN.CPP, 400-404
13.2 AUTOSRV.H, 407-408
13.3 AUTOSRV.CPP, 408-412
13.4 OBJECT.H, 413
13.5 OBJECT.CPP, 413-414
13.6 ODL File, 416-417
13.7 IAUTOSRV.H, 417-418
13.8 CLSID.C, 421
13.8 CLSID.H, 421
14.1 MYCLASS.H, 431
14.2 CDispatchDriver definition/DSPCALC2.H, 437-439
14.3 DSPCALCW.CPP, 440-441
15.1 XCLIENT.CPP, 449-452
15.2 Worksheet Class Definition, 454-456
15.3 COleDispatchDriver class, 457-458
15.4 Application class, 458-469
15.5 EXCEL.CPP, 470-475
15.5 EXCEL.H, 470-475
16.1 AUTOMFC.CPP, 481
16.10 Form_Load from the Visual basic test Script, 510

16.11 The Visual Basic for Applications test macro, 511-512
16.2 AUTOMVW.H, 484-488
16.3 SHAPE.H, 490-492
16.4 SHAPE.CPP, 492-495
16.5 CAUTODOC.H, 497-498
16.6 CAUTODOC.CPP, 498-502
16.7 IEnumVARIANT, 503
16.8 VARENUM.H, 506
16.9 VARENUM.CPP, 506-510
17.1 IDL file, 523-524
17.2 IUnknown IDL file, 525-547
17.3 BPS_P.CXX, 526-531
17.3 BPS_X.HXX, 526-531
17.4 BPS.H, 532-533
17.5 BPS_I.C, 533-534
17.6 make file for the proxy and stub DLL, 534-535
17.7 MAIN.CPP, 536-547
17.8 AUTOSRV.CPP, 540-547
17.8 AUTOSRV.H, 540-547
17.9 Client Application, 545-547
18.1 New Metafile Header, 577
18.2 Modified OLE 1.CPP, 579
18.2 Modified OLE1.CPP, 579-582
18.3 OLEDOC.H, 582-589
18.4 OLEDOC.CPP, 584-587

LoadFromStorage Method (listing 8.4), 258-259

loading
bitmaps, 292-303
component objects, 37
libraries, 168
objects, 93
servers, 519-520

local memory, 45

local objects, 592

local servers, 40, 50

LocalServer field, 40

locating
remote servers, 599
servers, 519-520

LockBytes objects, 26, 226-227

locks, 67-68

LockServer function, 406

LRPC (lightweight remote procedure call), 12-13
Message Monitor, 98-99
replacing with RPC, 598

M

macro languages, 345-347, 356

macros
CPP file macros, 433-436
DECLARE_DISPATCH_MAP macro, 432-436
DISP_FUNCTION macro, 489
IMPLEMENT_OLECREATE macro, 436
OLE headers, 59-60
OLECREATE macro, 431-432
SDK macros, 44
TCHAR macro, 563

MAIN.CPP (listing 13.1), 400-404

MAIN.CPP (listing 17.7), 536-547

make file for the proxy and stub DLL (listing 17.6), 534-535

mapping modes
GDI mapping modes, 265-266
MM_ANISOTROPIC mapping mode, 292
MM_HIMETRIC mapping mode, 265
Object Interface class, 337

marshaling, 518-520

MDI (Multiple Document Interface), 121, 305

measurement units, 265

memory
allocators, 44-45
containers, 282, 291, 336
local memory, 45
managing, 44-45
pages, 550
shared memory, 45, 576
subsegment-allocation schemes, 45

memory-mapped files (Win32), 555-556

menus
active object menus, 18
context menus, 179-190

message queues, 551-552
enlarging, 53, 372
Win32, 579

metafiles, 177, 266-267, 337
bitmaps, 337
creating, 142
formats, 576-577
in 32-bit OLE applications, 576-577
reference device context, 576
rendering objects, 291
scaling, 265-266, 291-292, 337

method stubs (ClassWizard), 436

methods
adding to classes, 428-429
adding with ClassWizard, 489-495
Application objects, 361-362
Automation, 382-395
calling, 457
collections (objects), 495-502
Create method (CDropTarget class), 70
CVarEnum methods, 505-512
Document objects, 363-365
DragEnter method (CDropTarget class), 72
DragLeave method (CDropTarget class), 75
DragOver method (CDropTarget class), 74
Draw method (component objects), 173
DrawGhostRect method (View class), 84
EnableAutomation method (AppWizard), 426, 488
exposed methods, 439-444
GetDragRect method (CDropTarget class), 71
GetIDsOFNames method
Automation, 382-383
IDispatch interface, 351
GetQuote method (CObject class), 412
GetShape method, 489
GetShapeCount method, 490
IEnumVARIANT methods, 503
Invoke method (IDispatch interface pointer), 383-388
OnChange method (COleClientItem class), 194
OnClone method, 505
OnCreate method (View class), 83
OnDestroy method (View class), 83
OnDragEnter method (drag-drop applications), 216-217
OnDragLeave method (drag-drop applications), 220

OnDraw method
  Object Interface class, 337
OnDraw method (Document class), 84-89
OnDraw method (Object Interface class), 291-292
OnDraw method (View class), 287, 331
OnEditBitmaps method (View class), 287
OnEditChangeTitle method (View class), 332-336
OnEditClear method (clipboard), 214-215
OnEditCopy method
  clipboard, 214-215
  View class, 331-332
OnEditCut method (clipboard), 214-215
OnEditPasteLink method (clipboard), 212
OnEditPasteSpecial method (clipboard), 212-213
OnGetEmbeddedItem method (Document class), 281-282
OnGetExtent method
  Document class, 282, 324
  Object Interface class, 291, 337
OnNewDocument method (Document class), 323
OnNext method, 505
OnOpenDocument method
  Document class, 323
  View class, 281
OnRest method, 505
OnSaveDocument method (Document class), 323
OnScrollBy method (drag-drop applications), 220-221
OnSetExtent method
  Document class, 282, 324
  Object Interface class, 291, 336
OnSetItemRects method (Document class), 280-281, 324
OnSetTitle method (Document class), 325-331
OnSkip method, 505
OnUpdatePaste method (clipboard), 213-214
parameters, 348, 429
RefreshWindow method, 490
return types, 429
Serialize method (Document class), 282-283, 324-325, 336
Serialize method (Object Interface Class), 291
SetContainerInfo method (application containers), 168-172
SetShape method, 490
UnRenderGlobalData method
  Object Interface class, 337-341
VARIANTs, 454-457

Methods/Properties list box, 359

MFC (Microsoft Foundation Classes), 53, 425-445
  Automation server, 479-512
  base classes, 122-127
  ClassWizard, 357, 453
  Document View architecture, 118-121
  library, 207-208
  OLE classes, 121-164
  OLE servers, 263-303

Microsoft System 7 OLE, 606

MIDL (Microsoft Interface Description
  Language), 518

miniservers, 305-306
  codes summary, 301-302
  creating, 267-301
  testing, 302-303

MiscStatus field, 41-42

MkTypLib application, 416

MM_ANISOTROPIC mapping mode, 266, 292

MM_HIMETRIC mapping mode, 265

Modified OLE1.CPP (listing 18.2), 579-582

modules, 110-111
  application modules, 168-200
  AUTOSRV.CPP module, 540-548
  document modules, 190-193
  object interface module, 193-200
  OLESRV2.CPP module, 306

monikers, 14, 340
  antimonikers, 22
  file monikers, 22
  item monikers, 22
  OLE stream, 239-240
  pointer monikers, 23

monitors, 98-99

Move method (COleClientItem class), 195

moving
  active objects, 280-281
  container objects, 160
  objects, 483

Multiple Document Interface, *see* MDI

mutexes (synchronization objects), 554

MYCLASS.H (listing 14.1), 431

MyTypLib (type library generator), 111

N

naming conventions, 234

nested classes, 503-505

new metafile header (listing 18.1), 577

NLS (National Language Support), 31

no-scribble state (embedded objects), 242

numbers (build numbers), 168

O

object browsers, 357-360

Object Description Language, *see* ODL

Object Descriptor fields, 95-96

object interfaces, 33-34
  constructor, 336
  models (Excel 5.0), 447-448
  module, 193-200
  Object Interface class, 287-292, 332-341

object servers, 596

object variables, 323

OBJECT.CPP (listing 13.5), 413-414

OBJECT.H (listing 13.4), 413

ObjectBroker technology, 597-598

objects
  access, 368-370
  Application object, 361-362
  applications, 404-405
  Automation, 347-355
  borders, 483
  calculating size, 71

class factory objects, 407-408
collections, 495-502
indices, 497
testing, 510
component objects, 34
creating, 129-137
CShape objects, 490-510
debugging, 113
distributed objects, 591-600, 608
Document objects, 362-364
methods, 363-365
properties, 362-364
document objects, 609-610
Documents collection object, 364-365
drawing, 287
embedded objects, 221
enumerator objects, 46
extended object layout, 602-603
Font objects, 365-366
HIMETRIC unit size, 282
irregularly shaped objects, 604-605
LockBytes objects, 26, 226-227
monikers, 14, 239-240
programmable objects, 30
rendering in metafiles, 291
Security objects, 368-370
synchronization objects, 554-555
tunneling, 603-604
waitable objects, 554
WordBasic objects, 376-377
see also component objects

Objects menu commands, 100
Objects/Modules list box, 359
ODL (Object Description Language), 369
ODL file (listing 13.6), 416-417
OFS (object file system), 14
OLB (object library), 453
OLE (object linking and embedding)
32-bit, 574-589
Distributed OLE, 598-600, 608
future development, 601-612
Microsoft System 7, 606
origins, 10-14
Windows NT 3.5, 606-607
Unicode, 577-578
OLE 1.0 libraries, 11
OLE 1.H (listing 3.1), 54-55
OLE Automation, 30-31
OLE Controls, 607-608
OLE dialog classes, 154-159
OLE formats, 202
OLE SDK (DISPTEST), 422
OLE streams (special OLE streams), 239-240
OLE1.CPP (listing 3.2), 55-58
OLE2.DLL defaults, 40
OLE2SRV.CPP (listing 10.1), 307-312
OLE2SRV.H (listing 10.1), 307-312
Ole2View (object browser), 358-359
Ole2View Utility, 100-110
OLECNDOC.CPP (listing 6.5), 191-193
OLECNDOC.H (listing 6.4), 191
OLECNT.CPP (listing 6.1), 169-172
OLECNT.CPP (listing 6.7), 196-200
OLECNVW.CPP (listing 6.3), 181-190
OLECNVW.H (listing 6.2), 180-181
OLECREATE macro, 431-432
OleCreateFromData function, 77
OLEDOC.CPP
listing 3.6, 79-82
listing 18.4, 584-587
OLEDOC.H
listing 3.5, 78-79
listing 18.3, 582-589
OleInitialize function, 168, 398
OleIPFrame class, 146-148
OleLoad function, 84-85
OleQueryCreateFromData function, 72
OleQueryLinkFromData function, 72
OleSave function, 77
OLESEDOC.CPP (listing 9.3), 275-280
OLESEDOC.H (listing 9.3), 275-280
OLESERV.CPP (listing 9.1), 268-280
OLESERV.H (listing 9.1), 268-280
OLESEVW.CPP (listing 9.4), 284-303
OLESEVW.H (listing 9.4), 284-303
OLESRDOC.CPP (listing 10.3), 317-322
OLESRDOC.H (listing 10.3), 317-322
OLESRV2.CPP module, 306
OLESRVW.CPP (listing 10.5), 327-331
OLESRVW.H (listing 10.5), 327-331
OleUninitialize function, 54
OLEVIEW.CPP (listing 3.8), 87-89
OLEVIEW.H (listing 3.7), 86-87
OMG CORBA (Object Management GroupCommon Object Request Broker Architecture), 596-597
OnChange method (COleClientItem class), 194
OnChangeItemPosition method (COleClientItem class), 178-179, 194
OnClone method, 505
OnCreate method (View class), 83
OnDeactivateUI method (COleClientItem class), 194-195
OnDestroy method (View class), 83
OnDragEnter method (drag-drop applications), 216-217
OnDragLeave method (drag-drop applications), 220
OnDragOver Method (listing 7.5), 218-220
OnDraw method
Document class, 84-89
Object Interface class, 291-292, 337
View class, 85, 287, 331
OnDrop Method (listing 7.6), 219-220
OnEditBitmaps method (View class), 287
OnEditChangeTitle method (View class), 332-336
OnEditClear Method (listing 7.3), 214-215
OnEditCopy method
clipboard, 214-215
View class, 331-332

OnEditCut method (clipboard), 214-215
OnEditPaste Method (listing 7.1), 209-212
OnEditPasteLink method (clipboard), 212
OnEditPasteSpecial method, 212-213
OnGetEmbeddedItem method (Document class), 281-282, 323-324
OnGetExtent method
- Document class, 282, 324
- Object Interface class, 291, 377

OnGetItemPosition method (COleClientItem class), 194
OnNewDocument method (Document class), 323
OnNext method, 505
OnOpenDocument method
- Document class, 323
- listing 8.3, 257-258
- View class, 281

OnRest method, 505
OnSaveDocument method
- Document class, 323
- listing 8.5, 259-261

OnScrollBy method (drag-drop applications), 220-221
OnSetExtent method
- Document class, 280-282, 324
- Object Interface class, 291, 336

OnSetItemRects method (Document class), 280-281, 324
OnSetTitle method (Document class), 325-331
OnSkip method, 505
OnStart command handler, 458
OnUpdatePaste method (clipboard), 213-214
OOP (object-oriented programming), 14, 46-47
Open command (File menu), 119-120
opening
- compound files, 233
- storages (compound files), 233-234

Options dialog box, 167
ORB (Object Request Broker), 596
OS (operating system), 14
OSF (Open Software Foundation), 37
OSF DCE (Open Software Foundation Distributed Computing Environment), 520, 592-596
OWL (ObjectWindows Library), 14

P

parameters
- /Embedding parameter, 268
- 32-bit programs, 557-558
- CreateStdDispatch function, 352
- messages (Win32), 558
- methods, 348, 429

Paste command (Edit menu), 209
Paste Link command (Edit menu), 212
Paste Special command (Edit menu), 339
Paste Special dialog box, 157, 212, 339
pointer monikers, 23
pointers
- CWnd pointer, 313
- embedded objects, 264
- IDispatch pointer, 476
- IDispatch pointers, 439
- interface pointers, 36-37, 48, 61, 76
- ITypeInfo pointer, 352-354
- retrieving, 281, 323
- storage pointers, 243

portable
- codes, 60
- type definitions (variables), 563
- versions, 560

prefixing application strings, 564-570
Presentation streams (special OLE stream), 240-262
ProgID field, 40
programmable objects, 30
programming (32-bit), 556-561
programming systems, 46
***Programming Windows*, 266**
Project Settings dialog box, 587
properties, 245
- Application objects, 361-362
- collections (objects), 495-502
- Document objects, 362-363
- Documents collection object, 364
- Font objects, 365-366
- RPCs (remote procedure calls), 594
- values 444
- Visible property (Excel 5.0 test application), 469

property inheritance of containers, 602
property sets, 244-256
protecting resources, 553-554
proxies
- codes, 516
- creating, 522-535
- objects, 50
- OLE distribution, 599
- registering, 547
- server substitute, 520

Proxy Manager, 520
ptd field (FORMATETC data structure), 203

Q–R

QueryInterface (COM), 35-36
quitting
- Excel 5.0, 448-452
- libraries, 400-404
- MFC Automation servers, 512

quotes, 423

radio buttons, 306
Read Type Library command button, 430, 453
Readable key (Conversion field), 40
reading type libraries, 437-439
Readwritable key (Conversion field), 40
real-time market data, 610-611
reference device context (metafiles), 576
RefreshWindow method, 490
REGEDIT file, 547
RegisterDragDrop function, 67, 83

registering
 32-bit OLE applications, 578-579
 class factories, 307, 399
 custom interfaces, 547
 drag-drop applications, 215-216
 proxies, 547
 servers, 547
 stubs, 547
 type libraries, 419-420
registration databases (updating), 136-137
Release function (IUnknown interface), 36
ReleaseStgMedium function, 72
remote objects, 592
remote servers, 50, 599
removing system modules, 111
resources
 active objects, 268
 protecting from corruption, 553
 serializing access, 553
restricting object access, 368-370
retrieving
 embedded object size, 324
 pointers, 281, 323
 quotes, 423
 storage information, 228
return codes, 42-44, 378
return types (methods), 429
returning errors to containers/ applications, 160
RevokeDragDrop function, 83
RIT (raw input thread), 551
root storage, 229, 237
ROT (running object table), 97, 341
RPC (remote procedure call), 50, 369, 575, 593-594
 properties, 594
 replacing LRPC, 598
RTF (Rich Text Format), 153-155
Run the Registry Editor command (File menu), 100
RunEmbedded function, 268, 307
running
 Automation servers, 421-423
 Excel 5.0 test application, 477

S

SaveToStorage Method (listing 8.6), 261-262
saving
 bitmaps, 292-303
 compound files, 259
 documents, 242
 embedded objects, 190-193, 195
 substorage objects, 77
scaling
 embedded objects, 324
 metafiles, 265-266, 292, 337
SCM (Service Control Manager), 519-520, 599
SCODE (status code), 42-44
script languages, 356
scrolling, 75
SDI (Single Document Interface), 121, 305, 448
SDK (Software Development Kit), 44, 91-114
searching
 component objects, 37-42
 streams (structured storage), 231
security
 32-bit OLE applications, 576
 Kerberos authentication system, 595
 objects, 368-370
 services, 595
SEH (structured exception handling), 572-575
Select Text button, 388
selecting type libraries, 430
semaphores (synchronization objects), 555
Serialize method
 COleClientItem class, 195
 Document class), 282-283, 324-325
 Object Interface Class), 291, 336
serializing resource access, 553
servers, 50
 architecture, 263-264
 Automation, 397-398
 Automation servers, 93-94, 397-423
 classes, 136-148
 client-server environments, 594
 code, 535-544
 full servers, 305-306
 implementing, 137
 in-proc (in-process), 40
 loading, 519-520
 locating, 519-520
 MFC OLE servers, 263-303
 miniservers, 305-306
 object servers, 596
 proxy (server substitute), 520
 registering, 547
 remote servers, 599
 server code, 535-544
 time servers, 596
Service Control Manager, *see* SCM
services
 DFS (Distributed File System), 595-596
 directory services, 594-595
 diskless support services, 596
 security services, 595
 time services, 596
SetContainerInfo method (application containers), 168-172
SetMessageQueue function, 53, 372, 579
SetProperty method (property values), 444
SetShape method, 490
setting property values, 444
severity field (SCODE), 42
SHAPE.CPP (listing 16.4), 492-495
SHAPE.H (listing 16.3), 490-492
shared memory, 45, 576
shared toolbars, 605
sharing
 compound files, 256-262
 storage objects, 26
shells (Windows 95), 612
Show CLDIS command (Objects menu), 100
Show Link Source Descriptor command (DataObject menu), 96
shutdown (applications), 54
signaled synchronization objects, 554
Single Document Interface, see SDI
SIZEL field, 72
sizing handles, 148, 483
software, 15-16
SOM (System Object Model), 49

special OLE streams, 238-240
special streams, 27
specifiers (type libraries), 370
SRVRITEM.CPP
- listing 9.5, 288-303
- listing 10.6, 332-336

SRVRITEM.H
- listing 9.5, 288-303
- listing 10.6 , 332-336

starting Excel 5.0, 448-452
static interfaces, 36
STATSTG structure, 228-229
status information (component objects), 41-42
StgCreateDocFile function, 76, 233
StgCreateDocFileOnILockBytes function, 233
StgIsStorageDocFile function, 76
StgIsStorageFile function, 249
STGMEDIUM data structure, 28, 205-208
StgOpenStorage function, 76
storage, 227-230, 233-234
- compound files, 235-236
- embedded objects, 241-243
- enumerators, 230
- naming conventions, 234
- objects, 26
- pointers, 243
- retrieving information, 228
- root storage, 229, 237
- structured storage, 13-14, 225-233
- transacted storage (compound files), 237

storing
- compound files data, 244-256
- DLLs, 377
- dropped component objects, 76-82
- Summary Information property set, 248

streams
- \2OlePres? (Special OLE stream), 240-262
- CompObj streams (Special OLE streams), 238-239
- compound files, 235-236
- debugging, 99
- Presentation streams (special OLE stream), 240-262
- special OLE streams, 238-240
- special streams, 27
- structured storage, 230-233
- Summary Information stream, 13

string enumerators (interfaces), 46
structured exception handling, *see* SEH
structures (application fields), 69-70
stubs (interfaces), 521-535
- codes, 516
- objects, 50
- OLE distribution, 599
- registering, 547

subsegment-allocation schemes, 45
subsets (Win 32), 549
substorage, 76-77
SUMINFO.CPP Module (listing 8.2), 253-255
SUMMADOC.CPP (listing 8.1), 250-252
SUMMADOC.H (listing 8.1), 250-252
Summary Information (property set), 245, 248
Summary Information stream, 13
synchronization objects, 554-562
synchronizing threads (Win32), 553-555
synchronous input, 552
SysAllocString function, 388

T

tables (vtables), 34
templates, 306-312, 448
termination handlers, 573
test application (Excel 5.0 object model), 448-452
testing
- collections (objects), 510-512
- custom interfaces, 547-548
- full server, 338-339
- MFC Automation server, 510
- miniservers, 302-303

text (Word file insertion), 388
TGS (Ticket Granting Server), 595
thread synchronization
- Critical sections, 553-554
- DCE service, 593
- Win32, 552-553

timestamps, 596
TITLE.CPP (listing 10.4), 325-327
TITLE.H (listing 10.4), 325-327
titles (pictures), 325-327
toolbar buttons (Excel 5.0), 476
toolbars, 605
tracker rectangles, 174, 483
tracking, 19-23, 609
transacted access (compound files), 237
true link tracking, 609
tunneling objects, 603-604
tymed field (FORMATETC data structure), 204-205
type identifier field, 245-247
type libraries, 415
- Excel 5.0, 453-477
- listing, 100
- MyTypLib generator, 111
- reading, 437-439
- registering, 419-420
- selecting, 430
- specifiers, 370

Type Library Browser, 112

U

UDT (Uniform Data Transfer), 11, 27-30, 148-154, 215-221
UI (user interface) dialog boxes, 154-159
Unicode
- applications, 562-572
- fonts, 572
- OLE (32-bit), 577-578

Unicode (Windows NT), 561-574
UnRenderGlobalData method (Object Interface class), 337-341
unsignaled synchronization objects, 554
Update dialog box, 158-159
UpdateAllViews function, 75
updating registration databases, 136-137
user feedback, 73-74, 218-219
user types, 41
UTC (Coordinated Universal Time), 596
utilities
- DISPTEST utility, 356
- Free Module Utility, 99-100

Ole2View Utility, 100-110
WPS (Windows Process Status) utility, 110-111
UUID (universally unique ID), 38, 96
UUIDGEN.EXE application, 38

V

values (type indicator), 245-247
VARENUM.CPP (listing 16.9), 506-510
VARENUM.H (listing 16.8), 506
variables
16-bit variables (32-bit conversion), 557
portable type, 563
protecting from corruption, 553
VARIANTARG variables, 384-387
VARIANTs, 454-457
VBA (Visual Basic for Applications), 30, 346
VBXs (Visual Basic custom controls), 607
Verb field, 40-41
VersionIndependentProgID field, 39-40
View Advise Sink (data changes), 173
View class, 172-190, 283-287, 327-332, 483-488
DrawGhostRect method, 84
OnCreate method, 83
OnDestroy method, 83
viewers
DocFile Viewer, 92-93
file viewers (Windows 95), 611
IDataObject Viewer, 95-96
IDispatch viewer, 101
interface viewers, 101
ROT (Running Object Table) Viewer, 97
virtual memory model (Win32), 550
Visible property (Excel 5.0 test application), 469
visual editing, 17-31
VMM (Virtual Memory Manager), 551
vtables (virtual function tables), 34

W-X-Y-Z

Win16, 560
Win32
asynchronous input model, 551-552
compound files, 576
DDE messages, 558
Developers Conference, 598
memory-mapped files, 555-557
message queues, 579
parameter messages, 558
portable versions, 560
subsets, 549
threads, 554-589
Window Application class, 267-272
windows
active objects frame windows, 272-275
Applications class, 306-312
in-place frame windows, 146
Windows 95, 611-612
Windows applications (executing from DOS boxes), 112
Windows NT, 549-589
Windows NT 3.5 OLE, 606-607
Word files, 388
WordBasic objects, 376-377
workbooks (Excel 5.0), 476-477
Worksheet class definition (listing 15.2), 454-456
WOSA/XRT (Windows Open Services Architecture Extensions for Real-time market data), 610-611
WPS (Windows Process Status) utility, 110-111
WriteClassStg function, 78
WXSRVR program, 112-113

XCLIENT.CPP (listing 15.1), 449-452